D1587438

THE OFFICIAL HISTORY OF

WEST HAM UNITED

1895–2001

Foreword by Trevor Brooking CBE

Adam Ward

Dedication
To Lindsay Johnson and my sons Joe and Tom

First published in Great Britain in 1999 Hamlyn, a division of Octopus Publishing Group Limited, 2–4 Heron Quays, Docklands, London, E14 4JP

This edition published in 2001

Copyright © 2001 Octopus Publishing Group Limited

All rights reserved. No part of this publication may be reproduced, stored in a retrieval system, or transmitted in any form or by any means, electronic, mechanical, photocopying, recording or otherwise, without the permission of Reed International Books Ltd and the copyright holder(s).

ISBN 0 600 60442 X

A catalogue record for this book is available from the British Library

Printed in Italy

FOREWORD

The history of West Ham United is quite unlike that of any other top-class football club. It is a tale not just of great matches and great personalities, successes and failures, but also of a very special tradition. Everybody associated with the Club – fans, directors, staff and players – is acutely aware of this tradition, and it is something which I feel proud to have contributed to. Football at Upton Park, you see, has always been about more than just results. It is about playing the game the right way, playing with style and flair. The Hammers fans, who are probably the most loyal and knowledgeable in English football, also insist that their team does things the 'right' way, and would never tolerate a change to a more pragmatic brand of football.

The passion of the West Ham United crowd is something I have experienced as both fan and player, and it was as an awe struck 10-year-old back in 1958 that I made my first trip to the Boleyn Ground. I can still clearly remember the game – the last home fixture of the 1957-58 promotion season – and the deafening roar which greeted John Bond's equalising goal against a highly fancied Liverpool team. Little did I know that seven years later I would be joining John on the Hammers staff, albeit as a teenage apprentice. My arrival at the Club came when the great triumvirate – Moore, Hurst and Peters – was on the verge of its zenith. The previous May, Hammers had defeated TSV Munich 1860 in the Cup Winners' Cup final and the following July, Bobby lifted the World Cup for England. It was a golden era for West Ham United.

Ron Greenwood, a great coach and tactical thinker, was Hammers manager when I joined the Club and it was he who gave me my first-team debut in October 1967. However, it was under Ron's successor, John Lyall, that I enjoyed my greatest successes. John was a tremendous motivator and it is often forgotten that he led the Club to four Cup finals in his reign as manager. There were many highlights during this period but, on a personal level, the 1980 FA Cup triumph over Arsenal was particularly memorable. And just for the record, yes, I did know what I was doing when I headed the game's only goal.

My playing days with the Hammers spanned 17 seasons and 636 matches, and I consider it a great honour that I ended my career as a one-club man. Throughout my time at the Boleyn Ground I enjoyed a special rapport with the crowd and I will never forget the tremendous send-off the fans gave me when I made my farewell appearance against Everton in 1984.

It is no longer possible for me to attend matches at Upton Park as regularly as I would like. My radio and television work, usually means I am either stuck in a press box or sat behind a video monitor in a TV studio on matchdays. However, you can rest assured that I am always kept informed of the slightest incident in every Hammers match. And I am pleased to say that a victory for my old team still gives me the same feeling of elation as when I wore the famous claret and blue shirt myself as a player. Fortunately, such moments are becoming ever more frequent and, after some difficult times in the early 1990s, the future now looks bright for the Hammers. With a host of talented players, many of whom have developed through the club's junior ranks, the West Ham United tradition is in safe hands.

Trevor Brooking, CBE.

CHAPTER 1
THE BIRTH OF THE IRONS

'Mr Taylor, who is working in the Shipbuilding Department, has undertaken to get up a Football Club for next winter...' *Thames Iron Works Gazette*, **June 1895.**

Arnold Hills

In June 1895 a new football team emerged from the docks of East London. The Thames Iron Works Football Club was not the first team to establish itself in the East End, but a wealthy benefactor gave it a major advantage over more experienced rivals. Arnold Hills was the owner of the Iron Works and a man passionately committed to enriching the lives of his workforce. To this end, Hills had set up a network of clubs and associations, taking in such disparate leisure pursuits as science and cycling. Music was considered particularly important, and the Works had a temperance choir, an operatic society and a military band. These clubs were Hills' attempt to foster good relations between management and workers. Hills was also acting out of a sense of paternalism toward his workers. He wanted to provide them with opportunities to enjoy wholesome leisure pursuits and so prevent them from spending their spare time on such evils as drink and gambling.

In his younger days, Hills had been a successful footballer. He represented Oxford University in the Varsity match, and later played for Old Harrovians with whom he won an international cap for England against Scotland in 1879. Given Hills' illustrious playing career, it is surprising that it took until 1895 for Thames Iron Works and Ship Building Company to add a football team to its growing list of clubs and associations.

On 29 June 1895 the *Thames Iron Works Gazette* carried a notice stating that Mr Hills had granted Dave Taylor – a foreman in the shipbuilding yard and also a local referee – permission to form a football team. Workers were invited to join the club and membership cost half a crown (12 ½p). Member subscriptions would help finance the new club, though much of the money would come direct from Hills.

Fifty applications for membership were received and Taylor immediately set about the business of arranging fixtures. Two teams were formed and the Thames Iron Works Football Club was affiliated to the Football Association. Taylor entered the teams in local cup competitions and arranged friendlies. But from the outset, the Irons were ambitious and, not content with testing themselves against local amateur teams, the club entered the FA Cup. The club secretary explained: 'Having some good men in the club, we somewhat presumptuously considered it would be wise to enter for the English Association Cup.'

The 'good men' referred to by the secretary were mainly recruited from leading local clubs including the Castle Swifts (reputed to be the first professional club in Essex), St Luke's and Anchor. The club was also quick to attract talent from outside its immediate catchment and on 20 September 1895, the *Kentish Mail and Greenwich and Deptford Observer* noted that, 'Robert Stevenson the late captain of the Arsenal team is coming from Scotland to play for the Thames Iron Works.'

The Thames Iron Works and Ship Building Company was one of the biggest and most important shipbuilding yards in Britain. The Iron Works began life on the Isle of Dogs at Blackwall, but switched to the banks of the River Lee in 1843.

Left: The financial backing of Arnold Hills was the key to the success of the Iron Works team.

Below: Tom Robinson, with his thick moustache and trademark cigar, was already one of the best-known figures in East London football when he became the Iron Works' first trainer in 1895.

The Irons played their home fixtures at the Hermit Road ground, known locally as Cinder Heap and previously home to the Castle Swifts. Training was held in a schoolroom in Barking Road and was taken by Tom Robinson, who was assisted by captain Bob Stevenson. Robinson was an experienced trainer and was well respected in East London, having previously worked with both St Luke's and the Castle Swifts. With the Irons now ready for their first season of football, Dave Taylor stood down from his position to concentrate on refereeing and was replaced by A.T. Harsent of Canning Town, who became the first club secretary. Chairman of the new Club was Iron Works secretary Francis Payne.

The Temperance team

Payne was involved in several of the other works' associations, most notably as vice-president of the Temperance League. This commitment to alcoholic abstinence was also shared by Hills, who was himself an active campaigner for the temperance movement. It is hardly surprising, therefore, that the first Iron Works teams were teetotal and also non-smokers. Five years later, when the Irons had become West Ham United, the *East Ham Echo* still referred to the team as 'the Teetotallers'.

In the spring of 1896, the Irons enjoyed their first major success, claiming the West Ham Charity Cup after a twice replayed final against Barking. The team group here shows the victorious Irons parading their trophy.

It was not only alcohol that Hills abhorred, he was also vehemently opposed to the growing tide of professionalism in Victorian sport. Hills' passionate advocacy of the virtues of sporting amateurism would be the cause of much tension during the club's formative years. The new club had already shown its ambition in recruiting top coaching and playing staff and by entering the FA Cup. Further evidence of a leaning toward professionalism came during 1895 when the players decided that the club's governing committee should be made up of non-players. 'The committee' would regularly find itself at loggerheads with Hills as they struggled to reconcile their different aims and ambitions for the football club.

Irons start strongly

The Irons played their first match on 7 September 1895, taking on Royal Ordnance at Hermit Road. The match ended in a 1–1 draw, a commendable result against experienced opposition. The second game, against Dartford A, brought the Irons' first victory, the *Thames Iron Works Gazette* commenting that the Kent side were given a 'licking of 4 to nil'. Results continued to improve and on 28 September the Irons played their first away game, taking on Manor Park and running out 8–0 victors. All too often during the club's first season they were forced to take on opposition that was vastly inferior, but this did not prevent the committee from continuing to strengthen the playing squad.

The first real test for the fledgling Irons came in October when they made their debut in the FA Cup. Their opponents were Chatham, one of the leading teams in the Southern League. The Irons had been drawn at home, but conceded this advantage and consented to the tie being played at Chatham in order to increase gate receipts. The Irons managed to compete well in the first half, but during the second period they were overrun and the game ended in a 5–0 victory for Chatham. *The Sportsman* noted that the 'goalkeeping and defence of the visitors was the best part of their play.' Aside from the result, the Irons' first FA Cup adventure had been a resounding success; the club had earned extra revenue as a result of switching the tie to Chatham and the game had helped raise the profile of the Thames Iron Works Football Club.

By November the committee's efforts to improve the team were paying dividends. The Irons took on Southern League Reading, considered to be one of the South's top club sides, and although they lost 3–2 the Londoners emerged with credit after dominating much of the game. This excellent display was followed by more impressive results during the winter of 1895–96, including a victory over St Luke's, a strong local club side. After these performances, it was widely speculated that the Irons would be elevated to the Southern League for the 1896–97 season.

Rudimentary illumination

The Irons also attracted much interest and a certain amount of notoriety by experimenting with floodlights during their first season. The lighting engineers from the Iron Works were given permission to rig up lights so that kick-off times could be put back to allow men from the works to attend games played during the week. The first game to enjoy this rudimentary illumination was a friendly against Old St Stephen's at Hermit Road on 16 December 1895. Twelve lights, each of 2,000 candle power, were mounted on poles. The results were far from perfect and the lights were unsteady and kept going out. One reporter commented that he heard Old St Stephen's complaining that 'the light always went out just when the Thames Iron Works men had taken a shot at goal.' The lights were gradually improved, though the ball still had to be regularly dipped in whitewash to make it visible, and at the end of January a report of a friendly against Barking Woodville in *The Sportsman* noted that 'the company [Thames Iron Works] have spared no expense,' adding that, 'the light gave a good view'.

By the end of 1895–96, the Irons were a match for any amateur side. The overall record for that first season stood at played 46, won 29, drawn five and lost 12, which according to secretary A.T. Harsent was 'a record to be proud of'. The Irons had rounded off the season by winning the West Ham Charity Cup, defeating Barking before a crowd of more than 3,000 in a tie that needed two replays, and they had also played a prestigious friendly against First Division West Bromwich Albion. There was clearly a need for the Irons to find regular competitive football for the 1896–97 season.

The Irons lost just one London League game during 1897–98 and were crowned champions at the end of the season. The Eastenders had been founder members of the League a year before, but now decided that the time was right to test themselves in the cut and thrust of the Southern League. It is interesting to note that, for this photograph, the team has been organised in formation, i.e. goalkeeper and full-backs at the back, the three-man half-back line in the middle and the five forwards at the front.

London League challenge

In March 1896 a meeting was held at Finsbury Barracks to discuss the formation of a London League. It was agreed that a new league should be formed, and that the league would comprise three divisions made up of both professional and amateur teams. Arnold Hills was elected as president of the new league and the Irons were initially placed in the second division, only to be elevated to the top division after the withdrawal of Royal Ordnance. It was hoped that the new league would help raise the standard of football in London at a time when the clubs of the Midlands and North West were dominating the professional game. A.T. Harsent declared in the *Thames Iron Works Gazette* that: 'The League will be a new feature in London football next season... it should raise the whole tone of football in the great city.'

As the 1896–97 season approached it seemed that Harsent's optimism was well placed. Club membership had increased and the Irons had attracted several new players. Included amongst the additions to the playing staff were a number of first-teamers from leading local club St Luke's, as well as four players from Reading. One player who was prevented from

joining the Irons at this time was an ex-Middlesbrough player called Wynn. Although Wynn was employed at the Iron Works, he was unable to play for the amateur Irons as he had previously been a professional footballer. Inevitably, rumours circulated that the Irons were preparing to turn professional – a notion that the club was quick to dismiss.

The Irons' first taste of League action came against Vampires at the Hermit Road ground on 19 September 1896 and resulted in a 3–0 victory which started a run of good League form. However, success in the FA Cup was not forthcoming, and an 8–0 defeat at the hands of Southern League Sheppey United brought elimination at the first hurdle. It was a defeat that was hard to take for the improving Eastenders, the sports reporter for the *Courier and Borough of West Ham News* commenting: 'I do not understand how Sheppey were able to run around Thames by 8–0. Surely the visitors must have been off colour.'

The bad news continued for the Irons when they discovered that they were to be evicted from Hermit Road in October 1896. Confusion reigned, with the club believing that they had been granted a new plot at the same site, only to discover that their ground developments were in breach of the tenancy agreement. The net effect was that the Irons were forced to play their games at the grounds of opponents until securing a temporary home at Browning Road, just off East Ham High Street.

The Irons' first-team enjoyed little luck in the local cup competitions, and were overshadowed by the reserves who progressed to a second consecutive West Ham Charity Cup final, losing 1–0 to West Ham Garfield before 6,000 fans at the Spotted Dog Ground in Forest Gate, East London. In the London League, however, the Irons made good progress, finishing as runners-up to Grenadier Guards. Much of the credit for this excellent showing was attributed to the generosity of Arnold Hills, and the *Courier and Borough of West Ham News* declared: 'Mr Hills is very liberal with the money and the satisfactory position of the club is almost entirely due to his judicial supervision.'

The Memorial Ground

Arnold Hills' generosity did not stop with investment in players, however, and in January 1897 he announced that he had found a new home for the Iron Works' football club and athletic societies. Mr Hills made his announcement at the Thames Iron Works Federated Clubs Annual Festival, remarking that he had 'secured a large piece of land for an athletic ground,' and that the 'ground would contain a cycle track equal to any in London [this comment was met with applause], and it would also be used for football, tennis, etc.' It is revealing that football is mentioned after cycling. The football club was not considered to be the most important of the Ironworks clubs and the cycling club seems to have been both more popular and more successful.

The new ground would be situated in Plaistow and was built in less than six months so that it could be opened in June 1897 to commemorate the 60th year of Queen Victoria's reign. The Memorial Ground could accommodate more than 100,000 spectators and was constructed at a cost of more than £20,000. The opening of the new ground attracted 8,000 people, who came to see a varied programme of events that included swimming, cycling, polo and cock fighting.

The football team made their debut at the Memorial Ground shortly after the grand opening, in a friendly against Northfleet, but the attendance was just 200 – a poor showing for a ground that the secretary described as being 'good enough to hold the English Cup final'. Disappointing support was something the Irons were growing used to. Before the 1897–98 season began, Taylor made a plea for support in the *Thames Iron Works Gazette*, expressing his disappointment that so few men from the Iron Works attended matches. But the club could hardly expect to be well supported by Iron Works employees when its path to professionalism was taking it ever further from any notion of a works team. Workers could still become members of the club at a cost of 2s 6d (12½p). Members were allowed to attend training on Tuesday and Thursday evenings and could take part in practice matches, but there was no suggestion that they would be considered for a place in the team.

Ambitious Irons

Despite this lack of support, the Irons maintained their grand ambitions and professional outlook. Six new players were signed for the 1897–98 season, and the committee took the bold step of insuring players against loss of earnings resulting from injuries. The Irons were also sporting a new kit when they kicked off their first season at the Memorial Ground. The new colours were Royal Cambridge blue shirts, white knickers, and red cap, belt and stockings. The *Thames Iron Works Gazette* commented that, when the new colours were worn on the field the 'contrast supplied by the delightful green turf is very pleasing.'

The Irons' results were also pleasing, and by November the East Londoners topped the London League having won their first six games. The first FA Cup-tie played at the Memorial Ground brought a 3–0 victory over Redhill, but after beating Royal Engineers in the next round the Irons were eliminated by Southern League St Albans. With the London League now their focus, the Irons swept to the title losing just one game, their penultimate fixture against rivals Brentford. The skipper of the title-winning side was Walter Tranter, who represented the London League against the London Football Association alongside team-mate George Neil in December 1897.

There was no resting on laurels for the Irons. With the London League title not yet dry from the celebratory cham-

In 1897 a new stadium opened at Canning Town. The Memorial Ground was a multi-sport arena and had been paid for by Arnold Hills at a pesonal cost of £100,000. The Iron Works football team was one of a number of sporting associations to benefit from the ground. Cycling was, however, the most popular sport hosted by the Memorial Ground in the early days and, as a result, the grandstand (seen on the left of the picture) was positioned to give the best sight of the home straight.

pagne, the committee secured a place in the second division of the Southern League for the 1898–99 season. Elevation to the Southern League meant the club required an even more professional approach. But the team was still struggling to attract big crowds. The new ground was difficult to get to and had no obvious catchment area. All too often the committee was forced to go cap in hand to Arnold Hills. A letter to the *Thames Iron Works Gazette* from the club secretary summed up the situation: 'I regret to say that from a financial point of view it has been a hard struggle. We are much indebted to the kindness of our President, who from time to time has assisted us in paying our debts, but it is very discouraging to us to feel that we have little or no support form the Works and that among the many admirers of football in... Canning Town, so few attend our matches.'

A lack of support, however, would not get in the way of the committee's ambition to reach the first division of the Southern League at the first attempt. Although Walter Tranter remained as skipper, he was one of only three players who were retained from the victorious London League campaign. Twenty-seven new players were engaged, many of them professionals, as the club's links with the Iron Works became ever more distant.

The new players were attracted from far and wide – among them were four Scots and a Welshman. It was also a young team by modern standards, with an average age of around 22; nevertheless, the youthful Irons set about their task with no shortage of confidence, taking the East Londoners to their second championship in consecutive seasons. By the end of the campaign, such was the Irons' superiority that a report of a match in April noted that 'Moore [the goalkeeper] had so little to do that he often left his goal unprotected and played up with the forwards.' The Irons completed their fixtures nine points ahead of their nearest rivals, winning 19, drawing one and losing just two of their matches. To secure promotion the Irons would have to take on Sheppey in a Test Match. The first match ended in a 1–1 draw, but before a replay could be held it was decided to expand the top division and both teams were admitted.

Shift toward professionalism

All seemed to be well for the Hammers and, according to the club secretary, 'nothing succeeds like success'; but beneath the surface, arguments about professionalism still simmered. The committee and president remained diametrically opposed on this issue. In June of 1899, Arnold Hills disapprovingly told the *Thames Iron Works Gazette*: 'In the developing of our Clubs, I find an increasing number of professionals who do not belong to our community but are paid to represent us in their several capacities.' But despite these protestations, it was Hills' money that provided the committee with the necessary capital to invest in new players.

For the Irons' first season in the top flight of the Southern League, Hills made substantial funds available to the committee to spend on players. Among the new signings was full-back Syd King, who arrived from New Brompton. King was joined by three players from Spurs, one of whom was former England winger Tom Bradshaw.

The new season got off to a bad start with a defeat away to Reading, and deteriorated further after a 7–0 reverse against Tottenham Hotspur. The Irons were struggling and were beginning to find life difficult in such exalted company as Millwall, Spurs and Southampton. Problems on the field were compounded when, on Christmas Day, the Irons received the devastating news that Tom Bradshaw had died of consumption at the age of just 26. Things got no better for the Irons in the new year, and, when struggling Cowes and Brighton United withdrew from the League, the East Londoners were left exposed at the foot of the table. The Irons finished bottom, having won only eight of their 28 games and were forced to contest a Test Match against Fulham to determine their fate. A 5–1 victory against the West Londoners ensured the Irons retained their top-flight status.

Crowds were still unimpressive but, with expenses rising, the club was forced to increase ticket prices. In the last two years of the 19th century, season ticket prices doubled from five shillings (25p) to 10 shillings (50p), and, although the committee attempted to minimise any ill-feeling by introducing concessions for 'ladies' and 'boys', gates were dwindling. The club was still reliant upon the finances of Arnold Hills. But the president remained unhappy about the committee's increasingly professional outlook. A crisis was brewing, and something would soon have to give.

The first team to bear the name West Ham United. The club's competitive debut came in the Southern League against Gravesend in September 1900. Inside-forward Billy Grassam (front row, second from right) was to be the hero for the fledgling Hammers, striking four goals in a resounding 7–0 win.

1895-1918

West Ham United

In 1900 the Iron Works became a public company in order to raise capital. Hills was now accountable to shareholders and the works could no longer retain a loss-making football club. The decision was made that the Iron Works and the football team would part company.

At the end of June 1900, the Thames Iron Works Football Club resigned from the Southern League and was wound up. Within days, the club was reformed under the name West Ham United and was elected to take the place of the Iron Works in the Southern League. In order to finance the new club, West Ham United was registered as a limited company and 4,000 ten shilling (50p) shares were issued. Despite his misgivings about the club's professional outlook, Arnold Hills continued to provide financial backing. Hills encouraged others to invest in the club, pledging to buy one share for every one sold to anybody else. Shares sold slowly and by 1902 only 1,777 shares had been sold, so once again Hills' generosity had provided the club with a lifeline. It seems that despite West Ham United's Articles of Association explicitly stating that they would 'employ and pay professional footballers,' Hills' primary concern was that the local community should have a football team. To this end, the new team was allowed to stay on at the Memorial Ground at a favourable rent.

The new club's board was made up of the seven subscribers to the Articles of Association plus an engineer and two local businessmen. The new secretary was L.M. Bowen. All the directors were from the surrounding areas of Canning Town, West Ham and Essex. AGMs were to be held, at which a third of the board had to resign each year – though directors stepping down were allowed to stand for re-election. None of the directors were to receive payment or even compensation for their work on the board.

West Ham United kicked off their first match on 1 September 1900 at the Memorial Ground before more than 2,000 fans. The new team got off to a flying start, defeating Gravesend 7–0, with Scottish inside-right Billy Grassam scoring four. Grassam was one of a number of Scots who had joined West Ham United during the summer. The next game brought a defeat at the hands of near-rivals Millwall, and such inconsistency would dog the East Londoners during their first season. A victory the following week had the *East Ham Echo* purring that West Ham's football was of the 'clear and clean order'. But by the middle of October the same paper was reporting that 'it doesn't seem as if the Teetotallers are going to maintain the high opinion formed earlier in the season.' The end of the season saw the Hammers finish in a comfortable sixth place out of 15 teams – a major improvement over the Irons' performance the previous year.

'Syd King is West Ham and West Ham is Syd King,' wrote Scribo in the *East Ham Echo* on the eve of the 1923 Cup final. In 1902 King, his playing career cut short by injury, was appointed Hammers' Secretary-Manager and for the next 30 years he ran the club from top to bottom.

Paynter makes his mark

In November 1900, West Ham United made one of their most important signings when they took on 21-year-old former Victoria Swifts player Charlie Paynter. Already a regular visitor to the Memorial Ground, he would work as an unpaid assistant trainer alongside Abe Morris until succeeding Tom Robinson as trainer in 1912. Paynter, who quickly became a popular figure with both players and fans, brought many qualities to his job with the Hammers, but chief among them was his unrivalled knowledge of local football.

Paynter's arrival coincided with the start of West Ham United's first FA Cup campaign, which kicked-off with a 1–0 victory over Olympic in the third qualifying round. After defeating New Brompton 4–1 in the next round, the Hammers were drawn against local rivals Clapton. The first game against Clapton ended in a draw in front of more than 10,000 fans at the Memorial Ground. A Billy Grassam hat-trick in the replay, before another sizeable crowd, saw the Hammers progress to the intermediate round of the Cup where they faced first division Liverpool who would go on to win the League Championship that season.

A disappointing crowd of 6,000 attended to see the Merseysiders visit the Memorial Ground on 9 January 1901. Although West Ham United were reputed to be a strong defensive team, they could not recover from the setback of losing goalkeeper Craig to injury and they eventually conceded a goal described by the *Canning Town Record* as 'flukey and debatable'. A narrow defeat was an impressive result against one of the top teams in England, and the Hammers emerged with much credit, which is more than can be said for the Liverpool secretary whose administrative error had forced the Merseysiders to contest the tie in the first place – Liverpool should have received a bye to the first round of the Cup.

The most significant development during West Ham United's first season was the opening of a new railway link to the Memorial Ground. Access to the ground had always been awkward and was widely blamed for poor gates. Attendances of around 2,000 were typical, although crowds could rise to around 5,000 for local derbies against the likes of Tottenham Hotspur or Millwall. The new line had been built by the London, Southend and Tilbury Railway Company and provided a direct connection from Fenchurch Street. The first game to benefit from the new station was that against Luton Town on 9 February 1901. The Hammers won 2–0, but the crowd was disappointingly small. The following week the Hammers faced Spurs and, despite a downpour just before kick-off, a crowd of around 6,000 turned up. However, by the end of the season it became clear that, although the new station had given a small boost to attendances, it had not solved the problem completely.

Hammers reach crossroads

The next three seasons would bring little progress for the Hammers. A small profit in 1900–01 was followed by two loss-making seasons, requiring the club to run up an overdraft. Gate receipts were unpredictable, but even crowds like the 17,000 that attended a match in 1901 against Spurs (who that season became the last team from outside the Football League to win the FA Cup) could not compensate for regular attendances of less than 5,000. New players were still being signed, although most made little impact, and although players like Craig and MacEachrane were sold to League clubs the balance sheet maintained an unhealthy look.

On the field, the team seemed to have reached a plateau and after finishing fourth in 1901–02 they made little progress in the League and failed to make any impression in the FA Cup. Bill Jones did at least become the first West Ham United player to win a full cap when he represented Wales against England in 1902. The most progressive step taken during this period was the appointment of Syd King as secretary/manager, also in 1902. King was a charismatic man who had the complete trust of the board to run the playing side of the club. As secretary/manager he spent much of his time looking after the players, most of whom were considered to lack the necessary moral wherewithal to resist temptation. To this end, the club adopted a very hard line on misconduct, particularly drinking which was punished by a heavy fine.

Above: Charlie Paynter, or Uncle Charlie as he became affectionately known, joined West Ham United in 1900 as an unpaid assistant trainer. It was the start of a 50-year association with the Hammers that would see Swindon-born Paynter serve the club as trainer, coach, scout, masseur and manager.

Above: In 1904 West Ham United moved to a new ground adjacent to Green Street House (pictured above) at Upton Park. The move was an unprecedented success and helped put an end to Hammers' long-standing financial struggles.

The move to Upton Park

But King's problems of maintaining order amongst his players paled into insignificance when compared with the troubles that were brewing in the boardroom. Tension was still evident between Arnold Hills and other members of the board. Hills was disappointed that several men he had nominated as directors had been rejected by the board and he was losing patience with the club's professional direction. The rent for the Memorial Ground had been another cause of argument, and the club had been considering moving when Hills forced their hand by asking them to vacate the Memorial Ground at the end of April 1904. Hills also requested that the club move out of offices at the Iron Works. With four months to go until the start of a new season, West Ham United was thrown into turmoil. Although the club had been looking at several new grounds around the East End, they had made no more than tentative enquiries.

During the course of the 1903–04 season, the board had been alerted to the possibility of building a new ground on a plot of land adjacent to Green Street House at Upton Park. Now homeless, the club agreed to rent the field, which had previously been used to grow potatoes. But turning a vegetable garden into a ground fit for Southern League football was not going to be cheap. So, with the ink barely dry on the lease for the Boleyn Ground, a million penny collection scheme was instigated. The board also asked local brewers for their support – thus further alienating the teetotal Arnold Hills.

The problems of moving to a new ground were compounded by the fact that the club had retained only five first-team players and just one professional – Tommy Allison – from the previous season. According to some reports, these difficulties made it far from certain that the club would be able to retain its place in the Southern League. Fortunately, new players were signed and the ground – which had 2,000 seats and a total capacity of 20,000 – was finished in time for the 1904–05 season. Unlike the Memorial Ground, the new site was easily accessible with better rail and tram connections and was close to the suburb of West Ham and the towns of East Ham, Ilford, Stratford and Barking. It would now be possible for the Hammers to attract bigger crowds and in so doing rid themselves of both their overdraft and their reliance upon Arnold Hills' generosity. Before long it became apparent that the move to Upton Park would be the making of West Ham United.

The Hammers took their bow at the new Boleyn Ground on 1 September 1904 against local rivals Millwall. A crowd of 10,000 fans watched the new look Hammers run out 3–0 winners, with local youngster Billy Bridgeman getting the first goal at the new ground. After the game, the Millwall 'keeper, 'Tiny' Joyce, was so disappointed with his team's performance that he put his fist through a dressing room door.

Goals would be hard to come by for the early part of the Hammers' first season at the Boleyn Ground. But on 28 January 1905, a run of nine successive defeats was ended with a 6–2 home victory over Luton Town, outside-left Christopher Carrick registering a hat-trick. Another Hammer showing goalscoring form that season was George Hilsdon, who had arrived at the club after impressing Syd King in a Sunday League match. Hilsdon, a former schoolmate of Billy Bridgeman, made his Hammers debut as an 18-year-old, scor-

ing four goals in a Western League match against Bristol City. An ankle injury would keep the young forward out of the Hammers team for much of his first season at Upton Park, and after just 16 Southern League appearances and seven goals he was transferred to Chelsea. Hilsdon would go on to establish himself as one of the leading goalscorers of the day and an England international before returning to the Hammers in 1912.

Back in the Black

An inconsistent season on the pitch ended with the Hammers in a comfortable 11th position, winning nine of their 30 league games. More significantly, and despite the obvious expense of moving ground, the club had turned an £800 loss into a £400 profit. The Hammers had worked hard to gain the support of the local people and gate receipts had increased as a result. Arnold Hills remained the club's majority shareholder but he no longer took an active role in the running of the club. Local businessmen and politicians were invited onto the board, bringing with them a network of potential investors. Before long, the re-election of directors became a formality and the board began to enjoy continuity. The club's balance sheet would also remain in credit until the First World War. This regular profit enabled the club to pursue its ambition, and before long the Hammers' sights were set on a place in the Football League. To this end, the club purchased more than 30 new players between 1904 and 1907.

The 1905–06 West Ham United team, photographed in the grounds of the Boleyn Castle. From left to right, back row: S Hammond, A McCartney, G Kitchen, C Cotton, D Gardner. Middle row: William White (Chairman), E.S. King (Secretary-Manager), T Allison, H Hindle, F Piercy, L Jarvis, T Robinson (Trainer), C Paynter (Assistant Trainer). Front row: W Ford, H Winterhalder, S McAllister, C Mackie, G Hilsdon, W Bridgeman, H Wilkinson, L Watson, F Blackburn, A Winterhalder.

Left: Wapping-born Danny Shea was West Ham United's first goalscoring hero. Danny was Hammers' top scorer for five consecutive seasons between 1908–09 and 1912–13.

Progress toward the Hammers' nirvana of a place in the Football League was slow. Any application for election to the League would need to be supported by a good placing in the Southern League, but during the first decade of the 20th Century the East Londoners failed to mount a serious challenge. For the supporters of West Ham United, however, there remained much to cheer as the board brought together many excellent players. Leading scorer for three seasons from 1905–06 was school teacher and amateur Harry Stapley. But even the goalscoring of Stapley could not surpass the achievements of goalkeeper George Kitchen. Signed from Everton at the end of the 1904–05 season, Kitchen was one of the leading keepers in the country, but it was his goalscoring rather than his shot stopping that caught the imagination of the fans. Penalties were Kitchen's speciality and, during his career at Upton Park, he scored five including one against Swindon Town on his debut.

The draw for the FA Cup did Hammers few favours in the early years at the Boleyn Ground. Although the team no longer had to compete in the Cup's preliminary rounds, they were handed a tough tie away to Woolwich Arsenal in 1906. A 1–1 draw with the Gunners was an excellent result for the Southern League side, but with the hard work seemingly done the Hammers let their London rivals off the hook, losing 3–2 at Upton Park. The following season, the draw was no kinder, pairing the Hammers with Everton at home. A 2–1 defeat saw the Hammers eliminated, while the Merseysiders made their first step toward the Cup final.

Shea and Piercy

The Hammers had many skilful players during the early years at the Boleyn Ground, but perhaps lacked a matchwinner to give them a chance against the top teams from the Football League. A player of just such calibre was to arrive in 1907. Danny Shea had been playing local football with Manor Park Albion when he was spotted by Charlie Paynter. The *East Ham Echo* was quick to appreciate Shea's virtues, eulogising in January 1908 that he had the 'makings of a really first-class player. He possesses plenty of dash and spirit, and is an excellent shot.' Shea adapted well to the demands of first-class football and in two of his five seasons as a Southern League player he finished as the league's top scorer.

If Shea provided the guile up-front, the man providing the steel for the Hammers during the first decade of the 20th Century was unquestionably centre-half Frank Piercy. Signed from Middlesbrough in 1904, Piercy became both skipper and hard man in Syd King's team. Piercy's 'competitive' displays earned him the adulation of the Boleyn crowd but the wrath of the FA, particularly after clashes with opponents against Swindon in 1907 and Millwall in 1908. The Teesider would enjoy a long association with the Hammers, and was employed as assistant trainer after retiring from playing in 1912, a position he held until his premature death in 1931. Piercy's commitment was never more clearly demonstrated than in 1908 when he took over in goal for an FA Cup tie against League Champions Newcastle United at St James' Park. Defeat was inevitable, but Piercy's endeavours restricted the Geordies' winning margin to just two goals.

Changing times

With gate receipts steadily rising, the Hammers continued to improve their playing squad, and among the new intake for the 1908–09 season was winger Herbert Ashton. A lightweight player who was nicknamed Tiddler, Ashton's frame belied a strong, competitive streak that would see him set a Hammers record for appearances in the tough environment of the Southern League between 1908 and 1915. The spring of 1908 also saw a local schoolboy forward catching the headlines.

Syd Puddefoot's hat-trick for Park School in the West Ham School's Cup final had served notice of a prodigious talent, and by 1913 he would be a regular in the Hammers first team.

Jack Foster, another of the new arrivals at Upton Park in the summer of 1908, got off to a scoring start on his debut against QPR in the first game of the season. QPR later provided the opposition for Hammers in the first round of the FA Cup. A 0–0 draw in West London brought Rangers to the Boleyn Ground where they were eliminated by a Danny Shea goal. The Hammers' reward was a tie away to Football League club Leeds City. A 31,000 crowd, Elland Road's biggest of the season, watched in disbelief as the Hammers held the Yorkshiremen to a 1–1 draw and took the tie back to the East End. Safely back in Upton Park, Danny Shea set to work on Leeds, striking a late equaliser and then firing home the winner in extra-time. Next up for the Hammers were Newcastle United, currently flying high in the First Division and on their way to a third Championship in five seasons. The Hammers, enjoying home advantage, managed to hold the Geordies to a 0–0 draw before more than 17,000 fans. The replay at St James' Park is reported to have been a classic encounter. The Hammers went behind to a penalty, equalising shortly afterwards through Shea, and were denied a giant killing when Anderson struck a late winner for the Geordies. Such fine fare in the Cup left the Hammers with little taste for the plain flavours of the Southern League and, with no away wins all season, the Eastenders finished the campaign in 17th place.

The 1909–10 season saw the arrival of the usual quota of new players, but the most significant change was in the boardroom. After three chairman in nine years, William White was elected chair of West Ham United in 1909. White, a barge builder, had been elected to the board in 1903. He would remain in office until his death in 1935, providing the club with much needed stability at boardroom level.

Above: In 1909 barge builder W.F. White was elected West Ham United Chairman. White, who had served on the Hammers board since 1903, enjoyed a successful 26-year tenure.

Cup tie specialists

On the pitch, the Hammers' attacking style was perfect for Cup football but was a disappointment in the league. A record of 69 league goals would equal that of Southern League Champions Brighton, but with 56 goals conceded Syd King's team were confined to mid-table, ending the season ninth out of 22 teams. However, the new chairman would no doubt have been more than happy with the Hammers' Cup exploits in 1909–10 which ensured that the club's finances retained their healthy glow.

The 1910 FA Cup campaign began disappointingly. A 1–1 draw against Carlisle United was far from the goal feast anticipated by most of the 11,000 fans inside the Boleyn Ground. But, with the resultant replay switched to Upton Park after the Cumbrians' decided to trade home advantage for a bigger gate, a crowd of 7,000, paying gate receipts of £241, watched the Hammers show their true form to record a 5–0 victory. The reward for Syd King and his team was a trip to the Black Country to take on Second Division Wolverhampton Wanderers at Molineux. During this era, it was the fashion for teams to travel away from home to prepare for Cup-ties the week before the match, and the Hammers followed the trend, heading for Droitwich. Wanderers were considered firm favourites, fielding ten of the 11 who had won the Cup two years before, and very few pundits gave Hammers a chance of victory. But the Londoners turned form on its head and ran out comfortable 5–1 victors. The *Sportsman* described the Hammers as 'unstoppable' and paid particular tribute to Danny Shea, who registered a hat-trick. The *Daily News* declared that 'West Ham's success constitutes the club's best achievement of their career.'

An away tie against QPR followed victory over the Wolves. West Ham stayed at home to prepare, but arranged a varied programme of relaxing events and excursions which included a day trip to Epping Forest and a visit to hot brine baths in Southend. Hammers were the underdogs once more, having already lost to Rangers in the League, and the *Daily News* correspondent predicted that the Eastenders would have to 'beat a retreat at Park

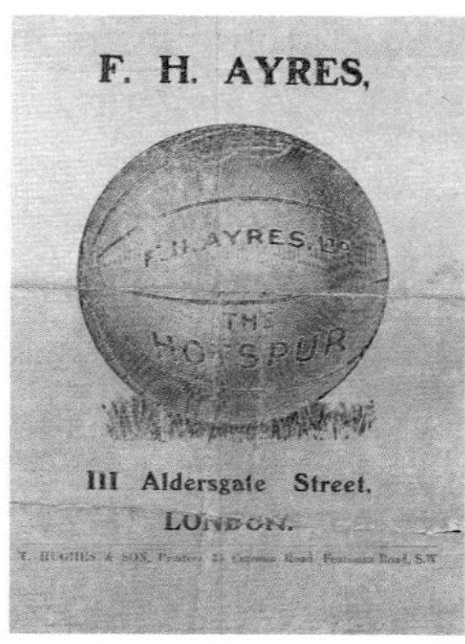

Above and right: *The Hotspur* from February 1909 included a song entitled 'Why Should Syd King's boys not beat the Tynesiders'. This encouraging ditty had been composed by Rhymster ahead of an FA Cup tie against the Magpies at Upton Park, but it failed to have the desired effect and after a 0–0 draw Hammers lost the replay 2–1 at St James' Park.

ENGLISH CUP TIE at WEST HAM.

NEWCASTLE v. WEST HAM,

FEBRUARY 20th, 1909.

Why should SYD KING'S BOYS not beat the Tynesiders.

How will it end ; is the general enquiry,
Will your prime favorites, Syd, "go all the way,"
Champions are they, lionhearted and wiry,
Ready for action, determined to "stay,"
Demons for trying, where'er they may be,
That is the local brigade to a T.

Here comes the "Geordies" as keen as they make 'em,
Down from the banks of historic old Tyne,
Stamp'd with a zeal that will never forsake 'em,
Men, who in one single object combine,
Still in this tussle, I'm tempted to say,
Newcastle won't have it all their own way.

Gird on your armour, boys, London confides in you,
Stand like the brave, with your face to the foe,
Strong in our confidence, still it abides in you,
This we desire to let the world know.
Go for your rivals again and again
And if you're vanquished, admit it, like men.

Strong are your foe, they're a clan well worth whacking,
You too, can boast eleven good men and true,
England will find 'tis not courage you're lacking,
Aim at the goal, my boys, keep it in view,
For full ninety minutes keep pegging in,
Remember 'tis goals wins the struggle—not din—

A.C., *Cricket Rhymster.*

Mr. Frank Matthews, BONE SETTER,
1 Melcombe Place, Dorset Square, N.W.
Specialist in the Treatment of Sprains, Displaced Joints, Injuries to Bones, Tendons and Joints, Rheumatism, Spinal Injuries, Gout, Paralysis, Nervous Disorders, and all forms of Lameness supposed to be incurable.
Book of Marvellous Cures on Application.

Spring Blinds, Roller Shutters, Tents, Flags & Tarpaulins. CHEAPEST & BEST HOUSE
Write for Terms to—
J. DEAN, Cromwell Works PUTNEY, S.W.
Telephones:—
251 Battersea. 254 Putney. 89 Finchley
5827 Central Manchester.
BRANCHES:—
96 High Street, Putney. 89 Aston Street, Birmingham. High Street, North Finchley. 316 Stretford Street, Manchester.

Royal'. A crowd of 31,000, paying receipts of £904, attended the match, and saw Hammers take a well deserved lead through Webb after good work from Shea. However, a dubious equaliser from Rangers' amateur centre-forward Steer sent the game into a replay at Upton Park. Another big crowd attended the mid-week fixture and most were disappointed when, just as the two clubs were discussing venues for a second replay, Steer struck a dramatic late, extra-time winner. Although they had not made it through to the latter stages of the competition, the Hammers had established their Cup credentials.

Cup success may have enhanced the club's reputation, but the Hammers still needed to prove themselves in the Southern League to gain support for election to the Football League. An improved performance in 1910–11 saw Danny Shea net 24 goals as the Hammers finished fifth in the table. Another forward who enjoyed a memorable season was Poplar-born striker George Webb. Having previously represented the England amateur team, Webb became the first West Ham United player to win a full England cap when he played against Scotland in 1911. Strong and quick, with a good shot, Webb remained an amateur for his whole career, and consequently work commitments restricted him to just 62 appearances (32 goals) in three-and-a-half years with the Hammers.

Fortunately for the Upton Park faithful, West Ham United's progress in the Southern League had no adverse effect upon the team's Cup form in 1911. First Division Nottingham Forest were Hammers' opponents in the first round of the Cup. A 2–0 victory at the Boleyn Ground eliminated the Midlanders, but the draw for the second round was no kinder to Syd King's team who would once again face top-flight opposition, on this occasion Preston North End. George Webb was Hammers' hero against the Lilywhites, registering a hat-trick to send his team into the third round and most of the 13,000 crowd home happy. A home draw against Manchester United, England's top side, gave the Hammers the perfect opportunity to prove their mettle. A full house at the Boleyn Ground, requiring the gates to be shut long before kick-off, witnessed the greatest result thus far in the Hammers' short history. With two minutes remaining and the scores level at 1–1, left-winger Tommy Caldwell struck a winner to send the crowd into ecstasy. When the whistle blew for full-time, Caldwell was duly mobbed as the fans invaded the pitch.

The final instalment in the East London v Lancashire FA Cup sideshow was against Blackburn Rovers in the quarter-final. On this occasion, however, the dramatic winner would go against the Hammers as defensive lapses denied the Southern League team a place in the last four of the competition. Two goals from George Butcher had pegged back the First Division side to 2–2, but just as it looked as if the match was heading for a replay, Rovers again profited from some poor defending to strike a late

Above: In 1912 Tom Robinson retired from his post as First Team Trainer and, for his long service, was rewarded with a benefit match against Southern League rivals Queens Park Rangers. The 1s ticket shown here gave admission to either stand or enclosure.

Above: Cover of a season ticket from 1913–14. The inside of the ticket is shown below and reveals that it belonged to 'J Casey... Player'. Casey was a Liverpool-born outside left who made 74 Southern League appearances for the Hammers between 1912 and 1915.

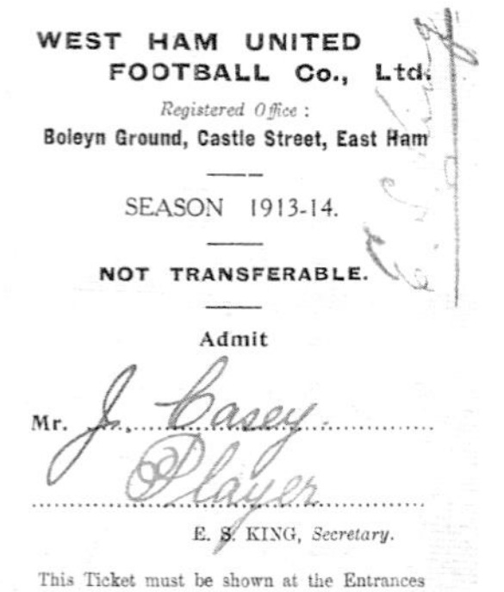

winner. For the board, at least, the disappointment of elimination from the Cup was tempered by the substantial income gained from four home ties against First Division opposition.

The move to Upton Park, allied with the Hammers' Cup adventures, had enabled the club to move onto a solid financial footing. In 1911, West Ham United's assets exceeded liabilities for the first time in the club's history. With Syd King's team acquitting themselves so well against Football League opposition in the FA Cup, nobody can have doubted that West Ham United would be able to raise themselves to Football League standard if elected. All that remained was for the board to improve the ground, and so from 1911 a concerted effort was made to develop the Boleyn Ground.

Shea sold for record fee

The 1911–12 season brought Hammers little success in either league or Cup, and saw Frank Piercy play his last game for the club. However, West Ham United would make a serious bid for the Southern League title during the following campaign. George Hilsdon had returned from Chelsea and Danny Shea was at the peak of his scoring power – notching 15 goals by 4 January. But Shea had been attracting interest from League clubs for some time, and with the board's priority now to develop the Boleyn Ground, Blackburn Rovers' world record bid of £2,000 was accepted in January 1913. With their talisman departed, Hammers faced a tricky away tie against West Bromwich Albion in the first round of the FA Cup. A 1–1 draw at the Hawthorns was followed by a draw at Upton Park, and so the teams faced a second replay at Stamford Bridge. Albion remained favourites, with the *Morning Leader* describing them as 'one of the fastest teams in their class', but two goals from Hilsdon and one from Denyer secured Hammers' passage to the second round.

Aston Villa away in the second round was not the draw that Hammers had hoped for. Villa were the top scorers in the Football League with 62 goals in 24 games, and though the Hammers were the top scorers in the Southern League they could not match the pedigree of the Midlanders who had won six League titles and four FA Cups. The *Morning Leader* attempted to find a grain of hope for Hammers prior to the game, declaring: 'If the ground were heavy and slippery it would be in favour of West Ham, whose forwards, light and fragile, can skip about much more effectively on a greasy surface.' We can only assume that the surface was hard and dry, as Villa ran out comfortable 5–0 victors and moved closer to their fifth FA Cup. Unfazed by the margin of defeat against Villa, the Hammers completed the rest of the season unbeaten and finished in third place, just two points behind Southern League champions Plymouth Argyle.

Ground developments gained momentum in 1913, with the club entering into contracts to build a new West Stand incorporating terracing in front and dressing rooms beneath the stand. West Ham United had enjoyed a vast improvement in support since moving to the Boleyn ground, and it was this enhancement in gate receipts that had paid for much of the ground development, a fact not wasted on the correspondent of the *Daily News and Leader*: 'Being fully aware of the constancy of their patrons the directors have made extensive ground improvements... these include a new grandstand, while the safety of the crowd in the neighbourhood of the south bank has been further ensured.'

Hammers hail new hero

On the field, however, there was great scepticism as to how well the team would fare in its first full season without Danny Shea. Alf Leafe had arrived from Sheffield United to try to fill the void left by Shea, but Hammers' problems remained in defence and not attack. A record of 61 goals scored was good enough, but a goals-against tally of 60 saw to it that Hammers failed to mount a challenge for the title, finishing sixth out of 20 teams. In the FA Cup, the Hammers kicked off with a memorable win over Chesterfield. An 8–1 victory over the Midland League team signalled the arrival of 18-year-old centre-forward Syd Puddefoot. The Bow-born striker scored five goals to set an FA Cup individual scoring record for the club. The *Athletic News* commented that 'Puddefoot, evidently born for the game, was far more sinister and dreadful than even the contorted spire under which they (Chesterfield) usually twist about.' Coincidentally, on the same day as the Chesterfield game, the Hammers reserves were also clocking up eight goals, in their fixture against Brentford. The reserves would win the South-Eastern League in 1913–14.

Victory over Chesterfield was followed by a home tie against Crystal Palace and again the salt baths at Southend were used as preparation. A crowd of 18,000 saw the Hammers run out 2–0 winners. Earlier in the season, Syd King's team had lost 2–1 to the Glaziers at Upton Park. The *Athletic News* put the improvement in Hammers' fortunes down to the colour of their shirts. When kits clashed (as they did when Palace and Hammers met) Southern League rules dictated that the home team had to change their shirts, but in the Cup it was the other way around so for the FA Cup-tie, Palace were forced into a white strip, while West Ham United stayed in their lucky claret and blue.

In the third round, Hammers faced Liverpool and Puddefoot was on the mark again, scoring Hammers' goal in a 1–1 draw, and though the youngster scored in the replay at Anfield, the home team scored five to take them through. Puddefoot went on to score 18 goals before being sidelined with an ankle injury.

Above: Syd Puddefoot made his Hammers debut in 1913, but it was following the club's election to the Football League after the First World War that he made his mark at Upton Park. The Bow-born striker was not only a great goalscorer but also an entertainer, and his assured skills brought him 60 goals in the first two seasons after the war. Puddy's talents, however, quickly came to the attention of bigger and richer clubs and in 1922 he was sold on to Falkirk for a record transfer fee of £5,000.

The emergence of Puddefoot had filled many Hammers fans with confidence, so it was with eager anticipation that West Ham United looked forward to the 1914–15 season. But, less than a month before the new football season was due to kick-off, football suddenly lost its importance. On 4 August 1914, Great Britain declared war on Germany. Few anticipated the carnage and human loss that would follow, many optimistically predicting a swift end to hostilities. After great debate, it was decided that the football season should go ahead as planned, and so it was that Hammers began their 15th and final season in the Southern League. Syd Puddefoot would continue his good form of the previous season, finishing top scorer with 15 goals as Hammers ended in fourth place.

League football suspended

For the remainder of the war, the FA Cup and national leagues were suspended and replaced with regional competitions. From 1915–16 to 1918–19 the Hammers would compete in the London Combination. Although up against five League sides, the Hammers flourished in the new competition. Success on the field, however, could not compensate for falling attendances and income. Costs inevitably had to be cut, particularly in view of the development work that had been started at the Boleyn Ground. A reduced rent was negotiated, but the highly valued manager Syd King was kept on, as was first-team trainer Charlie Paynter.

Throughout the war, players' contracts were suspended and they were free to play for who they liked. It was King's appreciation of this freedom of contract that brought Hammers much of their success during the war years. Though his approach was often criticised, King made good use of a number of high-profile guests, including Everton pair Chedgzoy and J MacConichie, Rangers' Andrew Cunningham, Blackburn's Percy Smith and Ted Hufton from Sheffield

West Ham United go on the attack during a Southern League match against Crystal Palace in 1914. The arrival of the First World War coincided with the formation of a team which at last looked fit for election to the Football League. The Hammers, however, would have to wait until 1919 to get their chance among English football's elite.

In 1919–20 the Hammers enjoyed their first season of League football. The photograph shown here was taken inside the Boleyn Ground and includes members of the board as well as both amateur and professional players. From left to right, back row: G F Davis (Director), G Handley (Director), H Igguldon (Director), W F White (Chairman), L Johnson (Vice-Chairman), JWY Cearns (Director), T Taylorson (Director), G F Fundell (Assistant Secretary), Unknown. Second row from back: E S King (Secretary), W Johnstone, W Cope, C Turner, G Kay, H Lane, P Griffiths, E Hufton, A Tirrell, J A Lee, J McCrae, A Fenwick, J Woodburn, Unknown. Third from back: C Paynter (Trainer), F Burton, D Smith, J Moyes, R Leafe, L Puddefoot, H Biggin, J Harris, J Tresadern, S Smith, F Murray, H Bradshaw. Front row: B Wolstenholme, H Ashton, E Worth, A Piggot, E Pettigan, T Green, R Morris, J Mackesy, J Thompson. Inset: Syd Puddefoot.

United. Several teams decided not to enter war competitions, preferring to wait for an early end to the war. Blackburn Rovers was one club to adopt this policy, and so in 1916 Danny Shea, now an England international, returned to Upton Park as a guest. The 1916–17 season gave King the opportunity to pair Shea with Puddefoot and the duo did not disappoint, registeranding 56 goals between them in Hammers' 40 games. Not surprisingly, West Ham United finished the season as champions. Puddefoot would later join the war effort, and though Hammers did not win the Combination title again, they remained among the competition's leading teams.

When war ended in 1918, Hammers' successes on the field were scant consolation for the lives of team-mates lost on the battlefield. Among the Hammers to die in action were Bill Kennedy, Fred Cannon, Frank Costello and Arthur Stallard.

Football would resume on a national level in September 1919. The new season would see the Football League expanded from 40 to 44 teams. West Ham United wasted little time in applying for election. Under chairman William White, the club's directors had worked hard to prepare the Hammers for League football and in March 1919 the case for election was put forward in the *Athletic News*. It was argued that West Ham United was a democratic club with shareholders drawn from the local area, that the club had a large and loyal fanbase and that the club's sound financial management had allowed the board to improve both the team and the ground. The arguments were heeded and, after a meeting in Manchester, West Ham United were elected to the Second Division of the Football League along with Coventry, Rotherham County and South Shields. A new challenge lay in wait.

During the first 30 years of the 20th century, West Ham United enjoyed the services of some of the greatest goalscorers ever to wear claret and blue. Three men in particular – Danny Shea, Syd Puddefoot and Vic Watson – went on to become Upton Park legends, but what is most remarkable is that in total they cost the club just £50.

Watson was the only one of the three for whom Hammers had to pay a transfer fee, while Shea and Puddefoot were products of East London's booming network of junior teams. The arrival of all three players, though, owed most to the astute judgment of Hammers' trainer and talent spotter Charlie Paynter.

Danny Shea 1908-13 and 1920-21
Born: Wapping, 1887
Southern League: 179 appearances (111 goals)
Football League: 16 appearances (1 goal)
England caps 1914: 2 appearances (0 goals)

Danny Shea was a winger, with local amateur side Manor Park Albion when he was spotted by Paynter, who quickly instigated a transfer for the Wapping-born forward. Danny was employed on the flanks during his early days at Upton Park, but it was following a move to inside-forward that he revealed his true talents. For five consecutive seasons Shea was Hammers' top goalscorer, and by the start of the 1912–13 season he had become one of football's most coveted stars. At that time West Ham United were still playing in the Southern League and, in an effort to further his international ambitions, Danny moved to League Champions Blackburn Rovers for a record transfer fee of £2,000. It proved a successful switch, and as well as making his senior debut for England he also picked up a League Champions medal during his time at Ewood Park. Shea would return to the Boleyn Ground in 1920, but after 16 games and one goal he moved on to Fulham before winding down his career with Coventry City and Clapton Orient.

Syd Puddefoot was not just a great goalscorer, he was also a great entertainer. Puddy was a favourite with the Upton Park crowd for almost ten years, and his trademark celebration – he would casually pick the ball from the net and hand it to the beaten goalkeeper – did much to endear him to Hammers fans. The Bow-born striker arrived at the Boleyn Ground in the same season that saw Danny Shea head for pastures new. However, Puddy was no instant success and it wasn't until his second season that he revealed his goalscoring expertise. He made up for lost time, though, and quickly established himself as the Hammers' most potent attacking weapon. In 1914 Syd set a Hammers FA Cup scoring record when he struck five times against Chesterfield. However, a year later football was put on hold because of the First World War. Puddy returned to Upton Park in 1919 and for the next three seasons was the club's top scorer. In 1922, the Hammers – who were counting the cost of lost revenue during the war years – accepted a record £5,000 bid for him from Scottish club Falkirk. The fans were incensed and accused the board of lacking ambition and of putting ground developments ahead of success on the field. Puddy was with Blackburn Rovers when he won his two England caps in 1926. Eventually he returned to West Ham United, but, after an absence of ten years, he was past his best and struggled to find the net.

Syd Puddefoot 1913-22 and 1932-33
Born: Bow, 1894
Southern League: 55 appearances (28 goals)
Football League: 125 appearances (67 goals)
England caps 1926: 2 appearances (0 goals)

No player has scored more goals for West Ham United than Victor Watson. To use a cliché, Watson was a 'natural born goalscorer'. Although neither the quickest nor the most skilful player, he made up for these deficiencies with a unique and priceless ability to find space in the penalty area.
The Cambridgeshire-born striker assumed the Hammers number nine shirt from Syd Puddefoot in 1922, and quickly made his mark. Watson, who retained an endearing modesty throughout his 14-year career in East London, would score the goals that took Hammers to promotion and the Cup final in the spring of 1923 and thereafter he was the star of Syd King's team. He was also something of a record breaker, and a six-goal haul against Leeds United in February 1929 was the first time a Hammers player had netted a double hat-trick in a First Division game. The following season, Vic continued to break records, striking 42 goals in 40 League matches, and he soon became a target for the so-called 'bigger clubs'. However, unlike his predecessors Shea and Puddefoot Vic Watson remained at the Boleyn Ground throughout his prime, and was in his late-30s when he finally left the club to play out his days on the south coast with Southampton in 1935.

Vic Watson 1921-35
Born: Cambridgeshire, 1897
Football League: 462 appearances (298 goals)
England caps 1923-30: 5 appearances (4 goals)

1895-1918

SEASON 1895-96
FRIENDLIES

THAMES IRONWORKS
All home games played at Hermit Road

Sep 7	(h)	Royal Ordnance	D	1-1
14	(h)	Dartford	W	4-0
28	(a)	Manor Park	W	8-0
Oct 5	(a)	Streatham	W	3-0
16	(a)	Old St Stephens	W	4-0
19	(h)	Erith United	L	1-2
Nov 2	(h)	Reading	L	2-3
9	(h)	Grenadier Guards	W	4-0
16	(h)	Charlton United	W	4-0
23	(h)	West Croydon	W	2-0
30	(h)	Coldstream Guards	W	3-1
Dec 7	(a)	Dartford	L	0-2
14	(a)	Millwall	L	0-6
16	(h)	Old St Stephens	W	3-1
21	(h)	Grenadier Guards	L	1-4
25	(h)	South West Ham	W	4-1
26	(h)	Wandsworth	W	5-1
28	(h)	Lewisham St Marys	W	7-1
Jan 4	(h)	Novacastrians	W	6-1
18	(h)	Upton Park	W	2-1
20	(h)	Barking Woodville	W	6-2
25	(h)	Civil Service	W	5-4
Feb 1	(h)	Manor Park	W	7-2
6	(h)	Royal Ordnance	W	2-1
8	(h)	Hornsey United	W	4-0
17	(h)	Vampires	L	1-3
22	(h)	St Lukes	W	1-0
29	(a)	Reading	L	2-4
Mar 7	(h)	Fulham	W	5-1
9	(h)	West Croydon	W	5-0
14	(a)	St Lukes	L	1-3
16	(h)	Woolwich Arsenal	L	3-5
20	(h)	West Bromwich Albion	L	2-4
28	(h)	Leyton	W	3-0
30	(h)	Royal Ordnance	L	0-4
Apr 3	(h)	St Lukes	D	1-1
4	(h)	Liverpool Casuals	W	3-1
6	(h)	Vampires	W	6-2
11	(h)	Commercial Athletic	W	3-1
18	(h)	South West Ham	W	3-4
25	(h)	Millwall Athletic	D	1-1

FA Cup

Oct 12	(a)	Chatham (Q1)	L	0-5

West Ham Charity Cup

Feb 15	(a)	Park Grove	W	1-0
Park Grove protested and forced a replay				
Mar 7	(a)	Park Grove	W	3-0
21	(a)	Barking	D	2-2
28	(a)	Barking	D	0-0
Apr 20	(a)	Barking	W	1-0

SEASON 1896-97
LONDON LEAGUE

THAMES IRONWORKS

Sep 19	(h)	Vampires	W	3-0
Oct 8	(h)	1st Scots Guards*	W	2-0
22	(a)	3rd Grenadier Guards	L	1-4
24	(a)	Crouch End	W	1-0
Nov 28	(a)	Ilford	D	2-2
Feb 27	(a)	Vampires	W	2-1
Mar 6	(h)	Ilford	W	3-2
13	(a)	Barking Woodville	L	0-1
Apr 1	(h)	3rd Grenadier Guards	L	0-5
3	(h)	Crouch End	W	4-1
8	(h)	Barking Woodville	D	1-1

	P	W	D	L	F	A	Pts
3rd Grenadier Gds	12	9	1	2	32	13	19
Thames Ironworks	12	7	2	3	17	17	16
Barking Woodville	12	6	3	3	20	11	15
Ilford	12	7	1	4	26	14	15
Crouch End	12	4	2	6	14	19	10
Vampires	12	3	1	8	10	28	7
London Welsh	12	0	2	10	9	26	2

*The 1st Scots Guards withdrew during the season and their record was deleted. London Welsh were suspended near the end of the season and as a result Thames Ironworks were awarded two wins.

FA Cup

Oct 10	(a)	Sheppey U	L	0-8

1st Qualifying round
West Ham Charity Cup

Mar 11	(h)	Manor Park	W	2-0
20	(n)	West Ham Garfield	L	0-1

London Senior Cup

Oct 17	(a)	West Norwood	W	2-1
Nov 7	(a)	Marcians	W	4-0
Jan 9	(h)	Wandsworth	W	3-1
16	(h)	Barking Woodville	W	2-0
30	(h)	Bromley	D	3-3
Feb 6	(a)	Bromley	D	2-2
13	(a)	Bromley	L	0-2

Essex Senior Cup

Dec 5	(a)	Leyton	L	2-3

SEASON 1897-98
LONDON LEAGUE

THAMES IRONWORKS
All home games played at Memorial Grounds

Sep 11	(h)	Brentford	W	1-0
Oct 2	(h)	Leyton	W	4-0
23	(a)	3rd Grenadier Guards	W	1-0
30	(a)	Leyton	W	3-1
Nov 13	(h)	Barking Woodville	W	3-0
Dec 2	(h)	2nd Grenadier Guards	W	5-1
11	(a)	Ilford	D	3-3
Jan 1	(h)	Ilford	W	4-0
8	(h)	Stanley	W	4-2
15	(h)	Bromley	W	7-3
Feb 26	(a)	Stanley	D	1-1
Mar 12	(a)	Barking Woodville	D	0-0
19	(a)	Bromley	W	5-1
Apr 2	(h)	3rd Grenadier Guards	W	3-1
23	(a)	Brentford	L	0-1
30	(a)	2nd Grenadier Guards	W	3-1

	P	W	D	L	F	A	Pts
Thames Ironworks	16	12	3	1	47	15	27
Brentford	16	12	2	2	43	17	26
Leyton	16	8	4	4	41	33	20
3rd Grenadier Gds	16	7	3	6	34	33	17
Ilford	16	5	7	4	33	25	17
Stanley	16	5	4	7	22	22	14
Barking Woodville	16	2	6	8	16	37	10
Bromley	16	4	2	10	20	49	10
2nd Grenadier Gds	16	0	3	13	17	42	3

FA Cup

Sep 18	(h)	Redhill	W	3-0
25	(h)	RE Training Battalion	W	2-1
Oct 16	(a)	St Albans	L	0-2

London Senior Cup

Nov 27	(a)	Novacastrians	W	1-0
Jan 15	(h)	2nd Grenadier Guards	W	*
*Walk-over after Guards withdrew				
22	(h)	Ilford	L	1-3

SEASON 1898-99
SOUTHERN LEAGUE

Sep 10	(a)	Shepherd's Bush	W	3-0
24	(h)	Brentford	W	3-1
Oct 8	(a)	Uxbridge	L	1-2
29	(a)	Wycombe	L	1-4
Nov 5	(h)	Shepherd's Bush	W	1-0
12	(a)	St Albans	W	4-1
26	(a)	Watford	D	0-0
Dec 3	(h)	Fulham	W	2-1
17	(h)	Watford	W	2-1
24	(a)	Chesham	W	3-0
31	(a)	Maidenhead	W	4-0
Jan 14	(h)	Wycombe	W	4-1
21	(a)	Wolverton	W	4-3
28	(h)	Chesham	W	8-1
Feb 11	(a)	Brentford	W	2-0
18	(h)	Uxbridge	W	4-0
Mar 4	(a)	Southall	W	2-0
11	(h)	St Albans	W	1-0
18	(h)	Wolverton	W	2-1
25	(h)	Southall	W	2-0
Apr 8	(a)	Fulham	W	1-0
15	(h)	Maidenhead	W	10-0

P	W	D	L	F	A	W	D	L	F	A	Pts	Pos
22	11	0	0	39	6	8	1	2	25	10	39	1st

FA Cup

1Q	Oct 1	(h)	RE Training Battn	W	2-0
2Q	15	(a)	Brighton U	D	0-0
R	19	(h)	Brighton U	L	1-4

Championship Decider (played at Millwall)

Apr 22	(n)	Cowes	W	3-1

Test Match (played at Chatham)

Apr 29	(n)	Sheppey U	D	1-1

SEASON 1899-1900
SOUTHERN LEAGUE

Sep 16	(a)	Reading	L	0-1
18	(h)	Chatham	W	4-0
Oct 7	(h)	Bedminster	W	1-0
Nov 4	(a)	Tottenham H	L	0-7
11	(h)	New Brompton	L	0-0
25	(h)	Swindon T	W	1-0
Dec 2	(a)	Bristol C	L	0-2
16	(a)	Southampton	L	1-3
23	(h)	Millwall	L	0-2
25	(a)	Queen's Park R	L	0-2
30	(h)	Queen's Park R	L	1-2
Jan 6	(a)	Chatham	L	1-3
13	(h)	Reading	L	0-1
15	(a)	Bristol R	L	1-1
20	(a)	Sheppey U	W	3-0
24	(a)	Gravesend	L	1-2
Feb 10	(a)	Bedminster	L	1-3
17	(h)	Bristol R	L	0-0
24	(a)	Portsmouth	L	0-2
Mar 10	(h)	Tottenham H	L	0-0
17	(a)	New Brompton	L	1-3
24	(h)	Gravesend	W	2-1
31	(a)	Swindon L	L	1-3
Apr 5	(h)	Portsmouth	L	2-4
7	(h)	Bristol C	L	0-0
9	(h)	Southampton	W	4-1
17	(h)	Sheppey U	W	4-2
28	(a)	Millwall	W	1-0

P	W	D	L	F	A	W	D	L	F	A	Pts	Pos
28	6	4	4	9	13	2	1	11	11	32	21	4th

FA Cup

P	Sep 23	(h)	Royal Engineers	W	6-0
1Q	30	(a)	Grays U	W	4-0
2Q	Oct 14	(h)	Sheppey U	W	4-2
3Q	28	(a)	Dartford	W	7-0
4Q	Nov 18	(a)	New Brompton	D	0-0
R	23	(h)	New Brompton	W	2-0
5Q	Dec 9	(h)	Millwall	L	1-2

Test Match (played at Tottenham)

Apr 30	(n)	Fulham	W	5-1

SEASON 1900-01
SOUTHERN LEAGUE

Sep 1	(h)	Gravesend	W	7-0
8	(a)	Millwall	L	1-3
15	(h)	Southampton	W	2-0
29	(h)	Bristol C	L	1-2
Oct 6	(a)	Swindon T	W	1-0
13	(h)	Watford	W	2-0
20	(a)	Luton T	L	0-2
27	(a)	Tottenham H	D	0-0
Nov 10	(a)	Portsmouth	L	2-3
24	(a)	Bristol R	L	0-2
Dec 1	(h)	Reading	W	1-0
15	(a)	Gravesend	D	0-0
29	(a)	Southampton	L	2-3
Jan 12	(a)	Bristol C	L	0-1
19	(h)	Swindon T	W	3-1
26	(a)	Watford	W	1-0
1Feb 9	(h)	Luton T	W	2-0
16	(h)	Tottenham H	L	1-4
23	(a)	Queen's Park R	W	2-0
Mar 2	(h)	Portsmouth	D	1-1
9	(a)	New Brompton	D	1-1
16	(h)	Bristol R	W	2-0
21	(h)	Millwall	W	1-0
23	(a)	Kettering T	W	1-0
30	(h)	Kettering T	D	1-1
Apr 5	(h)	Queen's Park R	W	2-1
10	(a)	Reading	L	1-3
20	(h)	New Brompton	W	2-0

P	W	D	L	F	A	W	D	L	F	A	Pts	Pos
28	10	2	2	28	10	4	3	7	12	18	33	6th

FA Cup

3Q	Nov 3	(h)	Olympic	W	1-0
4Q	17	(a)	New Brompton	D	1-1
R	21	(h)	New Brompton	W	4-1
5Q	Dec 8	(h)	Clapton O	D	1-1
R	12	(a)	Clapton O	W	3-2
1	Jan 5	(h)	Liverpool	L	0-1

SEASON 1901-02
SOUTHERN LEAGUE

Sep 7	(a)	Bristol R	W	2-0
14	(h)	Brentford	W	2-0
21	(a)	New Brompton	D	0-0
28	(h)	Kettering T	W	1-0
30	(h)	Wellingborough T	W	4-2
Oct 5	(a)	Northampton T	W	4-3
12	(h)	Luton T	W	4-1
19	(a)	Watford	D	0-0
26	(h)	Millwall	L	0-2
Nov 2	(h)	Tottenham H	L	0-1
9	(a)	Queen's Park R	L	1-2
23	(a)	Reading	L	0-3
Dec 7	(a)	Southampton	L	0-4
14	(h)	Swindon T	W	2-1
21	(h)	Bristol R	W	2-0
27	(a)	Wellingborough T	W	2-0
Jan 4	(h)	New Brompton	D	0-0
11	(a)	Kettering T	L	0-1
18	(h)	Northampton T	L	0-1
25	(a)	Luton T	W	3-0
Feb 1	(h)	Watford	W	3-2
8	(a)	Miliwall	D	1-1
15	(a)	Tottenham H	W	2-1
22	(h)	Queen's Park R	W	4-0
Mar 3	(a)	Brentford	W	2-0
8	(h)	Reading	W	2-1
15	(a)	Portsmouth	D	0-0
22	(h)	Southampton	W	2-1
29	(a)	Swindon T	W	1-0
Apr 12	(h)	Portsmouth	D	1-1

P	W	D	L	F	A	W	D	L	F	A	Pts	Pos
30	10	2	3	27	13	7	4	4	18	15	40	4th

FA Cup

3Q	Nov 2	(a)	Leyton	W	1-0
4Q	16	(h)	Grays	L	1-2

SEASON 1902-03
SOUTHERN LEAGUE

Sep 6	(h)	Reading	D	1-1
13	(a)	Queen's Park R	D	0-0
27	(a)	Wellingborough T	L	1-5
Oct 4	(h)	Bristol R	W	1-0
11	(a)	Northampton T	L	0-2
18	(h)	Watford	W	3-1
25	(a)	Brentford	W	3-0
Nov 1	(a)	Tottenham H	D	1-1
8	(h)	Millwall	L	0-3
Dec 6	(h)	Kettering T	D	1-1
20	(a)	Reading	L	0-6
25	(h)	Southampton	L	1-2
26	(a)	Portsmouth	L	0-2
27	(h)	Queen's Park R	W	2-0
Jan 10	(h)	Wellingborough T	W	3-0
17	(a)	Bristol R	D	1-1
24	(h)	Northampton T	W	3-2
31	(a)	Watford	L	1-2
Feb 7	(h)	Brentford	W	2-0
14	(h)	Tottenham H	W	1-0
Mar 7	(a)	New Brompton	L	0-2
14	(h)	Swindon T	D	1-1
23	(h)	New Brompton	D	1-1
28	(h)	Luton T	W	4-1
Apr 4	(a)	Swindon T	D	1-1
10	(h)	Portsmouth	D	1-1
13	(a)	Southampton	L	0-6
15	(a)	Kettering T	D	1-1
18	(a)	Luton T	L	0-4
25	(a)	Millwall	L	1-2

P	W	D	L	F	A	W	D	L	F	A	Pts	Pos
30	8	5	2	25	14	1	5	9	10	35	28	10th

FA Cup

1	Dec 13	(a)	Lincoln C	L	0-2

SEASON 1903-04
SOUTHERN LEAGUE

Sep 5	(a)	Millwall	L	2-4
7	(h)	Kettering T	W	4-1
12	(h)	Queen's Park R	W	1-0
19	(a)	Portsmouth A	L	0-2
24	(h)	Luton T	D	0-0
26	(h)	Reading	D	1-1
Oct 10	(h)	Bristol R	L	1-4
17	(a)	Brighton & HA	L	2-3
Nov 7	(h)	Brentford	L	0-1
21	(a)	Tottenham H	L	1-2
Dec 5	(a)	New Brompton	D	0-0
25	(h)	Southampton	W	2-1
26	(a)	Portsmouth	L	1-2
28	(h)	Fulham	W	2-0
Jan 2	(h)	Millwall	L	0-1
9	(a)	Queen's Park R	L	1-2
16	(h)	Plymouth A	D	1-1
30	(h)	Wellingborough T	W	4-1
Feb 6	(a)	Bristol R	L	0-4
13	(h)	Brighton & HA	W	5-0
27	(h)	Northampton T	W	2-0
Mar 2	(a)	Reading	L	0-1
5	(a)	Brentford	L	0-2
12	(a)	Swindon T	L	0-1
19	(h)	Tottenham H	L	0-2
26	(a)	Luton T	L	0-1
Apr 1	(h)	Portsmouth	W	3-0
2	(h)	New Brompton	D	0-0
4	(a)	Southampton	D	1-1
7	(a)	Northampton T	W	3-1
9	(a)	Kettering T	W	1-0
20	(a)	Wellingborough T	L	0-3
23	(a)	Fulham	D	1-1
30	(h)	SwindonT	L	0-1

P	W	D	L	F	A	W	D	L	F	A	Pts	Pos
34	8	4	5	26	14	2	3	12	13	30	27	12th

FA Cup

3Q	Oct 31	(h)	Brighton & HA	W	4-0
4Q	Nov 14	(a)	Clapton O	W	3-0
5Q	28	(a)	Chatham	W	5-0
1	Dec 12	(h)	Fulham	L	0-1

SEASON 1904-05
SOUTHERN LEAGUE

Sep 1	(h)	Millwall	W	3-0
3	(a)	Brentford	D	0-0

Syd Puddefoot challenges Crystal Palace's goalkeeper during a

Abbreviations:

Appearances (goals) refer to League games only

Figures shown as 2 etc. referto goals scored by individual players

* own-goal

	10	(h)	Queen's Park R	L	1-3
	17	(a)	Millwall	D	1-1
	24	(h)	Tottenham H	D	0-0
Oct	1	(a)	Luton T	W	2-0
	8	(h)	Swindon T	W	2-0
	15	(a)	New Brompton	L	0-3
	22	(h)	Wellingborough T	W	4-0
	29	(a)	Southampton	D	2-2
Nov	5	(h)	Fulham	D	0-4
	19	(h)	Plymouth A	W	2-0
	26	(h)	Bristol R	L	0-2
Dec	3	(a)	Reading	L	0-1
	17	(a)	Northampton T	L	0-1
	26	(a)	Portsrnouth	L	1-4
	27	(h)	Brighton & HA	L	0-1
	31	(h)	Brentford	L	0-1
Jan	7	(a)	Queen's Park R	L	0-1
	21	(a)	Tottenham H	L	0-1
	28	(h)	Luton T	W	6-2
Feb	4	(a)	Swindon T	D	3-3
	11	(h)	New Brompton	W	2-0
	18	(a)	Wellingborough T	L	0-3
	25	(h)	Southampton	W	2-1
Mar	11	(h)	Watford	W	2-0
	18	(a)	Plymouth A	L	0-2
	25	(a)	Brighton & HA	L	1-3
Apr	1	(h)	Reading	L	0-2
	8	(a)	Bristol R	D	2-2
	15	(h)	Northampton T	W	5-1
	17	(a)	Fulham	W	3-0
	21	(h)	Portsmouth	D	1-1
	25	(a)	Watford	W	3-0

P	W	D	L	F	A	W	D	L	F	A	Pts	Pos
34	9	3	5	30	15	3	5	9	18	27	32	11th

FA Cup

6Q	Dec 10	(h)	Brighton & HA	L	1-2

SEASON 1905-06
SOUTHERN LEAGUE

Sep	2	(h)	Swindon T	W	1-0
	9	(a)	Millwall	L	0-1
	16	(h)	Luton T	L	1-2
	23	(a)	Tottenham H	L	0-2
	30	(h)	Brentford	W	2-0
Oct	7	(a)	Norwich C	L	0-1
	14	(h)	Plymouth A	W	2-1
	21	(a)	Southampton	L	0-1
	28	(h)	Reading	L	2-3
Nov	4	(a)	Watford	L	1-3
	11	(h)	Brighton & HA	W	2-0
	18	(a)	Northampton T	L	1-2
	25	(a)	Fulham	L	0-1
Dec	2	(h)	Queen's Park R	W	2-0
	9	(a)	Bristol R	L	1-2
	16	(h)	New Brompton	W	1-0
	23	(h)	Portsmouth	W	1-0
	30	(a)	Swindon T	W	3-2
Jan	6	(h)	Millwall	W	1-0
	20	(a)	Luton T	D	1-1
	27	(h)	Tottenham H	L	0-1
Feb	10	(h)	Norwich C	W	6-1
	17	(a)	Plymouth A	L	2-4
	26	(h)	Southampton	W	3-0
Mar	3	(a)	Reading	L	1-2
	10	(h)	Watford	D	0-0
	17	(a)	Brighton & HA	D	0-0
	24	(h)	Northampton T	W	4-1
	31	(h)	Fulham	D	0-0
Apr	7	(a)	Queen's Park R	W	1-0
	14	(h)	Bristol R	W	2-0
	21	(a)	New Brompton	D	0-0
	23	(a)	Brentford	L	1-3
	28	(a)	Portsmouth	L	0-1

P	W	D	L	F	A	W	D	L	F	A	Pts	Pos
34	12	2	3	30	9	2	3	12	12	30	33	11th

FA Cup

1	Jan 13	(a)	W Arsenal	D	1-1
	18	(h)	W Arsenal	L	2-3

SEASON 1906-07
SOUTHERN LEAGUE

Sept	1	(a)	Tottenham H	W	2-1
	8	(h)	Swindon T	W	2-0
	15	(a)	Norwich C	L	2-3
	22	(h)	Luton T	W	5-1
	24	(a)	Bristol R	L	0-3
	29	(a)	Crystal P	D	1-1
Oct	6	(h)	Brentford	W	3-1
	13	(a)	Millwall	D	1-1
	15	(h)	Bristol R	L	0-1
	20	(h)	Leyton	W	3-0
	27	(a)	Portsmouth	L	3-4
Nov	3	(h)	New Brompton	D	1-1
	10	(a)	Plymouth A	D	0-0
	17	(h)	Brighton & HA	D	0-0
	27	(a)	Reading	D	2-2
Dec	1	(h)	Watford	D	1-1
	8	(a)	New Brompton	D	2-2
	22	(a)	Fulham	W	4-1
	25	(h)	Southampton	W	1-0
	29	(h)	Tottenham H	W	4-2
Jan	5	(a)	Swindon T	L	0-2
	19	(h)	Norwich C	W	3-1
	26	(a)	Luton T	D	1-1
Feb	9	(a)	Brentford	D	0-0
	16	(h)	Millwall	L	0-1
	23	(a)	Leyton	D	0-0
	25	(h)	Queen's Park R	W	2-1
Mar	2	(h)	Portsmouth	W	3-0
	7	(a)	Northampton T	D	0-0
	16	(h)	Plymouth A	D	0-0
	23	(a)	Brighton & HA	L	0-2
	25	(h)	Crystal P	D	1-1
	30	(h)	Reading	W	2-0
Apr	1	(a)	Southampton	W	3-2
	6	(a)	Watford	L	0-2
	13	(h)	Northampton T	W	4-0
	20	(a)	Queen's Park R	L	0-2
	27	(h)	Fulham	W	4-1

P	W	D	L	F	A	W	D	L	F	A	Pts	Pos
38	12	5	2	29	12	3	9	7	21	29	44	5th

FA Cup

1	Jan 12	(h) •	Blackpool	W	2-1
2	Feb 2	(h)	Everton	L	1-2

st-round tie at Upton Park in January 1914. The Hammers progressed as 2–0 winners, but were knocked out by Liverpool in the round three.

1895-1918

1895–1918

SEASON 1907-08
SOUTHERN LEAGUE

Date	Venue	Opponent	Res	Score
Sep 1	(h)	Swindon T	L	1-2
7	(h)	Tottenham H	D	1-1
14	(a)	Swindon T	D	1-1
21	(h)	Crystal P	W	1-0
28	(a)	Luton T	W	3-0
Oct 5	(h)	Brighton & HA	D	0-0
12	(a)	Portsmouth	W	2-0
19	(h)	Bradford	D	0-0
26	(a)	Millwall	L	0-1
Nov 2	(h)	Brentford	W	4-1
9	(a)	Bristol R	L	0-1
16	(h)	Leyton	L	0-2
23	(a)	Reading	W	1-0
30	(h)	Watford	W	2-0
Dec 7	(a)	Norwich C	D	1-1
14	(h)	Northampton T	D	1-1
21	(a)	Southampton	D	0-0
25	(h)	New Brompton	L	1-2
26	(h)	Queen's Park R	W	3-0
28	(h)	Plymouth A	D	1-1
Jan 4	(a)	Tottenham H	L	2-3
18	(a)	Crystal P	W	3-1
25	(h)	Luton T	W	1-0
Feb 8	(h)	Portsmouth	W	2-1
15	(a)	Bradford	W	1-0
22	(h)	Millwall	L	0-2
29	(a)	Brentford	L	0-4
Mar 7	(h)	Bristol R	D	0-0
14	(a)	Leyton	D	2-2
21	(h)	Reading	W	2-1
25	(a)	Brighton & HA	L	1-3
28	(a)	Watford	W	3-2
Apr 4	(h)	Norwich C	W	3-0
11	(a)	Northampton T	L	0-4
17	(a)	New Brompton	L	0-3
18	(h)	Southampton	W	4-2
20	(a)	Queen's Park R	L	0-4
25	(a)	Plymouth A	L	0-2

P	W	D	L	F	A	W	D	L	F	A	Pts	Pos
38	9	6	4	27	16	6	4	9	20	32	40	10th

FA Cup

Rd	Date	Venue	Opponent	Res	Score
1	Jan 11	(h)	Rotherham C	W	1-0
2	Feb 1	(a)	Newcastle U	L	0-2

SEASON 1908-09
SOUTHERN LEAGUE

Date	Venue	Opponent	Res	Score
Sep 1	(h)	Queen's Park R	W	2-0
5	(a)	Brighton & HA	L	2-3
12	(h)	Crystal P	L	0-1
19	(a)	Brentford	L	0-1
26	(h)	Luton T	W	4-0
30	(a)	Watford	L	1-2
Oct 3	(a)	Swindon T	L	0-3
10	(h)	Portsmouth	W	3-1
17	(a)	Queen's Park R	L	0-3
24	(h)	Northampton T	W	2-1
31	(a)	New Brompton	L	1-2
Nov 7	(h)	Millwall	W	1-0
14	(a)	Southend U	D	0-0
21	(h)	Coventry C	W	2-0
28	(a)	Bristol R	L	0-1
Dec 5	(a)	Plymouth A	L	0-2
12	(a)	Norwich C	L	3-6
19	(h)	Reading	W	2-1
25	(h)	Southampton	W	1-0
26	(a)	Leyton	L	0-1
28	(h)	Plymouth A	W	4-0
Jan 2	(h)	Brighton & HA	D	1-1
9	(a)	Crystal P	D	2-2
23	(h)	Brentford	W	3-0
30	(a)	Luton T	L	0-1
Feb 13	(a)	Portsmouth	L	1-4
27	(a)	Northampton T	L	0-6
Mar 6	(h)	New Brompton	L	0-1
8	(h)	Swindon T	W	4-2
13	(a)	Millwall	L	0-3
20	(h)	Southend U	W	4-0
27	(a)	Coventry C	L	1-3
Apr 1	(h)	Exeter C	W	4-1
3	(h)	Bristol R	L	0-2
9	(h)	Leyton	W	1-0
10	(h)	Watford	W	3-1
12	(a)	Southampton	D	2-2
17	(h)	Norwich C	W	2-1
21	(a)	Exeter C	L	0-1
24	(a)	Reading	L	0-1

P	W	D	L	F	A	W	D	L	F	A	Pts	Pos
40	16	1	3	43	13	0	3	17	13	47	36	17th

FA Cup

Rd	Date	Venue	Opponent	Res	Score
1	Jan 16	(a)	Queen's Park R	D	0-0
R	20	(h)	Queen's Park R	W	1-0
2	Feb 6	(a)	Leeds C	D	1-1
R	11	(h)	Leeds C	W	2-1
3	20	(h)	Newcastle U	D	0-0
R	24	(a)	Newcastle U	L	1-2

SEASON 1909-10
SOUTHERN LEAGUE

Date	Venue	Opponent	Res	Score
Sep 2	(h)	Exeter C	W	2-1
4	(a)	Norwich C	W	3-1
11	(h)	Brentford	W	3-2
13	(h)	Portsmouth	L	0-2
18	(a)	Covent C	D	2-2
25	(h)	Watford	W	2-0
29	(a)	Portsmouth	D	1-1
Oct 2	(a)	Reading	W	3-0
4	(h)	Bristol R	W	5-0
19	(h)	Southend U	D	0-0
16	(a)	Leyton	W	2-1
23	(h)	Plymouth A	W	4-1
25	(a)	Bristol R	L	0-1
30	(a)	Southampton	D	2-2
Nov 6	(h)	Croydon Com	W	5-1
13	(a)	Millwall	D	0-0
20	(a)	Plymouth A	D	0-0
27	(a)	Northampton T	L	1-3
Dec 4	(h)	Queen's Park R	L	1-2
11	(a)	Luton T	L	2-4
18	(h)	Swindon T	D	2-2
25	(h)	Brighton & HA	D	1-1
27	(a)	Brighton & HA	L	0-3
Jan 1	(h)	New Brompton	D	2-2
8	(h)	Norwich C	W	5-0
22	(a)	Brentford	D	0-0
29	(h)	Coventry C	W	3-2
Feb 12	(h)	Reading	D	1-1
26	(h)	Leyton	D	0-0
Mar 2	(a)	Watford	L	1-2
15	(a)	Exeter C	L	0-1
12	(h)	Southampton	D	1-1
19	(a)	Croydon Com	D	1-1
25	(h)	Crystal P	W	3-1
26	(h)	Millwall	L	1-2
28	(a)	Crystal P	W	4-2
29	(a)	Southend U	W	1-0
Ap r 2	(a)	New Brompton	L	0-1
9	(h)	Northampton T	W	1-0
16	(a)	Queen's Park R	D	3-3
23	(h)	Luton T	L	1-2
30	(a)	Swindon T	L	0-5

P	W	D	L	F	A	W	D	L	F	A	Pts	Pos
42	10	7	4	43	23	5	8	8	26	33	45	9th

FA Cup

Rd	Date	Venue	Opponent	Res	Score
1	Jan 15	(h)	Carlisle U	D	1-1
R	20	(h)	Carlisle U	W	5-0
2	Feb 5	(a)	Wolves	W	5-1
3	19	(a)	Queen's Park R	D	1-1
R	24	(h)	Queen's Park R	L	0-1

SEASON 1910-11
SOUTHERN LEAGUE

Date	Venue	Opponent	Res	Score
Sep 3	(h)	Southend U	D	3-3
10	(a)	Coventry C	L	0-3
12	(a)	Queen's Park R	W	2-0
17	(h)	New Brompton	W	2-0
24	(a)	Millwall	W	2-0
Oct 1	(h)	Queen's Park R	W	3-0
8	(a)	Norwich C	L	0-2
15	(a)	Luton T	D	1-1
22	(h)	Portsmouth	W	3-1
29	(a)	Northampton T	L	0-2
Nov 5	(h)	Brighton & HA	W	3-1
12	(a)	Exeter C	D	0-0
19	(h)	Swindon T	W	1-0
26	(a)	Bristol R	D	1-1
Dec 3	(h)	Crystal P	D	1-1
10	(a)	Brentford	L	0-3
17	(h)	Leyton	W	3-0
24	(a)	Watford	W	3-1
26	(h)	Plymouth A	W	4-0
27	(a)	Plymouth A	L	0-1
31	(a)	Southend U	W	6-0
Jan 7	(h)	Coventry C	D	1-1
21	(a)	New Brompton	D	1-1
28	(h)	Millwall	D	2-2
Feb 11	(h)	Norwich C	W	2-1
18	(h)	Luton T	W	2-0
Mar 4	(h)	Northampton T	L	1-2
18	(h)	Exeter C	W	4-1
25	(a)	Swindon T	L	1-4
29	(a)	Portsmouth	D	0-0
Apr 1	(h)	Bristol R	D	2-2
8	(a)	Crystal P	L	1-4
14	(h)	Southampton	W	4-1
15	(h)	Brentford	W	2-0
17	(a)	Southampton	W	1-0
22	(a)	Leyton	L	0-3
26	(a)	Brighton & RA	L	0-3
29	(h)	Watford	D	1-1

P	W	D	L	F	A	W	D	L	F	A	Pts	Pos
38	12	6	1	44	17	5	5	9	19	29	45	5th

FA Cup

Rd	Date	Venue	Opponent	Res	Score
1	Jan 14	(h)	Nottingham F	W	2-1
2	Feb 4	(h)	Preston NE	W	3-0
3	25	(h)	Manchester U	W	2-1
4	Mar 11	(h)	Blackburn R	L	2-3

SEASON 1911-12
SOUTHERN LEAGUE

Date	Venue	Opponent	Res	Score
Sep 2	(a)	Crystal P	L	0-1
9	(h)	Southampton	D	2-2
16	(a)	Plymouth A	D	0-0
23	(h)	Reading	W	5-0
30	(a)	Watford	L	0-2
Oct 7	(h)	New Brompton	D	0-0
14	(a)	Exeter C	D	3-3
21	(h)	Brentford	W	7-4
28	(a)	Queen's Park R	L	1-4
Nov 4	(h)	Millwall	W	2-1
11	(h)	Luton T	W	3-0
18	(a)	Bristol R	D	1-1
25	(h)	Swindon T	L	0-2
Dec 2	(a)	Northampton T	L	2-3
9	(h)	Brighton & HA	W	1-0
16	(a)	Stoke	L	3-4
23	(h)	Coventry C	L	0-1
25	(h)	Leyton	W	2-0
30	(h)	Crystal P	L	1-6
Jan 6	(a)	Southampton	W	2-1
20	(h)	Plymouth A	L	0-2
27	(a)	Reading	L	1-3
Feb 10	(a)	New Brompton	W	3-0
17	(h)	Exeter C	W	3-2
Mar 2	(h)	Queen's Park R	W	3-0
9	(a)	Millwall	L	1-5
11	(h)	Watford	L	1-3
16	(a)	Luton T	L	1-2
23	(h)	Bristol R	W	6-2
27	(a)	Brentford	W	2-1
Apr 5	(h)	Norwich C	w	4-0
6	(h)	Northampton T	L	0-2
8	(a)	Norwich C	D	2-2
9	(a)	Leyton	L	1-3
13	(a)	Brighton & HA	L	0-2
20	(h)	Stoke	D	0-0
22	(a)	Swindon T	L	1-3
27	(a)	Coventry C	L	0-2

P	W	D	L	F	A	W	D	L	F	A	Pts	Pos
38	10	3	6	40	27	3	4	12	24	42	33	13th

FA Cup

Rd	Date	Venue	Opponent	Res	Score
1	Jan 3	(h)	Gainsborough T	W	2-1
2	Feb 3	(a)	Middlesbrough	D	1-1
R	8	(h)	Middlesbrough	W	2-1
3	24	(h)	Swindon T	D	1-1
R	28	(a)	Swindon T	L	0-4

SEASON 1912-13
SOUTHERN LEAGUE

Date	Venue	Opponent	Res	Score
Sep 2	(h)	Exeter C	W	4-0
7	(h)	Coventry C	L	1-2
14	(a)	Watford	W	2-0
21	(h)	Merthyr T	D	1-1
28	(a)	Crystal P	D	1-1
Oct 5	(h)	Plymouth A	W	3-1
12	(a)	Southampton	W	3-1
19	(h)	Reading	L	1-2
26	(a)	Norwich C	L	0-2
30	(a)	Exeter C	D	0-0
Nov 2	(h)	Gillingham	W	4-0
9	(a)	Northampton T	L	3-4
16	(h)	Queen's Park R	W	1-0
23	(a)	Brentford	L	1-5
30	(h)	Millwall	D	1-1
Dec 7	(a)	Bristol R	L	1-2
14	(h)	Swindon T	W	4-1
21	(a)	Portsmouth	W	2-1
25	(h)	Stoke	W	5-0
26	(a)	Stoke	W	1-0
28	(a)	Coventry C	L	1-4
Jan 4	(b)	Watford	W	2-0
18	(a)	Merthyr T	L	2-6
25	(h)	Crystal P	D	1-1
Feb 8	(a)	Plymouth A	W	2-0
15	(h)	Southampton	D	1-1
Mar 1	(h)	Norwich C	W	2-1
8	(a)	Gillingham	D	2-2
15	(h)	Northampton T	D	0-0
21	(h)	Brighton & HA	D	1-1
22	(a)	Queen's Park R	W	1-0
24	(a)	Brighton & HA	D	0-0
29	(h)	Brentford	W	2-1
Apr 5	(a)	Millwall	W	3-1
12	(h)	Bristol R	W	3-1
19	(a)	Swindon T	D	1-1
23	(a)	Reading	D	1-1
26	(h)	Portsmouth	W	2-1

P	W	D	L	F	A	W	D	L	F	A	Pts	Pos
38	11	6	2	39	15	7	6	6	27	31	48	3rd

FA Cup

Rd	Date	Venue	Opponent	Res	Score
1	Jan 13	(a)	West Brom A	D	1-1
R	16	(h)	West Brom A	D	2-2
2R	22	(n*)	West Brom A	W	3-0
2	Feb 1	(a)	Aston Villa	L	0-5

*Played at Stamford Bridge.

SEASON 1913-14
SOUTHERN LEAGUE

Date	Venue	Opponent	Res	Score
Sep 1	(a)	Millwall	D	1-1
6	(h)	Swindon T	L	2-3
13	(a)	Bristol R	W	2-1
20	(h)	Merthyr T	W	3-1
27	(a)	Queen's Park R	D	2-2
Oct 4	(a)	Plymouth A	L	0-3
11	(h)	Southampton	W	5-1
18	(a)	Reading	L	0-2
25	h)	Crystal P	L	1-2
Nov 1	(a)	Coventry C	W	4-2
8	h)	Watford	D	1-1
15	(a)	Norwich C	L	0-1
22	(h)	Gillingham	W	3-1
29	(a)	Northampton T	D	0-0
Dec 6	(h	Southend U	L	0-1
13	a)	Brighton & A	W	1-0
20	(h)	Portsmouth	W	3-2
25	(h)	Exeter C	D	1-1
26	(a)	Exeter C	D	1-1
27	(a)	Swindon T	L	1-4
Jan 3	(h)	Bristol R	W	6-1
17	(a)	Merthyr T	W	2-1
24	(h)	Queen's Park R	W	4-1
Feb 7	(h)	Plymouth A	W	2-1
14	(a)	Southampton	W	3-2
28	(a)	Crystal P	W	2-1
Mar 7	(h)	Coventry C	W	1-0
21	(h)	Norwich C	D	1-1
23	(h)	Reading	D	0-0
28	(a)	Gillingham	L	1-3
Apr 1	(a)	Watford	L	0-6
4	(h)	Northampton T	D	1-1
10	(a)	Cardiff C	L	0-2
11	(a)	Southend U	D	1-1
13	(h)	Cardiff C	D	1-1
14	(h)	Millwall	W	3-2
18	(h)	Brighton & HA	D	1-1
25	(a)	Portsmouth	L	1-5

P	W	D	L	F	A	W	D	L	F	A	Pts	Pos
38	9	7	3	39	22	6	5	8	22	38	42	6th

FA Cup

Rd	Date	Venue	Opponent	Res	Score
1	Jan 10	(h)	Chesterfield	W	8-1
2	31	(h)	Crystal P	W	2-0
3	Feb 21	(h)	Liverpool	D	1-1
R	25	(a)	Liverpool	L	1-5

SEASON 1914-15
SOUTHERN LEAGUE

Date	Venue	Opponent	Res	Score
Se 1	(h)	Gillingham	W	2-1
5	(a)	Exeter C	L	1-3
9	(a)	Gillingham	L	0-4
12	(h)	Luton T	W	3-0
19	(a)	Portsmouth	L	1-3
26	(h)	Swindon T	D	1-1
Oct 3	(a)	Southend U	W	1-0
10	(h)	Queen's Park R	D	2-2
17	(a)	Millwall	L	1-2
24	(h)	Bristol R	W	4-1
31	(a)	Croydon Com	W	2-1
Nov 7	(h)	Reading	W	3-2
14	(a)	Southampton	L	1-3
21	(h)	Northampton T	W	1-0
28	(a)	Watford	W	1-0
Dec 5	(h)	Plymouth A	W	2-0
12	(h)	Crystal P	L	1-2
19	(a)	Norwich C	D	0-0
25	(a)	Brighton & HA	D	0-0
26	(h)	Brighton & HA	W	2-1
Jan 2	(h)	Exeter C	W	4-1
23	(h)	Portsmouth	W	4-3
30	(a)	Swindon T	D	1-1
Feb 6	(h)	Southend U	W	3-1
13	(a)	Queen's Park R	D	1-1
20	(h)	Millwall	D	1-1
27	(a)	Bristol R	L	0-1
Mar 6	(h)	Croydon Com	W	1-0
10	(a)	Luton T	W	2-1
13	(a)	Reading	L	1-3
20	(h)	Southampton	W	3-0
27	(a)	Northampton T	D	1-1
Apr 2	(h)	Cardiff C	W	2-1
3	(h)	Watford	W	2-0
5	(a)	Cardiff C	L	1-2
10	(a)	Plymouth A	L	0-1
17	(a)	Crystal P	L	1-2
24	(h)	Norwich C	D	1-1

P	W	D	L	F	A	W	D	L	F	A	Pts	Pos
38	14	4	1	42	18	4	5	10	16	29	45	4th

FA Cup

Rd	Date	Venue	Opponent	Res	Score
1	Jan 9	(h)	Newcastle U	D	2-2
R	16	(a)	Newcastle U	L	2-3

SEASON 1915-16
LONDON COMBINATION

Principal Tournament

Date	Venue	Opponent	Res	Score
Sep 4	(a)	Brentford	L	1-2
11	(h)	Chelsea	D	0-0
18	(h)	Tottenham H	D	1-1
25	(a)	Crystal P	L	0-2
Oct 2	(h)	Queen's Park R	W	2-1
9	(a)	Fulham	L	0-1
16	(h)	Clapton O	W	5-2
23	(a)	Watford	W	3-2
30	(h)	Millwall	W	2-1
Nov 6	(a)	Croydon	D	1-1
13	(h)	Brentford	W	4-1
20	(a)	Chelsea	L	2-5
27	(a)	Tottenham H	L	0-3
Dec 4	(h)	Crystal P	W	3-1
11	(a)	Queen's Park R	D	1-1
18	(h)	Fulham	L	2-3
25	(h)	Arsenal	W	8-2
27	(a)	Arsenal	L	2-3
Jan 1	(a)	Clapton O	W	2-1
8	(h)	Watford	W	5-1
15	(a)	Millwalll	L	0-1
22	(h)	Croydon	W	3-0

P	W	D	L	F	A	W	D	L	F	A	Pts	Pos
22	8	2	1	35	13	2	2	7	12	22	24	4th

Supplementary Tournament

Date	Venue	Opponent	Res	Score
Feb 5	(h)	Tottenham H	W	2-0
12	(a)	Millwall	L	0-1
19	(h)	Chelsea	W	2-0
Mar 4	(h)	Brentford	W	4-2
11	(a)	Reading	W	4-0
18	(h)	Millwall	W	2-1
25	(a)	Chelsea	L	0-4
Apr 1	(h)	Watford	D	2-2
8	(a)	Brentford	W	3-1
15	(h)	Reading	W	7-0
21	(a)	Clapton O	L	1-3
22	(h)	Clapton O	W	2-1
29	(a)	Tottenham H	D	1-1
May 6	(a)	Watford	W	2-0

P	W	D	L	F	A	W	D	L	F	A	Pts	Pos
14	6	1	0	21	6	3	1	3	11	10	20	2nd

SEASON 1916-17
LONDON COMBINATION

Date	Venue	Opponent	Res	Score
Sep 2	(h)	Arsenal	W	2-1
9	(a)	Luton T	W	4-3
16	(h)	Reading	W	5-1
23	(a)	Millwall	W	4-1
28	(a)	Tottenham H	W	2-1
30	(h)	Watford	D	2-2
Oct 7	(a)	Clapton O	W	4-0
14	(h)	Fulham	W	2-0
21	(a)	Queen's Park R	W	4-0
28	(a)	Southampton	L	0-3
Nov 4	(h)	Tottenham H	W	5-1
11	(a)	Crystal P	W	8-1
18	(h)	Brentford	W	4-0
25	(a)	Arsenal	W	2-0
Dec 2	(h)	Luton T	W	2-0
9	(a)	Portsmouth	W	2-1
23	(a)	Watford	W	3-1
25	(a)	Chelsea	D	1-1
26	(h)	Chelsea	W	2-0
30	(h)	Clapton O	W	6-1
Jan 6	(a)	Fulham	W	2-0
13	(h)	Queen's Park R	W	5-3
20	(h)	Southampton	D	1-1
27	(a)	Tottenham H	D	0-0
Feb 3	(h)	Crystal P	W	1-0
10	(a)	Brentford	D	1-1
17	(h)	Southampton	W	5-2
24	(a)	Clapton O	W	4-3
Mar 3	(a)	Crystal P	L	1-3
10	(h)	Arsenal	L	2-3
17	(a)	Portsmouth	W	5-2
24	(h)	Tottenham H	W	3-0
31	(a)	Southampton	W	2-1
Apr 6	(h)	Brentford	W	2-0
7	(h)	Clapton O	W	2-0
9	(a)	Brentford	W	2-1
10	(h)	Millwall	L	0-2
14	(h)	Crystal P	W	2-1
21	(a)	Arsenal	L	1-2
28	(h)	Portsmouth	W	5-2

P	W	D	L	F	A	W	D	L	F	A	Pts	Pos
40	16	2	2	58	20	14	3	3	52	25	65	1st

SEASON 1917-18
LONDON COMBINATION

Date	Venue	Opponent	Res	Score
Sep 1	(h)	Fulham	W	6-1
8	(a)	Queen's Park R	W	3-0
15	(h)	Clapton O	L	1-2
22	(a)	Millwall	W	3-2
29	(h)	Tottenham H	W	1-0
Oct 6	(a)	Chelsea	L	3-4
13	(h)	Brentford	W	8-3
20	(a)	Arsenal	D	2-2
27	(a)	Fulham	D	1-1
Nov 3	(h)	Queen's Park R	W	4-0
10	(a)	Clapton O	W	4-1
17	(h)	Millwall	D	0-0
24	(a)	Tottenham H	L	0-2
Dec 1	(h)	Chelsea	D	1-1
8	(a)	Brentford	L	2-3
15	(h)	Arsenal	W	3-2
22	(h)	Fulham	L	0-3
25	(h)	Crystal P	W	2-1
26	(a)	Crystal P	L	0-4
29	(a)	Queen's Park R	D	1-1
Jan 5	(h)	Clapton O	W	3-0
12	(a)	Millwall	W	1-0
19	(h)	Tottenham H	D	2-2
26	(a)	Chelsea	D	2-2
Feb 2	(h)	Brentford	W	7-2
9	(a)	Crystal P	D	1-1
16	(a)	Fulham	L	1-3
23	(h)	Queen's Park R	W	4-0
Mar 2	(a)	Clapton O	W	3-1
9	(h)	Millwall	W	2-0
16	(a)	Tottenham H	W	5-0
23	(h)	Chelsea	D	2-2
29	(h)	Arsenal	W	4-1
30	(a)	Brentford	W	7-3
Apr 1	(a)	Arsenal	W	3-1
6	(h)	Crystal P	W	11-0

P	W	D	L	F	A	W	D	L	F	A	Pts	Pos
36	12	4	2	61	20	8	5	5	42	31	49	2nd

SEASON 1918-19
LONDON COMBINATION

Date	Venue	Opponent	Res	Score
Sep 7	(a)	Brentford	L	0-2
14	(h)	Clapton O	W	3-1
21	(h)	Tottenham H	L	0-1
28	(a)	Chelsea	L	1-3
Oct 5	(h)	Arsenal	L	1-4
12	(a)	Crystal P	D	0-0
19	(h)	Queen's Park R	W	4-1
26	(a)	Fulham	D	2-2
Nov 2	(h)	Brentford	L	1-3
9	(a)	Clapton O	W	5-1
16	(a)	Tottenham H	W	4-1
23	(h)	Chelsea	W	3-1
30	(a)	Arsenal	W	2-0
Dec 7	(h)	Crystal P	W	2-0
14	(a)	Queen's Park R	L	0-1
21	(h)	Fulham	W	2-1
25	(a)	Millwall	W	2-0
26	(h)	Millwall	W	2-0
28	(a)	Brentford	L	1-3
Jan 4	(h)	Clapton O	W	7-0
11	(h)	Tottenham H	W	2-0
18	(a)	Chelsea	D	0-0
25	(h)	Arsenal	L	1-2
Feb 1	(a)	Crystal P	L	0-3
8	(h)	Queen's Park R	L	0-4
15	(a)	Millwall	D	2-2
22	(h)	Brentford	W	2-1
Mar 1	(a)	Clapton O	D	0-0
8	(a)	Tottenham H	W	1-0
15	(h)	Chelsea	D	3-3
22	(a)	Arsenal	L	2-3
29	(h)	Crystal P	L	1-3
Apr 5	(a)	Queen's Park R	W	3-1
12	(h)	Millwall	W	3-2
18	(a)	Fulham	D	1-1
21	(h)	Fulham	W	2-1

P	W	D	L	F	A	W	D	L	F	A	Pts	Pos
36	11	1	6	39	28	6	6	6	26	23	41	3rd

West Ham United at home to Reading in March 1914. The Southern League match ended in a 0-0 draw.

CHAPTER 2
RISE TO PROMINENCE

Syd King and Charlie Paynter can have had few worries as they prepared their team for its first taste of League football in the late summer of 1919. The Hammers had fared well in their regular encounters with League opposition during the war, and were confident that they could cope with the step up from the Southern League. The only real concern for West Ham United's management duo was that many of the guests who had appeared in claret and blue during the war were now returning to their previous clubs. However, King and Paynter wasted little time in re-signing several of their own pre-war stars, as well as adding a number of exciting new players to the Hammers staff.

The talismanic striker, Syd Puddefoot, was the most celebrated of the Upton Park returnees. Jack Tresadern – nicknamed the Mighty Atom – was another survivor of the Southern League days to arrive back in E13 in time for the Hammers' League debut. Popular full-back Frank Burton had re-signed too, and despite 'severe facial wounds' sustained during the war he went on to make 64 League appearances over the next two seasons. These familiar figures were joined by several new signings, one of whom would go on to establish himself as the cornerstone of the Hammers defence for many years to come. Manchester-born George Kay had guested for West Ham United during the war and had previously played for Bolton Wanderers. Kay, a tough uncompromising centre-half, had served in France and returned to England after being wounded and gassed. He would go on to make more than 200 League appearances for the Hammers.

Right: The caption on this cigarette card from the 1920s reads, 'Watson West Ham centre-forward about to score'. However, in the opinion of this caption-writer, a more accurate title might be 'Watson thwarted by defender'. But, whether he scored on this occasion or not, the inescapable fact is that Victor Watson was one of the greatest goalscorers ever to wear claret and blue. The Cambridge-born striker arrived at Upton Park in 1921 and was soon handed the difficult job of replacing outgoing hero Syd Puddefoot. It was a task which Vic took to with great gusto and his record of 298 League goals still stands.

Opposite: Billie the famous white horse clears the crowd from the pitch at Wembley in 1923.

Left: Jack Tresadern was a small, but extremely combative, wing-half who joined West Ham United from nearby Barking in 1913. Jack's all-action style of play earned him the nickname 'Mighty Atom', and by the early 1920s he had become a key player for Syd King's Hammers. His most successful season was 1922–23 when he played a key role in a campaign which ended with a Cup final appearance and promotion. Jack's efforts were further rewarded that season when he was called into the England team for matches against Scotland and Sweden.

The great Ted Hufton

The most significant new player to be signed ahead of the Hammers' League bow was unquestionably goalkeeper Ted Hufton. Joe Hughes had been the regular custodian around the time of Hufton's arrival, but after watching the new keeper in training, Hughes told Syd King that he couldn't compete with such an accomplished performer and asked to be put on the transfer list. Hughes was granted his wish and moved to Chelsea. Hufton – who had served in the Coldstream Guards – went on to establish himself as a Hammers legend, making more than 400 League appearances in a 13-year career at the Boleyn Ground.

Hammers fans, eager to get an early look at their refashioned team, attended the pre-season 'Trial' matches in large numbers. A typically optimistic report in the *East Ham Echo* of 29 August 1919 concluded its review of the Hammers' warm-up games with the assertion that: 'West Ham are going to have a team which ought to do well when they get together in full League trim.' The *Echo* also suggested that supporters would not be put off by increased admission prices. The war years had taken their toll on the club's coffers, but with the advent of League football the board had felt it prudent to invest in further stadium developments. By the time the League season kicked off, the Hammers had spent £4,000 on alterations and improvements to the ground. Most of the money was spent on moving the East stand back to allow standing room for nine more rows of spectators. The North Bank was also extended and raised. The net effect of all these developments was an increased capacity of around 30,000.

A crowd of 20,000 attended the opening fixture of the season at home to Lincoln City, and this impressive gate had one local reporter enthusing that 'the game is going to be more popular than ever this year'. A penalty gave the visitors the lead but the Hammers rallied in the second half and a clever header from Moyes earned them a well-deserved point. It would be the first and last goal scored by Moyes, a former Dundee player who had appeared as a wartime guest. The next match, the Hammers' first away fixture, brought a 7–0 thrashing at the hands of Barnsley. Fortunately, this result was no more than a blip, and in their remaining 40 League games, King's team conceded just 32 more goals. Goalkeeper Hufton deserved most credit for this impressive defensive record and his performances earned great acclaim. A review of a match at Leicester gave him a glowing report: 'It was Hufton's match all the time. He played a brilliant game saving shot after shot... He was quite on top of his form.'

During the early part of the 20th century East London had an unrivalled reputation for producing talented young footballers. East Ham's Central Park School was a particular soccer hot house, and between 1916 and 1919 it won the prestigious London Schools' Championship on four successive occasions. The undoubted hero of the 1919 success was Billy Williams (centre front row with largest display of medals). Williams would go on to become West Ham United's youngest ever professional when he joined the club in 1921 at the age of just 15.

Puddy hits form

At the other end of the field, Syd Puddefoot wasted no time recapturing his Southern League goalscoring touch, and after netting six times in the first eight games he finished the season as Hammers' top marksman with 21 goals in 39 outings. Puddy also became the first West Ham United player to score a hat-trick in a League game when he struck a triple against Port Vale in February 1920. The goal-grabbing exploits of the Hammers forward did not go unnoticed by the England selectors and during his first season of League football, Puddy was twice chosen for the national team. But, at the end of the season, the striker requested a transfer – a move which belies the commonly held notion that the players of this bygone era were loyal servants happy to play out their careers with their local clubs. Fortunately, Syd King managed to persuade his star player to sign a new deal which put him on top wages for the forthcoming season.

Hammers' first campaign in League football had been steady, offering just the occasional hint of the glories that were to come. Seventh place in the League was a respectable start, but the undoubted highlight for most Hammers' fans was the 2–1 victory over Spurs at Upton Park which was played out before a season's best crowd of 30,000 in March 1920. This victory went some way to avenging the FA Cup defeat inflicted by the North Londoners in the third round at White Hart Lane. The most disappointing result came in October 1919 when Hammers were eliminated from the London Challenge Cup by Southern League QPR. The *East Ham Echo* got rather carried away with its criticism of the Hammers' performance, stating: 'this defeat shows that Southern League football is of the standard which bears comparison with the Second League.' It seems probable that the *Echo* was overstating the case a little; the Hammers had merely had a bad day, with even Puddefoot having a quiet match. In fact, the *Echo*'s sports reporter took the unprecedented step of removing Puddy from his lofty pedestal to administer some rare criticism.

Despite the Hammers' Cup failures, the first season of League football had secured a much-needed profit after the lean years of the war. The bulk of this new-found wealth was spent on repairs to the Boleyn Ground, which was in a poor state after years of neglect during the war. Ground developments would become the board's priority throughout the inter-war period, as it was felt that the only sure route to the long-term success of the club was to develop a large, comfortable and modern stadium. With regard to the acquisition of new players, the board were happy to rely on the contacts, scouting and judgement of King and Paynter. There would be no expensive transfers.

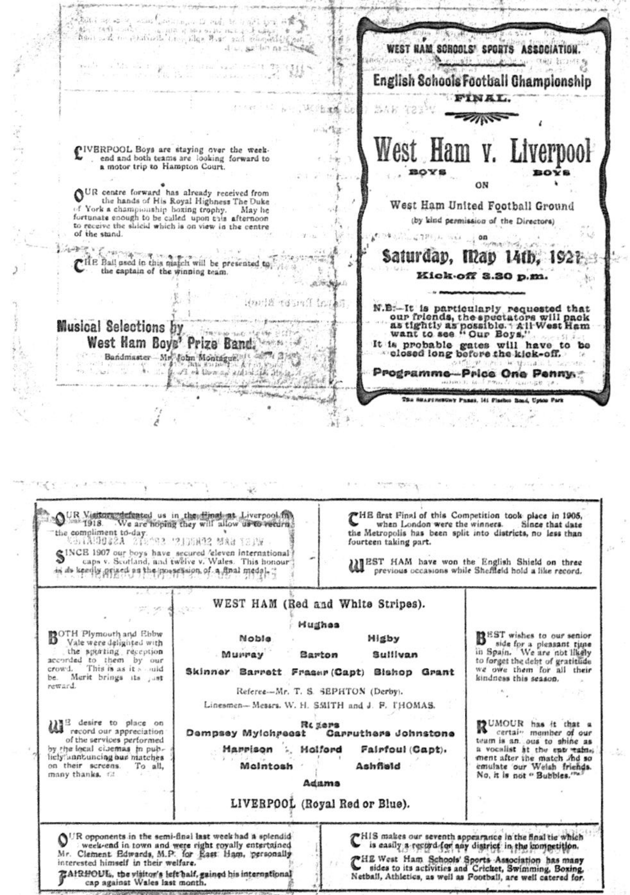

WEST HAM SCHOOLS' SPORTS ASSOCIATION.

English Schools Football Championship

FINAL.

West Ham v. Liverpool

BOYS BOYS

ON

West Ham United Football Ground

(by kind permission of the Directors)

on

Saturday, May 14th, 1921

Kick-off 3.30 p.m.

N.B.—It is particularly requested that our friends, the spectators will pack as tightly as possible. All West Ham want to see "Our Boys."

It is probable gates will have to be closed long before the kick-off.

Programme—Price One Penny.

The Shaftesbury Press, 141 Plashet Road, Upton Park

LIVERPOOL Boys are staying over the week-end and both teams are looking forward to a motor trip to Hampton Court.

OUR centre forward has already received from the hands of His Royal Highness The Duke of York a championship boxing trophy. May he fortunate enough to be called upon this afternoon to receive the shield which is on view in the centre of the stand.

THE Ball used in this match will be presented to the captain of the winning team.

Musical Selections by West Ham Boys' Prize Band.

Bandmaster—Mr. John Montague.

OUR Visitors defeated us in the Final at Liverpool in 1918. We are hoping they will allow us to return the compliment to-day.

SINCE 1907 our boys have secured eleven international caps v. Scotland, and twelve v. Wales. This honour is as keenly prized as the possession of a final medal.

THE first Final of this Competition took place in 1905, when London were the winners. Since that date the Metropolis has been split into districts, no less than fourteen taking part.

WEST HAM have won the English Shield on three previous occasions while Sheffield hold a like record.

BOTH Plymouth and Ebbw Vale were delighted with the sporting reception accorded to them by our crowd. This is as it should be. Merit brings its just reward.

WE desire to place on record our appreciation of the services performed by the local cinemas in publicly announcing our matches on their screens. To all, many thanks.

WEST HAM (Red and White Stripes).

Hughes

Noble Higby

Murray Barton Sullivan

Skinner Barrett Fraser (Capt) Bishop Grant

Referee—Mr. T. S. SEPHTON (Derby).

Linesmen—Messrs. W. H. SMITH and J. F. THOMAS.

Rogers

Dempsey Mylchreest Carruthers Johnstone

Harrison Holford Fairfoul (Capt).

McIntosh Ashfield

Adams

LIVERPOOL (Royal Red or Blue).

BEST wishes to our senior side for a pleasant time in Spain. We are not likely to forget the debt of gratitude we owe them for all their kindness this season.

RUMOUR has it that a certain member of our team is anxious to shine as a vocalist at the entertainment after the match and so emulate our Welsh friends. No, it is not "Bubbles."

OUR opponents in the semi-final last week had a splendid week-end in town and were right royally entertained. Mr. Clement Edwards, M.P. for East Ham, personally interested himself in their welfare.

FAIRFOUL, the visitor's left half, gained his international cap against Wales last month.

THIS makes our seventh appearance in the final tie which is easily a record for any district in the competition.

THE West Ham Schools' Sports Association has many sides to its activities and Cricket, Swimming, Boxing, Netball, Athletics, as well as Football, are well catered for.

A programme from the 1921 English Schools' Championship final between West Ham and Liverpool at Upton Park. The match, between district teams, was in theory nothing to do with West Ham United, but in reality the Hammers management would pay close attention to a team comprising the area's most talented young players. In 1921 the West Ham team included two names that would go on to enjoy long associations with the Upton Park club. Jim Barrett, a promising defender from West Ham, went on to play 467 games for the Hammers, while Bill Murray, with his curly hair, was the player who inspired the fans to adopt 'Bubbles' as the club's anthem.

Watson arrives for £50

One of a number of economy buys to arrive in time for the 1920–21 season was Cambridge-born striker Victor Watson, who was signed from Wellingborough in March 1920 for the princely sum of £50. The youngster, however, would have to wait for his chance in the first team. Puddefoot had kicked off the Hammers' second season of League football in sparkling form, delivering five goals in the first six games. Partnering Puddy in the Hammers' front line was returning hero Danny Shea who had arrived back at the Boleyn Ground after a war-disrupted seven-year spell at Blackburn Rovers. Sadly, the Shea of 1920 was a pale shadow of the powerful, all-action forward of the pre-war era, and in 16 League matches he added just one more strike to his Hammers' tally. Shea's final goal in claret and blue came in a match against Cardiff City in October, and two days later the old master watched as Watson, his rookie team-mate, struck the first of his 298 League goals. Watson enjoyed a four-match run in the first team during the Autumn of 1920, giving Hammers fans the opportunity to see the goalscoring legends of past, present and future play in the same forward line. But alas, the experiment did not work and December Shea had departed for Fulham and Watson had returned to the Hammers junior ranks to continue his football education.

Despite the wealth of attacking options at Syd King's disposal, his team struggled to find the net. A season's tally of 51 goals in 42 games would have been even more paltry had it not been boosted by heavy wins against Stockport (5–0) and Everton (7–0). Puddefoot finished as the division's top scorer with 29 and registered three hat-tricks in the League. At season's end, West Ham United occupied fifth place in the Second Division, a slight improvement over the previous campaign. More encouraging for the Hammers was the success of the West Ham junior team, which defeated Liverpool in the English Schools' Championships. It seemed that East London remained a good breeding ground for football talent, and among the victorious schoolboys was Jim Barrett, a player who would go on to replace George Kay as Hammers' centre-half.

Ruffell in – Puddy out

In the summer of 1921 a West Ham United squad toured Spain, and in the proceeding years these end-of-season European adventures became a regular feature on the club's calendar. At the other end of summer, the Trial matches were always eagerly anticipated by Hammers fans keen to catch an early viewing of any new signings. The usual intake of amateurs and budget signings was made, but among them were several top quality players. Right-back Billy Henderson joined from the Welsh club Aberdare and went on to make more than 150 League appearances. Henderson arrived at the same time as a prodigious 15-year-old forward, Billy Williams, who became the Hammers' youngest professional. But the most significant of Syd King's new boys for 1921–22 was Jimmy Ruffell, a winger from the Ilford Electricity Works team. Ruffell was arguably Syd King's greatest signing, and the pacy forward went on to become an England international before setting an appearance record for West Ham United which would stand for 37 years.

Whatever the quality of new signings made by King and Paynter, it was a familiar-looking Hammers line-up that began the 1921–22 season. Responsibility for goalscoring remained the preserve of Syd Puddefoot, although the potential of Vic Watson had become obvious and after the first few matches King endeavoured to perm his forward line to maximise the impact of his two born goalscorers. At the Boleyn Ground the Hammers were a match for all-comers and remained undefeated until March, but on their travels the Eastenders were vulnerable.

Fitful away form, however, could not deny the Hammers a place towards the top of the table, and at the season's halfway stage they were among the leading contenders for promotion. The FA Cup brought a three-match epic against Swansea in the third round which ended in a 1–0 defeat on Bristol City's heavily sanded pitch. The board had, no doubt, hoped for a lucrative run to the latter stages of the Cup, particularly as they had continued to invest in the ground. It became apparent in the early stages of 1922 that West Ham United was in need of an immediate cash injection. Syd Puddefoot would have to be sold. A £5,000 bid from Falkirk, with whom Puddy had played during the war, was too much to resist and the Hammers star headed north. This was a world record transfer fee, and meant that West Ham United became the first club to reach the £2,000 and £5,000 marks in selling players. Puddefoot had already notched 14 goals in his 26 games that season, and his departure left many Hammers fans feeling disgruntled and pessimistic about the team's chances of promotion. Vic Watson's good form went some way to pacifying them, and the youngster registered a goal in each of the three games after Puddefoot's transfer.

The Hammers managed to stay in the promotion race until the final weeks of the season, and the *East Ham Echo* of 14 April felt that, even with only six games to go, there was still a chance of elevation to the top division: 'West Ham since their famous centre-forward bade them good-bye, to join Falkirk... have made a very plucky fight of it, and their supporters still cling to the hope that they will bridge the gap, and beat Stoke for second place.' However, back-to-back defeats against struggling Blackpool ended the Hammers' ambition for First Division football and left them in fourth place at the end of the season.

King makes key signings

The disappointment of missing out on promotion was, however, short lived and by August it had been replaced by the warm glow of pre-season optimism. But even the most upbeat Hammers fan could not have predicted the glories that lay ahead in 1922–23. Supporters who wished to witness the events of this historic season were charged £4 4s plus 9s tax (£4.20 plus 45p) for a grandstand season ticket. Applications for tickets were to be made via Syd King in his capacity as club secretary, although it seems unlikely that King would have had time during pre-season to have dealt with enquiries personally. The secretary/manager had spent the summer tracking down his usual quota of amateurs and bargains, but had also invested in several more experienced players, most notably Billy Moore, an inside-forward from Sunderland, and Dick Richards, a Wales international inside-left from Wolves.

King's new signings, allied with Watson and Ruffell, gave the Hammers a formidable front line. However, in the opening fixtures West Ham United's form was unimpressive and it was only after they gained a 0–0 draw at home to Leeds in November that they finally moved into gear. By then, of course, the Hammers had fallen behind the Second Division leaders. But all was not lost, and at the turn of the year the Eastenders had closed the gap on second placed Leicester City to four points and were occupying seventh place. The West Ham United programme attributed Hammers' resurgence to a defensive change that had seen Jack Young and Billy Henderson take over the full-back positions.

Vic Watson had assumed Syd Puddefoot's mantle as the club's primary source of goals, registering 13 in 23 matches to the end of 1922, and he had been ably supported by new boy Billy Moore who was also finding the net with regularity. However, the most surprising feature of Hammers' upturn in form was that their best performances were reserved for away fixtures. By January, the Upton Park crowd was desperate to see their team show their best form at the Boleyn ground, so when Jack Tresadern struck a first-minute opener at home to

Coventry City, Hammers' fans eagerly awaited a goal feast against opposition that they had beaten 3–1 the previous week. Somewhat inevitably the score stayed unchanged for the remaining 89 minutes.

The pattern of home and away form persisted, and consecutive fixtures against Leicester City in February brought familiar results. A 2–2 draw at home against the Foxes left the *East Ham Echo* protesting that Hammers should have had both points after a performance described as 'their best game this year'. In the return at Filbert Street everything went right for the Hammers as they claimed their biggest victory of the season, scoring six without reply. West Ham United were now just three points behind the division's leading teams.

Cup contenders

Hammers' rise up the League table had been mirrored by good progress in the FA Cup. Syd King's team kicked off their Cup run away to Hull City, and within ten minutes they were two goals up. Hull pegged the visitors back, but with the score at 2–2, Vic Watson struck a 40th-minute winner to send the Hammers into the second round. The *East Ham Echo* was glowing in its praise after this triumph over fellow Second Division opponents with a reputation as 'Cup fighters', and declared: 'West Ham astonished the Doubting Thomases and pleased their supporters and friends mightily.' A replay was needed to dispose of Third Division Brighton and Hove Albion in the next round, but the Hammers had no such problem in the third round against another Third Division side, Plymouth Argyle, who were dispatched with a routine 2–0 win at the Boleyn Ground.

In March 1923 West Ham United entered the FA Cup fourth round draw for the first time in 12 years. And, just as they had done in the previous three rounds, Syd King's team avoided top-flight opposition, facing instead a trip to Second Division Southampton. The two teams had met twice in the League already that season, with the match at Upton Park ending in a draw, and Saints running out 2–0 victors in the return. A crowd of 22,000 packed into the Dell and saw Vic Watson open the scoring with a spectacular shot, only for Saints to snatch an equaliser and earn a replay in East London. The match at Upton Park also ended in a 1–1 draw, but a third game, this time at Villa Park, brought a conclusive result after inside-forward Brown slid home the only goal of the game to put Hammers into the semi-final.

The epic encounter against the Saints had left the Hammers with a fixture backlog in the League, and just five days to prepare for a Cup semi-final against Derby County. The Rams had disposed of Spurs in the competition's fourth round, and few pundits fancied Syd King's men to progress past the Midlanders when the teams met at Stamford Bridge on 24 March 1923. Derby had not conceded a goal thus far in their FA Cup campaign and had already defeated Hammers in the League, but within eight minutes County found themselves 2–0 down and were four goals behind before they managed to respond with a score of their own. A second Derby goal followed, but before the Rams could contemplate a fightback Ruffell scored the pick of the goals with a long-distance effort. It had been a breathtaking performance from a team playing its third game in an exhausting week and the press was unanimous in its praise. The *Daily Mail*'s review of the game appeared under the strapline 'How West Ham Electrified 50,000 Fans', and declared that 'never was a semi-final in modern times more emphatically won'.

The Hammers had earned a place in the FA Cup final for the first time in the club's history and would face First Division

Vic Watson employs the legitimate tactic of charging a goalkeeper. Watson was by no means a target man, but, like most players of the era, he was not averse to a physical challenge.

EDITORIAL TELEPHONES—CENTRAL 8000—PRIVATE EXCHANGE. LONDON, THE SUNDAY EXPRESS, MARCH 25, 1923.

West Ham to meet Bolton Wanderers in the

DERBY CITADEL RIDDLED BY QUICK FIRING

ELEVEN HAMMERS WITH THE SMILE THAT WON'T COME OFF.—Reading from left to right: Brown, Ruffell, Richards, Tresadern, Moore, Watson, Young, Henderson, Kay, Bishop, Hufton.

WATSON IN THE PICTURE.

LATEST SIPS FROM THE CUP.

Derby County went through four rounds without conceding a goal, but they could not resist the blows of the Hammers.

No fewer than 122,795 people watched the two games, and the gate money realised £13,440.

Old Trafford's gates were closed at 10.30 a.m., two hours before the advertised time of opening.

HOW WEST HAM ELECTRIFIED 50,000 FANS.

MASTER TACTICS IN A SEMI-FINAL TIE THAT CRUSHED DERBY COUNTY'S ASPIRATIONS.

LONDON CLUB FOR WEMBLEY.

West Ham United 5, Derby County 2.

NEVER has there been a greater surprise in a semi-final of the English Cup than that provided by West Ham United on Saturday at Stamford Bridge. They met Derby County, who had not lost a goal in the four previous rounds, but whose defence on this occasion was literally riddled. The result was a win for West Ham by five goals to two, but those who witnessed the game would not have been surprised if the margin in favour of the winners had been greater.

The match was a series of disasters for the midland club, relieved only in the middle of the second half, when the Hammers had established so pronounced a supremacy that nothing short of a miracle could save Derby from downfall. For three minutes there was a faint promise that the miracle would happen.

SEETHING EXCITEMENT.

With the United slackening their efforts when they were four goals in front, Derby twice found the net, and there was seething excitement. Would they make possible that which appeared impossible? West Ham soon answered the question by putting on another goal, and the passage of the East End club to Wembley Park was assured.

What is the explanation for the collapse of Derby? They had met in the road to the semi-final such well-known teams as Blackpool, Bristol City, The Wednesday, and Tottenham Hotspur. Not one of them could break down the Derby defence, but inside eight minutes of the start on Saturday West Ham had twice done so.

These early reverses must have had their effect on the County players, but if they did they did not betray it in their movements on the field. They showed a determination to repair their misfortunes that aroused the admiration of the unbiased onlooker, but the longer the game went on the more evident it became they had met their masters.

West Ham have never played finer football. It was intelligent, it was clever, and it was dashing. They were quick, they dribbled and swerved, and passed and ran as if the ball was to them a thing of life and obedient to their wishes. They were the master tacticians, and it was by their tactics that they gained, before ten minutes of the play had expired, a position which subsequently proved to be impregnable.

LIKE MACHINERY.

Every man always seemed to be in his place, and the manner in which the ball was flashed about from player to player—often without the man who parted from it taking the trouble to look—but with the assistance that his colleague was where he ought to be—suggested the well-assembled parts of a machine, all of which were in perfect working order.

Derby County were triers. It was not until victory for them was outside the region of practical football that they wavered, and then for a period West Ham toyed with them. They did a bit too much toying, as they lost a couple of goals through it, but there was never any danger that the County would get on terms, and never was a semi-final in modern times more emphatically won.

There has been a wider margin of goals, but not a game in which the superior tactics of one side against opponents who on form were at least their equals so effectually made the losers look second-raters. The fact is known to all who follow football; the explanation defies discovery.

Derby County on several previous occasions in the past have shown brilliant form up to the semi-final or final stages, and then have disappointed, but nobody expected they would be true to tradition on Saturday. The experts saw in them a team better armed at all points than West Ham, who had never had previous experience of the penultimate stage of the competition. But it was West Ham who played as if they were engaged in semi-final ties every week, and Derby County who were weak and uncertain.

Where the County were regarded as unbeatable they were unstable. Their defence, so much boomed, was their Achilles heel. With the defence shaky the forwards were patchy, and never did they show that brilliance that at Tottenham enabled them to defeat, on their merits, the premier Division club.

NO KICKING AND RUSHING.

With regard to West Ham, what need be said of them except that every player went to work as if his life depended on the result? Still, there was nothing suggesting random in their display. There was not a sign of the kick-and-rush order about what they did. They gave an exhibition of brainy football from goalkeeper to centre forward that few imagined them capable of giving.

The backs were always ready to deal with any dangerous situation that might develop; the half-backs were tenacious in defence and fine supporters in attack, and the forwards, led brilliantly by Watson, were a line good enough for any team in the country.

There were two goals in the first half, Brown driving the ball past Olney, at the end of five minutes, from a centre by Ruffell, and three minutes later, from a free kick taken by Tresadern, Moore kicked into the net with Olney lying on the ground.

The second half was three minutes old when Moore concluded a wonderful dribble by shooting the third goal, and Brown put his side

further ahead seventeen minutes later. After half an hour Henderson saw the ball screw back off his foot past Hufton, and then Moore (Derby) put on a second goal from Murphy's centre. Kay next made an opening for Ruffell, who finished the scoring with an unstoppable shot.

The gate was 50,795, and the takings £9,010.

Above and left: The press were unanimous in their praise for Syd King and his team after an emphatic 5–2 semi-final victory over Derby County in March 1923. Derby had been widely tipped to go through to the final, having kept clean sheets in all four of the previous rounds. 'West Ham have never played finer football. It was intelligent, it was clever, and it was dashing,' proclaimed the *Daily Mail*.

Right: After a delay of 44 minutes, the 1923 FA Cup final got underway. But with fans still lining, and often encroaching onto, the pitch the game was never likely to be a classic. The conditions would severely handicap West Ham United, whose game-plan relied upon the dribbling skills of Dick Richards and Jimmy Ruffell. Both wingers found themselves having to beat not only opponents but also supporters.

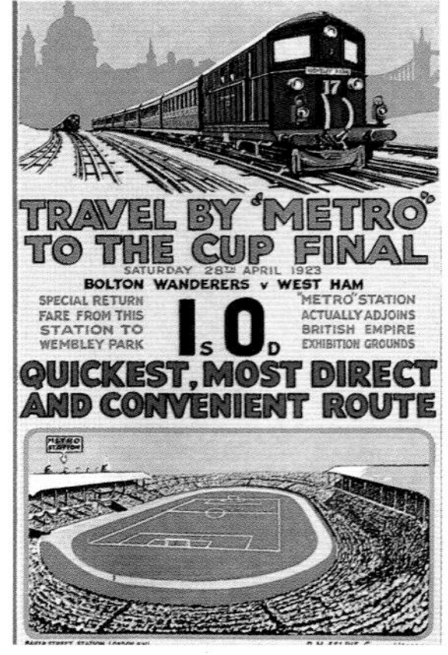

1919-31

Bolton Wanderers (their first top-flight opposition of the campaign) on 28 April at the new Wembley stadium, which had been constructed for the following year's British Empire Exhibition. But there would be no resting on laurels for West Ham United and in the five weeks between semi-final and final, Syd King's team had to cram in nine League games. Continued good form throughout the Easter fixtures brought the Hammers ten goals to keep them in the hunt for promotion. On Easter Monday the Hammers had travelled to Bury, and after going two goals behind, struck back with five of their own to stun the Shakers. The *East Ham Echo* reported that the game had been played before a number of Bolton scouts and declared that the Wanderers men 'went away profoundly impressed with the form of the Hammers, and cogitating on Bolton's chances against them in the final.'

Toward the end of April, the Hammers were faced with the awkward prospect of playing four League matches in eight days. Sandwiched between home and away fixtures against

WEST HAM'S
1923 WEMBLEY CUP FINAL SONG.

(To be sung to the refrain of "Till we meet again.")

There's a team that is true to its followers,
A team that have earned much renown,
They are here looking bright
In their Red, Blue and White
Worn by boys that are smartest in Town.

CHORUS.

All the while upon the field of play
Thousands cheer them gladly on their way;
Then you'll hear somebody say,
"Who can beat West Ham to-day"?
Every feat will leave a memory,
Every man will strive for victory.
So Kay! Here's luck – And bring the Cup
Back to London Town

They have taken a fancy to Wembley,
In fact, that is why they've come up;
But before home they go,
They mean England to know
That they really came here for the Cup.

CHORUS.

Extra Chorus to be sung when the lads have done the trick.

Now they've won it perhaps you'll understand
Why the lads are coming home so grand.
Now you'll hear all London say,
"None could beat West Ham to-day!"
Every feat will leave a memory,
Every man deserved the victory.
So Kay! Here's luck — You've brought the Cup
Back to London Town.

Fulham were difficult trips to Barnsley and Notts County. Despite the absence of Tresadern and Watson, who were on England duty, the sequence began with a 2–0 victory over Fulham which lifted Hammers to second place in the table. However, the trip to Barnsley ended with a first defeat in 15 matches and was followed by a reverse at Notts County two days later. It seemed the Hammers had lost form at the season's crucial point, but in the last match before the Cup final, Vic Watson struck a crucial winner at Craven Cottage to boost both confidence and promotion hopes.

Preparation for the Cup final consisted of the now-traditional trip to Southend to take the brine baths and a week of relaxation rather than exertion. Both teams were also invited to take a tour of the new stadium, and according to the *East Ham Echo*, the West Ham United players 'came to the unanimous and satisfactory conclusion that the green would suit them to a nicety'. Syd King's only major worry ahead of the final was Jimmy Ruffell, who had sustained a knee injury against Fulham in mid-April.

The Build-up

Syd King had become the focus of an unprecedented level of media exposure during the build up for the Cup final as journalists grew ever more preoccupied with the Hammers' bargain priced team. The team selected to contest the biggest match in the club's history had cost a mere £2,000. However, King believed they would be a match for their First Division opponents. The West Ham United manager told reporters: 'We have a level-headed lot of players who have not shown the least signs of kicking over the traces in spite of the hero-worship that has fallen to their lot... the directors with myself have every faith in the boys.'

Rival captains George Kay (West Ham United, left) and Joe Smith (Bolton Wanderers, right) in a nervous pose, before the 1923 Cup final.

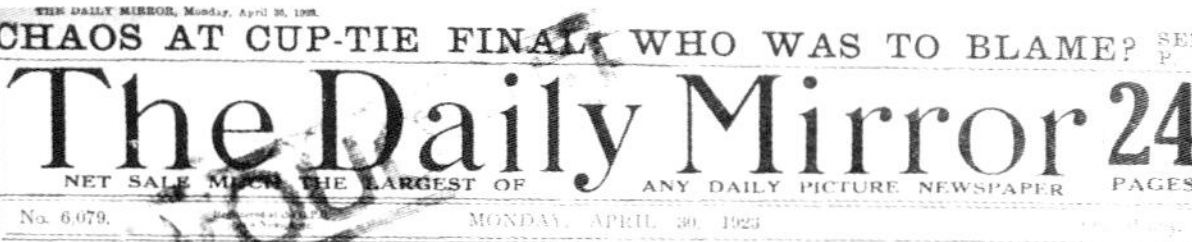

CHAOS AT CUP-TIE FINAL: WHO WAS TO BLAME? SEE P. 7

The Daily Mirror 24 PAGES

NET SALE MUCH THE LARGEST OF ANY DAILY PICTURE NEWSPAPER

POLICE v. CROWD: WEMBLEY'S FIRST CUP FINAL

The White Horse

In the days prior to the Cup final, posters around London began advertising the match and boasting that everybody was guaranteed a 'great view of the game' at the new stadium. Nobody was sure how much interest there would be for the first final played in suburban Wembley, although it seemed unlikely that demand would exceed space at the new arena. However, long before kick-off, and with supporters still arriving, it became apparent that the crowd was going to be greater than the stadium's 120,000 capacity. Panic began to spread as the fans inside realised that more and more spectators were flooding into an already full stadium. Eventually the gates were shut, but that did not put an end to the chaos, and the disappointed mob outside merely broke through the barriers and headed for any available space. Accounts from fans caught up in the mayhem describe a frightening scene with men climbing on one another and being crushed against iron railings in the shove to gain a vantage point. With nowhere else to go, many fans were forced to retreat from the crush of the terraces and head for the relative safety of the cinder track surrounding the pitch, or even the playing area itself.

There seemed little chance that the game would go ahead. But, in the words of one *East Ham Echo* reporter, 'then came the miracle. Half a dozen mounted policemen arrived on the scene, and working from the centre of the pitch by great efforts, filched a little more space from the crowd, which the cordon of police endeavoured to hold. ... But wonders of wonders was the work of an inspector on a dashing white horse. He rode here and there, everywhere, gaining a foot of ground now, and a yard then, the crowd giving way grudgingly.' The 'inspector' was, in fact, Constable G.A. Scorey, riding Billie, who became a legend of the FA Cup. By the time the King arrived to a rousing reception from the crowd just before 3pm, bedlam was slowly being replaced by a fragile order, with the fans on the pitch gradually being pushed back to form human touchlines.

When the match eventually got underway at 3.44pm, it was Bolton rather than West Ham United who adjusted more quickly

Squeak Plays Cricket: See Page 11

The Daily Mirror

NET SALE MUCH THE LARGEST OF ANY DAILY PICTURE NEWSPAPER

F.A. CUP FINAL PHOTOGRAPHS: SCENES ON AND AROUND THE FIELD OF PLAY

Right and top right: The 1923 Cup final was still dominating the news on the Monday after the game and *The Daily Mirror*, like most newspapers, devoted both front and back pages to telling the story of Wembley's first showpiece football match.

1919-31

to the unusual playing conditions. After just three minutes Wanderers took the lead, and though Hammers rallied with Watson missing a glorious chance to level, it was Bolton who finished the half the stronger, with J.R. Smith having a 'goal' disallowed for offside. In view of the discord on the terraces, the referee took the sensible step of omitting the half-time interval, and instead instructed the teams to turn around without delay. Eight minutes into the second period, the Cup final was all but over when Smith struck the Trotters' second goal. Many reasons and excuses were offered for Hammers' poor showing in their first major final, but in truth the Londoners had been beaten by opponents who adjusted more quickly to the bizarre circumstances surrounding the match. The Trotters' forwards had been more inventive and the Lancashire side's defence had also looked more resolute. Charlie Paynter blamed the pot-holes and divots left by fans and police horses prior to kick-off, but the Hammers' coach was also sporting enough to concede that his team had simply lost to the better team on the day.

Despite the disappointment of defeat, Hammers were not about to let their Cup final appearance pass without celebration. The illuminated tramcar (shown below) had been specially prepared and, after a dinner in Golders Green, transported the team to a civic reception at Canning Town.

Hammers pip Foxes

The disappointment of defeat, however, would not temper Hammers' celebrations and they returned to the East End to enjoy a civic reception and a tour through the streets in an illuminated tramcar. There was much talk of an appeal against the result, but after careful consideration West Ham United decided to let the matter rest. In any case, the club had to contend with the more pressing issue of promotion. Two days after the Cup final, Hammers were back in League action against The Wednesday in Sheffield. Promotion rivals Leicester had gone above West Ham United while the Londoners were engaged at Wembley, but a win at Wednesday would take Syd King's team to the top on goal average. Strikes from Brown and Watson did the trick and saw to it that Hammers took to the field in pole position for their final match of the season at home to second-placed Notts County. It could hardly be closer, with Hammers, County and Leicester all having 51 points, and only two to go up. Hammers needed just

a point to guarantee promotion and a win to make sure of the championship. But a tired Hammers eleven was frustrated by a hard-working County side who took a 1–0 lead. There seemed little chance of a Hammers' equaliser as the game entered its final phase with the home supporters musing over a season of near misses. And then, as hope was disappearing, came word of events in Bury to brighten the spirits of the crowd at the Boleyn Ground. Leicester had lost and Hammers were promoted as runners up to Notts County. Hammers' goal record was 63–38, while Leicester's was 65–44, so the Hammers' 6–0 defeat of Leicester earlier in the season was vital. Even 3–0 wouldn't have been enough.

W H U

WEST HAM UNITED FOOTBALL COMPANY, Ltd

Souvenir of the

DINNER

held at The "Princess Alice Hotel" Forest Gate, on Saturday, August 18th, 1923

TO COMMEMORATE Promotion to the First Division of the Football League and participation in the first Cup Final played on the Wembley Ground, 1923

Chairman . W. F. WHITE, Esq.

Above: Souvenir of the dinner, held at the Princess Alice Hotel in Forest Gate, commemorating promotion and participation in the 1923 Cup final.

Above, right: West Ham United's senior players and directors on the eve of the Club's First Division debut against Sunderland in 1923. Front row, from left to right: C Crossley, R Richards, W Brown, V Watson, W Moore, J Ruffell. Middle row: G Carter, W Henderson, S Bishop, P Allen, E Hufton, G Kay, J Tresadern, G Horler, J Young. Back row: T Williamson (committee), A N Searles (Assistant Secretary), G Handley (Vice-President), ES King (Secretary and Manager), L Johnson (Vice-Chairman), AC Davis (Director), H Iggulden (Director), F Piercy (Assistant Trainer), W F White (Chairman), C Paynter (Trainer), JWY Cearns (Director), J Holden (Director), GF Davis (Director), T Taylorson (Director), JE Johnson (Committee).

A Season to Remember

The 1922–23 season had been the greatest in West Ham United's short history. Syd King, with the help of Charlie Paynter, had constructed a team based around local talent, and the Hammers had come within a whisker of a rare promotion and Cup double. The murmurs of discontent caused by the sale of crowd-favourite Syd Puddefoot had disappeared following the emergence of new idols Vic Watson, Jimmy Ruffell, Dick Richards and Billy Moore. At the end of the season the club had made a record profit which would help finance the continued development of the Boleyn Ground. Unsurprisingly, every member of the 1922–23 playing staff was asked to re-sign for the Hammers' first campaign in English football's top flight. The 1922–23 season had seen the West Ham United board make an unprecedented investment in players, but there would be no repeat performance ahead of the team's First Division debut. The bulk of the new intake was made up of promising local youngsters and the only significant transfer fee paid was the £150 which secured the services of Hartlepool's Tom Yews. There was inevitable criticism of Hammers' transfer policy with several pundits predicting a 'rude awakening' for Syd King's boys. Scribbo, in the *East Ham Echo*, was, as usual, more optimistic: 'There is every reason why they [West Ham United] should do well in first-class company. They revealed themselves an exceptional side last year.'

Top-flight debut

An opening fixture away to Sunderland, whose line-up included the legendary Charlie Buchan, was a stern test of the Hammers' First Division credentials. A creditable 0–0 draw seemed to augur well for the campaign ahead, but the Hammers' first point had been achieved at a heavy cost. Striker Vic Watson had sustained a broken toe that would prevent him making a significant first-team contribution until April. The Cambridge-born forward would be sorely missed and no West Ham United player would make it into double figures for League goals during the 1923–24 season. Hammers' first goal in the top flight, struck against Arsenal to earn a 1–0 victory, came from the unlikely source of second-string player Albert Fletcher. Only Billy Moore would prove a regular source of goals, the inside-forward striking nine in 36 games.

By 1923 West Ham United's reputation for succeeding without spending was already well-established. But, even by Hammers' standards, the line-up for the Cup final that year was something of a bargain eleven. Only six of the players on show had cost more than £50, and in total the team had been assembled for just £2,025. To put this in perspective, the Upton Park club had sold Syd Puddefoot to Falkirk for a record transfer fee of £5,000 during the course of the previous season.

CUP FINAL TEAM

Bishop

Henderson

Kay

Hufton

Hufton – £300
Henderson – £650
Young – £300
Bishop – Nil
Kay – £100
Tresadern – Nil
Richards – £300
Brown – £25
Watson – £50
Moore – £300
Ruffell – Nil

The Hammers entered the First Division with a squad of 34 players and all are photographed here. Front row, left to right: G Howlett, JW Barrett, R Richards, V Watson, W Williams, W Moore, J Ruffell. Second row: P Kelly, TP Yews, L Robinson, N Proctor, W Brown, W Thirlaway, J Tresadern, H Hodges, WF Edwards. Third row: A R Leafe, PW Allen, A Fletcher, G Kay, G Eastham, G Carter, J Collins, A Cadwall, J Mackesy. Back row: J Hebden, T Hodgson, S Bishop, T Hampson, AE Hufton, WE Kaine, S Horler, J Young, W Henderson.

King leads England

It was to be a season of fitful form and indifferent results in the League, and although the Hammers' FA Cup run got off to a good start with a 5–0 victory over Aberdare, a second round defeat against Leeds United left Syd King's team with little to play for. With Watson already sidelined, Hammers' prospects were further hindered by injuries to Jack Tresadern and, most significantly, goalkeeper Ted Hufton. The Hammers custodian had sustained a triple fracture to his knee during a match at Nottingham Forest. A final placing of 13th in the First Division was a remarkable achievement given Hammers' poor luck with injuries. Syd King was rewarded for his efforts at club level when he was selected to take charge of the England team for an international at Wembley in 1924.

The now-traditional end of season summer tour took Hammers to Germany, Switzerland and France. It was the first time that a British football team had travelled to Germany since the war, and the club handbook reported that there was a certain amount of trepidation ahead of the tour. Fortunately, the Hammers were well received and enjoyed a successful trip, the high point of which was a match against the French national team in Paris. The hosts fielded a strong line up and Hammers were unlucky to lose 2–1, the decisive goal coming via an own goal from Henderson.

Inconsistent form

The only significant signing ahead of the 1924–25 season was that of Clapton's amateur inside-forward Stan Earle, a player who had previously represented Arsenal in the First Division. Earle would become a mainstay of the Hammers' forward line for eight seasons and enjoyed great success alongside fellow

Official Programme of the
WEST HAM UNITED
FOOTBALL Co. Ltd.
BOLEYN GROUND. CASTLE STREET. UPTON PARK.

19 Match No. November 27th, 1924 Price 2d.

WEST HAM UNITED
v.
CORINTHIANS
KICK-OFF 2.30 P.M.

BOLENIUM
(Pronounced BO-LENNY-UM)
Super-Garments
Worn by the man who knows

Made especially for ALL TRADES, including

ENGINEERS	PAINTERS	BOILER MAKERS	CHEMICAL WORKERS
CARPENTERS	PLUMBERS	BOILER SCALERS	GLASS WORKERS
SAWYERS	GROCERS	IRON FOUNDERS	PROVISION DEALERS
BUILDERS	BUTCHERS	PRINTING INK MAKERS	ETC., ETC.

Every Garment is Guaranteed for FIT, STRENGTH and LASTING WEAR

Ask your Outfitter, or write us direct
W. A. SMITH & Co., Ltd., Actual Manufacturers
BOLEYN CASTLE, UPTON PARK, E.13

England internationals Watson and Ruffell. This potent attacking trio took the field for the season's opening fixture at home to Preston North End and helped Hammers to a deserved win by a goal to nil. A second consecutive victory arrived courtesy of Earle's first West Ham United goal, but when Billy Moore regained his fitness the new man quickly found himself on the sidelines.

Hufton was still struggling to recover from his knee injury and made his first appearance of the season in April. By then, however, Hammers had become something of a Jekyll and Hyde team: formidable at home while struggling away from Upton Park. One of only three West Ham United away victories came against Huddersfield Town (in the middle of winning three successive Championships) in January, with Watson and Ruffell providing the decisive goals. Watson had returned to both fitness and form and registered 22 strikes in 41 games, a tally which had been boosted by a run of scoring in ten consecutive games from 20 December to 28 February. For the second season running Hammers finished in 13th place in the First Division, but in the FA Cup they enjoyed better luck, progressing to the third round where they were eliminated after a

Above: Jim Barrett snr, seen here as a 17-year-old in 1924, was born in West Ham and signed for his local team in 1923. 'Big Jim' took over from George Kay as the Hammers' regular centre-half in 1925 and went on to become one of the Club's best-loved players during the inter-war period.

Left: Matchday programme for a friendly against the famous amateur side Corinthians in 1924. Note the picture of the Boleyn Castle in the top left corner; it was an image which would continue to adorn West Ham United programmes until the 1950s.

Below: Stan Earle, who arrived at Upton Park in 1924. Although primarily a creative player, Stan was also a useful finisher and hit 56 League goals in his 258 appearances.

Left: The signing of goalkeeper Ted Hufton for just £350 in 1919 proved a master stroke on the part of Hammers manager Syd King. For 13 years, Hufton was West Ham United's first choice number-one and his assured handling was a key factor in the successful 1922–23 season. The Nottinghamshire-born custodian won six full England caps during his time at the Boleyn Ground.

replay against Blackpool. The FA Cup had provided the season's undoubted highlight, when Hammers overcame Arsenal after a three-match epic first round tie. The decisive clash had attracted a 40,000 crowd to Stamford Bridge, and the game was held up while many of the fans were cleared from the playing area. George Kay struck the winning goal, but according to a report of the match in the *Sunday People*: 'Arsenal should have made more of West Ham's defensive deficiencies.' The Achilles' heal in the Hammers' rearguard, however, was not a lack of organisation, aerial ability or pace, but instead that George Horler, the team's left-back, could not kick the ball far enough!

Trouble at the back

Whatever the inadequacies of the Hammers' defence, there would be no wholesale changes ahead of the 1925–26 campaign. The development of the Boleyn Ground remained the club's priority, and on 29 August 1925 the West Ham United board unveiled a new West Stand. The stand was reckoned to be one of the finest in the country, providing seating for 5,000 fans and giving shelter to 12,000 more on terraces below. The club programme trumpeted that the construction had taken 780 tons of steelwork as well as 2,700 cubic yards of ballast. The grand opening of the stand came in the season's opening fixture against newly promoted Manchester United. Chairman William White cracked a bottle of champagne and gave a speech just before the teams came out, but this would be the only celebratory bubbly enjoyed in E13 during a disappointing season.

2 BOYS' MAGAZINE. No. 419.

THIS WEEK'S GOAL-CRASHING FREE ART PLATE! Football Wizards of the Metropolis and the Greatest Seaport Vividly Depicted on a Two-Team Gem for Your Collections.

The Mighty Lads of West Ham and Liverpool Caricatured and Biographed by a Football Expert.

Liverpool (left): Hopkin, Hodgson, Jackson (capt.). West Ham: Earle (capt.), Watson, Yews, Earl (A.)

WEST HAM AND LIVERPOOL.

IF you ask people in East London which is the most popular footer club, ten out of every ten will answer, "West Ham, of course." There was a time—not so very long ago, either—when the Hammers played in the Southern League. But the club grew, their popularity increased, until, to-day, the Hammers have climbed from the lowest to the topmost rungs of the Football League ladder.

But, unlike the Arsenal, the management has not written out hefty big cheques for stars from other clubs. Manager Syd King, a former player with the club, has delved around among the junior sides in the district and has unearthed some of the country's finest players. Stanley Earle, the captain, Jimmy Barrett, Jim Collins, Alf Earl, Charlie Cox, Alf Cadwell, Vivian Gibbins—they were all found in the district where they were at one time schoolboy stars.

There are others in the side, of course, but they are all men who came to West Ham as almost unknown quantities—and they have made good. Teddy Hufton—England's best goalie—and one of the bravest!

There is Jimmy Ruffell, too, England's left winger; and Victor Watson, scorer of goals galore—another man with caps. Victor was a boxing instructor when he was in the Army. Perhaps that is why he has so much punch to-day—in his boots, of course!

Stanley Earle is one of the only two men in the country who won schoolboy, amateur, and full international caps. There is not a nicer chap playing football than Stan, whose father was a prominent player before him. Stan's greatest pal in the West Ham team is Vivian Gibbins, who is still an amateur and a schoolmaster in the West Ham district.

* * * * *

The Reds of Merseyside are not Bolsheviks, far from it. These Reds are much more popular, in fact thousands of people turn out every Saturda to see them play. They are the lads of the Liverpoo F.C., known as "The Reds" because they turn ou in shirts of that colour.

They are one of the best in the country—and hav been for years. Honours by the score have come the way—and plenty more will reach Anfield, th Liverpool club's headquarters, before long.

Now for the players—a collection of Scots, Irish men, Englishmen—and South Africans. Yes, South Africans. Riley, the goalie, and Hodgson, the burly inside-forward, were both born and bred in tha country.

The most popular man with the Anfield fans i Jim Jackson, Liverpool's sterling skipper, who i the only person in professional football. Jim is a fin player. His father was a star before him, his brothers too, and Jim is following in their footsteps.

Elisha Scott, the Irish goalkeeper, is another wh is travelling in brother's footsteps, for the first Scot was at one time on Everton's books. Elisha is a great lad. You should hear him cracking jokes in the dressing-room. The laughs nearly lift the roof of the grandstand.

There is a whole bunch of Scots at Anfield, too Tom Bradshaw—better known as "Tiny"—is the biggest of the lot. He only joined the club the other week from Bury. With him in the half-back line are Morrison and McDougal, two more of the best from the land of heather and bagpipes.

Several of the forwards are Scots, the best of them being Alec McPherson, from Glasgow Rangers, and Smith, the centre-forward, who scored lots of goals with Ayr United. These chaps are now doing the same thing in the Football League, and helping to make Liverpool one of the finest sides in the First Division.

NEXT WEEK—Another Splendid Two-team Art Photogravure Plate Presented Inside Every Copy of the Mag., Chums—

Right: This cartoon from the March 1930 edition of *Boys' Magazine* portrays West Ham United players Earle, Watson, Yews and Earl. The accompanying text profiles the Hammers as a team based upon local talent and the astute judgment of Syd King.

A Stan Earle goal gave Hammers an opening day victory, followed by three wins and a draw in the next four games. However, thereafter even the excellent form of Watson (20 goals), Ruffell (12 goals) and Earle (nine goals) could not compensate for defensive frailties that saw Hammers lose 7–1 to West Bromwich Albion and concede four goals on five further occasions. A change to the offside rule at the start of the season had made life easier for forwards, who now needed two, rather than three, defenders between them and goal. Clearly, the Hammers had struggled to adapt to this rule change and at season's end Syd King's side narrowly missed relegation to finish in 18th place.

Hammers' fortunes had not been helped by the declining form of the long-serving George Kay. The popular centre-half had been troubled by the change in the offside rule, but the end of his career had still come somewhat suddenly. The Hammers had travelled to Spain on tour in the summer of 1926 and Kay had sustained an injury which had led to a 'very severe illness' that sidelined him for many months. The arrival of the 'WM' formation to combat the new offside rule had also brought significant changes to the centre-half role, which had become more like that of a central full-back, or 'stopper', and by the time the veteran defender recovered his health he had lost his place to Jim Barrett. Kay would go on to enjoy a highly successful managerial career with Southampton and later Liverpool.

Below: The immaculate Jimmy Ruffell was West Ham United's most exciting and creative player throughout the inter-war period. Ruffell was Hammers outside-left for 16 seasons during which time he clocked up a then record 548 first-team appearances for the club.

Hard times

Off the pitch, Hammers were struggling to balance the books and in 1926 the board issued 100 debentures each costing £300. The club were still attracting large gates and the wage bill was not excessive, but the cost of continuing stadium developments was giving the West Ham United accounts an unhealthy hue. With no money available for new signings, Syd King continued to work his magic in the transfer market's bargain basement. Journeyman striker Joe Johnson arrived in time for the 1926–27 campaign and weighed in with seven goals in 14 appearances. Hammers at last enjoyed a season in the top half of the table, as a Watson-inspired forward line took the Eastenders to a best-ever finish of sixth, ten points behind Champions Newcastle United. Hammers struggled toward the end of the season, failing to win any of their last six games, but during a run of four consecutive wins in March, Syd King's team gave the crowd at the Boleyn Ground a memorable 7–0 victory over Arsenal, with Vic Watson grabbing a hat-trick.

Watson would provide most of the highlights during the next two seasons as Hammers struggled to survive in the top flight – ending in 17th place for two consecutive seasons. The Cambridge-born striker proved a regular source of goals and set a West Ham United individual League scoring record when he grabbed six in an 8–2 victory over Leeds United in February 1929.

The following season saw Watson register an amazing 42 League goals in 40 appearances, to set another record. Leeds United were once again significant victims of Watson's fire-power, with the striker hitting nine goals in three games against the Yorkshire side. At the other end of the pitch, Ted Hufton – the club's longest serving player – was back to his best form, helping Hammers to seventh place in the First Division.

However, the 1929–30 season proved to be a rare trip into the top half of the First Division for West Ham United, and the following campaign saw the club return to a more accustomed position toward the foot of the table. For many years the outstanding talent of players such as Watson, Hufton, Ruffell, Yews and Earle had helped make up for inadequacies elsewhere in the Hammers' squad, but toward the end of the 1920s it had become increasingly difficult for Syd King and Charlie Paynter to unearth cheap local talent to paper over the cracks. In 1928 *Magnet* magazine had run a feature on the Hammers, celebrating the club as the 'cheapest team in football', adding: 'they don't spend their cash on buying ready-made footballers. They hunt round home and make their own men.' But therein lay the problem. It was not always possible to replace experienced and skilful players with promising novices. Shortly after the start of the 1931–32 season the murmurs of discontent over a perceived lack of spending on players began to grow louder.

Left: Hammers players are introduced to the King of Denmark during a tour of Scandinavia in May 1927.

Downward spiral

The Hammers had got off to a good start in the League, taking maximum points from their first two matches, but they then began to struggle, suffering heavy defeats at the hands of Sheffield United (0–6), Aston Villa (2–5) and Leicester City (1–4). The arrival of winter brought a revival in West Ham United's fortunes, the highlight of which was a Jimmy Ruffell inspired 4–2 victory over Champions-elect Everton in December. For the second year running, Chelsea ended West Ham's involvement in the FA Cup, thus enabling Syd King and his team to complete their League programme without distraction. However, defeat against Chelsea had invoked a wave of criticism which even had the *East Ham Echo* declaring that: 'We have much admiration for the Hammers but precious little for their cheese-paring directors and it is high-time the latter looked to the interests of the club.'

At the start of March it appeared that the Hammers would avoid the relegation dogfight and finish in a low, mid-table position. Syd Puddefoot had returned to the club after an absence of 10 years in a move which helped appease many of the club's critics. But Puddefoot was not the same gifted goalscorer who had made the record move to Falkirk in 1922, and in any case Hammers were well served by the still prolific Watson and Ruffell in attack. As the season entered its final quarter West Ham United ran out of luck and form. An appalling run saw Syd King's team pick up just four points from ten games, and with two games remaining Hammers were in a perilous position. The situation deteriorated still further when the penultimate fixtures brought defeat for West Ham United at Sunderland, and victories for the other two relegation threatened clubs, Blackpool and Grimsby. Hammers travelled to Stamford Bridge to take on Chelsea in the final match of the season with the club programme describing the clash as 'of much more importance than... our Wembley match in 1923'. But it was a depleted Hammers team with little confidence who made the trip to West London. Goalkeeper Dixon had been injured at Sunderland and so Ted Hufton was recalled for his last West Ham appearance, despite the fact that he had already been granted a free transfer and would be moving on in the summer. In attack, Syd King was without Weldon, Earle and Puddefoot and so was forced to play Barrett out of position at centre-forward.

Hammers started the match against Chelsea well enough and looked like they were in control after taking the lead through their stand-in number nine. But in the second-half the home team struck back with three goals of their own and although Hammers scored a second through Yews it was not enough. West Ham United had finished bottom of the League and were relegated with Grimsby. The *East Ham Echo* laid the blame squarely on the shoulders of the board, and protested:

Right: Throughout Syd King's reign, West Ham United prepared for FA Cup matches with a visit to Southend and its famous brine baths. Here (from left to right) Tommy Yews, Jimmy Ruffell, Jim Collins, Jim Barrett, George Watson and Vic Watson take the sea air on the Pier ahead of the Cup match against Chelsea in 1931. This time the trip to the seaside failed to have the desired effect and Hammers lost 3–1 to the Blues.

'It is all very well for a football organisation to foster local soccer talent, but as has been proved, one should not venture to do so when in the First Division of the League, particularly when the other clubs in the Division are spending large sums to obtain at least one or more first rate players.' However, the *Echo* went on to say that Hammers should not be unduly worried by the slide into the Second Division, arguing that it was little more than a minor setback, and that 'both the management and the team have still plenty of "kick" left in them.' Alas it would be 26 years before this kick was again displayed in English football's top flight.

1919-1931

West Ham United 1919–20. Top row, left to right: J. Woodburn, G. Kay, J. McBrae, E. Hufton, T. Burton, A. Cope
Bottom row, left to right: H. Bradshaw, G. Butcher, S. Puddefoot, R. Leafe, J. Palmer

SEASON 1919-20
FOOTBALL LEAGUE (DIVISION 2)

Aug 30	(h)	Lincoln C	D	1-1
Sep 1	(a)	Barnsley	L	0-7
6	(a)	Lincoln C	W	4-1
8	(h)	Barnsley	L	0-2
13	(a)	Rotherham C	W	1-0
20	(h)	Rotherham C	W	2-1
27	(a)	Stoke	L	1-2
Oct 4	(h)	Stoke	D	1-1
11	(a)	Grimsby T	W	1-0
18	(h)	Grimsby T	W	1-0
25	(a)	Birmingham	W	1-0
Nov 1	(h)	Birmingham	L	1-2
8	(a)	Leicester C	D	0-0
15	(h)	Leicester C	W	1-0
22	(a)	Fulham	W	2-1
29	(h)	Fulham	L	0-1
Dec 6	(a)	Coventry C	D	0-0
13	(h)	Coventry C	W	2-0
20	(a)	Huddersfield T	L	0-2
25	(h)	Bristol C	W	2-0
26	(a)	Bristol C	D	0-0
27	(h)	Huddersfield T	D	1-1
Jan 3	(a)	Blackpool	D	0-0
17	(h)	Blackpool	W	1-0
24	(h)	Bury	W	1-0
Feb 7	(h)	Port Vale	W	3-1
11	(a)	Bury	L	0-1
14	(a)	Port Vale	L	0-1
28	(a)	Clapton O	L	0-1
Mar 4	(h)	Clapton O	L	0-1
13	(h)	Tottenham H	W	2-1
20	(a)	South Shields	L	0-3
22	(a)	Tottenham H	L	0-2
27	(h)	South Shields	W	1-0
Apr 2	(h)	Nottingham F	W	5-1
3	(a)	Wolves	D	1-1
5	(a)	Nottingham F	L	1-2
10	(h)	Wolves	W	4-0
17	(a)	Hull C	D	1-1
24	(h)	Hull C	W	2-1
26	(a)	Stockport C	L	0-1
May 1	(h)	Stockport C	W	3-0

P	W	D	L	F	A	W	D	L	F	A	Pts	Pos
42	14	3	4	34	14	5	6	10	13	26	47	7th

FA Cup

1	Jan 10	(a)	Southampton	D	0-0
R	15	(h)	Southampton	W	3-1
2	31	(h)	Bury	W	6-0
3	Feb 21	(a)	Tottenham H	L	0-3

SEASON 1920-21
FOOTBALL LEAGUE (DIVISION 2)

Aug 28	(h)	Hull C	D	1-1
30	(a)	Wolves	W	2-1
Sep 4	(a)	Hull C	L	1-2
6	(h)	Wolves	W	1-0
11	(a)	Fulham	D	0-0
18	(h)	Fulham	W	2-0
25	(a)	Cardiff C	D	0-0
Oct 2	(h)	Cardiff C	D	1-1
4	(a)	Coventry C	W	1-0
9	(a)	Leicester C	L	0-1
16	(h)	Leicester C	L	0-1
23	(a)	Blackpool	L	0-1
30	(h)	Blackpool	D	1-1
Nov 6	(a)	Sheffield W	W	1-0
13	(h)	Sheffield W	W	4-0
20	(a)	Stockport C	L	0-2
27	(h)	Stockport C	W	5-0
Dec 4	(a)	Stoke	L	0-1
11	(h)	Stoke	W	1-0
25	(h)	Birmingham	D	1-1
27	(a)	Birmingham	L	1-2
Jan 1	(h)	Coventry C	W	7-0
15	(a)	Clapton O	W	1-0
22	(h)	Clapton O	W	1-0
29	(a)	Leeds U	W	2-1
Feb 5	(h)	Leeds U	W	3-0
12	(a)	Bury	L	0-1
19	(h)	Bury	L	0-1
26	(a)	Bristol C	L	0-1
Mar 5	(h)	Bristol C	W	1-0
12	(a)	Barnsley	D	1-1
19	(h)	Barnsley	W	2-1
25	(h)	Notts C	L	0-2
26	(h)	Nottingham F	W	3-0
28	(a)	Notts C	D	1-1
Apr 2	(a)	Nottingham F	L	0-1
9	(h)	Rotherham C	W	1-0
16	(a)	Rotherham C	L	0-2
23	(h)	Port Vale	D	1-1
30	(a)	Port Vale	W	2-1
May 2	(h)	South Shields	W	2-1
7	(a)	South Shields	D	0-0

P	W	D	L	F	A	W	D	L	F	A	Pts	Pos
42	13	5	3	38	11	6	5	10	13	19	48	5th

FA Cup

1	Jan 8	(a)	Sheffield W	L	0-1

SEASON 1921-22
FOOTBALL LEAGUE (DIVISION 2)

Aug 27	(a)	Stoke	L	0-2
29	(h)	Bradford	W	1-0
Sep 3	(h)	Stoke	W	3-0
5	(a)	Bradford	L	0-2
10	(h)	Port Vale	W	3-0
17	(a)	Port Vale	L	1-2
24	(h)	South Shields	D	1-1
Oct 1	(a)	South Shields	L	0-1
3	(a)	Coventry C	L	0-2
8	(h)	Bristol C	W	3-0
15	(a)	Bristol C	W	1-0
22	(h)	Nottingham F	W	1-0
29	(a)	Nottingham F	L	0-2
Nov 5	(h)	Wolves	W	2-0
12	(a)	Wolves	W	1-0
19	(h)	Barnsley	W	4-0
26	(a)	Barnsley	D	1-1
Dec 10	(h)	Coventry C	W	3-0
17	(h)	Derby C	W	3-1
24	(a)	Derby C	L	1-3
26	(a)	Bury	W	1-0
27	(h)	Bury	W	3-2
31	(h)	Leicester C	W	1-0
Jan 14	(a)	Leicester C	L	1-2
21	(a)	Leeds U	D	0-0
28	(h)	Leeds U	D	1-1
Feb 4	(a)	Hull C	D	0-0
11	(h)	Hull C	D	1-1
25	(h)	Notts C	W	2-1
Mar 4	(a)	Crystal P	W	2-1
11	(h)	Crystal P	W	2-0
18	(h)	Rotherham U	L	1-2
25	(a)	Rotherham U	W	1-0
29	(a)	Notts C	D	1-1
Apr 1	(h)	Sheffield W	W	2-0
8	(a)	Sheffield W	L	1-2
14	(h)	Clapton O	L	1-2
15	(h)	Fulham	W	1-0
17	(a)	Clapton O	D	0-0
22	(a)	Fulham	L	0-2
29	(h)	Blackpool	L	0-2
May 6	(a)	Blackpool	L	1-3

P	W	D	L	F	A	W	D	L	F	A	Pts	Pos
42	15	3	3	39	13	5	5	11	13	26	48	4th

FA Cup

1	Jan 7	(a)	Swansea T	D	0-0
R	11	(h)	Swansea T	D	1-1
2R	16	(n*)	Swansea T	L	0-1

*Played at Bristol City

SEASON 1922-23
FOOTBALL LEAGUE (DIVISION 2)

Aug 26	(h)	Bradford C	L	1-2
28	(h)	Derby C	D	0-0
Sep 2	(a)	Bradford C	W	1-0
4	(a)	Derby C	L	1-2
9	(h)	Rotherham U	W	4-0
16	(a)	Rotherham U	D	2-2
23	(h)	Stockport C	L	0-1
30	(a)	Stockport C	L	1-2
Oct 7	(h)	Southampton	D	1-1
14	(a)	Southampton	L	0-2
21	(h)	Blackpool	W	2-0
28	(a)	Blackpool	L	1-4
Nov 4	(a)	Leeds U	L	1-3
11	(h)	Leeds U	D	0-0
18	(h)	Clapton O	W	1-0
25	(a)	Clapton O	W	2-0
Dec 2	(h)	South Shields	W	1-0
9	(a)	South Shields	D	0-0
16	(a)	Wolves	W	4-1
22	(h)	Wolves	W	1-0
25	(a)	Manchester U	W	2-1
26	(h)	Manchester U	L	0-2
30	(a)	Coventry C	W	3-1
Jan 6	(h)	Coventry C	W	1-0
20	(a)	Port Vale	W	3-1
27	(h)	Port Vale	D	0-0
Feb 10	(h)	Leicester C	D	2-2
15	(a)	Leicester C	W	6-0
17	(h)	Barnsley	D	0-0
Mar 3	(h)	Sheffield W	W	2-1
17	(a)	Hull C	D	1-1
30	(h)	Bury	D	0-0
31	(a)	Crystal P	W	5-1
Apr 2	(a)	Bury	W	5-2
7	(h)	Crystal P	D	1-1
9	(h)	Hull C	W	3-0

14 (a) Fulham W 2-0
16 (a) Barnsley L 0-2
18 (a) Notts C L 0-2
21 (h) Fulham W 1-0
30 (a) Sheffield W W 2-0
May 5 (h) Notts C L 0-1

P	W	D	L	F	A	W	D	L	F	A	Pts	Pos
42	9	8	4	21	11	11	3	7	42	27	51	2nd

FA Cup

1 Jan 13 (a) Hull C W 3-2
2 Feb 3 (a) Brighton & HA D 1-1
R 7 (h) Brighton & HA W 1-0
3 24 (h) Plymouth A W 2-0
4 Mar 10 (a) Southampton D 1-1
R 14 (h) Southampton D 1-1
2R 19 (n*) Southampton W 1-0
SF 24 (n**) Derby C W 5-2
F Apr 28 (n***) Bolton W L 0-2
* Played at Villa Park
** Played at Stamford Bridge
*** Played at Wembley

SEASON 1923-24
FOOTBALL LEAGUE (DIVISION 1)

Aug 25 (a) Sunderland D 0-0
27 (h) Arsenal W 1-0
Sep 1 (h) Sunderland L 0-1
8 (h) Cardiff C D 0-0
10 (a) Arsenal L 1-4
15 (a) Cardiff C L 0-1
22 (h) Middlesbrough D 1-1
29 (a) Middlesbrough W 1-0
Oct 6 (a) Newcastle U D 0-0
13 (h) Newcastle U W 1-0
20 (a) Chelsea D 0-0
27 (h) Chelsea W 2-0
Nov 3 (h) Birmingham W 4-1
10 (a) Birmingham L 0-2
17 (a) Burnley L 1-5
24 (h) Burnley D 0-0
Dec 1 (a) Bolton W D 1-1
8 (h) Bolton W L 0-1
15 (a) Nottingham F L 1-2
22 (h) Nottingham F W 3-2
25 (a) Aston Villa D 1-1
26 (h) Aston Villa W 1-0
29 (a) Liverpool L 0-2
Jan 1 (a) Sheffield U W 2-0
5 (h) Liverpool W 1-0
19 (a) Blackburn R D 0-0
26 (h) Blackburn R L 0-1
Feb 9 (h) Tottenham H D 0-0
16 (a) Huddersfield T D 1-1
Mar 1 (a) Notts C D 1-1
8 (h) Notts C D 1-1
15 (h) Everton W 2-1
22 (a) Everton L 1-2
27 (h) Huddersfield T L 2-3
29 (h) West Brom A W 1-0
Apr 5 (a) West Brom A D 0-0
12 (h) Preston NE W 3-1
19 (a) Preston NE L 1-2
21 (h) Sheffield U D 2-2
22 (a) Tottenham H W 1-0
26 (h) Manchester C L 1-2
May 3 (a) Manchester C L 1-2

P	W	D	L	F	A	W	D	L	F	A	Pts	Pos
42	10	6	5	26	17	3	9	9	14	26	41	13th

FA Cup

1 Jan 12 (h) Aberdare W 5-0
2 Feb 2 (h) Leeds U D 1-1
R 6 (a) Leeds U L 0-1

SEASON 1924-25
FOOTBALL LEAGUE (DIVISION 1)

Aug 30 (h) Preston NE W 1-0
Sep 6 (a) Blackburn R W 1-0
8 (h) Newcastle U D 0-0
13 (h) Huddersfield T D 0-0
17 (a) Newcastle U L 1-4
20 (a) Aston Villa D 1-1
22 (a) Sheffield U D 1-1
27 (h) Arsenal W 1-0
Oct 4 (a) Manchester C L 1-3
11 (h) Bury D 1-1
18 (a) Nottingham F L 1-2
25 (h) Burnley W 2-0
Nov 1 (a) Leeds U L 1-2
8 (h) Birmingham L 0-1
15 (a) West Brom A L 1-4
22 (h) Tottenham H D 1-1
29 (a) Bolton W L 0-5
Dec 6 (h) Notts C W 3-0
13 (a) Everton L 0-1
20 (h) Sunderland W 4-1
25 (h) Cardiff C W 3-2
26 (a) Cardiff C L 1-2
27 (a) Preston NE L 2-3
Jan 3 (h) Blackburn R W 2-0
17 (a) Huddersfield T W 2-1
24 (h) Aston Villa W 2-0
Feb 7 (h) Manchester C W 4-0
14 (a) Bury L 2-4
28 (a) Burnley L 4-5
Mar 7 (h) Leeds U D 0-0
14 (a) Birmingham D 1-1
21 (h) West Brom A W 2-1
23 (a) Arsenal W 2-1
28 (a) Tottenham H D 1-1
Apr 2 (h) Nottingham F D 0-0
4 (h) Bolton W D 1-1
10 (a) Liverpool L 0-2
11 (a) Notts C L 1-4
13 (h) Liverpool L 0-1
14 (h) Sheffield U W 6-2
18 (h) Everton W 4-1
25 (a) Sunderland D 1-1

P	W	D	L	F	A	W	D	L	F	A	Pts	Pos
42	12	7	2	37	12	3	5	13	25	48	42	13th

FA Cup

1 Jan 14 (h) Arsenal D 0-0
R 21 (a) Arsenal D 2-2
2R 26 (n*) Arsenal W 1-0
4 31 (a) Nottingham F W 2-0
5 Feb 21 (h) Blackpool D 1-1
R 25 (a) Blackpool L 0-3
* Played at Stamford Bridge

SEASON 1925-26
FOOTBALL LEAGUE (DIVISION 1)

Aug 29 (h) Manchester U W 1-0
31 (h) Cardiff C W 3-1
Sep 5 (a) Liverpool D 0-0
7 (a) Cardiff C W 1-0
12 (h) Burnley W 2-0
19 (a) Leeds U L 2-5
21 (a) Arsenal L 2-3
26 (h) Newcastle U W 1-0
Oct 3 (a) Bolton W L 0-1
5 (h) Arsenal L 0-4
10 (h) Notts C W 1-0
17 (h) Sheffield U L 1-3
24 (a) West Brom A L 1-7
31 (h) Manchester C W 3-1
Nov 7 (a) Tottenham H L 2-4
14 (h) Blackburn R W 2-1
21 (a) Sunderland L 1-4
28 (h) Huddersfield T L 2-3
Dec 5 (a) Everton L 0-2
12 (h) Birmingham D 2-2
19 (a) Bury L 1-4
25 (h) Aston Villa W 5-2
26 (a) Aston Villa L 0-2
Jan 2 (a) Manchester U L 1-2
16 (h) Liverpool L 1-2
23 (a) Burnley D 2-2
30 (h) Leeds U W 4-2
Feb 6 (a) Newcastle U L 1-4
13 (h) Bolton W W 6-0
27 (a) Sheffield U D 1-1
Mar 6 (h) West Brom A W 3-0
13 (a) Manchester C L 0-2
20 (h) Tottenham H W 3-1
22 (a) Notts C D 1-1
27 (a) Blackburn R L 0-1
Apr 2 (h) Leicester C D 1-1
3 (h) Sunderland W 3-2
5 (a) Leicester C D 1-1
10 (a) Huddersfield T L 1-2
17 (h) Everton W 1-0
24 (a) Birmingham L 0-1
May 1 (h) Bury L 0-2

P	W	D	L	F	A	W	D	L	F	A	Pts	Pos
42	14	2	5	45	27	1	5	15	18	49	37	18th

FA Cup

3 Jan 9 (a)
Tottenham H L 0-5

SEASON 1926-27
FOOTBALL LEAGUE (DIVISION 1)

Aug 28 (h) Leicester C D 3-3
Sep 4 (a) Everton W 3-0
6 (a) Sheffield W L 0-1
11 (h) Blackburn R L 1-5
18 (a) Huddersfield T L 1-2
25 (h) Sunderland L 1-2
Oct 2 (a) West Brom A W 3-1
4 (h) Sheffield W D 1-1
9 (h) Bury L 1-2
16 (a) Arsenal D 2-2
23 (a) Sheffield U W 2-0
30 (h) Manchester U W 4-0
Nov 6 (a) Bolton W L 0-2
13 (h) Aston Villa W 5-1
20 (a) Cardiff C W 2-1
27 (h) Burnley W 2-1
Dec 4 (a) Newcastle U L 0-2
11 (h) Leeds U W 3-2
18 (a) Liverpool D 0-0
25 (h) Birmingham W 1-0
27 (a) Birmingham W 2-0
28 (a) Derby C L 0-3
Jan 1 (h) Derby C L 1-2
15 (a) Leicester C L 0-3
22 (h) Everton W 2-1
Feb 5 (h) Huddersfield T W 3-2
12 (a) Sunderland W 3-2
14 (a) Blackburn R L 1-4
19 (h) West Brom A L 1-2
26 (a) Bury W 2-1
Mar 7 (h) Arsenal W 7-0
12 (h) Sheffield U W 3-0
19 (a) Manchester U W 3-0
26 (h) Bolton W D 4-4
Apr 2 (a) Aston Villa W 5-1
9 (h) Cardiff C D 2-2
15 (a) Tottenham H W 3-1
16 (a) Burnley L 1-2
18 (h) Tottenham H L 1-2
23 (h) Newcastle U D 1-1
30 (a) Leeds U L 3-6
May 7 (h) Liverpool D 3-3

P	W	D	L	F	A	W	D	L	F	A	Pts	Pos
42	9	6	6	50	36	10	2	9	36	34	46	6th

FA Cup

3 Jan 8 (h) Tottenham H W 3-2
4 29 (h) Brentford D 1-1
R Feb 2 (a) Brentford L 0-2

SEASON 1927-28
FOOTBALL LEAGUE (DIVISION 1)

Aug 27 (a) Derby C W 3-2
Sep 1 (h) Sunderland L 2-4
3 (h) Huddersfield T W 4-2
10 (h) Portsmouth W 4-2
17 (a) Leicester C W 3-2
24 (h) Liverpool W 3-1
Oct 1 (a) Arsenal D 2-2
8 (h) Burnley W 2-0
15 (a) Bury L 1-3
22 (a) Everton L 0-7
29 (h) Manchester U L 1-2
Nov 5 (a) Tottenham H L 3-5
12 (h) Cardiff C W 2-0
19 (a) Blackburn R L 0-1
26 (h) Middlesbrough L 4-5
Dec 3 (a) Sheffield W L 0-2
10 (h) Bolton W W 2-0
17 (a) Birmingham W 2-1
24 (h) Newcastle U W 5-2
26 (a) Sheffield U L 2-6
27 (h) Sheffield U D 1-1
31 (h) Derby C D 2-2
Jan 2 (a) Sunderland L 2-3
7 (a) Huddersfield T L 2-5
21 (a) Portsmouth L 1-2
Feb 4 (a) Liverpool W 3-1
11 (h) Arsenal D 2-2
18 (a) Burnley D 0-0
25 (h) Bury L 1-2
Mar 3 (h) Everton D 0-0
10 (a) Manchester U D 1-1
12 (h) Leicester C W 4-0
17 (h) Tottenham H D 1-1
24 (a) Cardiff C W 5-1
31 (h) Blackburn R W 4-3
Apr 6 (h) Aston Villa D 0-0
7 (a) Middlesbrough D 2-2
9 (a) Aston Villa L 0-1
14 (h) Sheffield W L 1-2
21 (a) Bolton W L 0-4
28 (h) Birmingham D 3-3
May 5 (a) Newcastle U L 1-3

P	W	D	L	F	A	W	D	L	F	A	Pts	Pos
42	9	7	5	48	34	5	4	12	33	54	39	17th

FA Cup

3 Jan 14 (a) Portsmouth W 2-0
4 28 (a) Huddersfield T L 1-2

SEASON 1928-29
FOOTBALL LEAGUE (DIVISION 1)

Aug 25 (h) Sheffield U W 4-0
Sep 1 (a) Bury W 3-0
3 (a) Burnley D 3-3
8 (h) Aston Villa W 4-1
10 (a) Cardiff C L 2-3
15 (a) Leicester C L 0-5
17 (h) Cardiff C D 1-1
22 (h) Manchester U W 3-1
29 (a) Leeds U L 1-4
Oct 6 (h) Liverpool D 1-1
13 (a) Arsenal W 3-2
20 (h) Everton L 2-4
29 (a) Blackburn R L 0-2
Nov 3 (h) Manchester C W 3-0
10 (a) Birmingham D 2-2
17 (h) Portsmouth L 0-1
24 (a) Bolton W L 1-4
Dec 1 (h) Sheffield W W 3-2
8 (a) Derby C L 0-6
15 (h) Sunderland D 3-3
22 (a) Huddersfield T L 0-4
25 (h) Newcastle U W 1-0
26 (a) Newcastle U L 0-1
29 (a) Sheffield U D 3-3
Jan 5 (h) Bury L 2-3
19 (a) Aston Villa L 2-5
Feb 2 (a) Manchester U W 3-2
9 (h) Leeds U W 8-2
23 (h) Arsenal L 3-4
Mar 4 (h) Leicester C W 2-1
9 (h) Blackburn R D 3-3
12 (a) Liverpool L 1-2
16 (a) Manchester C L 2-4
23 (h) Birmingham W 2-1
29 (h) Burnley W 4-0
30 (a) Portsmouth L 0-3
Apr 6 (h) Bolton W W 3-0
10 (a) Everton W 4-0
13 (a) Sheffield W L 0-6
20 (h) Derby C D 2-2
27 (a) Sunderland L 1-4
May 4 (h) Huddersfield T D 1-1

P	W	D	L	F	A	W	D	L	F	A	Pts	Pos
42	11	6	4	55	31	4	3	14	31	65	39	17th

FA Cup

3 Jan 12 (h) Sunderland W 1-0
4 26 (h) Corinthians W 3-0
5 Feb 16 (a) Bournemouth D 1-1
R 20 (h) Bournemouth W 3-1
6 Mar 2 (a) Portsmouth L 2-3

SEASON 1929-30
FOOTBALL LEAGUE (DIVISION 1)

Aug 31 (a) Blackburn R D 3-3
Sep 4 (a) Birmingham L 2-4
7 (h) Middlesbrough W 5-3
9 (h) Newcastle U W 5-1
14 (a) Liverpool L 1-3
16 (h) Birmingham L 0-1
21 (h) Derby C W 2-0
28 (h) Manchester U W 2-1
Oct 5 (a) Grimsby T D 2-2
12 (h) Leicester C L 1-2
19 (a) Manchester C L 3-4
26 (h) Portsmouth L 0-1
Nov 2 (a) Arsenal W 1-0
9 (h) Everton W 3-1
16 (a) Leeds U W 3-1
23 (h) Sheffield W D 1-1
30 (a) Burnley D 1-1
Dec 7 (h) Sunderland D 1-1
14 (a) Bolton W L 1-4
21 (h) Aston Villa W 5-2
25 (h) Huddersfield T L 2-3
26 (a) Huddersfield T L 0-3
28 (h) Blackburn R L 2-3
Jan 1 (a) Sheffield U L 2-4
4 (a) Middlesbrough L 0-2
18 (h) Liverpool W 4-1
Feb 1 (a) Manchester U L 2-4
5 (a) Derby C L 3-4
8 (h) Grimsby T W 2-0
20 (a) Leicester C W 2-1
22 (h) Manchester C W 3-0
Mar 8 (h) Arsenal W 3-2
12 (a) Portsmouth L 1-3
15 (a) Everton W 2-1
22 (h) Leeds U W 3-0
29 (a) Sheffield W L 1-2
Apr 5 (h) Burnley W 1-0
12 (a) Sunderland L 2-4
18 (h) Sheffield U W 1-0
19 (h) Bolton W W 5-3
26 (a) Aston Villa W 3-2
May 3 (a) Newcastle U L 0-1

P	W	D	L	F	A	W	D	L	F	A	Pts	Pos
42	14	2	5	51	26	5	3	13	35	53	43	7th

FA Cup

3 Jan 11 (h) Notts C W 4-0
4 25 (h) Leeds U W 4-1
5 Feb 15 (h) Millwall W 4-1
R Mar 1 (a) Arsenal L 0-3

SEASON 1930-31
FOOTBALL LEAGUE (DIVISION 1)

Aug 30 (h) Huddersfield T W 2-1
Sep 1 (h) Liverpool W 7-0
6 (a) Aston Villa L 1-6
8 (h) Middlesbrough L 0-3
13 (h) Chelsea W 4-1
17 (a) Middlesbrough D 2-2
20 (a) Newcastle U L 2-4
27 (h) Sheffield W D 3-3
Oct 4 (a) Grimsby T L 0-4
11 (h) Manchester U W 5-1
18 (h) Blackburn R W 4-3
25 (a) Arsenal D 1-1
Nov 1 (h) Sheffield U W 4-1
8 (a) Birmingham W 2-0
15 (h) Leeds U D 1-1
22 (a) Derby C D 1-1
29 (h) Leicester C W 2-0
Dec 6 (a) Blackpool W 3-1
13 (h) Manchester C W 2-0
20 (a) Sunderland L 1-6
25 (h) Portsmouth W 4-3
26 (a) Portsmouth L 0-2
27 (a) Huddersfield T L 0-2
Jan 3 (h) Aston Villa D 5-5
17 (a) Chelsea L 1-2
26 (h) Newcastle U W 3-2
31 (a) Sheffield W L 3-5
Feb 7 (h) Grimsby T L 3-4
14 (a) Manchester U L 0-1
21 (a) Blackburn R L 0-1
28 (h) Arsenal L 2-4
Mar 7 (a) Sheffield U W 2-1
16 (h) Birmingham L 1-2
21 (a) Leeds U L 0-3
28 (h) Derby C L 0-1
Apr 3 (h) Bolton W L 1-4
4 (a) Leicester C D 1-1
6 (a) Bolton W L 2-4
11 (h) Blackpool W 3-2
18 (a) Manchester C D 1-1
25 (h) Sunderland L 0-3
May 2 (a) Liverpool L 0-2

P	W	D	L	F	A	W	D	L	F	A	Pts	Pos
42	11	3	7	56	44	3	5	13	23	50	36	18th

FA Cup

3 Jan 10 (h) Chelsea L 1-3

SEASON 1931-32
FOOTBALL LEAGUE (DIVISION 1)

Aug29 (a) Bolton W W 1-0
31 (h) Chelsea W 3-1
Sep 5 (h) Middlesbrough L 0-2
7 (a) Sheffield U L 0-6
12 (a) Huddersfield T L 1-3
19 (h) Newcastle U W 1-2
21 (h) Sheffield U L 1-2
26 (a) Aston Villa L 2-5
Oct 3 (h) Leicester C L 1-4
10 (a) Liverpool D 2-2
17 (a) Manchester C W 1-0
24 (h) Portsmouth W 2-1
31 (a) Derby C L 1-5
Nov 7 (h) West Brom A L 1-5
14 (a) Arsenal L 1-4
21 (h) Blackpool D 1-1
28 (a) Blackburn R W 4-2
Dec 5 (h) Everton W 4-2
12 (a) Birmingham L 1-4
19 (h) Sunderland D 2-2
25 (a) Grimsby T L 1-2
26 (h) Grimsby T W 3-1
Jan 2 (h) Bolton W W 3-1
16 (a) Middlesbrough L 2-3
30 (a) Newcastle U D 2-2
Feb 1 (h) Huddersfield T D 1-1
6 (h) Aston Villa W 2-1
18 (a) Leicester C L 1-2
20 (h) Liverpool W 1-0
Mar 2 (h) Manchester C D 1-1
5 (a) Portsmouth L 0-3
12 (h) Derby C W 2-1
19 (a) West Brom A L 1-3
25 (h) Sheffield W L 1-2
26 (h) Arsenal D 1-1
28 (a) Sheffield W L 1-6
Apr 2 (a) Blackpool L 2-7
9 (h) Blackburn R L 1-3
16 (a) Everton L 1-6
23 (h) Birmingham L 2-4
30 (a) Sunderland L 0-2
May 7 (a) Chelsea L 2-3

P	W	D	L	F	A	W	D	L	F	A	Pts	Pos
42	9	5	7	35	37	3	2	16	27	70	31	22nd

FA Cup

3 Jan 9 (a) Charlton A W 2-1
4 23 (a) Chelsea L 1-3

CHAPTER 3
CHANGING TIMES

The fall from the First Division in 1932 did little to dampen the enthusiasm of most West Ham United fans. Evidence, if it were needed, of the loyal support still enjoyed by the Hammers came the following autumn when the pre-season matches attracted their usual large crowds. The match programme for the first of these practice fixtures noted 'with pleasure that our "long distance" ticket holders still consider that watching the Hammers is well worth the journey. Two come from Herne Hill, one comes from Surbiton, and another from Sudbury, in Suffolk.' But whether from East London or East Anglia, supporters of Syd King's team would have struggled to recognise any of the new signings that, it was hoped, would lead the Hammers out of the Second Division at the first attempt. King had persisted with his bargain transfers, and only one of his summer purchases – Arthur Wilson, a £500 buy from Southampton – had any League experience.

Above: Charlie Paynter instructs a group of first-team players, prior to a training session at the Boleyn Ground in the 1930s. Note the standard issue training kit of sweater, black shorts and running spikes.

Left: In the summer of 1939 West Ham United players signed up with the Territorial Army. The TA Hammers are seen here enjoying a sing-song while on camp at Ramsey, Hunts.

King's sad demise

Wilson was one of two debutantes, along with centre-forward Hugh Mills, when Hammers opened their League campaign away to Swansea Town on 27 August 1932, a game which the Welsh club won 1–0. For the most part of the early season Syd King relied upon the tried and trusted. Jim Barrett, Jimmy Ruffell, Syd Puddefoot and Vic Watson (who began the season on the injured list) formed the backbone of the team as they had done for many years in the First Division. The old guard, however, could not shake off the relegation form of the previous campaign, and after five games Hammers had collected just a single point and had conceded 15 goals. Problems on the pitch were matched by tensions between manager and board, as the directors became increasingly concerned about Syd King's drinking. King had developed quite a reputation around Upton Park, a fact supported by future Hammers manager Ted Fenton who recounts in his autobiography, *At Home With the Hammers*, how as a groundstaff boy one of his most important and regular errands was to visit the Boleyn pub to get the boss 'two dozen bottles of Bass'.

In November matters reached a head when King attended a board meeting while drunk. It was not unusual for him to be intoxicated, but when his replies to questions from directors were insulting and insubordinate, the board was left with little option but to take disciplinary action. The next day King was suspended without pay for three months. Alan Searles took over King's responsibilities as secretary, while Charlie Paynter assumed control of the playing side. The West Ham United directors had entered uncharted territory; King had been the club's only manager, but they now had to consider both his future and that of his assistant Charlie Paynter. On 3 January 1933 the board reached a somewhat inevitable decision and dismissed Syd King. Within a month King was dead, taking his own life by drinking a cocktail of alcohol and a 'corrosive substance'. The pressures of professional football had taken a heavy toll on West Ham United's first manager.

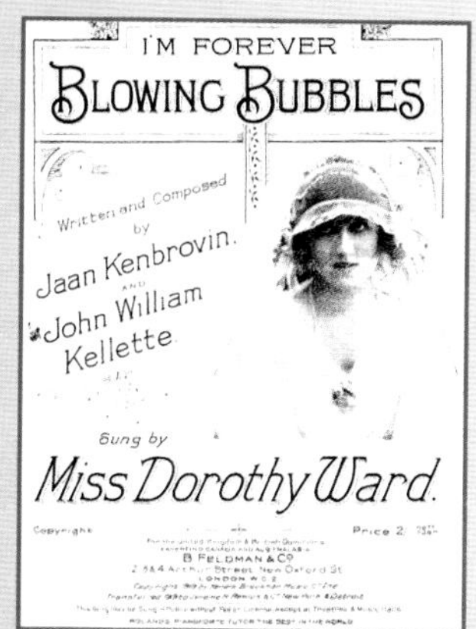

'I'm Forever Blowing Bubbles' was written by Jaan Kenbrovin and John William Kellette shortly after the First World War, and was adopted as the West Ham United theme tune in the late 1920s. The Club's association with this erstwhile music hall hit owes most to a curly haired boy called Billy Murray who played for West Ham schoolboys and, who it was said, resembled the character in a painting by Millais entitled 'Bubbles', which was used in the Pears Soap advert of the day.
The similarity between the character in Bubbles and young Murray prompted Cornelius Beal, a prominent figure in local junior football, to pen some new words to the tune and, before long, 'Bubbles' became a favourite song at schoolboy matches around the East End. As the twenties drew to a close, choruses of 'Bubbles' could also be heard at Hammers' first-team games, although with Corny Beal's words either forgotten or no longer appropriate, the fans reverted to the original lyrics.

Paynter takes charge

The question of a successor brought heated boardroom debate, with some directors uncertain about Paynter's ability to fulfil the manager's position permanently and others doubting the need for a manager at all. It was a difficult period for the caretaker boss, who had been put in an intolerable position by the club's decision to make no formal announcement to the press about King's situation. This lack of official information had led to feverish speculation in local papers. The board finally put an end to the whispering when they appointed Paynter as trainer and 'players' manager', with Leafe and Lidell in charge of scouting. It had been a protracted and tragic affair, which had done nothing to lift the team out of the doldrums. When Paynter finally got to hold the managerial reins unfettered, the spectre of relegation was rearing its head once more.

Above: Jackie Morton was a versatile and skilful forward who came from Midland League club Gainsborough Trinity for £600 in 1931. Jackie, who could play at inside-forward or on either wing, was most at home at outside-left and he won his only senior international cap in that position in 1937.

Left: This cartoon from 1933 shows West Ham United's management structure had changed following the demise of Secretary-Manager Syd King in 1932. Alan Searles, bottom left, had taken over as secretary, leaving Charlie Paynter, bottom right, to concentrate on the football side of the club.

The FA Cup provided welcome relief from the twin evils of off-field traumas and poor League form. Hammers made light work of their first two Cup ties, defeating the amateurs of Corinthians by 2–0 before dispatching West Bromwich Albion by the same score. A replay victory over Brighton was followed by Hammers' best performance at Upton Park against Birmingham City, who were sent back to the Midlands suffering a 4–0 defeat. A semi-final tie against Everton at Molineux followed, but the First Division side – who included the legendary Dixie Dean in their line-up – had too much quality for Charlie Paynter's boys. The match ended 2–1, with Vic Watson grabbing Hammers' consolation. Two days later Watson was again on the scoresheet, helping his team to a 2–1 victory over Bradford at Upton Park. But it was a rare League triumph for the East Londoners, who were beginning to look like relegation candidates for the second season in a row.

Three consecutive defeats in April left Hammers in a perilous position, and forced the new manager to make changes. Paynter had few options, and took the bold step of pitching two unproven youngsters into first-team action. Len Goulden was an inside-left who had played amateur football for Chelmsford and Leyton while Joe Cockroft was a wing-half recently signed from Midland League side Gainsborough Trinity. The Hammers fledglings were an immediate success and helped their team to four successive victories which guaranteed the club's status in the Second Division. All things considered, it was a satisfactory end to the most traumatic season in West Ham United's history.

Below: Len Goulden was one of the most gifted players of the 1930s. He formed a formidable partnership with Jimmy Ruffell on the left of Hammers' attack. Despite being a Second Division player, he won 14 England caps while at the Boleyn Ground.

Paynter mixes old and new

The 1933–34 season would bring little excitement to Upton Park, as the Hammers finished in a comfortable, and much-improved, seventh place in the League. More significantly, Charlie Paynter was beginning to build a new team, blending youngsters like Goulden, Cockroft, Jackie Morton and the versatile Ted Fenton with veterans Ruffell, Barrett and Vic Watson. At season's end, there was an air of optimism around Upton Park, with the final match programme declaring that: 'We look forward to next season with a great deal of confidence. Twenty-four of last season's men have re-signed, and we have one or two outstanding men in view to strengthen the weak spots. Most of our players are young, some very much so; and this fact forces us to contemplate an early return to the First Division with a side well able to hold its own.'

It is revealing that the club had recognised that it needed to 'strengthen the weak spots' by buying 'outstanding players'. Under Syd King there had been a reluctance to spend money, but with Charlie Paynter in place the club entered a new, more pragmatic era. Charles Korr, in his book *West Ham United, The Making of a Football Club,* argues that the change of manager helped facilitate an increase in expenditure on transfers. Korr points out that King had 'grown up with an impoverished West Ham United and... liked to point out that it had remained true to its old traditions'. The promotion of Charlie Paynter to manager provided the board with a fresh start, and a chance to show their commitment to gaining promotion by making high profile investments, which in turn helped maintain the fans' interest.

Despite the bold predictions, there were no big signings ahead of the 1934–35 season, and four defeats in the opening six fixtures left the Hammers well down the table. The club was further rocked by the deaths of long-serving chairman William F. White and former trainer Tom Robinson, in the autumn of 1934.

Hammers find form

By the end of November the Hammers were finding their form and had climbed towards the summit of the table. Veteran forwards Jimmy Ruffell (now 34 years old) and Vic Watson (37) were at the heart of the Hammers renaissance, and in December the pair struck a rich vein of scoring, each registering goals in six consecutive games. Paynter had also found a settled half-back line with Fenton at right-half, Cockroft on the left and 'Big' Jim Barrett in his familiar centre-half role. Albert Walker and Alfred Chalkley were the full-backs, while Goulden, Morton and Cockroft completed an exciting Hammers outfield line-up. West Ham United maintained their position around the promotion zone for the remainder of the season. However, in early March the Hammers suffered two consecutive defeats which saw them lose ground on the leaders. The board of directors responded to this setback and, as they had promised in the summer, made funds available for team strengthening.

Dr James Marshall, a Scotland international inside-forward, was signed from Arsenal for £2,000 and within days was joined by Dave Mangall, a centre-forward from Birmingham costing £780. Marshall was the club's record signing at the time, and was also a qualified medical practitioner. The pair were an immediate success for the Hammers, both scoring on their debut in a 2–2 draw away to Port Vale. However, the efforts of the new boys were in vain and defeat in the penultimate game of the season, away to promotion rivals Bolton Wanderers, would ultimately deny Charlie Paynter's team a swift return to the top flight. Bolton denied them the second promotion place on goal average.

Vic Watson had played his last game for the Hammers, and in the summer of 1935 the club's record goalscorer headed for Southampton where he linked up with former team-mate and Saints boss George Kay. Mangall took the place of the departing hero at centre-forward and finished his first full season with an impressive return of 22 goals from 25 League matches. Goulden, Ruffell and Marshall would all make it into double figures for goals as the Hammers made another serious challenge for promotion. Once again, though, a poor start hindered West Ham United's attempt to regain their First Division place, and it was only a run of six consecutive victories (including a 6–0 thrashing of Bury) during the winter which put the Eastenders back on track.

Above: Hammers players enjoy a break from training in the grounds of Green Street House, c1933. Jim Barrett snr holds the ladder supporting Jackie Morton (top), George Watson (middle) and Joe Musgrave (bottom).

West Ham United players and officials pose for a photograph on a tour of Sweden at the end of the 1934–35 season.

Promotion proves elusive

With promotion in their sights, the Hammers board once more made money available for the manager to strengthen the team. Bradford City captain Charlie Bicknell was the big signing in March 1936 that, it was hoped, would lead Hammers back to the top flight, but his arrival failed to have the desired effect and the team struggled in their final seven games of the season. The match against promotion rivals Charlton on 18 April was the Hammers' final hope of a top-two finish and elevation to the First Division. A record crowd of 43,000 attended the game, but even before such support the home team could not overcome their South London opponents, and lost 3–1. Charlton went up – a Hammers win would have put them up. For the second season running a single result had cost West Ham United promotion.

If the result of the Charlton game was painful for Hammers' fans, the post-match comments of director Bert Davis applied

the proverbial salt to some very sore wounds. Davis had suggested, within earshot of a reporter, that it was better, from a financial point of view, for the club to be successful in the Second Division, rather than struggling in the First. A terrible furore followed and the board – now under the chairmanship of W.J. Cearns – was forced to issue a statement explaining that they, like the fans, were anxious for promotion and that Davis had been misinterpreted. Whatever the truth, the Hammers' reputation would be tarnished in the eyes of many supporters, and the board's ambition would regularly be questioned henceforward.

On a brighter note, the 1935–36 season had seen the arrival of a young goalkeeper who would go on to establish a long-service record for West Ham United. Stratford-born Ernie Gregory had been a much-coveted junior footballer who had enjoyed great success with the West Ham regional teams, helping the borough's schoolboys to the final of the English Schools' Shield and earning the attention of many scouts. The young Gregory had been offered the chance to 'stay with uncle Charlie' after impressing the Hammers manager with his performance in a schoolboy game at Upton Park, and in November 1935 he joined the club as an amateur. More than 60 years on, the former Hammers keeper recalls the man who signed him with much affection: 'Charlie was number one, a marvellous man. He was a great motivator. If you were struggling for form and having a bad time on the pitch, he would take you in to the medical room and talk to you. When you came out, you'd feel so confident you'd feel like you could fight Jack Johnson.'

In 1940 Hammers returned to Wembley, after an absence of 17 years, to compete in the War Cup final. A goal from Sammy Small proved enough to claim the Cup and the West Ham United players are seen here celebrating with their prize. From left to right: Charlie Bicknell, Norman Corbett (in military uniform), Ted Fenton, Archie Macaulay, George Foreman and Stan Foxall.

For the remainder of the 1930s, however, transfer dealings rather than man-management would dominate Paynter's time. Arsenal full-back Albert Walker was the big signing ahead of the 1936–37 season, although his arrival was only financed by the controversial sale of leading goalscorer and fan's favourite Dave Mangall. With Mangall departed, scoring responsibilities were spread amongst Morton, Sam Small (a new signing from Birmingham), Foxall and Len Goulden, who had earned a well-deserved call-up to the England team in 1937. Goulden had become West Ham United's star player with his sparkling displays from inside-forward and in the remaining years before the war he would win a total of 14 England caps. At the other end of his Hammers career was groundstaff boy Eddie Chapman who began a 50-year association with the club in 1936.

Paynter completes building work

Comings and goings would continue apace during the 1937–38 season. Most significantly, defensive stalwart Jim Barrett relinquished his long-held number five shirt to 21-year-old Hackney-born stopper Dick Walker. The Hammers forward line was also changing following the departure of Mangall and the arrival of highly rated Scotsman Archie Macaulay from Rangers for £5,000. Most Hammers fans agreed that Paynter was bringing together an exciting line-up, but with so many personnel changes the East Londoners made little impression in the League, finishing in mid-table in both 1937–38 and 1938–39. All too often, the team's skilful, attacking style was easily bludgeoned by more down-to-earth, workmanlike opponents. A report of a home defeat against Spurs in 1939 brought typical criticism, with the writer asking: 'Is it any use telling West Ham that their frilly football habits... are developing into cables holding them down in the Second Division.' The 1939 FA Cup provided the only indication of Hammers' true ability as Paynter's squad swept to the fifth round before losing to the eventual winners, Portsmouth. The undoubted highlight of this run was a twice replayed tie against Spurs which was eventually won at Highbury courtesy of some bewitching forward play from Foxall, Small and Macaulay. By the season's end Paynter had made two final signings: Stan 'Dizzy' Burton, who was a top-class winger who had played for Wolves in the 1939 Cup final, and Cliff Hubbard. Ernie Gregory remembers these signings as the final pieces of West Ham's promotion jigsaw. The Hammers had also been boosted by the arrival in 1938 of first-team coach Bob John, a member of Arsenal's all-conquering side of the 1930s and a former Welsh international.

Charlie Paynter had finally assembled a team of undoubted ability and the Hammers were widely tipped for League success. From Harry Medhurst in goal to Cockroft, Foxall, Macaulay, Small and Goulden in the forward line, West Ham United had a team ready for a return to the top flight. Alas, there would be no chance for them to test their promotion credentials, as shortly after the start of the 1939–40 season England entered the war against Nazi Germany. Football would quickly pale into insignificance beside the atrocities that would follow in the next six years.

Above: James Marshall is the only medical doctor to have played in the West Ham United first team. 'Doc', as he was inevitably known, joined the Hammers from Rangers in 1935 and quickly established himself in Charlie Paynter's line-up at inside-right. Marshall's stay at the Boleyn Ground, however, was relatively short-lived and in 1938 he left to concentrate on his medical career.

Below: West Ham United take on Spurs at Upton Park in 1946. Archie Macaulay is the Hammers player challenging the keeper in a match that ended in a 2-2 draw. The picture also reveals the bomb damage to the Boleyn Ground which, owing to the shortage of materials and the need for a building licence, would take years to repair.

The 1940 War Cup

The outbreak of war in September 1939 brought the immediate suspension of national League and Cup competitions, and – as had been the case in the First World War – football was reorganised upon local lines. A pressing concern for all clubs was the potential disruption that conscription would cause. With this in mind, and before war had been declared, the Hammers squad volunteered for service; the first team with the Reserve Police and the second-string with the Territorials. Despite taking this initiative, it was not long before the Hammers' playing staff was scattered around the countryside as they made their contribution to the war effort. With so many of his players unavailable, Charlie Paynter was forced to pull the proverbial rabbit from his tin hat each week. Much of his time was spent negotiating with commanding officers for the release of his own players, or with other clubs for the service of guest players. And when petrol was available, he would drive around the countryside, ferrying players from their distant barracks back to Upton Park.

The first opportunity for Paynter to test his resourcefulness came with the 1940 War Cup, a hurriedly organised event that took place over nine weeks from 20 April. Hammers began in good form and made light work of disposing of Chelsea and Leicester in the competition's opening rounds. However Paynter's team required a replay at Upton Park to overcome Huddersfield Town. Another home victory, this time over Birmingham City, ensured West Ham United's passage to a semi-final against Fulham at Stamford Bridge. The Cottagers had already beaten Hammers in the regional league competition, but back on the ground where they had won their 1923 semi-final against Derby County, the boys in claret and blue found their true form to run out 4–3 victors.

The final, at Wembley Stadium, saw the Hammers come up against a strong Blackburn Rovers line-up in a match which

was played at 6.30pm to avoid high levels of absenteeism among war workers. The crowd was restricted to 50,000 – a far cry from the 1923 attendance – and to their credit, both clubs were able to name line-ups which were free from guests. The match programme listed five of the Hammers team as working in an aircraft factory, but it was ambulance builder Sammy Small who struck the game's only goal to earn West Ham United their first Wembley triumph. Ted Fenton, who was working as an army PT instructor at Aldershot, recalled in his book *At Home with the Hammers* that, although the competition was considered worth winning, victory 'was not followed by the customary high jinx... Austerity was the watchword... we players quietly split up and went straight back to our service units... it was as hilarious as a wet Sunday in Cardiff. But then the rest of the world wasn't exactly having a fancy-dress ball.'

Flame-haired inside-forward Archie Macaulay cost £5,000 when he arrived at Upton Park from Glasgow Rangers in 1937. Archie, however, fulfilled all expectation and made an excellent start to his West Ham United career, scoring 26 goals in his first two seasons. However, his spell in East London was interrupted by the Second World War, and when competitive football resumed Archie made just eight more appearances before signing for First Division Brentford.

Despite the best efforts of Charlie Paynter, the 1940 Cup was to be the only wartime silverware to make its way into the Boleyn Ground's trophy cabinet. Paynter had become a virtual one-man football club, and as well as looking after the team he was rolling the pitch, putting up the nets and keeping the books. As the war progressed it became more and more difficult for the manager to name anything approximating the team he would have liked. Only Len Goulden, Charlie Bicknell and Sam Small were able to turn out for the Hammers with any regularity and all too often Paynter was forced to rely on youngsters, players past their best or guests. On occasions the Hammers showed glimpses of their pre-war form and in 1944 and 1945 they finished as runners-up to Spurs in the wartime League South. The 1944–45 season also brought Hammers within a match of a second War Cup final, but a 2–1 defeat against Chelsea denied Charlie Paynter's boys a second Wembley appearance in five years. One Hammer who would play in the final was Len Goulden, who guested for the Blues and earned himself a £2 match fee, plus five Savings Certificates as a win bonus.

War hits Hammers hard

When the war came to a close in 1945 it had taken a heavy toll on the fortunes of West Ham United. Financially, the Hammers' predicament had been helped greatly by the Archdiocese of Westminster, which had reduced the rent for the Boleyn Ground in return for the club agreeing to allow the ground be used by the army for training. However, on the other side of the balance sheet, income had been reduced by rapidly falling gate receipts. These problems were compounded when in August 1944 the south-west corner of the ground was struck by a flying bomb, destroying a section of offices and blowing the roof from the South Bank. The ground was closed for four months, but it would be many years before the club was granted a licence to complete expensive ground repairs to this section of the stadium.

The Hammers' troubles also extended to the playing staff, where the team of 1939–40 were six years older and no longer the same focused, well-blended promotion hopefuls. Many players were still on active service as the 1945–46 season got under way, and the League retained its regional structure. Charlie Paynter would have been glad to welcome back his returning heroes, most notably Dick and Charlie Walker who had both enjoyed distinguished military careers, but the manager was dismayed to find that several of his players were set on departing from Upton Park. Len Goulden was the most notable of the post-war departees, heading for Chelsea after 14 years with the Hammers. Another Hammers favourite, Archie Macaulay, who was good enough to play for Scotland and for Great Britain against the Rest of Europe in 1947, followed

Goulden into the First Division, joining Brentford after serving as an army PTI. Senior players Ted Fenton and Charlie Walker also left, both taking up managerial posts – Fenton with Colchester and Walker with Margate. Paynter's misery was complete when promising young player Reg Atwell was sold to Burnley, Joe Cockroft returned to Sheffield and Jackie Morton was forced to retire with a knee injury.

Re-building begins

The long-serving Hammers manager was forced to embark upon a wholesale rebuilding programme, but with little money to pursue expensive transfers. The fans would have to be patient. Twelfth place in 1946–47 was followed by better entertainment the following season, with Hammers recovering after a poor start to finish in sixth. A new team was beginning to take shape. Ernie Gregory had taken over in goal and scout Ben Ives had started to tap into a rich pool of talent in the Republic of Ireland. The first of a number of top-class Irish players to make it into the Hammers first-team was Tommy Moroney a player who Gregory remembers as 'the best passer of a ball to come out of Ireland at that stage'.

The Irishmen continued to arrive in 1948–49 with Danny McGowan (an inside-forward), Freddy Kearns (a full-back) and John Carroll (a centre-forward) all making their way to London E13. However, the most significant signing in 1948 was that of Ted Fenton, who rejoined the club as assistant manager. Fenton had enjoyed great success as boss of Southern League Colchester, guiding the non-League outfit to the FA Cup fifth round after victories over Wrexham, Huddersfield and Bradford Park Avenue. He had quickly become the most highly sought after young manager in England and had been offered the manager's position at First Division West Bromwich Albion, before Charlie Paynter and W.J. Cearns moved to bring him home to the Hammers.

Fenton quickly became involved in West Ham United's junior teams, and while the first team made little impression toward the goal of promotion, youngsters like Andy Malcolm, Frank O'Farrell and Jim Barrett jnr were all nearing readiness for senior football.

The 1949–50 season was a deeply forgettable affair in terms of results, but it would offer an emotional finale. The goals of Bill Robinson, who had arrived from Charlton Athletic the previous January, were the only success in a dreary campaign which finished with Hammers in a lowly 19th place. But at season's end Hammers fans quickly forgot about results and promotion, and paid tribute to a man who had given their club 50 years of unbroken service. Charlie Paynter had decided to retire and to pass the managerial reins to his understudy Ted Fenton. The club granted the outgoing boss a well-earned

Right: Charlie Paynter (right) and Director Bert Davis survey the war damage to the Boleyn Ground in 1946. However, because of difficulties obtaining the necessary licence, it was not until the 1950s that the club was able to carry out much-needed repairs to both the stadium and the offices at Upton Park.

With the war over, West Ham United were able to embark on an end of season tour once more. The Hammers' destination for the summer of 1948 was Denmark and the booklet shown here was produced to commemorate the trip.

WEST HAM UNITED
Football Company Limited

Tour in
DENMARK
1948

FRIDAY, 21st MAY to
THURSDAY, 3rd JUNE

testimonial, but for many people it was difficult to perceive of West Ham United without the ubiquitous Paynter.

Fenton had a tough act to follow, but the departing manager was quick to offer words of encouragement in the *Stratford Express* on the eve of his retirement: 'It is a very trying moment for me and I suppose for a period I shall be at a loss to know what to do with myself now that I shall no longer have my regular daily chores. But there is one very great consolation and that is to know that I am handing over to Mr Ted Fenton... I have every confidence that he will strengthen the reputation he has already made for himself.'

1932-1950

SEASON 1932-33
FOOTBALL LEAGUE (DIVISION 2)

Date		Opponent	Res	Score
Aug 27	(a)	Swansea T	L	0-1
29	(h)	Bradford C	L	2-4
Sep 3	(h)	Notts C	D	1-1
7	(a)	Bradford C	L	1-5
10	(a)	Port Vale	L	0-4
17	(h)	Millwall	W	3-0
24	(a)	Southampton	L	3-4
Oct 1	(h)	Bury	L	0-1
8	(a)	Lincoln C	L	0-6
15	(h)	Oldham A	W	5-2
22	(a)	Preston NE	L	1-4
29	(h)	Burnley	D	4-4
Nov 5	(a)	Bradford	L	0-3
12	(h)	Grimsby T	W	5-2
19	(a)	Stoke C	D	0-0
26	(h)	Charlton A	W	7-3
Dec 3	(a)	Nottingham F	D	2-2
10	(h)	Manchester U	W	3-1
17	(a)	Tottenham H	D	2-2
24	(h)	Plymouth A	D	2-2
26	(a)	Fulham	L	2-4
27	(h)	Fulham	D	1-1
31	(h)	Swansea T	W	3-1
Jan 7	(a)	Notts C	L	0-2
21	(h)	Port Vale	W	5-4
30	(a)	Millwall	L	0-1
Feb 4	(h)	Southampton	W	3-1
11	(a)	Bury	L	1-6
Mar 6	(h)	Preston NE	D	1-1
11	(a)	Burnley	L	0-4
13	(a)	Oldham A	L	2-3
20	(h)	Bradford	W	2-1
25	(a)	Grimsby T	L	1-2
27	(h)	Lincoln C	D	0-0
Apr 1	(h)	Stoke C	L	1-2
8	(a)	Charlton A	L	1-3
14	(a)	Chesterfield	L	0-1
15	(h)	Nottingham F	W	4-3
17	(h)	Chesterfield	W	3-1
22	(a)	Manchester U	W	2-1
29	(h)	Tottenham H	W	1-0
May 6	(a)	Plymouth A	L	1-4

P	W	D	L	F	A	W	D	L	F	A	Pts	Pos
42	12	6	3	56	31	1	3	17	19	62	35	20th

FA Cup

Rd	Date		Opponent	Res	Score
3	Jan 14	(a)	Corinthians	W	2-0
4	28	(h)	West Brom A	W	2-0
5	Feb 18	(a)	Brighton & HA	D	2-2
R	22	(h)	Brighton & HA	W	1-0
6	Mar 4	(h)	Birmingham	W	4-0
SF	18	(n*)	Everton	L	1-2

* Played at Molineux

SEASON 1933-34
FOOTBALL LEAGUE (DIVISION 2)

Date		Opponent	Res	Score
Aug 26	(h)	Bolton W	W	4-2
30	(a)	Plymouth A	D	4-4
Sep 2	(a)	Brentford	L	1-4
4	(h)	Plymouth A	W	5-1
9	(h)	Burnley	L	1-2
16	(a)	Oldham A	L	1-4
23	(h)	Preston NE	W	6-0
30	(a)	Bradford	D	0-0
Oct 7	(h)	Grimsby T	W	3-1
14	(a)	Nottingham F	W	1-0
21	(a)	Millwall	D	2-2
28	(h)	Lincoln C	W	4-1
Nov 4	(a)	Bury	L	1-2
11	(h)	Hull C	W	2-1
18	(a)	Fulham	L	1-3
25	(h)	Southampton	D	0-0

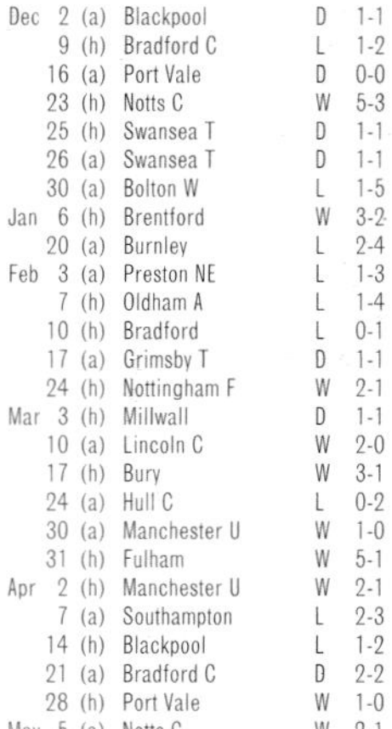

Date		Opponent	Res	Score
Dec 2	(a)	Blackpool	D	1-1
9	(h)	Bradford C	L	1-2
16	(a)	Port Vale	D	0-0
23	(h)	Notts C	W	5-3
25	(h)	Swansea T	D	1-1
26	(a)	Swansea T	D	1-1
30	(a)	Bolton W	L	1-5
Jan 6	(h)	Brentford	W	3-2
20	(a)	Burnley	L	2-4
Feb 3	(a)	Preston NE	L	1-3
7	(h)	Oldham A	L	1-4
10	(h)	Bradford	L	0-1
17	(a)	Grimsby T	D	1-1
24	(h)	Nottingham F	W	2-1
Mar 3	(h)	Millwall	D	1-1
10	(a)	Lincoln C	W	2-0
17	(h)	Bury	W	3-1
24	(a)	Hull C	L	0-2
30	(a)	Manchester U	W	1-0
31	(h)	Fulham	W	5-1
Apr 2	(h)	Manchester U	W	2-1
7	(a)	Southampton	L	2-3
14	(h)	Blackpool	L	1-2
21	(a)	Bradford C	D	2-2
28	(h)	Port Vale	W	1-0
May 5	(a)	Notts C	W	2-1

P	W	D	L	F	A	W	D	L	F	A	Pts	Pos
42	13	3	5	51	28	4	8	9	27	42	45	7th

FA Cup

Rd	Date		Opponent	Res	Score
3	Jan 13	(h)	Bradford C	W	3-2
4	27	(a)	Tottenham H	L	1-4

SEASON 1934-35
FOOTBALL LEAGUE (DIVISION 2)

Date		Opponent	Res	Score
Aug 27	(h)	Burnley	L	1-2
Sep 1	(h)	Nottingham F	W	3-1
3	(a)	Burnley	L	2-5
8	(a)	Brentford	L	1-4
15	(h)	Fulham	W	2-1
17	(a)	Hull C	L	0-4
22	(a)	Bradford	W	3-1
29	(h)	Plymouth A	W	2-1
Oct 6	(a)	Norwich C	W	2-1
13	(h)	Newcastle U	W	3-2
20	(h)	Swansea T	W	2-0
27	(a)	Manchester U	L	1-3
Nov 3	(h)	Port Vale	W	3-1
10	(a)	Barnsley	D	1-1
17	(h)	Sheffield U	W	2-0
24	(a)	Bradford C	W	2-0
Dec 1	(h)	Notts C	W	4-0
8	(a)	Southampton	D	2-2
15	(h)	Bolton W	W	4-1
22	(a)	Oldham A	W	2-1
25	(a)	Bury	W	4-2
26	(h)	Bury	W	3-0
29	(h)	Hull C	L	1-2
Jan 5	(a)	Nottingham F	L	0-2
19	(h)	Brentford	W	2-0
26	(a)	Fulham	L	0-3
Feb 2	(h)	Bradford	W	2-1
9	(a)	Plymouth A	W	1-0
18	(h)	Norwich C	W	1-0
23	(a)	Newcastle U	L	0-3
Mar 2	(a)	Swansea T	L	4-5
9	(h)	Manchester U	D	0-0
16	(a)	Port Vale	D	2-2
23	(h)	Barnsley	W	4-3
30	(a)	Sheffield U	W	2-1
Apr 6	(h)	Bradford C	W	1-0
13	(a)	Notts C	W	2-0
19	(a)	Blackpool	L	2-3
20	(h)	Southampton	W	2-1
22	(h)	Blackpool	W	2-1
27	(a)	Bolton W	L	1-3
May 4	(h)	Oldham A	W	2-0

P	W	D	L	F	A	W	D	L	F	A	Pts	Pos
42	18	1	2	46	17	8	3	10	34	46	56	3rd

FA Cup

Rd	Date		Opponent	Res	Score
3	Jan 12	(h)	Stockport C	D	1-1
R	16	(a)	Stockport C	L	0-1

SEASON 1935-36
FOOTBALL LEAGUE (DIVISION 2)

Date		Opponent	Res	Score
Aug 31	(a)	Norwich C	L	3-4
Sep 2	(a)	Bradford	L	0-2
7	(h)	Nottingham F	W	5-2
9	(h)	Bradford	W	1-0
14	(a)	Blackpool	L	1-4
16	(h)	Sheffield U	W	3-2
21	(h)	Doncaster R	L	1-2
28	(a)	Bury	L	0-3
Oct 5	(h)	Barnsley	W	2-0
12	(h)	Swansea	W	4-0
19	(a)	Plymouth A	L	1-4
26	(h)	Bradford C	D	1-1
Nov 2	(a)	Newcastle U	D	3-3
9	(h)	Tottenham H	D	2-2
16	(a)	Manchester U	W	3-2

Official Programme of the
WEST HAM UNITED FOOTBALL C^O L^TD
BOLEYN GROUND, GREEN STREET, UPTON PARK.

Directors
W. J. CEARNS (Chairman) F. R. PRATT (Vice-Chairman) A. C. DAVIS F. A. ENDERS J. H. ROOFF, J.P
Secretary A. N. SEARLES

Number 5 | 2nd September, 1939 | Price One Penny

WEST HAM UNITED
v
LEICESTER CITY

FOOTBALL LEAGUE — Division II | KICK-OFF 3.30 p.m

Football League, Div. II

	P	W	D	L	For	Ag.	Pts
Luton Town ...	2	2	0	0	6	0	4
West Ham United	2	2	0	0	5	2	4
Birmingham ...	2	1	1	0	3	1	3
Bury	2	1	1	0	4	2	3
Newport County	2	1	1	0	4	2	3
W Bromwich Alb	2	1	1	0	5	4	3
Chesterfield... ...	1	1	0	0	2	0	2
Millwall	2	1	0	1	3	2	2
Swansea Town ...	2	1	0	1	4	3	2
Barnsley	2	1	0	1	5	4	2
Tottenham H'spur	2	0	2	0	2	2	2
Coventry City ...	2	0	2	0	4	4	2
Plymouth Argyle	2	1	0	1	3	3	2
Leicester City ...	2	1	0	1	4	5	2
Sheff. Wednesday	2	1	0	1	3	4	2
Nott'gham Forest	2	1	0	1	3	4	2
Burnley	1	0	1	0	1	1	1
Manchester City...	2	0	1	1	4	5	1
Fulham	2	0	0	2	2	5	0
Southampton ...	2	0	0	2	2	6	0
Newcastle United	2	0	0	2	0	5	0
Bradford	2	0	0	2	0	5	0

Half-Time Score Board To-day

	Home Club	Away Club
A	Birmingham	Burnley ... ...
B	Bradford	Millwall ... ...
C	Coventry City	Barnsley ... ...
D	Fulham	Luton Town ... ...
E	Manchester City ...	Chesterfield ... ...
F	Newcastle United ...	Swansea Town... ...
G	Nottingham Forest...	Newport County ...
H	Sheffield Wednesday	Plymouth Argyle ...
J	Southampton	Bury ... ...
K	W. Bromwich Albion	Tottenham Hotspur
L	Arsenal	Sunderland ... ...
M	Brentford	Huddersfield Town...
N	Charlton Athletic ...	Manchester United...
O	Liverpool	Chelsea ... ...
P	Crystal Palace	Bristol Rovers... ...
Q	Reading	Southend United ...
R	Walsall	Queens Park Rangers
S	Watford	Clapton Orient... ...
T	Ipswich Town	Norwich City ... ...

Next Home Matches :

Monday, 4 Sept.	**TUNBRIDGE WELLS RGRS**	M.W.L	**6.0**
Saturday, 9 Sept.	**LEICESTER CITY Res**	Football Com.	**3.30**

Hellier & Sons, Printers, 237 Barking Road, London, E.13 Albert Dock 1905

This programme is from the Hammers final game before the League was suspended due to the Second World War.

23 (h) Hull C W 4-1
30 (a) Fulham L 2-4
Dec 14 (a) Charlton A D 2-2
21 (h) Port Vale W 4-0
25 (h) Southampton D 0-0
26 (a) Southampton W 4-2
28 (h) Norwich C W 3-2
Jan 4 (a) Nottingham F W 2-0
18 (h) Blackpool W 2-1
25 (a) Doncaster R W 2-0
Feb 1 (h) Bury W 6-0
3 (h) Burnley D 0-0
8 (a) Barnsley W 2-1
15 (a) Swansea T W 1-0
22 (h) Plymouth A W 4-2
29 (a) Burnley L 0-1
Mar 7 (h) Manchester U L 1-2
14 (a) Tottenham H W 3-1
21 (h) Newcastle U W 4-1
28 (a) Hull C W 3-2
Apr 4 (h) Fulham D 0-0
10 (h) Leicester C W 3-2
11 (a) Bradford C L 1-3
13 (a) Leicester C D 1-1
18 (h) Charlton A L 1-3
25 (a) Port Vale W 3-2
May 2 (a) Sheffield U L 2-4

P	W	D	L	F	A	W	D	L	F	A	Pts	Pos
42	13	5	3	51	23	9	3	9	39	45	52	4th

FA Cup
3 Jan 11 (h) Luton T D 2-2
R 15 (a) Luton T L 0-4

H. Lewis

SEASON 1936-37
FOOTBALL LEAGUE (DIVISION 2)

Aug 29 (h) Tottenham H W 2-1
31 (h) Newcastle U L 0-2
Sep 5 (a) Blackpool L 0-1
9 (a) Newcastle U L 3-5
12 (h) Blackburn R W 3-1
14 (a) Sheffield U L 0-2
19 (a) Bury D 1-1
26 (h) Leicester C W 4-1
Oct 3 (a) Nottingham F L 0-1
10 (a) Norwich C D 3-3
17 (h) Plymouth A D 1-1
24 (a) Coventry C I 0-4
31 (h) Doncaster R W 1-0
Nov 7 (a) Fulham L 0-5
14 (h) Burnley L 0-2
21 (a) Southampton W 2-0
28 (h) Swansea T W 2-0
Dec 5 (a) Bradford C L 1-2
19 (a) Chesterfield D 1-1
25 (a) Bradford L 1-2
26 (a) Tottenham H W 3-2
28 (h) Bradford W 1-0
Jan 2 (h) Blackpool W 3-0
9 (a) Blackburn R W 2-1
23 (h) Bury W 5-1
Feb 4 (a) Leicester C D 2-2
6 (h) Nottingham F D 2-2
13 (h) Norwich C W 4-1
20 (a) Plymouth A L 0-2
27 (h) Coventry C W 4-0
Mar 6 (a) Doncaster R W 4-1
13 (h) Fulham D 3-3
20 (a) Burnley L 1-2
26 (h) Barnsley D 0-0
27 (h) Southampton W 4-0
29 (a) Barnsley D 0-0
Apr 3 (a) Swansea T D 0-0
10 (h) Bradford C W 4-1
17 (a) Aston Villa W 2-0
24 (h) Chesterfield D 1-1
26 (h) Aston Villa W 2-1
May 1 (h) Sheffield U W 1-0

P	W	D	L	F	A	W	D	L	F	A	Pts	Pos
42	14	5	2	47	18	5	6	10	26	37	49	6th

FA Cup
3 Jan 16 (h) Bolton W D 0-0
R 20 (a) Bolton W L 0-1

SEASON 1937-38
FOOTBALL LEAGUE (DIVISION 2)

Aug 28 (a) Aston Villa L 0-2
30 (h) Swansea T W 2-1
Sep 4 (h) Bradford W 3-1
6 (a) Swansea T D 0-0
11 (a) Stockport C D 0-0
13 (h) Chesterfield w 5-0
18 (a) Southampton D 3-3
25 (h) Blackburn R W 2-0
Oct 2 (a) Sheffield W L 0-1
9 (h) Fulham D 0-0
16 (h) Barnsley W 4-1
23 (a) Luton T D 2-2
30 (h) Newcastle U W 1-0
Nov 6 (a) Nottingham F D 0-0
13 (h) Coventry C D 0-0
20 (a) Tottenham H L 0-2
27 (h) Burnley W 1-0
Dec 4 (a) Bury L 3-4
11 (h) Sheffield U L 0-2
27 (a) Norwich C D 2-2
28 (h) Norwich C D 3-3
Jan 1 (h) Aston Villa D 1-1
15 (a) Bradford L 1-2
22 (h) Stockport C W 1-0
29 (h) Southampton W 3-1
Feb 5 (a) Blackburn R L 1-2
12 (h) Sheffield W W 1-0
19 (a) Fulham D 1-1
23 (a) Manchester U L 0-4
26 (a) Barnsley L 0-1
Mar 5 (h) Luton T D 0-0
12 (a) Newcastle U D 2-2
19 (h) Nottingham F W 2-1
26 (a) Coventry C D 1-1
Apr 2 (h) Tottenham H L 1-3
9 (a) Burnley L 0-2
15 (h) Plymouth A L 0-1
16 (h) Bury W 3-1
18 (a) Plymouth A L 1-2
23 (a) Sheffield U L 1-3
30 (h) Manchester U W 1-0
May 7 (a) Chesterfield W 1-0

P	W	D	L	F	A	W	D	L	F	A	Pts	Pos
42	13	5	3	34	16	1	9	11	19	36	42	9th

FA Cup
3 Jan 8 (a) Preston NE L 0-3

SEASON 1938-39
FOOTBALL LEAGUE (DIVISION 2)

Aug 27 (a) Fulham L 2-3
29 (h) Blackburn R L 1-2
Sep 3 (h) Sheffield W L 2-3
7 (a) Manchester C W 4-2
10 (a) Bury D 1-1
17 (h) Coventry C W 4-1
19 (a) Blackburn R L 1-3
24 (h) Tranmere R W 6-1
Oct 1 (a) Chesterfield L 0-1
8 (h) Swansea T W 5-2
15 (a) Nottingham F D 0-0
22 (h) Newcastle U L 0-1
29 (a) Tottenham H L 1-2
Nov 5 (h) Norwich C W 2-0
12 (a) Luton T W 2-1
19 (h) Plymouth A W 2-1
26 (a) Sheffield U L 1-3
Dec 3 (h) Burnley W 1-0
10 (a) West Brom A L 2-3
17 (h) Southampton L 1-2
24 (h) Fulham W 1-0
27 (h) Millwall D 0-0
31 (a) Sheffield W W 4-1
Jan 14 (h) Bury D 0-0
28 (a) Tranmere R D 2-2
Feb 4 (h) Chesterfield D 1-1
16 (a) Swansea T L 2-3
18 (h) Nottingham F W 5-0
25 (a) Newcastle U L 0-2
Mar 4 (h) Tottenham H L 0-2
11 (a) Norwich C W 6-2
18 (h) Luton T L 0-1
25 (a) Plymouth A D 0-0
27 (a) Millwall W 2-0
Apr 1 (h) Sheffield U D 0-0
7 (h) Bradford L 0-2
8 (a) Burnley L 0-1
11 (a) Bradford W 2-1
15 (h) West Brom A W 2-1
22 (a) Southampton W 2-0
24 (a) Coventry C D 0-0
May 6 (h) Manchester C W 2-1

B. Fenton

P	W	D	L	F	A	W	D	L	F	A	Pts	Pos
42	10	5	6	36	21	7	5	9	34	31	44	11th

FA Cup
3 Jan 7 (a) Queen's Park R W 2-1
4 21 (h) Tottenham H D 3-3
R 30 (a) Tottenham H D 1-1
2R Feb 2 (n*) Tottenham H W 2-1
5 11 (a) Portsmouth L 0-2
* Played at Highbury Stadium London.

SEASON 1939-40
FOOTBALL LEAGUE (DIVISION 2)

Competition abandoned after three fixtures and deleted from records:
Aug 26 (a) Plymouth Argyle W 3-1
28 (h) Fulham W 2-1
Sep 2 (h) Leicester City L 0-2

Football League War Cup 1939-40
(1st leg)
1 Apr 20 (h) Chelsea W 3-2
(2nd leg)
27 (a) Chelsea W 2-0 (agg 5-2)
(1st leg)
2 May 4 (a) Leicester City D 1-1
(2nd leg)
11 (h) Leicester City W 3-0 (agg 4-1)
3 18 (a) Huddersfield T D 3-3
3R 22 (h) Huddersfield T W 3-1
4 25 (h) Birmingham W 4-2
SF June 1 (n*) Fulham W 4-3
F 8 (n**) Blackburn R W 1-0
*Played at Stamford Bridge
**Played at Wembley

Football League War Cup 1940-41
1st leg
1 Feb 15 (a) Norwich City L 1-2
2nd leg
22 (h) Norwich City W 4-1 (agg 5-3)
1st leg
2 Mar 1 (a) Southend United L 1-2
2nd leg
8 (h) Southend United W 3-1 (agg 4-3)
1st leg
3 15 (h) Arsenal L 0-1
2nd leg
22 (a) Arsenal L 1-2 (agg 1-3)

London War Cup "B" Division 1940-41
Jan 4 (a) Millwall W 2-1
11 (h) Millwall W 2-1
25 (h) Arsenal L 1-3
Feb 1 (a) Tottenham Hotspur W 2-1
8 (h) Tottenham Hotspur W 3-2
Mar 22 (h) Reading D 1-1
Apr 5 (a) Reading L 1-4
12 (h) Clapton Orient W 8-1
19 (a) Clapton Orient W 3-2
May 17 (a) Arsenal L 0-3

SEASON 1940-41
LEAGUE SOUTH

Aug 31 (a) Tottenham H W 3-2
Sep 7 (h) Tottenham H L 1-4
21 (h) Luton T W 3-0
28 (a) Clapton O D 3-3
Oct 5 (a) Chelsea D 1-1
12 (h) Miliwall W 3-2
19 (a) Miliwall D 2-2
26 (h) Southend U W 11-0
Nov 2 (a) Southend U L 1-3
16 (a) Brentford W 2-0
23 (h) Charlton A W 4-0
30 (a) Charlton A W 2-1
Dec 7 (h) Chelsea W 6-2
14 (h) Clapton O W 5-1
21 (a) Fulham W 2-1
25 (h) Arsenal W 4-2
28 (h) Fulham D 1-1
Apr 14 (h) Watford W 2-0
26 (h) Fulham L 0-1
May 3 (h) Brentford W 3-2
10 (a) Reading D 1-1
24 (h) Chelsea D 3-3
31 (a) Queen's Park R W 5-1
Jun 2 (h) Miliwall L 0-3
5 7 (h) Queen's Park R L 2-3

P	W	D	L	F	A	W	D	L	F	A	Pts	Pos
25	9	2	4	48	24	5	4	1	22	15	34	2nd

SEASON 1941-42
LONDON LEAGUE

Aug 30 (h) Portsmouth L 1-3
Sep 6 (a) Chelsea W 8-4
13 (a) Charlton A D 1-1
20 (h) Clapton O W 3-1
27 (a) Watford W 8-0
Oct 4 (h) Aldershot W 3-0
11 (h) Millwall W 4-2
18 (a) Arsenal L 1-4
25 (h) Queen's Park R W 2-0
Nov 1 (a) Reading L 2-3
8 (h) Brighton & HA W 4-0
2 15 (a) Brentford W 5-0
3 22 (h) Crystal P L 0-5
29 (a) Fulham W 3-1
Dec 6 (a) Tottenham H D 1-1
13 (a) Portsmouth L 0-1
20 (h) Chelsea W 5-0
25 (h) Charlton A D 2-2
27 (a) Clapton O L 1-3
Jan 3 (h) Watford W 4-1
10 (a) Aldershot W 5-1
17 (a) Millwall W 3-1
24 (h) Arsenal W 3-0
31 (a) Queen's Park R L 1-2
Feb 14 (a) Brighton & HA W 3-1
21 (h) Brentford W 2-1
28 (a) Crystal P D 1-1
Mar 7 (h) Fulham D 1-1
14 (h) Tottenham H L 2-3
Apr 25 (h) Reading W 2-1

P	W	D	L	F	A	W	D	L	F	A	Pts	Pos
30	10	2	3	38	20	7	3	5	43	24	39	3rd

London War Cup 1941-42 Group One
Mar 21 (a) Brighton & HA W 2-1
28 (h) Arsenal L 0-4
Apr 4 (h) Brighton & HA W 6-2
6 (a) Arsenal W 4-1
11 (h) Clapton Orient W 5-3
18 (a) Clapton Orient W 1-0

SEASON 1942-43
LEAGUE SOUTH

Aug 29 (h) Portsmouth W 5-4
Sep 5 (h) Luton T W 3-1
12 (h) Crystal P D 2-2
19 (h) Tottenham H W 3-1
26 (a) Clapton O W 5-0
Oct 3 (h) Chelsea L 0-1
10 (a) Brentford L 2-6
17 (a) Aldershot L 1-5
24 (h) Watford W 3-0
31 (a) Fulham W 3-2
Nov 7 (a) Queen's Park R L 2-5
14 (h) Millwall W 7-5
21 (a) Brighton & HA D 2-2
28 (h) Portsmouth W 2-1
Dec 5 (a) Luton T L 2-3
12 (a) Crystal P D 0-0
19 (a) Tottenham H L 0-2
25 (h) Charlton A L 1-3
26 (a) Charlton A D 4-4
Jan 2 (h) Clapton O W 10-3
9 (a) Chelsea W 3-1
16 (h) Brentford W 4-1
23 (h) Aldershot W 6-3
30 (a) Watford L 2-3
Feb 6 (h) Fulham W 2-1
13 (h) Queen's Park R L 1-3
20 (a) Millwall D 3-3
27 (h) Brighton & HA W 2-1

P	W	D	L	F	A	W	D	L	F	A	Pts	Pos
28	10	1	3	46	26	4	4	6	34	40	33	6th

Football League (South) Cup 1942-43
Group One
Mar 6 (h) Watford W 6-1
13 (a) Brighton & HA W 4-1
20 (h) Arsenal L 1-3
27 (a) Watford D 0-0
Apr 3 (h) Brighton & HA W 7-1
10 (a) Arsenal L 1-3

SEASON 1943-44
LEAGUE SOUTH

Aug 28 (a) Portsmouth L 0-2
Sep 4 (h) Luton T W 3-2
11 (h) Arsenal D 2-2
18 (h) Tottenham H D 3-3
25 (a) Clapton O W 4-0
Oct 2 (a) Crystal P W 6-1
9 (h) Brentford D 0-0
16 (a) Southampton W 4-2
23 (h) Reading W 1-0
30 (a) Fulham W 6-2
Nov 6 (h) Queen's Park R D 1-1
13 (h) Millwall W 3-0
20 (a) Brighton & HA W 2-1
27 (h) Portsmouth W 5-1
Dec 4 (a) Luton T W 1-0
11 (a) Arsenal D 1-1
18 (h) Charlton A L 0-1
25 (a) Chelsea D 3-3
27 (h) Chelsea W 3-0
Jan 1 (a) Tottenham H L 0-1
8 (a) Queen's Park R L 0-3
22 (h) Crystal P W 3-0
29 (a) Brentford L 1-2
Feb 5 (h) Southampton W 4-1
12 (a) Reading L 2-3
Apr 1 (h) Fulham W 3-2
10 (h) Clapton O W 3-1
22 (a) Charlton A D 1-1
29 (a) Millwall W 3-1
May 6 (h) Brighton & HA W 6-2

P	W	D	L	F	A	W	D	L	F	A	Pts	Pos
30	10	4	1	40	16	7	3	5	34	23	41	2nd

J. Morton

Football League (South) Cup 1943-44
Group B
Feb 19 (h) Watford L 1-2
26 (a) Southampton W 2-1
Mar 4 (a) Chelsea L 0-4
11 (a) Watford L 1-2
18 (h) Southampton W 5-1
25 (h) Chelsea W 6-1

SEASON 1944-45
LEAGUE SOUTH

Aug 26 (a) Tottenham H D 2-2
Sep 2 (a) Charlton A L 2-3
9 (a) Watford D 3-3
16 (a) Queen's Park R W 1-0
23 (a) Portsmouth W 3-1
30 (a) Brighton & HA W 1-0
Oct 7 (a) Aldershot W 3-2
14 (a) Luton T W 4-3
21 (a) Arsenal W 3-0
28 (a) Millwall W 3-0
Nov 4 (a) Clapton O W 3-0
11 (a) Fulham W 7-4
18 (a) Southampton L 1-2
25 (a) Crystal P L 0-3
Dec 2 (h) Tottenham H L 0-1
9 (h) Charlton A W 2-0
16 (h) Watford W 6-2
30 (h) Queen's Park R W 4-2
Jan 6 (h) Portsmouth W 4-0

13	(h)	Brighton & HA	W	5-4
20	(h)	Aldershot	W	8-1
Mar 24	(h)	Millwall	W	3-1
31	(h)	Clapton O	W	1-0
Apr 2	(a)	Chelsea	W	4-3
14	(h)	Fulham	W	3-2
21	(h)	Southampton	L	3-5
28	(h)	Crystal P	W	5-0
May 5	(a)	Arsenal	D	1-1
12	(h)	Luton T	W	9-1
19	(h)	Chelsea	W	2-1

P	W	D	L	F	A	W	D	L	F	A	Pts	Pos
30	12	1	2	56	21	10	2	3	40	26	47	2nd

Football League (South) Cup 1944-45
Group 3

Feb 3	(a)	Aldershot	W	3-1
10	(h)	Tottenham H	W	1-0
17	(a)	Queen's Park R	D	1-1
24	(h)	Aldershot	W	4-0
Mar 3	(a)	Tottenham H	L	0-4
10	(h)	Queen's Park R	W	5-0
17	(n*)	Chelsea (semi-final)	L	1-2

* Played at White Hart Lane

SEASON 1945-46
LEAGUE SOUTH

Aug 25	(a)	Birmingham C	W	1-0
27	(h)	Arsenal	D	1-1
Sep 1	(h)	Birmingham C	W	3-2
8	(h)	Tottenham H	D	1-1
10	(h)	Aston Villa	L	1-2
15	(a)	Tottenham H	W	3-2
22	(a)	Brentford	D	1-1
29	(h)	Brentford	L	0-2
Oct 6	(h)	Chelsea	L	2-4
13	(a)	Chelsea	W	2-1
20	(a)	Millwall	D	0-0
27	(h)	Millwall	W	3-1

R. Black

Nov 3	(h)	Southampton	W	3-1
10	(a)	Southampton	D	3-3
17	(a)	Derby C	L	1-5
24	(h)	Derby C	L	2-3
Dec 1	(h)	Leicester C	D	2-2
8	(a)	Leicester C	L	1-4
15	(a)	Coventry C	W	5-2
22	(h)	Coventry C	W	6-3
25	(h)	Luton T	L	3-4
26	(a)	Luton T	W	4-1
29	(a)	Aston Villa	D	2-2
Jan 12	(a)	Charlton A	L	0-3
19	(h)	Charlton A	W	2-0
Feb 2	(a)	Fulham	W	1-0
9	(a)	Plymouth A	W	2-1
16	(h)	Plymouth A	W	7-0
23	(h)	Portsmouth	W	3-1
Mar 2	(a)	Portsmouth	W	3-2
9	(a)	Nottingham F	I)	1-1
16	(h)	Nottingham F	L	1-3
23	(h)	Newport C	W	4-1
30	(a)	Newport C	D	2-2
Apr 6	(a)	Wolves	D	3-3
13	(h)	Wolves	W	2-1
19	(a)	Swansea T	W	3-2
20	(h)	West Brom A	D	1-1
22	(h)	Swansea T	W	3-0
27	(a)	West Brom A	W	2-1
29	(h)	Fulham	L	3-5
May 4	(a)	Arsenal	L	1-2

P	W	D	L	F	A	W	D	L	F	A	Pts	Pos
42	10	4	7	53	38	10	7	4	41	38	51	7th

FA Cup

3	Jan 5	(h)	Arsenal	W	6-0
	9	(a)	Arsenal	L	0-1
4	26	(a)	Chelsea	L	0-2
	30	(h)	Chelsea	W	1-0

SEASON 1946-47
FOOTBALL LEAGUE (DIVISION 2)

Aug 31	(a)	Plymouth A	L	1-3
Sep 2	(h)	Fulham	W	3-2
7	(h)	Leicester C	L	0-2
9	(a)	Fulham	L	2-3
14	(a)	Chesterfield	L	1-3
21	(h)	Millwall	W	3-1
28	(a)	Bradford	W	1-0
Oct 5	(h)	Manchester C	W	1-0
12	(a)	Burnley	L	1-2
19	(h)	Tottenham H	D	2-2
26	(a)	Swansea T	L	1-2
Nov 2	(h)	Newcastle U	L	0-2
9	(a)	West Brom A	W	3-2
16	(h)	Birmingham C	L	0-4
23	(a)	Coventry C	L	1-2
30	(h)	Nottingham F	D	2-2
Dec 7	(a)	Southampton	L	2-4
21	(a)	Barnsley	W	2-1
25	(h)	Luton T	W	2-1
26	(a)	Luton T	L	1-2
28	(h)	Plymouth A	W	4-1
Jan 1	(a)	Sheffield W	D	1-1
4	(a)	Leicester C	L	0-4
18	(h)	Chesterfield	W	5-0
25	(a)	Millwall	D	0-0
Feb 1	(h)	Bradford	D	1-1
8	(h)	Newport C	W	3-0
Mar 1	(h)	Swansea T	W	3-0
15	(h)	West Brom A	W	3-2
22	(a)	Birmingham C	L	0-3
29	(h)	Coventry C	L	1-2
Apr 4	(a)	Bury	L	0-4
5	(a)	Nottingham F	L	3-4
7	(h)	Bury	D	3-3
12	(h)	Southampton	W	4-0
19	(a)	Newport C	D	1-1
26	(h)	Barnsley	W	4-0
May 3	(h)	Sheffield W	W	2-1
17	(a)	Tottenham H	D	0-0
24	(a)	Manchester C	L	0-2
26	(a)	Newcastle U	W	3-2
31	(h)	Burnley	L	0-5

P	W	D	L	F	A	W	D	L	F	A	Pts	Pos
42	12	4	5	46	31	4	4	13	24	45	40	12th

FA Cup

3	Jan 11	(h)	Leicester C	L	1-2

SEASON 1947-48
FOOTBALL LEAGUE (DIVISION 2)

Aug 23	(a)	Bradford	L	1-4
25	(h)	Millwall	D	1-1
30	(h)	Nottingham F	W	2-1
Sep 1	(a)	Millwall	D	1-1
6	(a)	Doncaster R	L	0-1
8	(h)	Tottenham H	D	1-1
13	(h)	Southampton	W	2-0
15	(a)	Tottenham H	D	2-2
20	(a)	Bury	W	2-1
27	(h)	Coventry C	W	1-0
Oct 4	(h)	Chesterfield	W	4-0
11	(a)	Newcastle U	L	0-1
18	(h)	Birmingham C	D	0-0
25	(a)	West Brom A	W	2-1
Nov 1	(h)	Barnsley	W	2-1
8	(a)	Plymouth A	D	1-1
15	(h)	Luton T	D	0-0
22	(a)	Brentford	D	1-1
29	(h)	Leicester C	D	1-1
Dec 6	(a)	Leeds U	L	1-2
13	(h)	Fulham	W	3-0
20	(h)	Bradford	D	0-0
26	(a)	Sheffield W	L	3-5
27	(h)	Sheffield W	L	1-4
Jan 3	(a)	Nottingham F	L	1-2
24	(h)	Doncaster R	W	2-1
31	(a)	Southampton	L	1-3
Feb 7	(h)	Bury	W	2-0
14	(a)	Coventry C	W	1-0
28	(h)	Newcastle U	L	0-2
Mar 6	(a)	Birmingham C	W	1-0
13	(h)	West Brom A	L	0-2
20	(a)	Barnsley	D	1-1
26	(a)	Cardiff C	W	3-0
27	(h)	Plymouth A	D	1-1
29	(h)	Cardiff C	W	4-2
Apr 3	(a)	Luton T	D	0-0
7	(a)	Chesterfield	L	0-6
10	(h)	Brentford	L	0-1
17	(a)	Leicester C	W	3-1
24	(h)	Leeds U	W	2-1
May 1	(a)	Fulham	D	1-1

P	W	D	L	F	A	W	D	L	F	A	Pts	Pos
42	10	7	4	29	19	6	7	8	26	34	46	6th

L. Goulden

FA Cup

3	Jan 10	(a)	Blackburn R	D	0-0
R	17	(h)	Blackburn R	L	24

SEASON 1948-49
FOOTBALL LEAGUE (DIVISION 2)

Aug 21	(h)	Lincoln C	D	2-2
23	(a)	Sheffield W	L	0-3
28	(a)	Chesterfield	D	0-0
30	(h)	Sheffield W	D	2-2
Sep 4	(h)	West Brom A	W	1-0
6	(a)	Coventry C	L	0-1
11	(a)	Bury	L	0-2
13	(h)	Coventry C	D	2-2
18	(h)	Plymouth A	W	3-0
25	(h)	Tottenham H	W	1-0
Oct 2	(a)	Brentford	D	0-0
9	(a)	Blackburn R	D	0-0
16	(h)	Cardiff C	W	3-1
23	(a)	Queen's Park R	L	1-2
30	(h)	Luton T	L	0-1
Nov 6	(a)	Bradford	W	3-2
13	(h)	Southampton	D	1-1
20	(a)	Barnsley	W	3-2
Dec 4	(a)	Nottingham F	L	0-3
11	(h)	Fulham	W	1-0
18	(a)	Lincoln C	L	3-4
25	(h)	Leeds U	W	3-2
27	(a)	Leeds U	W	3-1
Jan 1	(h)	Chesterfield	L	1-2
15	(a)	West Brom A	L	1-2
22	(h)	Bury	W	2-1
Feb 5	(a)	Plymouth A	L	0-2
12	(h)	Grimsby T	W	1-0
19	(a)	Tottenham H	D	1-1
Mar 5	(h)	Blackburn R	W	2-1
12	(a)	Cardiff C	L	0-4
19	(h)	Queen's Park R	W	2-0
26	(a)	Luton T	W	1-0
Apr 2	(h)	Bradford	W	4-1
9	(a)	Southampton	W	1-0
15	(h)	Leicester C	W	4-1
16	(h)	Barnsley	W	2-0
18	(a)	Leicester C	D	1-1
23	(a)	Grimsby T	L	0-3
25	(h)	Brentford	D	1-1
30	(h)	Nottingham F	L	0-5
May 7	(a)	Fulham	L	0-2

P	W	D	L	F	A	W	D	L	F	A	Pts	Pos
42	13	5	3	38	23	5	5	11	18	35	46	7th

FA Cup

3	Jan 8	(a)	Luton T	L	1-3

SEASON 1949-50
FOOTBALL LEAGUE (DIVISION 2)

Aug 20	(a)	Luton T	D	2-2
22	(h)	Leeds U	W	3-1
27	(h)	Barnsley	W	2-1
31	(a)	Leeds U	D	2-2
Sep 3	(a)	Plymouth A	W	3-0
6	(h)	Southampton	L	1-2
10	(a)	Sheffield U	D	0-0
17	(h)	Grimsby T	W	4-3
24	(a)	Queen's Park R	W	1-0
Oct 1	(h)	Preston NE	L	0-3
8	(h)	Chesterfield	D	1-1
15	(a)	Bradford	L	1-2
22	(h)	Leicester C	D	2-2
29	(a)	Bury	L	1-3
Nov 5	(h)	Tottenham H	L	0-1
12	(a)	Cardiff C	W	1-0
19	(h)	Blackburn R	L	0-2
26	(a)	Brentford	W	2-0
Dec 3	(h)	Hull C	W	2-1
10	(a)	Sheffield W	L	1-2
17	(h)	Luton T	D	0-0
24	(a)	Barnsley	D	1-1
26	(h)	Swansea T	W	3-0
27	(a)	Swansea T	L	0-1
31	(h)	Plymouth A	D	2-2
Jan 14	(h)	Sheffield U	D	0-0
21	(a)	Grimsby T	L	0-2
Feb 4	(h)	Queen's Park R	W	1-0
18	(a)	Preston NE	L	1-2
25	(a)	Chesterfield	L	0-1
Mar 4	(h)	Bradford	W	1-0
11	(a)	Leicester C	L	1-2
18	(h)	Bury	W	4-0
25	(a)	Tottenham H	L	1-4
Apr 1	(h)	Brentford	D	2-2
8	(a)	Hull C	D	2-2
10	(h)	Coventry C	L	0-1
11	(a)	Coventry C	L	1-5
15	(h)	Cardiff C	L	0-1
22	(a)	Blackburn R	L	0-2
29	(h)	Sheffield W	D	2-2
May 6	(a)	Southampton	L	2-3

P	W	D	L	F	A	W	D	L	F	A	Pts	Pos
42	8	7	6	30	25	4	5	12	23	36	36	19th

FA Cup

3	Jan 7	(h)	Ipswich T	W	5-1
4	28	(h)	Everton	L	1-2

SEASON 1950-51
FOOTBALL LEAGUE (DIVISION 2)

Aug 19	(h)	Hull C	D	3-3
24	(h)	Luton T	W	2-1
26	(a)	Doncaster R	L	0-3
28	(a)	Luton T	D	1-1
Sep 2	(h)	Brentford	L	1-2
4	(a)	Cardiff C	L	1-2
9	(a)	Blackburn R	W	3-1
16	(h)	Southampton	W	3-0
23	(a)	Barnsley	W	2-1
30	(h)	Sheffield U	L	3-5
Oct 7	(h)	Queen's Park R	W	4-1
14	(a)	Bury	L	0-3
21	(h)	Leicester C	D	0-0
28	(a)	Chesterfield	W	2-1
Nov 4	(h)	Coventry C	W	3-2
11	(a)	Manchester C	L	0-2
18	(h)	Preston NE	W	2-0
25	(a)	Notts C	L	1-4
Dec 2	(h)	Grimsby T	W	2-1
9	(a)	Birmingham C	L	1-3
16	(a)	Hull C	W	2-1
23	(h)	Doncaster R	D	0-0
25	(h)	Leeds U	W	3-1
26	(a)	Leeds U	L	0-2
30	(a)	Brentford	D	1-1
Jan 13	(h)	Blackburn R	L	2-3
20	(a)	Southampton	D	2-2
Feb 3	(h)	Barnsley	W	4-2
17	(a)	Sheffield U	D	1-1
24	(a)	Queen's Park R	D	3-3
Mar 3	(h)	Bury	L	2-3
10	(a)	Leicester C	L	0-1
17	(h)	Chesterfield	W	2-0
23	(h)	Swansea T	D	1-1
24	(a)	Coventry C	L	0-1
26	(a)	Swansea T	L	2-3
31	(h)	Manchester C	L	2-4
Apr 7	(a)	Preston NE	W	1-0
14	(h)	Notts C	W	4-2
21	(a)	Grimsby T	W	1-0
28	(h)	Birmingham C	L	1-2
May 5	(h)	Cardiff C	D	0-0

P	W	D	L	F	A	W	D	L	F	A	Pts	Pos
42	10	5	6	44	33	6	5	10	24	36	42	13th

FA Cup

3	Jan 6	(h)	Cardiff C	W	2-1
4	27	(a)	Stoke C	L	0-1

WEST HAM UNITED FOOTBALL CO., LTD
Boleyn Ground, Green Street, Upton Park, E.13

West Ham Un. Res v Queens Pk. R. Res

LONDON JUNIOR FOOTBALL COMBINATION

Saturday, 18th May, 1940 Kick-off 3.15 p.m

WEST HAM UNITED Res

Colours: Claret and Blue

RIGHT LEFT

1 C. English

2 W. Lewis 3 A. Pope

4 W. Bricknell 5 A. Collier 6 D. Bailey or T. Fuller

7 R. Quickenden 8 E. Exton 9 E. Chapman (Captain) 10 A. Webber 11 B. Dowsett

Referee: Mr. H. BARNETT

Linesmen: Messrs. G. ROGERS (Red Stripe Flag) and W. J. DARLINGTON (Blue Stripe Flag)

11 F. Bevan 10 H. Daniels 9 D. Regan 8 J. Dumsday 7 J. Webb

6 F. Friend 5 L. Sneddon 4 F. Anderson

3 E. Barsham K. Wilson

1 H. Brown

LEFT RIGHT

QUEENS PARK RANGERS Res.

TO-DAY'S VISITORS

Our young Hammers extend a hearty welcome to the Queens Park Rangers second string.

Last week-end provided a reverse and a success for our lads. At the Valley last Saturday they found the Charlton Juniors too strong for them, but they gained a decisive victory over the Lions here on the Monday and added a further pair of points to keep company with those bagged at the Den.

CUP-TIE

Our first team faces a stiff task at Huddersfield to-day and the fact that in this round there is no second bite makes it the more interesting and keen. We are quite optimistic however

LAST SATURDAY

Our Cup XI beat Leicester City by a decisive score but there was plenty of the real cup fighting, and it was not an easy victory.

Following this they went to Portsmouth on the Monday and brought back a well-deserved point.

NEXT WEEK

We have an important Regional Competition match here on Monday when Millwall provide the opposition. Kick-off at 6.45 p.m.

On Wednesday our Junior XI visit Selhurst Park to meet Crystal Palace in the London Junior Football Combination.

In the event of our interest in the Football League Cup ending at Huddersfield to-day, we shall meet Charlton Athletic at the Valley next Saturday.

At the time of this programme being printed we have no match arranged for the Boleyn Ground next Saturday. Maybe we shall have a fourth round Cup match here. Any fixture that is arranged will be announced through the Press.

THANKS

Alderman Parsons asks us to tender her most grateful thanks for your truly magnificent effort last Saturday. The collection in aid of Comforts for the Troops was a bumper.

CHAPTER 4
THE TED FENTON ERA

The arrival of Ted Fenton as West Ham United manager attracted little coverage during the World Cup summer of 1950. Fenton, who had worked in tandem with predecessor Charlie Paynter for two years while waiting for his chance to take the managerial hotseat, was regarded as a conservative appointment who would make few significant changes. But despite his strong links with West Ham United's past, the new manager proved an open-minded and progressive coach, and was responsible for the modernisation of several key areas of the football club.

Fenton's youth policy

Fenton inherited a team that had narrowly avoided relegation the previous season, and which contained too many players well past their best. The Hammers were in desperate need of an injection of youth to shake them out of their Second Division slumbers. In his autobiography, *At Home with the Hammers*, Fenton recalled how, upon returning to Upton Park, he had found many of the men who had been his team-mates before the war, and that 'most of them were either past it, or getting near to that point'. But to replace these seasoned veterans with new, more youthful talent would be expensive and there was no money in the Hammers transfer kitty. If the club were to succeed they would need to establish a structured youth development programme. Fenton, together with new chairman Reg Pratt and chief scout Wally St Pier, worked tirelessly throughout the early 1950s to set up a proper youth section, but it would be several years before their labours bore fruit. In the meantime, the new manager would have to make do with the same squad of players that had flirted with the drop to the Third Division in 1949–50.

Allison arrives

The Fenton era kicked off with an entertaining 3–3 draw at home to Hull City before a crowd of 30,000, and Hammers' goals were scored by Gerry Gazzard and Bill Robinson. The same combination, ably supported by winger Terry Woodgate, would monopolise West Ham United's scoring throughout an otherwise inconsistent campaign, and the trio, who missed just three League games between them all season, claimed 51 of the club's 68 goals. But Hammers' biggest problems were in defence, and by mid-season the new manager had decided to make a significant change to his ageing rearguard. To facilitate this defensive reshuffle, however, Fenton needed money and so sold promising winger Eric 'Rabbit' Parsons to Chelsea for £22,500. With his new found transfer fund behind him, the Hammers boss made his first signing, paying Charlton Athletic £7,000 for 22-year-old centre-half Malcolm Allison in February 1950. It was a move which ended the Upton Park career of club captain Dick Walker who had made 287 League appearances since signing in 1934.

The arrival of Allison was hugely significant and represented a watershed in the history of the Hammers. Centre-half is a key position in any team, but at West Ham United this was particularly so. Between 1919 and 1951 only three men – George Kay, Jim Barrett and Walker – had worn the Hammers number five shirt with any regularity. Each member of this distinguished trio was recognised as the leader and standard-bearer of their team, and all three were imposing figures with powerful personalities. By installing his own number five, Fenton – who had enjoyed an uneasy relationship with Dick Walker since returning to the club in 1948 – was able to draw a line beneath the Charlie Paynter era and, at the same time, commence his own programme of team-building. The choice of Allison as the man to fulfil this role was also notable. The Kent-born defender was a hugely confident figure who was a keen student of modern, continental football and a man impatient for success. Despite their contrasting personalities, Allison and Fenton were united by ambition, and this unlikely combination would prove the driving force throughout a decade of great change at Upton Park.

League success, however, did not come quickly and in Ted Fenton's first four seasons the Hammers failed to finish in the top half of the table. With no money for big signings, it would take both time and ingenuity for the new manager to build a team which could challenge for promotion. Fortunately, there were a number of promising youngsters already playing in the Hammers junior teams. Harry Hooper jnr, Andy Malcolm and John Bond would all successfully make the step up to senior football, although all three would have their progress unavoidably interrupted by National Service in 1951. Southern Ireland would also continue to provide talent, with Frank O'Farrell the latest in a succession of Irishmen to break into the first team at Upton Park during the 1950s.

Right: Ireland was a rich source of talent for West Ham United throughout the 1950s. Manager Ted Fenton (second from the right) is seen here introducing Eire internationals Noel Cantwell (far right) and Frank O'Farrell (third from right) to newly recruited compatriots M McGuiness (second from left) and F Harvey (third from left) in the summer of 1955. The other figure (extreme left) is Mr E Davies, Hammers' representative in Ireland.

Above: Reg Pratt was West Ham United chairman from 1950 to 1979 and proved a key figure in the modernisation of the Club, in particular the development of the youth section.

Left: West Ham United have had few more influential players than Malcolm Allison. The Kent-born central defender was the leader of the famous Upton Park Academy and did as much as anybody to bring the Club into the modern era.

Fenton captures Cantwell

At the outset of the 1952–53 season the Chairman, Reg Pratt, explained that the club had been 'generally satisfied with the performance of our lads,' during the previous campaign, adding that it had provided 'valuable experience to our many young players'. There would, however, be one major signing at the start of Fenton's third campaign in charge. Former Hammer Johnny McGowan had alerted his old club to a talented young Irishman called Noel Cantwell, who had captained the Republic of Ireland youth team from left-back in 1951. Noel had moved to England to find work so the West Ham United boss had first to locate him at his digs in Birmingham. Eventually the two met and, according to Fenton, had a 'talk which was twice as long as it need have been because Noel was so darn modest'. A deal was agreed, with the Hammers paying Cork Athletic £750 for the services of the 20-year-old defender. It would prove a wise investment, and within six months of his arrival Noel had made his Second Division debut.

Noel Cantwell was one of three promising young defenders to break into the Hammers first team during 1952–53. John Bond, who had made his debut the previous season, got his chance in the number three shirt and made 14 appearances, while East London-born Ken Brown enjoyed a three-match run in the team at centre-half. Both Bond and Brown had joined the Club from amateur football, products of good scouting as opposed to professional coaching. Fenton had himself done much of the groundwork which led to the capture of Ken Brown, something which former Hammers goalkeeper Ernie Gregory remembers as typical: 'Ted was a man who knew his players, he would have made a great scout.'

Fenton's efforts to modernise his playing staff were matched by those of chairman Reg Pratt, who was doing his best to make sure that the club remained up-to-date in all other areas. In 1952 West Ham United took the bold step of installing floodlights at the Boleyn Ground, a move which harked back to the experiments of the Thames Ironworks team in 1896. This time the lights were supplied by GEC and were fitted to long wooden poles (steel was in short supply, and could only be used under licence), placed through the North and South Bank roofs. Results were impressive and, though it would be three years before League fixtures were played beneath the lights, two friendly matches brought in crowds in excess of 25,000.

Young Hammers shine

By 1953 the Hammers youth scheme was also beginning to take shape, and in that year the club's Colts progressed to the semi-final of the FA Youth Cup. Central to this success was Wally St Pier, whose honesty and integrity were key factors in the club's quest to attract top local talent to Upton Park. Never a man to adopt aggressive or dubious tactics, Wally was a well-respected and honest scout in a world dominated by unscrupulous sharks. West Ham United were now able to offer a complete network of teams from Frank Wilkins' 'Junior' side, which took boys at 14, through the Colts, B team and A team, into the Reserves and first team. Promising youngsters were trained by a coaching staff which included Bill Robinson, Albert Walker and Stan Wilcockson. Senior professionals were also becoming involved with training the youngsters and Malcolm Allison, already a qualified coach, was a regular contributor to the Tuesday and Thursday evening schoolboy sessions at Upton Park.

The success of the juniors, however, did little to satisfy short-term ambitions. With no change in financial circumstances there could be no big money signings to sweep the Hammers into the First Division. The chairman's programme notes ahead of the 1953–54 season spelled out the situation: 'The buying of high-priced stars is a privilege confined to a few of the present-day clubs... frankly we are not a rich club, and our future commitments mean that we must budget accordingly.' Two new signings who would make a big impact without breaking Ted Fenton's budget arrived in 1953. John Dick was a well-built inside-forward from Scotland, while Malcolm Musgrove was a winger who hailed from the north-east. Both men had been spotted playing amateur football for teams in the south of England while on National Service. Although there were no other clubs to negotiate with for the transfers of these two ex-servicemen, securing their signatures was far from simple. A chase around Glasgow was required before Fenton won the race for Johnny Dick, while an extended excursion to Newcastle was needed to convince Musgrove to head for E13.

New football, old problems

Dick was included in the Hammers line-up for the first match of the 1953–54 season, and played his part in a 5–0 home victory over Lincoln City. Fenton's team was beginning to take shape, and another convincing victory – 4–1 at home to Leicester City – in the next match raised hopes that this might be West Ham United's year. Alas, Hammers' third fixture ended in a 5–0 reverse at Rotherham United, and thereafter Ted Fenton's team reverted to their all-too – familiar inconsistent form of recent years. At season's end the Hammers occupied a disappointing 13th position, having lost more games than they had won.

The season had seen Ted Fenton embrace a new style of continental football which was to become an entrenched part of the now-famous West Ham United tradition. On 25 November 1953, Hungary crushed Walter Winterbottom's England 6-3 at Wembley. It was the first time that the home nation had lost to overseas opposition beneath the twin towers, and English football was stunned by the result. The Hungarians had played with a pace and fluency never before seen, and England had no answer to their measured, incisive football. Geoffrey Green of *The Times* wrote that Hungary were a team of 'progressive, dangerous artists who seemed able to adjust themselves at will to any demand'. Ted Fenton had become an instant convert to the Hungarian method and immediately set about introducing this exciting style of football at Upton Park. The Hammers boss watched the film of the England v Hungary match five times, and declared in his autobiography that he was, 'determined to milk that match dry of every possible lesson'. Attractive football based around short, quick passing would become the new Upton Park orthodoxy.

Fashion, fitness and flair

The influence of continental football, however, would extend beyond the style of play adopted by the Hammers. Both Ted Fenton and Malcolm Allison were keen that the club's new tactics should be matched by an equally modern kit. One of the first things that the West Ham United manager did was to replace the heavy old English boots worn by most players with lightweight footwear. Fenton contacted the Hungarian team to find out where they had got their boots from, and discovered that they had been made by a German company called Adidas. He immediately ordered two dozen pairs and told journalists that the difference was like that between 'clogs and ballet shoes'. Ernie Gregory remembers that Allison was the pioneer of this modern European football fashion: 'Malcolm was fascinated by the continental approach. He wore his socks pulled up, with no shin guards like the Italians, and he even took his shorts home and had them taken-up. Before long, we all turned out in the same style.' Eventually the West Ham United shirt was also updated from a jersey-style to a light, athletic v-neck. By the mid-1950s the Hammers looked every inch the modern European team, and their new appearance earned them the nickname Super Hammers from certain quarters of the media.

Fenton was also keen to improve the fitness of his team, and to this end he recruited the help of former weight-lifting champion Bill Watson. The players were sceptical about the benefits of weight-training at first, but gained enthusiasm after the manager helped break the ice by demonstrating each exercise himself. Watson would run sessions three afternoons a week, and Fenton claimed that the effects on both strength and fitness were marked. He had been an army PT instructor during the war and had an interest in what he called the 'scientific methods of physical education'. He believed that the old style training – sprinting and lapping with a session of ball work once a week – was outdated. Under Fenton, the Hammers would train for four instead of two hours a day combining both fitness and ball work.

John Bond (left) and Malcolm Allison (right) give piggy backs to Albert Foan and Jimmy Andrews during a typically unorthodox Hammers training session during 1955.

Despite their new found fashion and flair, the self-styled Super Hammers were still far from convincing on the pitch. The 1954–55 season kicked off with away fixtures against Swansea Town and Blackburn Rovers, and both matches ended in 5–2 defeats. A 3–0 home victory over Notts County in the next match temporarily raised Hammers' spirits, but two days later Blackburn completed a humiliating double over Ted Fenton's team by registering another 5–2 triumph. There were, however, mitigating factors. Goalkeeper Ernie Gregory was in the midst of an 18-month absence from the team with injury, and after the season's second match he was joined in the treatment room by key defenders Noel Cantwell and Malcolm Allison. The return of Cantwell and Allison in mid-season would trigger an upturn in fortune, and after a run of six consecutive victories the Hammers found themselves on the fringes of the promotion

Hammers go on the attack against Holland Sports during Upton Park's first live televised game. The match, which was played in 1955, was also memorable for the debut of a special 'TV-friendly' satin kit.

race at the end of March. Alas, the season's closing fixtures were an unmitigated disaster and five defeats in the last seven matches saw West Ham United finish in eighth place. 'We are disappointed, yes – but far from dismayed,' proclaimed the final matchday programme of the season, 'and despite all wild statements to the contrary we *do* want promotion.'

The 'Academy'

There would be no major signings ahead of the 1955–56 season, although one new arrival on the groundstaff – a local boy called John Lyall – was at the start of what would prove a long and illustrious Hammers career. Despite the absence of any major transfer activity, the summer months had not been a period of idleness for all at Upton Park. The most obvious change was that the Boleyn Castle had been demolished as part of extensive building work which would eventually result in a new and expensive main entrance on Green Street.

Away from E13, four first-team players – Malcolm Allison, Jimmy Andrews, Les Bennett and Dave Sexton – had used their summer break to good effect by taking coaching courses. Under Ted Fenton, the senior pros had begun to take a more active interest in tactics and training, and several players were involved in coaching schoolboys on Tuesday and Thursday evenings. Many of the players would also meet up at Cassattarri's Cafe after training where they discussed practice drills, patterns of play and all things football. Ideas would often find their way onto the football pitch on a Saturday afternoon, and by the mid-1950s it was apparent that player power was becoming increasingly influential at Upton Park.

Restless fans

But even the famous West Ham United Academy could not prevent a significant downturn in League form during 1955–56, and at season's end the Hammers occupied 16th place in the Second Division. The campaign had started badly, and after three defeats in the opening four fixtures, sections of the Upton Park crowd expressed their disquiet with behaviour which was described by the club programme as 'an appalling display of bad sportsmanship'. The expression of 'mob spirit' referred to, was of course 'that bane of modern soccer – the slow hand clap'. Supporters were advised to 'make fair criticism or please stay away'.

The Hammers' best form of 1956 was reserved for the FA Cup, and a run to the competition's sixth round had the fans applauding at full speed once more. Home victories against Preston North End (5–2) and Cardiff City (2–1), followed by a hard-fought replay triumph over Second Division rivals Blackburn Rovers, had guided Ted Fenton's team to a quarter-final tie against Tottenham Hotspur. The match at White Hart Lane provided a rare opportunity for West Ham United to show that they could still compete with the big clubs from the First Division. The boys in claret and blue did not disappoint, and produced a fine display of attacking football. A Johnny Dick hat-trick put the Hammers into a 3-1 lead, but by half-time they had been pegged back to 3-2, and with 15 minutes to go Len Duquemin struck an equaliser to earn Spurs a replay. West Ham United gave another polished performance at Upton Park, but after seeing a series of penalty appeals turned down by referee Joe Williams, Duquemin once more struck the decisive goal to claim a 2-1 victory for the North Londoners. The only consolation for the Hammers was that they had proved that they remained a quality team and, in particular, a potent attacking force.

Success in the Cup, however, was quickly forgotten in March when crowd favourite Harry Hooper was sold to Wolverhampton Wanderers for £25,000. The fans were incensed by the sale of a young player who they had hoped would play a key role in taking the club back to the First Division. Chairman Reg Pratt explained the circumstances which had necessitated Hooper's departure in the matchday programme: 'The directors of this club have for a long time had to face some very hard and disagreeable facts... we have never been "well off", in fact we have had an uphill struggle all the way.' Mr Pratt went on to explain that the club was facing a bill of £17,000 for the building work on a new main entrance at Upton Park and that with falling gate receipts, the Revenue account was £2,400 in the red. Put simply, the offer from Wolves was one which West Ham United could not afford to turn down. But the board did not keep all of the £25,000 fee, and granted Ted Fenton £8,500 to secure the services of a replacement outside-right. Mike Grice, a relative unknown, arrived from Fenton's former club Colchester United on the same day that Hooper was unveiled at Molineux.

By the start of the 1956–57 season, the Hammers squad had been trimmed from 37 to 33 full-time pros. Senior players including Dave Sexton, George Taylor, Jimmy Andrews and Harry Kinsell were among the departees as Ted Fenton pruned his large first-team pool. Another player on his way out of E13 was 43-year-old centre-half Dick Walker – hanging up his boots after 24 seasons with the Hammers. Walker, who had spent the last four years in the A team, was awarded a testimonial match against Sparta Rotterdam and would go on to work as a scout for Tottenham Hotspur. A benefit match was also arranged for injury victims Geoff Hallas and Brian Moore.

Despite their reduced playing staff, the Hammers enjoyed a much improved League campaign during 1956–57. A run of seven consecutive victories between Christmas Day and the middle of February even had Ted Fenton's team dreaming of a return to the top flight. However, poor form thereafter saw their hopes fade by Easter and they finished in eighth place in the League. It was still significant progress over recent performances, and there was now a belief that the club was at last moving into the ascendant.

Rising stars

But it was at youth rather than senior level that West Ham United enjoyed their greatest triumphs in 1957. The Hammers Colts had become London's leading junior team and boasted England youth internationals Johnny Cartwright and John Lyall in their line-up. It was a team dominated by local talent, and their appearance at the final of the FA Youth Cup was cause for much celebration at Upton Park. En route to the final, the Colts had smashed 14 goals past Briggs Sport and had defeated a highly fancied Arsenal team. Their opponents in the final were Manchester United, who had won all of the four previous Youth Cup competitions. John Lyall, in his autobiography *Just Like My Dreams*, recalls that the Reds were a 'superb side' who included two players – Dave Gaskell and Alex Dawson – with first-team experience in their line-up. A crowd of 15,000 attended the first leg of the final at Upton Park, and most were disappointed to see the home team go down 3-2. It was a deficit that the East Londoners were unable to reverse at Old Trafford, and after three hours of football the aggregate score stood at 8-2 in Manchester United's favour.

Although it was disappointing for the Hammers Colts to lose their Cup final, the primary objective of any youth programme is to develop players for the first team, and against that yardstick West Ham United's junior teams were proving a success. At the start of the 1957-58 season two more products of Wally St Pier's youth scheme, John Lyall and Joe Kirkup, signed on as pros. Both players had won England schoolboy caps and each looked forward to a bright future in the game. But as Lyall and Kirkup launched their careers, three other young Hammers – Brian Rhodes, Andy Nelson and Harry Obeney – had their football world severely disrupted by the call to national service.

Lyall and Kirkup apart, there were no new arrivals on the Upton Park professional staff during the summer of 1957, and it was a familiar looking West Ham United line-up which took the field for the opening fixture of the 1957–58 season at home to Lincoln City. The match ended in what Ted Fenton described as a 'fortunate draw', with Billy Dare and Malcolm Allison the Hammers scorers. Dare, a veteran forward who had arrived at Upton Park from Brentford in 1955, would enjoy a rich vein of form at the start of the season and he scored in each of West Ham United's first four matches – a sequence which included a hat-trick in the 3–1 victory at Bristol Rovers. Unfortunately, Hammers' results could not match their centre-forward's consistency, and at the end of August the team had won just one game. Things deteriorated in September, with Fenton's team losing four of their seven games. The manager would later reflect: 'If I say we made a moderate start to that season, I'd be overstating the case.' After 11 matches the Hammers were in seventh position, and had just three more points than last-placed Cardiff City.

Newcastle-born winger Malcolm Musgrove was one of a number of exceptional signings made by Ted Fenton during the early years of his reign at the Boleyn Ground. Musgrove, who was signed from Lynemouth Colliery in 1954, enjoyed a ten-season run in the Hammers line-up, scoring an impressive 89 goals in 301 appearances before joining Leyton Orient for £11,000 in 1962–63.

Shuffling the pack

West Ham United's ambitions were not helped when, at the end of September, Malcolm Allison was diagnosed as having tuberculosis. Allison, who was club captain and a vital figure in Fenton's plans, had begun to complain of chest pains and shortness of breath after an away fixture against Sheffield United. He was admitted to hospital and would only return to training following surgery and a long period of convalescence. The skipper's place at centre-half would go to Ken Brown, with Billy Lansdowne taking over at left-half. But, despite this defensive reshuffle, it was with his forward line that Fenton was most concerned.

The manager felt that the Hammers lacked a physical presence at centre-forward: a targetman who would complement the skilful Johnny Dick and who would profit from the service of wingers Malcolm Musgrove and Mike Grice. Newcastle striker Vic Keeble, who had played for Fenton at Colchester, was the man chosen to fill the Hammers number nine shirt. At 27 years old, he was an established first team regular and had scored 50 goals in his six years on Tyneside. Keeble's arrival at Upton Park, for a fee of £10,000, would prove hugely significant. It was a move which not only made the board's ambition patently clear to supporters but also helped put an end to criticism over the sale of Harry Hooper.

Buoyed by their expensive new signing, Hammers raised their sights toward promotion once more. Keeble did not disappoint and scored on his debut in a home fixture against Doncaster Rovers. There was, however, much to do if West Ham United were to recover after taking just 12 points from the same number of League games. Fourteen goals – including four each for Keeble and Dick – in the next four fixtures propelled Hammers up the table, and by the end of December they were third in the Second Division.

Cantwell and Bond

At last, Fenton's team had found the right blend of effective and entertaining football. The Hammers boss was now encouraging his players to mix their trademark short-passing game with a more direct approach, switching the ball quickly from defence to attack. Two players who did not always follow the plan, however, were full-backs Noel Cantwell and John Bond. Both men were committed to passing the ball out from the back and would only launch the ball forward if there was no other option. It was a practice shared by goalkeeper Ernie Gregory who had followed the lead of former England custodian Frank Swift – a goalie who would always throw the ball out rather than kick it. 'I could kick the ball as far as anyone, but it will just come straight back at you, so you don't give your defence the chance of a breather,' remembers Ernie. 'If it was on, I'd throw it. I threw more balls than I kicked, and I'd say to John and Noel: "If it's on to play football, why not play instead of keep hitting long balls."'

Cantwell had become team captain following Malcolm Allison's illness, and together with Bond, was one of eight regulars to make more than 30 League appearances during 1957–58. The Hammers full-backs were both skilful attackers and according to Fenton, they 'revelled in the promotion run, oozing confidence and getting away with things that weren't planned at any tactical meeting.' Ernie Gregory shares his former manager's view on the men charged with guarding the Hammers flanks: 'John and Noel had great ability and tremendous confidence. They would both bomb forward while Ken Brown kept things tight at the back. At the time, they were the greatest full-backs in Britain.'

Both Cantwell and Bond were among West Ham United's scorers during January 1958, a month which would bring four victories and 17 goals as Hammers enhanced their reputation as a team destined for the First Division. Two of these successes came in the FA Cup, but any hopes of a repeat of 1923's promotion and Cup final double were dashed when Johnny Haynes struck a memorable goal for Fulham to give the Cottagers a 3–2 victory in a fifth-round tie at Upton Park. Fenton reacted to this set-back with what he described as a 'psychological move... to combat depression,' ahead of the next match away to Leyton Orient. The manager's mind game was to change kits to the players' favoured white shirt with a claret and a blue hoop. It is impossible to gauge the effect of this sartorial switch — suffice to say that the Hammers ran out comfortable 4–1 victors thanks to goals from Smith, Dare, Keeble and Dick.

At boardroom level, the disappointment of elimination from the FA Cup was tempered by the news that Entertainment Tax was to be abolished. It was a move that, on the previous year's gate receipts, would save the club £16,000. According to the chairman, this change 'could not have been more timely,' as without it, the board would 'very soon have had to decide on a drastic curtailment of expenditure'. The Hammers were already committed to an extensive programme of rebuilding and repair at the Boleyn Ground, and it was only a transfer surplus of £17,500 which had kept the club in credit during 1957. Most of this surplus had been generated by the controversial sale of Harry Hooper to Wolves.

Malcolm Allison was a hugely influential figure for West Ham United both on and off the field. He took an active role not only in directing training but also in determining the kit and even the tactics employed by Hammers during the 1950s.

Life at the top

With West Ham United's accountants satisfied by the taxman's generosity, there would be no need to sell off prime assets for at least another year. Ted Fenton could now concentrate on the job of maintaining the club's position toward the summit of the Second Division, safe in the knowledge that none of his top stars would be sold to balance the books.

As the season entered its final quarter, Hammers enjoyed a rich vein of form, winning four successive matches to maintain their promotion push. It was a sequence which culminated in the 8–0 thrashing of Rotherham United at Upton Park – still the Club's record League victory. Four goals from Dick and two each for Keeble and Johnny Smith had earned a result which gave Fenton particular pleasure. The manager later commented that: 'The manner in which the goals came was the culmination of what we had been working on all season.' But after the sublime came the predictable, and a week later Hammers went down to their first League defeat of the year, a 3–1 reverse at Huddersfield Town. It was to be no more than a blip and the East Londoners returned to winning ways with victories in their next three games. There would be just one more defeat during 1957–58, coming at the hands of bottom-of-the-table Notts County courtesy of a hotly disputed penalty. It was, nevertheless, a result which unsettled the Hammers, and when, four days later, they made the trip to Cardiff City the players had become edgy and tense. A series of uncharacteristic mistakes in the game's opening stages left Fenton's team indebted to the assured goalkeeping of Ernie Gregory. Two goals from Johnny Dick and a rare strike from Andy Malcolm settled the nerves and ensured both points went to the men from Upton Park.

With two games to go West Ham United sat at the top of the table, but their lead was just a single point and there were still four other teams in with a chance of promotion. Among the contenders were Liverpool – Hammers' opponents in the season's penultimate match, the last at home. In a game played out before a crowd of 37,750, Billy Liddell, the visitors' 37-year-old skipper, struck the opening goal after 21 minutes. The home team pressed forward, urged on by their increasingly vocal support, and eventually got their reward. A foul on Johnny Dick had brought a free-kick on the edge of the area and John Bond – who was nicknamed Muffin the Mule because of his powerful kick – stepped forward to crash the ball home. It was a goal that ended Liverpool's hopes of promotion, and – according to the *Daily Express* – 'brought the wildest crowd enthusiasm Upton Park has seen for many a day'.

A long-awaited return

The final fixture of the season saw Hammers travel to Middlesbrough, while their rivals Blackburn and Charlton played one another at the Valley. In a tense encounter at Ayresome Park, Johnny Dick settled the visitors' nerves when he struck the game's first goal with a clever back-heel, before further strikes from Malcolm Musgrove and Vic Keeble earned Ted Fenton's team the victory they needed to claim not only promotion but also the Championship. After a 26-year absence, West Ham United were back in the First Division. Fenton described it as the 'dream of a life-time,' adding that the 'train journey back to London couldn't have been better had we done it in a Rolls Royce'. The Hammers team arrived back in London at 10pm to be met by a 1,000-strong crowd at King's Cross and as the players disembarked, top scorer Johnny Dick and skipper Noel Cantwell were carried down the length of the platform at shoulder height.

A celebratory dinner at the Cafe Royal followed, with 300 guests applauding the success of Ted Fenton and his players. Chairman Reg Pratt told reporters: 'Wise men, if they want to build something worthwhile, call in a good architect. We were fortunate to have with us Ted. There is no doubting that Ted Fenton has earned his particular laurel.' The manager, however, was quick to deflect this praise, claiming instead that 'success has been entirely due to wonderful team spirit,' adding: 'We have no temperamental stars at Upton Park. Every man is proud of his team.' Special mention was, though, reserved for the contribution of Vic Keeble who had struck 19 goals in his 29 games since arriving from Newcastle in October.

When the promotion celebrations had died down, Ted Fenton was left with the serious business of preparing West Ham United for their long-awaited return to the top flight. The Hammers had last played in the First Division in May 1932 when the team was managed by Syd King and included legendary goalscorer Vic Watson and goalkeeper Ted Hufton – a player who had appeared in the Club's very first League fixture in 1919. Much had changed during the East London club's 26-year spell in the Second Division, and it was not going to be easy for Fenton or his players to adjust to life alongside English football's elite. All the talk ahead of the new season was of consolidation for the Hammers, although mention was also made of several promising youngsters. Three 17-year-olds – Bobby Moore, Andy Scott and Andy Smillie – who had all risen through the youth ranks, were the only new professionals on the Upton Park staff in the summer of 1958. At the other end of his career was Malcolm Allison, who had returned to full-time training after recovering from tuberculosis.

Centre-forward Vic Keeble was considered something of a big-money signing when he arrived at Upton Park from Newcastle United in a £10,000 deal during October 1957. But the powerful targetman quickly proved a bargain, helping West Ham United to promotion during his first season with the Club. Keeble was the final piece in Ted Fenton's jigsaw, and provided a much need focal-point for the Hammers' attacking play.

Left: Left-back Noel Cantwell strides forward in typical fashion during a League match in 1954. The Irishman was one of the first full-backs to master the art of overlapping and his raids down the left flank proved a fruitful source of goals for Hammers during the 1950s.

Below: John Bond, like his full-back partner Noel Cantwell, was a formidable attacker and his powerfully shooting earned him the nickname 'Muffin the Mule'. So effective was Bond in attack, that he was even drafted in as an emergency centre-forward on occasions.

A bright start

The Hammers' pre-season preparation took place at Grange Farm in Chigwell, where the players were put through their paces by Fenton and his newly appointed number two, Bill Robinson. Assisting the coaching staff was chief trainer Billy Moore, who had been with the club since 1922. The role of trainer was a pseudo-medical one, and had previously been fulfilled by Charlie Paynter. Moore had learnt much from his predecessor who was regarded as a master of the magic sponge and a man with an excellent practical knowledge of physiotherapy. Fortunately, there was little call for the trainer's skills in the run up to the 1958–59 season and Ted Fenton was able to name his strongest team for the opening fixture away to Portsmouth.

Ten of the team who had played in the title decider at Middlesbrough in May 1958 took the field at Fratton Park, and from a familiar line-up came a familiar outcome with Johnny Dick and Vic Keeble striking the goals in a 2–1 win. Two days later the Hammers faced a stern test of their First Division credentials when reigning Champions Wolverhampton Wanderers made the trip to Upton Park. The match was a lock-out and the 37,500 lucky Hammers fans who managed to gain access to the Boleyn Ground were treated to an assured and skilful display from the home team who ran out comfortable 2–0 winners. Dick struck the opening goal, which he later claimed was the first he had ever scored with his right foot, while Johnny Smith grabbed the second. Victory over the mighty Wolves had the press in raptures, with one paper declaring: 'Wolves Crash to Fenton's Furies'.

A new 'Number 6'

As if to prove that their first two results were no fluke, the Hammers completed their August fixtures by crushing Aston Villa 7–2 at Upton Park. But the momentum could not be sustained. The next two matches brought just a single point, and so it was with a certain degree of trepidation that Ted Fenton's team prepared to face Manchester United at Upton Park on 8 September. West Ham United's plight was not helped by an injury to left-half Billy Lansdowne which forced Fenton to alter a line-up that had remained unchanged in the first five fixtures. Andy Nelson was the natural choice to come in for Lansdowne, but he too was injured, so the manager had to decide between giving a debut to 17-year-old Bobby Moore or recalling Malcolm Allison, a player who had worked tirelessly to recover after a season out of the game with tuberculosis. Fenton consulted with his captain, Noel Cantwell, and in the end decided to hand the number six shirt to the youngster. It was a painful blow for Allison, who had coached Moore when the defender had joined the club as a schoolboy. In his authorised biography, written by Jeff Powell, Bobby would later reflect that: 'I'd been a profes-

sional for two and a half months and Malcolm had taught me everything I knew. For all the money in the world I wanted to play. For all the money in the world I wanted Malcolm to play.'

The debutant rewarded his manager's faith and played his part in a dramatic 3–2 victory, which saw West Ham United take a three-goal lead before letting the Reds back into the game. Moore kept his place in the team for the next match, a 4–0 defeat away to Nottingham Forest – but thereafter he returned to the Hammers junior ranks to continue his footballing education. One man in need of no extra coaching was centre-forward Vic Keeble, who struck nine goals in the season's first 11 games. The highlight of this sequence was undoubtedly the four-goal haul which helped Hammers to a 6-3 victory at home to Blackburn Rovers on 4 October. It was a performance which earned Keeble the match ball and a £6 bonus. Also on the scoresheet against Blackburn was captain Noel Cantwell. But there would be no post-match celebration for the Hammers left-back who, along with Rovers' Mick McGrath, had to head to Liverpool to catch the boat to Dublin so that he could play for the Republic of Ireland against Poland the next day. The trip clearly did Noel no harm as he struck two goals from an unfamiliar centre-forward position to earn the boys in green a 2–2 draw.

Victory over Blackburn had been the Hammers' fifth consecutive home win. However, away from Upton Park, Ted Fenton's team was struggling and had taken just three points from six matches. At the start of the season the board had said that they intended to give the players who had won promotion the chance to prove themselves in the First Division, but they had also added that: 'If performances do not come up to what we believe possible then we shall have to take steps to try to remedy the situation.' In November the West Ham United directors proved as good as their word and sanctioned the purchase of Leyton Orient's Phil Woosnam for a club-record fee of £30,000. Woosnam was a skilful and inventive inside – forward who, according to Ted Fenton, was 'so West Ham he might have been moulded by us'.

Despite the manager's bold assertion, the Hammers' most expensive signing would take time to settle. Woosnam's arrival coincided with a disastrous run of form which brought a mere two points from six games. But just as it seemed that West Ham United were headed for a relegation battle, the club's fortunes moved into the ascendant with a 6–0 win over Portsmouth at Upton Park. Woosnam was among the scorers, opening his account with a spectacular strike from 25 yards which went some way to justifying Fenton's faith in the Welshman. The Hammers were at the start of a run of five consecutive victories that would lift them out of the lower reaches of the table and to within four points of leaders Arsenal. Woosnam, however, would miss two of these games after sustaining an injury in the 2–1 victory over Tottenham Hotspur at Upton Park on Christmas Day. In the absence of his record signing, Fenton would once more put his faith in youth, casting 17-year-old Andy Smillie into first-team action in the Boxing Day rematch against Spurs at White Hart Lane. The debutante excelled himself and played a key role in a 4–1 win before a crowd of 42,890.

Seniors fade as youth shine

Smillie was one of a number of promising young Hammers to gain international recognition during 1958, and in October, the Ilford-born inside-forward was selected along with Upton Park team-mates Bobby Moore, Peter Reader and Tony Scott to travel to Madrid as part of a 15-man England Youth squad. West Ham United's growing reputation for developing young players gained further recognition in November 1958 when the Boleyn Ground hosted a friendly match between an England Youth XI and the Hammers Colts. It would, however, prove something of a mismatch, and the home team crushed the England XI, which included Fulham's Alan Mullery, 8–1. The future certainly looked bright for the members of Hammers' successful junior teams, but for one senior player it held nothing but uncertainty. Malcolm Allison had failed in his bid to regain full fitness and announced that he was to hang up his boots. The board granted the 31-year-old, who had been with the Club since 1951, a testimonial match, which was duly arranged against an All Star XI for 17 November 1958.

Back in the cut and thrust of the First Division, Hammers were showing good form in front of goal but were far from convincing at the back. Away from home, they remained particularly vulnerable and would regularly engineer their own downfall with less than rigorous defending. The match against Birmingham City at St Andrews in February brought a distressingly familiar outcome – with the Londoners going down 3–0 – a result which had one reporter pleading: 'Don't hand out too many bouquets to the City forward line. Blame instead the West Ham defence which three times presented them with gift goals by loose marking.' Ted Fenton was livid with his team, and told the press that the Hammers had been beaten because they had shown a lack of heart.

Fair pay for footballers

The month of March would see an upturn in West Ham United's fortunes, with the East Londoners taking eight points from six games. But the big football story in the spring of 1959 concerned players' wages rather than team performances. The maximum wage had become an increasingly controversial subject, and the FA and Football League attempted to avert a crisis

The team that Ted built: In 1957-58 West Ham United won promotion to the First Division after an absence of 26 years, pictured here are 14 members of the triumphant Hammers squad. From left to right: Ernie Gregory, John Bond, Malcolm Pyke, Andy Nelson, Vic Keeble, Noel Cantwell, Johnny Dick, Ken Brown, Bill Lansdowne, Andy Malcolm, Mike Grice, Malcolm Musgrove, John Smith and Billy Dare.

by issuing a statement – a copy of which appeared in the West Ham United Club programme – proclaiming the virtues of the current system. In 1959 the maximum wage stood at £20 per week, while the ceiling on bonuses was £2 for a draw and £4 for a win. The situation was further complicated by an elaborate system of gratuities for success in various domestic and European Cup competitions. By printing these figures in newspapers and matchday programmes, football's authorities hoped to swing public opinion in their favour by establishing that there was 'every incentive for a player to reach the top and receive ample reward for his efforts from the game'. It was a move which would ultimately prove futile, as in 1961 the maximum wage was finally abolished.

But while players' salaries remained capped, talent money – which was awarded to teams finishing in the top five – would continue to act as a major incentive. As the 1958–59 season reached its closing stages, West Ham United were well placed to finish fifth and claim the last of the qualifying places which carried a team bonus of £220. The last home game of the season saw Hammers record a superb 5–1 victory over Manchester City. It was a win inspired by skipper Noel Cantwell who, playing as a stand-in striker, scored one goal and had a hand in each of the other four. Unfortunately, the final match of the season brought no glorious finale and a 1–0 defeat against Leeds United at Elland Road left the Hammers agonisingly just outside the talent money in sixth place. Despite this disappointment it had been an impressive season for the Hammers, who had confounded their critics to finish in the top half of the table.

Ted Fenton's job had been aided somewhat by five ever-presents in the West Ham United line-up. Ken Brown, John Bond, Noel Cantwell, Mike Grice and Andy Malcolm all finished the season without absences. Brown's efforts would be recognised by the club's fans who voted him Hammer of the Year in succession to Andy Malcolm, the first holder of that title.

The summer of 1959 would see several major changes at Upton Park. Firstly, the club announced that ticket prices were set to go up for the 1959–60 season. Terrace admission would rise by sixpence (2½p), while seats in the West Stand would jump by a shilling (5p). The second, and most significant, change in E13 went some way to explaining why these price increases were necessary. In May 1959, and after months of negotiation, the board announced that they had reached an agreement to buy the freehold of the Boleyn Ground from their landlords, the Archdiocese of Westminster, at a cost of £30,000. The club was also committed to cover the North Bank and carry out an extensive maintenance programme at Upton Park, so, in the short term, Ted Fenton would be unable to make any big money signings.

Keeble injury setback

Despite the lack of any fresh blood in the team, West Ham United got their 1959–60 League campaign off to a flying start with seven points from their opening four fixtures (two points for a win). Vic Keeble, who had missed the latter part of the previous season with injury, was among the scorers, having recovered from a summer operation on his knee. The return of the Colchester-born striker meant that the Hammers line-up boasted nine members of the promotion-winning squad from 1957–58 – record-signing Phil Woosnam and Republic of Ireland goalkeeper Noel Dwyer were the newcomers. Dwyer had arrived at the Club on the recommendation of his international team-mate Noel Cantwell, taking over the number one shirt from Ernie Gregory in March 1959. Ernie, who had been with West Ham United since 1936, would play his final first-team match in a 2–1 defeat at home to Leeds in September, and at the end of the season joined the Upton Park coaching staff.

The retirement of a veteran goalkeeper may not have caused too much disruption to Ted Fenton's plans, but the loss of his first-choice number nine was most certainly reason for concern. The match against Fulham at Craven Cottage on 31 October had left Vic Keeble nursing an Achilles tendon problem, and though he returned for one more first-team appearance in January, it was the start of an injury jinx which would force him to retire at season's end.

With no recognised centre-forward in his squad, Ted Fenton was forced to play winger Harry Obeney in the number nine jersey. It was a move which, initially at least, proved a startling success, with the deputy finding the net in both his first two games to help Hammers to consecutive victories over Manchester City and Arsenal. Obeney did not make it on to the scoresheet for the next match, at home to Champions Wolverhampton Wanderers, but a John Dick hat-trick secured another win which took West Ham United to the top of the First Division. However, just when it seemed that Ted Fenton's team had added much needed consistency and defensive fortitude to their conspicuous attacking talents, their title challenge blew up in most spectacular fashion. Having conceded just five goals in their previous six games, the Hammers made the trip to Sheffield Wednesday's Hillsborough ground in confident mood. But after eight minutes the East Londoners had shipped three goals and were on their way to a 7–0 thrashing. Ted Fenton's post-match analysis was simple and to the point: 'Sheffield Wednesday were magnificent. They gave us a jolly good whacking and that's all there is to it.'

The Hammers recovered from their humiliating defeat in Sheffield to beat Nottingham Forest 4–1 at home in their next match, but a week later were on the receiving end of another heavy reverse, losing 6–2 to Blackburn Rovers at Ewood Park. Fenton's team would struggle for the remainder of the season, winning just four of their final 22 League games. Centre-forward continued to be a problem position for the manager, and when the goal-trail ran dry for Obeney he experimented with first Noel Cantwell and then John Bond at number nine. Bond proved the more successful of the two converted full-backs, and grabbed a memorable hat-trick at home to Chelsea when he outshone the great Jimmy Greaves.

Moore and Hurst set out

A recognised striker at last arrived just ahead of the 1960 transfer deadline. David Dunmore was a 26-year-old, powerfully-built north-easterner who joined the Upton Park club from Spurs in exchange for England under-23 wing-half Johnny Smith. The new signing scored two goals in the remaining nine fixtures but could do little to improve Hammers' poor League position, and at the end of the campaign Fenton's team occupied a disappointing 14th place. The most significant aspect of the Smith/Dunmore transfer was that the departure of West Ham United's regular number six had created a gap in the half-back line which the club could not afford to fill with a costly signing. Eighteen-year-old Bobby Moore was the man handed the task of succeeding Smith, and so began a 14-year run in the first team for the most successful player in West Ham United's history.

Another soon-to-be famous Hammer had also made his mark in 1960. Like Moore, Geoff Hurst was an aspiring half-back and after impressive form as captain of the Colts he broke into the first-team reckoning to make three senior appearances in 1959–60. Among Hurst's colleagues in West Ham United's under-18s team were two more promising midfielders who could look forward to a bright future at Upton Park. Martin Peters and Ronnie Boyce would both play key roles in helping Hammers to the fifth round of the FA Youth Cup, and each was rewarded with England youth caps.

The 4-2-4 experiment

But despite the progress of the club's young players, the board was still criticised for a perceived lack of spending. By the outset of the 1960–61 season, the purchase of the Boleyn Ground and the signing of Phil Woosnam had long been forgotten. However, when the new campaign kicked off media attention quickly turned to the manager's dugout. Ted Fenton would become a source of great intrigue following his decision to employ the controversial 4-2-4 formation which had been used by Brazil to win the 1958 World Cup. The new look Hammers lined up with Ken Brown and Noel Cantwell in central defence; Bobby Moore and John Bond at full-back; Andy Malcolm and Phil Woosnam patrolling the midfield; and Mike Grice, Johnny Dick, David Dunmore and Malcolm Musgrove in attack. It was a system that proved popular with the players, but which brought a mixed reaction from media and supporters alike.

The season's opening match ended in a 4–2 defeat against

Inside-forward Phil Woosnam was Hammers record signing when he arrived from Leyton Orient for £30,000 in November 1958. Ted Fenton felt that Woosnam, a former PE teacher and a Bachelor of Science, would bring much needed craft to his team's midfield. And so it proved, the Wales international remained at Upton Park for four years and, in his early days at the Club was a revelation.

Wolverhampton Wanderers at Molineux, but despite the result West Ham United were given credit for their bright attacking football. The press would continue to celebrate Fenton's inventive new system after successive home victories over Aston Villa and Bolton Wanderers. However, when the Hammers went down to their third away defeat of the season, against Sheffield Wednesday, the story changed. 'West Ham's 4-2-4 formation is a negative type of soccer,' carped the Wednesday manager Harry Catterick, who had just seen his team win 1–0. 'You have to have two penetrative wingers to overcome it.' Fenton would begin to lose confidence in the new approach and was soon encouraging his team to get the ball forward more quickly. Bobby Moore would later comment in his authorised biography that initially the team was 'playing the way the players wanted... 4-2-4 with plenty of good football,' but the former skipper remembered that as things began to go wrong, 'we became the world's best hitters of long through balls to nobody... We seemed to lose every game 4–0.'

On 26 September 1960 the Hammers made their debut in the League Cup, and abandoned their 4-2-4 in favour of the old style WM formation. The switch proved a success and, before a crowd of only 12,496 at Upton Park, Fenton's team ran out comfortable 3–1 victors. The League Cup had been devised in an effort to boost flagging attendances, but the new competition struggled in its early years, with many top teams refusing to take part. Although Hammers were not among the boycotters, their interest in the new cup did not last long, as in the second round they were eliminated by Fourth Division Darlington.

Noel Cantwell goes north

Despite the reversion to a more conventional pattern of play, the media remained suspicious of West Ham United's tactics. The press would give Ted Fenton little credit for any successes, preferring instead to portray him as a compulsive tinkerer. In October the popularity of both the Hammers manager and the Club's board took a further knock when skipper Noel Cantwell was sold to Manchester United for £30,000. With crowds falling, the Club was keen to cash in on a player who was approaching 29 years old, and for whom there was a ready – made replacement in John Lyall.

Following the departure of Cantwell, Phil Woosnam was appointed Club captain, and the promotion of the Wales international coincided with the Hammers' best run of the season. One defeat in ten matches took the East Londoners into the top half of the table and, for a time at least, silenced the critics. The highlight of this sequence was a 6–0 victory over Arsenal at Upton Park, which saw David Dunmore grab a hat-trick and Bobby Moore take the plaudits for his polished display in defence. It was a rare clean sheet for the Hammers, who

Hammers players report back for pre-season training in July 1958. The photograph shows, from left to right: Ken Brown, Andy Malcolm, unknown player, Johnny Dick, Billy Dare, John Bond, Noel Cantwell and Ted Fenton.

Scottish international inside-forward Johnny Dick was West Ham United's most reliable goalscorer for nine seasons from 1953–54 onward. Tall and powerfully built, Dick enjoyed a particularly fruitful partnership with Vic Keeble, and the pair struck 40 League goals during Hammers, successful promotion campaign in 1957–58.

remained vulnerable at the back, as they proved in entertaining fashion when they made the trip to Newcastle United on 10 December. A half-time lead of five goals to two looked unassailable, but, in the words of one *Daily Express* correspondent: 'Fenton's men committed the dire sin of easing up too soon,' as the Magpies finished level at 5–5.

Fenton bows out

Three defeats over the Christmas and New Year period left West Ham United with nothing more to play for than their First Division survival. However, the situation deteriorated still further in February and March when Hammers embarked upon a sequence of five consecutive defeats. It was a run which would come to an end with a 0–0 draw at Highbury on 25 March, but by then the Upton Park career of Ted Fenton was already at an end. Nine days prior to the Arsenal fixture the club had issued a statement saying that the manager had been under great pressure and was taking some sick leave. Shortly afterwards, though, the true situation became apparent and it was announced that Fenton had left the club. The reasons for the dismissal of the long-serving manager have never been made clear and while it would be folly to suggest that Fenton's reign had been terminated because of a run of poor performances on the pitch, it is obvious that his cause had not been helped by two seasons spent in the lower reaches of the First Division. It was a somewhat low-profile ending to the tenure of a manager who had done much to establish the West Ham United tradition, and a man who should be given great credit for the successes that were to come in the following years.

THE FAMOUS ACADEMY

During the mid-1950s Upton Park was dubbed the 'Academy of football'. The nickname stuck and is still liberally used by journalists covering Hammers' games today. However, over the years the origins of this nickname have become somewhat blurred and, contrary to popular opinion, the Academy was neither a product of the 1960s nor the work of Ron Greenwood or Bobby Moore. Instead, it was a title which owed most to the fore-sight of Malcolm Allison, the tolerance of Ted Fenton and a cafe in the Barking Road.

The Academy was the name given to a group of like-minded West Ham United players who were brought together during Ted Fenton's time as Hammers manager, and who took a keen interest in the tactical side of the game. Central defender Malcolm Allison was the undisputed leader of this unofficial but increasingly influential group, and his powerful personality was to be its driving force. Allison was a hugely ambitious player who had been impressed by the professionalism and technical excellence of continental footballers. He believed that the British could learn much from their European neighbours and was determined that West Ham United should lead the way. It was the era of the maximum wage, and one of the few perks Hammers' players received was a lunch voucher which could be spent in several local cafes. The Academy members chose to eat at Cassatarri's Cafe on the Barking Road and met there each day after training. Ken Brown, John Bond, Noel Cantwell, Dave Sexton and Frank O'Farrell were among those who joined Allison in Cassatarri's and the assembled players would spend hours discussing tactics, formations and practice routines. It was unique for professional footballers to take such an active interest in coaching, and before long Allison and company were actively directing the occasional training session. Many managers would not have tolerated such a show of player power, but Ted Fenton, to his credit, made little effort to curtail the influence of his senior pros on the training ground.

The Academy was also instrumental in grooming the next generation of Hammers stars. On Tuesday and Thursday evenings at the Boleyn Ground experienced professionals ran coaching sessions for the Club's schoolboy players. Bobby Moore was among those to benefit from this arrangement and it was under the tutelage of Malcolm Allison that the future England skipper honed his skills as a youngster.

The coming together of so many prodigious football minds happened by coincidence rather than by design, but the Academy proved nonetheless to be a defining aspect of the West Ham United tradition. Neither before nor since have so many future coaches played in the same team and their talent soon became obvious as one-by-one they embarked upon successful careers in management.

ACADEMY GRADUATES

Malcolm Allison – Plymouth Argyle (1964-65 and 1978-79), Manchester City (1972-73 and 1979-80), Crystal Palace (1973-76 and 1980-81), Middlesbrough (1982-84), Bristol Rovers (1992-93)

John Bond – AFC Bournemouth (1970-73) Norwich City (1973-80), Manchester City (1980-83), Burnley (1983-84), Birmingham City (1986-87), Shrewsbury Town (1991-93)

Ken Brown – Norwich City (1980-87), Plymouth Argyle (1988-90)

Noel Cantwell – Coventry City (1967-72), Peterborough United (1972-77 and 1986-88)

Frank O'Farrell – Torquay United (1965-68 and 1981-82), Leicester City (1968-71), Manchester United (1971-72), Cardiff City (1973-74)

Dave Sexton – Leyton Orient (1965), Chelsea (1967-74), Queens Park Rangers (1974-77), Manchester United (1977-81), Coventry City (1981-83)

Members of the famous Hammers Academy return to Cassatarri's Cafe for a reunion in the late-1960s. From left to right: Malcolm Musgrove, Dave Sexton, Noel Cantwell, Malcolm Allison, Mr Cassatarri (standing), John Bond, Frank O'Farrell and John Lyall.

1951-1960

SEASON 1951-52
FOOTBALL LEAGUE (DIVISION 2)

Aug 18	(a)	Queen's Park R	L	0-2
23	(h)	Bury	D	1-1
25	(h)	Blackburn R	W	3-1
29	(a)	Bury	L	0-4
Sep 1	(a)	Hull C	D	1-1
5	(h)	Swansea T	D	2-2
8	(h)	Barnsley	W	2-1
13	(a)	Swansea T	L	1-2
15	(a)	Sheffield U	L	1-6
22	(h)	Leeds U	W	2-0
29	(h)	Coventry C	W	3-1
Oct 6	(a)	Rotherham U	L	1-2
13	(h)	Cardiff C	D	1-1
20	(a)	Birmingham C	L	1-2
27	(h)	Leicester C	L	2-3
Nov 3	(a)	Nottingham F	D	0-0
10	(h)	Brentford	W	1-0
17	(a)	Doncaster R	L	1-4
24	(h)	Everton	D	3-3
Dec 1	(a)	Southampton	W	2-1
8	(h)	Sheffield W	L	0-6
15	(h)	Queen's Park R	W	4-2
22	(a)	Blackburn R	L	1-3
25	(h)	Luton T	W	3-0
26	(a)	Luton T	L	1-6
29	(h)	Hull C	W	2-0
Jan 5	(a)	Barnsley	D	1-1
19	(h)	Sheffield U	W	5-1
26	(a)	Leeds U	L	1-3
Feb 9	(a)	Coventry C	W	2-1
16	(h)	Rotherham U	W	2-1
Mar 1	(a)	Cardiff C	D	1-1
8	(h)	Birmingham C	L	0-1
15	(a)	Leicester C	L	1-3
22	(h)	Nottingham F	W	3-1
Apr 5	(h)	Doncaster R	D	3-3
11	(h)	Notts C	W	2-1
12	(a)	Everton	L	0-2
14	(a)	Notts C	L	0-1
19	(h)	Southampton	W	4-0
21	(a)	Brentford	D	1-1
26	(a)	Sheffield W	D	2-2

P	W	D	L	F	A	W	D	L	F	A	Pts	Pos
42	13	5	3	48	29	2	6	13	19	48	41	12th

FA Cup

3	Jan 12	(h)	Blackpool	W	2-1
4	Feb 2	(h)	Sheffield U	D	0-0
R	6	(a)	Sheffield U	L	2-4

SEASON 1952-53
FOOTBALL LEAGUE (DIVISION 2)

Aug 23	(h)	Southampton	W	1-0
25	(a)	Hull C	L	0-1
30	(a)	Bury	D	1-1
Sep 1	(h)	Hull C	D	0-0
6	(h)	Birmingham C	L	1-2
8	(a)	Leicester C	D	0-0
13	(a)	Luton T	D	0-0
15	(h)	Leicester C	W	4-1
20	(h)	Leeds U	D	2-2
27	(a)	Plymouth A	D	1-1
Oct 4	(h)	Rotherham U	L	2-4
11	(a)	Blackburn R	L	0-3
18	(h)	Nottingham F	W	3-2
25	(a)	Everton	L	0-2
Nov 1	(h)	Brentford	W	3-1
8	(a)	Doncaster R	D	1-1
15	(h)	Swansea T	W	3-0
22	(a)	Huddersfield T	W	1-0
29	(h)	Sheffield U	D	1-1
Dec 6	(a)	Barnsley	L	0-2
13	(h)	Lincoln C	W	5-1
20	(a)	Southampton	W	2-1
25	(h)	Notts C	D	2-2
27	(a)	Notts C	D	1-1
Jan 3	(h)	Bury	W	3-2
17	(a)	Birmingham C	L	0-2
24	(h)	Luton T	L	0-1
Feb 7	(a)	Leeds U	L	2-3
18	(h)	Plymouth A	L	0-1
21	(a)	Rotherham U	D	1-1
28	(h)	Blackburn R	D	0-0
Mar 7	(a)	Nottingham F	D	0-0
14	(h)	Everton	W	3-1
21	(a)	Brentford	W	4-1
28	(h)	Doncaster R	L	1-3
Apr 3	(h)	Fulham	L	1-2
4	(a)	Swansea T	L	1-4
6	(a)	Fulham	W	3-2
11	(h)	Huddersfield T	L	0-1
18	(a)	Sheffield U	L	1-3
25	(h)	Barnsley	W	3-1
May 1	(a)	Lincoln C	L	1-3

P	W	D	L	F	A	W	D	L	F	A	Pts	Pos
42	9	5	7	38	28	4	8	9	20	32	39	14th

FA Cup

3	Jan 10	(h)	West Brom A	L	1-4

SEASON 1953-54
FOOTBALL LEAGUE (DIVISION 2)

Aug 19	(h)	Lincoln C	W	5-0
22	(h)	Leicester C	W	4-1
24	(a)	Rotherham U	L	0-5
29	(a)	Stoke C	D	1-1
Sep 3	(h)	Rotherham U	W	3-0
5	(h)	Fulham	W	3-1
10	(a)	Swansea T	D	1-1
12	(a)	Bristol R	D	2-2
14	(h)	Swansea T	W	4-1
19	(a)	Leeds U	W	2-1
26	(h)	Birmingham C	L	1-2
Oct 3	(a)	Nottingham F	L	0-4
10	(h)	Brentford	L	0-1
17	(a)	Derby C	L	1-2
24	(h)	Blackburn R	W	2-1
31	(a)	Doncaster R	L	0-2
Nov 7	(h)	Bury	W	5-0
14	(a)	Oldham A	L	1-3
21	(h)	Everton	D	1-1
28	(a)	Hull C	L	1-2
Dec 5	(h)	Notts C	L	1-2
12	(a)	Lincoln C	W	2-1
19	(a)	Leicester C	L	1-2
25	(h)	Luton T	W	1-0
27	(a)	Luton T	L	1-3
Jan 16	(a)	Fulham	W	4-3
23	(h)	Bristol R	D	1-1
Feb 6	(h)	Leeds U	W	5-2
13	(a)	Birmingham C	L	0-2
20	(h)	Nottingham F	D	1-1
27	(a)	Brentford	L	1-3
Mar 6	(h)	Derby C	D	0-0
13	(a)	Blackburn R	L	1-4
20	(h)	Doncaster R	W	2-1
27	(a)	Everton	W	2-1
Apr 3	(h)	Hull C	W	1-0
10	(a)	Bury	L	0-2
12	(h)	Stoke C	D	2-2
16	(h)	Plymouth A	D	2-2
17	(h)	Oldham A	L	0-1
19	(a)	Plymouth A	L	1-2
24	(a)	Notts C	L	1-3

P	W	D	L	F	A	W	D	L	F	A	Pts	Pos
42	11	6	4	44	20	4	3	14	23	49	39	13th

FA Cup

3	Jan 9	(h)	Huddersfield T	W	4-0
4	30	(h)	Blackpool	D	1-1
R	Feb 3	(a)	Blackpool	L	1-3

SEASON 1954-55
FOOTBALL LEAGUE (DIVISION 2)

Aug 21	(a)	Swansea T	L	2-5
23	(a)	Blackburn R	L	2-5
28	(h)	Notts C	W	3-0
30	(h)	Blackburn R	L	2-5
Sep 4	(a)	Liverpool	W	2-1
6	(h)	Hull C	D	1-1
11	(h)	Bristol R	W	5-2
13	(a)	Hull C	W	1-0
18	(a)	Plymouth A	D	1-1
25	(h)	Port Vale	W	2-0
Oct 2	(a)	Doncaster R	L	1-2
9	(h)	Nottingham F	W	2-0
16	(a)	Leeds U	L	1-2
23	(h)	Stoke C	W	3-0
30	(a)	Middlesbrough	L	0-6
Nov 6	(h)	Birmingham C	D	2-2
13	(a)	Ipswich T	W	3-0
20	(h)	Luton T	W	2-1
27	(a)	Rotherham U	D	2-2
Dec 4	(h)	Bury	D	3-3
11	(a)	Lincoln C	L	1-2
18	(h)	Swansea T	D	3-3
25	(h)	Derby C	W	1-0
27	(a)	Derby C	D	0-0
Jan 1	(a)	Notts C	L	1-5
22	(a)	Bristol R	W	4-2
Feb 5	(h)	Plymouth A	W	6-1
12	(a)	Port Vale	D	1-1
24	(h)	Doncaster R	L	0-1
Mar 5	(h)	Leeds U	W	2-1
12	(a)	Stoke C	W	2-0
19	(h)	Middlesbrough	W	2-1
26	(a)	Birmingham C	W	2-1
Apr 2	(h)	Ipswich T	W	4-0
8	(h)	Fulham	W	2-1
9	(a)	Luton T	L	0-2
11	(a)	Fulham	D	0-0
16	(h)	Rotherham U	L	1-2
23	(a)	Bury	L	1-4
27	(h)	Liverpool	L	0-3
30	(h)	Lincoln C	L	0-1
May 2	(a)	Nottingham F	D	1-1

P	W	D	L	F	A	W	D	L	F	A	Pts	Pos
42	12	4	5	46	28	6	6	9	28	42	46	8th

FA Cup

3	Jan 8	(h)	Port Vale	D	2-2
R	10	(a)	Port Vale	L	1-3

SEASON 1955-56
FOOTBALL LEAGUE (DIVISION 2)

Aug 20	(h)	Rotherham U	D	1-1
22	(a)	Port Vale	L	1-2
27	(a)	Swansea T	L	2-4
29	(h)	Port Vale	L	0-2
Sep 3	(h)	Notts C	W	6-1
6	(a)	Bristol C	L	1-3
10	(a)	Leeds U	D	3-3
17	(h)	Fulham	W	2-1
24	(a)	Bury	D	1-1
Oct 1	(h)	Barnsley	W	4-0
8	(h)	Plymouth A	W	4-0
15	(a)	Liverpool	L	1-3
22	(h)	Doncaster R	W	6-1
29	(a)	Lincoln C	D	1-1
Nov 5	(h)	Blackburn R	L	2-3
12	(a)	Hull C	L	1-3
19	(h)	Nottingham F	L	1-2
26	(a)	Sheffield W	D	1-1
Dec 3	(h)	Leicester C	L	1-3
10	(a)	Bristol R	D	1-1
17	(a)	Rotherham U	L	2-3
24	(h)	Swansea T	W	5-1
26	(a)	Middlesbrough	L	0-2
27	(h)	Middlesbrough	w	1-0
31	(a)	Notts C	W	1-0
Jan 14	(h)	Leeds U	D	1-1
21	(a)	Fulham	L	1-3
Feb 11	(a)	Barnsley	D	1-1
25	(h)	Liverpool	W	2-0
Mar 10	(h)	Bristol R	W	2-1
17	(a)	Blackburn R	L	1-4
19	(h)	Bury	W	3-2
24	(h)	Hull C	D	1-1
26	(a)	Doncaster R	L	1-2
30	(h)	Stoke C	W	2-0
31	(a)	Plymouth A	W	1-0
Apr 2	(a)	Stoke C	L	0-3
7	(h)	Sheffield W	D	3-3
14	(a)	Leicester C	L	1-2
18	(a)	Nottingham F	D	0-0
21	(h)	Lincoln C	L	2-4
28	(h)	Bristol C	W	3-0

P	W	D	L	F	A	W	D	L	F	A	Pts	Pos
42	12	4	5	52	27	2	7	12	22	42	39	16th

FA Cup

3	Jan 7	(h)	Preston NE	W	5-2
4	28	(h)	Cardiff C	W	2-1
5	Feb 18	(h)	Blackburn R	D	0-0

View from the North Bank, circa 1958. The picture is taken before A Block (top right-hand corner) was built. West Bromwich Albion are the visitors.

Hammers' prolific goal-scoring inside forward Johnny Dick during the 1953–54 season.

R		28	(a)	Blackburn R	W	3-2
6	Mar	3	(a)	Tottenham H	D	3-3
R		8	(h)	Tottenham H	L	1-2

SEASON 1956-57
FOOTBALL LEAGUE (DIVISION 2)

Aug	18	(a)	Fulham	W	4-1
	20	(h)	Blackburn R	L	1-3
	25	(h)	Swansea T	L	1-2
	27	(a)	Blackburn R	W	2-0
Sep	1	(a)	Lincoln C	W	2-0
	3	(h)	Liverpool	D	1-1
	8	(h)	Rotherham U	D	1-1
	15	(a)	Port Vale	D	0-0
	22	(h)	Barnsley	W	2-0
	29	(a)	Sheffield U	L	0-1
Oct	6	(a)	Leyton O	W	2-1
	13	(h)	Huddersfield T	L	0-2
	20	(a)	Bristol R	D	1-1
	27	(h)	Grimsby T	L	0-1
Nov	3	(a)	Doncaster R	L	0-3
	10	(h)	Stoke C	W	1-0
	17	(a)	Middlesbrough	L	1-3
	24	(h)	Leicester C	W	2-1
Dec	1	(a)	Bury	D	3-3
	8	(h)	Notts C	W	2-1
	15	(h)	Fulham	W	2-1
	22	(a)	Swansea T	L	1-3
	25	(h)	Nottingham F	W	2-1
	29	(h)	Lincoln C	W	2-1
Jan	12	(a)	Rotherham U	W	1-0
	19	(h)	Port Vale	W	2-1
Feb	2	(a)	Barnsley	W	2-1
	9	(h)	Sheffield U	W	3-2
	16	(h)	Leyton O	W	2-1
	23	(a)	Huddersfield T	L	2-6
Mar	2	(h)	Bristol R	L	1-2
	9	(a)	Grimsby T	L	1-2
	16	(h)	Doncaster R	D	1-1
	23	(a)	Stoke C	W	1-0
	30	(h)	Middlesbrough	D	1-1
Apr	6	(a)	Leicester C	L	3-5
	13	(h)	Bury	W	1-0
	15	(a)	Nottingham F	L	0-3
	19	(a)	Bristol C	D	1-1
	20	(a)	Notts C	L	1-4
	22	(h)	Bristol C	W	3-1
	27	(a)	Liverpool	L	0-1

P	W	D	L	F	A	W	D	L	F	A	Pts	Pos
42	12	4	5	31	24	7	4	10	28	39	46	8th

FA Cup

3	Jan	5	(h)	Grimsby T	W	5-3
4		26	(a)	Everton	L	1-2

SEASON 1957-58
FOOTBALL LEAGUE (DIVISION 2)

Aug	24	(h)	Lincoln C	D	2-2
	26	(a)	Blackburn R	L	1-2
	31	(a)	Bristol R	W	3-2
Sep	2	(h)	Blackburn R	D	1-1
	7	(h)	Derby C	W	2-1
	9	(h)	Sheffield U	L	0-3
	14	(a)	Swansea T	L	2-3
	16	(a)	Sheffield U	L	1-2
	21	(h)	Fulham	W	3-2
	28	(a)	Barnsley	L	0-1
Oct	5	(h)	Leyton O	W	3-2
	12	(a)	Charlton A	W	3-0
	19	(h)	Doncaster R	D	1-1
	26	(a)	Rotherham U	W	2-1
Nov	2	(h)	Huddersfield T	W	5-2
	9	(a)	Grimsby T	W	2-1
	16	(h)	Stoke C	W	5-0
	23	(a)	Bristol C	D	1-1
	30	(h)	Cardiff C	D	1-1
Dec	7	(a)	Liverpool	D	1-1
	14	(h)	Middlesbrough	W	2-1
	21	(a)	Lincoln C	W	6-1
	25	(h)	Ipswich T	D	1-1
	26	(a)	Ipswich T	L	1-2
	28	(h)	Bristol R	W	6-1
Jan	11	(a)	Derby C	W	3-2
	18	(h)	Swansea T	W	6-2
Feb	1	(a)	Fulham	D	2-2
	8	(h)	Barnsley	D	1-1
	20	(a)	Leyton O	W	4-1
	22	(h)	Bristol C	W	3-2
Mar	1	(a)	Doncaster R	W	2-1
	8	(h)	Rotherham U	W	8-0
	15	(a)	Huddersfield T	L	1-3
	22	(h)	Grimsby T	W	2-0
	29	(a)	Stoke C	W	4-1
Ap r	4	(h)	Notts C	W	3-1
	5	(h)	Charlton A	D	0-0
	8	(a)	Notts C	L	0-1
	12	(a)	Cardiff C	W	3-0
	19	(h)	Liverpool	D	1-1
	26	(a)	Middlesbrough	W	3-1

P	W	D	L	F	A	W	D	L	F	A	Pts	Pos
42	12	8	1	56	25	11	3	7	45	29	57	1st

FA Cup

3	Jan	4	(h)	Blackpool	W	5-1
4		25	(h)	Stockport C	W	3-2
5	Feb	15	(h)	Fulham	L	2-3

Hammer of the Year 1957-58

ANDY MALCOLM

SEASON 1958-59
FOOTBALL LEAGUE (DIVISION 1)

Aug	23	(a)	Portsmouth	W	2-1
	25	(h)	Wolves	W	2-0
	30	(h)	Aston Villa	W	7-2
Sep	3	(a)	Wolves	D	1-1
	6	(a)	Luton T	L	1-4
	8	(h)	Manchester U	W	3-2
	13	(a)	Nottingham F	L	0-4
	17	(a)	Manchester U	L	1-4
	20	(h)	Chelsea	W	4-2
	27	(a)	Blackpool	L	0-2
Oct	4	(h)	Blackburn R	W	6-3
	11	(h)	Birmingham C	L	1-2
	18	(a)	West Brom A	L	1-2
	25	(h)	Burnley	W	1-0
Nov	1	(a)	Bolton W	W	2-0
	8	(h)	Arsenal	D	0-0
	15	(a)	Everton	D	2-2
	22	(h)	Leicester C	L	0-3
	29	(a)	Preston NE	L	1-2
Dec	6	(h)	Leeds U	L	2-3
	13	(a)	Manchester C	L	1-3
	20	(h)	Portsmouth	W	6-0
	25	(h)	Tottenham H	W	2-1
	26	(a)	Tottenham H	W	4-1
Jan	3	(a)	Aston Villa	W	2-1
	31	(h)	Nottingham F	W	5-3
Feb	7	(a)	Chelsea	L	2-3
	16	(h)	Blackpool	W	1-0
	21	(a)	Blackburn R	W	2-1
	28	(a)	Birmingham C	L	0-3
Mar	7	(h)	West Brom A	W	3-1
	14	(a)	Burnley	L	0-1
	21	(h)	Bolton W	W	4-3
	27	(h)	Newcastle U	W	3-0
	28	(a)	Arsenal	W	2-1
	30	(a)	Newcastle U	L	1-3
Apr	4	(h)	Everton	W	3-2
	11	(a)	Leicester C	D	1-1
	13	(h)	Luton T	D	0-0
	18	(h)	Preston NE	D	1-1
	20	(h)	Manchester C	W	5-1
	25	(a)	Leeds U	L	0-1

P	W	D	L	F	A	W	D	L	F	A	Pts	Pos
42	15	3	3	59	29	6	3	12	26	41	48	6th

FA Cup

3	Jan	10	(a)	Tottenham H	L	0-2

Hammer of the Year 1958-59

KEN BROWN

SEASON 1959-60
FOOTBALL LEAGUE (DIVISION 1)

Aug	22	(h)	Leicester C	W	3-0
	25	(a)	Preston NE	D	1-1
	29	(a)	Burnley	W	3-1
	31	(h)	Preston NE	W	2-1
Sep	5	(h)	Leeds U	L	1-2
	9	(a)	Tottenham H	D	2-2
	12	(a)	Bolton W	L	1-5
	14	(h)	Tottenham H	L	1-2
	19	(a)	Chelsea	W	4-2
	26	(h)	West Brom A	W	4-1
Oct	3	(a)	Newcastle U	D	0-0
	10	(h)	Luton T	W	3-1
	17	(a)	Everton	W	1-0
	24	(h)	Blackpool	W	1-0
	31	(a)	Fulham	L	0-1
Nov	7	(h)	Manchester C	W	4-1
	14	(a)	Arsenal	W	3-1
	21	(h)	Wolves	W	3-2
	28	(a)	Sheffield W	L	0-7
Dec	5	(h)	Nottingham F	W	4-1
	12	(a)	Blackburn R	L	2-6
	19	(a)	Leicester C	L	1-2
	26	(a)	Birmingham C	L	0-2
	28	(h)	Birmingham C	W	3-1
Jan	2	(h)	Burnley	L	2-5
	16	(a)	Leeds U	L	0-3
	23	(h)	Bolton W	L	1-2
Feb	6	(h)	Chelsea	W	4-2
	20	(h)	Newcastle U	L	3-5
	27	(a)	Nottingham F	L	1-3
Mar	5	(h)	Everton	D	2-2
	9	(a)	West Brom A	L	2-3
	12	(a)	Blackpool	L	2-3
	19	(h)	Blackburn R	W	2-1
	30	(a)	Manchester C	L	1-3
Apr	2	(h)	Arsenal	D	0-0
	11	(a)	Wolves	L	0-5
	15	(h)	Manchester U	W	2-1
	16	(h)	Fulham	L	1-2
	18	(a)	Manchester U	L	3-5
	23	(a)	Luton T	L	1-3
	30	(h)	Sheffield W	D	1-1

P	W	D	L	F	A	W	D	L	F	A	Pts	Pos
42	12	3	6	47	33	4	3	14	28	58	38	14th

FA Cup

3	Jan	9	(h)	Huddersfield T	D	1-1
R		13	(h)	Huddersfield T	L	1-5

Hammer of the Year 1959-60

MALCOLM MUSGROVE

SEASON 1960-61
FOOTBALL LEAGUE (DIVISION 1)

Aug	20	(a)	Wolves	L	2-4
	22	(h)	Aston Villa	W	5-2
	27	(h)	Bolton W	W	2-1
	29	(a)	Aston Villa	L	1-2
Sep	3	(a)	Sheffield W	L	0-1
	5	(h)	Manchester U	W	2-1
	10	(a)	Chelsea	L	2-3
	14	(a)	Manchester U	L	1-6
	17	(h)	Blackpool	D	3-3
	24	(a)	Everton	L	1-4
Oct	1	(h)	Blackburn R	W	3-2
	8	(h)	Birmingham C	W	4-3
	15	(a)	West Brom A	L	0-1
	22	(h)	Preston N	W	5-2
	29	(a)	Fulham	D	1-1
Nov	5	(h)	Arsenal	W	6-0
	12	(a)	Manchester C	W	2-1
	19	(h)	Nottingham F	L	2-4
Dec	3	(h)	Cardiff C	W	2-0
	10	(a)	Newcastle U	D	5-5
	17	(h)	Wolves	W	5-0
	24	(a)	Tottenham 11	L	0-2
	26	(h)	Tottenham H	L	0-3
	31	(a)	Bolton W	L	1-3
Jan	14	(h)	Sheffield W	D	1-1
	21	(h)	Chelsea	W	3-1
Feb	4	(a)	Blackpool	L	0-3
	11	(h)	Everton	W	4-0
	25	(a)	Birmingham C	L	2-4
Mar	4	(h)	West Brom A	L	1-2
	11	(a)	Preston NE	L	0-4
	18	(h)	Fulham	L	1-2
	20	(a)	Blackburn R	L	1-4
	25	(a)	Arsenal	D	0-0
	31	(h)	Leicester C	W	1-0
Apr	1	(h)	Newcastle U	D	1-1
	3	(a)	Leicester C	L	1-5
	8	(a)	Nottingham F	D	1-1
	15	(h)	Manchester C	D	1-1
	18	(a)	Burnley	D	2-2
	22	(a)	Cardiff C	D	1-1
	29	(h)	Burnley	L	1-2

P	W	D	L	F	A	W	D	L	F	A	Pts	Pos
42	12	4	5	53	31	1	6	14	24	57	36	16th

FA Cup

3	Jan	7	(h)	Stoke C	D	2-2
R		11	(a)	Stoke C	L	0-1

League Cup

1	Sep	26	(h)	Charlton A	W	3-1
2	Oct	24	(a)	Darlington	L	2-3

Hammer of the Year 1960-61

BOBBY MOORE

CHAPTER 5

When Ted Fenton was dismissed from his position as West Ham United manager in March 1961, the Club's board of directors insisted they would not be rushed into appointing a successor. With no obvious internal candidate to fill the vacancy, the board decided that they should wait until the end of the season before resolving the situation. In the short term, Club captain Phil Woosnam and coach Albert Walker would look after team affairs, with chairman Reg Pratt undertaking the other duties previously fulfilled by Fenton. This stop-gap situation, however, did not last long. A 4–1 defeat against Blackburn Rovers at Ewood Park left the Hammers on the fringe of the relegation battle and, suddenly, finding a full-time manager became an urgent priority. On 13 April 1961 the Club announced that the Upton Park hot seat had been filled. Arsenal's assistant manager, Ron Greenwood, was to become the fourth manager in West Ham United's history in a move which broke with 61 years of tradition. Each of the three previous men in charge had enjoyed long associations with the Club prior to their appointment – Syd King and Fenton had been players, while Charlie Paynter was first-team trainer. For the first time, the Hammers had invited an outsider to lead their team.

The outsider takes charge

Although a relative unknown to most West Ham United fans, Lancashire-born Greenwood was a well-respected coach within the game. As a player he had enjoyed a long though unspectacular career as a centre-half with Brentford, Chelsea, Fulham and Bradford Park Avenue, before commencing his managerial career with non-League Eastbourne United. He had joined Arsenal in 1957 as chief coach and combined his position at Highbury with the role of manager of England's under-23 team. By the late 1950s, Greenwood had gained a reputation as an astute tactician who thought deeply about the game. He seemed the perfect choice to build upon the achievements of Ted Fenton, who had brought a host of promising youngsters to Upton Park, but who, many believed, had taken the Club as far as he could. Greenwood's great strength was his coaching and it was hoped that he would be able to maximise the effectiveness of the talented players at his disposal. According to former Hammers winger Peter Brabrook, 'Players liked the way Ron worked. He was years ahead of his time in terms of his coaching and tactics. He trained with a continental flair, and his methods are still being used in training sessions today.'

However, for the remaining four games of the 1960–61 season, pragmatism, rather than progressive coaching and entertaining football, was the order of the day. The priority for the new manager was to steady the ship and win enough points to remain in the First Division. Three successive draws proved sufficient to fend off the threat of relegation and, although they lost their final match of the campaign, West Ham United finished in a comfortable 16th position.

The arrival of Greenwood at Upton Park had coincided with the start of the era of unrestricted wage payments, and the new Hammers boss spent much of his first summer in E13 negotiating salaries and contracts. According to the club chairman, Reg Pratt, the new rule 'brought two assessments of a player's value – the player's and the management's'. Mr Pratt added that 'in a small minority of instances the sides have not reached complete agreement.' Seven fringe players, among them John Cartwright, Mike Grice and Andy Smillie, would depart the Club ahead of the 1961–62 season. Like any new manager, Greenwood was keen to begin his own team-building programme, but there would be no big-money signings during the summer of 1961. Two Scotsmen, winger Ian Crawford and goalkeeper Lawrie Leslie, were the only newcomers for whom Hammers paid transfer fees. Not for the first time, the board had directed its finances into ground developments. The North Bank had received its long-awaited roof, costing £20,000, and a new and expensive floodlight system had also been installed.

The Boleyn Ground now offered 'accommodation for over 33,000 [spectators] under cover,' but entertainment rather than

Left: Ron Greenwood goes to work on the training ground. Greenwood's great strengths were his coaching skills and tactical knowledge.

Right: In October 1962 Ron Greenwood bolstered his forward line with the £30,000 signing of England winger Peter Brabrook from Chelsea. Hammers had missed out on Brabrook, a former captain of East Ham Schools, when Ted Fenton hesitated over whether to sign him as an apprentice ten years earlier.

comfort was the chief priority for the 32,600 fans who attended the Hammers' opening fixture of the season, at home to Manchester United. The match ended in a 1-1 draw, with Johnny Dick's close range effort cancelling out an earlier strike from United's Nobby Stiles. In an exciting, end-to-end match, the home team had relied heavily upon the excellent goalkeeping of debutant custodian Lawrie Leslie and the defensive skills of Ken Brown, who had nullified the threat posed by David Herd, the visitors' expensive new striker.

The Hammers enjoyed a promising start to the season, losing just two of their opening 12 fixtures. It was a run that included a superb 4–2 victory away to Aston Villa which prompted Alan Williams of the *Daily Express* to declare that he would 'risk a modest bet that this poised and superbly schooled side will finish in a higher League position than any of their London rivals.' West Ham United's winning form continued a week later when they defeated Chelsea 2–1 at Upton Park. It had been a heroic performance by the Hammers, who had already lost Phil Woosnam to a gashed knee when Bobby Moore was forced to play the last half hour as an emergency goalkeeper because of an injury to Lawrie Leslie.

Alas, the onset of winter saw Hammers' form falter and, although their early season results had been good enough to keep them in the top-half of the table, they won just five of their 19 matches after the New Year. There was, however, much to be optimistic about. The Colts remained a particular source of pride at the club, and in October the youngsters beat Fulham 9–0 in the Youth Cup, with Brian Dear and John Starkey each grabbing hat-tricks. Another 9–0 victory was claimed in the competition's next round when Eton Manor were the vanquished team. Martin Peters and Johnny Sissons were key members of this successful junior line-up and both would soon make the step up to the first team. Ron Greenwood was already benefiting from several earlier graduates of Fenton's youth programme. The departure of Andy Malcolm to Chelsea in November had given young wing-half Geoff Hurst the chance of an extended run in the team and, together with Bobby Moore and Ken Brown, he formed part of a formidable half-back line. Eddie Bovington, a teak-tough ball winner from Edmonton, and the more attack-minded Ron Boyce were also on the fringe of the first team during 1961–62.

'Budgie' Byrne signs

If Hammers were to progress as Greenwood wanted, they would have to supplement their youth team products with more experienced additions to the playing staff. In March 1962 the new manager made his first, and arguably his most significant, major signing when he captured prolific Crystal Palace striker Johnny 'Budgie' Byrne. At £65,000 Byrne represented not only a then record signing for West Ham United but also a record deal between English clubs. Centre-forward had long been a problem position for the Hammers but, while few doubted Byrne's ability to score goals (he had netted 85 times in 203 League games for Palace), many were concerned as to whether he would be able to make the step up from Third to First Division football.

Hammers' new number nine had arrived in time to take part in the final 11 games of the season. However, he was so desperate to succeed that he tried too hard and struggled in front of goal; the fans grew impatient and at season's end he had scored just once. Despite his poor form with West Ham United, Byrne was selected, along with fellow Hammers Joe Kirkup and Bobby Moore, to play for a young England team in May 1962. Twenty-one-year-old Moore was the player who most caught the eye of England manager Walter Winterbottom though, and his efforts were rewarded with a shock call up to the squad for the 1962 World Cup finals in Chile. The Hammers defender made an impressive senior international debut in a warm-up friendly against Peru and retained his place in the line-up for all four of England's matches during the finals.

The World Cup adventures of the Hammers' international defender were, however, quickly forgotten when he reported back to Upton Park for pre-season training in July 1962. For Ron Greenwood the biggest worry ahead of the new season was not fitness levels or injury problems, but contract wrangles. Four senior players – Moore, Phil Woosnam, Ken Brown and Johnny Dick – had refused the Club's offer of terms. By the start of the season the situation was still not resolved. Moore and Dick were both placed on monthly contracts at £15 per week, while the other two players were left in the stand for the opening match of the season at Villa Park. There had been no new signings during the summer, so Greenwood was forced to shuffle his pack somewhat to cover for the absence of two of his most influential players. Ronnie Boyce took the place of Woosnam, while Billy Lansdowne deputised for Brown at centre-half. Predictably, the Hammers struggled and after three minutes they found themselves two goals down, eventually losing the game 3-1. For the next match two days later, against Wolverhampton Wanderers, Greenwood made extensive changes to his line-up. Woosnam and Brown were recalled, and John Lyall came in at left-back for Martin Peters, who moved into the half-back line to take the place of Geoff Hurst. The manager's efforts were, however, in vain and Hammers were swept aside by a breathtaking display from Stan Cullis's young Wolves team who ran out comfortable 4–1 victors. West Ham United's plight deteriorated still further with a humiliating 6–1 home defeat against Tottenham Hotspur which left Spurs manager Bill Nicholson commiserating that 'our opponents did not have one ounce of luck'.

Hurst steps forward

After five games of the season the Hammers were rooted to the bottom of the the First Division with just a single point to show for their efforts. The next match brought yet more changes to Greenwood's XI. Following the departure of Johnny Dick – the Club's most reliable goalscorer who had joined Brentford in September – West Ham United were in desperate need of a strike partner for Johnny Byrne. With few options, the manager produced a stroke of pure genius which proved of great significance to not only the Hammers but also to England. Geoff Hurst, an average and workmanlike wing-half, was pushed forward to wear the number ten shirt in a move which surprised both fans and players. Bobby Moore would later admit that 'none of us [the players] thought that Geoff was going to make the switch,' adding 'it took him years of hard work and patience to become the man who scored three goals in a World Cup final.'

In addition to the conversion of Hurst from half-back to forward, Greenwood made four other changes ahead of the match against Liverpool at Upton Park, and at last his tinkering paid dividends. A goal after just five minutes from recalled winger Tony Scott was enough to give the Hammers their first win of the season. A second victory arrived five days later when an unchanged line-up demolished Manchester City 6–1 at Maine Road. The result took West Ham United off the foot of the table and a month later Greenwood's team crashed five goals past Birmingham City to rise to a comfortable mid-table position. The match against the Midlanders was also notable as it saw Ken Brown score his first League goal after almost 300 matches for the Hammers. So elated was the experienced centre-half that he claimed he would buy 100 copies of the picture if any photographer had managed to capture his big moment on film.

Also among the scorers against the Blues was Johnny Byrne, who had struck five goals in six games, and was rumoured to be on the verge of a recall to the full England team. The former Palace striker was becoming an increasingly influential figure, and had added a new dimension to Hammers' attacking play. At a time when the average number nine remained a big, hulking six-footer who did little else but head the ball, Byrne was something of an anomaly. He stood at just 5 ft 7 in, but had great control, pace and passing ability. Greenwood encouraged his record signing to maximise his effectiveness by dropping deep to pick up the ball, and to link play by bringing the wingers and attacking midfielders into the game. With Byrne operating as a deep-lying centre-forward, in the style of the Hungarian master Hidegkuti, the more imposing frame of Geoff Hurst became the focus for many West Ham United attacking moves. The most famous and successful ploy used by the Hammers under Greenwood's tutelage was the near-post cross. Although not a new move, it was a tactic which had largely been forgotten. All too often a predictable cross to the far post gave the striker little chance, casting him against both goalkeeper and centre-half, whereas a ball whipped in at the near post could present an excellent opportunity to an attacker arriving late. Geoff Hurst became expert at timing his runs to profit from such centres.

In the autumn of 1962 Ron Greenwood took drastic action to solve a goalscoring crisis that saw Hammers net just three times in their first five games. Geoff Hurst, a workmanlike wing-half, was pushed forward to play up front alongside Johnny Byrne. It was an unexpected switch, as Hurst had shown no previous aptitude as a goalscorer, but it proved an inspired change. At season's end Hammers new number ten had scored 13 goals from 26 appearances in the forward line.

With Byrne and Hurst now installed as his first choice strike pairing, Ron Greenwood continued his team building in October 1962, by bolstering his forward line still further with the capture of Chelsea winger Peter Brabrook. A former captain of East Ham Schools, Brabrook had been keen to join the Hammers as an apprentice, but had ended up signing for the Stamford Bridge team when Ted Fenton decided against offering him a place on the groundstaff. Nine years later, West Ham

United were forced to pay £35,000 for a player who, along with Jimmy Greaves and Terry Venables, had been snapped up by Chelsea's master scout Jimmy Thompson. The signing of Brabrook was, however, a long drawn out affair and was only finally resolved after a League tribunal found no evidence of any wrongdoing on the part of West Ham United, who had been accused of unsettling the former Chelsea player.

The Hammers' new outside-right wasted little time making his mark, and after just 35 seconds of his debut delivered the killer-ball for Geoff Hurst to open the scoring at home to Burnley. The arrival of Brabrook would effectively sound the death knell on the Upton Park career of Malcolm Musgrove, who lost his place in the team when Tony Scott was switched from the right to the left wing in order to make space for the new man. Phil Woosnam, another of Fenton's forwards, was on his way out of E13 in the winter of 1962, joining Aston Villa after 134 League appearances for the Hammers. Greenwood had clearly been impressed by the form of the emergent Ronnie Boyce, who immediately assumed the former captain's number eight shirt. However, the Hammers boss had no ready-made replacement when goalkeeper and reigning Hammer of the Year, Lawrie Leslie, sustained a broken leg against Bolton Wanderers in November. Greenwood was forced, instead, to enter the transfer market and signed Luton Town's custodian Jim Standen for £7,000. Standen was a player the Hammers manager knew well, having worked with him in his time as Arsenal's reserve team coach, and the new goalie quickly proved himself a bargain buy.

Ronnie Boyce, or 'Ticker' as he was nicknamed, was an energetic midfielder whose contribution to Hammers' successful teams of the 1960s often went unrecognised. Boyce made his League debut against Preston North End as a 17-year-old in October 1960, but his greatest moment came against the same opponents four years later when he scored the winning goal in the FA Cup final.

With so many changes in personnel, it is hardly surprising that West Ham United struggled to find any consistent form throughout the 1962–63 season. Twelfth place in the League, however, was far better than could have been hoped for after the Club's disastrous start to the season. The FA Cup had provided the season's highlight, and it was only a late Roger Hunt goal at Anfield that denied the Hammers a well-earned quarter-final replay. Liverpool had also provided the opposition for West Ham United's Colts team in the two-legged final of the FA Youth Cup. The first match on Merseyside had ended in a 3–1 defeat for the Londoners and, when the Reds took an early lead in the return, it looked like the Hammers Colts were on the verge of losing their third Cup final. However, before a crowd of 13,200, Wally St Pier's youngsters staged a remarkable come-back to win 6–5 on aggregate. The Hammers line-up included Harry Redknapp (described by *The Evening Standard* as a 'darting flash of a right-winger'), John Dryden, Martin Britt and Bobby Howe and was captained by full-back John Charles.

International challenge

The summer of 1963 saw Ron Greenwood take his team across the Atlantic to compete in the 14-team American Challenge Cup. The Hammers began the tournament without Bobby Moore and Johnny Byrne, who were both on international duty, and it was only after the England duo arrived that the East Londoners showed their best form, recording victories over Mexican, German and French teams only to lose 2–1 in the final against Czech outfit Dukla Prague. The experienced eastern Europeans, however, proved too strong for a Hammers team with an average age of 23 and ran out 2–1 aggregate winners. Despite the disappointment of defeat, Ron Greenwood's men had gained valuable experience by competing against some of the strongest teams in world football, and had done much to enhance their reputation. One man in no doubt as to the bright future which lay ahead for the Hammers was Dukla's star player and goalscorer Joseph Masopust who declared: 'They are good, very good. I predict they will be a world-class team within two years.' The Czech's eulogising was dismissed as a victor's generous and completely insincere backslapping, but in the coming months his words were to prove more than a little prophetic.

By the start of the 1963–64 season Ron Greenwood had succeeded in building a Hammers team which bore little resemblance to that which he had inherited from Ted Fenton. The line-up which took the field for the opening fixture of the campaign, away at Chelsea, included just three players – Bobby Moore, Joe Kirkup and Ken Brown – who had survived from Fenton's final match in charge. Greenwood had, however, benefited greatly from the youth programme instigated by his predecessor, and five of the other stars on display at Stamford Bridge had been nurtured through the Club's junior ranks during the late 1950s. But whether bought or home-grown, all 11 West Ham United players toiled tirelessly against Tommy Docherty's talented Chelsea team and returned from their trip to West London with a valuable point.

The Hammers would remain unbeaten in their first four games of the season, and at the end of August were among the early front-runners in the race for the First Division Championship. However, five defeats in the next six matches put paid to any dreaming of title success, and for the remainder of the League campaign Greenwood's team were characteristically unpredictable. On their day, the Hammers remained formidable opponents, as they proved with celebrated victories at both Anfield and Old Trafford, but on other occasions, often against lesser opponents, they struggled inexplicably. The match against Blackburn Rovers at Upton Park on Boxing Day morning showed Greenwood's team at its very worst. On a heavy pitch, the home team failed to adapt to the conditions and were torn apart by England midfielder Bryan Douglas, who orchestrated Rovers' 8–2 victory. Two days later Hammers travelled to Ewood Park for the return match and, as if to reinforce their reputation for inconsistency, ran out comfortable 3–1 winners thanks to two goals from Byrne and one from Hurst. Greenwood had made just one change to his line-up for the trip to Lancashire, replacing the attack-minded Martin Peters with the more abrasive and tough-tackling Eddie Bovington. Peters would make just one more midfield appearance during the 1963–64 season.

Despite their erratic League form, the Hammers had made steady progress in the League Cup, and a 6–0 victory over Fourth Division Workington in December had earned Greenwood's team a semi-final clash with Leicester City. The first leg of the tie against the Midlanders saw West Ham United go three goals down inside 20 minutes, but two strikes from Geoff Hurst and one from Alan Sealey would eventually restrict the Foxes' advantage to just a single goal. However, it still proved an unassailable lead and, seven weeks later, the Hammers were unable to find a way past Leicester 'keeper Gordon Banks and conceded two further goals to crash out of the competition 3–6 on aggregate. By then though, the East Londoners were already in the midst of a glorious FA Cup run.

FA Cup glory

Hammers began their Cup campaign against Second Division Charlton Athletic, and goals from Hurst, Brabrook and Sissons proved enough to secure passage to a fourth round tie against local rivals Leyton Orient. For the match at Brisbane Road, Greenwood made no changes to his line up, which had remained unaltered since defeating Blackburn Rovers at Ewood Park in December. Standen played in goal; Bond and Burkett were the full-backs; Brown and Moore completed a four-man defence; Boyce and Bovington occupied the midfield; Sissons and Brabrook were the wingers; and Hurst and Byrne played up front. This formidable Hammers team, which would remain unchanged throughout the 1965 Cup run, could manage only a draw against the Orient, although they did secure a comfortable 3–0 victory in the replay at Upton Park four days later. Further triumphs, over Swindon Town and Burnley, took West Ham United into the last four of the FA Cup for the first time since 1933.

Hammers' opponents in the semi-final at neutral Hillsborough were title-chasing Manchester United. The Reds were the undoubted favourites to reach Wembley, and a week before the Cup clash, they reinforced their status with a 2–0 League victory at Upton Park. The legendary triumvirate of Law, Charlton and Best had been rested for the semi-final rehearsal, but all three were included in the line-up for the big match in Sheffield. With the odds so firmly stacked against their team, it was with much trepidation that Hammers fans made the long journey from East London to West Yorkshire. The players too had their concerns, and Peter Brabrook remembers: 'Manchester United were some team. On paper we had no chance.'

On the morning of the match, Sheffield was thoroughly soaked by torrential rain, and by the time three o'clock came the Hillsborough pitch had turned into a quagmire. Peter Brabrook recalls walking out on to the pitch and stepping up to his ankles in mud. Clearly it was not going to be a day for intricate passing or flashy dribbling. Despite the conditions, though, it was to be one of the greatest matches in the history of West Ham United. For much of the game, the Hammers defended, but with Bobby Moore at his most composed and constructive, the East Londoners gradually came into the game as an attacking force. All 11 West Ham United players worked tirelessly throughout the 90 minutes, but it was inside-forward Ronnie Boyce who proved the match winner, scoring twice in seven second-half minutes. Boyce's first goal arrived 11 minutes after the re-start when he let fly with a rasping 25-yard drive into the top left-hand corner of the Manchester United goal. His second, though, would have given Greenwood most pleasure as it came from a well-worked set-piece. From a corner on the left, John Sissons cut the ball back to Jackie Burkett who chipped a cross into the box for the Hammers number eight to head past the stranded United goalkeeper Dave Gaskell.

For the remaining half an hour of the match, Manchester United laid siege to Jim Standen's goal, but the Londoners defended stoutly, and it was not until 12 minutes from time that the Reds found a way through. The goal arrived when John Bond, normally a powerful striker of the ball, took a goal kick for Standen but mis-hit his clearance and sent the ball tamely into the path of George Best. The United winger advanced forward and, with chaos reigning in the Hammers' penalty area, Denis Law reduced the arrears to just the one goal. However, just as West Ham United's fans prepared for a nerve-racking final ten minutes, Bobby Moore calmly played the ball out of defence to start a move which resulted in a goal for Geoff Hurst. The game was over and West Ham United had reached their first FA Cup final for 41 years. It had been an epic encounter and the newspapers were full of kind words for Ron Greenwood's men, but no tribute was more eloquent or accurate than that of Brian Glanville: 'Under driving rain, on a cart track of a pitch, they [West Ham United] expertly contained Manchester United's attack, then proceeded to riddle their defence. It was a splendid team performance; but above all it was a captain's triumph for Bobby Moore... Moore played with transcendent authority; with poise strength, dexterity and anticipation.'

The Hammers skipper, who was also now captain of his country, had become the First Division's most accomplished defender, and shortly before the FA Cup final his conspicuous talent was recognised by the Football Writers' Association who duly named him their Footballer of the Year. However, while Bobby Moore enjoyed his success former team-mate John Lyall found himself in a rather different predicament. At the age of 23, Lyall's playing days had been brought to a premature halt by persistent injury problems and he faced an uncertain future. To ease his plight, the Club granted him a testimonial and the match, which was somewhat controversially played on the Monday before the Cup final, attracted a crowd of 18,000.

The 1964 FA Cup final:
Above: West Ham United skipper Bobby Moore shakes hands with his Preston North End counterpart Alex Dawson.

Right, top: West Ham United winger John Sissons (third from left) watches as his shot evades Preston 'keeper Alan Kelly.

Right, middle: Geoff Hurst (number ten) celebrates Hammers' second equaliser.

Right, bottom: Alan Kelly looks on as Ronnie Boyce's last-minute header moves goalward.

Return to the Twin Towers

West Ham United's opponents at Wembley were Second Division Preston North End, so it was in the unfamiliar role of favourites that the Hammers made their first FA Cup final appearance since 1940. Preston, however, belied their underdog status, making by far the stronger start to the final, and deservedly took the lead when Holden stabbed home after Standen had fumbled a shot from Dawson. It was a goal which spurred Greenwood's team into life, albeit temporarily, and four minutes later 18-year-old John Sissons broke forward before cutting inside from the left to unleash a shot which gave Alan Kelly, Preston's 'keeper, little chance. The score remained unchanged for half an hour, but Preston continued to boss the game, and it came as no surprise when they took

1961-73

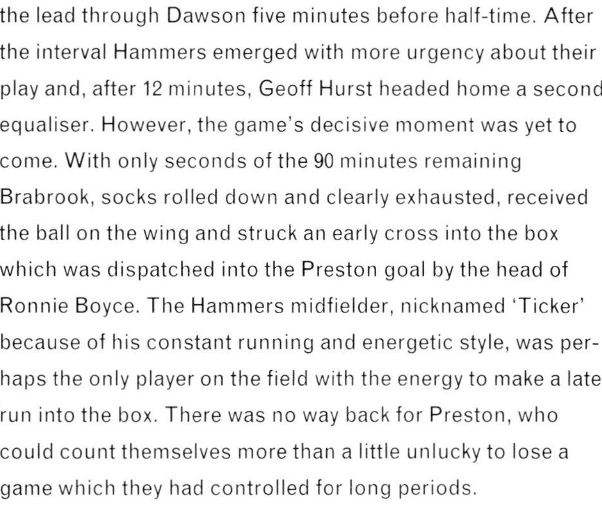

the lead through Dawson five minutes before half-time. After the interval Hammers emerged with more urgency about their play and, after 12 minutes, Geoff Hurst headed home a second equaliser. However, the game's decisive moment was yet to come. With only seconds of the 90 minutes remaining Brabrook, socks rolled down and clearly exhausted, received the ball on the wing and struck an early cross into the box which was dispatched into the Preston goal by the head of Ronnie Boyce. The Hammers midfielder, nicknamed 'Ticker' because of his constant running and energetic style, was perhaps the only player on the field with the energy to make a late run into the box. There was no way back for Preston, who could count themselves more than a little unlucky to lose a game which they had controlled for long periods.

After the game a delighted Ron Greenwood told reporters that he had not doubted his team's ability to win the match, commenting: 'To fight back twice means you are always in with a chance... we changed our tactics in the second half, with Bobby Moore watching Ashworth and Ken Brown taking Alex Dawson – they [previously] had too much room to work in.' But despite the dramatic finish and the elation of winning the most prestigous club competition in football, there is no doubt that the highlight of the Hammers' 1964 Cup run was the semi-final victory over Manchester United. At Wembley, Greenwood's team had played only in patches, whereas against United they produced a disciplined display which had enhanced their reputation as one of English football's emergent powers.

Next stop the Continent

West Ham United's FA Cup triumph of 1964 brought the club not only its first major silverware but also a passport to European competition. The Cup Winners' Cup – then the second most prestigious of Europe's three club Cups – would become Hammers' primary aim during the 1964–65 season. There would, however, be no new signings to boost Greenwood's squad and the only significant change of personnel at Upton Park during the summer of 1964 was the appointment of John Lyall as 'Official in Charge' of the youth team.

As FA Cup holders, Hammers began their 1964–65 season early contesting the Charity Shield, English football's traditional curtain-raiser. League Champions Liverpool provided the opposition in a match, somewhat unfairly, played at Anfield, but to their credit the East Londoners twice came from behind in an entertaining encounter which finished 2-2. It was a performance that earned Greenwood's team many plaudits and prompted Brian Glanville to write: 'West Ham are a consistently interesting side to watch because they are consistently trying to do something interesting. They are in the approved contemporary fashion a counter-attacking team, playing the ball out of a massed defence to an inventive forward line.'

Counter-attacking tactics were still widely frowned upon in the 1960s, and West Ham United would frequently be accused of adopting this approach. According to former Hammers outside-right Peter Brabrook, however, Greenwood never sent his teams out with a premeditated game-plan to hit their opponents purely on the break. Brabrook believes it was merely that more direct and physical opponents would often successfully pen the East Londoners in their own half, and with fast, incisive players like Byrne, Sissons and Boyce in the Hammers line-up, breakaway goals became a common occurrence. But whether by design or default, one fact not in dispute is that West Ham United's patient and calm style of play was well-suited to the challenge of European football.

By the time the Hammers kicked-off their European campaign in September 1964, they had already displayed their now-trademark erratic form in ten domestic fixtures. Impressive victories over Wolverhampton Wanderers, Manchester United and Tottenham Hotspur had been been interspersed with perplexing defeats against Stoke City, Burnley and Sunderland. So it was with much uncertainty that West Ham United fans waited to hear news of how their team had fared on their Cup Winners' Cup debut against Belgian club La Gantoise in Ghent. The news, when it arrived, was good, a Ronnie Boyce header had been the only goal of the game and gave Hammers a valuable lead for the return match at Upton Park two weeks later.

Far left: A youthful looking Bobby Moore – he was still just 24 years old – holds the FA Cup aloft so that Hammers fans who have scaled the windows of the Wembley dressing rooms can get a closer look at the silverware.

Left: Centre-half Ken Brown, still wearing his number five shirt, drinks milk from the FA Cup as John Sissons looks on.

Bottom, left: Johnny Byrne, himself something of a larger than life character, celebrates victory against Preston by carrying a gigantic Hammer on the post-match lap of honour.

Left: In August 1964 Hammers made their first appearance in the Charity Shield. An entertaining match, played somewhat unfairly at Anfield, ended 2–2 and the trophy was shared between the two clubs. Bobby Moore is shown here holding the Shield with Liverpool skipper Ron Yeats.

Below: Matchday programme from West Ham United's Cup Winners' Cup clash with Belgian side La Gantoise in October 1964. The tie was the Club's first competitive action in European competition.

Europe comes to E13

Confidence was high when the Belgian part-timers arrived in E13 for the first European fixture to be played at the Boleyn Ground. West Ham United were well placed in the First Division, having scored more goals than any other top-flight team, and in John Byrne the Club had a forward who had struck the net 12 times in ten games. A Hammers goal feast was eagerly anticipated. However, it failed to arrive and, when Martin Peters struck a back-pass beyond Alan Dickie for an own goal which put the Belgians back on terms, the Upton Park atmosphere became increasingly tense. Twelve minutes later, though, a strike from the predatory Byrne restored West Ham United's aggregate lead. It was enough to ensure

Midfielder Martin Peters, seen here heading goalwards in a match against Newcastle United, lost his place in the Hammers line-up to the more defensively-minded Eddie Bovington during 1963–64 and missed out on the Club's FA Cup triumph against Preston. However, Peters (who England manager Alf Ramsey would later describe as being 'ten years ahead of his time') responded in emphatic fashion to this set-back. The following season he played in nine of Hammers' ten European Cup Winners' Cup matches and began pushing for full international recognition.

Hammers' passage to the competition's second round – where they would face Spartak Prague – but it was not enough to prevent the home crowd from jeering a performance which had seen Greenwood's men struggle to break down the part-timers' well-organised and packed defence. Increased admission prices, which had brought record Upton Park receipts, had been a source of further criticism, although the club claimed that much of the £9,700 taken through the turnstiles would merely cover the considerable additional expenses of hosting a European tie.

Throughout Hammers' Cup Winners' Cup campaign, Greenwood relied heavily upon the team which had succeeded against Preston at Wembley. The manager would use just 14 outfield players throughout the campaign and, against Sparta Prague at Upton Park in the second round first leg, the value of this settled line-up was clearly apparent. The Czechs, top of their league and wily European competitors, arrived at the Boleyn Ground with a brief to defend deep and frustrate the Hammers. However, the patient and confident home team retained their composure and after a goalless first half overwhelmed Sparta. A long distance strike from John Bond opened the scoring, before Alan Sealey – in as a replacement for the injured Peter Brabrook – added a crucial second goal. It was a match which had provided rich entertainment for the 27,600 crowd, but the fans too had played their part and the club programme for the next home match applauded their contribution: 'The "chessboard" play was enthralling (if not pulsating) to watch but once we had the measure of the continentals the enthusiastic support did much to tip the scales in our favour.'

Victory over the Czechs had arrived with the Hammers in the midst of a rich vein of form, which would see them record impressive wins over Arsenal (3–0 at Highbury), Leeds United (3-1 at Upton Park) and Chelsea (3–0 at Stamford Bridge), so it was as confident favourites that a buoyant West Ham United line-up took the field for the return in Prague two weeks later. A well-taken goal from John Sissons after 14 minutes put the tie beyond the home team and, although two second-half goals from Sparta's Mraz set-up an unnecessarily tense finish, it proved enough to send the Hammers into the last eight of the Cup Winners' Cup.

The quarter-final draw paired Greenwood's team with Swiss side Lausanne, but, because of the competition's winter break, the tie was not scheduled until March; some three months away. It was a period which would see Hammers' early season from desert them – they lost nine of their 15 matches. By the time the Club returned to European action they had been been eliminated from the FA Cup (by Chelsea) and had slipped down the League. The Cup Winners' Cup now provided West Ham United's only realistic route back into

European competition for the 1965–66 season. The first leg of the quarter-final was played in Switzerland and a 2–1 victory for the Hammers (courtesy of goals from Brian Dear – on his European debut - and Johnny Byrne) gave no hint of the drama that was to unfold in the return at Upton Park. The second leg started slowly, but when the Swiss struck the opener after 37 minutes to draw level on aggregate, the game exploded into life. An own goal from Lausanne's Tacchella and Brian Dear's second goal of the tie gave Hammers what seemed an unassailable lead at the interval. But the goals kept coming and with ten minutes to go the aggregate score stood at 5–4 to West Ham United. In true schoolboy fashion it was quite simply a 'next goal wins' situation, and, much to the relief of most of the 31,800 crowd, it was the home team's Brian Dear who struck the decisive goal after 89 minutes. It had been a refreshingly open and entertaining Cup tie, but these qualities were lost on Hammers boss Ron Greenwood who declared: 'We kept putting Lausanne back into the game with silly goals. Against a better team that would be a tragedy.'

Two weeks later, that 'better team' arrived at Upton Park for the semi-final. Spanish Cup holders Real Zaragoza were by far the most talented and experienced side that West Ham United had faced, and a 35,000 crowd filled the Boleyn Ground to see the clash. Despite the pedigree of their visitors the Hammers were far from overawed and their fluent attacking play in the game's opening spell earned them a 2–0 lead. Brian Dear opened the scoring, registering his third goal in three European fixtures, with a well-taken header after just nine minutes, before John Byrne struck the goal of the game with a superb volley. The second half, however, was a rather different affair with Hammers keeping nine men behind the ball in an effort to protect their lead. It was an approach which, unsurprisingly, did not meet with the fans' approval, but more significantly it was a ploy which was also ultimately unsuccessful, and ten minutes after the break Zaragoza reduced the arrears to just a single goal for the return in Spain. The Spaniards were now the undoubted favourites to reach the final. Ron Greenwood was, nevertheless, upbeat, declaring: 'We produced an exhibition of soccer which had "out-continentalled" the continentals.' However, skipper Bobby Moore would later portray the true feeling in the Hammers camp: 'We put a brave face on it but none of us believed deep down that it [2–1] would be enough. They called the Zaragoza forward line the Magnificent Five and we knew they would give us a real going over in Spain.'

Moore's fears proved well-founded and after just 24 minutes of the return leg in Spain Zaragoza levelled the aggregate score with a goal from Lapetra. Thereafter the Spaniards laid

In 1965 West Ham United completed a long-awaited extension to the West Stand. The new section (A-block) is clearly visible on the left of this picture, as is the dilapidated roof of the Chicken Run on the opposite side of the ground.

siege to Jim Standen's goal. But, despite impassioned appeals for penalties on several occasions, the home team were unable to find a way through, and nine minutes after the interval John Sissons met a Brian Dear pass to strike the decisive goal. On this occasion the Hammers had truly 'out-continentalled the continentals'.

Victory over Zaragoza had arrived five days after the end of the English League season, leaving Greenwood's team with no competitive football for the three weeks ahead of the final against German outfit TSV Munich 1860. This lack of match practice, however, would prove far from decisive in the biggest game in the history of West Ham United. Wembley Stadium was to play host to the final in a move which, though seemingly unfair upon the Germans, had been decided long in advance. The Hammers line-up included seven of the XI who had been on duty at Wembley in the Cup final a year before, with Kirkup, Peters, Sealey and Dear coming in for the unlucky quartet of Bond, Bovington, Brabrook and Byrne. The loss of Byrne, who had not played since the semi-final first leg, was a huge blow to Greenwood's plans, although his replacement, Brian Dear,

Above: Alan Sealey (number seven) wheels away in delight after netting his second goal in the European Cup Winners' Cup final against TSV Munich 1860. Sealey, who played at outside-right, had scored just three goals all season and had spent most of the campaign as deputy to Ron Greenwood's favoured right-winger, Peter Brabrook.

Left: Munich keeper Radenkovic winces as Alan Sealey's shot finds the net for the opening goal of the 1965 Cup Winners' Cup final at Wembley. John Sissons, the Hammers player on the right of the picture is clearly enamoured with the contribution of his wing partner.

had shown excellent form in the League, scoring ten goals in ten games including a five-goal haul against West Bromwich Albion in April.

Victory in Europe

Dear would produce one of his finest performances in claret and blue during the final, and his powerful, surging runs into opposition territory were a key feature of the opening 45 minutes against the Germans. But it was not just Hammers' number ten who found form at the right time, the whole team it seemed had been lifted by the occasion and were immediately firing on all cylinders. The cagey, defensive play of the earlier rounds was quickly forgotten as the East Londoners set about attacking their opponents with a vigour which enthralled the 100,000 fans inside Wembley. But, despite the best efforts of both teams – Munich also had their chances – there had been no score at half-time. Fortunately, West Ham United's fluent football was not unduly affected by the interval and they continued with more of the same in the second period. The breakthrough finally arrived when, with 21 minutes to go, the unlikely figure of Alan Sealey popped up in the penalty area to fire home from a narrow angle. It was only his third goal of the season, and his first score since February. Two minutes later, as if to prove it had been no fluke, Sealey struck again, sending the ball past Radenkovic in the Munich goal to claim his place in West Ham United's history. There were no further additions to the scoreline, which by no means flattered the Hammers, who had also had a goal disallowed for hand ball and had seen John Sissons hit the frame of the goal twice.

The match had been screened live in 18 countries and West Ham United had done much to enhance their reputation as an exciting and effective team. Hans Bangerter, European FA Secretary, pronounced: 'There could not have been a finer advertisement for the game.' *The Evening Standard*'s Bernard Joy was equally complimentary: 'This is the day when England showed the world that we have absorbed lessons from our former pupils and are the masters again.' But perhaps the most prophetic testimony came from Brazil's Dr L. Murgel who eulogised: 'If the football of the England team is like this display by West Ham then England are the real danger in the World Cup. West Ham's football was brilliant – so clever and so quick.' The national team's prospects for 1966, however, were of little concern to Greenwood who, despite his team's victory, remained circumspect, commenting: 'We can't really be satisfied until we win the League. It is only a question of application... We have grown up a bit in this competition and proved our resolution in tough away matches in Prague and Zaragoza.' The manager did, though, reserve special praise for Bobby Moore, whom he described as 'technical perfection'.

Time for a change

According to the football truism which says that great teams last for just three years, 1965–66 should have been the final season for the Hammers line-up that Ron Greenwood had so carefully assembled during the early part of his reign. However, at the start of the League campaign it looked as though the manager had decided to commence his rebuilding programme ahead of time. With striker Johnny Byrne and veteran defenders Ken Brown and John Bond all absent it was a somewhat changed Hammers XI that kicked off the season away to West Bromwich Albion. But the changes did not end there, and a 3–0 defeat by the Baggies saw Greenwood continue to shuffle his pack in a way which he had not done since 1962. A new crop of youngsters had emerged through the Hammers' junior ranks and the boss, it seemed, was keen to give them all a chance in the first team. Dave Bickles, Peter Bennett, John Charles and Harry Redknapp would each play a part in a somewhat disappointing League campaign.

Below: Scenes of celebration as Hammers parade the Cup Winners' Cup outside East Ham Town Hall in May 1965.

The one bright spot during the early weeks of the season was the excellent form of Geoff Hurst and Martin Peters, both of whom were hotly tipped to win full England honours. Hurst and Peters would dominate Hammers' scoring in August and September, claiming 12 of the club's 14 goals. However, the good form of two players could not compensate for a general malaise which brought just seven points from ten games, and despite Greenwood's best efforts West Ham United occupied a perilous League position when they began their Cup Winners' Cup defence in November 1965. Fortunately, a home tie against Greek team Olympiakos proved far from taxing, and Hammers emerged with a 4–0 lead – courtesy of two goals from Hurst, a rare header from winger Peter Brabrook and Johnny Byrne's first strike of the season – to take into the second leg in Athens. It proved an unassailable advantage and, despite the intimidatory tactics of the Greek fans, the East Londoners added two more goals to their total in a game which finished in a 2–2 draw. Hammers' goals were both scored by Martin Peters, and the

first prompted the small band of travelling fans to celebrate with a chorus of *Bubbles*. It was a move, however, which met with the disapproval of the Greek police who immediately asked the Londoners to desist from their provocative chanting.

Victory over Olympiakos had ensured safe passage to a quarter-final tie against East German Cup holders Magdeburg in March, but during the interim the Hammers would have to forget the dramas of European competition and concentrate instead on improving their lowly League status. At the turn of the year, Greenwood's team remained dangerously on the fringes of the battle for First Division survival, and it was only a run of four consecutive victories in February and March which provided the necessary points to see them climb out of the relegation zone. Cup football would dominate the remainder of West Ham United's season.

Despite early elimination from the FA Cup, the Hammers had made good progress in the League Cup, although it has to be said that success in the competition's early rounds was more the result of fortune than form. Nevertheless, victories over Bristol Rovers, Mansfield Town, Rotherham United and Grimsby Town had taken West Ham United to a two-legged semi-final against Cardiff City. It was a match which would see Greenwood's team at last produce a display of style and confidence, recording ten goals from six different scorers to overcome their Welsh opponents. Hammers would now face West Bromwich Albion in their third Cup final in three years.

WEST HAM UNITED

BOLEYN GROUND : LONDON E.13

No. 47

WEST BROMWICH ALBION

FOOTBALL LEAGUE CUP: FINAL (First Leg)

WEDNESDAY 9th MARCH 1966 at 7.30 p.m.

OFFICIAL PROGRAMME 6d

Top: Future manager Harry Redknapp had been a member of Hammers' victorious 1963 FA Youth Cup winning team, and two years later he made the breakthrough into the senior line up.

Left: Jim Standen claims a cross during the away leg of the Cup Winners' Cup tie against Olympiakos in December 1965. The match ended in a 2–2 draw which gave Hammers a 6–2 aggregate victory.

Cup disappointments

At the start of March 1966 West Ham United's season lay firmly in the balance with four critical Cup ties to be played before the end of the month. First up was the home leg of the Cup Winners' Cup quarter-final against Magdeburg. Alas it was to be a largely frustrating night for Greenwood's men, who struggled to break down a stereotypically 'well-organised' German defence. The game's only goal came immediately after the interval when John Byrne eased a tense atmosphere by crashing home after good work from Geoff Hurst. Seven days later it was League Cup action which brought the fans (28,300) flocking back to Upton Park for the first of the two-legged final with West Brom. It was to be another difficult evening for Hammers fans who watched their strangely subdued team repeatedly surrender possession to the Baggies. The visitors took a deserved lead after 59 minutes, but goals from Bobby Moore and Johnny Byrne gave the Hammers a slim advantage for the return at the Hawthorns.

At the halfway stage, and despite holding a one goal lead in each match, West Ham United were now undoubtedly the underdogs for both their Cup Winners' Cup and League Cup ties. Given a choice, Hammers would probably have opted for success in Europe at the expense of victory in the League Cup – although it should not be forgotten that a win over Albion would have earned them a place in the Fairs Cup. So it was perhaps with one eye on their forthcoming match in East Germany, that Ron Greenwood's team travelled to the Midlands for the second leg of the match against West Bromwich Albion. According to former Hammers winger Peter Brabrook: 'We just weren't at the races that day, whereas West Brom most definitely were.' Albion struck four times in the first half to put the game beyond West Ham United's reach, and, despite an improved second-half display which saw Martin Peters reduce the arrears, the Londoners had lost their first

Cup final for 43 years. The following week did at least give Greenwood's men the chance to make amends in Cup Winners' Cup quarter-final against Magdeburg. And they did not disappoint.

Hammers had travelled to Germany with the intention of protecting their slender lead, and rarely ventured out of their own half during the first hour of the match. However, with just 12 minutes remaining the Ernst Grube stadium erupted with a deafening roar after Walter gave the home team the lead. Spurred into life, West Ham United struck back in dramatic fashion, cancelling out Magdeburg's goal through winger John Sissons. It proved the decisive strike of the tie and ensured Hammers' progress into the last four along with Celtic and Liverpool. Both British teams were successfully avoided in the semi-final draw, but a tie against West Germany's Borussia Dortmund looked equally perilous. And so it proved. The first leg at Upton Park started well enough, and a second-half goal from Martin Peters looked to have given Greenwood's team a lead to protect in Dortmund. However, as the game entered its last ten minutes Hammers pressed forward, clearly concerned that one goal would not be enough. The Germans, unsurprisingly, were quick to exploit the gaps that were suddenly appearing in the home team's defence and struck twice in two minutes to leave West Ham United needing nothing short of a miracle to progress to the Cup Winners' Cup final. Alas there was to be no divine intervention in Germany and a 3-1 defeat in the second leg completed a comprehensive Dortmund victory.

Elimination from the Cup Winners' Cup meant that a season of great promise ended without addition to the Upton Park trophy cabinet. But despite this disappointment, 1965–66 was not without its successes. The goalscoring form of Geoff Hurst had been a revelation and was a particular cause for optimism among Hammers' fans. Hurst was named Hammer of the Year – a fitting reward for a player who had struck 40 goals in 59 games – and in February he won his first senior cap for England. The powerful striker would be joined in Alf Ramsey's line-up by his West Ham United team-mate Martin Peters for the friendly against Yugoslavia, and both players, along with skipper Bobby Moore, would impress sufficiently to make it into the final squad for the 1966 World Cup finals.

World Cup winners

It was a source of tremendous pride to West Ham United that three of their players had been included in Ramsey's World Cup squad, but when the tournament kicked off on 11 July, only Moore was included in the manager's starting line-up. Peters, however, would win his fourth cap in England's second game, five days later, while Hurst would remain on the sidelines until an injury to Jimmy Greaves gave him his chance in the quarter-final against Argentina. England, as hosts, had been expected to do well in the World Cup, so it was no great surprise that Ramsey's 'wingless wonders' made it to the final. However, few Hammers fans could have predicted that three of their heroes would be included when England took on West Germany at Wembley on 30 July. It would prove to be English football's greatest success, and the contribution of West Ham United's famous trio cannot be overestimated. Geoff Hurst's famous hat-trick remains unequalled in a World Cup final, while Martin Peters' goal proved no less important in a 4-2 victory. It was a remarkable achievement for a club which at that point had spent most of its days in the Second Division, to provide not only the goalscorers but also the captain of a World Cup winning team. Two of Hurst's goals (his first and third) were also set up by the imperious Moore, and were the result of moves which appeared by kind permission of the Chadwell Heath coaching staff.

At the end of the World Cup, Bobby Moore was voted player of the tournament, and he returned to club duty in August as a national hero. He was unquestionably the most popular and successful footballer in West Ham United's history. But with his career at its zenith, the skipper had decided that the time was right to move on from Upton Park. Few people had realised that Moore's contract had expired at the end of the 1965–66 season, and prior to the World Cup finals he seemed destined for a switch to Tottenham Hotspur. Moore

Above: Johnny Byrne – who had taken over as Hammers skipper because of mounting speculation linking Bobby Moore with a move – leads Hammers out for the Cup Winners' Cup semi-final clash with Borussia Dortmund in April 1966.

Below: Bobby Moore with Eusebio and, from left to right: the BBC TV Team Award (won by Hammers in 1965), the World Cup and the BBC TV Sportsman of the Year award.

would later confess, in his authorised biography: 'I was itching to go there. Tottenham would have suited me down to the ground. They were *the* team of the 1960s.' However, following Moore's magnificent performances for England, there was no way that Greenwood was going to part with him – least of all to Bill Nicholson's Spurs team. In the end a new three-year deal was agreed which made Moore the club's top earner.

With their skipper now tied down to a new long-term contract, Hammers kicked off the 1966–67 season at home to Chelsea in confident mood. With three World Cup winners in the team, surely West Ham United would at last become a force to be reckoned with in the challenge for League honours? Alas it was not to be, and despite the conspicuous talent in Ron Greenwood's squad, the Hammers failed to make any significant impression on the title race. In attack West Ham United remained a potent force. Hurst would once more break the 40 goals mark, and Peters too would continue to provide a valuable source of goals from midfield. No team scored more on their travels, and only champions Manchester United bettered the Hammers' overall scoring record. Defensively, though, Greenwood's team was fundamentally flawed, conceding an average of two goals a game throughout the League campaign. The net effect of this entertaining combination of fluent forward play and weak defending was a disappointing 16th place in the First Division.

The League Cup did, however, provide some consolation for West Ham United's fans. Impressive victories over Tottenham Hotspur, at Upton Park, and Arsenal, at Highbury, were followed in the fourth round with a sensational 7–0 demolition of Leeds United in which both John Sissons and Geoff Hurst struck hat-tricks. But just when it seemed that Hammers were destined for another Cup final appearance, they drew bogey team West Bromwich Albion in the semi-final.

Above: A fee of £65,000 made Bobby Ferguson the most expensive goalkeeper in Britain when he arrived at Upton Park from Kilmarnock in May 1967.

Below: Hammers attack the Real Madrid goal during the prestigious friendly at the newly opened Houston Astrodome in April 1967. The Astrodome, which was described as the 'eighth wonder of the world' in the official programme, was the largest completely covered arena in the world.

Defensive errors proved the undoing for Greenwood's team once more, and a 4–0 first-leg defeat could not be overhauled in the return at Upton Park. League Cup elimination followed hot on the heals of a humiliating 3–1 FA Cup third round defeat against Swindon Town at the County Ground.

Despite current frustrations on the pitch, financially the Club was enjoying its best years. The chairman's report in March 1967 announced a record pre-tax profit of £96,000, much of which had been generated by successful runs in Cup competitions. The Club was also quick to highlight the money (£175,000) which had been spent on improving amenities over the preceding ten years, and the chairman concluded that: 'Our first priority is, and always will be, continued success on the field, and provided we secure this we hope to continue with our programme of steady improvement to the stadium.' However, by season's end there was little success on the field, and a run of seven successive defeats meant that there were only 17,186 fans enjoying the improved facilities at the Boleyn Ground for the final League game of the season against Manchester City.

Toughening up

There was one title, though, that was awarded to West Ham United in 1967 – the Hammers may not have accrued the most points in the race for the Championship, but according to the Football League they had enjoyed the best disciplinary record of any First Division team over the past five years. And, according to many pundits, therein lay the root of Hammers' problem. Ron Greenwood's team was too nice, it was too tame in defence. This was an era when men like Norman Hunter, Tommy Smith and Ron Harris bullied their opponents into submission. The tackle from behind was a key weapon for these no-nonsense stoppers, who really didn't mind if they kicked ball, man or both... as long as they kicked something. For the Hammers, Ken Brown and Bobby Moore were the men at the heart of the defence, and while both were strong players who were in no way shrinking violets when it came to tackling, neither had that extra, nasty edge which could terrify forwards.

Greenwood was acutely aware that he had a problem in defence and in the summer of 1967 he set out to toughen his defence with three new signings. Bobby Moore encouraged his manager to make a bid for Manchester United's Maurice Setters, but instead he went for John Cushley, a reserve team stopper from Celtic. Cushley was an educated man who was also a qualified teacher, but according to Moore, Greenwood was 'buying a compromise that satisfied his conscience,' adding that the Scotsman was 'a nice lad who could get stuck in.' At times, though, even Cushley was too forceful for the Corinthian ethics of the Hammers manager and he would fail to make a significant impression during his time in East London.

Record fee for Ferguson

Cushley was not the only new Hammer to arrive ahead of the 1967–68 season. In his attempts to bolster his leaky rearguard Greenwood made two more significant purchases. On 13 May Charlton right-back Billy Bonds arrived at the Boleyn Ground for what would prove a bargain £49,500, and within two weeks he was joined by Kilmarnock 'keeper Bobby Ferguson, signed for a then record fee for a goalkeeper of £65,000. All three would start the season in the Hammers line-up as Greenwood continued his efforts to build a second successful West Ham United team. The manager had seen many of the stars of his 1964 Cup winning team move on and he was in urgent need of top quality replacements. Defenders John Bond and Ken Brown had recently departed for Torquay United, while John Byrne had returned to Crystal Palace for £45,000, and winger Peter Brabrook would soon be on his way to Leyton Orient.

The departure of these seasoned veterans would accelerate the progress of several promising Hammers youngsters and Harry Redknapp, Trevor Brooking and Frank Lampard would all enjoy extended runs in the first-team during 1967–68. Midfielder Brooking, who was the youngest of the three, was handed the most difficult task, when for much of the season he was asked to fill-in wearing Hammers' number nine shirt. Brooking would finish the season with a respectable return of nine goals in 24 games from his sojourn at centre-forward, but it was a position which failed to maximise the impact of his prodigious ball skills and passing ability.

With so many changes in personnel, it is small wonder that West Ham United struggled for much of the season. At the start of December they found themselves in the bottom three of the First Division and facing an early season six-pointer against fellow-strugglers Sheffield United. Hammers won 3–0 – although the Blades would get their revenge with an FA Cup fifth round victory at Upton Park in February – and three further wins in December lifted the East Londoners away from danger. At the season's end West Ham United occupied a safe but unimpressive 12th place, and although the 'goals against' column had seen a significant improvement over the previous year, there had also been a serious reduction in the Club's goalscoring exploits.

The summer of 1968 would see no new major signings but one significant change at Upton Park. The famous Chicken Run, known officially as the East Terrace, was to be knocked down and replaced by a new £15,000 construction. The Chicken Run attracted the most committed and die-hard Hammers fans, and was a key aspect in the unique atmosphere generated at the Boleyn Ground. The Club, recognising the importance of the terracing on this side of the ground, made sure that the replacement East Stand still contained standing accommodation for 4,000 fans. The new stand would increase overall ground capacity to 41,000, and would be opened by former manager Charlie Paynter (then in his 90th year). However, the construction work would not be completed until January 1968, by which time most of the season's excitement had already passed. Hammers had kicked off the campaign in fine style, winning five of their opening seven games and remaining unbeaten until October. The run eventually came to an end with successive defeats against Burnley and Leeds United, but in the next game West Ham United produced their most emphatic First Division victory to overwhelm Sunderland 8–0 at Upton Park, equalling their best league win in any division. The match saw Geoff Hurst claim a hat-trick in each half to equal the record of Vic Watson set against Leeds United at the Boleyn Ground in February 1929 – although Hurst did later confess that he had punched his first goal into the net. The

Above: John Cushley (second from right) heads clear during a League match at Anfield in 1967. John, a centre-half who had previously played for Celtic, was one of Greenwood's more curious signings. He was bought to solve Hammers' vulnerability on crosses, but lacked the height to dominate in the air and ended up playing much of his football in the reserves.

Below: In January 1969 Hammers replaced the much-loved Chicken Run (shown here) with a new East Stand at a cost of around £150,000.

Left: Hammers players in relaxed mood ahead of a League match against Leeds United at Elland Road in October 1971. From left to right: John Ayres, Ronnie Boyce, Bryan Robson, Trevor Brooking, Clyde Best, Harry Redknapp and Geoff Hurst.

powerful Hammers striker would finish as the Club's top scorer with 31 goals in all competitions, but it was the goalscoring record of midfielder Martin Peters, who netted 24 times in 61 appearances, that was most eye-catching. Unfortunately, Peters' performances had been noted by several First Division rivals who promptly put his name to the top of their wanted lists.

Despite the presence of both Hurst and Peters, Hammers struggled to score goals in the later part of the season, hitting the net just four times as they failed to win any of their last nine games. They fell down the table to eighth position and prompted Ron Greenwood to comment: 'Of course, I'm disappointed. You cannot work as hard as we have or be as professional in this game if you are not disappointed when you end up winning nothing.' The FA Cup had remained Hammers' most realistic chance of success, but a 3–0 defeat away to Third Division Mansfield Town in the fifth round had provided another humiliating Cup elimination.

However, the disappointments of 1968–69 were quickly forgotten during a successful summer tour of the USA and a pre-season visit to Europe which left the club in buoyant mode for another League campaign. Unfortunately, any optimism soon proved misplaced and, after a third of the season, Hammers found themselves in a familiar position toward the foot of the table. The one bright spot for Ron Greenwood was the emergence of talented Bermudian forward Clyde Best, who had arrived at the club in April 1969. Best, who had been recommended to the Hammers by a contact of Greenwood's at the Bermudian FA, was only the second black player to appear in West Ham United's first team (full-back John Charles had been the first) and he unfortunately became the target for much racist abuse from opposing supporters. To his credit though, Clyde always remained focussed and his pace and power were vital to the Hammers team of the late 1960s and early 1970s.

Peters swapped for Greaves

By 1970 transfer deadline day, however, even the form of the club's new Bermudian star could not guide West Ham United away from the relegation zone. Greenwood decided that the time was right to act, and controversially made a deal with Tottenham Hotspur which saw World Cup hero Martin Peters move to White Hart Lane in exchange for £150,000 and striker Jimmy Greaves. The departure of Peters was a unpopular

Below: Jimmy Greaves shoots past Manchester City keeper Joe Corrigan to score in a 5–1 victory at Maine Road on his Hammers debut. Greaves had arrived from Tottenham Hotspur as part of the swap deal which saw Martin Peters move to White Hart Lane in March 1970.

move with the Upton Park crowd, who found it particularly galling that he had chosen to join London rivals Spurs. His place in the team would go to a then record signing Peter Eustace, who had arrived at the club in January from Sheffield Wednesday for £90,000.

The signing of Greaves was met with surprising optimism from most quarters, and despite a lack of match fitness – he had been out of the Spurs side since Christmas – he made an instant impact on his Hammers debut, scoring twice to help earn a valuable 5–1 win against Manchester City at Maine Road. The Dagenham-born striker would score two more goals by the end of the campaign as Greenwood's team secured their First Division status with three wins in the last six games. It had been a disappointing season for West Ham United, but the summer would at least provide the distraction of the World Cup finals in Mexico to help Hammers fans forget the woes of 1969–70. Geoff Hurst and Bobby Moore would of course play a key role in England's bid to retain the trophy they had won at Wembley in 1966. Ron Greenwood would also travel to Mexico as part of FIFA's technical committee, which was sent to make a study of the tactics and preparations made by each team. For Moore, pre-tournament preparations would largely take place in Bogota where the England skipper was held for more than a week after being falsely accused of stealing a bracelet from a shop in the Colombian City. The Hammers legend was eventually released and met up with his international team-mates to produce arguably his best display for England in the 1–0 defeat against Brazil. The reigning champions were later eliminated in the quarter-finals by Germany in a match which Hurst described as 'the worst of my career.' Defeat against a German team inspired by Franz Beckenbauer, however, would quickly be forgotten when Hurst and Moore returned to club action for a campaign which would prove to be the nadir in Ron Greenwood's 14-year reign as manager.

Season 1970–71 started brightly enough, with Hammers claiming a share of the spoils after a 2–2 draw against Tottenham Hotspur at White Hart Lane on opening day. It was a match which pitted Jimmy Greaves against his old team-mates for the first time, and in typical fashion the former Spurs star cut through the Lilywhite's defence to equalise after Alan Gilzean had given the home team the lead. It was a particularly sweet goal for the 30-year-old marksman, who had been written off by Bill Nicholson before the match when the Spurs boss told journalists: 'I would think he'd be on the fade out.'

The match was, however, marred by the abuse meted out to England skipper Bobby Moore by certain sections of the home crowd. Moore had long been a target for verbal abuse from the terraces. From the moment he had lifted the Jules Rimet trophy in 1966 Moore-baiting had become a popular 'sport' at most grounds visited by West Ham United. Former team-mate Peter Brabrook puts it down to no more than 'jealousy,' adding that 'they used to give him stick because he was too good'. But it was not just the Hammers number six who was targeted for sniping, and Brabrook remembers that at some grounds, particularly those in the north of England, the men in claret and blue would receive a merciless barracking: 'We'd get a lot of stick in Leeds and Manchester. They'd call us "southern pansies" because our kit was always immaculate. Style was important to us, we felt that if you looked right you'd feel good and you'd be confident in your football. Our shirts were always hung up and nearly every player would only put his shorts on at the last minute to avoid getting them dirtied or stained with greasy embrocation.' Brabrook attributes this sartorial preoccupation to Moore, but there can be no doubt that its origins came from the influence of Malcolm Allison in the 1950s.

However, despite their stylish appearance, Hammers remained far from convincing in their football. Three successive London derbies in August ended in draws and prompted

Bryan 'Pop' Robson – seen here hooking the ball goalward during a match against his former club, Newcastle United – proved an instant success after arriving at Upton Park for a fee of £120,000 in February 1971. Robson enjoyed his best season at the club in 1972–73 when he topped the scoring charts with 28 goals and was named Hammer of the Year.

In the summer of 1970 the floodlighting at the Boleyn Ground was completely replaced with a new system designed especially for colour television. The new lights, which were ten times as bright as the old ones, were installed by Thorn Lighting and cost the Club £30,000.

Maurice Smith of *The People* to write that: 'West Ham are a side of great potential with obvious weakness.' The team's biggest problem remained their defence, and in October Ron Greenwood completed a deal for promising Orient stopper Tommy Taylor. The 19-year-old was immediately drafted into first-team action and would retain his place in the line-up for the remainder of the season. Taylor made his debut in a 2–2 draw against Spurs at Upton Park before the Boleyn Ground's record attendance of 42,322. It was a match which saw Geoff Hurst grab a late equaliser to surpass Jimmy Ruffell's record of 165 Hammers goals and thus become the Club's second highest goalscorer behind the legendary Vic Watson (who scored 306).

The Blackpool affair

Despite Hurst's career achievements, it was to be his worst season in front of goal for seven years and with Greaves also proving uncharacteristically profligate, Hammers would struggle to find the net all season. Five victories in their first 33 League matches was an unmitigated disaster for Greenwood's team, but his problems were compounded when, in January, the club endured its most humiliating FA Cup exit. A third round draw against fellow First Division strugglers Blackpool did not look to be too much of a banana skin. However, while the two teams may have been in the same division, West Ham United's reputation was significantly greater than that of their Lancashire opponents, as were the expectations of their fans. A 4–0 defeat at Bloomfield Road was too much to bear for many supporters, who immediately called for Greenwood to resign. It was not the first time the Club had been eliminated from the Cup by less-fancied opposition, and 370 fans signed a petition demanding that the chairman sack the manager. But it was not just Greenwood who bore the brunt of the criticism. In an unnecessary, not to say unsporting, outburst the victorious Blackpool manager Jimmy Meadows slammed the contribution of the West Ham United captain. Meadows told reporters that: 'For my money Moore is the worst defender in the world. He just can't tackle. We all saw the result. Green [Blackpool's young striker] ran away with the game.' He claimed that his team had targeted Moore as 'the weak link', adding that 'you have only to look at the result to see that we were right.'

After the match, Ron Greenwood somewhat diplomatically declined to comment, but his chairman was quick to offer support for both team and manager, declaring: 'There is no panic here... we have full confidence in the manager... no one could do more... we are all in the fight together.' However, just as the club prepared to regroup and rebuild, the situation deteriorated still further when allegations were made that four West Ham United players had been seen out drinking in the early hours of the morning prior to the match at Blackpool. The four accused, Bobby Moore, Jimmy Greaves, Brian Dear and Clyde Best, admitted their wrongdoing and a board meeting was hastily arranged to determine an appropriate punishment. Each was fined a week's wages and, with the exception of Best, they were suspended for two weeks. Chairman Reg Pratt told reporters: 'I gather they were not drinking heavily, just a beer or two. But even if they had only had a lemon squash it would have been the same. In view of all the problems we have been facing and the position we are in, we can imagine no more irresponsible behaviour.' Of course, had West Ham United beaten Blackpool this late night drinking episode would, no doubt, have been quickly forgotten. But the Hammers had lost, and the fall-out from the incident would dominate the rest of the season.

Ron Greenwood reacted to the Blackpool debacle by dropping Bobby Moore (the first time the skipper had been left out for 12 years). It was a move which would alienate the manager from both press – Moore had many friends in the media – and fans. But after two games out of the Hammers line-up the England captain was given a place on the bench for the match against Derby County at Upton Park, and with the visitors leading 3–0 at half-time he was brought on. An improved performance in the second period prompted one reporter to ask Greenwood if he was pleased with the impact his substitution had made. It was a question which brought a somewhat unexpected and uncharacteristic answer from the normally reserved manager: 'Moore coming on was immaterial to the side's improvement. We played well for ten minutes before he even touched the ball.' It was a view not shared, however, by goalkeeper Peter Grotier who countered: 'I don't agree... he has a steadying influence on colleagues just by being there with them on the field.' Despite Greenwood's post-match comments Moore was restored to the starting line-up for the next game, and kept his place for the rest of the season. It would, however, prove to be something of an uneasy truce and there is no doubt that whole the episode irrevocably damaged the relationship between manager and captain.

These internal wranglings had damaged West Ham United's hopes of avoiding the drop into the Second Division, and with the season entering its final quarter the Hammers were among the favourites for relegation. But on 22 February the team's salvation arrived in the shape of striker Bryan Robson, who signed from Newcastle United in a £120,000 deal. For much of the season Geoff Hurst had lacked any support in the front line, and he told the club programme: 'When I heard he [Robson] was coming I thought "Hallelujah! Reinforcements at last"'. Hammers' new look strike force was an instant success, and both Robson and Hurst scored in a 2–0 victory over Nottingham Forest at Upton Park in their first match together. Brian James of the *Daily Mail* wrote that Robson had 'dropped like a stone into West Ham's pool of recent misery, and the ripples spread out to swamp Forest'.

Right: Bermudian international striker Clyde Best strides purposefully forward during an FA Cup tie against Hereford in 1972. Best, who packed a powerful and accurate long-range shot, arrived at Upton Park in August 1969 after Ron Greenwood had received a tip from a contact at the Bermudian FA.

Below: Bobby Moore, immaculate as ever, prepares to pass the ball out of defence. Moore's form remained consistently high throughout his 16-year run in the Hammers first team; however, during the early 1970s he was frequently linked with a move away from Upton Park.

Brooking on the list

The signing of Robson had visibly lifted Hammers, and in the final nine games of the campaign they claimed five victories – the same number they had recorded in the previous 33 matches – to maintain their First Division status. Despite this late rally, though, it had been a disastrous season for the Hammers who had registered their lowest points tally since winning promotion in 1958. Changes were clearly needed, and at season's end Ron Greenwood announced a mass clear-out. Jimmy Greaves decided that the time was right to retire, while seven players were given free transfers and four others made available for transfer. Somewhat surprisingly, the name of 22-year-old midfielder Trevor Brooking featured on the transfer list. Brooking's talent was obvious, but after six months out of the team he had become racked with self-doubt and would happily have accepted a step down into the Second Division for the chance of regular first team football. Although the Club would have accepted a fee of around £40,000 for him, no firm offers arrived and Brooking remained at Upton Park.

With so many players departing in the summer of 1971, it was a relatively new look Hammers team that kicked off the 1971–72 League campaign with a home match against West Bromwich Albion. However, despite several changes in personnel, Greenwood's team continued to struggle and a 1–0 defeat against Albion filled West Ham United supporters with trepidation for the season ahead. John Moynihan in the *Sunday Telegraph* wrote: 'From West Ham's point of view, the opening of a new season was only a sad reminder of their recent past. Their old disorders obviously remain.' It would prove an accurate analysis and, although Greenwood enjoyed the luxury of a relatively settled team in which eight players made more than 35 League appearances, Hammers finished a disappointing 14th position in the First Division. Fortunately, the League Cup at least provided moments of excitement and entertainment for followers of the men in claret and blue.

In the early rounds of the competition West Ham United had disposed of both Cardiff City and Championship-chasing Leeds United, but a fourth round tie against Bill Shankley's Liverpool offered an even sterner test. A 40,000 crowd packed into the Boleyn Ground to see the match, and few were disappointed when goals from Geoff Hurst and Bryan Robson secured safe passage to a quarter-final tie against Sheffield United. The match against the Blades saw Hammers produce their most convincing performance of the season, and a hat-trick from Bryan Robson and two goals from Clyde Best earned Greenwood's men a place in the last four.

With both Chelsea and Spurs in the semi-final draw, West Ham United were probably somewhat relieved to be paired with struggling Stoke City. However, it would prove no easy option, and over four matches and 420 minutes there was precious little to choose between the two teams. The first leg of this epic semi-final was played at the Boleyn Ground and, although Stoke took a deserved lead, Hammers rallied to finish the game with a one goal advantage courtesy of a Hurst penalty and a volley from Best. At the Victoria Ground, West Ham United were awarded another penalty, but on this occasion Gordon Banks pulled off a sensational save to deny his England colleague what would surely have been a decisive goal. Stoke responded to this scare with an equaliser through Ritchie, but that was to be the end of the scoring despite half an hour of extra time. A replay at neutral Hillsborough followed, but when that too finished goalless the combatants moved across the Pennines to decide matters once and for all at Old Trafford. The game's crucial moment arrived in the first half, when Terry Conroy's crude challenge on Bobby Ferguson left the Hammers 'keeper concussed and out of the game. Clyde Best was the appointed stand-in goalie but, when he declined the offer to take over, responsibility was taken by Bobby Moore. The skipper gave an accomplished performance between the posts, and even saved a penalty from Bernard – although he was beaten on the rebound. Hammers responded with goals from Billy Bonds, who was now operating in midfield, and Trevor Brooking, but Greenwood's team was unable to hold its lead and conceded twice in the second half to bow out of the competition.

Above: In February 1973 Greenwood paid a Club record fee of £170,000 for Manchester United striker Ted MacDougall. However, after six goals in 25 games he moved on to Norwich.

Below: A youthful looking Trevor Brooking surveys his options during a League match at Upton Park in 1971.

Brooking the new hero

At season's end Trevor Brooking was named Hammer of the Year, thus completing an incredible turn around which had seen him go from a transfer-listed reserve to become the most creative and influential player in Ron Greenwood's first team. The Hammers manager was no longer concerned with finding a buyer for the talented midfielder, his priority now was to try to hang on to him. During 1972–73 Derby County manager Brian Clough would make a £400,000 joint bid for both Brooking and Moore which, although accepted in principle by the West Ham United board, was rejected out of hand by Greenwood. The manager had already sold three of his most experienced players – Geoff Hurst (to Stoke City), Harry Redknapp (to Bournemouth) and Alan Stephenson (to Portsmouth) – and was in no position to part with either his captain or his star midfielder.

The only new arrival ahead of the 1972–73 season had been winger Dudley Tyler who was signed from Hereford United for £25,000 to take the place of the recently departed Harry Redknapp. Tyler would join a new look Hammers front line which was now based around the comprehensive talents of Bryan Robson and the invention of Brooking. The subtle skills of this exciting West Ham United attack would provide rich entertainment for the Upton Park crowd, but most significantly would inspire Greenwood's team to sixth place in the First Division, thus equalling the Club's highest finish. Four consecutive victories in March and April had done much to boost Hammers' League standing, and this well-timed run of form had arrived shortly after the purchase of club record signing Ted MacDougall. The well-travelled striker had joined from Manchester United in a £170,000 deal and struck four goals in ten matches to help maintain the Hammers' position in the top half of the table.

The 1972–73 season had been one of welcome, though unexpected, League success, and the match programme for the final home game was full of optimism, declaring: 'The tendency since the opening month of 1973 has been one of increasing confidence, and we hope to set new marks in the next campaign.' However, 1973–74 brought nothing more than a return to the familiar territory of the First Division relegation zone. For the first time, the League had introduced 'three up, three down', and there was much discussion about whether the old safety mark of 36 points would still be enough to guarantee survival. The Hammers, it seemed, were determined to test the theory, and accrued just 37 points to finish in 18th place.

There were of course, mitigating factors behind West Ham United's slump in form. The prolific Bryan Robson would spend much of the campaign in the treatment room, and despite his tinkering Greenwood was unable to find an adequate deputy. Record signing Ted McDougall was one of several strikers who failed to provide a regular source of goals, and in December 1973 he was sold to Norwich City. Bobby Ferguson would also miss much of the season, although in teenage custodian Mervyn Day, Hammers did at least find an able replacement.

The FA Cup saw West Ham United enjoy no better fortune and, on 5 January, Greenwood's team endured another humiliating third round exit – this time at the hands of Third Division Hereford. It was a match which brought the manager predictable criticism, but most significantly saw Bobby Moore make his last appearance in claret and blue. Moore twisted his knee against Hereford and by the time he had recovered, Mick McGiven had taken his place in the line up. The impressive Billy Bonds – who was enjoying his best season in front of goal, even registering a hat-trick against Chelsea at Upton Park – was installed as skipper.

Mooro signs off

Greenwood had promised Moore a free transfer at the end of the season, but with Hammers enjoying their best run of form during the spring, and seemingly out of relegation trouble, the Club decided that they would let the skipper go ahead of schedule. The catch, however, was that the directors now wanted a fee for the man who had played more games for West Ham United than any other. Nevertheless, at a price of just £25,000 there were still many willing takers, and eventually Moore decided to join Fulham where he linked up with his former England team-mate Alan Mullery. On 16 March, Moore attended the home match against Coventry City and said farewell to the Hammers fans who had idolised him since he had made his debut as a prodigiously gifted 17-year-old in 1958. It was most definitely the end of an era at Upton Park.

Below: Ron Greenwood (right) appointed John Lyall (left) as Hammers assistant manager in August 1971. Lyall would hone his coaching and management skills while working alongside Greenwood, and in 1974 he succeeded his mentor as team manager.

Below, right: Bobby Moore is congratulated by former Hammers winger Jimmy Ruffell after breaking the Club's League appearance record in February 1973. Ruffell had, himself, been the previous record-holder, having played 505 times between 1921 and 1937.

SEASON 1961-62
FOOTBALL LEAGUE (DIVISION 1)

Month	Day	Venue	Opponent	Res	Score
Aug	19	(h)	Manchester U	D	1-1
	23	(a)	Tottenham H	D	2-2
	26	(a)	Wolves	L	2-3
	28	(h)	Tottenham H	W	2-1
Sep	2	(h)	Nottingham F	W	3-2
	4	(a)	Blackpool	L	0-2
	9	(a)	Aston Villa	W	4-2
	16	(h)	Chelsea	W	2-1
	18	(h)	Blackpool	D	2-2
	23	(a)	Sheffield U	W	4-1
	30	(h)	Leicester C	W	4-1
Oct	7	(a)	Ipswich T	L	2-4
	14	(h)	Burnley	W	2-1
	21	(a)	Fulham	L	0-2
	28	(h)	Sheffield W	L	2-3
Nov	4	(a)	Manchester C	W	5-3
	11	(h)	West Brom A	D	3-3
	18	(a)	Birmingham C	L	0-4
	25	(h)	Everton	W	3-1
Dec	2	(a)	Arsenal	D	2-2
	9	(h)	Bolton W	W	1-0
	16	(a)	Manchester U	W	2-1
	18	(h)	Wolves	W	4-2
	26	(h)	Blackburn R	L	2-3
Jan	13	(a)	Nottingham F	L	0-3
	20	(h)	Aston Villa	W	2-0
Feb	3	(a)	Chelsea	W	1-0
	10	(h)	Sheffield U	L	1-2
	17	(a)	Leicester C	D	2-2
	24	(h)	Ipswich T	D	2-2
Mar	3	(a)	Burnley	L	0-6
	17	(a)	Sheffield W	D	0-0
	24	(h)	Manchester C	L	0-4
	28	(a)	Blackburn R	L	0-1
	31	(a)	West Brom A	W	1-0
Apr	6	(h)	Birmingham C	D	2-2
	14	(a)	Everton	L	0-3
	20	(h)	Cardiff C	W	4-1
	21	(h)	Arsenal	D	3-3
	23	(a)	Cardiff C	L	0-3
	28	(a)	Bolton W	L	0-1
	30	(h)	Fulham	W	4-2

P	W	D	L	F	A	W	D	L	F	A	Pts	Pos
42	11	6	4	49	37	6	4	11	27	45	44	8th

FA Cup

Month	Day	Venue	Opponent	Res	Score
Jan	6	(a)	Plymouth A	L	0-3

League Cup

Month	Day	Venue	Opponent	Res	Score
Sep	11	(h)	Plymouth A	W	3-2
Oct	9	(h)	Aston Villa	L	1-3

Hammer of the Year 1961-62

LAWRIE LESLIE

SEASON 1962-63
FOOTBALL LEAGUE (DIVISION 1)

Month	Day	Venue	Opponent	Res	Score
Aug	18	(a)	Aston Villa	L	1-3
	20	(h)	Wolves	L	1-4
	25	(h)	Tottenham H	L	1-6
	29	(a)	Wolves	D	0-0
Sep	1	(a)	Leyton O	L	0-2
	3	(h)	Liverpool	W	1-0
	8	(a)	Manchester C	W	6-1
	12	(a)	Liverpool	L	1-2
	14	(h)	Blackpool	D	2-2
	22	(a)	Blackburn R	W	4-0
	29	(h)	Sheffield U	D	1-1
Oct	6	(h)	Birmingham C	W	5-0
	13	(a)	Arsenal	D	1-1
	22	(h)	Burnley	D	1-1
	27	(a)	Manchester U	L	1-3
Nov	3	(h)	Bolton W	L	1-2
	10	(a)	Leicester C	L	0-2
	17	(h)	Fulham	D	2-2
	24	(a)	Sheffield W	W	3-1
Dec	1	(h)	West Brom A	D	2-2
	8	(a)	Everton	D	1-1
	15	(h)	Aston Villa	D	1-1
	22	(a)	Tottenham H	D	4-4
	29	(a)	Nottingham F	W	4-3
Feb	16	(a)	Sheffield U	W	2-0
Mar	2	(h)	Arsenal	L	0-4
	9	(a)	Burnley	D	1-1
	18	(h)	Manchester U	W	3-1
	23	(a)	Bolton W	L	0-3
	30	(h)	Sheffield W	W	2-0
Apr	6	(a)	Fulham	L	0-2
	12	(h)	IpswichT	L	1-3
	13	(h)	Leicester C	W	2-0
	15	(a)	Ipswich T	W	3-2
	20	(a)	West Brom A	L	0-1
	22	(h)	Nottingham F	W	4-1
	27	(h)	Everton	L	1-2
May	1	(a)	Birmingham C	L	2-3
	4	(h)	Blackburn R	L	0-1
	11	(h)	Leyton O	W	2-0
	13	(a)	Blackpool	D	0-0
	18	(h)	Manchester C	W	6-1

P	W	D	L	F	A	W	D	L	F	A	Pts	Pos
42	8	6	7	39	34	6	6	9	34	35	40	12th

FA Cup

	Month	Day	Venue	Opponent	Res	Score
	Feb	4	(h)	Fulham	D	0-0
R		20	(a)	Fulham	W	2-1
	Mar	4	(h)	Swansea T	W	1-0
		16	(h)	Everton	W	1-0
		30	(a)	Liverpool	L	0-1

League Cup

Month	Day	Venue	Opponent	Res	Score
Sep	26	(h)	Plymouth A	W	6-0
Oct	16	(a)	Rotherham U	L	1-3

Hammer of the Year 1962-63

BOBBY MOORE

SEASON 1963-64
FOOTBALL LEAGUE (DIVISION 1)

Month	Day	Venue	Opponent	Res	Score
Aug	24	(a)	Chelsea	D	0-0
	26	(h)	Blackpool	W	3-1
	30	(h)	Ipswich T	D	2-2
Sep	2	(a)	Blackpool	W	1-0
	7	(h)	Sheffield U	L	2-3
	9	(h)	Nottingham F	L	0-2
	14	(a)	Liverpool	W	2-1
	17	(a)	Nottingham F	L	1-3
	21	(h)	Aston Villa	L	0-1
	28	(a)	Tottenham H	L	0-3
Oct	5	(h)	Wolves	D	1-1
	7	(h)	Burnley	D	1-1
	12	(a)	Sheffield W	L	0-3
	19	(h)	Everton	W	4-2
	26	(a)	Manchester U	W	1-0
Nov	2	(h)	West Brom A	W	4-2
	9	(a)	Arsenal	D	3-3
	16	(h)	Leicester C	D	2-2
	23	(a)	Bolton W	D	1-1
	30	(h)	Fulham	D	1-1

Bobby Moore after the 1964 FA Cup final victory.

A photocall for the playing staff at the Chadwell Heath training ground ahead of the 1964–65 season.

Dec 7 (a) Birmingham C L 1-2
14 (h) Chelsea U 2-2
20 (a) Ipswich T L 2-3
26 (h) Blackburn R L 2-8
28 (a) Blackburn R W 3-1
Jan 11 (a) Sheffield U L 1-2
18 (h) Liverpool W 1-0
Feb 1 (a) Aston Villa D 2-2
8 (h) Tottenham H W 4-0
17 (a) Wolves W 2-0
22 (h) Sheffield W W 4-3
Mar 3 (a) Burnley L 1-3
7 (h) Manchester U L 0-2
18 (a) Leicester C D 2-2
21 (h) Arsenal D 1-1
27 (h) Stoke C W 4-1
28 (a) West Brom A W 1-0
31 (a) Stoke C L 0-3
Apr 4 (h) Bolton W L 2-3
11 (a) Fulham L 0-2
17 (h) Birmingham C W 5-0
25 (a) Everton L 0-2

P	W	D	L	F	A	W	D	L	F	A	Pts	Pos
42	8	7	6	45	38	6	5	10	24	36	40	14th

FA Cup
Jan 4 (h) Charlton A W 3-0
25 (a) Leyton O D 1-1
29 (h) Leyton O W 3-0
Feb 15 (a) Swindon T W 3-1
29 (h) Burnley W 3-2
Mar 14 (n*) Manchester U W 3-1
May 2 (n**) Preston NE W 3-2
*Played at Hillsborough
** Played at Wembley

League Cup
Sep 25 (h) Leyton O W 2-1
Oct 16 (a) Aston Villa W 2-0
Nov 19 (a) Swindon T D 3-3
25 (h) Swindon T W 4-1
Mar 23 (a) Burnley L 1-3
Dec 16 (h) Workington T W 6-0
Feb 5 (a) Leicester C L 3-4
Mar 23 (h) Leicester C L 0-2

Hammer of the Year 1963-64
JOHNNY BYRNE

SEASON 1964-65
FOOTBALL LEAGUE (DIVISION 1)

Aug 22 (a) Fulham W 2-1
24 (h) Manchester U W 3-1
28 (h) Nottingham F L 2-3
Sep 2 (a) Manchester U L 1-3
5 (a) Stoke C L 1-3
7 (h) Wolves W 5-0
12 (h) Tottenham H W 3-2
14 (a) Wolves L 3-4
19 (a) Burnley L 2-3
26 (h) Sheffield U W 3-1
Oct 3 (a) Everton D 1-1
10 (h) Aston Villa W 3-0
17 (a) Liverpool D 2-2
24 (h) Sheffield W L 1-2
31 (a) Blackpool W 2-1
Nov 7 (h) Blackburn R D 1-1
14 (a) Arsenal W 3-0
21 (h) Leeds U W 3-1
28 (a) Chelsea W 3-0
Dec 5 (h) Leicester C D 0-0
12 (h) Fulham W 2-0
19 (a) Nottingham F L 2-3
26 (h) Birmingham C L 1-2
28 (h) Birmingham C W 2-1
Jan 2 (h) Stoke C L 0-1
16 (a) Tottenham H L 2-3
23 (h) Burnley W 3-2
Feb 6 (a) Sheffield U L 1-2
13 (h) Everton L 0-1
20 (a) Sunderland L 2-3
27 (h) Liverpool W 2-1
Mar 6 (a) Sheffield W L 0-2
13 (h) Sunderland L 2-3
20 (a) Blackburn R L 0-4
27 (h) Arsenal W 2-1
31 (a) Aston Villa W 3-2
Apr 3 (a) Leeds U L 1-2
12 (h) Chelsea W 3-2
16 (h) West Brom A W 6-1
17 (a) Leicester C L 0-1
19 (a) West Brom A L 2-4
23 (h) Blackpool W 2-1

P	W	D	L	F	A	W	D	L	F	A	Pts	Pos
42	14	2	5	48	25	5	2	14	34	46	42	9th

FA Cup
Jan 9 (h) Birmingham C W 4-2
30 (h) Chelsea L 0-1

League Cup
Sep 30 (a) Sunderland L 1-4

F.A. Charity Shield
Aug 15 Liverpool D 2-2

European Cup - Winners Cup
Sep 23 (a) La Gantoise W 1-0
Oct 7 (h) La Gantoise D 1-1
Nov 25 (h) Sparta Prague W 2-0
Dec 9 (a) Sparta Prague L 1-2
Mar 16 (a) Lausanne W 2-1
Mar 23 (h) Lausanne W 4-3
Apr 7 (h) Real Zaragoza W 2-1
Apr 28 (a) Real Zaragoza D 1-1
May 19 (n) TSV Munich 1860 W 2-0

Hammer of the Year 1964-65
MARTIN PETERS

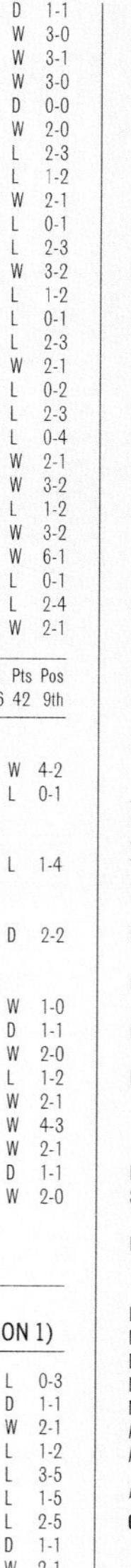

SEASON 1965-66
FOOTBALL LEAGUE (DIVISION 1)

Aug 21 (a) West Brom A L 0-3
23 (h) Sunderland D 1-1
28 (h) Leeds U W 2-1
Sep 1 (a) Sunderland L 1-2
4 (a) Sheffield U L 3-5
6 (h) Liverpool L 1-5
11 (h) Leicester C L 2-5
15 (a) Liverpool D 1-1
18 (a) Blackburn R W 2-1
25 (h) Blackpool D 1-1
Oct 2 (a) Fulham L 0-3
9 (a) Nottingham F L 0-5
16 (h) Sheffield W W 4-2
23 (a) Northampton T L 1-2
30 (h) Stoke C D 0-0
Nov 6 (a) Burnley L 1-3
13 (h) Chelsea W 2-1
20 (a) Arsenal L 2-3
27 (h) Everton W 3-0
Dec 4 (a) Manchester U D 0-0
11 (h) Newcastle U W 4-3
18 (a) Sheffield W D 0-0
Jan 1 (h) Nottingham F L 0-3
8 (a) Newcastle U L 1-2
11 (a) Everton D 2-2
15 (h) Northampton T D 1-1
29 (h) West Brom A W 4-0
Feb 5 (a) Leeds U L 0-5
7 (a) Aston Villa W 2-1
19 (h) Sheffield U W 4-0
Mar 5 (h) Aston Villa W 4-2
12 (h) Blackburn R W 4-1
19 (a) Blackpool L 1-2
26 (h) Fulham L 1-3
Apr 2 (h) Burnley D 1-1
8 (a) Tottenham H W 4-1
9 (a) Chelsea L 2-6
16 (h) Arsenal W 2-1
25 (h) Tottenham H W 2-0
30 (h) Manchester U W 3-2
May 7 (a) Stoke C L 0-1
9 (a) Leicester C L 1-2

P	W	D	L	F	A	W	D	L	F	A	Pts	Pos
42	12	5	4	46	33	3	4	14	24	50	39	12th

FA Cup
Jan 22 (a) Oldham A D 2-2
R 24 (h) Oldham A W 2-1
Feb 12 (h) Blackburn R D 3-3
R 16 (a) Blackburn R L 1-4

League Cup
Sep 21 (a) Bristol R D 3-3
R 29 (h) Bristol R W 3-2
Oct 13 (h) Mansfield T W 4-0
Nov 3 (a) Rotherham U W 2-1
17 (a) Grimsby T D 2-2
R Dec 15 (h) Grimsby T W 1-0
SF 20 (h) Cardiff C W 5-2
Feb 2 (a) Cardiff C W 5-1
F Mar 9 (h) West Brom A W 2-1
23 (a) West Brom A L 1-4

European Cup - Winners Cup
Nov 24 (h) Olympiakos W 4-0
Dec 1 (a) Olympiakos D 2-2
Mar 2 (h) F.C. Magdeburg W 1-0
Mar 16 (a) F.C. Magdeburg D 1-1
Apr 5 (h) Borussia Dortmund L 1-2
Apr 13 (a) Borussia Dortmund L 1-3

Hammer of the Year 1965-66
GEOFF HURST

SEASON 1966-67
FOOTBALL LEAGUE (DIVISION 1)

Aug 20 (h) Chelsea L 1-2
23 (a) Arsenal L 1-2
27 (a) Leicester C L 4-5
29 (h) Arsenal D 2-2
Sep 3 (h) Liverpool D 1-1
7 (a) Manchester C W 4-1
10 (h) Stoke C D 1-1
17 (a) Sheffield W W 2-0
24 (h) Southampton D 2-2
Oct 1 (a) Sunderland W 4-2
8 (h) Everton L 2-3
15 (a) Fulham L 2-4
26 (h) Nottingham F W 3-1
29 (a) Sheffield U L 1-3
Nov 5 (h) Fulham W 6-1
12 (a) Tottenham H W 4-3
19 (h) Newcastle U W 3-0
26 (a) Leeds U L 1-2
Dec 3 (h) West Brom A W 3-0
10 (a) Burnley L 2-4
17 (a) Chelsea D 5-5
26 (a) Blackpool W 4-1
27 (h) Blackpool W 4-0
31 (h) Leicester C L 0-1
Jan 7 (a) Liverpool L 0-2
14 (a) Stoke C D 1-1
21 (h) Sheffield W W 3-0
Feb 4 (a) Southampton L 2-6
11 (h) Sunderland D 2-2
25 (a) Everton L 0-4
Mar 18 (a) Nottingham F L 0-1
24 (h) Aston Villa W 2-1
25 (h) Burnley W 3-2
28 (a) Aston Villa W 2-0
Apr 1 (a) Manchester U L 0-3
4 (h) Sheffield U L 0-2
22 (h) Leeds U L 0-1
26 (a) Newcastle U L 0-1
28 (a) West Brom A L 1-3
May 6 (h) Manchester U L 1-6
9 (h) Tottenham H L 0-2
13 (h) Manchester C L 1-1

P	W	D	L	F	A	W	D	L	F	A	Pts	Pos
42	8	6	7	40	31	6	2	13	40	53	36	16th

FA Cup
Jan 28 (h) Swindon T D 3-3
R 31 (a) Swindon T L 1-3

League Cup
Sep 14 (h) Tottenham H W 1-0
Oct 5 (a) Arsenal W 3-1
Nov 7 (h) Leeds U W 7-0
Dec 7 (a) Blackpool W 3-1
SF Jan 18 (a) West Brom A L 0-4
Feb 8 (h) West Brom A D 2-2

Hammer of the Year 1966-67
GEOFF HURST

SEASON 1967-68
FOOTBALL LEAGUE (DIVISION 1)

Aug 19 (h) Sheffield W L 2-3
21 (h) Burnley W 4-2
26 (a) Tottenham H L 1-5
29 (a) Burnley D 3-3
Sep 2 (h) Manchester U L 1-3
5 (a) Everton L 0-2
9 (a) Sunderland W 5-1
16 (h) Wolves L 1-2
23 (a) Fulham W 3-0
30 (h) Leeds U D 0-0
Oct 7 (h) Stoke C L 3-4
14 (a) Liverpool L 1-3
23 (h) Southampton L 0-1
28 (a) Chelsea W 3-1
Nov 11 (a) Newcastle U L 0-1
18 (h) Manchester C L 2-3
25 (a) Arsenal D 0-0
Dec 2 (h) Sheffield U W 3-0
8 (a) Coventry C D 1-1
11 (h) West Brom A L 2-3
16 (a) Sheffield W L 1-4
23 (h) Tottenham H W 2-1
26 (h) Leicester C W 4-2
30 (a) Leicester C W 4-2
Jan 6 (a) Manchester U L 1-3
20 (a) Wolves W 2-1
Feb 3 (h) Fulham W 7-2
10 (a) Leeds U L 1-2
26 (a) Stoke C L 0-2
Mar 16 (a) Southampton D 0-0
23 (h) Chelsea L 0-1
29 (h) Arsenal D 1-1
Apr 6 (h) Newcastle U W 5-0
12 (h) Nottingham F W 3-0
13 (a) Manchester C L 0-3
16 (a) Nottingham F P 1-1
20 (h) Liverpool W 1-0
24 (h) Sunderland D 1-1
27 (a) Sheffield U W 2-1
Mar 1 (a) West Brom A L 1-3
4 (h) Coventry C P 0-0
11 (h) Everton P 1-1

P	W	D	L	F	A	W	D	L	F	A	Pts	Pos
42	8	5	8	43	30	6	5	10	30	39	38	12th

FA Cup
Jan 27 (a) Burnley W 3-1
Feb 17 (a) Stoke C W 3-0
Mar 9 (h) Sheffield U L 1-2

League Cup
Sep 13 (a) Walsall W 5-1
Oct 11 (h) Bolton W W 4-1
Nov 1 (a) Huddersfield T L 0-2

Hammer of the Year 1967-68
BOBBY MOORE

SEASON 1968-69
FOOTBALL LEAGUE (DIVISION 1)

Aug 10 (a) Newcastle U D 1-1
14 (a) Stoke C W 2-0
17 (h) Nottingham F W 1-0
19 (h) Everton L 1-4
24 (a) Coventry C W 2-1
26 (h) Burnley W 5-0
31 (h) West Brom A W 4-0
Sep 7 (a) Manchester U D 1-1
14 (h) Tottenham H D 2-2
21 (a) Chelsea D 1-1
28 (h) Sheffield W D 1-1
Oct 5 (h) Southampton D 0-0
8 (a) Burnley L 1-3
12 (a) Leeds U L 0-2
19 (h) Sunderland W 8-0
26 (a) Arsenal D 0-0
Nov 2 (h) Queen's Park R W 4-3
9 (a) Wolves L 0-2
16 (h) Leicester C W 4-0
23 (a) Ipswich T D 2-2
30 (h) Manchester C W 2-1
Dec 7 (a) Liverpool L 0-2
14 (h) Leeds U D 1-1
21 (a) Sunderland L 1-2
26 (a) Southampton D 2-2
Jan 11 (a) Queen's Park R D 1-1
Feb 1 (a) Leicester C D 1-1
22 (h) Liverpool D 1-1
Mar 1 (h) Newcastle U W 3-1
8 (a) Nottingham F W 1-0
14 (h) Coventry C W 5-2
21 (h) Ipswich T L 1-3
24 (h) Wolves W 3-1
29 (h) Manchester U D 0-0
Apr 1 (a) Everton L 0-1
5 (a) Sheffield W D 1-1
8 (h) Stoke C D 0-0
12 (h) Chelsea D 0-0
14 (a) West Brom A L 1-3
19 (a) Tottenham H L 0-1
21 (h) Arsenal L 1-2
30 (a) Manchester C D 1-1

P	W	D	L	F	A	W	D	L	F	A	Pts	Pos
42	10	8	3	47	22	3	10	8	19	28	44	8th

FA Cup
Jan 4 (h) Bristol C W 3-2
25 (a) Huddersfield T W 2-0
Feb 26 (a) Mansfield T L 0-3

League Cup
Sep 4 (h) Bolton W W 7-2
25 (h) Coventry C D 0-0
R Oct 1 (a) Coventry C L 2-3

Hammer of the Year 1968-69
GEOFF HURST

SEASON 1969-70
FOOTBALL LEAGUE (DIVISION 1)

Aug 9 (h) Newcastle U W 1-0
11 (h) Chelsea W 2-0
16 (a) Stoke C L 1-2
20 (a) Chelsea D 0-0
23 (h) West Brom A L 1-3
25 (h) Arsenal D 1-1
30 (a) Nottingham F L 0-1
Sep 6 (h) Tottenham H L 0-1
13 (a) Everton L 0-2
20 (h) Sheffield W W 3-0
27 (a) Manchester U L 2-5
Oct 4 (h) Burnley W 3-1
6 (h) Stoke C D 3-3
11 (a) Coventry C D 2-2
18 (a) Wolves L 0-1
25 (h) Sunderland D 1-1
Nov 1 (a) Southampton D 1-1
8 (h) Crystal P W 2-1
15 (a) Liverpool L 0-2
22 (h) Derby C W 3-0
29 (a) Ipswich T L 0-1

Munich left-half Luttrop challenges Alan Sealey during the Cup Winners' Cup final 1965.

1961-1973

Billy Bonds in action during a 3–1 victory away to Hereford United in the FA Cup, February 1972.

Month	Day	Venue	Opponent	Res	Score
Dec	6	(h)	Manchester C	L	0-4
	13	(h)	Everton	L	0-1
	17	(a)	Leeds U	L	1-4
	20	(a)	Tottenham H	W	2-0
	26	(a)	West Brom A	L	1-3
	27	(h)	Nottingham F	D	1-1
Jan	10	(a)	Sheffield W	W	3-2
	17	(h)	Manchester U	D	0-0
	31	(a)	Burnley	L	2-3
Feb	11	(h)	Coventry C	L	1-2
	21	(a)	Sunderland	W	1-0
	28	(h)	Southampton	D	0-0
Mar	2	(a)	Newcastle U	L	1-0
	7	(a)	Derby C	L	0-3
	14	(h)	Ipswich T	D	0-0
	21	(a)	Manchester C	W	5-1
	24	(a)	Crystal P	D	0-0
	28	(h)	Liverpool	W	1-0
	31	(h)	Wolves	W	3-0
Apr	2	(h)	Leeds U	D	2-2
	4	(a)	Arsenal	L	1-2

P	W	D	L	F	A	W	D	L	F	A	Pts	Pos
42	8	8	5	28	21	4	4	13	23	39	36	17th

FA Cup

Month	Day	Venue	Opponent	Res	Score
Jan	3	(a)	Middlesborough	L	1-2

League Cup

Month	Day	Venue	Opponent	Res	Score
Sep	3	(h)	Halifax T	W	4-2
	23	(a)	Nottingham F	L	0-1

Hammer of the Year 1969-70

BOBBY MOORE

SEASON 1970-71
FOOTBALL LEAGUE (DIVISION 1)

Month	Day	Venue	Opponent	Res	Score
Aug	15	(a)	Tottenham H	D	2-2
	17	(h)	Arsenal	D	0-0
	22	(h)	Chelsea	D	2-2
	26	(a)	Leeds U	L	0-3
	29	(a)	Manchester U	D	1-1
	31	(h)	Southampton	D	1-1
Sep	5	(h)	Everton	L	1-2
	12	(a)	West Brom A	L	1-2
	19	(h)	Newcastle U	L	0-2
	26	(a)	Huddersfield T	D	1-1
Oct	3	(h)	Burnley	W	3-1
	10	(a)	Stoke C	L	1-2
	17	(h)	Tottenham H	D	2-2
	24	(a)	Crystal P	D	1-1
	31	(h)	Blackpool	W	2-1
Nov	7	(a)	Ipswich T	L	1-2
	14	(h)	Wolves	D	3-3
	21	(a)	Manchester C	L	0-2
	28	(h)	Coventry C	L	1-2
Dec	5	(a)	Derby C	W	4-2
	12	(h)	Liverpool	L	1-2
	19	(a)	Chelsea	L	1-2
Jan	9	(a)	Arsenal	L	0-2
	16	(h)	Leeds U	L	2-3
Feb	6	(h)	Derby C	L	1-0
	9	(a)	Coventry C	W	1-0
	16	(a)	Liverpool	L	0-1
	20	(h)	Manchester C	D	0-0
	24	(h)	Nottingham F	W	2-0
	27	(a)	Blackpool	D	1-1
Mar	6	(h)	Crystal P	D	0-0
	13	(a)	Wolves	L	0-2
	20	(h)	Ipswich T	D	2-2
	30	(a)	Everton	W	1-0
Apr	3	(h)	Manchester U	W	2-1
	9	(h)	West Brom A	W	2-1
	10	(a)	Nottingham F	L	0-1
	13	(a)	Burnley	L	0-1
	17	(h)	Stoke C	W	1-0
	24	(a)	Newcastle U	D	1-1
	27	(a)	Southampton	W	2-1
May	1	(h)	Huddersfield T	L	0-1

P	W	D	L	F	A	W	D	L	F	A	Pts	Pos
42	6	8	7	28	30	4	6	11	19	30	34	20th

FA Cup

Month	Day	Venue	Opponent	Res	Score
Jan	2	(a)	Blackpool	L	0-4

League Cup

Month	Day	Venue	Opponent	Res	Score
Sep	9	(h)	Hull C	W	1-0
Oct	6	(a)	Coventry C	L	1-3

Hammer of the Year 1970-71

BILLY BONDS

Clyde Best tussles with Leeds' Billy Bremner in 1973.

SEASON 1971-72
FOOTBALL LEAGUE (DIVISION 1)

Month	Day	Venue	Opponent	Res	Score
Aug	14	(h)	West Brom A	L	0-1
	18	(a)	Derby C	L	0-2
	21	(a)	Nottingham F	L	0-1
	23	(h)	Ipswich T	D	0-0
	28	(h)	Everton	W	1-0
	30	(h)	Coventry C	W	4-0
Sep	4	(a)	Newcastle U	D	2-2
	11	(h)	Chelsea	W	2-1
	18	(a)	Manchester U	L	2-4
	25	(h)	Stoke C	W	2-1
Oct	2	(a)	Leeds U	D	0-0
	9	(h)	Leicester C	D	1-1
	16	(a)	West Brom A	D	0-0
	23	(h)	Wolves	W	1-0
	30	(a)	Crystal P	W	3-0
Nov	6	(h)	Sheffield U	L	1-2
	13	(a)	Huddersfield T	L	0-1
	20	(h)	Manchester C	L	0-2
	27	(a)	Liverpool	L	0-1
Dec	4	(h)	Arsenal	D	0-0
	11	(a)	Southampton	D	3-3
	18	(h)	Newcastle U	L	0-1
	27	(a)	Tottenham H	W	1-0
Jan	1	(h)	Manchester U	W	3-0
	8	(a)	Everton	L	1-2
	22	(h)	Derby C	D	3-3
	29	(a)	Ipswich T	L	0-1
Feb	12	(a)	Wolves	L	0-1
	19	(h)	Crystal P	D	1-1
	29	(a)	Sheffield U	L	0-3
Mar	4	(h)	Huddersfield T	W	3-0
	11	(a)	Leicester C	L	0-2
	18	(h)	Nottingham F	W	4-2
	21	(a)	Coventry C	D	1-1
	25	(a)	Chelsea	L	1-3
	31	(h)	Leeds U	D	2-2
Apr	1	(h)	Tottenham H	W	2-0
	4	(a)	Stoke C	D	0-0
	8	(a)	Manchester C	L	1-3
	15	(h)	Liverpool	L	0-2
	22	(a	Arsenal	L	1-2
May	1	(h)	Southampton	W	1-0

P	W	D	L	F	A	W	D	L	F	A	Pts	Pos
42	10	6	5	31	19	2	6	13	16	32	36	14th

FA Cup

Rd	Month	Day	Venue	Opponent	Res	Score
	Jan	15	(h)	Luton T	W	2-1
	Feb	9	(a)	Hereford U	D	0-0
R		14	(h)	Hereford U	W	3-1
		26	(a)	Huddersfield T	L	2-4

League Cup

Rd	Month	Day	Venue	Opponent	Res	Score
	Sep	8	(h)	Cardiff C	D	1-1
R		22	(a)	Cardiff C	W	2-1
	Oct	6	(h)	Leeds U	D	0-0
R		20	(a)	Leeds U	W	1-0
		27	(h)	Liverpool	W	2-1
	Nov	17	(h)	Sheffield U	W	5-0
SF	Dec	8	(a)	Stoke C	W	2-1
		15	(h)	Stoke C	L	0-1
R	Jan	5	(n*)	Stoke C	D	0-0
2R		26	(n**)	Stoke C	L	2-3

*Played at Hillsborough,Sheffield
**Played at Old Trafford, Manchester

Hammer of the Year 1971-72

TREVOR BROOKING

SEASON 1972-73
FOOTBALL LEAGUE (DIVISION 1)

Month	Day	Venue	Opponent	Res	Score
Aug	12	(a)	West Brom A	D	0-0
	14	(h)	Coventry C	W	1-0
	19	(h)	Leicester C	W	5-2
	22	(a)	Wolves	L	0-3
	26	(a)	Liverpool	L	2-3
	29	(a)	Arsenal	L	0-1
Sep	2	(h)	Manchester U	D	2-2
	9	(a)	Chelsea	W	3-1
	16	(h)	Norwich C	W	4-0
	23	(a)	Tottenham H	L	0-1
	30	(h)	Birmingham C	W	2-0
Oct	7	(a)	Ipswich T	D	1-1
	14	(h)	Sheffield U	W	3-1
	21	(a)	Manchester C	L	3-4
	28	(h)	Crystal P	W	4-0
Nov	4	(h)	Wolves	D	2-2
	11	(a)	Coventry C	L	1-3
	18	(h)	Derby C	L	1-2
	25	(a)	Everton	W	2-1
Dec	2	(h)	Newcastle U	D	1-1
	9	(a)	Leeds U	L	0-1
	16	(h)	Stoke C	W	3-2
	23	(a)	Southampton	D	0-0
	26	(h)	Tottenham H	D	2-2
	30	(a)	Leicester C	L	1-2
Jan	6	(h)	Liverpool	L	0-1
	20	(a)	Manchester U	D	2-2
	27	(h)	Chelsea	W	3-1
Feb	10	(a)	Norwich C	W	1-0
	17	(h)	West Brom A	W	2-1
	24	(a)	Stoke C	L	0-2
Mar	2	(h)	Ipswich	L	0-1
	10	(a)	Sheffield U	D	0-0
	17	(h)	Manchester C	W	2-1
	24	(a)	Crystal P	W	3-1
	31	(h)	Everton	W	2-0
Apr	7	(a)	Newcastle U	W	2-1
	14	(h)	Leeds U	D	1-1
	20	(h)	Southampton	W	4-3
	21	(a)	Derby C	D	1-1
	23	(a)	Birmingham C	D	0-0
	28	(h)	Arsenal	L	1-2

P	W	D	L	F	A	W	D	L	F	A	Pts	Pos
42	12	5	4	45	25	5	7	9	22	28	46	6th

FA Cup

Month	Day	Venue	Opponent	Res	Score
Jan	13	(a)	Port Vale	W	1-0
Feb	3	(a)	Hull C	L	0-1

League Cup

Month	Day	Venue	Opponent	Res	Score
Sep	6	(h)	Bristol C	W	2-1
Oct	4	(a)	Stockport C	L	1-2

Hammer of the Year 1972-73

BRYAN ROBSON

SEASON 1973-74
FOOTBALL LEAGUE (DIVISION 1)

Month	Day	Venue	Opponent	Res	Score
Aug	25	(h)	Newcastle U	L	1-2
	27	(h)	Ipswich T	D	3-3
Sep	1	(a)	Norwich C	D	2-2
	4	(a)	Queen's Park R	D	0-0
	8	(h)	Tottenham H	L	0-1
	10	(h)	Queen's Park R	L	2-3
	15	(a)	Manchester U	L	1-3
	22	(h)	Leicester C	D	1-1
	29	(a)	Stoke C	L	0-2
Oct	6	(h)	Burnley	L	0-1
	13	(a)	Everton	L	0-1
	20	(a)	Coventry C	W	1-0
	27	(h)	Derby C	D	0-0
Nov	3	(a)	Leeds U	L	1-4
	10	(h)	Sheffield U	D	2-2
	17	(a)	Wolves	D	0-0
	24	(h)	Arsenal	L	1-3
Dec	1	(a)	Liverpool	L	0-1
	8	(h)	Manchester C	W	2-1
	15	(a)	Birmingham C	L	1-3
	22	(h)	Stoke C	L	0-2
	26	(a)	Chelsea	W	4-2
	29	(a)	Tottenham H	L	0-2
Jan	1	(h)	Norwich C	W	4-2
	12	(h)	Manchester U	W	2-1
	19	(a)	Newcastle U	D	1-1
Feb	2	(h)	Birmingham C	D	0-0
	5	(a)	Ipswich T	W	3-1
	9	(a)	Leicester C	W	1-0
	16	(h)	Everton	W	4-3
	23	(a)	Burnley	D	1-1
Mar	2	(h)	Chelsea	W	3-0
	9	(a)	Derby C	D	1-1
	16	(h)	Coventry C	L	2-3
	23	(a)	Sheffield U	L	0-1
	30	(h)	Leeds U	W	3-1
Apr	6	(a)	Arsenal	D	0-0
	12	(h)	Southampton	W	4-1
	13	(h)	Wolves	D	0-0
	15	(a)	Southampton	D	1-1
	20	(a)	Manchester C	L	1-2
	27	(h)	Liverpool	D	2-2

P	W	D	L	F	A	W	D	L	F	A	Pts	Pos
42	7	7	7	36	32	4	8	9	19	28	37	18th

FA Cup

Rd	Month	Day	Venue	Opponent	Res	Score
3	Jan	5	(h)	Hereford U	D	1-1
R		9	(a)	Hereford U	L	1-2

League Cup

Rd	Month	Day	Venue	Opponent	Res	Score
2	Oct	8	(h)	Liverpool	D	2-2
R		29	(a)	Liverpool	L	0-1

Watney Cup

Month	Day	Venue	Opponent	Res	Score
Aug	11	(a)	Bristol Rovers (lost 5-6 on pens)	D	1-1

Hammer of the Year 1973-74

BILLY BONDS

A youthful Mervyn Day makes a save during a London derby at White Hart Lane.

CHAPTER 6
LYALL TAKES CHARGE

The summer of 1974 brought few significant changes and little by way of transfer activity to suggest the dawning of a new era at Upton Park. Star striker Bryan Robson had been sold to Sunderland, but apart from that the West Ham United first-team pool was unaltered, and the line-up which opened the new season away at Manchester City was identical to that which had closed the previous campaign with a 2–2 draw at home to Liverpool. However, as the team made their way to Maine Road they were informed of a change which was to have a marked effect on the club's fortunes for the next 16 years. John Lyall – former player, wages clerk and youth team boss, and current assistant manager – had been promoted to the position of Team Manager, and would take responsibility for the day-to-day running of the senior squad from Ron Greenwood, who had moved 'upstairs' to become general manager. The change had come about on Greenwood's recommendation, and the board, ever keen to maintain continuity, were happy to comply.

Search for a striker

It had long been speculated that Lyall was to be the next incumbent of the Upton Park hotseat, so his appointment was not entirely unforeseen. However, the timing of this managerial switch was somewhat surprising. The new boss inherited a team in transition, which had struggled to survive in the First Division the previous season, and which was clearly lacking in confidence. The three World Cup stars had all departed but had not been adequately replaced, sparking criticism that the club had not invested sufficiently in its playing staff. In this context, it was hard to see how Lyall could be expected to bring glory back to Upton Park, and a poor start to the season saw Hammers claim just three points from their opening seven games.

Lyall's biggest problem was the lack of an effective strikeforce. The departure of Bryan Robson had left Hammers without a recognised goalscorer and, by the end of August, frontmen Bobby Gould and Clyde Best had failed to hit the net in five games. Reinforcements were clearly needed, but there would be no big name signing to solve this or any other problem at Upton Park. West Ham United's policy of dealing at the lower end of an inflated transfer market, though, did not meet with the approval of either fans or players. 'I certainly felt that in the late 1960s and early 1970s we didn't ever compete for a big name signing,' remembers Trevor Brooking, adding that: 'Most of the players who came to the club at that time, without being unkind, were either bargains or players at the end of their careers.'

Striker Billy Jennings was the first signing of the John Lyall era. Jennings, who arrived from Watford for £110,000 in September 1974, had been brought in to solve a goalscoring crisis which had afflicted Hammers since the departure of Bryan Robson the previous season. The new boy would make a bright start to his career in claret and blue, striking five goals in his first five games.

Hammers manager John Lyall (second from left) and his Arsenal counterpart Terry Neil lead the teams out at Wembley ahead of the 1980 FA Cup final.

Jennings and Robson

The autumn of 1974 would see the Hammers head for the bargain counter once more, as the new management duo attempted to find a pair of strikers to lift the club away from the relegation zone. Ron Greenwood, now free from his coaching duties, was able to spend valuable time looking at the various cut-price options available, and after careful consideration signed Watford's promising 22-year-old forward Billy Jennings in a £110,000 deal. Jennings, who had scored 33 goals in 93 games while at Vicarage Road, was drafted straight into first team action for the home fixture against Sheffield United on 7 September. And the new boy made a solid start to his Upton Park career, netting the opening goal after 19 minutes. However, the match was to end in familiar fashion with Hammers conceding two second-half goals to go down 2–1. The poor results continued, and by the time West Ham United made their next appearance at the Boleyn Ground, two weeks later, they were bottom of the league. The good news, though, was that the home crowd had another new forward to cheer on. Twenty-one-year-old Keith Robson had arrived from Newcastle United in a £45,000 switch, and was accommodated in a three-man front line along with Bobby Gould and Billy Jennings. It proved a devastating combination, and visitors Leicester City were swept aside in a 6–2 victory which saw all three Hammers forwards get on the scoresheet.

The arrival of Billy Jennings and Keith Robson – who each struck five goals in their first five matches in claret and blue – had coincided with an upturn in form which saw Lyall's team climb out of the bottom half of the table with four wins and three draws during September and October. So impressive was the turnaround, that there were even whispers of League Championship success following an excellent run in November when Hammers claimed nine points from a possible ten. Middlesbrough, Carlisle United, Wolves, QPR and Leeds United were duly beaten; however, indifferent results in December saw any hope of League glory disappear, and by the turn of the New Year even a place in the Uefa Cup had become a far-fetched fantasy.

Left: Warrior in white. Billy Bonds, under pressure from Arsenal's Brian Kidd, staggers through Highbury's mud during the 1975 FA Cup quarter-final as a weary looking Trevor Brooking ambles forward. West Ham United won the game 2–0, with Alan Taylor scoring both goals in a victory which earned Hammers a semi-final clash with Bobby Robson's Ipswich Town.

Below: Matchday programme from Hammers' 1975 FA Cup semi-final replay against Ipswich Town at Stamford Bridge. The first game, played at Villa Park, ended goalless but when the teams reconvened in West London, Alan Taylor secured John Lyall's team a place at Wembley with a goal in each half.

Path to Wembly Taylor-made

The FA Cup provided West Ham United's only realistic route to Europe for 1975–76, but, having already suffered defeat by Second Division Fulham in the League Cup, the East Londoners were not among the favourites to make it to Wembley in May. Hammers, who had failed to win a match for almost a month, kicked-off their Cup run with a tricky away tie against Southampton in the third round. First-half goals from Lampard and Gould, though, were enough to secure a 2–1 victory and passage to a fourth round clash with Swindon Town. The Hammers had met the Wiltshire side on route to the 1964 Cup final, and, as on that occasion, a replay was needed to separate the two teams. A goal from Pat Holland, with just four minutes remaining, proved decisive in a 2–1 victory at Swindon's County Ground, and the Poplar-born midfielder was again on the scoresheet in the next round as West Ham United came from a goal down to beat Queens Park Rangers at Upton Park. However, Holland was on the injured list as preparations began for the quarter-final against Arsenal at Highbury and, in his absence, Lyall choose to revert to a three-man front line, which he believed would upset a Gunners' defence that was palpably lacking in pace. Rookie striker Alan Taylor, who had made just one appearance in the Hammers starting line-up since arriving from Fourth Division Rochdale in a £40,000 deal in November, was the man chosen to step into the attack alongside Jennings and Robson.

It proved an inspired tactical change and, after just 15 minutes, Taylor claimed his first Hammers goal to open the scoring following excellent approach play from Graham Paddon. Lyall's team were good value for their lead at the break, but still had to survive a spirited penalty appeal shortly before the interval when Mervyn Day appeared to fell Ronnie Radford. A minute into the second half, though, Taylor struck his second goal with a powerful right-footed shot to put the game beyond the Gunners and send West Ham United into the last four of the FA Cup for the first time in 11 years.

Bobby Robson's title-chasing Ipswich Town provided Hammers' opposition in the semi-final at Villa Park. The Suffolk club were the undoubted favourites to make it to Wembley and, in truth, had much the better of the first match, which ended 0–0, thanks in no small part to a last-minute goal-line clearance from Billy Jennings. Fortune would again favour the Hammers in the replay at Stamford Bridge when, with the score at 0–0, Bryan Hamilton had a goal ruled out for offside. Despite this disappointment, Ipswich continued to enjoy the greater share of possession, and it was somewhat against the run of play that West Ham United opened the scoring after 29 minutes. Inevitably, the goal owed much to the creative talents of Trevor Brooking, whose dangerous cross arrived at the far post via the head of Bobby Gould whereupon it was

Left: This cartoon from *The Sun* newspaper on the eve of the 1975 Cup final reveals the dilemma facing many Hammers fans. For once, Bobby Moore and West Ham United could not both be Wembley winners.

despatched past the Ipswich keeper by Alan Taylor. The lead, however, was short-lived and 15 minutes later Town got back on terms when Billy Jennings – Hammers' hero in the first match – sliced a clearance into his own net. The second half brought more Ipswich pressure, but with only seven minutes to go John Wark's poor clearance fell to Alan Taylor 25 yards from goal. The West Ham United striker took aim and fired an unerring shot in off a post to claim the game's winning goal.

Below: Alan Taylor, seen here tricking his way past Fulham defenders John Lacey and John Fraser, was the undoubted hero of Hammers' 1975 Cup final triumph. Not only did Alan score a brace of goals in the final, he also struck twice in both the quarter- and semi-final.

One Moore final

The Hammers were through to the FA Cup final for the third time in the club's history and, as in 1964, they would face a team from the Second Division. The difference was that this time Bobby Moore – now of Fulham FC – would be playing for the opposition. The Cottagers, who also included former Spurs and England midfielder Alan Mullery in their line-up, were the the underdogs and the neutral's choice. However, the West Londoners had already beaten the Hammers in the League Cup and would not be underestimated by John Lyall and his team.

The press billed it as the Cockney Cup final, a clash of East and West London, but there was no doubt that the real story was the contest between East London's favourite son and its favourite team. Loyalties were torn for many Hammers fans, and the emotion of the occasion undoubtedly affected several senior West Ham United players who had spent their youth looking up to a man they were now competing against. It is hardly surprising, therefore, that the match itself was far from a classic.

The first 45 minutes brought few chances for either team, although at half-time Fulham would probably have been slightly the happier, having tested Mervyn Day with shots from John Mitchell and John Lacey. Trevor Brooking, though, was still confident that West Ham United would improve in the second half: 'I always felt that we were going to end up creating chances because I knew we still had more to offer,' recalls the former Hammers midfielder. Brooking was to be proved right after just 16 minutes of the second period. Pat Holland, who had regained his place in the team following an injury to the unlucky Keith Robson, won the ball in midfield and passed to Billy Jennings whose driven shot from the edge of the box was fumbled by Fulham keeper Peter Mellor. The ball spun loose and Alan Taylor was quickest to react, driving the ball between Mellor's legs to open the scoring. Three minutes later Taylor once more profited from an error by the Fulham number one, who this time spilled a Graham Paddon strike to present an opportunity which was eagerly snapped up by the former Rochdale forward. There would be no more goals, and at the final whistle Alan Taylor was proclaimed as West Ham United's hero. Donald Saunders in the *Daily Telegraph* wrote that: 'His [Taylor's] decisive five-minute intervention at Wembley rendered much that had gone before and all that followed more or less meaningless,' adding that: 'It is encouraging to know that West Ham will be in Europe next season. At their best, they are worthy of lining up with Derby and Ipswich as English soccer's ambassadors to the continent.'

John Lyall's first season in charge had ended with glorious success, and, although the Hammers had finished in a disappointing 13th position in the League, this too represented an improvement over the previous campaign. The arrival of Jennings, Robson and Taylor during the season's early weeks had, no doubt, played a significant role in West Ham United's improving fortunes, but credit must also go to the coaching and interpersonal skills of the new manager. Trevor Brooking believes that: 'John [Lyall] took on the West Ham reputation for playing attractive, attacking football, but what he also added was that little bit of drive and edge. He didn't stand any nonsense. If he didn't feel you were putting in the effort that he thought you should – irrespective of who you were – he would let you know in no uncertain terms.'

Above: Alan Taylor (third from left) is congratulated by skipper Billy Bonds after scoring his second goal during the 1975 FA Cup final. The other Hammers in the picture are, from left to right: Graham Paddon, Frank Lampard, Kevin Locke and Billy Jennings.

Below: Alan Taylor enjoys his moment of fame as Billy Bonds salutes the Wembley crowd.

Home made Hammers

Another of Lyall's qualities which Brooking is quick to applaud was his willingness to give young players a chance. The new manager, like his predecessors, did not have a significant transfer fund at his disposal, so would have to rely upon the club's youth development programme for new talent. Fortunately, the Upton Park production line was stilling working efficiently, and as well as winning the FA Cup final in 1975 the Hammers had also been runners-up in the Youth Cup, losing out to a strong Ipswich Town team over two legs. For Lyall at least, the disappointment of the Colts' defeat was tempered by the knowledge that several of the youngsters on display would soon be pushing for places in the first team.

Alvin Martin and Paul Brush had both been members of the 1975 Youth Cup final side, but it was midfielder Geoff Pike who was first to make his debut in the senior line-up. Pike, who took his bow as a substitute at Leeds United in February, was one of only two newcomers to the West Ham United team during 1975–76 (Cypriot striker Yilmaz Orhan was the other). So despite a season which would see Hammers play 58 matches and compete for four trophies, John Lyall's squad was not significantly strengthened from the previous campaign. This lack of fresh blood, though, did not seem to hinder West Ham United's efforts in the early weeks of the season, and after three wins in the first four games Hammers were at the top of the table. Lyall's men maintained their form throughout the autumn, and, following a 1–0 victory over Arsenal at Upton Park, found themselves in third place at the end of November. However, after such a promising start came a dramatic decline: the first 18 matches had brought an impressive 11 wins, but the ensuing 24 fixtures saw Hammers claim just two more victories, and at season's end the East Londoners occupied a disappointing 18th position in the First Division. Injuries to Billy Bonds and Billy Jennings had, no doubt, contributed in part to this fall from grace, but the club's European adventures had also become something of a preoccupation.

Return to Europe

West Ham United kicked off their 1975–76 Cup Winners' Cup campaign with a trip to Helsinki's Olympic Stadium and a clash with unfancied minnows Lahden Reipas. It proved, however, to be a disappointing night for the Hammers who twice had to come from behind to secure a 2–2 draw against their part-time opponents. The second-leg did at least see a somewhat improved performance, and goals from Keith Robson, Pat Holland and Billy Jennings ensured safe passage to the second round. The Soviet Union, or more precisely Armenia, was the destination for West Ham United's next European away day where they would face a somewhat unknown quantity in the shape of Ararat Erevan. The match, played out before a crowd of 60,000, sprang into life in the second half when, 11 minutes after the break, Alan Taylor opened the scoring. The lead, however, was short-lived and the home-team struck back on 66 minutes with a goal which owed most to the German referee, who let Petrosian's equaliser stand, despite the fact that the striker had clearly headed the ball out of Mervyn Day's hands. There would be no such controversy in the second leg at Upton Park on Bonfire Night, and first-half goals from Paddon and Robson ended any hopes for the Armenians in a match which ended 3–1.

For the third time in the club's history West Ham United had made it to the last eight of the Cup Winners' Cup. However, because of the competition's winter break the quarter-final against Dutch team Den Haag could not take place until March. In the interim, Hammers' form had slumped alarmingly, so it was with no little trepidation, and on the back of a run of six games without a win, that the East Londoners headed for Holland for the first leg. Preparations were also hindered when John Lyall was laid low by flu shortly before the match, forcing the experienced Ron Greenwood to take charge of team affairs. However, there was precious little that even he could do to counter a disastrous first half which saw Hammers concede four goals as German referee Rudi Glockner took it upon himself to upstage all 22 players. The game had started badly for the visitors when Den Haag's skipper Aad Mansveld had shot the home team into

Bobby Moore is consoled by former team-mate Kevin Lock after the 1975 Cup final. Lock, who had worn the number-six shirt at Wembley, was the first in a long-line of Hammers defenders to be unfairly burdened with the 'New Moore' tag.

the lead after just 13 minutes, but from thereon it was Herr Glockner who stole the show. First he awarded a penalty against Mick McGiven for hand ball when clearly no offence had taken place, then he pointed to the spot again after a foul by Kevin Lock was wrongly adjudged to have occurred inside the penalty area, and then, with three minutes to go to half-time, the ever-innovative referee compounded Hammers' misery by presenting a bizarre drop ball to Shoenmacker who went on to hit the fourth goal. But the Londoners were far from beaten, and spurred on by a half-time pep talk from Greenwood and the injustices of the first 45 minutes, they mounted a stirring comeback. Two goals for Billy Jennings put the Hammers right back in the tie, and, had it not been for an incorrect offside decision, the striker would have completed a famous hat-trick.

After the game, the normally affable Ron Greenwood was uncharacteristically incensed and, while he knew that there was little prospect of getting the match replayed, he was intent upon lodging a formal complaint. The West Ham United general manager told reporters: 'We don't see much point complaining about the referee's decisions regarding the three goals. Our complaint would not stop those goals counting. But where I do think we can lodge a valid protest is on Glockner's determination to stop the game at will for his own ideas of behaviour.' Greenwood was referring to the East German referee's frequent practice of holding up play to insist that the Hammers' players pulled up their socks. Such was Glockner's preoccupation with West Ham United's hosiery that he even sent Kevin Lock to the touchline to get tie-ups.

Fortunately a new referee was engaged for the return leg at Upton Park, and a 29,000 crowd created a charged atmosphere on a memorable night at the Boleyn Ground. Hammers started strongly, but gained no reward for their enterprising attacking play until the 29th minute when rebound specialist Alan Taylor was on hand to open the scoring after Trevor Brooking's shot was spilled by the Den Haag keeper. Two more Hammers goals followed in quick succession, and at the interval the home team were ahead 5–4 on aggregate. But after the high jinx of the first half, the second period proved a tense affair, and when the Dutchmen grabbed a goal after 59 minutes Hammers were ahead only by virtue of the away goals rule. For the remaining half an hour the home team were forced to live on their nerves, and the final whistle was greeted with cheers of relief. West Ham United had won their first match since January and would now face Eintracht Frankfurt in the Cup Winners' Cup semi-final.

As in all three previous rounds of the competition, Hammers were drawn away for the first leg of the tie against Eintracht, and it was as underdogs that the East Londoners travelled to Frankfurt for the match on 31 March. West Ham United's domestic form was still poor, and away defeats against Arsenal (6–1) and Norwich (1–0) in the ten days ahead of the semi-final had done nothing to boost confidence. But League results have never been an accurate indicator for Cup form, and Lyall's team confounded their domestic status to produce a disciplined and accomplished performance which frustrated their German opponents. A spectacular 30-yard shot from Graham Paddon after nine minutes gave the Hammers a valuable away goal, and although Eintracht struck back with one goal in each half, a 2–1 defeat gave West Ham United a great chance of progressing to the final.

Eintracht KO'd

Defenders Billy Bonds – who had moved into the back-four in place of the injured Kevin Lock – and Tommy Taylor had been the heroes of the first leg, but the bottom line was that West Ham United had to score to make it to the final in Brussels, but with the pitch at the Boleyn Ground at its worst, conditions did not favour the home team's trademark short-passing game. The first half brought few clear cut chances and, although Hammers did have a goal ruled out when Keith Robson fired home after the ball had got stuck in a muddy penalty area, the aggregate score was unchanged at the interval. Lyall's half-time team talk, though, quickly worked the miracle and after four second half minutes the home fans knew it would be their night when a header from Trevor Brooking opened the scoring. Eighteen minutes later Hammers' number ten turned provider, playing a defence-splitting pass to Keith Robson who checked inside before despatching a powerful left-footed shot into the corner of the Eintracht goal. Brooking was at his devastating best and with the game seemingly won, he produced a party piece. 'I knew exactly what I was doing,' remembers the Hammers midfielder. 'I came inside, shaped to shoot and, as the keeper came out, I curled it round him into the far corner.' The drama, however, was not yet over, and with three minutes remaining Eintracht struck back to take the score to 3–1 on the night. Players and fans were on tenterhooks for the last few moments of the match, knowing that another goal from the Germans would see Hammers eliminated. Seconds before the final whistle, Mervyn Day found himself stranded out of his goal with the ball heading toward the net, but to the relief of most of the 39,000 crowd, Tommy Taylor produced a match-winning goal-line clearance to save the day.

John Lyall described the semi-final as 'the greatest performance in the club's history,' adding that: 'Everything I hoped for came true tonight. This was a performance to climax months of hard work by the players. People say that English football is not skilful and yet we produced a performance tonight to equal anything you will see. I don't think you could possibly see a better match than that.' Lyall was also quick to applaud former Spurs boss Bill Nicholson, who had been working as an advisor to Ron Greenwood since leaving White Hart Lane in 1974.

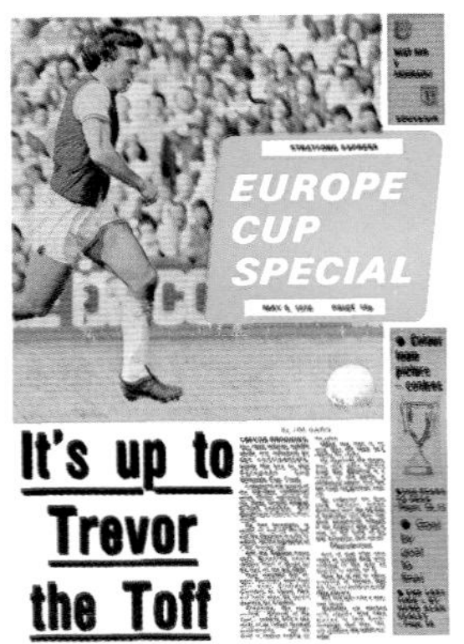

EUROPE CUP SPECIAL

It's up to Trevor the Toff

EUROPE CUP SPECIAL

HERE'S TO THE FANS WHO BURST WITH PRIDE

Above: Newspaper cuttings from the *Stratford Express* on the eve of the 1976 European Cup Winners' Cup final against Anderlecht.

Below: The 1975 Cup Winners' Cup final was held at the Heysel Stadium in Brussels but, just as they did for each of Hammers' European away matches, Club printers Helliar and Sons produced a special matchday programme for West Ham United fans.

WEST HAM UNITED F.C.
OFFICIAL
SOUVENIR EDITION
FIFTEEN PENCE

EUROPEAN CUP WINNERS CUP 1975-76 FINAL

Heysel Stadium Brussels, Belgium WEDNESDAY 5 MAY 1976 at 20.15

R.S.C. ANDERLECHT
BELGIUM
versus
WEST HAM UNITED
ENGLAND

Lampard's lament

Hammers opponents in the Cup Winners' Cup final were Belgian side Anderlecht, a team with an excellent European pedigree who possessed several world class players. The Belgians would also enjoy the benefit of home advantage since, by coincidence, the match was to be held at the club's Heysel stadium. Ahead of the final, the *Stratford Express* interviewed former Luton player Peter Anderson, who was then playing for FC Antwerp. Anderson was in no doubt who the Anderlecht danger man was, and warned Hammers that: 'No one can play without a man on Rensenbrink for the full 90 minutes. He is capable of appearing from nowhere if he doesn't have a tight marker all the time.' In the early stages of the match, though, it was West Ham United who looked the more dangerous, and after 29 minutes Pat Holland headed the Londoners into a deserved 1–0 lead. However, three minutes before half-time disaster struck. In attempting a routine back pass, Frank Lampard got his studs stuck in the turf and succeeded only in nudging the ball into the path of Haan, who

squared to Rensenbrink to grab an equaliser that left the Hammers bench fuming.

Lampard's misery was compounded by the fact that he had also injured himself in his efforts to pass back to Mervyn Day, and the full-back did not reappear for the second half. Alan Taylor was brought on, and the resultant reshuffle saw Holland move into midfield with John McDowell filling in at full-back. 'It was,' said Geoffrey Green, 'a harsh penance for Lampard. Up to that point Anderlecht looked a well-beaten side and yet they rose out of nothing as if at the touch of a magic wand.' And the man waving the wand for the Belgians was unquestionably Robbie Rensenbrink, who gave a superb display of attacking play throughout the second half. The Anderlecht forward began his masterclass with a defence-splitting pass to Francois van der Elst, who despatched the ball past Mervyn Day to give the home team a one-goal lead. Hammers did, though, strike back on 69 minutes with Keith Robson heading home a Brooking cross to level at 2-2. But Rensenbrink was in devilish mood, and four minutes later he tempted Holland into an unnecessary tackle, earning a penalty which he duly converted. Another goal from van der Elst arrived 12 minutes later – with the pass coming, somewhat predictably, from Rensenbrink – and at 4–2 down with just five minutes to play there was to be no dramatic fightback for Lyall's team.

Above: Trevor Brooking picks his way through the Anderlecht defence during the 1976 Cup Winners' Cup final.

Below: Keith Robson celebrates after levelling the scores at 2–2 during the second half of the Cup Winners' Cup final.

Defeat in Rotterdam had brought an exciting season to a disappointing conclusion. However, given their dismal domestic form, West Ham United's European run represented a remarkable achievement and much credit was due to the club's youthful manager. In his first two years in charge at Upton Park, Lyall had guided Hammers to two Cup finals and had enjoyed far more success than could have been anticipated when he had taken over the managerial reigns in 1974. However, the club's progress in knockout competitions had papered over some deep cracks. In particular, the first team squad continued to lack depth and, despite the manager's best efforts, Hammers would struggle against relegation for the next two seasons.

Robson pops back

The 1976–77 campaign started badly with a 4–0 defeat at Aston Villa and, although Hammers won their next game at home to Queens Park Rangers, things would get worse before they got better. The summer break had seen Lyall make just one signing, centre-half Bill Green arriving from Carlisle United in an £80,000 deal. But it was in attack that West Ham United were most in need of reinforcements. Hammers' dearth of forwards became patently obvious when, in the early weeks of the season, Lyall was forced to experiment with Tommy Taylor in the front line. By the end of September the East Londoners had won just one League game, had scored only four goals and were stuck in 20th place in the First Division. Every striker who was available – and many who were not – was linked with a switch to Upton Park. Plymouth's Paul Mariner seemed the most likely to make the move to E13, but at the start of October Lyall revealed that he was putting his trust in a more experienced and familiar goalscorer. After two years away from the Boleyn Ground, Bryan 'Pop' Robson was returning to the club and would be charged with the task of scoring the goals to shoot the Irons to safety.

However, by the time Robson arrived back in East London, Hammers' problems had extended beyond the forward line. Confidence was low, the defence was leaking goals at an average of two a game, and the team's plight had not been helped by a serious injury to midfielder Patsy Holland. Holland had sustained a broken shin in a clash at Bristol City in September and would miss the remainder of the season, forcing Lyall to enter the transfer market once more. This time, though, the manager opted for youth over experience, paying non-League

Southall £5,000 for the services of former Crystal Palace apprentice Alan Devonshire. The signing of the gangly, 20-year-old midfielder owed much to Hammers' new scouting combination of Eddie Baily and Charlie Faulkner, whose judgment was soon proved sound when Devonshire made his senior debut against West Bromwich Albion at the Hawthorns in October.

The comings and goings would continue throughout the first half of the season as Lyall sought to find the right blend of youth and experience to lift Hammers away from the relegation zone. In October, winger Graham Paddon joined Norwich City for £100,000 and within days the manager had reinvested half that fee to sign 20-year-old Barnsley midfielder Anton Otulakowski. A further £80,000 was spent bringing John Radford across London from Arsenal, and the powerful striker took his Hammers bow against Liverpool at Upton Park in a team which included just five of the line-up that had kicked off the season against Aston Villa in August. But despite Lyall's wheeling and dealing, the poor League form persisted and at the turn of the year West Ham United were one place off the bottom of the table having won just four of their 20 games. The early part of 1976 brought still more misery and, after a run of three defeats and one goal in four games, Hammers looked certainties for the drop.

February did, at least, see Lyall's new-look team record their first League win of the year – Bryan Robson netting the only goal of the game against Stoke City at Upton Park. It was the start of a three-match winning streak which took Hammers to the relative safety of 18th place at the end of the month. The highlight of this sequence was a 3–2 win at Highbury which prompted Lyall to remark: 'It was the sort of performance that gives us hope... it has come at the right time... we showed a lot of qualities, the kind we really need to get us out of trouble.' *The Sunday Express* described the display against Arsenal as 'a great Hammers show of blood and guts,' and a week later a similarly committed display earned a valuable 2–0 victory over fellow-strugglers Bristol City. However, just as it seemed that the corner had been turned, West Ham United travelled to Roker Park and found themselves on the receiving end of a 6–0 defeat against relegation-threatened Sunderland. It proved, though, to be no more than a blip and for the remainder of the season, Hammers tightened up their act, playing a careful, often defensive style, which prompted journalist John Sadler in *The Sun* to quip: 'It looks as if the academy has gone comprehensive.'

But despite improving results, which saw Lyall's team lose just two of their last 18 games, West Ham United were perilously placed in 19th position at the start of May. A victory over lowly-placed Coventry City did much to release the pressure, but a disappointing home draw against Derby County meant

Expectation was immense when Bryan Robson returned to Upton Park after a two-year sojourn in his native North East with Sunderland.

Bryan 'Pop' Robson (number eight) was a hugely popular figure with both players and supporters at Upton Park. Billy Bonds, seen here congratulating the Geordie striker after a goal in 1977, is clearly among Bryan's fans.

that results were needed from the final two matches of the season... Liverpool at Anfield and Manchester United at Upton Park. Bob Paisley's Reds would finish the season as League Champions and European Cup winners, so it was with much credit that Hammers returned from their trip to Merseyside having claimed a point after a 0–0 draw. However, there was no time for self-congratulation, and two days after the match at Anfield, Hammers entertained Manchester United. 'It's up to us now,' declared John Lyall, 'we reckon we need to win to stay up.' But after just 30 seconds Gordon Hill opened the scoring for the Red Devils to send West Ham United supporters reaching for their matchday programmes to check points tallies and goal difference columns. However, there would be no need for any complex arithmetic, and a first-half equaliser from Frank Lampard eased the faithful's nerves before two goals from Pop Robson and one from Geoff Pike gave Hammers a deserved victory.

Greenwood's England call-up

It had been a season of few highlights for West Ham United and, with no sign of an increased transfer budget for John Lyall, it was difficult to see how a similar struggle could be averted in 1977–78. Hammers' prospects were also not helped by Ron Greenwood's decision to accept the FA's offer to become England manager. Greenwood had been the most successful coach in West Ham United's history and, while it was a source of great pride to the club that he had been chosen to take charge of the national team, his presence at Upton Park would be sorely missed.

Transfer activity during the summer of 1977 was minimal, and the departure of Keith Robson to Cardiff City was the only deal to affect Hammers' first-team pool. So with no new signings to call upon, John Lyall named a familiar looking line-up – in which youngster Paul Brush was the only debutant – for the season's opening fixture at home to Norwich City. But from a well-known cast came a well-known and disappointing performance. The home team were second to everything, and Norwich ran out comfortable 3–1 victors. It was the first of three successive defeats for West Ham United who occupied 21st place in the First Division at the end of August.

Relegation looms

Hammers would continue to struggle throughout the season, and with just six victories in their first 33 games, Lyall's team quickly became a popular tip for relegation. Defensive errors became commonplace and by mid-season the confidence of 22-year-old goalkeeper Mervyn Day was in tatters. Veteran custodian Bobby Ferguson was eventually recalled, but there was

1974-85

little he could do to halt Hammers' slide. The problems were not, however, confined to defence, and despite the enterprising forward play of Bryan Robson the team also lacked goals. John Radford had started the League campaign in the number nine shirt, but he was destined never to score for the club, and Billy Jennings' season was brought to a premature end by an achilles' injury after just two appearances. In September Lyall acted to bolster his front line by signing Derby County striker Derek Hales for £110,000. Hales would prove a moderate success, but it was not until he was joined at Upton Park by the formidable figure of David Cross that the Hammers revealed any true potency in attack.

At Easter West Ham United were still occupying the last of the three relegation places, although with nine games left to play they were at least masters of their own destiny. A David Cross hat-trick against Ipswich Town at Upton Park ensured a bright start to Hammers' run-in, and victory over Chelsea the following day lifted Lyall's team to the dizzy, and safe, heights of 19th place. Trevor Brooking was now at his peak and his incisive and inventive attacking play would prove a major consolation in an otherwise disappointing season. However, even Mr Brooking could not inspire his team to victory over Birmingham City, and a 3–0 defeat did nothing for Hammers' survival hopes. The drama was not yet over, though, and three consecutive wins – against Coventry City, Leeds United and Derby County – raised hopes of a dramatic revival. The East Londoners' next game was against Manchester United at Old Trafford, but with rookie centre-half Alvin Martin ruthlessly exposed by the experienced Stuart Pearson, Hammers could do nothing to prevent a 3–0 reverse. Victory over Middlesbrough at Ayrsome Park three days later left Lyall's men needing to win their final game of the season against Liverpool.

It was a similar situation to that which had concluded the previous campaign, but this year there was to be no happy ending. The Merseysiders needed to win the match to finish in second place and, despite a string of early chances for the home team, the visitors took the lead in the first-half through McDermott before clinching victory with a David Fairclough goal 13 minutes from time. Hammers' only hope of survival now was for fellow strugglers Wolves to lose both their two remaining games. John Lyall, however, was already convinced of his team's fate, declaring: 'It looks as though we have had it – we have got to set ourselves a new target and hope that this time next season we can be knocking on the door for promotion back from the Second Division.' The manager's appraisal of the situation was of course accurate. Wolves won the points they needed and West Ham United entered the Second Division after a run of 21 years in the top flight. Only Arsenal and Everton, of the current membership, had enjoyed a longer unbroken run among English football's elite.

Loyalty a bonus

Relegation, however, did not bring an end to John Lyall's worries. The manager would now have to convince Trevor Brooking, Hammers' most gifted and influential player, to remain at Upton Park. Brooking, who was 29-years-old and at his undoubted peak, was naturally concerned that playing in the Second Division would harm his England career. But West Ham United's chief creator was not about to turn his back on the club he had joined as a teenager. 'I felt that, although we had conceded some shocking goals, we shouldn't have gone down in the first place. I remember saying to John [Lyall] that surely we would bounce back at the first attempt.' However, it was not only his confidence in Hammers' ability to quickly regain top-flight status that had swayed Trevor to stay. 'Ron Greenwood had been appointed England manager, so because I knew him well from our days together at West Ham, I was able to ask him whether he would pick me even though I was playing in the Second Division. Ron said that he would provided he was happy with my form.' Brooking had also been moved by the size of the crowd which had attended his testimonial at season's end: 'It was a time filled with economic and political problems, and I remember driving through Ilford on my way to the game to find that all the electricity had been turned off. I thought that the game would be postponed, but it went ahead, and despite these problems and the disappointment of relegation, 23,000 people attended the match.'

With their adroit playmaker now committed to the fight for promotion, Hammers were further buoyed by the news that, despite much speculation to the contrary, striker Bryan Robson

In December 1977, with West Ham United languishing in 20th place in the First Division, John Lyall splashed out £200,000 on West Bromwich Albion striker David Cross. A quirk of the fixture list saw Cross, who would soon earn the nickname 'Psycho', make his Hammers debut against his old team-mates at The Hawthorns, and he is seen here looking forlorn as Albion celebrate the only goal of the game.

Phil Parkes hones his skills on the training pitch at Chadwell Heath as former Arsenal and Scotland keeper Bob Wilson looks on. Parkes, who had joined the Hammers for £565,000 (then a world record fee for a goalkeeper), was a key figure in John Lyall's team-building programme of the late 1970s.

was also happy to remain at the Boleyn Ground. Lyall would make no summer signings but, with youngsters Alvin Martin, Nicky Morgan and Billy Lansdowne all now on the fringe of the first team, West Ham United were installed as 5-1 favourites to win the Second Division title. And the opening game of the season gave no reason to doubt the bookmakers. Four goals in the first 20 minutes against Notts County at Upton Park set the home team on route to a breathtaking 5–2 victory. David Cross netted a hat-trick, and Eric McManus, the beleaguered County keeper told reporters 'their football was five-a-side-stuff. They tapped in all five and there was nothing I could do.' However, it was not all one-way traffic and two second-half goals for the visitors exposed the defensive vulnerability which had cost Hammers so dearly the previous season. Lyall was clearly concerned after the match, and fumed: 'I am disappointed with the two sloppy goals we gave away after our exciting attacking display in the first half – they took the edge off our win.'

David Cross was again on the scoresheet in the next match, claiming the second goal in a 3–0 Hammers victory at Newcastle United. A draw against Crystal Palace followed and at the end of August, West Ham United were just a point behind leaders Stoke City. However, September saw a return to the fitful form of previous seasons, and three defeats in five games pushed Lyall's team out of the promotion picture. The most galling of these three reverses came at Burnley, where Hammers surrendered a 2–0 lead to lose 3–2. It was a result which left Billy Bonds, who was now playing in the back four alongside Tommy Taylor, exasperated. 'We give everyone value for money except ourselves,' exclaimed the skipper. 'We've got to stop this habit of playing well, but losing.' It was, however, a compulsion that West Ham United could not break and for the remainder of the season they provided excellent entertainment but inconsistent results.

Upton Parkes new keeper

Bryan Robson and David Cross had forged a superb understanding in the forward line and both strikers were in double figures for goals by the end of November, but at the back Hammers still had their problems. The goalkeeper's position, in particular, had become a major cause for concern, and with neither Mervyn Day nor Bobby Ferguson showing their best form, it became clear that a new custodian was needed. This time, though, Lyall would not be shopping for a short-term, cut-price bargain. The West Ham United manager had his eye on Queens Park Rangers' Phil Parkes – an England international and one of the most highly-rated keepers in English football. Not since the signing of Phil Woosnam had the club competed for such a high-profile player, but in February 1979 Lyall got his man, paying Rangers £565,000 for the 6ft 2in goalie. It was a world record fee for a goalkeeper and went a long way to helping Hammers shake off their thrifty image. 'I was surprised he came to us,' remembers Trevor Brooking. 'I couldn't believe that John [Lyall] had managed to sign him and I told them that, I didn't know how he'd done it, but he'd signed a truly top-class keeper.' Brooking also believes that had it not been for the presence of Peter Shilton and Ray Clemence, Parkes would have enjoyed a long and successful international career. 'He was as good a keeper as I played with. He was Mr Reliable, he never gave the ball away and when he came out he always got the ball.'

However, by the time Parkes arrived, Hammers had already been eliminated from both domestic cup competitions, losing out in humiliating fashion to Third Division Swindon Town in the League Cup and Fourth Division Newport County in the FA Cup. Promotion would also elude the Upton Park club, who drew eight of their last 15 games to finish six points adrift of the three teams who made it into the top flight. The absence of Trevor Brooking – who sustained ankle ligament damage against Newcastle United in March – for ten of the last 11 games was a key factor in West Ham United's failure to mount a late push for promotion. However, despite the disappointment of failing to bounce back to the First Division at the first attempt, season 1978–79 had been far from a disaster and the most pleasing aspect of the campaign was undoubtedly the progress made by several of the club's young players. Alvin Martin had featured in the starting line-up for the last 18 games and the 21-year-old stopper had impressed with his confident and committed displays. Geoff Pike and Paul Brush had also both made significant contributions, but it was midfielder Alan Devonshire who had made the greatest impact. The lightly built schemer had missed just one of Hammers' 42 League game and at season's end was named Hammer of the Year. Devonshire had been blessed with both pace and skill and his beguiling ball skills made him a hugely popular figure with the Upton Park crowd.

Out with the old

The emergence of a new crop of talented youngsters had helped John Lyall's team-building efforts immeasurably, and in the summer of 1979 the manager accelerated his restructuring programme by purging his first-team squad of all those considered surplus to requirements. Mervyn Day, Billy Jennings and Tommy Taylor were all despatched to Leyton Orient, while Jon McDowell and Alan Taylor found a new home at Norwich City. Alan Curbishley and Bryan Robson would also depart the Boleyn Ground ahead of the new season.

It was a period of great change in the boardroom too, and in May 1979 Reg Pratt retired as chairman after a 29-year tenure. Pratt had overseen the defining era in West Ham United's history and his role in bringing the club into the modern age cannot be underestimated.The outgoing chairman was, however, somewhat modest about his contribution and in an interview for the club's official annual he declared: 'I always say there's been three things I've done for the club, if nothing else. The first was to buy the freehold of the ground in the 1950s. The second was bringing Ron Greenwood to the club as manager. And the third – and most recent – was making the decisive vote for the purchase of Phil Parkes.'

Pratt's replacement as chair of the West Ham United board was Len Cearns, whose father W.J. Cearns had also held the position from 1935 to 1950. The new chairman would be assisted by Eddie Chapman, who became the club's first chief executive in July 1979, and the pair were quickly called upon to oversee their first transfer purchase when experienced striker Stuart Pearson arrived at the Boleyn Ground from Manchester United for £220,000. However, Pearson was to be the only newcomer signed ahead of the 1979–80 season, which kicked off in all-too familiar fashion with defeats – against Wrexham and Chelsea – in the opening two games. A win at home to Oldham Athletic, courtesy of a Pat Holland goal, in the next fixture provided Hammers' first points of the season, but defeats against Watford and Queens Park Rangers left Lyall's team languishing in the bottom of the table. It was time for the manager to enter the transfer market once more, and with the cash from his summer sale still burning a hole in his pocket, Lyall signed defender Ray Stewart from Dundee United. Stewart was one of Scottish football's most highly rated youngsters, and it cost the Hammers all £400,000 of their transfer profit to bring him to Upton Park. It was a fee which also made the 19-year-old right-back the most expensive teenager in British football. Stewart – who was nicknamed 'Tonka' because of his penchant for driving the ball with power and pace – made his debut at centre-half alongside Alvin Martin in a 1-1 draw at Preston North End. However, after three games in the middle of the defence, the young Scot switched to the number two shirt and it was from the right flank that he made his mark with Hammers.

Lyall's back-four

Lyall had started his rebuilding from the back, and he now had a defence which boasted both steel and skill. With the excellent Phil Parkes already *in situ*, Stewart forged a superb full-back partnership with the experienced Frank Lampard, while in the heart of the back four veteran skipper Billy Bonds kept his eye on the gifted, though occasionally overly ambitious, Alvin Martin. 'I think that was by far and away the best back-four unit the club has ever had,' offers Trevor Brooking, adding: 'All of them could play, but they could also put it about too.'

By November 1979 the new look West Ham United backline was beginning to knit together, and this new-found defensive security provided the foundation for a run of four wins in five games which lifted the Upton Park team to the fringes of the promotion race. Hammers had also been making good progress in the League Cup, and victories against Barnsley, Southend and Sunderland had earned a quarter-final clash with European champions Nottingham Forest at the Boleyn Ground. The match against the Midlanders saw Lyall's team show that they could still compete with best the First Division had to offer. However, despite enjoying by far the greater share of possession, Hammers were unable to score and the game went to a replay which Forest won 3–0. The consolation for West Ham United was that the club's League Cup run had been a fruitful source of revenue, since the nine matches played had been watched by a total crowd of more than 200,000.

Twin Towers beckon

There was, of course, still the chance of Wembley glory in the FA Cup, although having failed to progress past the fourth round in four attempts, few pundits gave the Hammers more than an outside chance of reaching the twin towers in May. The draw for the third round of the Cup handed Lyall and his team a seemingly difficult trip to First Division West Bromwich Albion. With former Albion striker David Cross injured for the clash at the Hawthorns, utility man Geoff Pike was handed the number nine shirt. Pike would play alongside Stuart Pearson, with Jimmy Neighbour – who had joined the club from Norwich City in November – and Alan Devonshire manning the flanks. A header from Pearson opened the scoring after 33 minutes, but thereafter Hammers were forced to rely on the fortitude of their defence and the agility of Phil Parkes. Eventually, though, the Baggies found a way through, and a goal from Cyril Regis took the tie to a replay at Upton Park. Stand-in striker Geoff Pike struck the first goal in the return, with Brooking adding a second in a 2–1 win. The next two rounds saw Hammers take on Second Division opposition, and both Leyton Orient and Swansea were despatched to earn a quarter-final tie against

Championship-chasing Aston Villa.

West Ham United went into the clash against Ron Saunders' Villa in confident mood, following a 12-match unbeaten run which had taken the club to fifth place in the Second Division. However, the Midlanders were an emergent power in English football – they would win the League Championship and European Cup during the next two and a half years – and were the pundit's favourites to progress to the competition's last four. It proved a hard-fought and tense encounter, and after 88 minutes the score still stood at 0–0. Hammers, though, had a corner, and when Trevor Brooking swung the ball in toward a crowded penalty area, Alvin Martin challenged with Villa's Ken McNaught who, according to the referee, put hand to ball. Responsibility for the resultant spot-kick fell on the shoulders of 20-year-old Ray Stewart, who had assumed penalty-taking duties from Geoff Pike in September. Stewart had scored five times from the spot already in 1979–80 but his nerve had not yet been tested under such intense pressure. If he scored Hammers would be one match away from Wembley, if he missed they would face an uphill struggle in the replay at Villa Park. To the relief of the majority of the 36,000 fans inside the Boleyn Ground, the young Scot made no mistake.'I rate that as my greatest-ever penalty,' wrote Stewart in his biography *Spot on with Tonka*. 'When the ball struck the back of the net, and the fans went wild, I truly felt I had been accepted by the West Ham supporters.'

Cup success, though, was not without its costs and Hammers failed to win any of their five League matches during March. On the back of such a run, the East Londoners were easily the least fancied side in a semi-final draw which paired Arsenal with Liverpool and West Ham United with Everton. Fortunately, though, by the time Hammers met the Toffeemen at Villa Park their form had improved slightly, and they began the semi-final strongly. However, after 42 minutes Alan Devonshire's challenge on Andy King brought a hotly disputed penalty which was despatched by Brian Kidd to give Everton the lead. Devonshire and Ray Stewart were both booked for their protestations, and thereafter the match became ill-tempered. In the second half Kidd was involved in a fracas with Stewart and, to the relief of the Hammers fans in the 47,000 crowd, the Everton man was shown the red card. The drama continued and, with 20 minutes remaining, Stuart Pearson finished a move fashioned by the impeccable Trevor Brooking to earn a replay. Four days later the combatants reconvened at Elland Road to resume hostilities. Both teams made changes for the replay, with Ratcliffe and Latchford replacing Megson and Kidd for Everton, and Lampard and Pike taking the places of Martin and Holland for the Hammers. The most significant change, however, was the tactical switch which saw John Gidman redeployed to the right of midfield to man-mark Alan Devonshire. It proved an impossible mission for the Everton number two, who could neither match the pace, nor master the trickery of Hammers' most exciting player. Devonshire ran his marker ragged throughout the game, although through a combination of resolute defending and profligacy before goal, the game was still scoreless after 90 minutes. At the start of extra time, John Lyall gave his star player a pep talk: 'I told him that if he scored in the next 30 minutes it would cap the best midfield performance I have seen from anyone in a match like this.' Devonshire was clearly paying attention, and after just four minutes he struck the goal that his display had merited. However, as the game entered its final ten minutes Everton hit back with an equaliser from Bob Latchford and it seemed that the tie was destined for a second replay. But with only two minutes to go a ball to the far post found the unlikely figure of Frank Lampard lurking in the penalty area. The veteran full-back launched himself at the cross to score what was reportedly the first headed goal of his career. He would later confess: 'I thought about a volley and then just flung myself at it. I can't describe the feeling when it went in. It must be the best moment of my life.' Lampard's joy, though, was clearly apparent and as the ball hit the net he headed for the corner flag where he celebrated with a victory jig. 'I was embarrassed about that part,' revealed the former England defender. 'I've got the game on video... and I always shut it off immediately I score. I can't bear to watch myself behaving like a madman.'

Lampard's goal had secured West Ham United a place in the Cup final in May, but before anybody could get carried away with thoughts of Wembley, Hammers still had seven League matches to complete. 'I haven't given up hope of promotion yet,' Lyall told reporters. 'But the fact is that if you play as we do against Second Division teams, who use six or eight men in defence, then some of them will nick a goal or two and beat you... but we are not prepared to compromise our principles, to start kicking because others say you have to in order

There were just two minutes of the 1980 FA Cup semi-final remaining when the unlikely figure of veteran full-back Frank Lampard popped up in the Everton penalty area to score one of the most celebrated goals in West Ham United history.

Now a stinging view of butterfly Brooking

Brooking — floats and stings like a butterfly

TREVOR BROOKING floats like a butterfly . . . and stings like one.

I have never had a high opinion of him as a player. He has been lucky enough to become a member of teams that he shouldn't really have had a sniff at.

Lack of application

I believe his lack of application and that of other players like him have meant relegation for West Ham in the past and the failure to win promotion this time.

Wembley is made for a player like Alan Devonshire. He is young, in form and full of enthusiasm.

Brooking will only be able to have an influence on this Cup Final when Devonshire or another of his willing team-mates has battled to win it at the front or at the back so that he can pick it up in midfield.

The West Ham skipper, Billy Bonds, is the luckiest man alive to be even playing in this match. There is no way we at Forest would have wanted to deprive him of his Cup Final place.

He has had a magnificent career and there are not many more honest men in the game.

But when we saw he had escaped suspension while we had Larry Lloyd banned before the League Cup Final by Bert Millichip, the top man in the FA Disciplinary Commission, we felt entitled to wonder where justice had gone.

I'm baffled

We saw in two League Cup battles with West Ham this season that they had obviously set out their stall to capture a cup.

It baffles me now to hear some of their players bleat on about preferring promotion.

They should have thought about that in January. If they had channelled as much energy into getting out of the Second Division as they have into reaching Wembley, they would have done it.

It is a tremendous indictment of them, because in my opinion they were most certainly good enough to get out. But I knew after we had played them, they were not going to do it.

to get promotion. I would rather remain in the Second Division than sacrifice what we believe in.' Hammers did indeed maintain their principles, but alas they also maintained their League status. The home game against promotion rivals Birmingham City at Upton Park had been critical, but, despite a season's best crowd of 37,167, Lyall's team suffered a 2–1 reverse which left them in eighth place and with too much ground to make up. Hammers' disappointments were further compounded by the sending-off of Billy Bonds, who had been shown the red card after a clash with Birmingham's Colin Todd. Bonds' dismissal took him past 20 disciplinary points and left him facing a possible suspension for the Cup final. The West Ham United skipper attended a hearing at Lancaster Gate ten days before the final but, after a frenzy of media interest, he was relieved to escape with a warning. Bonds was now free to lead his team at Wembley.

The butterfly stings

Arsenal, who had triumphed in an epic semi-final against Liverpool, would be Hammers' opponents in the Cup final. The Gunners were the Cup holders, and were inevitably installed as the bookmakers' favourites. West Ham United were 12/1 to win the game 1-0, while odds of 7/1 were being offered on the same score in Arsenal's favour. Similarly, Frank Stapleton and Alan Sunderland were favourites to score first, both at 7/1, but the generous price of 25/1 was on offer to those who thought Trevor Brooking would open the scoring. The pundits shared the view of the bookmakers, and the Gunners were universally tipped to win. John Lyall, though, was in confident mood. 'We haven't come this far to lose. Second Division club we may be, but we have several players who have already appeared at Wembley and we like to think we play First Division football. If there is any doubt about that just ask the three First Division teams we knocked out on our way here.'

For the final, the West Ham United manager made one change to the team which had defeated Everton in the semi-final, with Alvin Martin returning to the line-up at the expense of the unlucky Paul Brush. Pat Holland, who had played in 1975, and Jimmy Neighbour were also unfortunate to miss out. But, while the personnel bore few changes, the tactics would be markedly different from those employed at Elland Road. Arsenal's great strength was their defence, so rather than play

Trevor Brooking stoops to conquer as he heads the winner in the 1980 Cup final. Despite the fact that the goal came in open play, the Gunners have already put a defender on each post. Trevor, seen wheeling away (right) with Geoff Pike, instigated the move which led to the goal when he fed the ball out to Devonshire on the left wing. When Stuart Pearson's misguided shot flashed across the box, Brooking was on hand to divert the ball past Pat Jennings.

straight into that strength, Lyall decided to employ just one out-and-out striker. David Cross was to be the lone frontman, with Stuart Pearson playing in a withdrawn role amongst the midfield. It meant that Gunners defenders Willie Young and David O'Leary were left marking one man, while in midfield their team-mates were outnumbered. The tactics would not make for an open, attacking game but after 13 minutes Hammers got their reward when Trevor Brooking scored with his famous 'rare header'. Brooking refutes claims that it was a goal that owed more to luck than judgment: 'Everybody says it just hit me on the head, but I did know what was happening. It was a controlled header, but the lucky part was that Stuart [Pearson] wasn't crossing – he was actually shooting for goal. If I'd have stayed still it would have clipped me somewhere about the right ear, but by falling back and just steering it with my forehead the power of the shot meant it had to beat Pat Jennings. It was instinctive more than anything but I did know what was happening.'

Lucky or not, Brooking's goal gave Hammers a valuable half-time lead. But with the Arsenal defence still marking just one player, everybody expected Terry Neill to push men forward in the second period and go all out for an equaliser. The anticipated change, though, never came and throughout the 90 minutes the Gunners stuck rigidly to their 4-4-2. In the end it was West Ham United who came closest to scoring, with Willie Young committing a cynical, professional foul on Paul Allen as the young midfielder closed in on Pat Jennings' goal. It was an offence which was all the more galling since it denied Allen, who at 17 years and 256 days was the youngest player to appear in an FA Cup final, the chance to become also the youngest Cup final scorer. Fortunately, though, Young's tackle had no bearing on the game's result and in the end Brooking's header proved decisive. For the second time in five years Billy Bonds lifted the FA Cup.

Above: Alan Devonshire leaps over the challenge of Arsenal's David Price during the first half of the 1980 Cup final.

Above: Billy Bonds lifts the FA Cup while Ron Greenwood (top of picture) applauds the contribution of a player he brought to the Club in 1967.

Victory against Arsenal was made all the sweeter by the fact that Hammers had confounded the pundits, and after the game Lyall told reporters: 'It suited us to be the underdogs. Reading what all the experts thought helped to create the spirit to respond to the challenge. I always said it would be a cat and mouse business, but we were the cats today.' Brooking had been the undoubted man of the match, but before the game he had been singled out for particular criticism from Nottingham Forest manager Brian Clough, who wrote that: 'Trevor Brooking floats like a butterfly... and stings like one.' The England midfielder had provided the perfect retort with a goal which had not only won the Cup but had also taken Hammers back into European competition.

Forward planning

Season 1980–81 would see West Ham United competing for four major trophies; however, no amount of silverware would

East End boys done good. Trevor Brooking (Barking) and Frank Lampard (East Ham) hold aloft the FA Cup and savour the adulation of the Hammers fans in the 100,000 Wembley Crowd.

be able to compensate if the club missed out on promotion for the third year running. After two seasons in the second tier of English football, regaining top-flight status was the number one priority. If Hammers were to achieve their aim they would need to improve upon the scoring record of the previous League campaign which had seen them net just two more goals than when they had been relegated in 1977–78. So with a transfer fund boosted by the revenue from two highly profitable cup runs, Lyall swooped for a new striker, signing 21-year-old Paul Goddard from Queens Park Rangers for a club record fee of £800,000 in August. Trevor Brooking believes the arrival the Harlington-born forward was the key to what would prove one of the club's most successful seasons: 'Once we got Paul Goddard, I'd have put my house on us going up. He was an excellent signing and his arrival made me think that we would be a good First Division side when we went back up, rather than strugglers. He was the final cutting edge we needed.'

Goddard, however, had not been signed in time to make his debut in the Charity Shield, and without him West Ham United suffered their first defeat at Wembley since 1923, losing 1–0 to Liverpool. A week later, Hammers opened their League programme with a home fixture against Luton Town. This time Lyall's new signing was in the team, but the outcome was no better with two late Luton goals negating a Ray Stewart penalty. Consecutive away draws against Bristol City and Preston North End followed, and with three games played Hammers looked anything but promotion favourites as they languished in 17th place. However, things were about to change and the last match of August saw West Ham United record their first win of the season, crushing high-flying Notts County 4–0 at Upton Park. It was the start of an eight-match winning sequence that would take Hammers to second place in the League and the fourth round of the League Cup by the end of September. The new look strike force of Goddard and Cross had provided the springboard for this dramatic rise, and between them they struck 14 times in the season's first 11 games.

Behind closed doors

September had also seen Lyall's team return to European action with a Cup Winners' Cup first round tie against Castilla of Spain. Castilla were the nursery club for Real Madrid and, with Hammers' domestic form fast improving, the East Londoners were in confident mood for the first leg of the match at the giant Bernabeu stadium. It was, however, to be a disastrous night for West Ham United. The match had started well enough when David Cross opened the scoring with a first-half header, but three goals from the Spaniards in the second period left Hammers with a difficult task for the return. However, the problems did not end there, and following crowd trouble the club was left facing Uefa disciplinary action. The media had a field day, reporting rioting, and portraying the English supporters as violent hooligans. In reality, though, only five fans were detained by police and just two were formally arrested. A week later Uefa announced that West Ham United were to be fined £7,700 and ordered that the second leg of the tie be played 186 miles away from Upton Park. The club appealed against their punishment, and were eventually allowed to stage the return at the Boleyn Ground provided the game was played behind closed doors.

Castilla arrived in E13 determined to protect their first-leg advantage, but goals from Pike, Cross and Goddard gave Hammers an aggregate lead at the break. However, without the benefit of a home crowd to urge them on, Lyall's team could not maintain their momentum in the second half and, as the shouts of the respective coaches rang around the ground, Castilla's Miguel Bernal struck home a superb long-range shot to take the game into extra time. But in the final analysis Hammers were just to strong for their Spanish opponents, and two more goals from David Cross ensured passage to a second round tie against Romania's Poli Timisoara. On this

occasion the first leg was to be played at the Boleyn Ground, where thankfully the doors were open to supporters. Hammers' defence, however, was not quite so accommodating, and Phil Parkes – who had not conceded a goal in 436 minutes of football ahead of the match against Poli – kept another clean sheet to frustrate the Romanians. Meanwhile, at the other end, goals from Bonds, Goddard, Stewart and Cross secured an unassailable lead ahead of the return. The second leg proved remarkably uneventful, and ended in a 1–0 defeat for Lyall's team which was enough to ensure that Hammers retained an interest in the Cup Winners' Cup throughout the winter break.

European football would return to Upton Park in March, but in the meantime West Ham United had much to occupy themselves on the domestic stage. A hard-fought victory over Barnsley at the Boleyn Ground had earned a place in the League Cup quarter-finals, while a 1–0 win at Bristol Rovers was enough to take Hammers top of the table at the start of November. The other Bristol club would also fall victim to the fluent skills of Brooking and company, crashing to a 5–0 defeat which had John Lyall talking about 'total football'. November, though, would also bring two defeats in the League – away at Luton Town and Derby – but such anomalies were not enough to knock the Hammers off the top of the table.

Top: David Cross heads West Ham United into a 17th-minute lead against Spanish side Castilla at the giant Bernabeu Stadium in the first round of the 1980–81 Cup Winners' Cup. However, despite Cross's early score, things quickly deteriorated and after conceding three second half goals, John Lyall's team were left with the proverbial mountain to climb. Their plight was also not helped when UEFA ordered that the return at Upton Park be played behind closed doors after crowd trouble in Madrid. The smaller of the two pictures above reveals the empty Boleyn Ground which greeted both teams on 1 October 1980. Fortunately Hammers were not adversely affected by the spooky atmosphere inside the stadium and ran out 5–1 victors.

The Boleyn Fortress

Upton Park was becoming something of a fortress, and it was on the back of a run of 11 consecutive home wins that Lyall prepared his team for the visit of Tottenham Hotspur in the League Cup quarter-final. Spurs had not played a competitive match at the Boleyn Ground since 1976, and the majority of the 36,000 crowd were delighted to see David Cross strike the only goal of the game from a Brooking pass to earn Hammers a place in the last four of the competition.

West Ham United's excellent form, however, did not extend to their defence of the FA Cup, and a twice replayed third-round tie against Wrexham eventually ended in a 1–0 defeat at the Racecourse Ground. In the League, though, Lyall's team had maintained their momentum and, two days prior to their Cup elimination, Hammers travelled to Notts County for a League match against their closest rivals in the race for promotion. The game ended in a 1–1 draw and interrupted what would otherwise have been a run of nine successive victories. However, there were more serious things to worry about than a mere dropped point. Midfielder Pat Holland had struck the opening goal of the match, but in doing so had collided with the County keeper, sustaining a serious knee injury which would ultimately end his playing career.

Holland's poor luck would give Jimmy Neighbour the chance of an extended run in the Hammers line-up during the winter of 1981, and the former Norwich winger found his name on the teamsheet for the first leg of the League Cup semi-final against Coventry City at Highfield Road. Despite home advantage, the Sky Blues would not be underestimating their Second Division opponents, and Terry Yorath told reporters: 'They are not a nice team any more... they don't shirk the physical side of the game now. They are hard and determined and tackle as though they want to win things.' Yorath's analysis seemed reasonably accurate in a first half which saw Hammers take a 2–0 lead through Billy Bonds and a Thompson own goal. However, in the second period, Lyall's team showed all their old fragility and conceded three goals to let the Midlanders back in the tie. Fortunately, West Ham United were able to make amends in the return and two superb goals from Goddard and Neighbour booked Hammers a third Wembley appearance in two years.

With so much success on the pitch, attendance figures were inevitably on the up, and on six occasions home League matches attracted gates in excess of 30,000. But it was not just supporters who were taking a keen interest in the club's progress. International scouts had also become regular visitors to E13, and as a result both Ray Stewart and Alvin Martin made their full international debuts during 1981. Paul Allen, Mark Schiavi and Bobby Barnes were also included in England youth squads, while veteran midfielder Trevor Brooking enjoyed one of his finest moments in international football, striking two superb goals against Hungary in Budapest to keep England's World Cup hopes alive. Brooking would also net two of his best goals in claret and blue during a 5–0 win over Chelsea at Upton Park on St Valentine's Day. The first was a left-footed shot from outside the area, while the second was a right-footed long-distance curler which even had Blues' Yugoslavian goalkeeper Petar Borota applauding.

Record points total

At the start of March, Hammers were already eight points clear of their nearest rivals in the race for the Second Division Championship, so it was with much confidence that the East Londoners returned to Cup Winners' Cup action with a home tie against Georgian side Dynamo Tbilisi. The only problem was that since the draw had been made, Dynamo had been on their winter break, so it had been impossible for Lyall or any of his scouts to watch the Georgians play live. It put West Ham United at a distinct disadvantage, making it difficult for the Hammers manager to decide upon his tactics. However, even with detailed inside knowledge of his opponents, it is doubtful that Lyall would have been able to conceive a plan which could have combated Dynamo's superb attacking play. By half time West Ham United were two goals down, and although David Cross struck a goal back after the break, the visitors added two

more to secure a comfortable advantage for the second leg. Dynamo were quite simply the best side Hammers had met in European competition. 'Even though they were the away team, their sweeper Chivadze kept surging out from the back and he opened the scoring with a 30-yard screamer,' remembers Trevor Brooking. 'We lost four goals, but it could have been many more. In the end we came off shell-shocked and knowing that we had little chance in the second leg. But you couldn't feel sour about it afterwards because it wasn't as if we had played badly. All you could do was admire the quality of the opposition.' In the return, Hammers did, though, achieve an

Above: Ray Stewart courteously enquires as to why the linesman did not raise his flag against Sammy Lee, who had been in an offside position when Liverpool opened the scoring in the 1981 League Cup final.

Left: John Lyall and Liverpool manager Bob Paisley lead their teams out ahead of the 1981 League Cup final. The two white-shirted Hammers players in the picture are Billy Bonds and David Cross.

Below: Tonka shows his mettle. With just two minutes of extra-time remaining, Ray Stewart crashes home the equalising goal from the penalty spot in the 1981 League Cup final. From left to right: David Cross, Stuart Pearson and Geoff Pike can't wait to share their delight with Hammers' goalscoring hero.

unlikely victory with Stuart Pearson striking the game's only goal after 88 minutes.

The disappointment of defeat against Dynamo (who would go on to win the Cup Winners' Cup) had, however, been tempered by the prospect of the forthcoming League Cup final on 14 March. Bob Paisley's Liverpool team would provide the opposition at Wembley, and the Reds – who were at the peak of their powers having won two consecutive League titles – were predictably installed as the favourites for the competition. Hammers, though, were also in the winning habit, and with nine of their triumphant 1980 Cup team in the side, the Londoners were not to be underestimated. But, despite both teams' excellent League form, the match remained scoreless at the end of 90 minutes. In extra time, however, a previously uneventful final exploded into life, and with just three minutes to go, a shot from Alan Kennedy hit the net. Without hesitation, referee Clive Thomas awarded a goal, but on its way past Phil Parkes, the ball had travelled over the prostrate and rotund figure of Sammy Lee who had been forced to duck out of the way at the last minute. Lee had clearly been lying in an offside position, but according to Thomas he was not interfering with play. It was a decision which incensed the West Ham United players who implored the referee to consult with his linesman. Thomas declined to get a second opinion and made his way back to the halfway line.

But whether Kennedy's goal had been legitimate or not, Hammers had just three minutes to get back in the game. The Londoners were clearly shaken by the controversial opening goal, and it seemed unlikely that they would be able to snatch a last gasp equaliser. As the match entered its final seconds West Ham United had a corner. Brooking sent over a perfect centre and Alvin Martin rose above the Liverpool defence to send a header goalward. But before the ball could reach the net, Liverpool midfielder Terry McDermott fisted it away from

Left: David Cross follows Billy Bonds out of the tunnel for the final match of the 1980–81 season against Sheffield Wednesday at Hillsborough. Hammers would win the match 1–0 and ended the campaign as Second Division Champions with a record points total.

danger. It was one decision that required no debate, and Clive Thomas pointed to the spot. Ray Stewart was handed the job of taking the penalty, and even under such intense pressure the Scot retained his cool nerve. For once Stewart decided against his trademark 'tonk', and instead placed the ball past Ray Clemence to send the Hammers contingent in the 100,000 crowd wild with ecstasy.

Liverpool and West Ham United would have to meet again to decide who would claim the last League Cup trophy which was free from a sponsor's name. The replay was to be played on 1 April at Villa Park but, in the interim, John Lyall would have to motivate his team to maintain their push for promotion. In truth, though, Hammers were simply too good for the Second Division and draws against Oldham and Bolton proved enough to guarantee a return to the top flight. With seven games to play there seemed little doubt that the Upton Park club would be crowned as Champions. However, any flickering hopes of a Second Division and League Cup double were extinguished at Villa Park on April Fools' Day. Hammers did, at least, put up an excellent fight against an in-form Liverpool team, with Paul Goddard hitting the opening goal to have West Ham United supporters dreaming of a famous victory. Alas it was not to be, and first-half strikes from Kenny Dalglish and Alan Hansen clinched the trophy for the Reds, leaving John Lyall with just the Second Division title to concentrate on.

Despite the disappointment of defeat at Villa Park, there was to be no Cup final hangover for West Ham United, and Hammers dropped just one point from their final seven games. It was a run which saw Lyall's team travel to Sheffield Wednesday for the last game of the season as Champions, knowing that a win against the Owls would also establish a new record points total for the Second Division. It was to be a match of few chances, but after 64 minutes rookie striker Nicky Morgan struck the only goal of the game to ensure a winning end to an exciting season. However, the match at Hillsborough was not all good news for West Ham United. Before the game, Ron Greenwood had telephoned John Lyall to tell him that Alvin Martin and Billy Bonds would be in the line-up for England's next match against Brazil. For 34-year-old Bonds it represented probably his last chance to gain a full England cap. However, during the game in Sheffield, the Hammers skipper found himself crushed in a challenge between Wednesday centre-forward Andy McCulloch and Phil Parkes, and for his trouble ended up with two broken ribs. Bonds was forced to withdraw from the squad and was never given another chance to represent his country. Fortunately for fans of West Ham United, though, Bonzo would continue to provide stalwart service at Upton Park for many years to come.

Above: The goals of Paul Goddard – seen here celebrating with Geoff Pike – were a key factor in the 1980–81 promotion season. Paul had arrived at Upton Park for a club record £800,000 in August 1980, and ended his first campaign with 17 goals from 37 League appearances.

Below: Hammers skipper Billy Bonds holds aloft the Second Division Championship trophy at the end of the 1980–81 season.

Top flight return

The 1980–81 season had been a campaign of great drama at the Boleyn Ground, and a return to the First Division was the least West Ham United deserved for their enterprising and entertaining football. The club was now in a far healthier position than it had been at any time during John Lyall's seven-year reign. One clear sign of this progress was the Hammers youth team, which had at last recaptured the success of years gone by to claim the FA Youth Cup with a 2–1 aggregate victory over Tottenham Hotspur. Lyall was clearly optimistic about the prospects for the club's youngsters, and in the summer of 1981 he made no significant moves on the transfer market. It was, therefore, a familiar looking line-up which took the field for Hammers' top-flight return against big-spending Brighton and Hove Albion at the Boleyn Ground. Lyall made just two changes to the team which had played the final game of the promotion season – Allen and Goddard replacing Brooking and Morgan – and a combination of resolute defending and a Ray Stewart penalty earned the East Londoners a creditable 1–1 draw.

West Ham United were optimistic about their prospects for their first season back amongst English football's elite, and were looking to achieve more than just mere First Division survival. Confidence was high, and with good reason. Lyall's carefully constructed defence of Parkes, Stewart, Lampard, Martin and Bonds was now matched by an equally impressive array of talent in midfield and attack. An increasingly important influence upon Hammers' attacking play was the form of Alan Devonshire, who had struck up an understanding with Trevor Brooking which was nothing short of transcendental. The considerable creative talents of 'Trev and Dev' would catch the headlines, but they were ably supported by a fine supporting cast which included the promising Paul Allen and much-underrated Geoff Pike. The line up was completed by strikers David Cross and Paul Goddard who, between them, had netted 48 goals during the promotion season. It was a team which Trevor Brooking believes was the best he played in during his 16-year career at the Boleyn Ground. 'We had a very strong starting eleven,' remembers the Barking-born midfielder, 'although the squad didn't have a lot of depth.'

The fragility of Lyall's squad would take its toll during the 1981–82 season, although in the early weeks of the League campaign there was little cause for concern. The manager's only real worry was an injury to Brooking which would keep the midfielder's name from the teamsheet for the first six games. But, despite the absence of their star player, Hammers made an impressive start, and were still unbeaten after the first nine games. It was a run which took in a memorable 4–0 victory against Tottenham Hotspur at White Hart Lane, with David Cross hitting all the goals. The big number nine struck the net eight times in the first ten matches, and his rich scoring form was instrumental in taking West Ham United to the giddy heights of fifth place in the table by mid-October. However, it was a situation which could not last and, throughout the remainder of the season, Hammers' results came in patches which fluctuated from sensational to aberrational.

By the turn of the year the lack of depth in the first-team squad had become all too apparent, and following a run of four successive defeats Lyall entered the transfer market. First to sign was Belgian international striker Francois van der Elst, a player who had lined-up against the Hammers in the 1976 Cup Winners' Cup final. Van der Elst was a skilful and pacy forward who could play anywhere across the frontline, and he quickly became a big hit with the fans at the Boleyn Ground. The Belgian was joined in E13 by another versatile performer in the shape of Scot Neil Orr who signed from Morton. Both new players would make significant contributions to an impressive late run which saw West Ham United make a spirited challenge for a Uefa Cup place in March and April. In the end, though, Hammers failed to win any of their last five matches and finished in a creditable ninth position.

New Year's Day 1983 saw the arrival of a new hero at Upton Park. Tony Cottee had been a prolific goalscorer in the Hammers youth team, but few could have anticipated the start he would make to his senior career. After 25 minutes of his debut against Tottenham Hotspur, the diminutive striker pounced to score when Ray Clemence failed to hold on to a header from Joe Gallagher.

Striking vacancy

The final game of the 1981–82 League campaign had seen David Cross make his last appearance in a claret and blue shirt, and at season's end the popular striker – who was nicknamed Psycho because of his 'full-blooded' approach to the game – moved on to Manchester City. John Lyall would waste little time finding a replacement for Cross, and in June the West Ham United manager snapped up 25-year-old Sandy Clark from Airdrie for £200,000. Clark would struggle to come to terms with life in the First Division, and lasted less than a year at Upton Park, but he did enjoy a rich vein of form during the Autumn of 1981, netting five goals in five games. It was a scoring sequence which coincided with Hammers' best run of the season and after five successive victories the Upton Park club in second place by mid-October. Lyall's team would struggle to find any consistent form for the remainder of the League programme, while in the Cup competitions they were unfortunate to meet both the eventual winners – Manchester United in the FA Cup and Liverpool in the League Cup.

The Hammers did, however, maintain their presence in the top half of the table throughout most of the season, and a Uefa Cup place remained a realistic target until the final week. But points dropped in a disastrous run of four consecutive defeats over the festive period could not be made up and, despite a strong finish which saw Lyall's team win seven of their last ten games, there would be no return to European competition in 1983. Any disappointment, however, was tempered by the progress made by two young players who had risen through the youth ranks at Upton Park. Midfielder Alan Dickens made his senior debut against Notts County at Meadow Lane on 18 December, and after just six minutes struck the game's opening goal. Two weeks later, Lyall included another debutante in the Hammers line-up. Tony Cottee had been a prolific striker in

the youth team, and like Dickens the diminutive 17-year-old wasted little time opening his scoring account, striking after 25 minutes of the New Year's Day derby match against Tottenham Hotspur at Upton Park. Cottee, who had been an avid West Ham United supporter as a youngster, finished the season with a record of five goals from three starts and it quickly became apparent that Hammers had unearthed a natural-born goalscorer. But despite the progress of the West Ham-born forward, Lyall still felt the need to buy an experienced centre-forward to fill the void which Cross had left the previous summer, and signed Derby County's Dave Swindlehurst in March.

One man at a rather different stage in his Upton Park career to Cottee and Swindlehurst was Billy Bonds, and after 15 years at the club 'Bonzo' made his 545th appearance against Ipswich Town in September to break Bobby Moore's West Ham United first-team appearance record. By now Bonds was nothing short of a Hammers legend, and even at the age of 35 he remained an integral part of John Lyall's team for the 1983–84 season. However, another Upton Park veteran, Frank Lampard, would miss much of the campaign through injury. Lampard's number three shirt would go to summer signing Steve Walford, who had arrived from Norwich City in a £165,000 deal. Lyall had made another signing during the close season, bringing in Coventry winger Steve Whitton as a replacement for the outgoing Francois van der Elst. Both newcomers would make impressive starts to their time at the Boleyn ground, and both played key roles as Hammers flew out of the blocks to record victories in each of their five opening games.

Sponsored football

The prolific strike partnership of Tony Cottee – who had taken the place of the injured Paul Goddard – and Dave Swindlehurst was the key factor behind West Ham United's early season form, and the duo struck nine goals in the first five fixtures. But the Hammers were unable to maintain their high aspect, and three defeats in five matches saw them drop to third in the table at the end of October. Lyall's team had, though, made progress in the League Cup, defeating Bury 10–0 to establish the club's record victory. The League Cup was now sponsored by the Milk Marketing Board and, although the name change seemed insignificant, it hinted at the growing tide of commercialism that was sweeping through professional football. Hammers, of course, were making every effort to keep up in this changing world of marketing men and financial brinkmanship. In October, the club entered into its first-ever shirt sponsorship agreement. The deal with American finance company Avco Trust was said to be worth as much as £300,000, depending on performance related bonuses, and when the

A legend departs. Trevor Brooking retired as a player at the end of 1983–84 season and his farewell game, against Everton at Upton Park, brought a flood of emotion from Hammers supporters.

team took the field for the home match against Norwich City their shirts were emblazoned with their new sponsor's name. Fresh sources of income were developing elsewhere, too, and West Ham United hoped to earn around £200,000 from merchandising, while extra revenue was also to be gained from VIP entertainment.

Football's new money would, at least, help compensate for Hammers' failures in both domestic Cup competitions. Defeats in the Milk Cup against Everton in the quarter final, and versus Birmingham City in the fifth round of the FA Cup, had left Lyall's team with just the League to concentrate upon from the middle of February onwards. Dreams of the title, though, had all but faded following defeats in three of December's six games. Lyall's ambitions had also been hit by injuries to three key players. The most serious and devastating blow had arrived in an FA Cup match against Wigan Athletic when Alan Devonshire sustained a serious knee injury which would keep him out of the game for more than a year. There was no way the West Ham United manager could compensate for the loss of such an influential player as Devonshire, and shortly afterwards his problems were compounded when he learned that both Alvin Martin and Steve Whitton had been involved in a car accident. Martin would miss the remainder of the season, while Whitton would make just four more appearances. Lyall attempted to resolve at least one of his problems by signing centre-half Paul Hilton. It was, however, a transfer which perplexed many supporters since, only four months earlier, Hilton had been a member of the Bury defence which had conceded ten goals at Upton Park earlier in the League Cup.

Brooking bids farewell

With three of their most influential players missing, Hammers began to struggle and at season's end had slid down the League to finish in ninth place. However, any disappointments were temporarily forgotten during the final match of the season which saw Everton visit the Boleyn Ground on an emotional afternoon in E13. Hammers' former England midfielder Trevor Brooking had decided to hang up his boots, and the match against the Toffeemen was to bring the curtain down on the career of a player who had provided rich entertainment in his 16 years at Upton Park. A crowd of 25,500 (8,000 more than the previous home fixture) attended an otherwise meaningless match. The game ended in defeat for the Hammers, but the crowd cared little for the result and waited waited patiently for their hero to return for a richly deserved lap of honour. Lyall would now have to contemplate life without his most gifted and influential player, and the manager was only too aware that Brooking's departure had left a gaping chasm in his team. 'You don't replace people like him,' lamented the Upton Park boss.

Brooking's departure had also prompted fellow veterans Billy Bonds and Frank Lampard to contemplate their futures, and at the end of 1983–84 both defenders announced that they would be standing down as regulars in the first team. 'We have certainly reached the end of what I would call a memorable era,' declared Lyall, before adding: 'Next season we must try and build a side with the object of playing regularly in Europe.' However, there would be no mass influx of expensive signings and, with one exception, the Hammers manager started his rebuilding work with youngsters already at the club. The odd man out was central defender Tony Gale who arrived from Fulham for a tribunal-set fee of £200,000. It would prove a bargain price and Tony, who had previously been linked with a big-money move to Liverpool, was drafted straight into first-team action for the opening game of the season at home to Ipswich. The match against the Suffolk club ended in a 0–0 draw and although Hammers won their next three games, a growing injury list would soon take its toll. Among those receiving treatment from physio Rob Jenkins in the early weeks of the season were Phil Parkes, Alan Devonshire, Steve Whitton and Neil Orr. With Hammers' playing resources stretched to the limit, John Lyall somewhat inevitably turned to the ever-reliable Billy Bonds, who was recalled from his semi-retirement to take up a position in midfield for much of the season.

Despite their autumnal injury crisis, West Ham United maintained a place in the top five of the First Division until the end of November, but thereafter League form deserted Lyall's team. Tom McAllister, who had got his chance in the line-up because of Phil Parkes' injury, had been Hammers' hero in the club's good start to the season, but there was little that even he could do to halt a slide which saw the East Londoners drop to 16th place at the end of February. The club now faced a battle to maintain First Division status. However, it was not all doom and gloom in E13, and in March John Lyall signed a new four-year contract to end speculation linking him with moves to Queens Park Rangers and Tottenham Hotspur. The Hammers' cause was also boosted by the return to fitness of Alan Devonshire, who made his first-team comeback in an FA Cup fifth round clash against Wimbledon at Plough Lane. It was the first of three Cup matches in five days for West Ham United and a Tony Cottee goal earned Hammers a 1–1 draw. Cottee was also among the scorers in the replay at Upton Park two days later, netting a hat-trick in a 5–1 win which ensured passage to a quarter-final tie away to Ron Atkinson's Manchester United. However, the exertions of the previous five days caught up with Lyall's team at Old Trafford and they crashed out of the Cup 4–2.

In the summer of 1985 John Lyall paid St Mirren £340,000 for little-known attacking midfielder Frank McAvennie. However, when Paul Goddard was injured in the first game of the 1985–86 season, McAvennie was pushed into the forward line. It proved an inspired switch and the Glaswegian, seen here scoring his first Hammers goal, against Queens Park Rangers at Upton Park, ended the season as the team's top scorer with 26 League goals.

For the remainder of the season, West Ham United were concerned only with maintaining their First Division status. The trouble was, though, that Hammers were unable to string together the run of two or three victories needed to lift the club away from danger. Injuries had continued to frustrate Lyall's efforts, with Alan Devonshire returning to the treatment room after the FA Cup replay with Wimbledon. At the start of May the League situation had become critical with Hammers occupying 19th position, having won just two First Division games since the turn of the year. Defeats away to Everton and Sheffield Wednesday did nothing to enhance survival hopes but, with three games to go, Lyall's team at last succeeded in winning two consecutive games. The first match saw Billy Bonds hit two goals in a 5–1 demolition of bottom-of-the-table Stoke City, and Hammers followed up with a 1–0 away victory – courtesy of a Tony Cottee goal – at Ipswich Town. The win at Portman Road allowed West Ham United the luxury of knowing that they could lose their final fixture at home to Liverpool, and they duly took advantage of their new found security by losing 3–0. The final League table of the season showed the Hammers in the relative comfort of 16th place, but they had finished the season with just two more points than relegated Norwich City.

McAvennie heads south

Season 1984–85 had also brought to a close the Upton Park careers of Frank Lampard and Paul Allen. At the age of 36, Lampard's decision to end his First Division career was far from unexpected, but the news that Allen was looking to get away from E13 was rather more disappointing for John Lyall. The versatile 22-year-old – who was one of several midfielders to benefit from the departure of Brooking – had enjoyed his

Tony Cottee may have lacked height, but he proved himself a goalscorer of enormous talent during the 1985–86 season. Tony ended the campaign with 26 goals in all competitions.

best season at the Boleyn Ground but was out of contract and keen to move on in the summer of 1985. His wish was eventually granted and a move to Tottenham Hotspur earned the club £400,000 for a player who had been nurtured through the Hammers' junior ranks. Allen's choice of destination, though, would do little for his Upton Park popularity.

The disastrous League campaign of the previous season and the departure of key players had left John Lyall's squad in urgent need of an injection of fresh talent. And during the summer of 1985 the manager acted decisively, signing two players whose success in E13 would quickly surpass all expectations. Mark Ward, a diminutive but tigerish midfielder, was brought in as a replacement for the outgoing Paul Allen, and arrived from Oldham Athletic for a modest fee of £220,000. For his second signing, though, the Hammers boss headed North of the border. 'I needed a player who could operate just behind the front two of Goddard and Cottee, and score goals, too,' wrote Lyall in his autobiography. 'The player I wanted was Frank McAvennie.' A fee of £340,000 proved sufficient to secure the services of the St Mirren forward, and both McAvennie and Ward were included in a new look Hammers line-up for the opening game of the season away to Birmingham City. The match against the Blues would also see the return to League action of Alan Devonshire, who was now fully recovered from his serious knee injury. Devonshire took his place in an attacking midfield quartet which was completed by McAvennie, Ward and Neil Orr. However, despite this array of talent, Hammers rarely troubled home keeper David Seaman and were defeated 1–0. The West Ham United cause had not been helped when, in the first half, Paul Goddard had to be taken off with a dislocated shoulder. Lyall was forced to reshuffle his team, with Alan Dickens coming on in midfield and Frank McAvennie moving into the forward line.

Goddard's injury would keep him out of the Hammers line-up for several months, and with little alternative Lyall kept faith with his new strike pairing of Cottee and McAvennie. Dickens, too, would maintain his place in the team, and after 24 minutes of the home match against Queens Park Rangers, he struck his first goal of the season. But the young midfielder was to be upstaged by Frank McAvennie who, on his Upton Park debut, scored the first and last goals in a 3–1 victory. Nobody, however, was getting carried away with a win over a team who had finished just one point away from relegation the previous May. The match had been watched by a disappointing crowd of just 15,530, but even fewer people – 14,040 – attended the next home fixture against Luton Town, which ended in a 1–0 reverse courtesy of a Mick Harford penalty. Two days later, Lyall's team were on the end of another defeat, this time against early leaders Manchester United at Old Trafford, and after four games Hammers occupied 17th place in the First Division. Another relegation battle looked to be in prospect, but a 2–2 draw against Kenny Dalglish's Liverpool at the end of August hinted at a somewhat brighter future. McAvennie was Hammers' hero once more, netting twice against a Reds defence which included both Mark Lawrenson and Alan Hansen. But after the match, Lyall's team were disappointed not to have claimed all three points, particularly since Tony Cottee's seemingly legitimate goal had been ruled out in the dying moments. Cottee was struggling to find his goalscoring touch, though, and after six matches he was still waiting to open his account fo was right to rest his talented young striker, who was given the number 12 shirt for the trip to Southampton on 6 September. This short spell on the bench proved the perfect tonic, and Cottee returned to the starting line-up against Sheffield Wednesday to strike a late equaliser in a 2–2 draw.

Dev the difference

Hammers' form was beginning to improve, although, even after three successive draws, there was little to suggest that the East Londoners were at the start of an unbeaten run which would take them into the top half of the table in mid-October. Progress had been gradual, but by the end of September the new players had settled in, and confidence was growing. Cottee and McAvennie were now working as an effective partnership and the goals were beginning to flow. However, it was not just in attack that Lyall's team were showing signs of improvement. The defence bore no significant changes in personnel from the previous season – with Ray Stewart and Steve Walford the full-backs and Tony Gale and Alvin Martin the central defenders – but was now playing with a previously unseen assurance. In midfield, too, there was a growing sense of confidence, and Mark Ward, Alan Dickens and Neil Orr were all showing impressive form. But the undoubted inspiration for Hammers' resurgence was the revitalised Alan Devonshire. The languid wide man had added an extra dimension to West Ham United's play with his sublime dribbling skills and intelligent distribution. Tony Gale is in no doubt about Devonshire's contribution to a memorable season in E13:' I think the most important change to the squad was not a new signing but the return to the team of Dev. I'd played against Alan when I'd been with Fulham and I knew he was good, but his injury had seemed to last for an eternity. When he did come back, he'd lost some of his pace, but he was still one of the best players I've ever played with or against – he was fantastic. It was such a big lift for the whole club when he came back.'

Title aspirations

West Ham United began October in 11th place in the First Division, and made the trip to Newcastle's St James' Park in confident mood. McAvennie opened the scoring against the Magpies after just 12 minutes, netting his 10th League goal of the season, before Cottee added a second midway through the first half. The home team did manage to grab a consolation goal six minutes from time, but with Martin and Gale in superb form at the back, the points were never really in danger. A goalless home draw against Arsenal followed, but a week later Hammers gained a memorable victory over Aston Villa which took them into the top of half of the table. Cottee and McAvennie were at their irrepressible best against the Midlanders, and each grabbed two goals in a 4–1 win. But victory over Villa was just the beginning, and by Christmas a record-breaking run of nine successive victories had propelled West Ham United into the Championship race. The highlight of Hammers' glorious run was the win against reigning Champions Everton at Upton Park in November. A goal from Trevor Steven had given the Toffeemen the lead, but two McAvennie strikes secured a victory which went a long way to raising West Ham United's status from perennial strugglers to title contenders.

The winning streak eventually came to an end on 21 December with Hammers held to a 0–0 draw on Luton Town's notorious plastic pitch. Boxing Day brought further disappointment when Spurs stalwart Steve Perryman struck his first goal in two years to earn the North Londoners a 1–0 victory at White Hart Lane. It was West Ham United's first League defeat since August, but because of poor weather they would have to wait 16 days before they could get back on the winning trail. In the interim there was the small matter of an FA Cup third round clash against Charlton Athletic at Selhurst Park with which to contend. A late Tony Cottee goal proved enough to defeat the Robins, and earned Lyall's team a tie against First Division strugglers Ipswich Town in the fourth round. Next up for Hammers, though, was a trip to Leicester City in the League and though the East Londoners won the match 1–0, they were flattered by a result which owed much to a penalty save from Phil Parkes and some stout defending from Alvin Martin and Tony Gale.

With their form beginning to falter, a trip to Anfield could hardly have come at a worse time for Lyall's team. However, the Hammers began the match against the Reds with all their pre-Christmas verve, and enjoyed the better chances in a goalless first half. Twelve minutes into the second period, though, came a moment which would ultimately prove decisive in the title race. A challenge between Paul Walsh and Alvin Martin resulted in the Liverpool striker falling to the ground, and, without hesitation, Referee G. Tyson pointed to the spot. The Hammers players were incensed and Ray Stewart led the protests. The referee, however, was not amused by this challenge to his authority and pointed his red card in the direction of Stewart. Jan Molby duly converted the penalty and 10-man West Ham United eventually went down 3–1.

Frank McAvennie heads for the South Bank to celebrate his 15th goal of the 1985–86 season in the match against Watford at Upton Park in November.

According to the press Hammers' title challenge had reached the end of the road. In reality, though, it had merely pulled onto the hard shoulder for a well earned rest, and in the next eight weeks inclement weather would see the East Londoners play just one League game. The match which interrupted West Ham United's First Division sabbatical was a home fixture against second-placed Manchester United. The Hammers' indifferent results and infrequent appearances since Christmas had seen the club slip down to fifth place in the table, but, with a television dispute now resolved, the match against United was still deemed of sufficient interest to merit live broadcast. The judgment of the TV executives proved sound, and the match was an engaging encounter, with the Reds taking a first-half lead through Robson before Hammers fought back to win 2–1, courtesy of goals from Ward and Cottee.

Four days after defeating Manchester United in the League, Lyall's team earned an FA Cup fifth round tie against the Reds with a 1–0 victory over Ipswich Town in a twice-replayed fourth round encounter. The Cup clash with Ron Atkinson's team, however, would be held up by poor weather and was eventually played on 5 March. It was the fourth time the two sides had met during 1985–86, and United had enjoyed the better of the three previous encounters, having beaten Hammers at Old Trafford in both the League and the League Cup. Upton Park, however, was the venue for the FA Cup match and West Ham United, who had not lost a home match since August, took the lead after 25 minutes when Frank McAvennie applied the finishing touch to a Tony Cottee pass. United struck back in the second half, though, and a Frank Stapleton header took the game to a replay. The return at Old Trafford saw Hammers treat a Sunday afternoon TV audience to one of their best performances of the season, and a Geoff Pike header from the edge of the box and a Ray Stewart penalty gave John Lyall's team a well-deserved victory. A fixture backlog was becoming something of a problem though, and the West Ham United manager had just three days to prepare his team for an FA Cup quarter-final against Sheffield Wednesday at Hillsborough. It proved a game too far for the Hammers who were unable to recover after conceding two first half goals.

Fixture pile up

With the cold weather now passed, and no more Cup ties to offer distraction, West Ham United were able to concentrate on cramming their remaining 16 League fixtures into the final eight weeks of the season. The Hammers occupied seventh position in the table in mid-March, but with so many games in hand over their rivals there was every chance of a much higher finish... some optimists were even still talking about the title. Consecutive away defeats at Arsenal and Aston Villa, though, did nothing to help the cause, but three victories in March's remaining matches lifted Lyall's team to fifth place and saw the optimists find their voice once more. It was a run which included a superb 4–1 victory over high-flying Chelsea at Stamford Bridge. 'If West Ham keep playing like that, they'll win the Championship, ' declared defeated Blues skipper Colin Pates, 'They are the best side we've seen at Stamford Bridge for a long time. There is not a weakness – they are a good, strong, all-round team.' Tony Cottee had struck two of the goals in the win against Chelsea and at the end of March he was named PFA Young Player of the Year.

Cottee's name was again on the scoresheet in the match against Nottingham Forest on 5 April, but the striker's goal turned out to be no more than a consolation this time, with Brian Clough's team claiming a 2–1 victory with a strike from Brian Rice two minutes from time. Hammers would, however, still claim the League if they were able to win their final ten matches of the season. The only problem was that they had little more than five weeks to complete their fixtures. The first two games, against Southampton and Oxford, brought the required victories, but uncharacteristic defensive mistakes saw Hammers surrender a second-half lead to lose 2–1 against Chelsea at Upton Park. It was not all over yet though, and a victory at Watford saw Lyall's team keep up the pressure on the leaders. There were still six games to play and a win in the next match at home to Newcastle would put West Ham United in third place. The Magpies arrived at the Boleyn Ground to find the Hammers at the peak of their form, and after three minutes found themselves a goal down. By half-time the home team held a 4–0 advantage, and Newcastle goalkeeper Martin Thomas, who had been carrying an injury, decided not to come out for the second half, leaving first Hedworth and later Peter Beardsley to take guard between the posts. Hammers took full advantage, with Alvin Martin collecting a hat-trick and Paul Goddard scoring his only goal of the season in an 8–1 victory.

Three consecutive home matches in the space of five days concluded West Ham United's fixtures for April, and though 1–0 wins over Coventry and Manchester City were achieved with a minimum of fuss, the clash with struggling Ipswich Town proved a rather more tense encounter. After 63 minutes the Suffolk side took the lead, but an Alan Dickens goal got Hammers back on terms, and with four minutes to go Mark Ward won a hotly disputed penalty which Ray Stewart duly despatched past Cooper in the Ipswich goal. With two games to go, West Ham United were in second place and along with Liverpool and Everton could still win the League Championship. However, Hammers' fate was no longer in their own hands and, as they travelled to the Hawthorns to take on West Bromwich Albion, Lyall's team knew that if Liverpool won at Chelsea the title would go to Anfield. West Ham United began strongly, and goals from Cottee and McAvennie gave them a comfortable lead after 24 minutes. Events at Stamford Bridge would preoccupy both fans and players for the remainder of the match. Tony Gale remembers that, throughout the game, he and his team-mates were getting bogus scores from the crowd. In fact, so distracting were these progress reports from West London, that Hammers let Albion back into the match in the second half, and needed a late Ray Stewart penalty to claim a 3–2 victory. However, it was not enough, and when the players reached the dressing-room they discovered that Liverpool had won the match against Chelsea and with it the League Championship.

West Ham United still had one game left to play but, although the result of the clash with Everton at Goodison Park would determine which team finished as runners-up, it was difficult for the players to rouse themselves after the disappointment of losing the title race. And, because of a Uefa ban on English teams in European competition following the Heysel disaster in 1985, there was not even the consolation of a place in the Uefa Cup to look forward to. 'We were all exhausted and it was only the adrenalin of winning all the time that had carried us through the run-in,' remembers Tony Gale, 'But after the West Brom game there was no chance of us winning the title and it was impossible to maintain the same level of adrenalin.' Hammers lost the game at Goodison, and so finished in third place. It is easy to look at the 'what ifs', but had it not been for a poor start which brought just three points in the opening four games Upton Park would undoubtedly have been celebrating its first League Championship. It was, nevertheless, the highest League placing in the club's history and represented a tremendous achievement for Lyall and his players. The goalscoring feats of Frank McAvennie and Tony Cottee, who as a partnership netted 54 times in all competitions, would grab the headlines, but Hammers' success had been the result of the efforts of a skilful and, perhaps more importantly, settled side. Nine players appeared in 38 or more League matches, and in total Lyall used just 17 outfield players all season. The big question now was whether West Ham United could build upon their success and continue to challenge for League honours in the years to come.

So near but yet ... Hammers finished third in 1985–86. It was the Club's best ever League placing, but the disappointment of missing out on the League title – which had remained a possibility until the last week of the season – is clearly apparent from the expressions etched onto the player's faces after the season's final game at Everton. The disappointed Hammers are, from left to right: Ray Stewart (number two), Paul Goddard (number 12), Tony Cottee, Tony Gale, George Parris (number three) and Alan Devonshire.

1974-1985

Alan Devonshire foils an attack from Newcastle winger Stewart Barrowclough at Upton Park in 1978.

SEASON 1974-75
FOOTBALL LEAGUE (DIVISION 1)

Aug 17	(a)	Manchester C	L	0-4
19	(h)	Luton T	W	2-0
24	(h)	Everton	L	2-3
28	(a)	Luton T	D	0-0
31	(a)	Newcastle U	L	0-2
Sep 7	(h)	Sheffield U	L	1-2
14	(a)	Tottenham H	L	1-2
21	(h)	Leicester C	W	6-2
25	(h)	Birmingham C	W	3-0
28	(a)	Burnley	W	5-3
Oct 5	(h)	Derby C	D	2-2
12	(a)	Coventry C	D	1-1
15	(a)	Everton	D	1-1
19	(h)	Ipswich T	W	1-0
26	(a)	Arsenal	L	0-3
Nov 2	(h)	Middlesborough	W	3-0
9	(a)	Carlisle U	W	1-0
16	(h)	Wolves	W	5-2
23	(a)	Liverpool	D	1-1
30	(a)	Queen's Park R	W	2-0
Dec 7	(h)	Leeds U	W	2-1
14	(h)	Manchester C	D	0-0
21	(a)	Chelsea	D	1-1
26	(h)	Tottenham H	D	1-1
28	(a)	Stoke C	L	1-2
Jan 11	(a)	Leeds U	L	1-2
18	(h)	Queen's Park R	D	2-2
Feb 1	(h)	Carlisle U	W	2-0
8	(a)	Middlesborough	D	0-0
19	(h)	Liverpool	D	0-0
22	(a)	Wolves	L	1-3
28	(h)	Newcastle U	L	0-1
Mar 15	(h)	Burnley	W	2-1
18	(a)	Birmingham C	D	1-1
22	(a)	Sheffield U	L	2-3
28	(h)	Stoke C	D	2-2
29	(h)	Chelsea	L	0-1
Apr 1	(a)	Leicester C	L	0-3
12	(a)	Derby C	L	0-1
19	(h)	Coventry C	L	1-2
26	(a)	Ipswich T	L	1-0
28	(h)	Arsenal	W	1-0

P	W	D	L	F	A	W	D	L	F	A	Pts	Pos
42	10	6	5	38	22	3	7	11	20	37	39	13th

FA Cup

	Jan 4	(a)	Southampton	W	2-1
	25	(h)	Swindon T	D	1-1
R	28	(a)	Swindon T	W	2-1
	Feb 15	(h)	Queen's Park R	W	2-1
	8	(a)	Arsenal	W	2-0
SF	Apr 5	(n*)	Ipswich T	D	0-0
R	9	(n**)	Ipswich T	W	2-1
F	May 3	(n***)	Fulham	W	2-0

*Played at Villa Park
**Played at Stamford Bridge
***Played at Wembley

League Cup

	Sep 11	(a)	Tranmere R	D	0-0
R	18	(h)	Tranmere R	W	6-0
	Oct 3	(a)	Fulham	L	1-2

Texaco Cup

Aug 3	(h)	Leyton Orient	W	1-0
Aug 7	(h)	Luton Town	L	1-2
Aug 10	(a)	Southampton	L	0-2

Hammer of the Year 1974-75

BILLY BONDS

SEASON 1975-76
FOOTBALL LEAGUE (DIVISION 1)

Aug 16	(a)	Stoke C	W	2-1
19	(a)	Liverpool	D	2-2
23	(h)	Burnley	W	3-2
25	(h)	Tottenham H	W	1-0
30	(a)	Queen's Park R	D	1-1
Sep 6	(h)	Manchester C	W	1-0
13	(a)	Leicester C	D	3-3
20	(h)	Sheffield U	W	2-0
27	(a)	Wolves	W	1-0
Oct 4	(h)	Everton	L	0-1
11	(h)	Newcastle U	W	2-1
18	(a)	Middlesborough	L	0-3
25	(h)	Manchester U	W	2-1
Nov 1	(a)	Birmingham C	W	5-1
8	(h)	Coventry C	D	1-1
15	(a)	Derby C	L	1-2
22	(h)	Middlesborough	W	2-1
29	(h)	Arsenal	W	1-0
Dec 6	(a)	Norwich C	L	0-1
13	(a)	Burnley	L	0-2
20	(h)	Stoke C	W	3-1
26	(a)	Aston Villa	L	1-4
27	(h)	Ipswich T	L	1-2
Jan 10	(h)	Leicester C	D	1-1
17	(a)	Manchester C	L	0-3
24	(h)	Queen's Park R	W	1-0
31	(h)	Liverpool	L	0-4
Feb 7	(a)	Tottenham H	D	1-1
14	(a)	Coventry C	L	0-2
21	(h)	Derby C	L	1-2
23	(h)	Leeds U	D	1-1
28	(a)	Manchester U	L	0-4
Mar 6	(h)	Birmingham C	L	1-2
9	(a)	Leeds U	D	1-1
13	(a)	Newcastle U	L	1-2
20	(a)	Arsenal	L	1-6
27	(h)	Norwich C	L	0-1
Apr 3	(h)	Wolves	D	0-0
10	(a)	Sheffield U	L	2-3
17	(h)	Aston Villa	D	2-2
19	(a)	Ipswich T	L	0-4
24	(a)	Everton	L	0-2

P	W	D	L	F	A	W	D	L	F	A	Pts	Pos
42	10	5	6	26	23	3	5	13	22	48	36	18th

FA Cup

Jan 3	(h)	Liverpool	L	0-2

League Cup

	Sep 9	(h)	Bristol C	D	0-0
R	24	(a)	Bristol C	W	3-1
	Oct 8	(h)	Darlington	W	3-0
	Nov 12	(a)	Tottenham H	D	0-0
R	24	(h)	Tottenham H	L	0-2

F.A. Charity Shield

Aug 9	(n)	Derby County	L	0-2

Anglo-Italian Cup-Winners' Cup

Sep 3	(a)	Florentina	L	0-1
Dec 10	(h)	Florentina	L	0-1

European Cup-Winners Cup

Sep 17	(a)	Lahden Reipas	D	2-2
Oct 1	(h)	Lahden Reipas	W	3-0
Oct 22	(a)	Ararat Erevan	D	1-1
Nov 5	(h)	Ararat Erevan	W	3-1
Mar 3	(a)	FC Den Haag	L	2-4
Mar 17	(h)	FC Den Haag	W	3-1
	(won on away goals rule)			
Mar 31	(a)	Eintracht Frankfurt	L	1-2
Apr 14	(h)	Eintracht Frankfurt	W	3-1
May 5	(n)	Anderlecht	L	2-4

Hammer of the Year 1975-76

TREVOR BROOKING

SEASON 1976-77
FOOTBALL LEAGUE (DIVISION 1)

Aug 21	(a)	Aston Villa	L	0-4
23	(h)	Queen's Park R	W	1-0
28	(h)	Leicester C	D	0-0
Sep 4	(a)	Stoke C	L	1-2
11	(h)	Arsenal	L	0-2
18	(a)	Bristol C	D	1-1
25	(h)	Sunderland	D	1-1
Oct 2	(a)	Manchester C	L	2-4
6	(h)	Leeds U	L	1-3
16	(h)	Ipswich T	L	0-2
23	(a)	Everton	L	2-3
30	(a)	West Brom A	L	0-3
Nov 6	(h)	Tottenham H	W	5-3
10	(a)	Norwich C	L	0-1
20	(h)	Newcastle U	L	1-2
27	(a)	Manchester U	W	2-0
Dec 4	(h)	Middlesborough	L	0-1
18	(h)	Liverpool	W	2-0
27	(a)	Birmingham C	D	0-0
Jan 1	(a)	Tottenham H	L	1-2
3	(h)	West Brom A	D	0-0
22	(h)	Aston Villa	L	0-1
Feb 5	(a)	Leicester C	L	0-2
12	(h)	Stoke C	W	1-0
19	(a)	Arsenal	W	3-2
26	(h)	Bristol C	W	2-0
Mar 5	(a)	Sunderland	L	0-6
12	(h)	Manchester C	W	1-0
22	(a)	Ipswich T	L	1-0
Apr 2	(h)	Everton	D	2-2
4	(a)	Queen's Park R	D	1-1
8	(h)	Birmingham C	D	2-2
9	(a)	Coventry C	D	1-1
11	(h)	Norwich C	W	1-0
16	(a)	Newcastle U	L	0-3
20	(a)	Derby C	D	1-1
26	(a)	Leeds U	D	1-1
29	(a)	Middlesborough	D	1-1
May 4	(h)	Coventry C	W	2-0
7	(h)	Derby C	D	2-2
14	(a)	Liverpool	D	0-0
16	(h)	Manchester U	W	4-2

P	W	D	L	F	A	W	D	L	F	A	Pts	Pos
42	9	6	6	28	23	2	8	11	18	42	36	17th

FA Cup

Jan 4	(h)	Bolton W	W	2-1
29	(a)	Aston Villa	L	0-3

League Cup

Sep 1	(h)	Barnsley	W	3-0
21	(a)	Charlton A	W	1-0
Oct 27	(h)	Queen's Park R	L	0-2

Hammer of the Year 1976-77

TREVOR BROOKING

SEASON 1977-78
FOOTBALL LEAGUE (DIVISION 1)

Aug 20	(h)	Norwich C	L	1-3
24	(a)	Leicester C	L	0-1
27	(h)	Manchester C	L	0-1
Sep 3	(a)	Newcastle U	W	3-2
10	(h)	Queen's Park R	D	2-2
17	(a)	Bristol C	L	2-3
24	(h)	Everton	D	1-1
Oct 1	(a)	Arsenal	L	0-3
3	(h)	Middlesborough	L	0-2
8	(h)	Nottingham.F	D	0-0
15	(a)	Wolves	D	2-2
22	(h)	Aston Villa	D	2-2
29	(a)	Ipswich T	W	2-0
Nov 5	(a)	Coventry C	L	0-1
12	(h)	West Brom A	D	3-3
19	(a)	Derby C	L	1-2
26	(h)	Leeds U	L	0-1
Dec 3	(a)	Liverpool	L	0-2
10	(h)	Manchester U	W	2-1
17	(a)	West Brom A	L	0-1
26	(h)	Birmingham C	W	1-0
27	(a)	Chelsea	L	1-2
31	(h)	Leicester C	W	3-2
Jan 2	(a)	Norwich C	D	2-2
14	(a)	Manchester C	L	2-3
21	(h)	Newcastle U	W	1-0
Feb 11	(h)	Bristol C	L	1-2
18	(a)	Everton	L	1-2
25	(h)	Arsenal	D	2-2
Mar 4	(a)	Nottingham F	L	0-2
11	(h)	Wolves	L	1-2
14	(a)	Queen's Park R	L	0-1
18	(a)	Aston Villa	L	1-4
24	(h)	Ipswich T	W	3-0
25	(h	Chelsea	W	3-1
28	(a)	Birmingham C	L	0-3
Apr 1	(h)	Coventry C	W	2-1
8	(a)	Leeds U	W	2-1
15	(h)	Derby C	W	3-0
22	(a)	Manchester U	L	0-3
25	(a)	Middlesborough	W	2-1

	Date	Venue	Opponent	Res	Score
	29	(h)	Liverpool	L	0-2

P	W	D	L	F	A	W	D	L	F	A	Pts	Pos
42	8	6	7	31	28	4	2	15	21	41	32	20th

FA Cup

	Date	Venue	Opponent	Res	Score
	Jan 7	(h)	Watford	W	1-0
	28	(h)	Queen's Park R	D	1-1
R	31	(a)	Queen's Park R	L	1-6

League Cup

	Date	Venue	Opponent	Res	Score
	Aug 30	(a)	Nottingham F	L	0-5

Hammer of the Year 1977-78

TREVOR BROOKING

SEASON 1978-79
FOOTBALL LEAGUE (DIVISION 2)

Date	Venue	Opponent	Res	Score
Aug 19	(h)	Notts C	W	5-2
23	(a)	Newcastle U	W	3-0
26	(a)	Crystal P	D	1-1
Sep 2	(h)	Fulham	L	0-1
9	(a)	Burnley	L	2-3
16	(h)	Bristol R	W	2-0
23	(h)	Sheffield U	W	2-0
30	(a)	Sunderland	L	1-2
Oct 7	(h)	Millwall	W	3-0
14	(a)	Oldham A	D	2-2
21	(h)	Stoke C	D	1-1
28	(a)	Brighton & HA	W	2-1
Nov 4	(h)	Preston NE	W	3-1
11	(a)	Notts C	L	0-1
18	(h)	Crystal P	D	1-1
21	(a)	Fulham	D	0-0
25	(a)	Leicester C	W	2-1
Dec 2	(h)	Cambridge U	W	5-0
9	(a)	Wrexham	L	3-4
16	(h)	Charlton A	W	2-0
26	(h)	Orient	L	0-2
30	(h)	Blackburn R	W	4-0
Jan 20	(a)	Bristol R	W	1-0
Feb 10	(h)	Sunderland	D	3-3
24	(h)	Oldham A	W	3-0
26	(a)	Luton T	W	4-1
Mar 3	(a)	Stoke C	L	0-2
10	(h)	Brighton & HA	D	0-0
17	(a)	Preston NE	D	0-0
24	(h)	Newcastle U	W	5-0
26	(h)	Leicester C	D	1-1
Apr 2	(a)	Sheffield U	L	0-3
7	(a)	Cambridge U	D	0-0
9	(h)	Luton T	W	1-0
14	(a)	Orient	W	2-0
16	(h)	Cardiff C	D	1-1
2!	(a)	Charlton A	D	0-0
24	(h)	Burnley	W	3-1
28	(h)	Wrexham	D	1-1
May 5	(a)	Blackburn R	L	0-1
11	(a)	Cardiff C	D	0-0
14	(a)	Millwall	L	1-2

P	W	D	L	F	A	W	D	L	F	A	Pts	Pos
42	12	7	2	46	15	6	7	8	24	24	50	5th

FA Cup

Date	Venue	Opponent	Res	Score
Jan 9	(a)	Newport C	L	1-2

League Cup

Date	Venue	Opponent	Res	Score
Aug 30	(h)	Swindon T	L	1-2

Hammer of the Year 1978-79

ALAN DEVONSHIRE

SEASON 1979-80
FOOTBALL LEAGUE (DIVISION 2)

Date	Venue	Opponent	Res	Score
Aug 18	(a)	Wrexham	L	0-1
20	(h)	Chelsea	L	0-1
25	(h)	Oldham A	W	1-0
Sep 1	(a)	Watford	L	0-2
8	(a)	Preston NE	D	1-1
15	(h)	Sunderland	W	2-0
22	(a)	Queen's Park R	L	0-3
29	(h)	Burnley	W	2-1
Oct 6	(h)	Newcastle U	D	1-1
13	(a)	Leicester C	W	2-1
20	(h)	Luton T	L	1-2
27	(a)	Notts C	W	1-0
Nov 3	(h)	Wrexham	W	1-0
10	(a)	Fulham	W	2-1
14	(a)	Chelsea	L	1-2
17	(h)	Swansea C	W	2-4
24	(h)	Cardiff C	W	3-4
Dec 1	(a)	Charlton A	L	0-1
8	(h)	Bristol R	W	2-1
15	(a)	Shrewsbury T	L	0-3
21	(h)	Cambridge U	W	3-1
Jan 1	(a)	Orient	W	4-0
12	(h)	Watford	D	1-1
19	(h)	Preston NE	W	2-0
Feb 9	(h)	Queen's Park R	W	2-1
19	(a)	Burnley	W	1-0
23	(h)	Leicester C	W	3-1
Mar 1	(a)	Luton T	D	1-1
11	(h)	Notts C	L	1-2
15	(a)	Newcastle U	D	0-0
22	(h)	Fulham	L	2-3
29	(a)	Swansea C	L	1-2
Apr 1	(a)	Cambridge U	L	0-2
5	(h)	Orient	W	2-0
7	(a)	Birmingham C	D	0-0
19	(a)	Cardiff C	W	1-0
22	(h)	Birmingham C	L	1-2
26	(h)	Shrewsbury T	L	1-3
29	(a)	Oldham A	D	0-0
May 3	(a)	Bristol R	W	2-0
5	(h)	Charlton A	W	4-1
12	(a)	Sunderland	L	0-2

P	W	D	L	F	A	W	D	L	F	A	Pts	Pos
42	13	2	6	37	21	7	5	9	17	22	47	7th

FA Cup

	Date	Venue	Opponent	Res	Score
	Jan 5	(a)	West Brom A	D	1-1
R	8	(h)	West Brom A	W	2-1
R	8	(h)	West Brom A	W	2-1
	26	(a)	Orient	W	3-2
	Feb 16	(h)	Swansea C	W	2-0
	Mar 8	(h)	Aston Villa	W	1-0
SF	Apr 12	(n*)	Everton	D	1-1
R	16	(n**)	Everton	W	2-1
F	May 10	(n***)	Arsenal	W	1-0

*Played at Villa Park, Birmingham
**Played at Elland Road, Leeds
***Played at Wembley Stadium

League Cup

	Date	Venue	Opponent	Res	Score
	Aug 28	(h)	Barnsley	W	3-1
	Sep 4	(a)	Barnsley	W	2-0
	25	(h)	Southend U	D	1-1
R	Oct 1	(a)	Southend U	D	0-0
2R	8	(h)	Southend U	W	5-1
	31	(a)	Sunderland	D	1-1
R	Nov 5	(h)	Sunderland	W	2-1
	Dec 4	(h)	Nottingham F	D	0-0
R	12	(a)	Nottingham F	L	0-3

Hammer of the Year 1979-80

ALVIN MARTIN

SEASON 1980-81
FOOTBALL LEAGUE (DIVISION 2)

Date	Venue	Opponent	Res	Score
Aug 16	(h)	Luton T	L	1-2
19	(a)	Bristol C	D	1-1
23	(a)	Preston NE	D	0-0
30	(h)	Notts C	W	4-0
Sep 6	(a)	Chelsea	W	1-0
13	(h)	Shrewsbury T	W	3-0
20	(h)	Watford	W	3-2
27	(a)	Cambridge U	W	2-1
Oct 4	(a)	Newcastle U	D	0-0
7	(h)	Cardiff C	W	1-0
11	(h)	Blackburn R	W	2-0
18	(a)	Oldham A	D	0-0
25	(h)	Bolton W	W	2-1
Nov 1	(a)	Bristol R	W	1-0
8	(h)	Grimsby T	W	2-1
11	(h)	Bristol C	W	5-0
15	(a)	Luton T	L	2-3
22	(h)	Swansea C	W	2-0
26	(a)	Derby C	L	0-2
29	(a)	Wrexham	D	2-2
Dec 6	(h)	Sheffield W	W	2-1
13	(a)	Blackburn R	D	0-0
20	(h)	Derby C	W	3-1
26	(a)	Queen's Park R	L	0-3
27	(h)	Orient	W	2-1
Jan 10	(a)	Swansea C	W	3-1
17	(a)	Notts C	D	1-1
31	(h)	Preston NE	W	5-0
Feb 7	(a)	Shrewsbury T	W	2-0
14	(h)	Chelsea	W	4-0
21	(h)	Cambridge U	W	4-2
28	(a)	Watford	W	2-1
Mar 7	(h)	Newcastle U	W	1-0
21	(h)	Oldham A	D	1-1
28	(a)	Bolton W	D	1-1
Apr 4	(h)	Bristol R	W	2-0
11	(a)	Grimsby T	W	5-1
18	(a)	Orient	W	2-0
21	(h)	Queen's Park R	W	3-0
May 2	(h)	Wrexham	W	1-0
6	(a)	Cardiff C	D	0-0
8	(a)	Sheffield W	W	1-0

P	W	D	L	F	A	W	D	L	F	A	Pts	Pos
42	19	1	1	53	12	9	9	3	26	17	66	1st

FA Cup

	Date	Venue	Opponent	Res	Score
	Jan 3	(h)	Wrexham	D	1-1
R	6	(a)	Wrexham	D	0-0
2R	19	(a)	Wrexham	L	0-1

League Cup

	Date	Venue	Opponent	Res	Score
	Aug 26	(a)	Burnley	W	2-0
	Sep 2	(h)	Burnley	W	4-0
	23	(a)	Charlton A	W	2-1
	Oct 28	(h)	Barnsley	W	2-1
	Dec 2	(h)	Tottenham H	W	1-0
SF	Jan 27	(a)	Coventry C	L	2-3
	Feb 10	(h)	Coventry C	W	2-0
F	Mar 14	(n*)	Liverpool	D	1-1
R	Apr 1	(n**)	Liverpool	L	1-2

*Played at Wembley Stadium
**Played at Villa Park, Birmingham

F.A. Charity Sheild

Date	Venue	Opponent	Res	Score
Aug 9	(n)	Liverpool	L	0-1

European Cup-Winners' Cup

Date	Venue	Opponent	Res	Score
Sep 17	(a)	Castilla	L	1-3
Oct 1	(h)	Castilla	W	5-1
Oct 22	(h)	Poli Timisoara	W	4-0
Nov 5	(a)	Poli Timisoara	L	0-1
Mar 4	(h)	Dynamo Tbilisi	L	1-4
Mar 18	(a)	Dynamo Tbilisi	W	1-0

Hammer of the Year 1980-81

PHIL PARKES

SEASON 1981-82
FOOTBALL LEAGUE (DIVISION 1)

Date	Venue	Opponent	Res	Score
Aug 9	(h)	Brighton & HA	D	1-1
Sep 2	(a)	Tottenham H	W	4-0
5	(a)	Sunderland	W	2-0
12	(h)	Stoke C	W	3-2
19	(a)	West Brom A	D	0-0
22	(h)	Southampton	W	4-2
26	(h)	Liverpool	D	1-1
Oct 3	(a)	Birmingham C	D	2-2
10	(h)	Everton	D	1-1
17	(a)	Aston Villa	L	2-3
24	(a)	Notts C	D	1-1
31	(h)	Middlesborough	W	3-2
Nov 7	(a)	Nottingham F	D	0-0
21	(h)	Coventry C	W	5-2
28	(a)	Leeds U	D	3-3
Dec 5	(h)	Arsenal	L	1-2
Jan 5	(a)	Liverpool	L	0-3
16	(a)	Brighton & HA	L	0-1

Frank Lampard clashes with Liam Brady during the 1980 Cup final.

1974-1985

Hammers Scotland international right-back Ray Stewart crashes home a penalty in the 4–0 destruction of Poli Timisoara during the 1980–81 Cup Winners' Cup campaign.

27	(a)	Manchester U	L	0-1
30	(h)	West Brom A	W	3-1
Feb 2	(h)	Manchester C	D	1-1
6	(a)	Stoke C	L	1-2
13	(h)	Birmingham C	D	2-2
20	(a)	Southampton	L	1-2
27	(a)	Everton	D	0-0
Mar 2	(h)	Ipswich T	W	2-0
6	(h)	Aston Villa	D	2-2
13	(h)	Notts C	W	1-0
20	(a)	Middlesborough	W	3-2
27	(h)	Nottingham F	L	0-1
30	(a)	Swansea C	W	1-0
Apr 3	(a)	Manchester C	W	1-0
6	(h)	Wolves	W	3-1
10	(h)	Swansea C	D	1-1
13	(a)	Ipswich T	L	2-3
17	(a)	Coventry C	L	0-1
24	(h)	Leeds U	W	4-3
May 1	(a)	Arsenal	L	0-2
4	(h)	Sunderland	D	1-1
8	(h)	Manchester U	D	1-1
10	(h)	Tottenham H	D	2-2
15	(a)	Wolves	L	1-2

P	W	D	L	F	A	W	D	L	F	A	Pts	Pos
42	9	10	2	42	29	5	6	10	24	28	58	9th

FA Cup

	Jan 2	(h)	Everton	W	2-1
	23	(a)	Watford	L	0-2

League Cup

	Oct 7	(a)	Derby C	W	3-2
	27	(h)	Derby C	W	2-0
	27	(h)	Derby C	W	2-0
	Nov 10	(h)	West Brom A	D	2-2
R	24	(a)	West Brom A	D	1-1
2R	Dec 1	(h)	West Brom A	L	0-1

Hammer of the Year 1981-82

ALVIN MARTIN

SEASON 1982-83
FOOTBALL LEAGUE (DIVISION 1)

Aug 28	(h)	Nottingham F	L	1-2
31	(a)	Luton T	W	2-0
Sep 4	(a)	Sunderland	L	0-1
7	(h)	Ipswich T	D	1-1
11	(h)	Birmingham C	W	5-0
18	(a)	West Brom A	W	2-1
25	(h)	Manchester C	W	4-1
Oct 2	(a)	Arsenal	W	3-2
9	(h)	Liverpool	W	3-1
16	(a)	Southampton	L	0-3
23	(a)	Brighton & HA	L	1-3
30	(h)	Manchester U	W	3-1
Nov 6	(a)	Stoke C	L	2-5
13	(h)	Norwich C	W	1-0
20	(a)	Tottenham H	L	1-2
27	(h)	Everton	W	2-0
Dec 4	(a)	Aston Villa	L	0-1
11	(h)	Coventry C	L	0-3
18	(a)	Notts C	W	2-1
27	(h)	Swansea C	W	3-2
29	(a)	Watford	L	1-2
Jan 1	(h)	Tottenham H	W	3-0
4	(h)	Luton T	L	2-3
15	(a)	Nottingham F	L	0-1
22	(h)	West Brom A	L	0-1
Feb 5	(a)	Birmingham C	L	0-3
26	(h)	Southampton	D	1-1
Mar 5	(h)	Brighton & HA	W	2-1
12	(a)	Liverpool	L	0-3
19	(h)	Stoke C	D	1-1
22	(a)	Manchester U	L	1-2
26	(a)	Norwich C	D	1-1
Apr 2	(h)	Watford	W	2-1
5	(a)	Swansea C	W	5-1
9	(h)	Sunderland	W	2-1
16	(a)	Manchester C	L	0-2
23	(h)	Aston Villa	W	2-0
30	(a)	Everton	L	0-2
May 3	(a)	Ipswich T	W	2-1
7	(h)	Notts C	W	2-0
10	(h)	Arsenal	L	1-3
14	(a)	Coventry C	W	4-2

P	W	D	L	F	A	W	D	L	F	A	Pts	Pos
42	13	3	5	41	23	7	1	13	27	39	64	8th

FA Cup

	Jan 8	(a)	Manchester U	L	0-2

League Cup

	Oct 6	(a)	Stoke C	D	1-1
	26	(h)	Stoke C	W	2-1
	Nov 10	(a)	Lincoln C	D	1-1
R	29	(h)	Lincoln C	W	2-1
	Dec 7	(a)	Notts C	D	3-3
R	21	(h)	Notts C	W	3-0
	Jan 18	(a)	Liverpool	L	1-2

Hammer of the Year 1982-83

ALVIN MARTIN

SEASON 1983-84
FOOTBALL LEAGUE (DIVISION 1)

Aug 27	(h)	Birmingham C	W	4-0
29	(a)	Everton	W	1-0
Sep 3	(a)	Tottenham H	W	2-0
6	(h)	Leicester C	W	3-1
10	(h)	Coventry C	W	5-2
17	(a)	West Brom A	L	0-1
24	(h)	Notts C	W	3-0
Oct 1	(a)	Stoke C	L	1-3
15	(h)	Liverpool	L	1-3
22	(h)	Norwich C	D	0-0
29	(a)	Watford	D	0-0
Nov 5	(h)	Ipswich T	W	2-1
12	(a)	Wolves	w	3-0
19	(a)	Sunderland	W	1-0
27	(h)	Manchester U	D	1-1
Dec 3	(a)	Aston Villa	L	0-1
10	(h)	Arsenal	W	3-1
17	(a)	Nottingham F	L	0-3
26	(h)	Southampton	L	0-1
27	(a)	Luton T	W	1-0
31	(h)	Tottenham H	W	4-1
Jan 2	(a)	Notts C	D	2-2
14	(a)	Birmingham C	L	0-3
21	(h)	West Brom A	W	1-0
Feb 4	(h)	Stoke C	W	3-0
7	(h)	Queen's Park R	D	1-1
11	(a)	Coventry C	W	2-1
21	(h)	Watford	L	2-4
25	(a)	Norwich C	L	0-1
Mar 3	(a)	Ipswich T	W	3-0
10	(h)	Wolves	D	1-1
17	(a)	Leicester C	L	1-0
31	(h)	Queen's Park R	D	2-2
Apr 7	(a)	Liverpool	L	0-6
14	(h)	Sunderland	L	0-1
17	(h)	Luton T	W	3-1
21	(a)	Southampton	L	0-2
28	(a)	Manchester U	D	0-0
May 5	(h)	Aston Villa	L	0-1
7	(a)	Arsenal	D	3-3
12	(h)	Nottingham F	L	1-2
14	(h)	Everton	L	0-1

P	W	D	L	F	A	W	D	L	F	A	Pts	Pos
42	10	4	7	39	24	7	5	9	21	31	60	9th

FA Cup

	Jan 7	(h)	Wigan A	W	1-0
	28	(a)	Crystal P	D	1-1
R	31	(h)	Crystal P	W	2-0
	Feb 18	(a)	Birmingham C	L	0-3

League Cup

	Oct 4	(a)	Bury	W	2-1
	25	(h)	Bury	W	10-0
	Nov 8	(h)	Brighton & HA	W	1-0
	30	(h)	Everton	D	2-2
R	Dec 6	(a)	Everton	L	0-2

Hammer of the Year 1983-84

TREVOR BROOKING

SEASON 1984-85
FOOTBALL LEAGUE (DIVISION 1)

Aug 25	(h)	Ipswich T	D	0-0
27	(a)	Liverpool	L	0-3
Sep 1	(a)	Southampton	W	3-2
4	(h)	Coventry C	W	3-1
8	(h)	Watford	W	2-0
15	(a)	Chelsea	L	0-3
22	(h)	Nottingham F	D	0-0
29	(a)	Newcastle U	D	1-1
Oct 6	(h)	Leicester C	W	3-1
13	(a)	Manchester U	L	1-5
20	(a)	Stoke C	W	4-2
27	(h)	Arsenal	W	3-1
Nov- 3	(a)	Aston Villa	D	0-0
10	(h)	Everton	L	0-1
17	(h)	Sunderland	W	1-0
24	(a)	Luton T	D	2-2
Dec 1	(h)	West Brom A	L	0-2
8	(a)	Norwich C	L	0-1
15	(h)	Sheffield W	D	0-0
22	(h)	Southampton	L	2-3
6	(a)	Tottenham H	D	2-2
29	(a)	Coventry C	W	2-1
Jan 1	(h)	Queen's Park R	L	1-3
Feb 2	(h)	Newcastle U	D	1-1
23	(h)	Aston Villa	L	1-2
Mar 2	(a)	Arsenal	L	1-2
15	(h)	Manchester U	D	2-2
23	(a)	leicester C	L	0-1
30	(a)	Nottingham F	W	2-1
Apr 2	(a)	Watford	L	0-5
6	(h)	Tottenham H	D	1-1
8	(a)	Queen's Park R	L	2-4
13	(h)	Chelsea	D	1-1
20	(a)	Sunderland	W	1-0
27	(h)	Luton T	D	0-0
May 4	(a)	West Brom A	L	1-5
6	(h)	Norwich C	W	1-0
8	(a)	Everton	L	0-3
11	(a)	Sheffield W	L	1-2
14	(h)	Stoke C	W	5-1
17	(a)	Ipswich T	W	1-0
20	(h)	Liverpool	L	0-3

P	W	D	L	F	A	W	D	L	F	A	Pts	Pos
42	7	8	6	27	23	6	4	11	24	45	51	16th

FA Cup

	Jan 5	(h)	Port Vale	W	4-1
	Feb 4	(h)	Norwich C	W	2-1
	Mar 4	(a)	Wimbledon	D	1-1
R	6	(h)	Wimbledon	W	5-1
	9	(a)	Manchester U	L	2-4

League Cup

	Sep 25	(a)	Bristol C	D	2-2
	Oct 9	(h)	Bristol C	W	6-1
	31	(a)	Manchester C	D	0-0
R	Nov 6	(h)	Manchester C	L	1-2

Hammer of the Year 1984-85

PAUL ALLEN

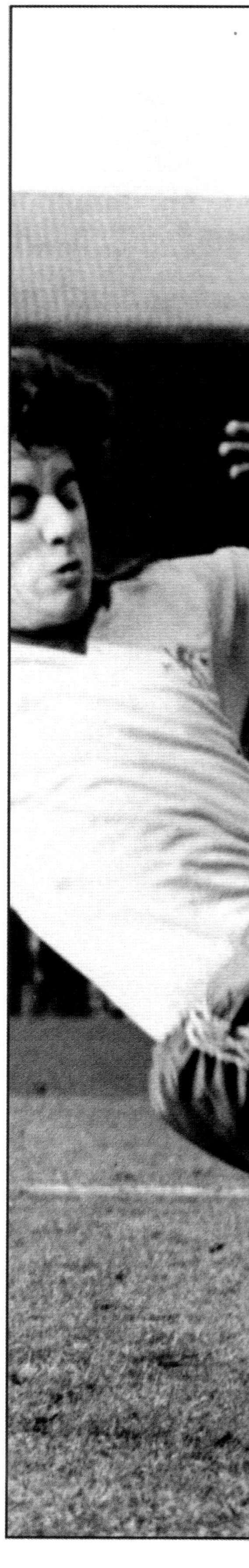

Billy Bonds during a Second Division clash against Chelsea at Upton Park on Valentine's Day, 1981.

CHAPTER 7

AN ERA OF UNCERTAINTY

'Our target is easily defined,' declared John Lyall on the eve of the 1986–87 season, 'we have to carry on where we left off.' Hammers had, of course, 'left off' the previous campaign in third position in the First Division – their best ever top-flight finish. Lyall tried to bring in new talent, but told reporters in November: 'We never spend money just for the sake of doing so. It is all a question of whether a player we feel will fill the bill becomes available at the price we are ready to pay.' It was a common-sense approach, but the logic of Lyall's argument would do little to placate fans who had watched as rivals made expensive signings during the close season.

Head start for Ince

All criticism of the Club's transfer policy was temporarily forgotten, though, when the Hammers made an uncharacteristically bright start to their League campaign. A Tony Gale free-kick from the edge of the area was enough to earn all three points from the opening fixture against Coventry City at Upton Park, and two days later a trip to Manchester United also ended in victory – two goals from Frank McAvennie and one from Alan Devonshire securing a 3–2 scoreline. A goalless draw at Oxford United followed and, when the first League tables were published, West Ham United occupied third place.

Hammers' form faltered during the remainder of 1986, however, and by the turn of the year the East Londoners had slipped down to 12th in the table. Injuries and suspensions would hinder Lyall's efforts throughout the season and the manager was frequently unable to name his preferred eleven. The previously prolific Frank McAvennie was struggling to find his goal touch and a run of nine games without a League goal had done little to enhance Hammers' League position. McAvennie's strike partner Tony Cottee was at least finding the net with regularity, scoring 11 times in the first 22 League games. Cottee would also shoot Hammers to the last eight of the League Cup, netting four goals in four games as West Ham United progressed past Preston, Watford and Oxford to earn a quarter-final tie against Spurs at Upton Park. There were other 'pluses' for Lyall too, not least the emergence of talented youngsters Steve Potts, Kevin Keen and Paul Ince, who all made their debuts in the West Ham United starting line-up during 1986. Ince had looked the most impressive of the newcomers, marking his first full appearance with a brilliant diving header past Southampton goalkeeper Peter Shilton in a 3–1 win at Upton Park.

Paul Goddard was sold to struggling Newcastle United in November for £415,000. Lyall had not wanted to release Goddard, but after a year spent watching Cottee and McAvennie from the sidelines, he was keen to move on in an effort to find first-team football. The sale of Goddard meant that there were only two strikers with any first-team experience in the Hammers squad. But, despite this glaring weakness, Lyall choose to invest the bulk of his transfer fund in a midfielder – signing Arsenal's Stewart Robson for £600,000 – rather than a forward. Robson was a highly rated and versatile performer who had twice been named in the England squad, but he arrived at Upton Park having only recently recovered from a serious pelvic injury. 'This has been a difficult year, but I am on my way back,' declared Hammers' new signing. 'I like West Ham's style and the way the club is run.'

Left: New Hammers manager Lou Macari meets the press outside the Boleyn Ground in 1989. Macari's Upton Park reign was to last just seven months, ending in traumatic fashion in February 1990.

Robson's debut came in a League match at Coventry City, but it was Tony Cottee who stole the show at Highfield Road, scoring a hat-trick in a 3–1 win to take his tally against the Sky Blues to ten goals in nine games. Cottee was again on target three days later when Hammers took on fifth-placed Tottenham Hotspur in the League Cup quarter-final at Upton Park. This time, though, the striker's goal was only enough to earn his team a draw and a replay at White Hart Lane. Lyall's plans for the return match were hit by another bout of injuries and with both Steve Walford and Alan Dickens out of action Neil Orr and 40-year-old Billy Bonds were recalled. For Bonds it was yet another remarkable comeback – he had been absent from the starting line-up for 18 months.

But there was little that even Bonzo could do to stop rampant Spurs, who opened the scoring after just five minutes and completed a 5–0 rout with four goals in the last 19 minutes. February would also see Hammers eliminated from the FA Cup following a 2–0 home defeat against Sheffield Wednesday – the same opponents who had knocked Lyall's team out of the Cup in 1986. It was the first time West Ham United had lost an FA Cup tie at Upton Park since 1976, but Lyall refused to dwell on the defeat and told *Hammers News*: 'Every team wants to finish in the top six and that must now be our aim for the rest of this season... it is up to us to lift ourselves and start playing.'

Below: Paul Ince marks his first appearance in the Hammers starting line-up by scoring with this diving header against Southampton in December 1986. Ince was one of precious few players to emerge through the Club's junior ranks during the late 1980s.

Brady chooses Hammers

Alas, the manager's rallying cry fell on deaf ears and, following their double Cup elimination, Hammers embarked upon a run of five consecutive defeats and in March the Hammers boss entered the transfer market once more – signing Lincoln Town skipper Gary Strodder and Aberdeen full-back Tom McQueen in an effort to bolster his rearguard. But it was the purchase of former Arsenal midfielder Liam Brady which attracted most attention. Brady had spent seven years playing in Italy and although he was now 31 years old, he remained a gifted playmaker, and at a fee of £100,000 there was interest from several other First Division clubs. But Brady was in no doubt where he wanted to play out his career. 'West Ham were my first choice,' declared the talented Dubliner. 'I have always admired West Ham because they try to play the same way regardless of whether they win trophies. They are having a bad time right now but they have some fine players and a win will start things going.' That win did eventually arrive, in a home match against Watford at the end of March, but it failed to trigger a revival and for the remainder of the season Hammers were unable to establish any consistent form. The only consolation for the fans was that both of West Ham United's victories in April came against London rivals.

Billy Bonds greets fellow midfield veteran Liam Brady who joined the Hammers from Italian club Ascoli in March 1987. Brady would prove a popular figure with the Upton Park faithful, making 89 League appearances for the Club before retiring as a player at the end of the 1989–90 season.

However, despite the glory of victories over Arsenal and Spurs, Hammers' League position remained unaltered and at season's end the Club occupied a disappointing 15th place. To the supporters, it seemed unfathomable that the fluent, exciting line-up which had finished third in the spring of 1986 had now metamorphosed into a disjointed, struggling team in the space of just 12 months. Two factors had contributed to Hammers' decline. Firstly, Frank McAvennie had not been able to emulate his goalscoring form of 1985–86 (he ended the season with just seven League goals compared to 26 a year before), and secondly, a spate of injuries had exposed the lack of depth in the first-team squad. The fragility of Lyall's playing resources was clearly apparent by the fact that he had needed to call upon Billy Bonds, who was supposedly semi-retired, to make 17 League appearances. It would be wrong, though, to write off Bonds as a mere has-been, and such was the quality of his play that he was voted Hammer of the Year and rewarded with a new one-year contract. Lyall said of Bonds: 'He is such a great competitor and so committed in his attitude to training and playing that his value to the side is immense.'

Another player whose value to the side was undeniable was Tony Cottee, who had enjoyed his best season in front of goal (scoring 28 times in all competitions), so it was with shock and concern that most Hammers fans learned that the 21-year-old striker had submitted a written transfer request. 'This was my way of showing John Lyall and the club how frustrated I was that their ambitions did not seem to me like they matched my own,' wrote Cottee in his autobiography, *Claret and Blues*, in 1995. Fortunately, Lyall was able to convince his star striker that the 'grass isn't always greener' and Cottee withdrew the transfer request. There would, though, be one departure from Upton Park in the summer of 1987. Geoff Pike had given the Hammers sterling service during an 11-year spell with the club, but following the arrival of Stewart Robson – who had been bought to take over the midfield anchor role – he decided that the time was right to move on and joined Notts County in a £50,000 deal. Another player on his way out of E13 was utility man Neil Orr who signed for Hibernian shortly after the start of the season. Despite these departures, John Lyall was in confident mood on the eve of the Football League's centenary season. The Hammers manager was still able to call upon 23 players with first-team experience, and told reporters it was the 'strongest squad I can recall,' before adding: 'While there are no guarantees we should have every hope of regaining a top six place this season.'

The Bhoy McAvennie departs

Unfortunately, John Lyall's hopes were not to be realised, though, and West Ham United began their League programme in disastrous fashion; after ten games they found themselves in familiar territory, hovering just above the relegation zone in 17th place. Lyall attempted to avert a further slide down the table by employing Paul Ince as a sweeper, but the manager's most urgent problem was in the forward line rather than the defence. After much speculation and rumours in the newspapers of a rift with Tony Cottee (which have always been denied), Frank McAvennie was sold to Celtic for £750,000. It was at that time the biggest transfer fee received by the club and represented a significant profit on a player who had cost £340,000 in 1985 and who had failed to find the net in any of his last 13 games. 'We are after a replacement as soon as possible... but it's all a question of valuation and availability,' declared the Hammers boss. Meanwhile, midfielder Alan Dickens was redeployed to play alongside Tony Cottee in attack.

Despite their makeshift strikeforce, Hammers enjoyed their best League form of the season during November and December – winning three home matches and drawing away at both Chelsea and Coventry to move up to tenth place in the First Division by Christmas. The League Cup, though, had ended in disappointment with a 5–2 extra-time defeat against Barnsley at Upton Park. The game had been played out before a meagre crowd of just 12,403 and, at half-time, Hammers had led 2–0 only to surrender their advantage in the second period before collapsing in extra time. It was too much for many fans to bear and after the game there was an impromptu demonstration calling for Lyall to resign.

The New Year brought no better luck in cup competition and although West Ham United started their FA Cup campaign in good style – winning 2–0 win away to Charlton Athletic – a fourth-round defeat against Queens Park Rangers at Loftus Road left them with only First Division survival to play for during the remainder of the season.

As the March transfer deadline day loomed, John Lyall did eventually manage to sign a forward, but his transfer capture was not the type of high-profile proven striker that the fans had been craving for. Tony Cottee's new strike-partner was to be Leroy Rosenior, a £275,000 buy from Fulham, who had already netted 20 League goals for the Cottagers during 1987–88. Rosenior proved an immediate success for the Hammers, scoring the only goal of the game on his debut against Watford at Upton Park to give West Ham United their first win for more than two months. The new boy was again on target in the next two matches – away fixtures against Manchester United and Sheffield Wednesday – unfortunately, both of these games ended in defeat.

Above: Plaistow-born Midfielder Alan Dickens made his Hammers debut in 1982, but it it was not until 1984–85 that he won a regular place in John Lyall's line-up. Expectations, however, were sky high for Alan who was charged with the impossible task of filling the number-ten shirt which had so long been worn by Trevor Brooking.

Dicks signs

After the game at Hillsborough Billy Bonds told reporters: 'We are in the mire. We've enough ability but we lack confidence.' One player who Lyall hoped would help improve the Hammers' self-belief was new signing Julian Dicks, who had made his debut against Wednesday following a £300,000 move from Birmingham City. Dicks had been bought to play at left-back, a position which had become something of a problem since the departure of Frank Lampard in 1985. But even with their new number three in the team, Hammers were unable to win any of their six matches in April and with just two games to play they were in 18th place, facing the prospect of a play-off match to maintain their First Division status. The penultimate fixture of the season brought fellow strugglers Chelsea to Upton Park. Only a win would do for the Hammers, and Lyall's patched-up team did not disappoint, winning 4–1. West Ham United completed their League programme with a trip to Newcastle United and could only be relegated if they lost by more than seven goals and Chelsea drew their match with Charlton Athletic. It was a very unlikely prospect, but Lyall was taking no chances and named Phil Parkes as a substitute – the first time a goalkeeper had fulfilled such a role in Football League history.

Right: In March 1988 Hammers boss John Lyall paid Birmingham City £300,000 for 19-year-old left-back Julian Dicks. The Bristol-born defender would become one of the most popular players in West Ham United history.

Fortunately, Parkes was able to remain on the bench and the match ended in a 2–1 defeat which left Hammers safe by virtue of goal difference.

'It has easily been the worst season since I took over,' confessed Lyall. 'The trouble has been that countless injuries have stopped us from naming a full strength team... it has been a nightmare, and I don't want another season like it.' But the summer of 1988 brought no end to Lyall's problems, and shortly after the end of the season it became clear that Tony Cottee would be leaving Upton Park. The England striker quickly became the subject of feverish transfer speculation and eventually joined Everton in a record-breaking £2m deal at the end of July. This time, though, the Hammers boss did at least have a replacement lined up; paying £600,000 to sign promising Walsall striker David Kelly. Both Spurs and Bayern Munich had been chasing Kelly, who Lyall described as 'the most exciting player outside the top division.' But the prolific Midlander had opted to come to Upton Park, as had Celtic reserve team keeper Allen McKnight, who arrived in a £250,000 deal. Lyall was optimistic about the prospects for both new signings and wrote in West Ham United's handbook for 1988–89 that 'in young David Kelly and Allen McKnight, I believe we have signed two very promising prospects who have the ability to serve this club well for many seasons to come.' One player who had already given the club sterling service was Billy Bonds who, at the age of 41 had decided to call a halt to his playing career and take up a position on the Hammers coaching staff. 'That's it. I won't be playing again and this time I mean it,' declared Bonds.

In the space of just two years the Hammers' line-up which had finished third in 1986 had all but disappeared. Cottee, McAvennie, Orr, Walford and Pike had departed, while Devonshire's influence was waning and Parkes was struggling to contend with advancing years and persistent knee trouble. Lyall, though, remained upbeat: 'Let us look forward to better things in the season ahead. In many ways it is the dawning of a new era,' wrote the Upton Park boss on the eve of the 1988–89 season.

However, a run of four consecutive defeats left the Club bottom of the table at the start of October. On 22 October Hammers clashed with struggling Newcastle United at Upton Park in a match which already carried the 'six-pointer tag'. A predictably tense first half ended goalless, but, in the second period, quick thinking from Alan Devonshire created a goal for Alan Dickens and, with nine minutes to play, Ray Stewart completed the scoring with a penalty won by Stuart Slater. The result lifted Hammers to the dizzy heights of 18th place. However, the ascent up the table was to be shortlived and, with just one win in the next 11 League games, the club was soon back at the foot of the table.

Ince sees off Liverpool

The League Cup did at least provide a welcome distraction from First Division struggle and, with the pressure off, Lyall's team responded with some of their best performances in an otherwise disappointing season. Sunderland had provided the opposition in the second-round, and a 5–1 aggregate victory earned West Ham United a home tie against Champions Liverpool. The pundits gave Hammers no chance against Kenny Dalglish's Reds, but Lyall's team had clearly not read the script for a match which would see Paul Ince give his finest display in claret and blue. The 21-year-old midfielder fired in the opening goal with a superb volley after 21 minutes and followed up with a header three minutes later. Liverpool struck back via an Aldridge penalty but a Steve Staunton own goal and a strike from the fit-again Tony Gale gave Hammers a well-deserved 4–1 victory and a place in the quarter-finals. It was Liverpool's heaviest Cup defeat since the War, but it was the performance of Ince which caught the headlines. 'This lad [Ince] will surely play for England by the end of the season,' eulogised Lyall after the game.

Hammers' victory over Liverpool was followed by a 1–0 win against bitter rivals Millwall at the Den. But at the turn of the year the club were firmly rooted to the bottom of the First Division, and John Lyall was coming under increasing pressure from the terraces. Tony Gale told *Hammers News* that the cat-calls were premature: 'It's hard for the fans... but I hope they can be patient because I think we'll soon be back on the right track... It hurts when you hear them shout things like "Lyall Out" and "One McAvennie".' But Lyall was not the only target for Hammers' hecklers, and new signings Allen McKnight and David Kelly soon came under fire too. 'They were on a hiding to nothing,' remembers Tony Gale: 'They were seen as replacements for two exceptional players – David taking over from Tony Cottee and Allen coming in for Phil Parkes – and they could only fail. Allen actually started very well, but then he made a few mistakes, his confidence began to go and the crowd got on his back. The situation was also made worse because his rickets always seemed to happen in televised games.'

Leroy's golden goal

Cup football would continue to offer Hammers' only respite from the pressures of the relegation battle, although an FA Cup third round tie against League leaders Arsenal at Upton Park hardly seemed an opportunity to rebuild flagging confidence. But, just as they had done against Liverpool in the League Cup, Hammers belied their lowly position to take a two-goal lead. Arsenal, though, were dogged opponents and struck back with a goal in each half from Paul Merson to level

In his efforts to save Hammers from relegation, John Lyall paid Celtic £1.2m to secure the return of fans' favourite Frank McAvennie in March 1989. It was a last, desperate throw of the dice and one which was destined to fail. McAvennie made nine appearances in 1988–89, failing to score in any of them, and Hammers were relegated.

the scores and take the tie to a replay at Highbury three days later. 'Hammers have had their chance', carped the experts. 'This time the Gunners will prevail'. The second meeting proved a tense encounter and at half-time the game was still goalless. Lyall's team was growing in confidence, though, and with just 13 minutes left to play, Leroy Rosenior ghosted into the penalty area to take advantage of an error from Tony Adams and score the game's only goal with a superb header.

Victory against Arsenal was followed by Hammers' first League win of the year, with goals from Kelly and Brady securing a 2–1 success against Derby County at the Baseball Ground. Four days later Lyall's team completed a hat-trick of victories when they defeated Aston Villa 2–1 in a League Cup quarter-final at the Boleyn Ground. However, Hammers' good run was to come to a disappointing end in the next match when mistakes from Allen McKnight proved decisive in a 3–1 reverse against Manchester United at Upton Park. The rookie keeper responded to this set-back with clean sheets in his next two appearances – both against Swindon Town in the FA Cup fourth round – but his confidence had been damaged and his errors would again prove costly in a 2–1 defeat at Highbury on 4 February. Hammers' next fixture was the first leg of the League Cup semi-final against Luton Town at Upton Park, and there was much media speculation that Lyall was set to recall veteran custodian Phil Parkes. In the end the manager kept faith with McKnight, but it was a decision which he would soon regret, as in the space of ten second-half minutes the young keeper was twice beaten on his near post. Hammers crashed to a 3–0 defeat and after the match McKnight told reporters: 'I feel happier playing away. There are too many hecklers out there. It's a pity when your own fans turn against you.' The Northern Ireland international keeper would never play at Upton Park again. Thirty-eight-year-old Phil Parkes was recalled for the second leg of the semi-final on Luton Town's infamous plastic pitch, but Hammers were unable to master the difficult conditions and crashed out of the competition 5–0 on aggregate.

It was a huge disappointment to both fans and players that the club had fallen when so close to Wembley, but they were in the last eight of the FA Cup and had a home tie against Norwich City. The Canaries were in second place in the First Division and were the undoubted favourites to progress to the semi-finals, but Hammers matched the East Anglians at the Boleyn Ground and the game ended in a goalless draw. Four days later the two teams reconvened at Carrow Road, where Norwich ran out comfortable 3–1 victors. Hammers now had only their League status to play for and, with just 13 matches left to play, time was fast running out.

Frank McAvennie returns

As transfer deadline day approached, Lyall made his last throw of the dice. Hammers had lacked a proven goalscorer all season and, in the eyes of the fans, there was only one man who could fill the gap. Frank McAvennie had been a hugely popular during his first spell at Upton Park and in March 1989, he returned for a club record £1.2m fee. Arsenal had also been keen, but Frank opted to rejoin the Hammers, and when asked why he had signed for a club at the foot of the table McAvennie simply said: 'They won't be [there] at the end of the season,' before adding 'perhaps my arrival has given the club the lift it needs.' West Ham United's most expensive player made his second debut for the club away to Aston Villa, but it was Paul Ince who took the plaudits at Villa Park. The promising midfielder picked up the ball in his own half and carried it forward for more than 50 yards, before despatching a long-range shot past the Villa keeper to earn Hammers their first League win for two months. Welcome as this result was, it was not enough to lift the club off the foot of the table, and a disastrous run of four defeats in the next five games did nothing to enhance West Ham United's survival prospects.

But with seven games remaining Lyall was not about to give up, and for the home match against Millwall the manager moved Julian Dicks into the middle of the defence alongside Tony Gale. It proved a master stroke and the converted full-back gave a superb display, even venturing forward to score the opening goal in a 3–0 win for Hammers. It was the start of a run of four consecutive victories which lifted the club to 19th place and gave the fans hope that there might yet be a remarkable recovery. However, the winning sequence came to an end at Goodison Park where Everton came back from an early goal from Stuart Slater to win 3–1. Hammers had two games left to play and would need to win both of them to have any chance of survival. The penultimate fixture took Lyall's team to third-placed Nottingham Forest where a goal from Leroy Rosenior after just 19 seconds gave West Ham United the perfect start. Rosenior was again on target 17 minutes later and, although Lee Chapman struck back with a goal before half-time, Hammers held on to win 2–1.

Relegation heartache

With one game left the situation was simple. West Ham United had to win against title-chasing Liverpool to send Aston Villa down. If they did not claim all three points at Anfield they would be relegated themselves. Hammers made a good start to the game, and though they went a goal down after 20 minutes, they struck back quickly, with Rosenior scoring his fourth goal in as many matches. For the remainder of the first-half it was impossible to tell which team were title favourites and which relegation tips. But when Paul Ince failed to emerge for the second half, following a heavy challenge with Steve McMahon, Hammers began to fade. The eventual 5–1 scoreline undoubtedly flattered the Reds, but the inescapable fact was that West Ham United were relegated. Liverpool manager Kenny Dalglish offered words of encouragement to his devastated opponents. 'Personally I think they are a great club and it's a disappointment that they have to go out of the First Division.'

It had been a disastrous season for West Ham United and John Lyall told reporters: 'Our best form came too late in the season. We had some problems in fielding a settled side through injuries, but in the end we have to look at our home form in particular and realise we just didn't get enough points at Upton Park.' It was the third time that the club had been relegated in its 94-year history, but this time the board of directors took unprecedented action in an effort to ensure a swift promotion. At the end of the season John Lyall's contract had come to an end, but after 15 years in charge, the First Division's longest serving manager could not have anticipated what was about to come. On Monday 5 June, Lyall was informed that his contract would not be renewed. For the first time in 27 years West Ham United had sacked their manager. Lyall was one of the most popular men in football and his departure shocked both players and staff. 'When I found out about John leaving the club, it really felt like there had been a death in the family,' remembers Tony Gale. 'John had run the club from top to bottom, but football was changing. I personally think that Upton Park is a worse place without John Lyall.'

Above: Lou Macari's ill-fated tenure as Hammers boss came to an unceremonious end when he left the Club shortly after the 6–0 League Cup semi-final defeat against Oldham in February 1989.

Below: Lou Macari's final transfer deal as Hammers manager was to sign Czech international keeper Ludek Miklosko from Banik Ostrava for £300,000 in January 1990. Ludo, who was named Hammer of the Year in his first full season at Upton Park, was one of West Ham United's most consistent performers throughout the 1990s.

Macari: The Outsider pt II

There was much speculation about who would succeed Lyall in the Upton Park hotseat, with both Billy Bonds and Tony Carr strongly tipped to take over. However, the board opted to bring in an outsider – just as they had done with Ron Greenwood in 1961 – and appointed Swindon Town boss Lou Macari. The new boss was quick to dismiss claims that he was a 'long-ball coach' and he told reporters: 'You play to your strengths, which at Swindon had to be fitness and the will to win.' But as Macari settled in to his new job, it was his man-management skills rather than tactical brain that was most in demand. Several Hammers players had been unsettled by the combination of relegation and Lyall's sacking. Among those unhappy in E13 were: Paul Ince, who was reigning Hammer of the Year; England international Alvin Martin; and midfielders Mark Ward and Alan Dickens. Macari would struggle to hang on to this talented quartet and Ince, in particular, would provide the new West Ham United manager with an especially tricky problem. The promising midfielder had long been linked with a move to Manchester United and during the summer of 1989 a photo of him in a Red Devils kit appeared in *The Sun* newspaper. It was an incident which would anger Hammers' supporters who would never forgive Ince for wearing the shirt of another team while still a West Ham United player. The move to Old Trafford did eventually materialise, but the fee proved to be something of a disappointment. The Hammers had wanted £2m for their midfield protegee, but, when a routine medical found an apparently worrying hip injury, the price was reduced to just £800,000 plus additional payments of £5,000 per game for the next five years.

Ince made his final appearance in claret and blue away to Stoke City in the opening game of the 1989–90 season. The match proved largely forgettable, but was marred when a second-half challenge from City's Chris Kamara left Frank McAvennie with a broken leg. McAvennie would be absent from Hammers' starting line-up for the remainder of the League campaign. It was a bitter blow for Macari, whose plans had already been hit by the sale of Alan Dickens and the impending departure of Paul Ince. 'I have got no magic wand, which can transpose last season's failure into success,' wrote the new Hammers boss in his programme notes for the season's first game at the Boleyn Ground. 'All I can do is generate the enthusiasm for everyone to work hard... My intention is to knock a group of good players into a good team, which is not what they were last season for one reason or another.'

The manager was also beginning to bring in new players with the money earned from the sale of Alan Dickens (who joined Chelsea for £600,000) and Ince. First to sign was Queens Park Rangers midfielder Martin Allen, who arrived in a £600,000 deal and marked his debut at home to Plymouth with a headed goal in a 3–2 victory. Central defender Colin Foster, a £750,000 buy from Nottingham Forest, was next to join and he too enjoyed a winning start to his Upton Park career when a penalty from skipper Julian Dicks earned a 1–0 victory at home to Watford. Hammers' next fixture also ended in a 1–0 win, with Leroy Rosenior, who was making his first appearance of the season, scoring the only of the goal of the game after 89 minutes. It was a victory which took West Ham United second in the League table, but successive defeats against West Bromwich Albion and Leeds United dropped Macari's team back down to tenth position.

Bishop and Morley arrive

In November Macari signed former Nottingham Forest forward Justin Fashanu on a short-term loan deal. In December came Jimmy Quinn, Ian Bishop and Trevor Morley. Bishop, a midfielder, and Morley, a striker, arrived from Manchester City in a £1m swap deal which saw Mark Ward travel in the opposite direction, while much-travelled centre-forward Quinn signed from Bradford City. All three players made their home debuts in a 3–2 win against Barnsley on New Year's Day – Hammers' first League victory in six weeks – and the trio were also included in the team which travelled to Fourth Division Torquay United for the third round of the FA Cup five days later. However, the trip to Devon was to prove an unmitigated disaster. Prior to the game the FA announced that they were to investigate allegations made against Macari concerning his spell in charge at Swindon Town, and on a muddy Plainmoor pitch Hammers crashed to a humiliating 1–0 defeat to compound the manager's misery.

Hammers were still in with a chance of Wembley glory, having for the second year in succession reached the quarter-finals of the League Cup. In typical style they shrugged off the disappointment of their FA Cup debacle with victory in their twice-replayed quarter-final against First Division Derby County. Second Division rivals Oldham Athletic would provide Hammers' opposition in the semi-final, and Macari's men travelled to Lancashire for the first leg on the Latic's notorious plastic pitch in confident mood, buoyed by a 3–1 victory over Brighton and Hove Albion four days earlier. However, Tony Gale remembers that the manager, who was by now coming under increasing pressure as a result of an alleged betting scandal at Swindon, made a surprising change for the game. 'Macari decided to play five at the back against Oldham, but we really weren't happy playing that system. We'd been playing 4-4-2 all season and I felt that by using five defenders we would hand the initiative to Oldham, which would make life very awkward on their plastic pitch.' It is difficult to assess the bearing that this tactical switch had on the result, but it was undoubtedly a factor in a game which finished with a crushing 6–0 defeat for the Hammers.

Billy Bonds, seen here collecting one of his three Barclays Manager of the Month awards during 1990–91, made a bright start to his managerial career, leading Hammers to promotion in his first full season in charge.

Bonzo takes charge

West Ham United's next match was away to Lou Macari's former club Swindon Town. But the Hammers boss failed to make the team coach for the game at the County Ground, and in his absence Billy Bonds assumed control. Two goals from Jimmy Quinn and some excellent goalkeeping from Czech international Ludek Miklosko, who was making his debut following a £300,000 move from Banik Ostrava, earned Hammers a share of the points. However, all the talk after the game was of management changes rather than goals and saves, and the following day the club announced that Macari had tendered his resignation. Ronnie Boyce was put in temporary charge and

speculation mounted as to who would get the job on a permanent basis. This time, the board wasted little time deliberating and, after the failure of 'Macari the outsider', they opted for Billy Bonds. It was a move which was popular with both players and supporters. 'There was a round of applause in the dressing room when we were told the news,' remembers Tony Gale.

The managerial career of Billy Bonds began with a 1–1 draw at home to Blackburn Rovers, with in-form striker Jimmy Quinn grabbing Hammers' goal. The next match, away to Middlesbrough, brought Hammers' first away win in the League since October and did much to build confidence ahead of the League Cup semi-final second leg against Oldham Athletic. With the Latics holding a six-goal advantage – which Bonds described as an 'insurmountable deficit' – Hammers had only pride to play for, but they nevertheless produced a fluent display to win 3–0.

West Ham United had fallen to 14th place when Billy Bonds took charge, but the new manager quickly renewed his team's self-belief and they made a spirited ascent up the table to challenge for a play-off place. Three consecutive victories at the start of April gave hope, but defeats by Oldham and Newcastle proved costly and, although they won seven of their last 12 games, Hammers finished in seventh place just two points adrift of the play-off zone. Despite this disappointment, the closing stages of the 1989–90 season had given much cause for optimism. Trevor Morley had found his goal touch, scoring nine times in the last 14 games, and Hammers had also recorded an impressive 5–0 victory over First Division-bound Sheffield United. The season had ended in fine style too, with a 4–0 win against Wolves at Upton Park, in which Liam Brady signed-off his playing career with a scintillating long-range goal on a sunny afternoon at Upton Park.

The summer of 1990 brought the dawn of a new era in British football. The exploits of Bobby Robson's England team at Italia 90 would see soccer return to fashion. West Ham United were also entering a new era. The Hammers had a new chairman, Martin Cearns, and a new manager, and were working on plans to redevelop the Boleyn Ground to comply with the Taylor Report. The net result of this change in E13 was a growing mood of optimism, which provided support for the bookmakers' view that West Ham United were favourites for promotion in 1990–91.

Above: Midfield playmaker Ian Bishop arrived at Upton Park, along with striker Trevor Morley, in a £1m swap deal which took Mark Ward to Manchester City in December 1989. Bishop would quickly become one of the most popular and influential players at the Club.

Left: Hammers skipper Julian Dicks began the 1990–91 season in excellent form, scoring three times in the first ten matches. However, in the next game, away to Bristol City the powerful left-back suffered a cruciate ligament injury which would sideline him for more than a year.

Hammers on promotion trail

After an uncertain start, Hammers finally revealed their true potency with a 7–1 victory over Hull City at Upton Park on 6 October. Both Julian Dicks and Jimmy Quinn scored twice against Hull, but the game will always be remembered for Steve Potts' first goal in senior football. 'People were just getting out of my way,' remembers the versatile defender. 'I got to the edge of the box and the shot wasn't the best, but the keeper did me a huge favour and let it in. I've taken loads of stick since then, but a second goal would be nice and it would take the pressure off too.' But the elation of the emphatic win against Hull was short lived and the following week disaster struck at Ashton Gate where Hammers' skipper Julian Dicks sustained a serious knee injury. Remarkably, Dicks played out the rest of the game, which finished in a 1–1 draw, and was even in the line-up for the next two matches. However, the combative and skilful left-back was unable to complete the 90 minutes in either game and shortly afterwards the full extent of his knee injury became apparent. He had ruptured the cruciate ligament in his left knee and would be out of the game for more than a year.

Ian Bishop, who was becoming an increasingly influential presence in Hammers' midfield, assumed the captaincy from Dicks, and the long-haired Liverpudlian led the team out for the first time when Charlton Athletic visited Upton Park on 27 October. Two long-distance goals from Martin Allen proved enough to earn all three points against the Robins. It was a third successive League win for West Ham United, who were now up to second place in the table and playing with great assurance. The undoubted key to Hammers' success was the fortitude of their defence. Goalkeeper Ludek Miklosko was in breathtaking form, conceding just 12 goals in the first 20 games, and in front of him central defenders Alvin Martin and Colin Foster were also both playing with great confidence.

In October Bonds bolstered his already impressive defence by buying a pair of new full-backs. Tim Breacker, a £600,000 buy from Luton Town, was to be the first signing during Bonds' reign, and two weeks later he was joined by Tottenham Hotspur's veteran left-back Chris Hughton, signed initially on a month's loan to cover for the injured Julian Dicks. Hughton later made the switch to Upton Park permanent and played in all 39 of Hammers' remaining fixtures. Both new defenders wasted little time settling in, and each played their part in extending West Ham United's unbeaten run throughout November. In the forward line, Stuart Slater, now playing on the left wing, was winning the plaudits for his exciting dribbling skills, which had brought him obvious comparison with the now-departed Alan Devonshire. The young striker had hit his first goal of the season against Brighton at Upton Park and was fast becoming a huge favourite with the fans at the Boleyn Ground. However, still top of the popularity stakes in E13 was

Frank McAvennie and against Plymouth on 24 November the Scotsman struck the only goal of the game to take Hammers to the top of the Second Division for the first time in 1990–91.

West Ham United's remarkable unbeaten sequence continued into the start of December, but on the last Saturday before Christmas the run came to an abrupt end with a 1–0 reverse against Barnsley at Oakwell. Hammers' first defeat in 21 League games also saw them lose top spot to Oldham Athletic. However, on Boxing Day the top two met at Upton Park and Bonds' men reclaimed pole position with a comfortable 2–0 win, courtesy of goals from Morley and Slater. Victory against the Latics brought the first of five consecutive clean sheets for Ludek Miklosko and, from this sound foundation, Hammers claimed 13 points from a possible 19 to establish a five-point lead over their promotion rivals at the end of January.

However, despite their impressive League form it was Cup football that would preoccupy West Ham United during the first two months of 1991. Bonds' team began their FA Cup run with a seemingly straightforward tie against Fourth Division strugglers Aldershot at Upton Park, but after 90 minutes of deeply forgettable football the match finished 0–0. Fortunately the replay, 11 days later, provided rather more incident and a 6–1 victory earned Hammers the dubious privilege of a fourth round tie on Luton Town's plastic pitch, upon which they had lost 5–1 in the Zenith Data Systems Cup in December. This time, though, Bonds fielded a full-strength line-up and a goal from the in-form George Parris proved enough to take the tie to a second match at Upton Park. Parris was again on target in the return, netting the first goal in a 5–0 win which ensured safe passage to an inviting home tie against Third Division Crewe Alexandra. However, the match against the Alex proved rather tougher than expected and it was only a hotly disputed strike from substitute Jimmy Quinn that saved Hammers' blushes and booked a place in the last eight of the FA Cup.

Slater chews up Toffees

West Ham United's quarter-final opponents were First Division Everton, conquerors of League Champions and neighbours Liverpool in the fifth round. The Toffeemen were, somewhat inevitably, installed as the favourites for a Monday evening game which was to be played out beneath the floodlights at a packed Upton Park. Hammers were in the winning habit though and, inspired by a charged atmosphere inside the Boleyn Ground, they made by far the brighter start to the game. After 33 minutes the home team got the reward that their adventurous play deserved, when the unlikely figure of Colin Foster swivelled to strike a volley on the turn past Neville Southall. Upton Park erupted in celebration, but the best was yet to come. Stuart Slater had been giving the Everton defence palpitations throughout the first half, and 14 minutes after the interval the pacy forward picked up the ball on the left flank, cut inside his marker and sent a low right-footed shot inside Southall's near post. Hammers maintained their two-goal lead until Dave Watson pulled a goal back for the Mersey giants four minutes from time, but this proved to be no more than a consolation and the home team were deserved winners on a night of rich entertainment in E13.

After the high jinx of their Cup quarter-final, West Ham United lost their next two games as they struggled to readjust to the plain fare of League football. It was the first and last time Hammers would lose two consecutive League matches during 1990–91, and with 13 fixtures still to play they dropped to second place in the table. Billy Bonds responded to this setback by signing striker Iain Dowie from Luton Town in a £500,000 deal. Dowie's arrival coincided with an upturn in League form and his first four games brought eight points for Hammers. It was a run which included a vital away draw against Oldham Athletic on Good Friday and an impressive win at Port Vale eight days later. Hammers were now back at the top of the Second Division, but after a frustrating defeat away to Brighton and Hove Albion they returned to FA Cup action against Nottingham Forest at Villa Park in the semi-final.

Above: Suffolk-born forward Stuart Slater reached his zenith during the 1991 FA Cup quarter-final against Everton in March 1991. After 59 minutes he cut in from the left flank and unpacked a low driven shot inside Neville Southall's post.

Below: The combative George Parris provided an unexpected source of goals during the 1990–91 promotion season, scoring five times in the League.

Hackett's big day

The match at Villa Park kicked off at 3.30pm, by which time the other semi-final, between Arsenal and Tottenham, had been completed. Hammers knew that if they could overcome Forest they would face Spurs at Wembley in May. However, it was a somewhat depleted line-up which began the match in Birmingham. Iain Dowie was Cup-tied, Frank McAvennie suspended and Tim Breacker injured, while Trevor Morley made only his second appearance after recovering from stab wounds sustained in a 'domestic incident'. Despite these problems, Hammers began the match well enough and looked to be the equals of their First Division opponents. But a controversial decision from referee Keith Hackett after 26 minutes ended the game as a meaningful contest. Defender Tony Gale appeared to do no more than challenge shoulder-to-shoulder with Forest's Gary Crosby, but when both players picked themselves up from a challenge devoid of any malice, Hackett showed the Hammers stopper the red card. 'I just remember the ball being knocked over my head and thinking I had more time than I probably did have,' recalls Gale. 'I had to wait to see which way the ball bounced because it was quite an uneven surface. As the ball popped up Crosby was there on my shoulder. He tried to come across me and I tried to get in front of him, and we both fell to ground. As I got up, I really didn't know which way the ref was going to give the free-kick. Then, all of a sudden, he's gone to get out a card. I said to him, "I can't believe you're booking me," but to my complete amazement he showed me the red card and didn't say a word.'

The Hammers rallied for the remainder of the first half, and at the interval the match was still goalless. However, Forest's precise passing game was too much for West Ham United's ten men to contend with, and the Midlanders struck four times in the second period to claim a place in the final. But while Forest may have won, it was the West Ham United fans who took the plaudits. The injustice of their team's defeat had inspired the travelling Hammers to give an unprecedented display of support, and as each goal went in the chants of 'Billy Bonds' claret and blue army' grew louder and louder. 'It was great to hear the fans give that kind of support,' remembers Steve Potts, 'but it was also disappointing because it made you think about what it would have been like if we'd actually won and made it to Wembley.'

Despite the disappointment of defeat at Villa Park, within a week Hammers had guaranteed their promotion with wins over John Lyall's Ipswich Town and Glenn Hoddle's Swindon. All that was left now was for West Ham United to clinch the Second Division Championship. When they began their last match of the season, against Notts County at Upton Park, the only way they could be pipped to the Second Division crown was if they lost to County and rivals Oldham won at third-placed Sheffield Wednesday. Confidence was high. But, on a glorious sunny day in E13, Billy Bonds' team went down 2–1. However, with Oldham trailing 2–1 at Hillsborough, Hammers thought they had done enough to claim the Championship. The celebrations began and fans duly rushed onto the pitch to proclaim their heroes. But as the players contemplated their lap of honour, news filtered through that Oldham were level at 2–2. Nerves began to jangle and as the game at Hillsborough entered injury time the news got worse. With just seconds to play Oldham's Neil Redfearn scored from the penalty spot to give his team victory and the Second Division title. In an instant Upton Park swapped noisy celebration for stunned silence. It was a hugely anticlimactic end to a season which had been high on both drama and entertainment. Steve Potts remembers the flatness in the Hammers dressing room after the game: 'It felt like we'd been beaten in a Cup final rather than the last game of a promotion season.'

Above: Tony Gale is controversially sent off by referee Keith Hackett in the 1991 FA Cup semi final at Hillsborough. Hackett would not referee another Hammers match until September 1993.

The disappointment of missing out on the Second Division Championship quickly subsided during the summer of 1991, and thoughts inevitably turned to Hammers prospects for their first season back in the top flight. Survival was to be the aim for the 1991–92 League campaign and, with this in mind, Billy Bonds attempted to improve his squad. Striker Mike Small arrived from Brighton and Hove Albion and Mitchell Thomas, who could play at full-back or in midfield, made the switch from Spurs. Both players were signed for fees in the region of £500,000. The only other significant close-season signing was Plymouth right-back Kenny Brown – son of former Hammers legend Ken Brown – who joined initially on a one-month loan, but later made the switch permanent for a fee of £175,000. There were also major departures. Ray Stewart, who had regained his fitness after a long absence through injury, joined St Johnstone after more than ten years at Upton Park; Jimmy Quinn headed for Harry Redknapp's AFC Bournemouth; and Iain Dowie signed for Southampton in a £550,000 deal. The big question was would the net effect of all this transfer activity be enough to ensure Hammers' survival in the top division. The pundits said no, and made Hammers favourites for relegation. Tony Gale was more optimistic: 'I thought we were going to stay up, I definitely thought we were good enough. We had a lot of players with First Division experience.' Unfortunately, Gale's confidence was misplaced.

By the end of October the Hammers had slumped to 18th position in the League table. The goals of new signing Mike Small were at least providing reason for optimism, and the 29-year-old striker scored eight times in a nine-game spell to earn himself a call up to the standby list for the England B squad in November. Small's goals had also inspired a mini-revival for Hammers, and victories over Spurs at home and Arsenal at Highbury lifted the club away from the relegation places and to the relative safety of 14th place. The good run continued with an impressive, and surprisingly entertaining, goalless draw against Liverpool in a live TV game at Upton Park. But from then on the season descended into disaster both on and off the pitch.

Below: Centre-forward Mike Small joined Hammers in the summer of 1991 for a fee of around £500,000 and proved a revelation in his first few months at the Club. Small would score eight goals in a nine-game run, the highlight of which was a superb solo-effort in the 1–0 victory over Arsenal at Highbury in November.

1986-92

Bond scheme controversy

The home match against Liverpool had seen West Ham United unveil controversial plans for the redevelopment of the Boleyn Ground, which was to be made all-seater by 1995 in compliance with the Taylor Report. The planned redevelopment involved the demolition of the North and South Bank terraces and the building of replacement cantilever stands. The work would cost an estimated £15m and in order to raise the money the Club issued the now-infamous Hammers Bond. 'The Bond is, in effect, a non-returnable, unsecured loan to the Club,' explained the matchday programme. According to newly appointed Managing Director Peter Storrie, it was a preferable option to the uncertainty of a Stock Exchange flotation. Storrie declared: 'The debenture route offers everything that we are looking for in our fund-raising... we raise the money, the Club remains under internal control, we do not take on huge debt, and monies for the team are not affected.' It might have been everything that the club was looking for, but, to the fans the Bond was rather less appealing. The supporters argued that in return for a minimum investment of £500 they would receive little more than the right to buy their season ticket in the future. There were precious few subscribers to the Hammers Bond. West Ham United's form rapidly deteriorated following the launch of the Bond scheme and, after a run of six defeats in seven games, Hammers found themselves in 21st place on New Year's Day 1992. The only consolation in this appalling run was the long-awaited return to fitness of Club captain Julian Dicks. The combative left-back made his comeback in the home match against Sheffield United on the last Saturday before Christmas, and marked the occasion with a goal from the penalty spot in a 1–1 draw. However, even the return of Dicks could not halt the descent toward the foot of the table and, despite wins against fellow strugglers Luton Town and Oldham Athletic, the Hammers hit rock-bottom after a 1–0 defeat at Southampton on 3 March. It was unquestionably the worst of times for West Ham United. Dismayed by the Bond Scheme and unhappy with the performance of their team, the supporters began to organise protests at home games. There was a pitch invasion and a one-man centre-circle sit-in against Everton, balloons were released when Arsenal visited the Boleyn Ground and for the match against Southampton some fans chose to express their dissatisfaction by walking out at half-time. 'It was a really negative atmosphere at Upton Park,' remembers Steve Potts. 'We weren't playing well, the supporters weren't happy – and quite rightly so in my opinion – and for a long time it just seemed that relegation was inevitable.' Despite the club's deep-rooted problems, Billy Bonds continued to do his best to lead the Hammers out of the mire. And on transfer deadline day the manager made his last throw of the dice, signing much-travelled Chelsea striker Clive Allen in a £250,000 deal. It was, however, too little too late and four defeats in the final six matches ensured West Ham United made an immediate return to English football's second tier. There had, at least, been two highly entertaining victories at Upton Park in the closing weeks of the season. Firstly, Championship-chasing Manchester United were sent back to Lancashire empty-handed after Kenny Brown's somewhat fortuitous goal had earned Hammers an unlikely 1–0 victory and then, on the last day of the season, came Frank McAvennie's farewell to E13. The Scottish striker, who had been granted a free transfer, sat out a goalless first-half against Brian Clough's Nottingham Forest but made a typically dramatic entrance after the interval. As the crowd urged him not to go, McAvennie struck a superb hat-trick to evoke memories of 1985–86.

Trevor Morley enjoyed his best season for the Hammers in 1992–93, striking 20 League goals to help the Club to promotion and a place in the new Premiership.

Harry comes home

Despite the glorious finale to their relegation season, there was no disguising the fact that Hammers were at their lowest ebb. 'There wasn't the same optimism that there had been when we'd last been in the Second Division,' remembers Steve Potts, 'and the problems didn't just stop with the first team, there were no kids coming through either.' Billy Bonds would face a difficult task to rally his forlorn players ahead of the 1992–93 season and to help him he enlisted former Hammers winger and long-serving Bournemouth manager Harry Redknapp. The arrival of Redknapp as assistant manager was one of a number of changes to the Upton Park coaching staff during the 1992 close season. Ronnie Boyce, who had been assistant manager, became chief scout; Paul Hilton switched from youth team coach to reserve team manager; and Tony Carr took charge of the youth section. But the changes didn't end in the boot room, and in July the West Ham United board elected Terence Brown as its new chairman in succession to Martin Cearns. Behind-the-scenes comings and goings, though, were of little interest to the fans who were more concerned with the club's transfer dealings. However, since relegation had cost Hammers a place in the lucrative new Premier League and a share of the League's £304m satellite television deal, Billy Bonds would be given precious little money for team building.

The one big-money transfer deal to take place at Upton Park during the summer of 1992 was the sale of 23-year-old forward Stuart Slater to Celtic for £1.5m. Slater had been a popular figure with Hammers fans, but his form had slumped alarmingly during the relegation season and after a run of 55 games without a goal he was judged to be expendable. In Slater's place arrived former Spurs winger Mark Robson, signed on a free transfer after an injury-ravaged spell at White Hart Lane.

Robson was joined by two other new signings: Matt Holmes, a £75,000 buy from Bournemouth, and Peter Butler, a £175,000 capture from First Division rivals Southend. However, it was confidence rather than personnel that was West Ham United's greatest problem. Harry Redknapp, in his autobiography, wrote: '... morale was at a low ebb and I remember thinking from the first minute I arrived, "this is going to be tough". Things were bad... and the general confidence level was zero.'

Despite losing two early games, a 2–1 home win over Watford at the start of September put West Ham United on an ascendant path. Steve Potts is in no doubt that West Ham United's revival owed most to the influence of Harry Redknapp. 'He brought a fresh approach,' remembers the long-serving defender. 'He was exactly what was needed to lift the club. And he and Billy worked well together.' A run of six victories in eight games, which included an impressive 5–1 win at Bristol City and a memorable 6–0 triumph over Sunderland at the Boleyn Ground, established Hammers' promotion credentials. The only real problem for West Ham United's management duo was Julian Dicks' disciplinary record. The Club captain was sent off twice in the first nine games and earned suspensions totalling eight games. However, Dicks apart, Bonds and Redknapp were able to name a settled line-up during the first half of the season, and the forward line of Mark Robson, Trevor Morley, Clive Allen and Kevin Keen was proving a particular revelation – striking 32 goals in the first 20 games. At the turn of the year, and despite an indifferent run of form which had seen them lose four of their last 12 games, Hammers were third in the table – just three points behind Tranmere Rovers and an automatic promotion place.

Above: Loan signing David Speedie scores the first of his two goals in the 3–1 victory over Leicester City in April 1993. Speedie would score three times during his short stay in E13, but was unable to win over the crowd at the Boleyn Ground who had taken an instant dislike to the former Chelsea and Liverpool striker.

Below: An emotional afternoon at Upton Park. The game against Wolverhampton Wanderers on 6 March 1993 was the first match to be played at the Boleyn Ground since the tragic death of Bobby Moore ten days before. Martin Peters, Ron Greenwood and Geoff Hurst are seen here carrying a floral tribute to the former Hammers skipper out onto the pitch ahead of kick-off.

Another promotion drive

A live-TV match away to big-spending Derby County provided West Ham United's first League action of the season, and Bonds' team arrived at the Baseball Ground knowing that a win would take them up to second place. Hammers made an impressive start to the game against the Rams and, on a difficult, muddy surface, took a 2–0 lead inside 15 minutes, with goals from Robson and Morley. However, the first-half drama was far-from over and, prior to the interval, Julian Dicks earned his third red card of the season for a reckless challenge on Ted McMinn. For the remainder of the game, Hammers were forced to fight a rearguard action in an effort to protect their lead. But, with the unlikely duo of Morley and Kevin Keen helping out in defence, Derby were held at bay and Ludek Miklosko was able to record his ninth clean sheet of the season. Victory, however, had been achieved at a cost, and in addition to Julian Dicks' three-match ban for his sending off, Alvin Martin had sustained an achilles' injury which would keep him out of the side for the remainder of the season. Transfer-listed Tony Gale came in for the next match, against sixth-placed Portsmouth, and Hammers recorded a 2–0 win which would prove decisive at season's end. Pompey manager Jim Smith had no complaints about his team's defeat and he told reporters. 'They [West Ham United] are the best team we've played this season. We were beaten at Newcastle but on the evidence of the two games we've had with West Ham, I am convinced that they are favourites to take second place.'

Hammers would suffer ignominious defeats in both domestic Cup competitions – losing out to Crewe in the League Cup and going down 4–1 to Barnsley in the FA Cup – but throughout January and February 1993 their League form was both impressive and consistent. Even an injury to veteran goalscorer Clive Allen could not interrupt a 15-match unbeaten run which saw West Ham United take a firm grip on the second automatic promotion place. In Allen's absence new signing Alex Bunbury was called into action, but the Canadian international failed to impress in a home match against Bristol City and another newcomer, Steve Jones, was given his chance. Jones had arrived at Upton Park on the recommendation of former Hammers winger and current Billericay Town manager Peter Brabrook, and the young striker proved an immediate crowd favourite after scoring in each of his first two appearances in the starting line-up.

Tribute to a legend

All thoughts of promotion were quickly forgotten, though, on Wednesday 24 February 1993. At 6.30am, Bobby Moore OBE, the most successful player in West Ham United's 93-year history, died at his Putney home after a two-year fight against cancer. The tributes to England's World Cup winning captain were overwhelming and football supporters from all clubs flocked to the Boleyn Ground to leave flowers, scarves and messages of condolence. Hammers' first home match after Moore's death was against Wolves and it proved an emotional occasion. Prior to kick-off Ron Greenwood, Geoff Hurst and Martin Peters placed a floral tribute to their former colleague in the centre of the pitch, which was then encircled by the players for an impeccably observed minute's silence. Hammers also played the entire game without a number six shirt, Ian Bishop wearing number 12 instead. The result of the game against Wolves seemed of minor consequence on such a sad day, but, as Moore would have wished, West Ham United retained their professionalism to win 3–1.

Victory over Wolves was followed, three days later, by a 2–1 win over Grimsby Town but, for the remainder of March, Hammers' form was far from convincing. Bonds was struggling to compensate for the continued absence of Clive Allen and, as transfer deadline day approached, signed much-travelled Southampton striker David Speedie on loan. Speedie, who had not endeared himself to the Boleyn Ground faithful during his time with Chelsea, was unable to find the net in his first five games and, with goals in short supply, Hammers took just seven points from a possible 15. The situation was not helped by the astonishing form of Jim Smith's Portsmouth who had won seven of their last eight games. On 6 April, Pompey won 4–0 at home to Peterborough to take second place from Billy Bonds' team who responded to this setback with a disappointing 1–0 reverse at Southend. However, with six games left to play, and only 'goals scored' separating the two teams there was still, to use a cliché, 'everything to play for'.

David Speedie scored twice in Hammers' next match, against Leicester City, but with Portsmouth winning too, there was no change at the top of the table. Pompey played next and claimed a 3–0 home victory over Derby County to open up a three-point lead. West Ham United would now need to win 5–0 away to struggling Luton Town the following evening to reclaim second place. However, it was to be a disastrous night in Bedfordshire for Billy Bonds' team, who went behind to a hotly disputed penalty after 84 minutes and eventually lost 2–0 after conceding a soft goal following a Luton counter-attack. Portsmouth now held the advantage and needed only to match the results of their rivals to ensure promotion. Both teams won their next two fixtures, but significantly Hammers outscored Pompey by six goals to three.

Pompey pipped to promotion

The penultimate Saturday of the season saw Portsmouth travel to relegation-threatened Sunderland while, the following day, Hammers faced a tough trip to Swindon Town. The match on Wearside was to prove decisive, and after a run of 11 wins in 12 games, Pompey's promotion push blew up in spectacular fashion, with two players sent off in a 4–1 reverse. West Ham United would now move into second place if they could beat Glenn Hoddle's Swindon by three or more goals at the County Ground. It seemed an unlikely prospect given the Robins' excellent home record of just two defeats in 22 games, but after a nervous start, Hammers grew in confidence and strikes from Trevor Morley and substitutes Clive Allen and Kenny Brown earned a celebrated 3–1 win.

The tension, however, was not yet over. Hammers' advantage was just one goal and, with both teams facing home matches on the final day of the season, little could be taken for granted. Cambridge United would provide West Ham United's opposition at the Boleyn Ground while Grimsby Town made the trip to Fratton Park. Radio commentaries kept supporters up-to-date with events in both matches, and at half-time the scores were very much in Hammers' favour. Pompey were trailing by one goal, while at Upton Park the match remained goalless. And after two minutes of the second half the situation improved still further, with David Speedie hooking home the ball following a penalty-area scramble. However, as West Ham United's match entered its final ten minutes the fans were on tenterhooks. First, Cambridge winger Chris Leadbitter had a seemingly legitimate goal ruled out for offside and then, as the tension mounted, news filtered through that Portsmouth had pulled back to 1–1. Billy Bonds, no doubt feeling the strain more than anybody else, played his last card and threw on substitute Clive Allen. The former England striker quickly proved Hammers' promotion winner and, following a surging run from Julian Dicks, struck home a second goal to spark wild celebrations and a mini-pitch invasion from the South Bank. The match at Portsmouth ended in a 2–1 victory for Pompey, but it was not enough to deny West Ham United promotion by virtue of a superior goalscoring record. Hammers had scored 81 times to Portsmouth's 80.

Above: Hammers players celebrate promotion at the end of the 1992–93 season. From left to right: Mark Robson, Martin Allen (standing), David Speedie, Trevor Morley (standing), Steve Potts, Peter Butler and Kevin Keen.

Below: The West Ham United management duo of Harry Redknapp and Billy Bonds reflect on the 1992–93 season after clinching promotion in the final match against Cambridge United.

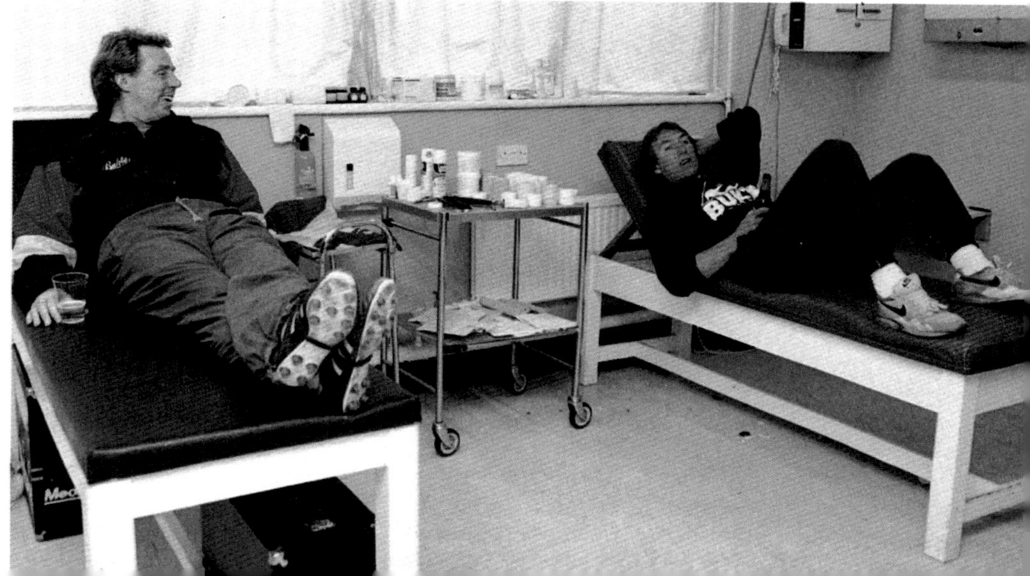

1985-1992

SEASON 1985-86 FOOTBALL LEAGUE (DIVISION 1)

17 Aug	Birmingham C	A	L	0-1	Parkes	Stewart	Walford	Gale	Martin	Devonshire	Ward	McAvennie	Goddard*	Cottee	Orr	Dickens
20 Aug	Queens Park R	H	W	3-1	..	..	..	..	..	..	..	..2	Dickens1	..	..	
24 Aug	Luton T	H	L	0-1	..	..	..	..	..	..	..	..	..	..*	..	Campbell
26 Aug	Manchester U	A	L	0-2	..	..	..	..	..	..	..	..	..	..*	..	..
31 Aug	Liverpool	H	D	2-2	..	..	..	..	..	..	..	..2	..	..	..	
3 Sep	Southampton	A	D	1-1	..	..	..	..	..	..	..	..1	..	Campbell*	..	Cottee
7 Sep	Sheffield W	A	D	2-2	..	..	..	..	..	Parris	..	..*1	..	Cottee1	..	Barnes
14 Sep	Leicester C	H	W	3-0	..	..	..	..	..	Devonshire1	..	..1	..	..1	..	
21 Sep	Manchester C	A	D	2-2	..	..	..	..	..	..	..	..	..	..1	..	(McCarthy og)
28 Oct	Nottingham Forest	H	W	4-2	..	..	..	..	..	..	..	..2	..1	..1	..	
5 Oct	Newcastle U	A	W	2-1	..	..	..	..	..	..	..	..1	..	..1	..	
12 Oct	Arsenal	H	D	0-0	..	..	..	..	..	..	..	..	..*	..	..	Parris
19 Oct	Aston Villa	H	W	4-1	..	..	..	..	..	..	..	..2	Parris	..2	..	
26 Oct	Ipswich T	A	W	1-0	..	Parris	..	..	..	..*	..	..	Dickens	..1	..	Potts
2 Nov	Everton	H	W	2-1	..	Stewart	..*	..	..	..	..	..2	..	..	..	Parris
9 Nov	Oxford U	A	W	2-1	..	..	..	..	..	..	..1	..	..	..1	..	
16 Nov	Watford	H	W	2-1	..	..	..	..	..	..	..1	..1	..	..	..	
23 Nov	Coventry C	A	W	1-0	..	..	..	..	..	..	..	..1	..	..	..	
30 Nov	West Brom A	H	W	4-0	..	..	..	..	..	..1	..	Parris1	..	..1	..1	
7 Dec	Queens Park R	A	W	1-0	..	..	..	..	..	..	..	McAvennie1	..	..	..	
14 Dec	Birmingham C	H	W	2-0	..	..1	..*	..	..	..	..	..1	..	..	..	Parris
21 Dec	Luton T	A	D	0-0	..	..	..	..	..	..	..	..	..	..	..	
26 Dec	Tottenham H	A	L	0-1	..	..	..	..	..	..	..	..	..	..	..	
11 Jan	Leicester C	A	W	1-0	..	..	..	..	..	..	..	..1	..	..	Parris	
18 Jan	Liverpool	A	L	1-3	..	..(so)	..	..	..	..	..	..	..1	..	..	
2 Feb	Manchester U	H	W	2-1	..	Parris	..	..	..	..	..1	..	..	..1	Pike	
15 Mar	Arsenal	A	L	0-1	..	Stewart	Parris	..	..(so)	..	..	..	..	..	..	
19 Mar	Aston Villa	A	L	1-2	..	Parris	Walford	..	..	Orr	..	..	..	..*	..	Goddard (Hunt og)
22 Mar	Sheffield W	H	W	1-0	..	Stewart	Parris	..	..	..	..	..1	..	..*	..	..
29 Mar	Chelsea	A	W	4-0	..	..	..	..	Hilton	Devenshire*1	..	..1	..2	..	..	Orr
31 Mar	Tottenham H	H	W	2-1	..	..	..	..	..	..*	..1	..1	..	..	..	..
2 Apr	Nottingham F	A	L	1-2	..	..	..	..	Martin	Orr	..	..	..	..1	..	
8 Apr	Southampton	H	W	1-0	..	..	..	..	..1	Devonshire	..	..	..	..	..	
12 Apr	Oxford	H	W	3-1	..	..1	..	..	..	..	..	..1	..	..	..	(Trewill og)
15 Apr	Chelsea	H	L	1-2	..	..	..	..*	..	..	..	..	..	..1	..	Orr
19 Apr	Watford	A	W	2-0	..	..	..	..	..	..	..	..1	..	..1	Orr	
21 Apr	Newcastle U	H	W	8-1	..	..1	..	..	..3	..	..	..1	..*	..	..1	Goddard1 (Roeder og)
26 Apr	Coventry C	H	W	1-0	..	..	..	..	..	..	..	..	..	..1	..	
28 Apr	Manchester C	H	W	1-0	..	..1	..	..	..	..	..	..	..	..	..	
30 Apr	Ipswich T	H	W	2-1	..	..1	..	..	..	..	..	..	..1	..	..*	Goddard
3 May	West Brom A	A	W	3-2	..	..1	..	..	..	..	..	..1	..	..1	..	
5 May	Everton	A	L	1-3	..	..	..	..	..	..	..	..	..*	..1	..	Goddard
	Milk Cup															
24 Sept	Swansea (2:1)	H	W	3-0	..	..1	Walford	..	..	..	..	..1	..	..1	..	
8 Oct	Swansea (2:2)	A	W	3-2	..	..2	..	..	..	..	..	..*	..	..1	..	Parris
29 Oct	Manchester U (3)	A	L	0-1	..	..	..	..	..	..	..	..	..*	..	..	..
	FA Cup															
5 Jan	Charlton (3)	A	W	1-0	..	..	..	..	..	..	..	..	..	..1	Parris	
25 Jan	Ipswich T (4)	H	D	0-0	..	..	..*	..	..	..	..	..	..	..	..	Goddard
4 Feb	Ipswich T (4R)	A	D	1-1	..	Parris	..*	..	..	..	..	..	..	..1	Pike	Orr
6 Feb	Ipswich T (4RR)	A	W	1-0	..	Stewart	Parris	..	..	Orr	..	..	..	..1	..	
5 Mar	Manchester U (5)	H	D	1-1	..	..	..	..	..	Devonshire	..	..1	..	..	..	
9 Mar	Manchester U (5R)	A	W	2-0	..	..1	..	..	..	..	..	..	..	..	..1	
12 Mar	Sheffield Wed (QF)	A	L	1-0	..	..	..	..	..	..	..	..	..	..1	..	

Hammer of the Year 1985-86
TONY COTTEE

	P	W	L	D	F:A	Pts	Pos
Liverpool	42	26	6	10	89:37	88	1st
West Ham	42	26	6	10	74:40	84	3rd

Alan Devonshire (v. Man United, FA Cup 5th Round replay 1986)

SEASON 1986-87 FOOTBALL LEAGUE (DIVISION 1)

23 Aug	Coventry C	H	W	1-0	Parkes	Stewart	Parris	Gale1	Martin	Devonshire	Ward	McAvennie	Dickens	Cottee	Orr	
25 Aug	Manchester U	A	W	3-2	..	..	..	Hilton	..	..1	..	..2	..	..	..	
30 Aug	Oxford U	A	D	0-0	..	..	..	Gale	..	..	..	..	..	..	..	
2 Sep	Nottingham Forest	H	L	1-2	..	..	..	..	..	..*	..	..1	..	..	..	Goddard
6 Sep	Liverpool	H	L	2-5	..	..1	..	..	..	Pike*	..	..	..	..1	..	Keen
13 Sep	Queens Park R	A	W	3-2	..	..	..	..	..	Walford	Keen	..	..	..3	..	
20 Sep	Luton T	H	W	2-0	..	..	Walford	..1	..(so)	Parris1	..	..	..*	..	..	Pike
27 Sep	Sheffield W	A	D	2-2	..	..	Parris	..	..1	Walford	Ward	..	..	..	..1	
4 Oct	Watford	A	D	2-2	..	..	..	..	Hilton	..	..	..1	..1	..	..*	Keen
11 Oct	Chelsea	H	W	5-3	..	..2	..	..	..	Keen	..	..*1	..	..2	..	Bonds
18 Oct	Norwich C	A	D	1-1	..	..	..	..	..	..	..*	Goddard1	..	..	..	Bonds
25 Oct	Charlton	H	L	1-3	..	..	..	..	..	Devonshire*	..	..	..	..1	..	Keen
2 Nov	Everton	H	W	1-0	..	..	..	..	..	..	..	..	..1	..	..	
8 Nov	Arsenal	A	D	0-0	..	..	..	..	..	..	..	McAvennie	..	..	Walford	
15 Nov	Wimbledon	A	W	1-0	..	..	..	..	..	..*	..	..	..	..1	Orr	Walford
22 Nov	Aston Villa	H	D	1-1	..	Walford	..	..	..	..	..	..	..	..1	Keen*	Bonds
30 Nov	Newcastle U	A	L	0-4	..	Stewart.	..	..	..	..	..	..	..*	..	Orr	Ince
6 Dec	Southampton	H	W	3-1	..	Potts	..	..	Martin	..1	..	..	Ince1	..1	..	
13 Dec	Manchester C	A	L	1-3	..	..	..	..	..1	..	..	..	..	..	..*	Dickens
20 Dec	Queens Park R	H	D	1-1	..	..	..	..	..	..	..	..	Dickens	..1	..	
26 Dec	Tottenham H	A	L	0-4	..	..	..	Walford*	..	..	..	..	..	..	..	Hilton
27 Dec	Wimbledon	H	L	2-3	..	..	..	Hilton1	..	Ince	..	..	Keen*	..1	Pike	Dickens
1 Jan	Leicester C	H	W	4-1	..	Walford	..	..	..	Devonshire	..	..1	Dickens1	..2	..	
3 Jan	Liverpool	A	L	0-1	..	..	..	..	..	..	Orr	..	..*	..	..	Ince
24 Jan	Coventry C	A	W	3-1	..	..	..	..	..	..	Ward	..	..	..3	Robson	
7 Feb	Oxford U	H	L	0-1	..	Stewart	..	Gale	Hilton	..	..	..	..*	..	..	Bonds
14 Feb	Nottingham F	A	D	1-1	..	..1	..	..	Bonds	Walford	..	..	Pike	..	..	
28 Feb	Luton T	A	L	1-2	..	..	Walford*	..	..	Dickens	..	..	..	..1	..	Ince
7 Mar	Charlton A	A	L	1-2	..	..	..	..	..	..	..	..*	..	..	..1	Parris
14 Mar	Norwich C	H	L	0-2	..	..	Parris	..	..	..	Brady	Ince	..*	..	..	Keen
21 Mar	Chelsea	A	L	0-1	..	..	..	..	Strodder	Brady	Ward	McAvennie	..	..	..	
24 Mar	Sheffield W	H	L	0-2	..	..*	..	..	..	..	..	..(so)	Dickens	..	..	Keen
28 Mar	Watford	H	W	1-0	..	Bonds	McQueen	..	..	..	..	..	Parris1	..	..*	Dickens
8 Apr	Arsenal	H	W	3-1	McAlister	..	..	..	..	..1	..	Dickens	..	..2	..	
11 Apr	Everton	A	L	0-4	..	..	..	..*	..	..	Pike	..	..	..	..	Orr
14 Apr	Manchester U	H	D	0-0	..	Parris	..	Bonds	..	..	Ward	McAvennie	Dickens	..	..	
18 Apr	Leicester C	A	L	0-2	..	Bonds	..	Gale	..	..	..	..	Parris*	..	..	Dickens
20 Apr	Tottenham H	H	W	2-1	..	..	..	..	..	Devonshire	..	..1	Brady	..1	..	
25 Apr	Aston Villa	A	L	0-4	..	..*	..	..	..	..	..	..	..	..	..	..
2 May	Newcastle U	H	D	1-1	..	Potts	..*	Bonds	..	Ince	..1	..	Dickens	..	..	Keen
4 May	Southampton	A	L	0-1	..	Bonds	..	Potts	..	..	..	..	Brady	..	..	
9 May	Manchester C	H	W	2-0	..	Potts	Orr	Keen	..	Brady1	..*	..	Robson	..1	Ince	Dolan
	Littlewoods Cup															
23 Sept	Preston (2:1)	A	D	1-1	Parkes	Stewart	Parris	Gale	Martin	Walford	..1	..	Pike	..	Orr	
7 Oct	Preston (2:2)	H	W	4-1	..	..	..	Keen	Hilton	..	..	..	Dickens*1	..3	..	Bonds
29 Oct	Watford (3)	A	W	3-2	..	..	..	Gale	..*	Devonshire	..1	Goddard1	..1	..	..	Walford
18 Nov	Oxford (4)	H	W	1-0	..	Walford*	..	..	..	..	..	McAvennie	..	..1	Keen	Bonds
27 Jan	Tottenham H (QF)	H	D	1-1	..	..	..	Hilton	Martin	..	..	..	..	..1	Robson	
2 Feb	Tottenham H (QF)	A	L	0-5	..	Bonds	..*	Gale	..	..	..	..	Orr	..	..	Hilton
	FA Cup															
10 Jan	Orient (3)	A	D	1-1	..	Walford	..	Hilton1	..	..	..	..	Ince	..	Pike	
31 Jan	Orient (3R)	H	W	4-1	..	..*	..1	..	Gale	Keen2	Dickens	..1	Dickens	..1	Orr	Bonds
9 Feb	Sheffield U (4)	H	W	4-0	..	Bonds	..	Gale1	Stewart	Devonshire*	Ward	..2	Pike	..	Robson1	Keen
21 Feb	Sheffield W (5)	A	D	1-1	..	Stewart	..	..	Bonds	Walford	..	..1	..	..	..	
25 Feb	Sheffield W (5R)	H	L	0-2	..	..	..*	..	..	Devonshire	..	..	..	..	..	Dickens
	Full Member's Cup															
Nov 25	Chelsea	H	L	1-2	..	Walford*	..	..	Hilton	Ince	..	..	Dickens	..1	Keen	Potts

Hammer of the Year 1986-87
BILLY BONDS

	P	W	L	D	F:A	Pts	Pos
Everton	42	26	8	8	76:31	86	1st
West Ham	42	14	18	10	52:67	52	15th

Abbreviations:

Figures shown as 2 etc. refer to goals scored by individual players

* own-goal
(so) sent off

SEASON 1987-88 FOOTBALL LEAGUE (DIVISION 1)

15 Aug	Queens Park R	H	L	0-3	McAlister	Stewart	McQueen	Orr	Martin	Devonshire*	Ward	McAvennie	Brady	Cottee	Robson	Dickens/Strodder
22 Aug	Luton T	A	D	2-2	..	..1	..	Strodder	..	Brady1	..	..	Ince	..	..	
29 Aug	Norwich C	H	W	2-0	..	..	..	..	..	..	..	..	..	..2	..	
31 Aug	Portsmouth	A	L	1-2	..	..*	..	..1	..	..	..	..	..	..	..	Parris
5 Sep	Liverpool	H	D	1-1	..	..	..	..	..	..	..	..	..	..1	..	..
12 Sep	Wimbledon	A	D	1-1	..	..	Parris	..	..	..	..(so)	..	..	..1	..	
19 Sep	Tottenham H	H	L	0-1	..	..	..	..*	..	..	..	..	..	..	..	Hilton
26 Sep	Arsenal	A	L	0-1	..	..	..	..	..	..	Keen	..	..	..	..	
3 Oct	Derby	H	D	1-1	..	..*	McQueen	..	..	..1	..	Parris	..	..	..	Hilton/Slater
10 Oct	Charlton	H	D	1-1	..	..	Parris	Keen	..	..	Ward	Dickens	..1	..	..	
17 Oct	Oxford U	A	W	2-1	..	..	..	Dickens	..	..	Keen	Ward	..	..1	..	(Canton og)
25 Oct	Manchester U	H	D	1-1	..	..1	..	Keen	..	..	Ward	Dickens	..	..	McQueen	
31 Oct	Watford	A	W	2-1	..	..	..	..	..	..	..	..1	..	..1	Robson	
7 Nov	Sheffield W	H	L	0-1	..	..	..	..*	..	..	..	..	..	..	..	Dolan
14 Nov	Everton	A	L	1-3	..	Bonds	..*	Hilton1	..*	..	..	..	..	..	..	Strodder/Keen
21 Nov	Nottingham F	H	W	3-2	..	..	..	..	Stewart1	Keen	..	..	..	..2	..	
28 Nov	Coventry C	A	D	0-0	..	..	..	..	..	..	..	..	..	..	..	
5 Dec	Southampton	H	W	2-1	..	..	..	Strodder	..	..1	..(so)	..1	..	..	..	
12 Dec	Chelsea	A	D	1-1	..	..	..1	..	..	..	..	..	Hilton	..	..	
19 Dec	Newcastle	H	W	2-1	..	..*	..	..	..	..	Brady	..	Ince1	..	..1	Hilton
26 Dec	Wimbledon	H	L	1-2	..	..1	..*	..	..	..	Ward	..*	..	..	..	Hilton/Brady
28 Dec	Tottenham H	A	L	1-2	..	..	..	Hilton1	..	..	..*	Brady	..	..	..	Strodder
1 Jan	Norwich C	A	L	1-4	..	..	..	..	..	..	..	Dickens	..*	..1	..	Gale/Dolan
2 Jan	Luton T	H	D	1-1	..	..	..*	Strodder	..	Potts	..	Gale	Hilton	..	..	Ince1
16 Jan	Queens Park R	A	W	1-0	..	Stewart	McQueen	Bonds	Strodder	Gale	..	Brady	Dickens1	..	..	
6 Feb	Liverpool	A	D	0-0	..	..	Ince	..	..	..	..	..	..*	..	Robson	McQueen
13 Feb	Portsmouth	H	D	1-1	..	Stewart	..	..	..	..	..	..	..	..1	..	
27 Feb	Derby C	A	L	0-1	..	..	..	..	..	..	..	..*	..*	..	..	Keen/McQueen
5 Mar	Oxford	H	D	1-1	..	Stewart	McQueen	..	..	..	..1	Keen	Ince*	..	..	Dolan
12 Mar	Charlton	A	L	0-3	..	..	..	..	..	..	..	Dickens*	Dolan	..	..	Keen
19 Mar	Watford	H	W	1-0	..	..	Potts	..	..	..	..	Keen	Rosenior1	..	..*	Dickens
26 Mar	Manchester U	A	L	1-3	..	..	..	..	..	..	..	..*	..1	..	Dickens	Parris
2 Apr	Sheffield W	A	L	1-2	..	..	Dicks	..*	..	..	..	Parris	..1	..	Robson	Dickens/Potts
4 Apr	Everton	H	D	0-0	..	..*	..	Parris	..	..	..	Dickens	..	..	..	Ince
12 Apr	Arsenal	H	L	0-1	Parkes	Potts*	..	Bonds	..	..	..	Parris	..	..	..	Keen
20 Apr	Nottingham F	A	D	0-0	McAlister	Parris	..	..	..	..	..	Dickens	..	..	Robson	
23 Apr	Coventry C	H	D	1-1	..	..	..	Keen	..	..	..	..	Ince*	..1	..	Hilton/Slater
30 Apr	Southampton	A	L	1-2	..	Potts	..	Bonds	..	..	..	..	Rosenior	..1	Parris	
2 May	Chelsea	H	W	4-1	..	Parris	..	Potts	Hilton1	..	..	..	..(so)2	..1	Robson	
7 May	Newcastle U	A	L	1-2	..	..	..	..	..	..	..	..	..	..	..1	
	Littlewoods Cup															
22 Sep	Barnsley (2:1)	A	D	0-0	..	Potts*	Parris	Strodder	Martin	Brady	..	McAvennie	Ince	..	..	McQueen
6 Oct	Barnsley (2:2)	H	L	2-5	..	Parris*	McQueen	..	..	..	..	Keen1	..	..	..1	Dickens/Hilton
	FA Cup															
9 Jan	Charlton (3)	H	W	2-0	..	Potts	Stewart	Bonds	Strodder	Gale	..	Brady*1	Hilton	..1	Robson	Ince
30 Jan	Queens Park R (4)	A	L	1-3	..	Stewart	McQueen*	..	..	..	..	..	Dickens	..1	..	Hilton
	Simod Cup															
Nov 10	Millwall	H	L	1-2	McAlister	Potts *	Parris	Hilton	Martin	Brady	Ward	Dickens1	Ince	Dolan	Robson	Keen

Hammer of the Year 1987-88
STEWART ROBSON

	P	W	L	D	F:A	Pts	Pos
Liverpool	40	26	2	12	87:24	90	1st
West Ham	40	9	16	15	40:52	42	16th

Liam Brady (v. Watford in 1987)

SEASON 1988-89 FOOTBALL LEAGUE (DIVISION 1)

27 Aug	Southampton	A	L	0-4	McAlister	Potts	Dicks	Gale*	Martin	Keen	Ward	Parris	Slater	Kelly	Robson	Hilton/Dickens
3 Sep	Charlton	H	L	1-3	..	..*	..	Dickens	..	..1	..	..	..	..	..	Ince/Devonshire
10 Sep	Wimbledon	A	W	1-0	McKnight	Parris	..	Hilton	..	Ince	..1	Kelly*	Rosenior	Dickens	..	Devonshire
17 Sep	Aston Villa	H	D	2-2	McKnight	..	..	Strodder*	..	..	..	..1	..	..	..	.. (Mountfield og)
24 Sep	Manchester U	A	L	0-2	..	..	..	..	Hilton	..	..	..	..	..	..	..
1 Sep	Arsenal	H	L	1-4	..	..*	..	Hilton	Martin	..	..	..	..	..1	..	Strodder/Devonshire
8 Oct	Middlesbrough	A	L	0-1	..	Potts*	..	Gale	Hilton	Devonshire	..	..	Parris	..	Ince	Keen
15 Oct	Queens Park R	A	L	1-2	..	..	..	..	..	..*	..	..1	Rosenior	..	..	..
22 Oct	Newcastle	H	W	2-0	..	Stewart1	..	..	Martin	..*	..	..	Slater	..1	..	Keen
29 Oct	Liverpool	H	L	0-2	..	..	..	..	..	..	..	..*	..	..	..	Rosenior
5 Nov	Coventry	A	D	1-1	..	Potts	..	..	..	Keen	..	..1	Resenior	..	..	
12 Nov	Nottingham F	H	D	3-3	..	..	..	..	..	..	..	..*2	..1	..	..	Brady/Parris
19 Nov	Luton T	A	L	1-4	..	..	..	..	..1	..*	..	Brady	..	..	..	Parris/Hilton
26 Nov	Everton	H	L	0-1	..	..	..	..	..	..	..*	..	..	..	..	Devonshire
3 Dec	Millwall	A	W	1-0	..	..	..	..	..	Devonshire	Brady	Kelly	..	..	..1	
10 Dec	Sheffield W	H	D	0-0	..	..	Parris	..	..	..	..	..	..	..	..	
17 Dec	Tottenham H	H	L	0-2	..	..	..	..	..	..*	..	..	..	..	..	Keen
27 Dec	Norwich C	A	L	1-2	..	Potts	..	..	..*	..	..	..	..	..	..	Stewart1/Keen
31 Dec	Charlton	A	D	0-0	..	..	Dicks	..	..	Stewart	..*	..	..	..	Keen	Parris
2 Jan	Wimbledon	H	L	1-2	..	..	..	..	..	..	..	..	..1	..	..	
14 Jan	Derby C	A	W	2-1	..	Stewart*	..	..	Potts	Devonshire	..1	..1	..	..	Ince	Strodder/Keen
21 Jan	Manchester U	H	L	1-3	..	Potts	..	..	Martin	..	..1	..*	..	Ward	..	..
4 Feb	Arsenal	A	L	1-2	..	..	..1	..	Stodder	..*	Ward	Dickens	..	Brady	..	Kelly
25 Feb	Queens Park R	H	D	0-0	Parkes	..	..	..	Martin	..	..	..*	Slater	..	..	Parris
11 Mar	Coventry C	H	D	1-1	..	..	..	..	..	..	Kelly	..	..	..	..1	
24 Mar	Aston Villa	A	W	1-0	..	Parris	..	Gale	Hilton	..*	Ward	McAvennie	..	..	..1	Dickens
27 Mar	Norwich C	H	L	0-2	..	..	..	..	..	Dickens	..	..	..	..*	..	Rosenior
1 Apr	Tottenham H	A	L	0-3	..	..	..	..	Strodder*	Potts	..	..	..	..	..	Dickens
8 Apr	Derby C	H	D	1-1	..	..	..	..	Martin	Dickens	..	..	Rosenior1	..	..	Potts/Slater
11 Apr	Middlesbrough	H	L	1-2	..	..	..	Potts	Hilton	..	..	..	..	..1	Keen	
15 Apr	Southampton	H	L	1-2	..	..	Keen	..	..	..	..	..	..	..*1	Ince	Slater/McQueen
22 Apr	Millwall	H	W	3-0	..	..1	Dicks1	Gale	Potts	..1	..	..	Slater	Keen	..*	McQueen
3 May	Newcastle U	A	W	2-1	..	..	..	..	Martin	..	..1	..	Slater	..1	..	Kelly
6 May	Luton T	H	W	1-0	..	..	..	..*	..	..1	..	Slater	Rosenior	..	..	Potts/Kelly
9 May	Sheffield W	A	W	2-0	..	..	..	..*	..	..1	..	..	..1	..	..	Potts
13 May	Everton	A	L	1-3	..	..	..	..	..	..	..	..1	..	..	..*	Potts/Kelly
18 May	Nottingham F	A	W	2-1	McKnight	..	..	..	..	..	..	..1	..1	..	Brady*	Potts
23 May	Liverpool	A	L	1-5	..	..	..	..	..	..	..	..	..1	Brady*	Ince	McAvennie/Keen
	Littlewood Cup															
27 Sept	Sunderland (2:1)	A	W	3-0	..	..	..	Hilton	..*	Ince	..	Kelly2	..1	Dickens	Robson	Potts
12 Oct	Sunderland (2:2)	H	W	2-1	..	Potts	..	Gale	Hilton	Devonshire*	..	..1	Parris	..1	Ince	Keen
1 Nov	Derby C (3)	H	W	5-0	..	Stewart1	..	..	Martin2	Keen1	..	..*	Rosenior1	..	..	Brady
30 Nov	Liverpool (4)	H	W	4-1	..	Potts	..	..1	..	Devonshire	Brady	..	..	..	..2	(Staunton og)
18 Jan	Aston Villa (QF)	H	W	2-1	..	..	..	..	Strodder	..	..	..1	..	..*	..1	Ward
12 Feb	Luton T (SF)	H	L	0-1	..	..	..	Gale	Martin	..	Ward	Dickens	..	Brady*	..	Kelly
1 Mar	Luton T (SF)	A	L	0-1	Parkes	..	..	..	..	Kelly	..	Parris	Slater	..	..	
	FA Cup															
8 Jan	Arsenal (3)	H	D	2-2	McKnight	Stewart	..	Potts	..	Devonshire*	Brady	Kelly	Rosenior	Dickens1	..	Keen (Bould og)
11 Jan	Arsenal (3R)	A	W	1-0	..	..	..	..	..*	..	..	..	..1	..	..	Strodder/Keen
28 Jan	Swindon (4)	A	D	0-0	..	Potts	..	Gale	..	..*	Ward	..	..	Brady	..	Dickens
1 Feb	Swindon (4R)	H	W	1-0	..	..	..	..	..*	..	..	..	..1	..	..	Strodder/Dickens
18 Feb	Charlton (5)	A	W	1-0	Parkes	..	Parkes	..	..	..*	..(so)	Dickens	Slater1	..	..	Keen
18 Mar	Norwich C (QF)	H	D	0-0	..	..	Dicks	..	Strodder	..*	Kelly	..	..	..	..	Keen
22 Mar	Norwich C (QF)	A	L	1-3	..	..	..*	..	..	..*	..	..	..	..	..1	Hilton/Keen
	Simod Cup															
9 Nov	West Bromwich Albion	H	W	5-2	McKnight	..	..	..	Hilton	Keen	Ward	Kelly 1	Rosenior 4	..*	..	Parris
22 Nov	Watford	A	L	1-1 (1-4 on pens)	..	..	..	..	Martin *	..	..	Brady	..	Dickens	..1	Hilton

Hammer of the Year 1988-89
PAUL INCE

	P	W	L	D	F:A	Pts	Pos
Arsenal	38	22	6	10	73:36	76	1st
West Ham	38	10	20	8	37:62	38	19th

1985-1992

SEASON 1989-90 FOOTBALL LEAGUE (DIVISION 1)

19 Aug	Stoke C	A	D	1-1	Parkes	Potts	Parris	Gale	Martin	Keen1	Ward	McAvennie*	Slater	Brady	Ince	Kelly
23 Aug	Bradford C	H	W	2-0	..	..	Dicks	..	..	..	..	Kelly	..2	..	Parris	
26 Aug	Plymouth	H	W	3-2	..	..	..	..	..	..1	..	..1	Allen M1	..	..	
2 Sep	Hull	A	D	1-1	..	..	..	..	..	..	..1	..(so)	Allen	..*	Slater	Devonshire
9 Sep	Swindon	H	D	1-1	..	..	..	..	..	..	..	..*	..1	..	Parris	Dolan/Devonshire
16 Sep	Brighton	A	L	0-3	..	..	..	..	..	..	..	Slater	..	..	..	
23 Sep	Watford	H	W	1-0	..	..	..1	..	..	..	Allen	..	Dolan*	Foster	..	Rosenior
26 Sep	Portsmouth	A	W	1-0	..	..	..	..	..	..	..	..	Rosenior1	..	..	
30 Sep	West Brom A	H	L	2-3	..	..	..1	..	..	..	..	..	Kelly*	..	..	Dolan1
7 Oct	Leeds U	H	L	0-1	..	..	..	..*	..	..	..	..	Ward	..	..	Brady
14 Oct	Sheffield U	A	W	2-0	..	..	..	Strodder	..	..	Ward2	..	Dolan	..	..	
18 Oct	Sunderland	H	W	5-0	..	..	..*	..	..	..1	..	..1	..2	Allen1	..	Brady
21 Oct	Port Vale	A	D	2-2	..	..	..	..	..	..1	..	..1	..	..	..	
28 Oct	Oxford	H	W	3-2	..	..	..1	..	..	..	Brady	..	..1	..	..1	
1 Nov	Bournemouth	A	D	1-1	..	..	..	..1	..	..*	..	..	..	..	..	Ward
4 Nov	Wolves	A	L	0-1	..	..	..	..	..	..*	..	..	..	..	..	Ward/Foster
11 Nov	Newcastle	H	D	0-0	..	..	..	..	..	..*	..*	..	..*	Ward	..	Devonshire/Kelly
18 Nov	Middlesbrough	H	W	2-0	..	..	..1	Foster	..	..	..	..1	Allen	..	..	
25 Nov	Blackburn	A	L	4-5	..	..	..1	Strodder	..	Devonshire	..1	..1	..	..1	Fashanu	
2 Dec	Stoke	H	D	0-0	..	..	..	..	..	..*	..	..	Keen	..	..	Kelly/Foster
9 Dec	Bradford C	A	L	1-2	..	..	McQueen	..	..	Gale	..	..	..	..1	Allen	
16 Dec	Oldham	H	L	0-2	Suckling	..	Dicks	..*	..	..	..	..	Foster	..	..	Keen/Devonshire
26 Dec	Ipswich T	A	L	0-1	..	..	..	..	..	..	..*	..	Keen	..	..	Parris/Kelly
30 Dec	Leicester C	A	L	0-1	..	..	..	..	..	..	Allen	Bishop	Morley	Kelly	Parris	
1 Jan	Barnsley	H	W	4-2	..	..	..1	Parris	..	..	Quinn	..	Keen*2	Morley	Allen1	Kelly
13 Jan	Plymouth	A	D	1-1	..	..	..	Gale	..	Devonshire*	Allen	..	..	..	Quinn1	Brady/Parris
20 Jan	Hull	H	L	1-2	..	..*	McQueen	Strodder	..	Gale	Brady	..	Quinn	..1	Keen	Kelly P/Kelly D
10 Feb	Brighton	H	W	3-1	Parkes	Robson	Dicks1	Parris*	..	..	..	..	Kelly	Slater	..	Quinn2
18 Feb	Swindon	H	D	2-2	Miklosko	..	..	..	..	..	..	Allen	Quinn2	..*	..	Bishop/Kelly
24 Feb	Blackburn	H	D	1-1	..	..*	..	..	..	..	..	..	..1	..	..	Kelly/Bishop
3 Mar	Middlesbrough	A	W	1-0	..	..	..	..	..	..	..*	..	..1	..	..	Bishop/Morley
10 Mar	Portsmouth	H	W	2-1	..	Slater	..1	..	Foster	..	..*	..1	Rosenior	Keen	Kelly	Quinn/Bishop
13 Mar	Watford	A	W	1-0	..	..	..	..	..	..	Bishop	..	Quinn	..	Morley1	
17 Mar	Leeds U	A	L	2-3	..	..	McQueen	..*	..	..	..	..	..	..	..1	Brady, (Chapman og)
21 Mar	Sheffield U	H	W	5-0	..	..	..	..	..	..	..	..1	..3	..	..1	
24 Mar	Sunderland	A	L	3-4	..	..	..	..	Strodder	..	..	..	..2	..*	..1	Brady
31 Mar	Port Vale	H	D	2-2	..	..	Dicks	..1	Foster	..	..	..	..*	..	..1	McAvennie/Brady
4 Apr	West Brom A	A	W	3-1	..	..	..	..	Strodder	..	..1	..	..1	Keen1	..	
7 Apr	Oxford U	A	W	2-0	..	..	..	..	Foster	..	..	..	..1	..*	..1	McQueen
11 Apr	Bournemouth	H	W	4-1	..	..	..1	..*	..	..	..1	..1	..	..	..*	Potts/McAvennie (Miller og)
14 Apr	Barnsley	A	D	1-1	..	..	..	..	..	..	Keen	..	..	Morley1	Brady	
17 Apr	Ipswich T	H	W	2-0	..	..	..	..	..	..	Brady	..1	..	Keen1	Morley*	McAvennie/Potts
21 Apr	Oldham	A	L	0-3	..	..	..	..	..	..	..	..	..	..	..	McQueen
28 Apr	Newcastle U	A	L	1-2	..	..	..1	Potts	..	..	Robson	..	..*	..	..	McAvennie/Parris
2 May	Leicester	H	W	3-1	..	..	..	..	..	..	..	..	Rosenior1	..*1	..1	Brady
5 May	Wolves	H	W	4-0	..	..	..	..	..	..	..1	..	..	..*1	..1	Brady1/Quinn
	Littlewoods Cup															
19 Sept	Birmingham (2:1)	A	W	2-1	..	Potts	..	Gale	Martin	Keen	Ward*	Slater1	Allen1	Dolan	Parris	Brady
4 Oct	Birmingham (2:2)	H	D	1-1	..	..	..1	..	..	..	Allen	..	Dolan*	Ward	..	Kelly/Brady
25 Oct	Aston Villa (3)	A	D	0-0	..	..	..	Strodder	..	..	Brady*	..	..	Allen	..	Kelly
8 Nov	Aston Villa (3R)	H	W	1-0	..	..	..1	..	..	..	..	..	..	Ward	..	
22 Nov	Wimbledon (4)	H	W	1-0	..	..	..(so)	..	..	..*	..	..	Allen1	..	..	Fashanu/Devonshire
17 Jan	Derby C (QF)	H	D	1-1	..	..	..1	Parris	..	Gale	..	Kelly	Resenior*	Allen (so)	Keen	Slater
24 Jan	Derby C (QF)	A	D	0-0	..	Strodder	McQueen	..	..	..	..	..	Slater	Robson	..	Milne/Devonshire
31 Jan	Derby C (QF)	H	W	2-1	..	..	..	..	..	..	..*	..	..1	..	..1	McQueen
14 Feb	Oldham (SF)	A	L	0-6	..	Robson	Dicks	..	..	..	..	Slater	Strodder*	Kelly	..	Devonshire
7 Mar	Oldham (SF)	H	W	3-0	Miklosko	Slater	..1	..	..1	..	..	Allen	Resenior	..1	..	McQueen
	FA Cup															
6 Jan	Torquay (3)	A	L	0-1	Parkes	Potts	..	Parris*	..	..	Quinn	Bishop	Keen	Morley	Allen	Resenior
	Zenith Data Systems Cup															
29 Nov	Plymouth Argyle	H	W	5-2	..	..	..1	Strodder	Martin 1	Keen 1	Devonshire	Slater1	Allen	Ward*	Kelly*	Foster/Dolan1
22 Dec	Chelsea	A	L	3-4	..	..	..	..	Keen 1	Gale	Brady*	..1	Foster	..	Allen	Kelly1

Hammer of the Year 1989-90
JULIAN DICKS

	P	W	L	D	F:A	Pts	Pos
Leeds	46	24	8	13	79:51	85	1st
West Ham	46	20	14	12	80:57	52	7th

SEASON 1990-91 FOOTBALL LEAGUE (DIVISION 1)

25 Aug	Middlesbrough	A	D	0-0	Miklosko	Potts	Dicks	Foster	Martin	Keen	Bishop	McAvennie	Slater	Allen	Morley	
29 Aug	Portsmouth	H	D	1-1	..	..	..	..	..	..	..	..1	..	..	..	
1 Sep	Watford	H	W	1-0	..	..	..1	..	..	..	..	..	..	..	..	Quinn/Parris
8 Sep	Leicester	A	W	2-1	..	..	..	..	..	..	..	..*	..	..	..1	.. (James og)
15 Sep	Wolves	H	D	1-1	..	..	..	..	..1	..	..	..	Livett*	..	..	Parris
19 Sep	Ipswich T	H	W	3-1	..	..	..	..	..	..	..1	..*	Slater	..	..1	Quinn1/Parris
22 Sep	Newcastle	A	D	1-1	..	..	..	..	..	..	..	Quinn*	..	..	..1	McAvennie/Parris
29 Sep	Sheffeild W	A	D	1-1	..	..	..1	..	..	..	..	..	..	..	..	
3 Oct	Oxford	H	W	2-0	..	..	..	..1	..	..	..	..	..*	..	..1	Parris
6 Oct	Hull	H	W	7-1	..	..1	..2	..	..	..*	..	..2	Parris1	..	..1	McAvennie/Rush
13 Oct	Bristol City	A	D	1-1	..	..	..	..	..	Parris	..	..	Slater*	..	..	McAvennie1
20 Oct	Swindon	A	W	1-0	..	..	..	..	..	..	..	..*	Gale	..	..	McAvennie1/Breacker
24 Oct	Blackburn	H	W	1-0	..	Breacker	..	..	..	..	..1	..*	..	..	..	McAvennie/Slater
27 Oct	Charlton	H	W	2-1	..	..	Keen	..	..	..	..	McAvennie	Slater*	..2	..	Rush
3 Nov	Notts Co	A	W	1-0	..	..	Parris	..	..	Hughton	..	Keen	Rush	..	..1	
10 Nov	Millwall	A	D	1-1	..	..	..	..	..	..	..	..	McAvennie1	..*	..	Rush
17 Nov	Brighton	H	W	2-1	..	..	..	..1	..	..	..	McAvennie.	Rush*	Keen	..	Slater1
24 Nov	Plymouth	A	W	1-0	..	..	..	..	..	..	..	..1	Slater	..	..	
1 Dec	West Brom A	H	W	3-1	..	..	..1	..	..	..	..	..1	..	..*	..1	Allen
8 Dec	Portsmouth	A	W	1-0	..	..	..	..	..	..	..	..*	..	Allen	..1	Quinn/Gale
15 Dec	Middlesbrough	H	D	0-0	..	..	..	Gale	Potts	Hughton	Keen	McAvennie	..	..	..*	Quinn
22 Dec	Barnsley	A	L	0-1	..	..	..	..	..	..	..	..*	..	..	..	..
26 Dec	Oldham	H	W	2-0	..	..	..	..	Foster	..	..	Quinn	..1	..	..1	
29 Dec	Port Vale	H	D	0-0	..	..	..	..	..	..	..	..	..	..	..	Potts
1 Jan	Bristol Rov	A	W	1-0	..	..	..	..	..	..	..	Potts	Quinn1	Slater	..	
12 Jan	Watford	A	W	1-0	..	..	..	..	..	..	..	Slater	..*	Potts	..1	Clarke/Robson
19 Jan	Leicester	H	W	1-0	..	..	..1	..	Bishop	..	..	..*	..	..	..	McAvennie
2 Feb	Wolves	A	L	1-2	..	..	..	..	..	..	..	McAvennie1	Slater*	..	..	Allen/Quinn
24 Feb	Millwall	H	W	3-1	..	..	..	..	..	..	..	..2	..	..	..1	Allen
2 Mar	West Brom A	A	D	0-0	..	..	..	..	..	..	..*	..	..	..	..	
5 Mar	Plymouth	H	D	2-2	..	..1	..	Foster	..	..*	..	..	..	..	Quinn	Allen (Marker og)
13 Mar	Oxford	A	L	1-2	..	..*	..	Gale	Foster	..	Bishop	..	Carr	..	..1	Keen/Slater
16 Mar	Sheffield Wed	H	L	1-3	..	Potts	..	..	..	..*	..	..	Slater	Keen	..1	Allen/Carr
20 Mar	Bristol City	H	W	1-0	..	..	..	..1	..	..	..	..(so)	..*	..	..	Allen/Rosenior
23 Mar	Hull	A	D	0-0	..	..	..	..	..	..	..	..*	Dowie	..	Allen	Carr/Rosenior
29 Mar	Oldham	A	D	1-1	..	..	..	..	..	..	..1	..	..	Slater	..	
1Apr	Barnsley	H	W	3-2	..	..	..	..	..1	..*	..	..1	..1	..	..	Keen
6 Apr	Port Vale	A	W	1-0	..	..	..	..	..	..	..1	Slater	..	Keen	..	
10 Apr	Brighton	A	L	0-1	..	..	..	Stewart	..	..	..	Keen	..*	Morley	Slater	Allen/Quinn
17 Apr	Ipswich T	A	W	1-0	..	..	..	Gale	..	..	..	Slater	..*	Keen	Morley1	McAvennie/Allen
20 Apr	Swindon	H	W	2-0	..	..	..1	..	Stewart	..	..	..	..1	..*	..	Allen
24 Apr	Newcastle U	H	D	1-1	..	..	..	..	..	..	..	..	..1	..	..	..
27 Apr	Blackburn	A	L	1-3	..	..	..	..	..	..	..	Keen	..1	Slater*	..	Allen/Quinn
4 May	Charlton	A	D	1-1	..	..	..	Breacker	..	..	..	Allen1	..*	..	..	Quinn
8 May	Bristol Rov	H	W	1-0	..	Breacker	..	Potts	Foster	..	..	Slater1	..*	Allen	..	McAvennie/Keen
11 May	Notts Co	H	L	1-2	..	Potts	..1	Breacker	..	..	..	..	..*	..	..	McAvennie/Keen
	Rumbelows Cup															
26 Sept	Stoke C (2:1)	H	W	3-0	..	..	Dicks1	Foster	Martin	Keen1	..	Quinn1	Slater	..*	..	Parris
10 Oct	Stoke C (2:2)	A	W	2-1	..	..	..	..	..	..*	..	Parris	Quinn	..2	..	Gale/McAvennie
31 Oct	Oxford (3)	A	L	1-2	..	Rush	Keen	..	..	Parris	..	Quinn	Slater	..	..1	
	FA Cup															
5 Jan	Aldershot (3R)	A	D	0-0	Miklosko	Breacker	Parris	Gale	Foster*	Hughton	Keen	Slater	Quinn	Potts	Morley	Livett
16 Jan	Aldershot (4)	H	W	6-1	..	..	..1	..	Robson*	..	..	..1	..1	..	..2	Bishop 1
26 Jan	Luton T (5)	A	D	1-1	..	..	..1	..	Bishop	..	..*	..	Allen	..	..	McAvennie
30 Jan	Luton T (5R)	H	W	5-0	..	..	..1	..	..1	..	..	McAvennie1	Slater	..	..2	
16 Feb	Crewe A (6)	H	W	1-0	..	..	..	..	..	..	..	..*	..	..	..	Quinn1
11 Mar	Everton (QF)	A	W	2-1	..	..	..	..	Foster1	..	Bishop	..	..1	..	Quinn*	Keen
14 Mar	Nottingham F (SF)	H	L	0-4	..	Potts	..	..(so)	..	..	..	Slater	Allen*	Keen	Morley*	Stewart/Quinn
	ZENITH DATA SYSTEMS CUP															
19 Dec	Luton Town	A	L	1-5	McKnight	Kelly	..	..	Potts	Livett	Allen	Quinn	Slater	..1	..	

Hammer of the Year 1990-91
LUDEK MIKLOSKO

	P	W	L	D	F:A	Pts	Pos
Oldham	46	25	8	12	83:53	88	1st
West Ham	46	24	7	15	60:37	87	2nd

Julian Dicks against Bristol City in 1990.

SEASON 1991-92 FOOTBALL LEAGUE (DIVISION 1)

17 Aug	Luton T	H	D	0-0	Miklosko	Brown	Thomas	Breacker	Foster	Parris	Bishop*	Slater	Small	Rosenior	Allen M	Keen
20 Aug	Sheffield U	A	D	1-1	..	..	..	..	..	..	..	..	..1	..*	..	Morley/Keen
24 Aug	Wimbledon	A	L	0-2	..	..	..	..	..	..	..	..	..	..	..*	Morley/Rush
28 Aug	Aston Villa	H	W	3-1	..	..1	..	..	..	..	..	..	..1	..1	..*	Rush
31 Aug	Notts Co	H	L	0-2	Parks	..	..	..	..	..	..	..	..	..*	Rush	Morley/Hughton
4 Sep	Queen Park R	A	D	0-0	..	..	..	..	..	..	..	..	..*	Potts	Morley	Rush/Rosenior
7 Sep	Chelsea	H	D	1-1	Miklosko	..	..	..	..	..	..	..	..1	..	..	
14 Sep	Norwich	A	L	1-2	..	..	..	..	..	..*	..	..	..1	..	..	Rush/Rosenior
17 Sep	Crystal Palace	A	W	3-2	..	..	Parris	Thomas1	..	Breacker	..	..	..1	..	..1	
21 Sep	Manchester C	H	L	1-2	..	..1	..	Breacker	..(so)	Parris	..	..	..	..	..*	Rosenior
28 Sep	Nottingham F	A	D	2-2	..	Breacker	Thomas	Gale	..	..	..	..	..*2	..	..	..
5 Oct	Coventry	H	L	0-1	..	..	..*	..	Brown	..	..	..	..	..	..	Allen M/Keen
19 Oct	Oldham	A	D	2-2	..	..	..	..	Potts	..	..	..*	..1	Keen	..	Allen M/McAvennie1
26 Oct	Tottenham H	H	W	2-1	..	..	..1	..	..	..	..	McAvennie	..1	..*	Slater	Allen M
2 Nov	Arsenal	A	W	1-0	..	..	..	..	..	..	..	..	..1	..	..	
17 Nov	Liverpool	H	D	0-0	..	..	..	..	..	..	..	..	..	..	..	
23 Nov	Manchester U	A	L	1-2	..	..	..	..	..	..	..	..1	..	..*	..	Allen M
30 Nov	Sheffield Wed	H	L	1-2	..	..1	..	..	..	..	..	..	..	..*	..	..
7 Dec	Everton	A	L	0-4	..	..(so)	..	..	..	..*	..	..	..	Allen M	..	Keen
21 Dec	Sheffield U	H	D	1-1	..	Brown	Dicks1	..	..	Foster	..	..	..*	..	..	..
26 Dec	Aston Villa	A	L	1-3	..	Breacker	..	..	..	Parris	..	..1	..*	Keen	..	Morley
28 Dec	Notts Co	A	L	0-3	..	..	..	..	..	Foster	..	..	..	..	..	
1 Jan	Leeds U	H	L	1-3	..	..	..1	..	..	Thomas	..	..	..*	..	..	Morley
11 Jan	Wimbledon	H	D	1-1	..	..	..	..	Foster	..*	..	..	Brown	..	..	Morley1/Small
18 Jan	Luton T	A	W	1-0	..	..	..	Potts	..	..	..	..	..	Morley	..	Keen/Small1
1 Feb	Oldham	H	W	1-0	Parks	..	..1	..	..	..	Keen	..	..	..*	..	Small
22 Feb	Sheffield Wed	A	L	1-2	..	..	..	..	..	Atteveld	Bishop	Keen*	Small1	Allen M	..	Brown
29 Feb	Everton	H	L	0-2	..	..	..	..	..	Thomas	..	Brown	..	..	..*	Morley/Rush
3 Mar	Southampton	A	L	0-1	..	Potts	..	Gale	..	..*	..	..	..	..	..	..
11 Mar	Liverpool	A	L	0-1	Miklosko	Brown	..	..	Potts	..*	..	Keen	..	..	..	Rush
14 Mar	Arsenal	H	L	0-2	..	..	..	..	Foster	Keen	..	McAvennie*	..	..	..	Morley/Parris
21 Mar	Queen Park R	H	D	2-2	..	..	..	..	..	..	..*	..	..1	..	..	Thomas/Breacker1
28 Mar	Leeds U	A	D	0-0	..	..	..	Breacker	..	Potts	..	Thomas	..	..	..*	McAvennie/Gale
1 Apr	Tottenham F	A	L	0-3	..	..*	..	Gale	..	Breacker	..	..	..	..	..	McAvennie/Keen
4 Apr	Chelsea	A	L	1-2	..	..	..	..	..	Potts	..	McAvennie	Thomas	Allen C1	Keen*	Morley
11 Apr	Norwich	H	W	4-0	..	Breacker	..1	Potts	Martin A	Thomas	..1	Rush2	Small*	..	Slater	Keen
14 Apr	Southampton	H	L	0-1	..	..	Gale	Hughton	..	Morley	..	..*	..	..	..	..
18 Apr	Manchester C	A	L	0-2	..	..	Dicks	Potts	..	Keen	..	Gale	..*	Morley	..	Clarke
20 Apr	Crystal Palace	H	L	0-2	..	..*	..	..	..	Thomas	..	Keen	Morley	Allen C	..	Brown
22 Apr	Manchester U	H	W	1-0	..	Potts	..	Gale	..	..	..	..	Small	Brown1	..	
25 Apr	Coventry	A	L	0-1	..	..	..	..	..	..	..	..	..	..*	..	Morley/Martin D
2 May	Nottingham F	H	W	3-0	..	..	..	..	..	..*	..	Allen M	..	Martin D	..	McAvennie3

Rumblelows Cup

24 Sept	Bradford C (2:1)	A	W	1-1	..	Brown	Parris	Thomas	Foster	Breacker	..	Slater	..1	Potts	Morley*	Gale
9 Oct	Bradford C (2:2)	H	W	4-0	..	Breacker	Thomas	Gale	..	Parris1	..	..	..*1	Keen1	..1	McAvennie
29 Oct	Sheffield U (3)	A	W	2-0	..	..	..	..*	Potts	..	..	McAvennie1	..1	..	Slater	Allen M
4 Dec	Norwich (4)	A	L	1-2	..	..	..	..	..	..	..	..	..1	Allen M	..	

FA Cup

4 Jan	Farnborough (3)	A	D	1-1	..	..	Dicks1	Gale	..*	Thomas	Bishop	McAvennie	Small	Keen	..	Morley
14 Jan	Farnborough (3R)	H	W	1-0	..	..	..	..	Foster	..	..	..	Brown	Morley1	..	
25 Jan	Wrexham (4)	H	D	2-2	..	..	..	Potts1	..	..	Keen	..*	..	..1	..	Small
4 Feb	Wrexham (4R)	A	W	1-0	Parks	..	..	..	..1	..	..	..	..	Small	..	Martin D/Morley
15 Feb	Sunderland (5)	A	D	1-1	Parks	..	..	..	..	Atteveld	..	Brown	Small1	Allen M	..	
26 Feb	Sunderland (5R)	H	L	2-3	Parks	..	..	..	..	..*	Bishop	Keen	..	..2	..	Morley

ZENITH DATA SYSTEMS CUP

22 Oct	Cambridge United	H	W	2-1	Miklosko	Breacker	Hughton	Gale	Potts	Parris 1	Bishop	McAvennie 1	Small	Keen	Allen M	
26 Nov	Brighton & Hove Albion	H	W	2-0	Miklosko	Breacker	Thomas	Gale	Potts	Parris	Bishop	McAvennie 2	Small	Keen	Slater	
7 Jan	Southampton	A	L	1-2	Miklosko	Breacker	Dicks	Gale	Foster	Thomas	Bishop 1	McAvennie	Brown	Keen *	Slater	Morley

Hammer of the Year 1991-92

JULIAN DICKS

	P	W	L	D	F:A	Pts	Pos
Leeds U	42	22	4	16	74:37	82	1st
West Ham	42	9	22	11	37:59	38	22nd

SEASON 1992-93 FOOTBALL LEAGUE (DIVISION 1)

16 Aug	Barnsley	A	W	1-0	Miklosko	Breacker	Dicks	Potts	Martin	Parris	Bishop	Butler	Small(so)	Allen C*1	Keen	Gale/Robson
22 Aug	Charlton A	H	L	0-1	..	..	..	..	..	..	..*	..	..	..	..	Robson
29 Aug	Newcastle U	A	L	0-2	..	..	..(so)	..	..	Holmes*	..	..	Allen M	..	..	Small
5 Sep	Watford	H	W	2-1	..	..	..	..	..	Allen M1	Robson*	..	Morley	..1	..	Parris
12 Sep	Peterborough	A	W	3-1	..	..	Thomas	..	..	..1	..	..	..1	..*	..1	Small
15 Sep	Bristol C	A	W	5-1	..	..	..	..	..	..	..*1	..	..2	..2	..	..
20 Sep	Derby C	H	D	1-1	..	..	..	..	..	..	..*	..	..1	..	..	..
27 Sep	Portsmouth	A	W	1-0	..	..	Dicks	..	..	..	..*	..	..	..1	..	Holmes
4 Oct	Wolves	A	D	0-0	..	..	..(so)	..	..	..	..*	..	..	..	..	Holmes/Gate
11 Oct	Sunderland	H	W	6-0	..	..	..	..	..1	..1	..2	..	..1	..	..1	
17 Oct	Bristol R	A	W	4-0	..	..	..1	..	..	..	..	..	..1	..1	..1	
24 Oct	Swindon	H	L	0-1	..	..	Parris(so)	..	..	..	..	..	..	..	..	
31 Oct	Cambridge	A	L	1-2	..	..	..	..	..	..	..	..	..1	..	..	
3 Nov	Grimsby	A	D	1-1	..	..	..	..	..	..	..*	..	..1	..	..	
7 Nov	Notts Co	H	W	2-0	..	..	Brown	..	..	..	..	..	..1	..1	..	
15 Nov	Millwall	A	L	1-2	..	..	..	..	..	Parris	..1	Holmes	..	..	..*	Clarke
21 Nov	Oxford	H	W	5-3	..	..1	Dicks2	..	..	..	..	..	..1	..1	..*	Brown
28 Nov	Birmingham	H	W	3-1	..	..	..	..	Foster	..	..	..	..1	..2	..*	Bishop
4 Dec	Tranmere	A	L	2-5	..	..	..	..	Martin	Allen M	..	Parris*	..1	..1	..	Bishop/Foster
12 Dec	Southend	H	W	2-0	..	..	..	..	..	Parris*	..	Allen M	..1	..1	..	Bishop
20 Dec	Brentford	A	D	0-0	..	..	..	..	..	Allen M	..	Bishop	..	..	..	Bunbury
26 Dec	Charlton	A	D	1-1	..	..	..1	..	..	..	..	..*	..	..	..	..
28 Dec	Luton T	H	D	2-2	..	..1	..1	..	..	..	..	Butler	..	..	..	
10 Jan	Derby	A	W	2-0	..	..	..(so)	..	..	..	..*1	..	..1	..*	..	Foster/Parris
16 Jan	Portsmouth	H	W	2-0	..	..	..	..	Foster1	..	..	..	..1	..	..	Holmes/Parris
27 Jan	Bristol City	H	W	2-0	..	..	Brown	..	Gale	..	..*1	..	..1	Bunbury*	..	..
30 Jan	Leiecester	A	W	2-1	..	..	..	..	..1	..	..*1	..	..	Holmes	..	Parris/Jones
6 Feb	Barnsley	H	D	1-1	..	..	Dicks	..	..	..	..	..	..	Jones1	..	
9 Feb	Peterborough	H	W	2-1	..	..	..	..	..	..	..	..1	..	..1	..*	Holmes
13 Feb	Watford	A	W	2-1	..	..	..	..	..	..	..*2	..	..	..	..	Holmes/Bishop
21 Feb	Newcastle	H	D	0-0	..	Brown	..	..	..	..	..	..	..	Bishop	..*	Jones
27 Feb	Sunderland	A	D	0-0	..	..	..	..	..	Bishop	..	..	..	Bunbury*	..	Parris/Holmes
6 Mar	Wolves	H	W	3-1	..	..	..1	..	..	..	..	..	..1	Small	..	Holmes 1
9 Mar	Grimsby	H	W	2-1	..	..	..2	..	..	Allen M	..	..	..	..*	..	Bishop
13 Mar	Notts Co	A	L	0-1	..	..	..	..	..	..	..*	..	..	..	..	Bishop
20 Mar	Tranmere	H	W	2-0	..	..	..2	..	..	..	..*	..	Speedie	Morley	..	Holmes
23 Mar	Oxford	A	L	0-1	..	..	..	..	..	..	Holmes	..	..	..	..*	Robson
28 Mar	Millwall	H	D	2-2	..	Breacker	Brown	..	..	Bishop	Robson	..	..	..1	..1	
3 Apr	Birmingham	A	W	2-1	Miklosko	Breacker	Brown1	Potts	Gale	Bishop1	Robson*	Butler	Speedie	Jones	Keen	Holmes/Foster
7 Apr	Southend	A	L	0-1	..	..	Dicks	..	..	..	..	..	..	Foster	..	
11 Apr	Leicester	H	W	3-0	..	..	..	..	..	..	..	..	..2	Morley	..1	
13 Apr	Luton T	A	L	0-2	..	..	..	..	..	..	Allen M*	..	..	..	..	Holmes
17 Apr	Brentford	H	W	4-0	..	..	..	..	..	Allen M1	Robson	..1	..	..1	..1	
24 Rpr	Bristol Rov	H	W	2-1	..	..	..1	..	..	..	..*	..	..1	..	..	Bishop
2 May	Swindon	A	W	3-1	..	..	..	..	..	Bishop	..*	..	..	..1	..	Allen C1/Brown1
8 May	Cambridge U	H	W	2-0	..	..	..	..	..	..	..*	..	..1	..	..	Allen C1/Allen M

Coca-Cola Cup

23 Sep	Crewe (2:1)	H	D	0-0	..	..	Thomas	..	Martin	Allen M	..	..	Morley	Allen C	..*	Small
7 Oct	Crewe (2:2)	A	L	0-2	..	..	Dicks	..	..	..	..	..	..	..	..	

FA Cup

2 Jan	West Brom A (3)	A	W	2-0	..	..	Dicks	..	Martin	..	..1	..	..	..1	..	
24 Jan	Barnsley (4)	A	L	1-4	..	..	Brown	..	Foster	..	..*	..	..1	Holmes	..	Bunbury

ANGLO ITALIAN CUP WINNERS CUP

2 Sep	Bristol Rovers	H	D	2-2	Banks	Potts	Dicks 2	Gale	Martin	Allen M	Robson *	Butler	Morley	Allen C	Keen	Rush
30 Sep	Southend United	A	W	3-0	Miklosko	Breacker	Dicks 1	Potts	Martin	Allen M	Robson	Holmes 1	Morley 1	Allen C	Keen	
11 Nov	Cremonese	A	L	0-2	Miklosko	Brown	Dicks	Potts	Martin	Allen M	Robson	Parris *	Morley	Allen C	Holmes	Keen
24 Nov	Reggiana	H	W	2-0	Miklosko	Breacker	Dicks	Potts	Martin *	Allen M	Robson *	Holmes	Morley	Allen C 2	Keen	Brown/Bishop
8 Dec	Cosenza	A	W	1-0	Miklosko	Breacker	Dicks	Potts	Martin	Allen M	Rush	Parris	Jones	Allen C 1 *	Keen *	Foster/Brown
16 Dec	Pisa	H	D	0-0	Miklosko	Breacker	Dicks	Potts	Martin	Allen M	Rush	Bishop	Bunbury	Allen C *	Keen	Jones/Robson

Hammer of the Year 1992-93

STEVE POTTS

	P	W	L	D	F:A	Pts	Pos
Newcastle U	46	29	8	9	92:38	96	1st
West Ham	46	26	10	10	81:48	88	2nd

Frank McAvennie against Millwall, 1991.

1985-1992

CHAPTER 8
INTO THE PREMIERSHIP

'Consolidation' was the buzz word around Upton Park as Hammers prepared for their first season in the FA Carling Premiership during the summer of 1993. Painful memories of the Club's recent ignominious relegation were still fresh in the minds of both players and supporters, and the undoubted aim for season 1993–94 was to avoid a repeat performance. But with work on the redevelopment of the South Bank already underway, the West Ham United board could not afford to grant Billy Bonds the sort of transfer budget that would let him buy his way to safety. Instead the manager would have to spend carefully, and his most expensive summer buy was Rangers winger Dale Gordon, who arrived at Upton Park for £750,000. Gordon would take the place of Kevin Keen, who had been sold to Wolverhampton Wanderers for £600,000 despite playing a key role in the Hammers' promotion campaign.

Bonds made two other significant signings ahead of the new season, bringing in utility player Keith Rowland, from AFC Bournemouth, for a fee of £175,000, and centre-half Simon Webster from Charlton Athletic for £500,000. Webster, however, was to suffer a disastrous start to his career at Upton Park, sustaining a broken leg after a challenge with Julian Dicks during pre-season training. The 29-year-old stopper, who had been widely tipped to become Club captain, would never fully recover from this injury and, after just five substitute appearances in 1995, was forced to retire. Without Webster, and with no new strikers signed during the close season, changes to the Hammers line-up were confined to midfield. Peter Butler and Martin Allen remained Bonds' first-choice pairing in the middle of the pitch, but wingers Kevin Keen and Mark Robson (who would soon join Charlton Athletic) were replaced with Matt Holmes and Dale Gordon on the flanks. It was hoped that this change would give Hammers more resilience without detracting from the team's attacking threat. The theory, however, proved flawed when Wimbledon visited Upton Park for the season's opening game and claimed a relatively straightforward 2–0 win.

Early season struggles

Hammers followed their disappointing defeat against the Dons with an equally forgettable performance against Leeds United at Elland Road. This time the margin of defeat was just one goal, but for much of the game the travelling fans had to endure watching the ungainly Colin Foster attempt to play as an emergency striker. A trip to Coventry City was next on the agenda, and the match against the Sky Blues brought Hammers not only their first Premiership point but also their first goal in the new League – scored by Dale Gordon. Four days later, Sheffield Wednesday visited Upton Park and two late goals from Clive Allen proved enough to secure all three points. However, victory over the Owls served only to paper over some deep cracks, and in their next three games Hammers failed to score and claimed just one point. An injection of fresh talent was clearly needed, but with no money available Bonds would have to sell before he could buy.

Despite his chequered disciplinary record, Julian Dicks remained Hammers' most saleable asset, and – following a chance conversation with Harry Redknapp – Liverpool manager Graeme Souness expressed his interest in the England B defender. Souness initially proposed a straight swap deal for Reds' left-back David Burrows, but after much bartering he was persuaded to include midfielder Mike Marsh and a cash adjustment of £200,000 in the deal. 'The money was very important,' wrote Harry Redknapp in his autobiography. 'We hadn't got a striker who could score goals. Clive Allen was out injured, and we were desperate for a scorer. I knew Lee Chapman was available and I believed he could do a job for us, with £200,000 enough to sign him.' Chapman had turned down a move to the Boleyn Ground during the summer of 1993, preferring instead to join First Division Portsmouth, but after just five games he was desperate for a return to the top-flight and this time he signed. For the price of one player the Hammers had brought in a top-class defender, a promising midfielder and a striker whose goals had shot Leeds United to the Championship in 1991–92. It seemed an amazing coup, but the fans would reserve judgment on a deal which had seen terrace idol Julian Dicks depart E13. Fortunately for Harry Redknapp – a well known horse-racing fan and the man behind this transfer bonanza – the gamble paid off.

Below: Former Leeds United striker Lee Chapman arrived at Upton Park in September 1993. He would score 11 goals in 39 appearances during 1992–93 but was often a target for the terrace boo boys.

Above: Left-back David Burrows joined the Hammers in the swap deal that took the hugely popular Julian Dicks to Anfield in Autumn 1993.

Chapman, Marsh and Burrows

All three new signings made their debuts in the match against Blackburn Rovers at Ewood Park. Blackburn were 11 places above the Hammers in the League table, and were on the brink of mounting a Championship challenge that would see them lose just two League games at home all season. Even with their

Right: Alvin Martin, second from left, challenges for a loose ball in the FA Cup quarter-final against Luton Town in March 1994.

Left: Veteran central-defender Alvin Martin celebrates the opening goal of Hammers' 2–0 victory over Oldham Athletic in November 1993. Alvin's appearances during 1993–94 would be restricted by injuries, but he still impressed Billy Bonds sufficiently to earn a new one-year contract at season's end.

trio of new signings, Billy Bonds' team was given little chance. However, a 33rd minute goal from Lee Chapman and a second-half header from Trevor Morley gave Hammers an unlikely, but well-deserved, 2–0 victory. It was just the boost that West Ham United's flagging fortunes needed and, although they lost their next match away to Newcastle – where £250,000 new signing Jerome Boere was sent off minutes after making his debut as a substitute – confidence began to grow. From the start of October, Hammers embarked upon a steady climb up the table and, after a run which brought just one defeat (away to Liverpool) in nine games, reached the dizzy heights of tenth place in the table.

By December, Billy Bonds' team were basking in the glorious inconsistency of a true mid-table team and, following an entertaining 3–2 home victory over Coventry City, suffered a 5–0 thrashing against Sheffield Wednesday at Hillsborough. It was a defeat, though, which had little effect on Hammers' League position and it was from the relative security of 11th place in the Premiership table that Bonds prepared his team for FA Cup action in January. First Division Watford provided the opposition in a third-round match at Upton Park, but it took second-half goals from Martin Allen and Mike Marsh to spare the blushes of the home team who had fallen behind after 27

Below: Rookie striker Steve Jones slides the ball past Norwich City goalkeeper Bryan Gunn during a thrilling 3–3 draw against the East Anglians in January 1994. Jones, who had joined Hammers from non-League Billericay Town in November 1992, proved a big hit with supporters at the Boleyn Ground.

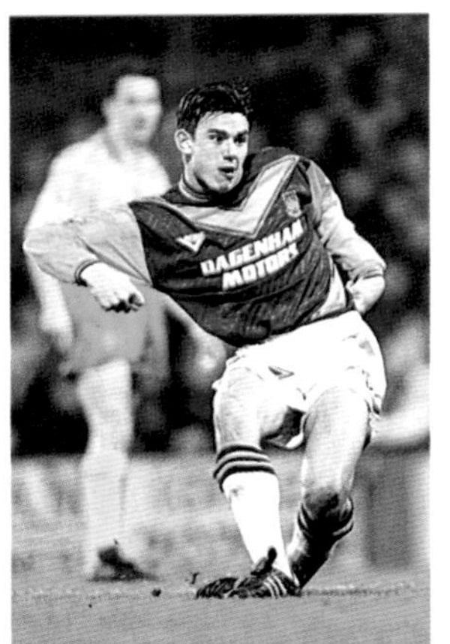

minutes. Hammers' reward was a fourth round trip to First Division Notts County where a goal from Steve Jones earned a 1–1 draw and a replay at Upton Park. The rematch proved a dull and disappointing encounter, and was most memorable for the barracking directed at striker Lee Chapman who had gone seven games without a goal. The cat-calls, however, were brought to an abrupt end in the second period of extra-time when Chapman headed home Tim Breacker's cross for the only goal of the game. Hammers were again grateful for the aerial ability of the veteran striker in the fifth round, when his finish from Keith Rowland's looping centre earned victory over Vauxhall Conference side Kidderminster Harriers.

Potts' blunder proves costly

West Ham United had made it to the quarter-finals of the Cup and would now face David Pleat's Luton Town – conquerors of Newcastle United in the fourth round. The first match, at Upton Park, proved a cagey encounter and ended goalless, but nine days later at Kenilworth Road a rather more engaging match was played out. Hammers enjoyed the brighter start to the game, and after half an hour Martin Allen struck the opening goal when he broke the offside trap to fire past Hatters keeper Jurgen Sommer. However, the lead was to be short-lived, and two goals in 17 minutes from Scott Oakes put the Hatters in the driving seat. The excitement continued throughout the second half, but after Ian Bishop had got Hammers back on terms, following a smart counter-attack, disaster struck. Steve Potts, reigning Hammer of the Year, stepped forward to control a clearance as it bounced inside the Luton half, but succeeded only in standing on the ball which squirted free and fell to the on-rushing Scott Oakes. The Luton forward ran unchallenged through the Hammers half before completing his hat-trick with a right-footed shot past Ludek Miklosko. The match ended 3–2 and Potts still recalls with anguish the moment which cost West Ham United a Wembley semi-final with Chelsea: 'It was definitely the worst point in my footballing career. I can remember running behind him [Scott Oakes] and just thinking "miss, miss, miss" but he didn't. There was still 15 minutes left to play, though, and for the rest of the match I was just praying we were going to get another goal.'

Despite the disappointment of their defeat at Luton, Hammers had enjoyed an exciting Cup run, but in the League their form had slumped alarmingly. At the end of March – after a run of nine games without a win – the Club was down to 15th in the table and on the fringes of the relegation battle. However, while results had been poor, Hammers were still providing great entertainment to the Upton Park faithful, with exciting draws against Norwich City and Manchester United proving particular highlights. The game against United – which ended 2–2 after former Hammer Paul Ince scored a late equaliser after receiving a 'warm' reception on his return to the Boleyn Ground – had also seen the opening of the new Bobby Moore stand. The stand would be formally unveiled on 7 March in the Bobby Moore Memorial Match, which saw George Graham select a Premiership XI that included both Tony Cottee and Julian Dicks.

Spurs and Arsenal defeated

Hammers began April just five points clear of the relegation places, but returned to winning ways with a 2–1 success against Ipswich Town at the Boleyn Ground. Winger Matthew Rush, who had recently returned from a loan spell with Swansea City, was to prove the hero against Town, netting a 30-yard volley to open the scoring and winning the free-kick that led to Trevor Morley's decisive goal after 75 minutes. Relegation worries were further eased two days later, when Hammers produced their most emphatic victory of the season to crush Tottenham Hotspur 4–1 at White Hart Lane. Morley, who would end the campaign as top scorer with 13 League goals, was again on the mark, netting twice between strikes from Steve Jones and Mike Marsh. A win against Oldham in Hammers' next away match left little to play for, but there was still time for a much lauded victory over Arsenal at Highbury on the penultimate Saturday of the season. George Graham's Gunners had the meanest defence in the Premiership, but goals from Trevor Morley and the in-form Martin Allen – his fourth in four games – earned a well-deserved 2–0 win. Victory at Highbury was followed by draws against Queens Park Rangers and Southampton, and at season's end Hammers occupied a creditable 13th place in the Premiership.

West Ham United's first campaign back in the top division had been a resounding success. On the field, the Club had finished in a comfortable League position and had made it to the quarter-finals of the FA Cup, while off the field, the first stage in the redevelopment of the Boleyn Ground was now complete. The challenge for Billy Bonds and Harry Redknapp was to maintain this momentum, though, and in his final programme notes of the 1993–94 season Bonds wrote: 'We need to strengthen the squad in a couple of areas and we are very much aware of this.'

The manager's first close-season action, however, was to grant a free transfer to long-serving defender Tony Gale. The former Fulham centre-half had made 35 appearances in the previous campaign but, on the day of his testimonial against an Ireland International XI, he was given the news that he was to be released. It was a huge disappointment to Gale, but he would recover from this setback in fine style, collecting a League Championship medal with Blackburn Rovers the following May.

Tony Cottee returned to Upton Park in September 1994, ending a six-year sojourn on Merseyside with Everton. His second spell as a Hammer would start tentatively with just one goal in his first 12 games, but he soon returned to more familiar form and struck 12 times in his next 19 appearances. He would end the season as the Club's top scorer with 15 goals in all competitions.

Billy Bonds departs

The departure of Tony Gale had left a huge void in the Hammers squad; not only had the team lost one of its most experienced defenders but also its number one dressing-room joker. Bonds acted quickly to fill the gap left by Gale – nick-named Reggie after Reggie Kray because of his evil sense of humour – and signed the equally quick-witted John Moncur from Swindon Town for £1m. As well as his sense of humour, Moncur would bring a good measure of both skill and industry to the Hammers midfield. Bonds made one other big-money signing ahead of pre-season training, paying Oxford United £850,000 for the services of talented winger Joey Beauchamp. It was a transfer, though, which quickly descended into farce. After one day's training Beauchamp told Harry Redknapp that he had made the wrong decision in joining the Hammers. He said that London was too far from his Oxford home and that he was unhappy making the long journey to and from training. It was an unprecedented situation and eventually the PFA were called in to mediate, but first Beauchamp would travel with the rest of the first-team squad on a pre-season tour of Scotland. And just when Hammers thought their preparations could get no worse a disastrous sequence of events began to unfold.

While in Scotland, Harry Redknapp was approached by former AFC Bournemouth chairman Geoffrey Hayward, who was contemplating buying the Hampshire club and wanted Redknapp to become his managing director. It was an offer which appealed to the Hammers assistant manager who still lived in Bournemouth. Redknapp immediately informed Billy Bonds and the pair met with Club chairman Terry Brown and managing director Peter Storrie. What exactly was said at the meeting will never be known by outsiders, but it is clear that a new management structure was proposed, with Bonds 'moving upstairs' to become director of football and Redknapp taking over as team manager. It was an arrangement, though, which did not appeal to Bonds, who interpreted the proposal as a snub, and decided to leave the Club altogether. Redknapp was immediately offered the job of replacing his friend and former boss, and after much soul-searching agreed to take the post. Bonds' departure was, according to Hammers skipper Steve Potts, 'a shot out of the blue,' coming, as it did, after a 'successful campaign and with plenty to look forward to in the following season.'

Harry Redknapp's first task as West Ham United manager was to sort out the increasingly embarrassing Beauchamp farce. The situation had reached a head when the 23-year-old malcontent appeared in a friendly at Southend and was booed by Hammers supporters throughout the match. Beauchamp clearly had no future in E13. The problem, however, was that he would only move to a club which was nearer to his Oxford home. Eventually Redknapp managed to strike a deal with Swindon Town that brought defender Adrian Whitbread and a cash adjustment to Hammers in exchange for the Club's most disastrous and short-lived signing. Redknapp made one other capture ahead of the new season, appointing brother-in-law and former Upton Park legend Frank Lampard as his assistant.

Redknapp rings the changes

Following the traumas of pre-season, Hammers made a predictably poor start to season 1994–95, and after four-and-a-half hours of League football they had gained just one point and were still waiting for their first goal of the campaign. The previous season's top scorer Trevor Morley was injured, and neither Lee Chapman nor Steve Jones looked likely to provide the answer to Hammers' goal famine. Harry Redknapp took decisive action, and swooped to sign Liverpool's goalscoring midfielder Don Hutchison in a club record £1.5m deal. With no real alternative, Redknapp cast his new signing straight into the forward line for a debut against top-of-the-table Newcastle at Upton Park on 31 August. But, although Hutchison marked his first appearance with a goal from the penalty spot, it was to prove no more than a consolation in a 3–1 reverse. Ahead of Hammers' next match, against Liverpool at Anfield, Redknapp would again enter the transfer market as he attempted to solve the Club's striker crisis. This time the manager opted for the proven talents of Tony Cottee and struck a deal with Everton which took David Burrows to Goodison Park in a straight swap. Cottee's second debut for the Hammers was to prove a disastrous occasion though, and after 55 minutes of a match which ended 0–0, the diminutive striker was sent off for a late lunge on Reds defender Rob Jones. The next fixture, against Aston Villa at Upton Park, did at least bring better fortunes, and with just four minutes remaining, Cottee struck the game's only goal with a sharp finish that gave Mark Bosnich no chance.

Changing the old guard. In the summer of 1994 Billy Bonds departed West Ham United after 27 years of unbroken service. Harry Redknapp took over as Hammers manager and immediately appointed former Upton Park legend Frank Lampard as his assistant.

Two wins in October lifted Hammers to the relative comfort of 13th place in the Premiership, but Redknapp was still looking to improve his squad and on 21 October the manager announced a signing which excited the Upton Park faithful more than probably any other in the Club's history. Julian Dicks was coming 'home'. And the good news was that his return would cost Hammers an initial fee of just £100,000 with further payments dependent upon appearances. Dicks made his return in the a 2–0 home victory against Southampton on 22 October, and the terrace idol looked to have lost none of his skill or confidence despite his disappointing sojourn on Merseyside.

Victory over Southampton had taken Hammers up to 12th place in the Premiership; however, thereafter the Club began to slide down the table and by Christmas Hammers were just one place above the relegation zone. Despite Redknapp's efforts on the transfer market, goalscoring remained a problem, and the situation was not helped when Don Hutchison was forced to sit out three games after being sent off against Leicester City on Bonfire Night. The only consolation against Leicester was that ten-man Hammers had rallied to claim an unlikely victory, with Julian Dicks slamming home the game's only goal from the penalty spot 13 minutes from time. Four consecutive defeats followed the win against the Foxes and Redknapp again acted to bolster his line-up. This time, though, the manager had no money to make permanent signings, so moved to bring in two players on loan deals. First, Northern Ireland international winger Michael Hughes arrived from French club Strasbourg and then, a week later, Denmark centre-half Marc Rieper joined from Brondby. Hughes and

Rieper were both in the Hammers team which made the trip to Elland Road for a match against Leeds United on 10 December, and each played their part in a comeback that saw Jeroen Boere net a brace of headers to claw back a two-goal deficit which earned Hammers their first away point for two months.

Cottee too hot for City

West Ham United returned to winning ways with a 3–0 success against Manchester City at Upton Park on the last Saturday before Christmas – Tony Cottee netting a hat-trick to end an 11-game barren spell without a goal. Hammers' form continued to show signs of improvement over the festive period, and a stylish 3–1 win at home to fourth-placed Nottingham Forest on New Year's Eve did much to boost confidence. However, at the turn of the year, Hammers were still languishing in 16th place and during January the situation deteriorated. Three defeats in the League were accompanied by an FA Cup exit away to Queens Park Rangers in the fourth round, and as February commenced Harry Redknapp was forced to contemplate a relegation battle. There were encouraging signs, however, not least the goalscoring form of the revitalised Tony Cottee. The diminutive striker scored his 100th goal for West Ham United in a 2-1 win at Leicester City, and followed up with a brace in a 2–2 draw at home to his former Club Everton. The match against the Merseysiders also marked the official unveiling of the Centenary stand, which had replaced the old North Bank to provide seating for 5,686 fans. The Club had spent £11.5m on modernising the Boleyn Ground, and the opening of the new stand completed phase one of the redevelopment programme.

Hammers now had a stadium fit to grace the Premiership, but, with just nine games to play, they had fallen back to 19th place in the table. However, just when it seemed that the Club's top-flight status was in jeopardy, Harry Redknapp's team at last found their form. Thirteen points from six games – including memorable victories against Aston Villa (away) and Champions-elect Blackburn Rovers (home) – pulled Hammers clear of the mire. It was a terrific performance but, with three games to go, safety was by no means guaranteed. Points were still needed from tough fixtures against fellow-strugglers Crystal Palace, high-flying Liverpool and title-chasing Manchester United in order to secure Premiership survival.

Mattie and Hutch the heroes

The run-in started badly with a beleaguered Hammers line-up producing a listless display against Crystal Palace to lose 1–0. The following Tuesday, Palace met Leeds United at Elland Road knowing that victory would push Hammers into the relegation zone, but Leeds were too strong for the Eagles and won 3–1. West Ham United were now back in the driving seat. Twenty-four hours later, Hammers played Liverpool at Upton Park knowing that a win would take them four points clear of Palace with just one game to play. The pressure was immense, but Redknapp's team rose to the occasion. Matt Holmes opened the scoring with a neatly taken first-half goal which eased the tension, before Don Hutchison struck twice in a minute to give Hammers a 3–0 victory which preserved the Club's place in the Premiership. The relief was overwhelming. 'To stay up was a great achievement.' remembers Steve Potts, 'We all dug in and stuck together as a team. After beating Liverpool I remember sitting in the dressing room and just feeling completely drained. It had been so intense – needing to win every game out of the last ten. The pressure was incredible, but after the result against Liverpool we knew we could go into the last game and just enjoy ourselves.'

The final match of the season brought Alex Ferguson's Manchester United to Upton Park, and the Reds were looking for the win which, they hoped, would take them to a second consecutive Premiership title. Hammers, though, were in buoyant mood following their win against Liverpool and after 31 minutes Michael Hughes opened the scoring with a well-taken volley from Matt Holmes' cross. Manchester United did manage to net an equaliser in the second half but, despite several clear cut chances, they could not beat the impressive Ludek Miklosko

Right: Denmark international centre-back Marc Rieper brought both power and athleticism to the West Ham United defence following his loan move from Brondby in December 1994. He eventually joined the Club on a permanent basis for a fee of £800,000 during the summer of 1995, and made more than 100 first-team appearances before signing for Celtic in August 1997.

Below: Don Hutchison was one of the heroes of Hammers' miraculous escape from relegation during the Spring of 1995. The former Liverpool midfielder, who had arrived at Upton Park as the Club's record signing in August 1994, proved a revelation when he was switched to the forward line for the run-in, scoring seven goals in the last 14 games.

for a second time. The result meant that Blackburn Rovers, who lost their final match against Liverpool at Anfield, had won their first title for 81 years. Hammers' committed display was a testament to the integrity of the Premier League, but Blackburn were nonetheless grateful and choruses of 'I'm Forever Blowing Bubbles' were heard to emanate from the Rovers dressing room... no doubt directed by former Hammer Tony Gale.

Boogers makes his mark

After the drama of the previous 12 months, the summer of 1995 was pleasantly free from drama for Harry Redknapp. The Hammers boss made just one major signing ahead of pre-season training, paying Sparta Rotterdam £800,000 for striker Marco Boogers. Redknapp explained the reasoning behind his decision to buy Boogers in his programme notes for the first home match of the season: 'Unless you have four or five million [pounds] to spend on a striker you have to take a gamble. I couldn't find anyone in this country I fancied with the sort of money I had to spend. So, we have taken a chance on Boogers... with the hope he'll do well for us.' For once, however, the gamble did not pay off. In the second game of the season, away at Manchester United, Boogers came off the bench and within minutes was shown the red card for an ugly, two-footed lunge on United's Gary Neville. He would make just two more substitute appearances for Hammers and, while serving his suspension, returned home to Holland where he was alleged to be suffering from stress and living in a caravan.

Julian Dicks brushes aside Nottingham Forest's Steve Stone during Hammers' 1–1 draw at the City Ground in April 1995. The popular left-back had returned to the Club the previous October after a short spell with Liverpool.

Both of Redknapp's other summer deals involved Australians. First, promising 23-year-old left-winger Stan Laziridis signed for £300,000 after impressing against Hammers in the Club's end of season tour of Australia. And then, just days before the start of the new season, Redknapp swapped Mattie Holmes for Blackburn's Aussie midfielder Robbie Slater and a £600,000 cash adjustment.

Neither of Hammers' two Antipodeans were included in the line-up for the opening game of the Club's centenary season, and it was left instead to E13-born Danny Williamson to get the campaign off to a flying start with a goal after just five minutes. However, the home team's advantage lasted for just 43 minutes, and in the second half Leeds' Ghanian international Tony Yeboah struck two superb goals to earn his team a 2-1 win. Defeat against Leeds was to prove the sign of things to come, and in a disappointing opening to the season, Hammers failed to win any of their first six games. But Harry Redknapp had proved during his first year in charge that he was not afraid to move players around when the need arose, and he continued with this practice during the autumn of 1995. Midfielder Martin Allen (Portsmouth) and reserve goalkeeper Ian Feuer (Luton Town) both left on loan deals, which were later made permanent for fees of around £500,000, while Matthew Rush headed for Norwich City and Jeroen Boere joined Crystal Palace in a swap deal that saw Iain Dowie return to Upton Park. Dowie had enjoyed little success during his first spell with the Hammers, but Redknapp had no doubts that the industrious target-man would win the supporters over second time around. The manager's judgment proved true and, although the Northern Ireland international was far from prolific in front of goal, his work-rate and selfless running earned him the respect of both fans and team-mates.

Dowie made his return in a televised match against Chelsea at Upton Park. However, the game – which ended in a disappointing 3–1 defeat – would attract most headlines for an incident involving Julian Dicks and John Spencer. Midway through the first half the two players tangled on Chelsea's right flank, Spencer fell to the ground and Dicks, who failed to jump over the grounded Scot, put his studs down on his opponent. The Hammers full-back claimed that his momentum had made it impossible to avoid stamping on Spencer but, despite evidence from a sports scientist, the FA disciplinary committee didn't believe him. Dicks, whose case was not helped by a sending-off against Arsenal just five days after the Spencer incident, received a three-match suspension. It was an unfortunate blot on the copybook of the former Hammers captain who had played with both skill and restraint since his return from Liverpool.

A successful run-in

West Ham United's long-awaited League win arrived against Everton at Upton Park in late September, with two penalties from Julian Dicks proving decisive in a 2–1 success. It was the start of a five-match unbeaten run which propelled Hammers from 19th place to 12th in the space of just five weeks. The ascent continued in November when, despite a season's worst defeat (4–1) at home to Aston Villa, wins against Bolton Wanderers (3–0) and Queens Park Rangers (1–0), lifted Redknapp's team to 10th place. However, the resurgence was set to come to a dramatic end with a run of six defeats in seven games from the start of December, and by the end of January Hammers were just three points clear of the relegation places.

Redknapp, never one to stand by and wait for luck to intervene, entered the transfer market once more. Don Hutchison, who had struggled to recapture the form of the previous season, was sold to Sheffield United for £1.2m, and in his place came Spurs' Romanian World Cup star Ilie Dumitrescu for £1.5m. Dumitrescu would be joined at Upton Park by another non-EC player in the shape of Croatian central-defender Slaven Bilic, who joined from German side Karlsruhe SC for a fee of around £1.5m. Both new players would require work permits, so neither was available for the vital clash against Coventry City at Upton Park on the last day of January. It proved a match of great entertainment, with Hammers taking a deserved 2–0 lead through Rieper and Cottee, only to be hit by two goals in ten minutes from City, who were inspired by the appearance of their player-coach Gordon Strachan as a second-half substitute. Strachan had been introduced to the fray at the same time as Hammers debutant Frank Lampard jnr, a player with an unrivalled Upton Park pedigree, who had shown impressive form at both youth and reserve team level. However, it was Iain Dowie, rather than Lampard or Strachan, who struck the decisive goal of the game five minutes from time.

Victory against Coventry was the start of a run of five consecutive League successes. It was a sequence which took in wins away to both Tottenham Hotspur and Chelsea and at home against leaders Newcastle United. The match at Spurs saw two new foreign players make their debuts in the Hammers starting line-up. After a wait of several weeks, Slaven Bilic had received his work permit and the powerful Croat made up for lost time with a polished debut against the North Londoners. The other newcomer was Portuguese youngster Dani, a player best remembered for his film star good looks, who had arrived on loan from Sporting Lisbon until the end of the season. Although still only 19 years old, Dani was already a full international and after just four minutes against Spurs he showed his talent to head home the only goal of the game.

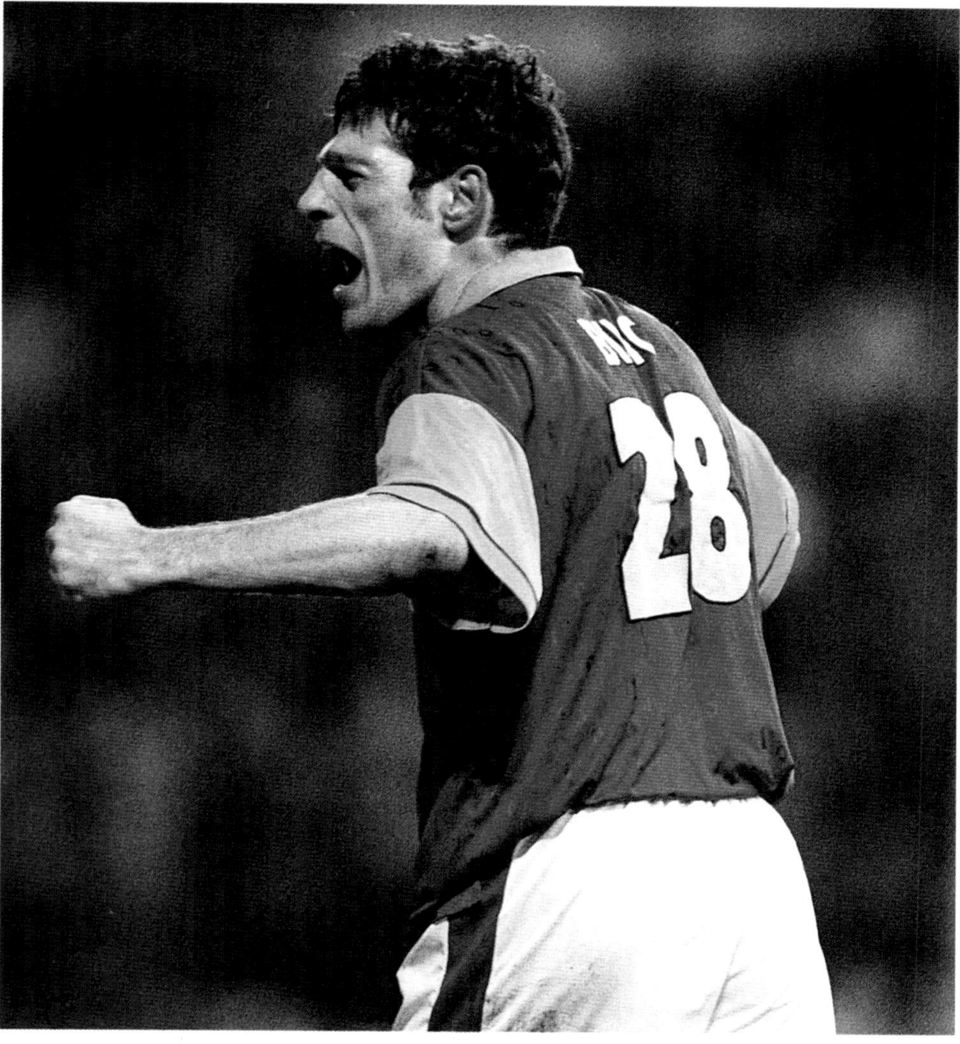

Above: Charismatic Croat Slaven Bilic proved a big hit with the Upton Park faithful after his £1.6m move from German club Karlsruhe in February 1996. He would make 48 League appearances for the Hammers before moving to Everton for £4.5m – then a British record fee for a defender – in the summer of 1997.

Left: Nineteen-year-old Portuguese wonderkid Dani was already a full international when he arrived at Upton Park for a nine-match loan spell during the Spring of 1996. However, it was his pretty-boy looks rather than his two goals or mesmeric skills which attracted most newspaper headlines.

The sight of Paulo Futre running with the ball in a Hammers shirt – albeit a beige one – was a joy to behold for any true West Ham United supporter. The man once dubbed the European Maradona, however, arrived at Upton Park with a history of knee complaints and managed just nine appearances before departing for semi-retirement with Atletico Madrid.

Two days after their win at White Hart Lane, Hammers travelled to Grimsby Town for an FA Cup fourth round replay. Redknapp's team had already been knocked out of the League Cup by Southampton but against the Mariners suffered the indignity of losing 3–0 to a struggling First Division team. West Ham United's disappointment was compounded by the news that Ilie Dumitrescu's application for a work permit had been turned down by the Department of Employment on the grounds that he had failed to play in 75 per cent of Tottenham's games over the previous year. West Ham United immediately lodged an appeal, as did Everton who were suffering a similar problem with regard to Swiss full-back Marc Hottiger. After much debate, the DoE finally granted both players a second work permit, and on 9 March Dumitrescu made his long-awaited debut as a substitute in a 2-0 win against Middlesbrough at Upton Park.

At the start of March, Hammers were in the unusual position of having already guaranteed their top-flight status. With the pressure off, Redknapp's team produced some of their best performances of the campaign, and wins against Bolton Wanderers and Manchester City gave the Club its highest finish to a League season for ten years. The progress of the senior team, however, was more than matched by Tony Carr's Youth team who claimed the South East Counties Championship and reached the final of the FA Youth Cup. Hammers were prevented from claiming a rare youth double when they ran into a Liverpool team inspired by Michael Owen in the final of the Youth Cup. However, for youngsters Frank Lampard and Rio Ferdinand, the disappointment of losing the Cup was somewhat tempered by substitute appearances in the final game of the season. For Ferdinand, a tall and elegant central defender, the match against Sheffield Wednesday on 5 May represented his senior debut. However, as one promising career started, the playing days of one of Upton Park's all-time greats drew to a close. Alvin Martin, who had won 17 England caps and had made 486 first team appearances during his 20 years at the Boleyn Ground, joined Leyton Orient at season's end.

After the successes of 1995–96, Harry Redknapp went into the summer break in optimistic mood. 'This whole club is on the way up,' wrote the Hammers boss in his final programme notes of the season. But Redknapp was not about to rest on his well-earned laurels. He would be looking to improve his squad even more during the close season and he declared: '... I know the areas that need strengthening and hope to sign the players the fans will enjoy watching.' The supporters, though, would have looked on in surprise at the first of Redknapp's new intake. Steve Jones had been a hugely popular figure during his first spell at Upton Park, but he had been unable to establish himself in the first team and, despite hitting 20 goals in his first full season with Bournemouth, there was little to suggest that he could now become Tony Cottee's long-term successor.

Harry's foreign legion

Jones, who re-signed in May for a fee of around £200,000, was the first of five new arrivals at Upton Park during the summer of 1996. The remainder of Redknapp's new recruits, though, did not arrive until July, as the Hammers boss took the opportunity to assess several of his potential signings at the European Championships, which were held in England for the first time in June. Romanian striker Florin Raducioiu was the player most strongly linked with a move to West Ham United and, although he failed to show his best form during the competition, Redknapp was still impressed enough to make the Español forward a Club record signing at a cost of £2.4m. However, while Raducioiu was a player of undoubted pedigree, he was neither the most famous nor the most accomplished newcomer to E13. 'Legend' is an oft-overused word in football, but there was no more appropriate description for Paulo Futre who signed for the Hammers on a free transfer from AC Milan. Futre's reputation was immense. As a teenager he had played for Portugal against England in the 1986 World Cup finals, and a year later he had been instrumental in Porto's European Cup final victory against Bayern Munich. There was no doubting the ability of a player once dubbed the European Maradona. However, he was now 29 years old, and after ten years of close attention from Europe's most brutal markers he arrived with a history of knee complaints.

Redknapp made one other expensive summer signing, paying Southampton £1.9m for 24-year-old centre-half Richard Hall. The Hammers boss was keen to persist with the 3-5-1-2 system which he had employed during the Spring of 1996 and to this end he needed to increase the number of central defenders at the club. Hall was regarded as a great prospect, having narrowly missed out on inclusion in Terry Venables' squad for the European Championships. The summer intake was completed with the free-transfer signings of winger Michael Hughes and Wales international full-back Mark Bowen. The signing of Hughes would go largely unnoticed, though, since the Northern Ireland cap had already spent the better part of two seasons on loan at Upton Park.

Goal famine

The arrival of six new players – four of them full internationals – did much to raise aspirations ahead of the 1996–97 season. For the first time since they had returned to the top division, Hammers were no longer among the favourites for relegation, and there was even whispered talk of a top-six finish and a Uefa Cup place. However, pre-season was to take a heavy toll on West Ham United's new signings, and Steve Jones was the only newcomer fit enough to appear in the starting line-up on opening day against Arsenal at Highbury. Paulo Futre had been included in the squad for the match against the Gunners, but had felt insulted when told he would wear the number 16 shirt rather than his favoured number ten. After a heated argument with Redknapp, Futre stormed away from Highbury in a taxi, forcing the manager to make a late change to his line-up. A frustrating day quickly got worse for the Hammers – who were without Dumitrescu, Raducioiu, Hall, Bishop, Moncur, Cottee and Bowen – and first-half goals from John Hartson and Dennis Bergkamp gave the Gunners a straightforward 2–0 victory.

Right: Romanian forward Ilie Dumitrescu carries the ball forward during the 2–2 draw against Manchester United in December 1996. Dumitrescu, a player of undoubted talent, would inexplicably fail to play to his potential during a nine-month stay at Upton Park and after just 13 first-team appearances he left the Club.

Below: Harry Redknapp's obsession with tricky left-sided Portuguese forwards (he had previously brought both Dani and Paulo Futre to the Club) continued in the Autumn of 1997 when he drafted in Hugo Porfirio on loan from Sporting Lisbon. Hugo was undoubtedly the pick of the bunch, and his bewitching ball skills and electric pace made him an instant hit with Hammers fans.

West Ham United's injury list gradually improved during the early weeks of the season – although Richard Hall's foot problem would continue to baffle the specialists for many years to come – but even the return to fitness of star forwards Dumitrescu and Raducioiu could do little to avert a disappointing start to the season. Victories against Southampton (at home) and Nottingham Forest (away) had hinted at a revival; however, after eight games Hammers were down to 15th in the table. The team simply was not coming together. Futre had shown only flashes of brilliance – most notably on his debut against Coventry City – while Dumitrescu and Raducioiu had contributed little, and the latter had seemed both shocked and terrified by the merest physical challenge. With so many foreign players in his squad, Harry Redknapp came, somewhat prematurely, under fire for the failure of what the tabloids described as his 'Foreign Legion'. The Hammers boss had not been put off buying continental, though, and in September signed Portuguese forward Hugo Porfirio on loan from Sporting Lisbon. Porfirio's arrival coincided with the departure of Tony Cottee, who was sold to Malaysian side Selangor after 279 games and 115 goals during his two spells at Upton Park.

In the League Cup, Hammers kicked-off with a narrow 2–1 aggregate victory over Barnet, but in the third round produced their most fluent display thus far to beat Nottingham Forest 4–1 at Upton Park. New signing Hugo Porfirio was the man most responsible for this emphatic win, and Forest simply had no answer to the winger's bewitching skills which saw him score once and create two goals for Iain Dowie. The diminutive Portuguese was also the architect of League successes against Leicester City and Blackburn Rovers which arrived either side of the match against Forest. However, three victories could not disguise the problems facing Harry Redknapp. Quite simply, Hammers could not find a strikeforce that could score goals. After 16 League games none of the front-line centre-forwards had found the net. Both Iain Dowie and Steve Jones had been given their chance but neither had the guile to find a way past

Premiership defences. The fans were desperate to see Florin Raducioiu given an extended run in the team, but Redknapp had reservations about the Romanian international.

In December, Raducioiu gave weight to the fans' view that he should be given a starring role, when he came off the bench to score a superb goal in a 2–2 draw at home to Manchester United. But one goal was not enough to persuade Redknapp to put his record signing in the team. Hammers' next game was a fourth round League Cup replay away to Second Division Stockport County and when Raducioiu learned that he would not be in the starting line-up he decided not to join the team for the trip to Lancashire. Redknapp was incensed and, from then on, the Romanian's days in E13 were numbered. The manager's troubles continued, though, and on a disastrous night at Stockport's Edgeley Park ground, Hammers crashed to an embarrassing 2–1 defeat, with Iain Dowie heading a spectacular own goal to help County on their way.

In December Harry Redknapp attempted to resolve his striker crisis by taking former Blackburn Rovers centre-forward Mike Newell on loan from Birmingham City. However, Newell enjoyed no better fortune than the other strikers on West Ham United's books, and five of the seven games in which he

Above: The formidable frame of David Unsworth thundering down the left-flank is enough to give any right-winger palpitations. The versatile and highly competitive Scouser arrived at Upton Park as part of a swap deal which took Danny Williamson to Everton in August 1997 and, while Williamson struggled with injuries at Goodison Park, Unsworth enjoyed a superb first season in E13. Alas, his first was also to be his last and in the summer of 1998 he departed on a truncated return trip to Everton, via a short spell at Aston Villa.

Left: Centre-forward Paul Kitson, who scored eight times in his first 14 appearances for West Ham United, played a key role in Hammers' successful battle to avoid relegation in 1996–97. Kitson, who signed from Newcastle United in a £2.3m deal, arrived at Upton Park just two days before fellow striker John Hartson and the pair struck up an immediate rapport.

appeared ended in defeat. By the turn of the year, Redknapp's much vaunted Foreign Legion had all but disbanded. Futre had been forced to retire, Dumitrescu – with his work permit again in jeopardy – had left for Mexican club Futbal America and Raducicioou had been returned to Español. Hammers, as Redknapp was wont to say, were down to the bare bones. The situation finally reached its nadir on 25 January when Second Division Wrexham came to the Boleyn Ground for an FA Cup third round replay. Hammers, who had failed to score in three matches, struggled to create any chances against their Welsh opponents and in injury time conceded a goal which led to an ignominious Cup exit.

Hartson and Kitson

West Ham United's problems, though, were not confined to the pitch, and following the defeat against Wrexham the media began to speculate that wealthy businessman Michael Tabor was set to take over the Club. There were also reports that the board had refused offers of financial assistance from a mystery benefactor. The fans, who were already frustrated by the team's performances, grew restless and staged a demonstration during the 2–1 reverse against Arsenal at Upton Park on 29 January. The poor results continued, though, and with 16 games left to play, Hammers had dropped to 18th place in the Premiership. With crisis point reached, the Board gave Harry Redknapp the green light to sign the strikers he needed to shoot the Club to safety. Both Dean Holdsworth and Pierre van Hooijdonk had been linked with moves to Upton Park, but it was Newcastle United centre-forward Paul Kitson who was first to arrive, joining Hammers in a £2.3m deal. Strikers work in pairs, though, and Kitson told reporters: 'Ideally, I'd like to play alongside someone who holds the ball up. I like to play off their flick-ons – that's my sort of game.' Within days, Kitson's perfect partner had arrived in the shape of Welshman John Hartson, who signed from Arsenal for an initial fee of £3.3m.

West Ham United's new-look all-British strikeforce made its debut against Derby County at the Baseball Ground on 15 February, but there was to be no instant solution to Hammers' goal shortage, and a somewhat debatable penalty earned the Rams a 1–0 victory. The match against Derby had seen John Hartson make a particularly inauspicious start to his Hammers career when he received a booking for a foul on Igor Stimac which earned him a two-match suspension. However, before taking his enforced break, the Wales international striker faced Tottenham Hotspur at Upton Park, and this time he did not disappoint. Both Hartson and Kitson found their way onto the scoresheet in an entertaining match which also saw Julian Dicks net twice in a 4-3 victory. Confidence quickly returned and, although they lost their next game 1-0 away to Leeds

United, Hammers collected eight points in March to rise to the relative security of 15th place in the table. The goals of Kitson and Hartson would continue to help West Ham United climb to safety and at season's end the pair had struck 13 times in 25 games. In his final programme notes of the season, Harry Redknapp paid tribute to his two strikers: 'Without them and their 13 goals, I doubt we would have survived. They were magnificent against Wednesday [Hammers beat Sheffield Wednesday 5–0 on the penultimate Saturday of the season].'

However, while Hartson and Kitson had undoubtedly contributed greatly to the end of season rally, credit for West Ham United's survival was not entirely due to the efforts of the Club's expensive new strikers. The ever-dependable Julian Dicks had also been magnificent throughout the season, topping the statistical averages for Premiership defenders, and scoring six crucial goals. Dicks had played much of the season as part of a three-man central defence and at the end of the campaign was named Hammer of the Year for the second year in succession. The combative defender had, however, sustained another serious injury to his troublesome left knee, which would keep him out of not only the final seven games of 1996–97 but also the whole of the following season. Dicks' successor as Hammers skipper would be midfielder Steve Lomas, who had arrived from Manchester City on transfer deadline day for a fee of £1.6m.

Throughout season 1996–97 there had been much speculation about the possible departure of centre-half Slaven Bilic, and in June the Croatian international joined Everton in a £4.5m deal. It was a huge setback for Harry Redknapp, who had lost one of his most accomplished players, but there was at least the compensation that, in the immensely promising Rio Ferdinand, Hammers had an obvious replacement. Another player on the move from Upton Park in the summer of 1997 was Hugo Porfirio. The Portuguese forward had beguiled the Boleyn crowd with his dribbling skills, but had chosen to reject Hammers' offer of a permanent contract in favour of a move to Spain. Harry Redknapp, whose tactics relied upon an attacking free spirit to play behind the main strikers, acted quickly to find a replacement. On 2 June, the Hammers boss swooped ahead of Tottenham Hotspur to sign Israeli international Eyal Berkovic for a cut-price £1.75m. Hammers' only other major summer signing was Ipswich Town's Canadian goalkeeper Craig Forrest, who arrived in a £500,000 deal to provide competition for established number one Ludek Miklosko.

West Ham United kicked off the 1997–98 season with a trip to newly-promoted Barnsley. It was a game which cast Hammers in the role of gate crashers on a big day at Oakwell and, after Barnsley had taken a first-half lead through Neil Redfearn, Harry Redknapp's team ruined the party with goals from John Hartson and substitute Frank Lampard. Hartson was again on the score sheet four days later when Tottenham

Above: The inimitable Samassi Abou celebrates one of his two goals against Barnsley in January 1998.

Below: When Hugo Porfirio decided against signing permanently in the summer of 1997, Redknapp signed Israeli playmaker Eyal Berkovic to fill the 'free role' in his 5-2-1-2 formation. Berkovic, who joined for £1.5m from Maccabi Haifa, proved a more than adequate replacement.

Hotspur visited the Boleyn Ground for a match which saw the adroit Eyal Berkovic mark his home debut with the decisive goal in a 2–1 victory. Two wins in the opening two fixtures gave West Ham United their best start to a League season since winning promotion. However, while the attacking trio of Hartson, Kitson and Berkovic was proving a potent combination, Harry Redknapp faced problems in defence. Julian Dicks and Richard Hall would both miss the entire season through injury and Marc Rieper, who was in the final year of his contract, was sold to Celtic for £1.2m to avoid losing him on a Bosman-style free transfer at season's end.

The Hammers boss acted quickly to avert a defensive crisis by signing two players of immense promise. First, Redknapp swapped midfielder Danny Williamson for Everton's 23-year-old England cap David Unsworth in a deal which also netted Hammers £1m. The cash adjustment from the Unsworth transfer was then added to the money from Rieper's sale to finance the purchase of Blackburn Rovers central defender Ian Pearce. These two deals meant that by mid-September Harry Redknapp had assembled a new-look rear-guard in which Rio Ferdinand was given the pivotal role of sweeper with Unsworth to his left and Pearce on his right. This youthful back three (average age

22), was given its first outing in the home match against Newcastle United, but an unfortunate mix-up between Pearce and Unsworth let in John Barnes to strike the only goal of the game and give the Magpies a somewhat undeserved victory. The defensive teething troubles continued in the next match at Highbury where Hammers suffered a disappointing 4–0 reverse. However, three days later, and back on home ground, Redknapp's new look team produced a superb display to overcome Liverpool with goals from Berkovic and Hartson. The match against the Reds was also notable for the long-awaited debut of new signing Andy Impey, whose £1.2m transfer from Queens Park Rangers had been in jeopardy for several months following a troublesome toe injury. Impey's arrival would provide Harry Redknapp with much needed options on the flanks – an area that had been weakened greatly by the sale of Michael Hughes to Wimbledon in September for £800,000.

At the end of October Hammers were eighth in the table and, in John Hartson, had one of the Premiership's most feared strikers. Hartson would net 11 goals in the first 16 League games of the season, profiting greatly from the midfield invention of Eyal Berkovic. However, with his regular strike partner Paul Kitson out with a groin injury, the powerful Welshman was ploughing something of a loan furrow in attack. Iain Dowie was recalled from the reserves to fill in, but when he failed to score in ten games, Redknapp entered the transfer market once more. This time the Hammers boss opted for a foreign import, signing former France Under-21 striker Samassi Abou from AS Cannes for a fee of around £250,000. Abou, who quickly became something of a favourite at Upton Park, made his debut as a substitute in a televised game against Crystal Palace on 3 November. The match against Palace proved an engaging encounter and, although the visitors took a swift two-goal lead, Hammers hit back with strikes from John Hartson and Frank Lampard to level the score early in the second half. However, as the ball nestled in the back of the net following Lampard's equaliser, the Boleyn Ground was hit by a floodlight failure which sent the stadium into darkness. The match was eventually abandoned after unsuccessful efforts to resolve the problem.

Above: Harry Redknapp's peerless ability for wheeling and dealing brought Trevor Sinclair to Upton Park in a cash-plus-players deal which saw Iain Dowie and Keith Rowland move across London to Queens Park Rangers.

Below: Hammers skipper Steve Lomas (second from right) heads off after scoring the decisive penalty in the shoot-out against Blackburn Rovers in the fifth round of the FA Cup in 1998. Lomas is pursued by (from left to right): John Moncur, John Hartson and Frank Lampard.

The emergence of Rio

The rematch against Crystal Palace took place on 3 December, but this time Hammers were at their incisive best, with goals from Hartson, Berkovic, Unsworth and Lomas earning a deserved 4–1 victory. By now, West Ham United's results were following a clear pattern. At Upton Park, Hammers were a match for all comers, and their first ten home fixtures brought nine victories. However, away from E13, the story was rather different, and the club's first ten matches on the road brought eight defeats and just one win. It was, therefore, somewhat propitious that, after beating Huddersfield Town over two legs, the draw for the League Cup gave Hammers home advantage against Aston Villa in the third round. Two goals from Hartson – one an exquisite header from a perfect Tim Breacker cross – and a neatly taken strike from Frank Lampard, earned an impressive 3–0 victory and another home tie, this time against Second Division Walsall. Hartson and Lampard were again the scorers, but on this occasion it was the young midfielder who took the plaudits netting a clinical hat-trick in a 4–0 win. Lampard was rapidly maturing into a key player for the Hammers and his progress was acknowledged in November when he was called into the England Under-21 line-up for a match against Greece. Rio Ferdinand was also establishing a reputation as one of the brightest talents in the Premiership, and in November the 19-year-old sweeper became the youngest West Ham United player to win a senior England cap when he came off the bench against Cameroon at Wembley.

Victory against Walsall had taken Hammers into the quarter-finals of the League Cup, and for the third time in succession their name was drawn out of the hat first. The bad news was that they were paired against title-chasing Arsenal. Confidence, though, was high and after a run of three successive victories, the popular view was that if anybody could beat the Gunners it was West Ham United at Upton Park. The opening stages of the game gave further cause for optimism and after ten minutes, David Seaman hauled down Paul Kitson in the penalty area. Referee G. Barber had no hesitation and immediately pointed to the spot. In the absence of Julian Dicks, John Hartson had assumed penalty-taking duties and the Wales international now had the chance to put Hammers in the lead if he could beat his former team-mate David Seaman from 12 yards. It was a contest that had no doubt been played out many times on Arsenal's training pitch and as Hartson prepared to take the kick another of his former colleagues, Ian Wright, offered him a 'friendly' word of advice. The tension was unbearable and, as Hartson ran in to take the kick, Upton Park took a deep breath... waited... and then groaned in despair. Hammers' top-scorer had scuffed his shot and Seaman had made a simple save. It was to be the turning point of the match, Hartson bowed his head and for the remainder of the 90 minutes the powerful Welshman was uncharacteristically quiet. Goals from Ian Wright and Marc Overmars gave the Gunners a two-goal lead, and although Samassi Abou came off the bench to strike his first goal for the Hammers, there was to be no dramatic fight-back.

League Cup elimination was a great disappointment to West Ham United, but there was little time for commiseration. Four days later, Hammers – who were in eighth position in the Premiership and challenging for a Uefa Cup place – returned to League action with a home match against bottom-of-the-table Barnsley. It was the perfect opportunity for Harry Redknapp's team to rebuild their confidence, and they did not disappoint, with Samassi Abou giving his best performance since arriving at Upton Park, scoring twice and laying on two more goals in a season's best 6–0 win. Abou again grabbed the headlines a week later, following a 1–0 defeat against Tottenham Hotspur at White Hart Lane, but this time he was making the news for the wrong reasons. The popular striker had taken exception to some rough treatment from Spurs' Ramon Vega and was sent off for lashing out at the Swiss defender. Abou would now face a three-match suspension and with Paul Kitson again on the injured list, Harry Redknapp was left with few attacking options. It was time for the manager to shuffle his pack once more. Queens Park Rangers forward Trevor Sinclair was the player Redknapp wanted, and after much negotiation a deal was agreed which saw Iain Dowie and Keith Rowland move to Loftus Road in part-exchange.

Any tricky Trev

Sinclair, who could operate anywhere across the forward line, made a sensational start to his Hammers career, scoring twice on his debut against Everton before adding three more goals in his next five appearances. The bad news, however, was that the Dulwich-born striker was Cup-tied and would have to sit out his new team's FA Cup campaign. Hammers had kicked off the competition with a somewhat taxing 2–1 home victory over non-League Emley in the third round, for which they had been rewarded with an awkward away tie against First Division strugglers Manchester City. The match at Maine Road was chosen for live television broadcast and provided great entertainment. A goal from Eyal Berkovic put Hammers into the lead early in the first half, but the advantage was to be short-lived and a superb solo effort from Georgiou Kinkladze ensured that City were back on terms at the interval. The home team rallied in the second half and when Kinkladze won a penalty City had the perfect opportunity to establish a lead. However, German striker Uwe Rösler was unable to convert the chance and ballooned his spot kick over the bar. It was to prove the game's decisive moment, and shortly afterwards Steve Lomas fired through a crowded goalmouth to strike the winner against his old club.

Title-chasing Blackburn Rovers provided the opposition in the fifth round of the Cup, and after a bad-tempered match at the Boleyn Ground, which ended in a 2–2 draw, the combatants moved to Ewood Park for the replay. After 90 minutes the match remained goalless and, although John Hartson netted in extra-time, his effort was cancelled out by a late Blackburn equaliser that took the tie to a penalty shoot-out. After four successful penalties from each team, the spotlight fell on the two captains,

Hammers' promising young defender Rio Ferdinand hooks the ball clear during a League match against Liverpool at Upton Park in September 1997.

with Rovers' Colin Hendry shooting first. The Scotland defender, however, was unable to beat Hammers keeper Craig Forrest, who saved well with his legs. Steve Lomas now had the chance to play the hero for the second successive Cup tie and, despite kicking into the Blackburn end, he held his nerve to strike the ball calmly into the top left-hand corner.

West Ham United were now through to the last eight of the FA Cup where they would face Double-chasing Arsenal in a repeat of January's League Cup quarter-final. This time, however, it was the Gunners who would enjoy home advantage in a match which was predictably chosen for live television broadcast. By a quirk of the fixture computer, the Cup clash at Highbury was also given a dress rehearsal in a League encounter at Upton Park six days prior to the main event. It was match of few chances though, ending goalless and notable only for the debut of Hammers' France international goalkeeper Bernard Lama who had joined on loan until the end of the season. Lama would retain his place in a somewhat weakened West Ham United team which was without David Unsworth, John Hartson and Frank Lampard for the Cup tie at Highbury. However, despite these notable absentees, Hammers produced a committed and enterprising display against the Gunners and took the lead via a well-taken Ian Pearce goal. Shortly after Pearce's strike, Eyal Berkovic had a superb opportunity to increase the lead, but for once the talented Israeli scuffed his shot. It was to prove a costly miss, though, and a Dennis Bergkamp penalty took the tie to a replay.

The fifth meeting between West Ham United and Arsenal began at great pace, and after 32 minutes referee Mike Reed sent off Dennis Bergkamp for elbowing Steve Lomas. The home team were visibly lifted by the sending-off of Arsenal's most influential player, and they strode forward, relieved that their chief tormentor had departed. Hammers' sense of security, though, was ill-founded and deep into first-half injury time, Nicolas Anelka pinched the ball from the boot of a team-mate and curled an exquisite shot into the left-hand corner of Lama's goal. The second-half brought a characteristically resolute defensive display from Arsenal, but with six minutes to go John Hartson at last escaped the close attentions of Martin Keown, bludgeoned his way into the penalty area and struck a low drive inside Alex Manninger's near post. Upton Park erupted in relief and the game entered extra time. With the teams flagging, gaps began to appear at both ends, but amazingly the scores remained unaltered. For the second time in the competition Hammers faced a penalty shoot-out, but on this occasion there was to be no glorious ending. Hartson, Eyal Berkovic and Samassi Abou all failed to find the net with their spot-kicks and at the end of a draining evening in E13 it was Arsenal's supporters who were again celebrating Cup success inside the Boleyn Ground.

Left: Joe Cole (English football's most hyped teenager) takes on Jaap Stam (football's most expensive defender) on his League debut against Manchester United at Old Trafford in January 1999.

Push for Europe

There were no Premiership fixtures for the weekend following West Ham United's FA Cup exit, but when Hammers did return to League action, with a home match against Leeds United, they showed no signs of any hangover from their shoot-out misery. Goals from Abou, Ian Pearce – who played as an attacking right wing-back – and Hartson secured a 3–1 victory and a step up the table to seventh place. At the start of April, Hammers were still in with an excellent chance of qualifying for European football in 1998–99. However, a disappointing defeat away to resurgent Aston Villa and a goalless draw at home against Derby County did little to enhance prospects of a Uefa Cup debut for West Ham United. The match against Derby had also been marred by the sending-off of John Hartson who had struck out at Croat defender Igor Stimac to earn his second dismissal in the space of seven weeks. Hartson would now be suspended for the final four games of the season and, although he signed off with a superb performance against Blackburn Rovers – netting both goals in a 2–1 win – his presence would be sorely missed.

Hammers' form during the run-in became uncharacteristically erratic, and consecutive defeats against Southampton (4–2) and Liverpool (5–0) dropped them to tenth in the table. But even after Redknapp's team had only managed a draw away to First Division-bound Crystal Palace in the penultimate fixture, Europe remained a distinct possibility. The situation going into the last game of the season was simple. West Ham

Frank Lampard lets fly with a long-range shot in the 2–0 victory against Coventry City in December 1998. Lampard had been captain of Hammers' successful Youth team which won the South East Counties Championship and made it to the final of the FA Youth Cup in 1995–96.

United needed to win their match at home to Leicester City, and hope that Aston Villa failed to beat newly crowned Champions Arsenal at Villa Park. The first half of this combination was achieved via an entertaining 4–3 victory – which saw former Upton Park favourite Tony Cottee net twice for the visitors – but, with Villa also claiming three points against the Gunners, the European dream was over. Hammers had ended the season in eighth place, just two points away from a Uefa Cup place. It was, however, difficult to feel too disappointed after a season of both progress and entertainment at Upton Park. 'It's been a great season overall for the Club,' wrote Harry Redknapp in his programme notes for the match against Leicester. 'We've made massive strides over the past year. New players have come in and strengthened the squad, young players have emerged and there are more coming through.'

The pick of Hammers' young players was undoubtedly Rio Ferdinand, and at season's end the immensely gifted teenager was named Hammer of the Year. Ferdinand's progress was further rewarded when he was included in Glenn Hoddle's 22-man squad which travelled to the World Cup finals in France. Harry Redknapp would also make the short trip across the Channel to assess the talent on display during the World Cup. One player whom Redknapp had his eye on in particular, was Chile's experienced centre-half Javier Margas, who had been impressive against England at Wembley in February. Polished performances against both Italy and Brazil proved enough to convince the Hammers boss that Margas was a player of genuine talent and, at the end of the tournament, Redknapp moved in to sign his man in a £2.3m deal. The South American stopper was one of five new arrivals at Upton Park during the summer of 1998. French midfielder Marc Keller had been first to arrive, signing on a Bosman-style free-transfer from German club Karlsruhe SC in May. Newcastle goalkeeper Shaka Hislop was also brought in without a transfer fee and Liverpool defender Neil Ruddock cost just £500,000, but it was the signing of Arsenal's 34-year-old record goalscorer Ian Wright that attracted most attention. Wright was a player whom Harry Redknapp had been keen on for several years, and when it became clear that he would be departing Highbury, Hammers made an immediate enquiry which was followed up by a successful bid of around £600,000. The transfer activity at Upton Park, however, was not all incoming and, despite a successful first season in E13, David Unsworth left to join Aston Villa in a £3m deal after his family had failed to settle in the south.

Just did it. Ian Wright milks the applause after scoring on his Hammers debut against Sheffield Wednesday at Hillsborough in August 1998.

The close season also saw West Ham United announce a lucrative new shirt sponsorship deal with footwear giants Dr Martens. Hammers' kits had been bereft of a sponsor's branding throughout 1997–98, but the agreement with Dr Martens would make amends, and was said to be among the top ten shirt deals in the Premiership. The Club was further buoyed by the news that season ticket sales had hit an all-time high, and that all the executive boxes and lounges had been sold for the entire season. This increased revenue would go some way to paying for a state-of-the-art playing surface which was installed at the Boleyn Ground during June 1998. New head groundsman Simon Jacobs was the man overseeing work that cost Hammers around £800,000 and which incorporated a revolutionary drainage and heating system. The pitch itself had been completely relaid and was now reinforced by man-made fibres, stitched eight inches downwards into the ground to bind natural grass roots. There were further improvements at the Boleyn Ground, with the installation of a new PA system and new video screens, but these changes were of minor interest to the supporters' who were more concerned with the Club's latest signings.

Wright on the mark

After a summer of frenzied transfer activity, which had seen Hammers add four full internationals to their already impressive playing ranks, confidence was booming. 'Our target is to finish high enough in the League to ensure we secure a place in Europe... if we don't, then our supporters will perceive the 1998–99 season as disappointing,' declared Director of Football Peter Storrie on the eve of the new campaign. Storrie, who had worked tirelessly to help Harry Redknapp bring in the players he wanted, added: '...the quality of our summer signings proves the Club is determined to compete with the best... Stars do not come much bigger, or brighter than Ian Wright.' Despite his advancing years, Wright had impressed the Hammers coaching staff with his energy and enthusiasm during pre-season, and the veteran striker made his Hammers debut against Sheffield Wednesday on the opening day of the Premiership campaign. Wright told reporters: 'The boys have made me so welcome. It's just unbelievable. They are working very hard for me, I'm working hard for them and if I can just score a goal and repay the faith Harry has shown in me then I'll be well happy.' At the end of the game Wright wore a revealing and broad smile. Six minutes from time he had received the ball inside the penalty area – 'it had to fall to him,' rued Wednesday boss Danny Wilson – and made no mistake, crashing a goal which gave his new team a 1–0 win.

Victory against Wednesday was followed by two consecutive goalless draws – at home to Manchester United and away at Coventry City – to leave West Ham United in eighth place in the Premiership table at the end of August. New signing Shaka Hislop had proved a revelation in Hammers' goal and after 270 minutes of football the 6ft 5in custodian remained unbeaten. In attack, though, Hammers had been less impressive, scoring just once and creating few chances. However, with Harry Redknapp's preferred strikeforce of Ian Wright and John Hartson making its Upton Park debut against Wimbledon on 9 September, the popular view was that this problem would soon be resolved. And so it proved. Within the first 25 minutes of the clash with the Dons, Hammers surged into a 3–0 lead with two goals from stand-in skipper Ian Wright and one from John Hartson. Wimbledon, though, refused to accept what seemed certain defeat and a header from Marcus Gayle reduced arrears ahead of the interval. In the second half the Hammers goal came under a prolonged aerial bombardment, and when Jason Euell closed the gap to just one goal after 65 minutes, nerves began to fray. The home defence, which was without the injured Rio Ferdinand, gave a home debut to Javier Margas, but the Chilean was left bemused and floundering by Wimbledon's direct tactics. Twelve minutes from time, the Dons struck a somewhat inevitable equaliser, and then two minutes later they delivered the coup de grace when substitute Efan Ekoku headed home the game's winning goal.

Dicks returns

As is so often the case with West Ham United, the ridiculous was swiftly followed by the sublime and three days after their disastrous defeat against the Dons, Harry Redknapp's team claimed a 2–1 victory against Liverpool at Upton Park. It was the start of an impressive run of League form which saw Hammers climb from 11th to fourth place in the Premiership during September. However, despite this upturn in League form, Second Division Northampton Town were too strong for Redknapp's high-flyers in the Worthington Cup. A 2–0 deficit from the first leg gave the Midlanders what proved an unassailable lead and, although Frank Lampard scored in the return at Upton Park, Hammers crashed out of the competition at the first hurdle.There was, however, one consolation which could be gleaned from this humiliating defeat. After several operations and 16 months on the sidelines, Julian Dicks had made his long-awaited return to first-team action. For the second time in his career the popular full-back had confounded the experts to recover from a horrific knee injury. Former team-mate Tony Gale commented: 'Dicksy is a one-off. Most players would not have had the courage or strength of character to come back from the kind of injuries he's had.' Dicks completed his remarkable recovery when he skippered West Ham United to a 1–0 victory against Southampton at the Boleyn Ground on 28 September.

The month of October began badly for the Hammers – with a 3–0 defeat against struggling Blackburn Rovers – and then got worse. On the Wednesday after the Blackburn game the *Daily Mirror* ran a story, complete with damning photographs, of a clash between John Hartson and Eyal Berkovic at the Hammers training ground. The pictures clearly showed that Hartson had kicked the Israeli midfielder in the head, and although the Club acted to fine the firebrand Welshman, the incident continued to dominate tabloid backpages for more than a week. Hartson, who was eventually charged by the FA with bringing the game into disrepute, apologised to Berkovic and the two players made peace ahead of the home game against Aston Villa on 17 October. 'Everything is OK now,' claimed Berkovic. 'It was an accident and it is finished.' On the pitch, though, problems still remained and a lacklustre Hammers performance in the match against Villa, which ended

John Hartson had been Hammers hero in 1997–98, finishing the campaign as top scorer with 24 goals. But the following season he adopted the role of villain and, after a training ground assault on Eyal Berkovic and just four goals in 17 appearances, the firebrand Welshman was sold on to Wimbledon for £7.5m.

0–0, was followed by a hugely disappointing 4–2 reverse away to struggling Charlton Athletic.

Defeat against Charlton dropped West Ham United six places down the table to 14th position. But, just as Hammers fans began to nervously contemplate the possibility of a season of struggle, their team embarked upon a five-match unbeaten run. It was a sequence that began with a sensational 3–0 away win against big-spending Newcastle United, and which also included further victories over Leicester City, Derby County and Tottenham Hotspur. However, the win against Derby County at Pride Park – which had seen Marc Keller strike his first goal for the Club with a blistering 20-yard drive – had been marred by a spat between Harry Redknapp and Hammers' Director of Football Peter Storrie. Redknapp had been incensed by the way that the Club had conducted the £1.3m sale of utility player Andy Impey to Leicester City, and had vented his fury with a public outburst. The Hammers boss had been forced to withdraw Impey from his line-up for the match at Pride Park and had felt that, since the player had not yet signed for Leicester, he should have been made available for selection. Storrie, meanwhile, contended that Redknapp had known well in advance that the Club needed to sell a player to balance the books, and explained that he had merely followed standard practice by insisting that Impey be left out of the squad.

The sublimely talented Rio Ferdinand had developed into one of the most accomplished defenders in Europe by the start of the 1998–99 season. Rio, who had made his senior England debut in November 1997, was included in Glenn Hoddle's squad which travelled to the World Cup finals in France during the summer of 1998.

Although Storrie and Redknapp did eventually resolve their differences, the debacle at Derby fuelled rumours of an impending financial crisis at Upton Park. According to the media, West Ham United would soon be looking to sell off their top stars and there was much speculation that both Rio Ferdinand and Frank Lampard would soon depart E13. Several of Hammers' Premiership rivals would test the water with speculative enquiries for the Club's key players, and Spurs were reported to have made a somewhat derisory bid of £4.3m for Lampard. The offer was immediately rejected, and Peter Storrie declared: 'Some people might have been under the misapprehension that we are fair game but they are badly mistaken... We have built a good squad of players at West Ham and we certainly don't intend to see it broken up now.' Storrie would prove as good as his word, and there would be no enforced departures from Upton Park during the remainder of the season.

Hammers upset at the Vetch

At the turn of the year, Hammers' form had reverted to the pattern of the previous season – impressive at home but vulnerable away from the Boleyn Ground. However, despite this lack of success on the road, West Ham United ended 1998 in sixth place in the Premiership to keep alive their dream of Uefa Cup qualification. There was also still the possibility of a route into Europe via the FA Cup, and a home draw against Third Division Swansea City seemed to offer straightforward passage to the competition's fourth round. However, West Ham United's propensity for failure against lower League opposition is legendary, and after 61 minutes an increasingly confident Swansea team took the lead through defender Jason Smith. Hammers had created few clear cut chances but, faced with a second humiliating Cup exit inside four months, Redknapp's team rallied and, four minutes from time, Julian Dicks struck a 25-yard shot which deflected off a defender before trickling underneath City goalkeeper Roger Freestone. The two teams would now face a replay at Swansea's Vetch Field ground, but

Frank Lampard surges through midfield during West Ham United's 2–0 victory against Spurs at White Hart Lane in April 1999. Lampard's consistent form as skipper of the England Under-21 team would see him elevated to Kevin Keegan's senior squad at the end of the 1998–99 season.

this time Hammers would be without star striker Ian Wright, who had sustained an injury which would keep him out of first-team action for more than three months.

The match against Swansea City had, however, provided one moment to remember for West Ham United supporters when, late in the second half, Harry Redknapp had given a senior debut to 17-year-old midfield prodigy Joe Cole. Media interest in the England Youth player had been unprecedented and, long before his first-team bow, Cole had variously been compared to Pele, Michael Owen, Trevor Brooking and Paul Gascoigne. 'It would have been nice if I'd been able to come on and make my debut as an unknown,' reflected Cole in an interview with *Hammers News*. 'I just tried to play how I usually do but I certainly didn't come on and change the game.' The teenager had shown enough talent though, to ensure he kept his place on the bench for Hammers' next match, against Manchester United at Old Trafford. However, the clash against title-chasing United, proved a disappointment, ending in a 4–1 reverse, which did little to build confidence ahead of the Cup showdown with Swansea City. The match against the Welshmen rapidly turned into the giant-killing that all Hammers fans had feared, and, after 29 minutes, Swansea midfielder Martin Thomas struck the game's decisive goal. 'There really was no lack of effort,' claimed Harry Redknapp after the match. 'But yes, there was a lack of quality in front of goal.'

A lack of goals was also becoming a problem for the Hammers in the Premiership. So, with the season now past the halfway mark, Redknapp busied himself on the transfer market. First to sign was wing-back Scott Minto, who arrived from Benfica just days after the FA Cup defeat at Swansea for a fee of around £1m. However, for Redknapp to further bolster his squad, he would need to generate revenue through sales. John Hartson had been struggling throughout the season, and by his own admission had 'gone off the boil' – netting just four goals in 17 League appearances – so when Wimbledon manager Joe Kinnear made a £7.5m offer for the powerful Welshman,

Redknapp gladly accepted. The Hammers boss would be given all of the money from Hartson's sale to reinvest in players, but, with no time to make any new signings ahead of the home match against Sheffield Wednesday, he was forced to send out a somewhat weakened line-up against the Owls. It proved a disaster. Scott Minto, making his debut at left-back, struggled to readjust to the pace of English football, while the makeshift strikeforce of Abou and Sinclair lacked both service and enterprise. The game ended in a humiliating 4–0 defeat and increased the pressure on Harry Redknapp to bring in fresh talent.

After two weeks of speculation, linking Hammers with almost every available forward in Europe, West Ham United announced one of most controversial signings, in the Club's 104-year history. 'I don't care what anybody says, I've not gone potty... I've signed a football genius,' declared a buoyant Harry Redknapp. The subject of his eulogy was Italian forward Paolo Di Canio, who had arrived from Sheffield Wednesday in a £1.5m deal. Nobody doubted Di Canio's footballing talent, but, the former Juventus and AC Milan player was considered to be of suspect temperament following his push on referee Paul Alcock earlier on in the season which had earned him a 12-match suspension. Redknapp, was unconcerned by his new signing's reputation: 'This is not a gamble for the club in any shape or form... The crowd here will love him. I have no worries about his temperament as he is a first-class professional.'

Above: Cameroon midfielder Marc-Vivien Foe became Hammers' record signing when he joined the Club for £3.5m from French Champions Lens in January 1999.

Left: Goalkeeper Shaka Hislop joined the Hammers from Newcastle United under the Bosman ruling during the summer of 1998. The 6ft 5in custodian quickly endeared himself to the Upton Park faithful with a series of superb performances, and at the end of his first season was named Hammer of the Year.

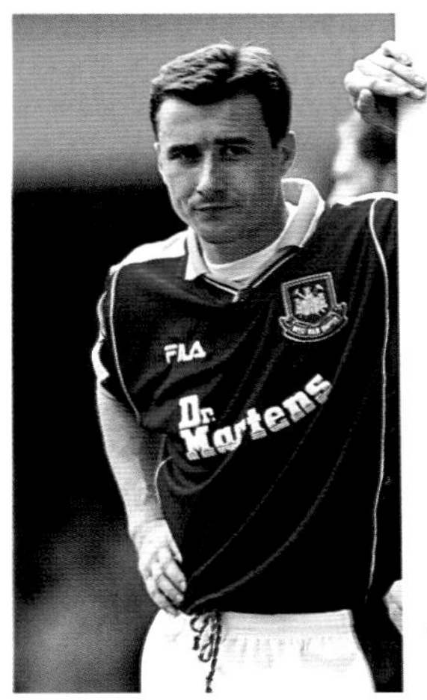

Below: French midfielder Marc Keller, who arrived at Upton Park from German club Karlsruhe in June 1998, quickly proved himself a player of both skill and industry during his first season in E13.

The transfer activity did not end with the signing of Di Canio, though, and the Italian's arrival coincided with the capture of 22-year-old Cameroon midfielder Marc-Vivien Foe, who joined Hammers for a club record £3.5m. Redknapp was equally pleased with the signing of Foe and told reporters: 'He's a monster of a player... He is big and powerful – in the Patrick Vieira mould.' Di Canio and Foe would make their Hammers debuts away to Wimbledon in a match which saw John Hartson take the field against his former team. However, the game could not live up to its billing and ended goalless. Next on the agenda was a clash with Arsenal at Upton Park, but for the second home game in succession Hammers suffered a 4–0 reverse. Dreams of Europe were now beginning to fade. Di Canio, though, would become an increasingly creative influence during February and, after home wins against Nottingham Forest and Blackburn Rovers, and an impressive 2–2 draw at Anfield, Hammers moved back up the table to sixth position.

During March, Harry Redknapp began to experiment with his formation, and for several key away fixtures switched from his long-favoured 5-2-1-2 system to a more traditional 4-4-2. One casualty of this tactical change – which brought impressive performances at Chelsea (1–0) and Aston Villa (0–0) – was Eyal Berkovic who was not suited to the defensive responsibilities of 4-4-2. However, Berkovic remained a key figure in Redknapp's plans and his incisive attacking play was instrumental in a 5–1 victory over Derby County at Upton Park. The Israeli playmaker was the architect of another Hammers success seven days later, when George Graham's Tottenham Hotspur were defeated 2–1 at White Hart Lane. Ian Wright, who was making his first appearance in the starting line-up after recovering from injury, had opened the scoring against Spurs, before Marc Keller added a well-crafted second goal. Victory at the Lane had left Hammers in sixth place in the Premiership with four games to play. The bad news, however, was that because of radical changes to the format of both the Uefa Cup and the Champions League, West Ham United would now need to finish fourth to be guaranteed a place in Europe for 1999–2000. Hammers' only other route into

Europe was via the Inter-Toto Cup, although they would still need to finish fifth to qualify for that.

Fourth-placed Leeds United visited Upton Park on the 1 May. It was a match which West Ham United had to win to stand any chance of gaining a Uefa Cup berth. However, with Rio Ferdinand and Ian Pearce both injured, Harry Redknapp was forced to deploy Marc-Vivien Foe as an emergency defender. It proved a disastrous tactic though, and after two minutes Foe was ruthlessly exposed as Jimmy Floyd Hasselbaink strode forward to smash the game's opening goal past Shaka Hislop. Hammers' problems were further compounded when Ian Wright was sent off for a second bookable offence later in the first half. Leeds were buoyed and seconds before the break, they extended their advantage with a goal from Alan Smith. Paolo Di Canio did manage to pull a goal back after the interval, but as Hammers pressed forward looking for an equaliser they were hit on the counter-attack, and as Hasselbaink broke clear he was felled by the outrushing Shaka Hislop. Referee Rob Harris brandished his red card and pointed to the penalty spot. Craig Forrest was brought on, but could do nothing to prevent Ian Harte's spot-kick. Hammers' misery was completed by a late goal from Lee Bowyer and an even later sending-off for skipper Steve Lomas.

Hammers go Inter-Toto

West Ham United's disastrous performance against Leeds was followed by an equally disappointing 6–0 reverse against perennial strugglers Everton at Goodison Park. The good news, however, was that, while Hammers now had no chance of taking fourth place, they could still qualify for the Inter-Toto Cup, although, for the second year in succession their fate would depend upon a match between Aston Villa and Arsenal. If Arsenal avoided defeat against Villa at Highbury and Hammers beat Middlesbrough at Upton Park, West Ham United would claim fifth place and enter the Inter-Toto Cup. This time Arsenal obliged with a 1–0 win, while at the Boleyn Ground, two goals from Trevor Sinclair and one each for Lampard and Berkovic completed a 4–0 victory.

It had been a season of great excitement at Upton Park, and, for once the entertainment had been matched by the team's achievements. Fifth place in the Premiership represented West Ham United's second highest League finish, and meant that for the first time in the Club's history, Hammers had qualified for European competition via the League. Harry Redknapp, who deserved great credit for leading his team into the Inter-Toto Cup, told reporters: 'It doesn't get much better than this at West Ham – to finish fifth and win the FA Youth Cup. We are in good shape.' Director of Football Peter Storrie had also played a key role in Hammers' success, but, after nine years service his tenure at Upton Park came to an end. Storrie's duties would now be shared between Chairman Terry Brown and incoming Club Secretary Graham Mackrell.

The signing of Paolo Di Canio from Sheffield Wednesday in January 1999 brought raised eyebrows from some quarters. The critics questioned Redknapp's judgment for investing £1.5m in a player who had recently served a 12-match ban for pushing a referee. But the skilful Italian forward, would reward his new manager's faith with four goals and consistently entertaining performances.

West Ham United had come a long way in 104 years and would go into the new millennium as one of English football's leading lights. The Club's founder, Arnold Hills, could scarcely have predicted the meteoric rise of an East End institution which began life as no more than an amateur works team in 1895. And, although Hills' Corinthian ethics would, no doubt, be appalled by the commercialisation which has beset football in recent years, he would have found much consolation in the triumphs and entertaining football which West Ham United have brought to their supporters throughout the 20th century.

YOUTH SUCCESS

West Ham United's FA Youth Cup winning team of 1963. Included in the line-up are: future Hammers manager Harry Redknapp (bottom, left); the Club's first black player, John Charles (bottom, centre); and winger John Sissons, who would score in the 1964 FA Cup final (second from right).

Since the early-1950s West Ham United have had a reputation for finding and developing youth talent. From the legendary Bobby Moore to the prodigiously talented Joe Cole, Upton Park has been graced by a succession of home-grown stars who have all enjoyed a special bond with the Hammers faithful.

West Ham United's youth movement, as it was called in the early days, only really got going when Ted Fenton returned to the Boleyn Ground as assistant manager in 1948. Fenton had seen the progress made by rival clubs, most notably Chelsea, and immediately set about reorganising Hammers' scouting and coaching set-up. Wally St Pier, a former player and long-serving coach, was appointed as the Club's chief scout and it is he who deserves most credit for the early successes of the youth movement. St Pier was a man of immense integrity and his refreshingly honest, straight-talking approach secured the signatures of many talented youngsters. Fenton and St Pier were also well-supported by Club chairman Reg Pratt, who was equally committed to the development of an effective junior set-up.

By the mid-1950s the efforts of the Hammers management were beginning to bear fruit, and in 1957 the Colts reached the final of the FA Youth Cup for the first time where they lost to Manchester United (who were on a run of five successive Cup wins). The Colts were again in the final two years later, but again lost to Lancashire opposition, this

The 1981–82 Hammers Youth team display the trophies won during the course of the previous season. From left to right: the ADO trophy, the South East Counties Division One Cup and the FA Youth Cup.

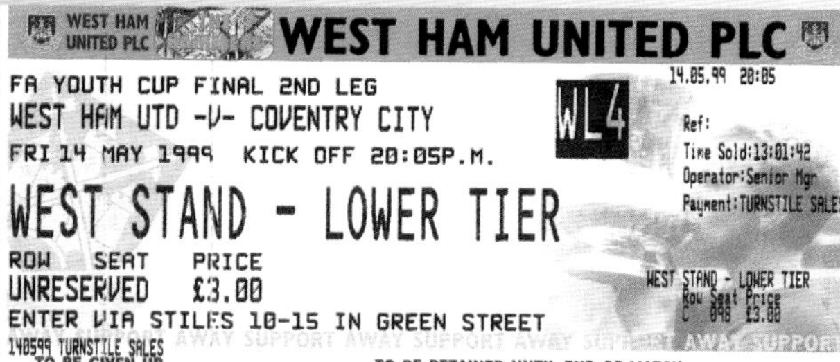

time Blackburn Rovers. Hammers did at last claim victory in the FA Youth Cup in 1963, when they defeated Liverpool 6-3 in a thrilling final. However, the success of a youth system is judged not on silverware but on how many players progress to first team level. And by this yardstick Hammers' set-up was a resounding success. In 1964, the Club won the FA Cup for the first time and seven of the 11 players in Ron Greenwood's team on duty against Preston North End at Wembley had progressed through the Upton Park junior ranks.

Hammers' youth set-up continued to bring forth a procession of talented individuals throughout the 1960s and 1970s, with Trevor Brooking, Frank Lampard and Alvin Martin all going on to collect senior England honours. There was also further success in 1981, when a team which included Paul Allen and Alan Dickens triumphed in the FA Youth Cup final against Tottenham Hotspur. However, during the late-1980s and early-1990s Hammers' youth system entered the doldrums, with only a handful of youngsters making the grade. It was a desperate time for the Club, and it was only after a reorganisation following the appointment of Harry Redknapp as manager in 1994 that the situation began to improve.

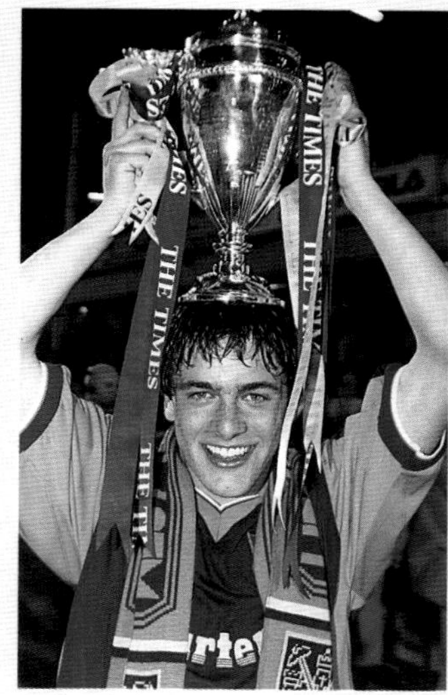

Joe Cole, Hammers' star of the successful 1998–99 season holds the FA Youth Cup aloft.

The resurgence of West Ham United's youth section in the 1990s has been due, in the main, to the efforts of the Club's Academy director, Tony Carr, and his talented and dedicated staff, which also includes former England winger Peter Brabrook. In 1996 Carr led Hammers to the South East Counties League title and the final of the FA Youth Cup, with a team which included future first-team players Rio Ferdinand and Frank Lampard. But two years later this achievement was surpassed by an unprecedented 'double' of Youth Cup and Academy Under-19 Championship. 'This has been a massive achievement by the lads,' said Carr after Hammers had claimed the Academy Championship in the final minute of extra-time, ' and what an act to follow next season... the lads have shown what they can do and won some silverware but the test comes over the next 18 months to two years. We'll see how many can follow the likes of Rio Ferdinand and Frank Lampard into the first team.' Time will, of course, tell for the class of 1999, but there can be few doubts that West Ham United will continue to be among youth football's leading lights in the new millennium.

FA YOUTH CUP FINALS

1957
First leg
West Ham United 2 (John Cartwright, George Fenn)
Manchester United 3

Second leg
Manchester United 5
West Ham United 0

1959
First leg
West Ham United 1 (Andy Smillie)
Blackburn Rovers 1

Second leg
Blackburn Rovers 1
West Ham United 0

1963
First leg
Liverpool 3
West Ham United 1 (Martin Britt)

Second leg
West Ham United 5 (Martin Britt 3, Trevor Dawkins, John Dryden)
Liverpool 2

1975
First leg
West Ham United 1 (Terry Sharpe)
Ipswich Town 3

Second leg
Ipswich Town 2
West Ham United 0

1981
First leg
West Ham United 2 (Bobby Barnes, Wayne Reader)
Tottenham Hotspur 0

Second leg
Tottenham Hotspur 1
West Ham United 0

1996
First leg
West Ham United 0
Liverpool 2

Second leg
Liverpool 2
West Ham United 1 (Frank Lampard)

1999
First leg
Coventry City 0
West Ham United 3 (Adam Newton, Stevland Angus, Bertie Brayley)

Second leg
West Ham United 6 (Bertie Brayley 2, Richard Garcia 2, Adam Newton, Michael Carrick)
Coventry City 0

The 1998–99 West Ham United Youth team celebrate their 9–0 aggregate victory over Coventry City in the final of the FA Youth Cup.

1993-1995

SEASON 1993-94 FA CARLING PREMIERSHIP

14 Aug	Wimbledon	H	L	0-2	Miklosko	Breacker	Dicks	Potts	Gale	Allen M	Gordon	Butler	Morley	Allen C	Holmes*	Rowland
17 Aug	Leeds U	A	L	0-1	..	..	..	..*	Foster	Gale	..	..	..	..*	Allen M	Rowland/Robson
21 Aug	Coventry C	A	D	1-1	..	..	..	..	..	Allen M	..1	..	..	..	Rowland	
25 Aug	Sheffield Wed	H	W	2-0	..	..	..	..	..	..	..*	..	..	..2	..	Holmes
28 Aug	Queens Park R	H	L	0-4	..	..	..	..	..	..	Robson	..	..	..	..	
1 Sep	Manchester U	A	L	0-3	..	..	..	..	..	..*	Gordon*	Holmes	..	..	..	Gale/Robson
11 Sep	Swindon T	H	D	0-0	..	..	..	..	Gale	Bishop	..*	..	..	Jones	..	Rush
18 Sep	Blackburn R	A	W	2-0	..	Rowland	Burrows	..	..	..	..	..	Chapman 1	Marsh*	Morley 1	Allen M
25 Sep	Newcastle U	A	L	0-2	..	Brown*	..	..	..	..	..	Morley*	..	..*	Holmes	Allen M/Boere (so)
2 Oct	Chelsea	H	W	1-0	..	Breacker	..	..	..	..	Butler	..1	..	..*	..	Allen M
16 Oct	Aston Villa	H	D	0-0	..	..	..	..	..	..	..	..	..	..	..	
23 Oct	Norwich C	A	D	0-0	..	..	..	..	..*	..	..	..	..	..	..	Rowland
1 Nov	Manchester C	H	W	3-1	..	..	..1	..	Martin	..	..	..	..1	..	..1*	Rowland
6 Nov	Liverpool	A	L	0-2	..	..	..	..	..	..	..	..	..	..	..	
20 Nov	Oldham A	H	W	2-0	..	..	..	..	..1	..	..	..1	..	..	..	
24 Nov	Arsenal	H	D	0-0	..	..	..	..	Gale	..	..	..	..	..	..	
28 Nov	Southampton	A	W	2-0	..	..	..	..	..	..	..	..1	..1	Allen M	..	
4 Dec	Wimbledon	A	W	2-1	..	..	..	..	..	..	..	..	..2	..	..	
8 Dec	Leeds U	H	L	0-1	..	..	..	..	..	..	..	..*	..	Marsh	..	Boere
11 Dec	Coventry C	H	W	3-2	..	..	..	..	..	..*	..	..	..	..	..	Allen M
18 Dec	Sheffield Wed	A	L	0-5	..	..	..	..	..	..*	..	..	..	..	..*	Allen M/Boere
27 Dec	Ipswich Town	A	D	1-1	..	..	..	..	..	..	..	..1	..	..	..*	Rowland
28 Dec	Tottenham H	H	L	1-3	..	..	..	..	..	..	..	..	..	..	..1*	Jones
1 Jan	Everton	A	W	1-0	..	..1	..	..	..	..	..	..	..	..	..*	Rowland
3 Jan	Sheffield Wed	H	D	0-0	..	..	..	..	..	..	..	..*	..	..	Rowland	Jones
15 Jan	Aston Villa	A	L	1-3	..	..	Rowland	..	..	..	Allen M 1	..*	..	..	..	Jones
24 Jan	Norwich City	H	D	3-3	..	..	..	..	..*	..	..	Jones 1	..*	..	..	Morley 1/Brown (Sutton 1og)
12 Feb	Manchester C	A	D	0-0	..	..	..	..	Brown	..	..	Marsh*	..	Allen C*	Holmes	Morley/Marquis
26 Feb	Manchester U	H	D	2-2	..	..	..	..	Martin	..	..	Morley 1	..1	Marsh	..	
5 Mar	Swindon T	A	D	1-1	..	..	..	..	..	..	..	..1	..	..	..*	Rowland
19 Mar	Newcastle U	H	L	2-4	..	..1	..	..	..1	..	Butler	..*	..	..	..	Boere
26 Mar	Chelsea	A	L	0-2	..	..	Burrows*	..	Gale	..	Allen M*	Butler	..	..	Rowland	Morley/Jones
29 Mar	Sheffield U	A	L	2-3	..	..	Rowland	..	..	..1	Butler	Morley	..	..*	Holmes 1*	Allen M/Brown
2 Apr	Ipswich T	H	W	2-1	..	..	..	..	..	..	..	Rush 1*	Morley 1	..	..	Brown
4 Apr	Tottenham H	A	W	4-1	..	..	..	..	..	..	..*	..	..2	..1	..	Jones 1
9 Apr	Everton	H	L	0-1	..	..	..*	..	..	..	Jones	..	..	..	..	Martin
16 Apr	Oldham A	A	W	2-1	..	..	Burrows	Brown	..	..	Allen M 1	..	..1	..	..	
23 Apr	Liverpool	H	L	1-2	..	..	..	Potts	..	..*	..1	..	..	..	..	Chapman
27 Apr	Blackburn R	H	L	1-2	..	..	Brown	..	..	..	..1	..*	..	..	..*	Chapman/Mitchell
30 Apr	Arsenal	A	W	2-0	..	..	Burrows*	..	..	..	..1	..	..1	..	Brown	Williamson
3 May	Queens Park R	A	D	0-0	..	..	Brown	..	..	..	..	..*	..	..	Williamson	Chapman
7May	Southampton	H	D	3-3	..	..	Burrows	..	..	..*	..1	..	..	..	..1	Chapman (Monkou 1og)
	Coca-Cola Cup															
22 Sep	Chesterfield	H	W	5-1	..	Rowland	..1	..	..	..	Gordon	Morley 2	Chapman 2	Holmes	Marsh	
5 Oct	Chesterfield	A	W	2-0	..	Breacker	..	..	..	..	Butler*	..	..*	Marsh	Holmes	Allen M 1/Boere 1
27 Oct	Nottingham F	A	L	1-2	..	..	..	..	Martin	..	..*	..1	..	..	..	Allen M
	FA Cup															
1 Jan	Watford	H	W	2-1	..	..	..*	..	Gale	..	Allen M 1	Morley*	..	Marsh 1	Rowland	Brown/Jones
29 Jan	Notts C	A	D	1-1	..	..	Rowland	..	Brown	..	..	Jones 1	..	..	Holmes	
9 Feb	Notts C	H	W	1-0	..	..	..	..	..	..	..	..*	..1	..	..	Allen C
19 Feb	Kidderminster Harriers	A	W	1-0	..	..	..	..	Martin	..	..	Marsh	..1	Allen C*	..	Morley
14 Mar	Luton T	H	D	0-0	..	..	Burrows	..	..	..	..	Morley	..*	Marsh	..	Allen C
23 Mar	Luton T	A	L	2-3	..	..	Burrows	..	..	..1	Butler	..	..	..*	Allen M 1	Jones

Hammer of the Year 1993-94
TREVOR MORLEY

	P	W	L	D	F:A	Pts	Pos
Manchester U	42	27	4	11	80:38	92	1st
West Ham	42	13	16	13	47:58	52	13th

SEASON 1994-95 FA CARLING PREMIERSHIP

20 Aug	Leeds U	H	D	0-0	Miklosko	Breacker	Burrows	Potts*	Martin	Allen	Bishop	Butler	Morley	Chapman	Holmes*	Whitbread/Marsh
24 Aug	Manchester C	A	L	0-3	..	..	..	..	..	..	..	Butler*	..	..*	..	Marsh/Whitbread
27 Aug	Norwich C	A	L	0-1	..	..	..	..	..	..	..	Marsh*	Moncur	Jones	Rowland*	Chapman/Whitbread
31 Aug	Newcastle U	H	L	1-3	..	..	..	..	..	..*	Hutchison 1	..	..	Butler	Holmes	Jones
10 Sep	Liverpool	A	D	0-0	..	..	Rowland	..	..	..	Butler	..	..	Rush	Cottee (so)	
17 Sep	Aston Villa	H	W	1-0	..	..	..	..	..	..	Butler*	..	..	..	..1	Chapman
25 Sep	Arsenal	H	L	0-2	..	..	..	..	..	..	Hutchison	..	..	Chapman	Holmes*	Rush
2 Oct	Chelsea	A	W	2-1	..	..	..	..	..	..1	..	..	..1	..	Rush	
8 Oct	Crystal P	H	W	1-0	..	..	..	..	..	..	..1	..	..	..*	Cottee	Rush
15 Oct	Manchester U	A	L	0-1	..	..	..	..	..	..	..	..	..	Rush	..	
22 Oct	Southampton	H	W	2-0	..	..	Dicks	..	..	..1	Bishop	Marsh	Rush 1	Chapman	..	
29 Oct	Tottenham H	A	L	1-3	..	Rowland	..	..	..	Allen*	..*	..	Hutchison	Rush 1	..	Whitbread/Chapman
1 Nov	Everton	A	L	0-1	..	Whitbread	..	..	..	Rush	..	..	..	Chapman	..	
5 Nov	Leicester C	H	W	1-0	..	..	..1	..	..	Morley	..	Moncur	..(so)	Rush	..*	Brown
19 Nov	Sheffield W	A	L	0-1	..	Brown	..	..	..	Allen*	..	..	Morley	..	..	Marsh
26 Nov	Coventry C	H	L	0-1	..	..	..	..	Whitbread	Holmes	..*	Marsh	Moncur	Morley	..	Rush
4 Dec	Queens Park R	A	L	1-2	..	..	..	..	Rowland	Rush	Hughes	..	..	Boere 1	..	
10 Dec	Leeds U	A	D	2-2	..	..	..	..	Rieper	Rowland*	Bishop	Holmes	Rush	..2	..	Hughes
17 Dec	Manchester C	H	W	3-0	..	Breacker	..	..	Martin	Holmes	..	Hughes	..	..	..3	
26 Dec	Ipswich T	H	D	1-1	..	..	..	..*	..	..	..	..	..	..	..1	Rieper
28 Dec	Wimbledon	A	L	0-1	..	Brown	..	..	..	Rieper*	..	..	Holmes	..	..	Rush
31 Dec	Nottingham F	H	W	3-1	..	Breacker	..	..	Martin	Holmes	..1	..1	Moncur*	..*	..1	Rush/Rieper
2 Jan	Blackburn R	A	L	2-4	..	..	..1	..	Rieper	..*	..	..	..	..	..1	Rush
14 Jan	Tottenham H	H	L	1-2	..	..	Brown	..	Martin	..*	..	..*	..	..1	..	Allen/Morley
23 Jan	Sheffield W	H	L	0-2	..	..(so)	..	..	..(so)	..*	..	..*	..	..	..	Rieper/Allen
4 Feb	Leicester C	A	W	2-1	..	..	Dicks 1	..	..	Allen	Moncur	..	Hutchison*	Williamson	..1	Boere
13 Feb	Everton	H	D	2-2	..	Brown	..	..	..	..	..	..*	..	..	..2	Boere
18 Feb	Coventry C	A	L	0-2	..	Breacker	..	..	..*	..	Holmes*	Moncur	..	Williamson	..	Rieper/Boere
25 Feb	Chelsea	H	L	1-2	..	..	..	..	Rieper	..	Bishop	..	..1	Morley	..	
5 Mar	Arsenal	A	W	1-0	..	..	..	..	..	..	..	..	..1	..*	..	Rush
8 Mar	Newcastle U	A	L	0-2	..	..	..	..	..	..	..	Hughes	..	Rush*	..	Morley
11 Mar	Norwich C	H	D	2-2	..	..	..	..	..	Williamson	..	Moncur*	..	Morley	..2	Hughes
15 Mar	Southampton	A	D	1-1	..	..	..	..	..	Rush*	..	..	..1	Holmes	..	Boere
18 Mar	Aston Villa	A	W	2-0	..	..	..	..	..	Allen	..	..1	..1*	..*	..	Rowland/Boere
8 Apr	Nottingham F	A	D	1-1	..	Brown	..1	..	..	..	..	Hughes	Holmes*	Boere	..	Whitbread
13 Apr	Wimbledon	H	W	3-0	..	Breacker	..1	..	..	..	..	..	..	..1	..1	
17 Apr	Ipswich T	A	D	1-1	..	..	..	..	..	..*	..	Moncur	Hutchison	..1	..	Hutchison
30 Apr	Blackburn R	H	W	2-0	..	..	..	..	..1	..	..	..	..1	..*	Holmes	Rush/Webster
3 May	Queens Park R	H	D	0-0	..	..	..	..	..	..(so)	..	..	..	..*	..	Morley/Webster
6 May	Crystal P	A	L	0-1	..	..	..	..	..	..*	..	..	..*	..	..	Morley/Webster
10 May	Liverpool	H	W	3-0	..	..	..*	..	..	Moncur	..	Hughes	..2	Morley	..1	Webster
14 May	Manchester U	H	D	1-1	..	..	Rowland	..	..	..	..	..1*	..*	..	..	Allen/Webster
	Coca-Cola Cup															
20 Sep	Walsall	A	L	1-2	..	..	..	..	Martin	Allen*	Moncur	Marsh	Hutchison	Rush*	Cottee	Chapman/Whitbread (Newmark 1og)
5 Oct	Walsall	H	W	2-0	..	..	..	..	Moncur 1*	..	Bishop	..	..1	Whitbread	Chapman	Brown
26 Oct	Chelsea	H	W	1-0	..	..	..	..	Martin	..	..	..	..1	Rush	Cottee	
30 Nov	Bolton W	H	L	1-3	..	Brown	..	..	Whitbread	Rush	..	Holmes*	Moncur	Boere	..1	Morley
	FA Cup															
7 Jan	Wycombe W	A	W	2-0	..	Breacker	..	..	Martin	Moncur	..	Hughes	Holmes*	Boere*	..1	Brown 1/Morley
28 Jan	Queens Park R	A	L	0-1	..	..	..	..	..	..	..*	..	Allen	..	..	Hutchison

Hammer of the Year 1994-95
STEVE POTTS

	P	W	L	D	F:A	Pts	Pos
Blackburn R	42	27	7	8	80:39	89	1st
West Ham	42	13	18	11	44:48	50	14th

Abbreviations:

Figures shown as 2 etc. refer to goals scored by individual players

* own-goal
(so) sent off

Matty Holmes away to Liverpool in 1993.

SEASON 1995-96 FA CARLING PREMIERSHIP

19 Aug	Leeds U	H	L	1-2	Miklosko	Breacker	Dicks	Potts	Rieper	Williamson 1*	Moncur	Bishop	Cottee	Hutchison	Rowland*	Martin/Boogers
23 Aug	Manchester U	A	L	1-2	..	..	..	..	..	Allen	..	..	..	..	Williamson*	Boogers (so) (Bruce 1og)
26 Aug	Nottingham F	A	D	1-1	..	..	..	..	..	.. 1	..	..	..*	..	Slater	Martin
30 Aug	Tottenham H	H	D	1-1	..	..	..	..	..	..	..	..	..	.. 1*	..	Boere
11 Sep	Chelsea	H	L	1-3	..	..	..	..	..	Bishop*	..	Dowie	..	.. 1	..	Lazarides
16 Sep	Arsenal	A	L	0-1	..	..	..(so)	..	..	..	..*	..	..*	..*	..	Martin/Laz/Sealy
23 Sep	Everton	H	W	2-1	..	..	.. 2	..*	Martin	..	..	..	..*	Lazarides	..	Rieper/Williamson
2 Oct	Southampton	A	D	0-0	..	..	Rowland	..	..	..	..	Lazarides*	Dowie	Hutchison	..	Cottee
16 Oct	Wimbledon	A	W	1-0	..	Potts	Dicks	Rieper	..	..	..	Dowie	Cottee1	Slater	Hughes	
21 Oct	Blackburn R	H	D	1-1	..	..	..	..	..	..	..	.. 1	..	..*	..	Hutchison
28 Oct	Sheffield W	A	W	1-0	..	..	..	..	..	..	..*	.. 1	..	..*	..	Hutchison/Harkes
4 Nov	Aston Villa	H	L	1-4	..	..	.. 1	..	..	..	Slater*	..	..	Hutchison*	..	Boogers/Harkes
18 Nov	Bolton W	A	W	3-0	..	..	Rowland	..	..	.. 1	Harkes	..	..1	Williamson 1	..	
22 Nov	Liverpool	H	D	0-0	..	..	..	..	..	..	..	..	..		..	
25 Nov	Queens Park R	H	W	1-0	..	..	..*	..	..	..	..*	..	..1	..	..	Brecker/Slater
2 Dec	Blackburn R	A	L	2-4	..	Breacker	Dicks 1	Potts	Rieper	..*	..*	..	..*	..	..	Hutchison/Slater1/Boogers
11 Dec	Everton	A	L	0-3	Miklosko (so)	..	..	..	..	..	Slater	..	..*	..	..	Rowland
16 Dec	Southampton	H	W	2-1	..	Potts	..	Rieper	Martin*	..	Moncur*	.. 1	..1	..	..	Breacker/Slater
23 Dec	Middlesbrough	A	L	2-4	..	Breacker*	.. 1	Potts	Rieper	..	..*	..	..1	..	..*	Rowland/Slater
1 Jan	Manchester C	A	L	1-2	Finn	Harkes	..	..	..	..	..	Slater	Dowie 1	..*	..	Hutchison
13 Jan	Leeds U	A	L	0-2	Miklosko	Potts	Rowland*	Williamson	..	Dicks	..	Bishop	Cottee	Dowie	..	Slater
22 Jan	Manchester U	H	L	0-1	..	Brown	Dicks	Potts	..	Bishop	..	Dowie	..	Williamson	Slater*	Rowland
31 Jan	Coventry C	H	W	3-2	..	..	..	..	.. 1	..	..*	.. 1	.. 1*	..	Hughes	Whitbread/Lampard
3 Feb	Nottingham F	H	W	1-0	..	..	..	..	..	..	Slater 1*	..	..*	..	..	Whitbread/Dani
12 Feb	Tottenham H	A	W	1-0	..	Potts	..	Bilic	..	..	Hughes*	..	Dani 1*	..	Rowland	Cottee/Harkes
17 Feb	Chelsea	A	W	2-1	..	..	.. 1	..	..	..	..	..	..*	.. 1	..	Cottee
21 Feb	Newcastle U	H	W	2-0	..	..	.. 1	..*	..	..	..	..*	Cottee 1*	..	..	Harkes/Gprdon
24 Feb	Arsenal	H	L	0-1	..	Harkes*	..	Potts	..	..	..	..	..	..	..	Dani
2 Mar	Coventry C	A	D	2-2	..	Potts	..	Bilic	.. 1	..	..	..	.. 1*	..	..	Harkes
9 Mar	Middlesbrough	H	W	2-0	..	Breacker	.. 1	Potts	Bilic	..	..	.. 1	..*	..	..	Dumitrescu
18 Mar	Newcastle U	A	L	0-3	..	Potts	..	Bilic	Rieper	..*	..	..	Dumitrescu*	..	..	Breacker/Dani
23 Mar	Manchester C	H	W	4-2	..	Breacker	.. 1	..	..	..	..	.. 2	..*	..	..	Dani 1
6 Apr	Wimbledon	H	D	1-1	..	..	.. 1	..	..	..	..	..	Dani	..	..*	Slater
8 Apr	Liverpool	A	L	0-2	..	..	..	..	..	..	..*	..	Slater	..	..	Dani
13 Apr	Bolton W	H	W	1-0	..	..	..	..	..	..	Slater*	..	Cottee 1	..	Hughes*	Moncur/Rowland
17 Apr	Aston Villa	A	D	1-1	..	..	..	Potts*	..	Bilic	Moncur	..	..1	..	Rowland	Dani
27 Apr	Queens Park R	A	L	0-3	..	..	..	..	..	..	Hughes	Moncur*	..	..	..	Watson
5 May	Sheffield W	H	D	1-1	..	..	.. 1	..	..	..	..	Dowie*	..*	..	..*	Martin/L'pard/Ferd'
	Coca-Cola Cup															
20 Sep	Bristol R	A	W	1-0	..	..	..	..	Martin	Bishop	Moncur 1	..*	..	Lazarides	Slater*	Rieper/Williamson
4 Oct	Bristol R	H	W	3-0	..	..	.. 1	..	Rieper	.. 1	..	..	.. 1	Slater	Hughes	
25 Oct	Southampton	A	L	1-2	..	Potts	..	Rieper	Martin	..	..	..	.. 1	..	..	
	FA Cup															
6 Jan	Southend U	H	W	2-0	..	Harkes	..	Potts	Rieper .	..	.. 1	..	..	Williamson	Hughes 1	
7 Feb	Grimsby T	H	D	1-1	..	Potts	..	Rieper	Whitbread	..	Slater*	.. 1	..	..	..	Lazarides*/Rowland
14 Feb	Grimsby T	A	L	0-3	..	..	..	..	Martin*	..	Hughes	..	..	..	Rowland*	Gordon/Harkes

Hammer of the Year 1995-96
JULIAN DICKS

	P	W	L	D	F:A	Pts	Pos
Manchester U	38	25	6	7	73:35	82	1st
West Ham	38	14	15	9	43:52	51	10th

1993-1999

SEASON 1996-97 FA CARLING PREMIERSHIP

17 Aug	Arsenal	A	L	0-2	Miklosko	Breacker	Dicks	Rieper	Bilic*	Williamson	Hughes	Rowland*	Lampard*	Dowie	Jones	Ferdinand/Lazarides/Slater
21 Aug	Coventry C	H	D	1-1	..	..*	..	..1	..	..	..	Lazarides	Slater	..	Jones*	Futre/Bowen
24 Aug	Southampton	H	W	2-1	..	Slater*	..1	..	..	..	..1	..*	Futre	..	Bowen	Breacker/Radu/Dumit
4 Sep	Middlesbrough	A	L	1-4	..	Breacker	..	Potts*	..	..	..1	..*	..	Raducioiu*	..	Dowie/Dumit/L'pard
8 Sep	Sunderland	A	D	0-0	..	..	..	Rieper	..	..	..	Dumitrescu*	..*	Raducioiu*	..	Rowland/Ferd/Jones
14 Sep	Wimbledon	H	L	0-2	..	..*	..	..	..	..	..	..*	..*	Dowie	..	Laz/Moncur/Cottee
21 Sep	Nottingham F	A	W	2-0	Mautone	Bowen 1	..	..(so)	..	Lazarides	..1	Bishop*	Moncur	..	Cottee	Lampard
29 Sep	Liverpool	H	L	1-2	Miklosko	Breacker	..	..	..1	Bowen*	..	..	..	..	..*	Porfirio/Dumitrescu
12 Oct	Everton	A	L	1-2	..	..	..1	Potts*	..	Rowland	..	..*	..	..	Porfirio	Raducioiu/Dumitrescu
19 Oct	Leicester C	H	W	1-0	..	Bowen*	..	Rieper	..	Porfirio	..	..	..1	..	Raducioiu*	Breacker/Lazarides
26 Oct	Blackburn R	H	W	2-1	..	..*	..	..	..	Lazarides	..	..	..*	..	Porfirio 1*	Braeck/Futre/L'pard (Berg 1og)
2 Nov	Tottenham H	A	L	0-1	..	Breacker	..	..	..	..	..	..	..*	..	Porfirio	Futre
16 Nov	Newcastle U	A	D	1-1	..	..	..	Potts	..	Rowland 1	..	..	..	..	Raducioiu*	Futre
23 Nov	Derby C	H	D	1-1	..	..	..	..	..	Lazaridis*	..	..1	..	..	Porfirio	Futre
30 Nov	Sheffield W	A	D	0-0	..	..	..	..	..	..	..*	..	..	..	Rowland	Lazaridis
4 Dec	Aston Villa	H	L	0-2	..	..*	..*	Rieper	..	Rowland*	..	..	..	..	Raducioiu	Bowen/Lazaridis
8 Dec	Manchester U	H	D	2-2	..	Bowen	..1	..	..*	..*	..	..	..	..	Dimitrescu	Potts/Raducioiu 1
21 Dec	Chelsea	A	L	1-3	..	..	..	..	..	..*	..	..*	..*	Porfirio1	Newell	Radu/L'pard/W'mson
28 Dec	Sunderland	H	W	2-0	..	..	..	..	..1	Williamson	..	..	..*	..	..	Lampard/Raducioiu 1
1 Jan	Nottingham F	H	L	0-1	..	..*	..	..	..	..	..	..	Porfirio	Raducioiu	..*	Potts/Lampard/Jones
11 Jan	Liverpool	A	D	0-0	..	Breacker	..	..	..	..*	..	..	Moncur	Porfirio*	Jones*	Potts/Newell/Lazaridis
20 Jan	Leeds U	H	L	0-2	..	..	..	..	..	..	..	..	Lazaridis*	Jones	Newell	Porfirio
29 Jan	Arsenal	H	L	1-2	..	..	..	..	..	..	..	Rowland*	Moncur*	Porfirio	..	Jones/Lampard (Rose 1og)
1 Feb	Blackburn R	A	L	1-2	Sealey	..	..	..	..	..	..	Bishop	Rowland*	Jones*	..	Lazaridis/Ferdinand 1
15 Feb	Derby C	A	L	0-1	Miklosko	..	..	..*	Potts	..	Roland*	..	Ferdinand	Hartson	Kitson	Porfirio/Lampard
24 Feb	Tottenham H	H	W	4-3	..	..	..2	Ferdinand	..	Bowen	Hughes	..	Moncur	..1	..1*	Dowie
1 Mar	Leeds U	A	L	0-1	..	..*	..	..	Bilic	..*	..(so)	..*	..	Dowie	..	Omoy/Rowland/Lampard
12 Mar	Chelsea	H	W	3-2	..	..	..1	..*	..	Potts	..	..*	..	..	..2	Williamson/L'pard/Porfirio
15 Mar	Aston Villa	A	D	0-0	..	..	..	Potts	..	Lampard*	Lazaridis	..	..	Hartson	..	Ferdinand
18 Mar	Wimbledon	A	D	1-1	..	..	..	Rieper	..	Potts*	Ferdinand	..*	..	..	..	Porfirio/Lazaridis1
22 Mar	Coventry C	A	W	3-1	..	..*	..	..	..	..	..1*	..*	..	..2	..	Rowland/Dowie/Porfirio
9 Apr	Middlesbrough	H	D	0-0	..	Potts	Hall	..	..	Lomas	Lazaridis*	..	Hughes	..	..	Porfirio
12 Apr	Southampton	A	L	0-2	..	..	..	..*	..	..	Rowland*	Bishop*	..	..	..	Dowie/Lazaridis/Porfirio
19 Apr	Everton	H	D	2-2	..	..	..	Ferdinand	..	..	Porfirio*	Moncur*	..	..	..2	Rieper/Bishop
23 Apr	Leicester C	A	W	1-0	..	..	..	..	Rieper	..	..*	..1	..	..	..	Rowland/Dowie
3 May	Sheffield W	H	W	5-1	..	..	..	..	Bilic*	..*	..	..	Lazaridis*	..2	.. 3	Rieper/Boylan/Bishop
6 May	Newcastle U	H	D	0-0	..	..	..	..	..	..	..*	..*	..	..	..	Hughes/Bishop
11 May	Manchester U	A	L	0-2	..*	..	..	..*	..	..	..	..	..	Dowie	..	Sealey/Hughes
	Coca-Cola Cup															
18 Sep	Barnet	A	D	1-1	Mautone	Breacker*	Dicks	Rieper	..	Bowen	Hughes	Bishop	Moncur*	..	Cottee 1	Lazaridis/Lampard
25 Sep	Barnet	H	W	1-0	Mautone	..	..	..	..1	Moncur	Lazaridis*	..	Dimitrescu	..	..*	Ferdinand/Jones
23 Oct	Nottingham F	H	W	4-1	Miklosko	Bowen	..1	..	..	Lazaridis	..	..	Moncur	..2	Porfino 1	
27 Nov	Stockport C	H	D	1-1	..	Breacker	..	Potts	..	..*	..	..	Lampard	..	Raducioiu 1	Dumitrescu
18 Dec	Stockport C	A	L	1-2	..	Bowen	..1	Rieper	Bilic	Moncur	..	..	Dimitrescu	..*	Porfirio	Williamson
	FA Cup															
4 Jan	Wrexham	A	D	1-1	..	Breacker	..	Rieper	Potts	Williamson	..	..	Moncur	Porfirio 1	Jones	
25 Jan	Wrexham	H	L	0-1	..	..	..	Ferdinand	Bilic	..	..	..	Lampard	Lazaridis*	Jones	Porfirio

Hammer of the Year 1996-97
JULIAN DICKS

	P	W	L	D	F:A	Pts	Pos
Manchester U	38	21	5	12	76:44	75	1st
West Ham	38	10	16	12	39:48	42	14th

SEASON 1997-98 FA CARLING PREMIERSHIP

9 Aug	Barnsley	A	W	2-1	Miklosko	Breacker*	Potts	Rieper	Ferdinand	Lomas	Hughes	Kitson*	Hartson 1	Berkovic*	Moncur	LazaridisLampard 1/Terrier
13 Aug	Tottenham H	H	W	2-1	..	..	..	..	..	..	Lazaridis	..*	..1*	..1	..*	Hughes/Dowie/Lampard
23 Aug	Everton	A	L	1-2	..	..*	Unsworth	..	..	..	..	..*	..	..*	..*	Dowie/Hughes/Lampard (Watson og)
27 Aug	Coventry C	A	D	1-1	..	..	..	..	..	..	..	..1*	..	..	..	Dowie
30 Aug	Wimbledon	H	W	3-1	..	..	..	..1	..	..	..	Dowie	..1	..1	..	
13 Sep	Manchester U	A	L	1-2	..	..	..	Potts	..	..	Hughes	Kitson	..1	..	..*	Lampard
20 Sep	Newcastle U	H	L	0-1	..	..*	..	Pearce	..	..	Lazaridis	Dowie	..	..*	Lampard	Hughes/Potts
24 Sep	Arsenal	A	L	0-4	..	..	..	..	..*	..	..	..	..	Lampard	Bishop	Potts
27 Sep	Liverpool	H	W	2-1	..	..	..	..	..	..	Impey	..	..1	Berkovic 1	Lampard	
4 Oct	Southampton	A	L	0-3	..	..	..	..	..	..	..	..*	..	..	Bishop	Moore
18 Oct	Bolton W	H	W	3-0	Forrest	Potts	..	Lampard	..	..	Dowie	Hartson 2	Berkovic 1	Moncur	Rowland	
27 Oct	Leicester C	A	L	1-2	..	..	..	..	..	..	..	..	..1	..	..	
3 Nov	Crystal P	H	Abnd	2-2	..	..*	..	Pearce	..	..	Moncur	Lampard 1	..	Hartson 1	Dowie	Impey/Abou
9 Nov	Chelsea	A	L	1-2	..	Rowland	..*	..	..	..	Impey	Berkovic	Hartson 1	Moncur*	Lampard	Potts/Abou
23 Nov	Leeds U	A	L	1-3	Miklosko	Breacker	..	..	Potts	..	..	..*	..	Abou*	..1	Dowie/Moncur
29 Nov	Aston Villa	H	W	2-1	..	..	..	..	Ferdinand	Potts	Berkovic	Abou*	..2	Lomas	Rowland	Alves
3 Dec	Crystal P	H	W	4-1	Forrest	..	..1	..	..	Lomas 1	..1	Abou*	..1	Moncur	Lazaridis*	Rowlands/Alves
6 Dec	Derby C	A	L	0-2	Miklosko	..*	..	..	..	..	..	Lampard	..	..	..*	Abou/Alves
13 Dec	Sheffield W	H	W	1-0	Forrest	Pearce	..	Lampard	..	..	Impey*	Berkovic	..	Kitson 1*	Rowland	Breacker/Abou
20 Dec	Blackburn R	A	L	0-3	..	..	..	..	..	..(so)	..	..	..	..*	..	Abou
26 Dec	Coventry C	H	W	1-0	..	..	..	..	..	..	..	..*	..	..1	Lazaridis	Potts
28 Dec	Wimbledon	A	W	2-1	..	Breacker	..	Pearce	..	..	..	Lampard	..	..1	..	(Kimble og)
10 Jan	Barnsley	H	W	6-0	..	Pearce	..	Potts	..	Lampard 1	..*	Berkovic	..1	Abou 2	..1	Moncur 1
17 Jan	Tottenham H	A	L	0-1	..	..	..	..	..	..	Berkovic*	Abou so	..	Moncur	..*	Dowie/Hodges
31 Jan	Everton	H	D	2-2	..	Breacker	Pearce	..	..	Lomas	Sinclair 2*	Berkovic	..	Lampard	..*	Hodges
7 Feb	Newcastle U	A	W	1-0	..	..	..	Impey*	..	..	..	Hartson	Kitson*	Moncur	..1	Berkovic/Potts
21 Feb	Bolton W	A	D	1-1	..	Pearce	Unsworth	..	..	..	..1	Berkovic	Hartson (so)	..	..	
2 Mar	Arsenal	H	D	0-0	Lama	Breacker*	..	..	Pearce	..	..	..	..	Lampard	..	Potts
11 Mar	Manchester U	H	D	1-1	..	Potts	Pearce	..	Ferdinand	..	..1	..	Abou	..	..	
14 Mar	Chelsea	H	W	2-1	..	Pearce	Unsworth 1	..*	..	Lampard	..1	..	Abou	Bishop	..	Potts
30 Mar	Leeds U	H	W	3-0	..	Potts	..	Pearce 1	..	Moncur	..	..*	Hartson 1	Abou 1*	..	Mean/Omoyinmi
3 Apr	Aston Villa	A	L	0-2	..	Potts*	..	..	..	Lomas	..	Lampard	..	Moncur	..	Abou
11 Apr	Derby C	H	D	0-0	..	Pearce*	..	Impey*	..	..	..	Berkovic*	.. so	Lampard	..	Abou/Potts/Moncur
13 Apr	Sheffield W	A	D	1-1	..	..	..	..	..	..	Berkovic 1	Abou*	..	..	..	Omoyinmi
18 Apr	Blackburn R	H	W	2-1	..	..	..	..	..	..	Sinclair	Berkovic*	..2	..	..	Potts
25 Apr	Southampton	H	L	2-4	..	..	Potts*	Impey	..	..1	..1	..	Abou	..	..	Kitson
2 May	Liverpool	A	L	0-5	..	..	Unsworth	Lampard	..	..	..	..	Kitson*	Moncur*	..	Mean/Abou/Omoyinmi
5 May	Crystal P	A	D	3-3	..	..	.. (so)	Impey	Lampard	..	..	..	..	Abou*	..	Omoyinmi 2 (Curcic og)
10 May	Leicester C	H	W	4-3	..	..	..	Lomas	Ferdinand	Lampard 1	..1	..*	Omoyinmi	Abou 2	..	Mean
	Coca-Cola Cup															
16 Sep	Huddersfield T	A	L	0-1	Miklosko	Breacker	..	Potts	..	Lomas	Hughes	Kitson*	Hartson	Berkovic	Lampard	Dowie
29 Sep	Huddersfield T	H	W	3-0	..	..	..	Pearce	..	..	Impey*	Dowie	.. 3	..	..	Potts
15 Oct	Aston Villa	H	W	3-0	Forrest	..*	..	Potts	..	..	..	..*	..2	..	..1	Rowland/Bishop
19 Nov	Walsall	H	W	4-1	..	..	..	Pearce	..	..	Abou	Berkovic	..1	Moncur	.. 3	
6 Jan	Arsenal	H	L	1-2	..	Pearce*	..	Potts	..	Lampard	Impey	..	..	Kitson*	Lazaridis	Abou 1

Iain Dowie against Chelsea, March 1997.

Ian Wright celebrates his goal against Southampton (1998) with Julian Dicks who was making his first league appearance after more than a year out.

Date	Opponent		Result												Subs
	FA Cup														
3 Jan	Emley T	H	W 2-1	..	Breacker*	..	Pearce	..	..1	Potts	Berkovic	..1	..	..	Abou
25 Jan	Manchester C	A	W 2-1	..	Pearce	..*	Potts	..	Lomas 1	Berkovic1	Abou*	..	Lampard	..	Breacker/
14 Feb	Blackburn R	H	D 2-2	..	Breacker*	Pearce	Impey	..	..	Lampard	Berkovic 1	..	Kitson 1*	..	Potts/Hodges
25 Feb	Blackburn R	A	D1-1 AET (W 5-4 on pens)	..	Pearce	Unsworth	..	..	..	..	..*	..1	Moncur	..	Abou
8 Mar	Arsenal	A	D 1-1	Lama	Potts	Pearce 1	..	..	..	..	..*	Abou	..	..	Hodges
17 Mar	Arsenal	H	D1-1 AET (L 3-4 on pens)	..	Pearce*	Unsworth	Potts*	..	Lomas	Berkovic	Abou	Hartson 1	Lampard	..	Moncur/Hodges

Hammer of the Year 1997-98
RIO FERDINAND

	P	W	L	D	F:A	Pts	Pos
Arsenal	38	23	6	9	68:33	78	1st
West Ham	38	16	14	8	56:57	56	8th

SEASON 1998-99 FA CARLING PREMIERSHIP

Date	Opponent		Result												Subs
15 Aug	Sheffield W	A	W 1-0	Hislop	Pearce	Ruddock	Impey	Ferdinand	Lomas	Sinclair	Berkovic*	Wright 1	Lampard	..	Moncur
22 Aug	Manchester U	H	D 0-0	..	..	..	..	..	..	..	..*	Hartson	..	..	Abou
29 Aug	Coventry C	A	D 0-0	..	Margas	..	..	..	..*	Lampard	..	..	Wright	..	Moncur
9 Sep	Wimbledon	H	L 3-4	..	Pearce	..	Lampard	Margas	Moncur	Sinclair	..*	..1	..2	..	Impey
12 Sep	Liverpool	H	W 2-1	..	..	..	..	Potts	..	..	..1*	..1*	..	..	Breacker/Keller
19 Sep	Nottingham F	A	D 0-0	..	..	Impey	Potts	..	Lampard	..	..	Abou*	..	Keller	Omoyinmi
28 Sep	Southampton	H	W 1-0	..	..	Dicks	Ruddock	..	..	..	..*	Hartson	..1*	..*	Lazaridis/Moncur/Potts
3 Oct	Blackburn R	A	L 0-3	..	..	..	Potts*	..*	..	..	Moncur	..	..	Impey	Keller/Hodges
17 Oct	Aston Villa	H	D 0-0	..	..	..	Lomas	..	..*	..	Berkovic	..	..*	Lampard	Impey/Kitson
24 Oct	Charlton A	A	L 2-4	..	..	..	..	..	..	..	..1	..	..*	..	Moncur/Kitson (1og)
31 Oct	Newcastle U	A	W 3-0	..	..	Impey*	..	..	Ruddock	..1	Lampard	Wright 2	Kitson*	Keller	Potts/Hartson
8 Nov	Chelsea	H	D 1-1	..	..	Ruddock 1	Lampard	..	Lomas	..	Berkovic*	..	..	..	Potts
14 Nov	Leicester C	H	W 3-2	..	..	Dicks	..1	..	..1	..	..	..	..1*	..	Moncur
22 Nov	Derby C	A	W 2-0	..	..	Ruddock		..	..	..	..	Hartson 1	..	..1*	Potts
28 Nov	Tottenham H	H	W 2-1	..	..	..	..	..	..	..2	..*	..	..	Lazaridis	Potts
5 Dec	Leeds U	A	L 0-4	..	..	..(so)	..	Margas	..	..	Wright	..	Keller	..*	Moncur
12 Dec	Middlesbrough	A	L 0-1	..	..	Potts	..	Ferdinand	..	..	..	..	..*	..*	Moncur/Omoyinmi
19 Dec	Everton	H	W 2-1	..	..	Dicks	Lomas	..	Lampard	..1	Berkovic	Wright	Hartson	Keller 1	
26 Dec	Arsenal	A	L 0-1	..	..	Potts	..	..	..	..	..	..	..	..*	Lazaridis
28 Dec	Coventry C	H	W 2-0	..	..	Dicks	..	..	..	..	..*	..1*	..1	Lazaridis	Potts/Omoyinmi
10 Jan	Manchester U	A	L 1-4	..	..	Ruddock	Potts	..	..1	..*	..	Hartson	Lomas	..	Cole
16 Jan	Sheffield W	H	L 0-4	..	..	Minto	Lampard	..	Ruddock*	Keller	..*	Sinclair	Abou	Lomas	Cole/Kitson
30 Jan	Wimbledon	A	D 0-0	..	Breacker	Dicks	Ruddock	..	Moncur	Foe	Cole*	Kitson	Lampard	Minto	Di Canio
6 Feb	Arsenal	H	L 0-4	..	..*	..	Pearce	..	Foe	Sinclair	Kitson	Di Canio	..	..	Berkovic
13 Feb	Nottingham F	H	W 2-1	..	Pearce 1	Ruddock	Lomas	..	Lampard 1	..	Berkovic*	..	Kitson	Lazaridis*	Cole/Minto
20 Feb	Liverpool	A	D 2-2	..	Potts	Pearce*	Foe	..	Lomas	..	..	Cole*	Lampard 1	Minto*	Lazaridis/Keller1 /Holligan
27 Feb	Blackburn R	H	W 2-0	..	Pearce 1	Potts	Lomas	..	Foe	..	..	Di Canio 1	..	Keller	
6 Mar	Southampton	A	L 0-1	..	..	Ruddock	..	..	..*	..	..	..	..	..	Kitson
13 Mar	Chelsea	A	W 1-0	..	..	Minto	Ruddock	..	..	..	Lomas	Kitson 1	..	..*	Potts
20 Mar	Newcastle U	H	W 2-0	..	..	..	..	..	..	..	..	..1	Di Canio 1	Lampard	
2 Apr	Aston Villa	A	D 0-0	..	..	..	Foe	..*	Ruddock	..	..	..	Lampard	Di Canio	Potts
5 Apr	Charlton A	H	L 0-1	..	..	..	..	Ruddock	Lomas	..	Di Canio	..*	..	Keller	Berkovic
10 Apr	Leicester C	A	D 0-0	..	..	..	Potts	..	..	..	Berkovic	Di Canio*	Kitson*	Lampard	Wright/Moncur
17 Apr	Derby C	H	W 5-1	..	..	..	Foe	..1	Potts*	..1	..1	..1	Lomas*	..	Wright1/Cole
24 Apr	Tottenham H	A	W 2-1	..	Lomas	..	Pearce	Ferdinand	Moncur (so)	..	..	Wright1*	Lampard	Keller 1	Lazaridis
1 May	Leeds U	H	L 1-5	..(so)	..(so)	..	Foe	Ruddock	..	..*	..*	*(so)	Di Canio*1	Lampard	Cole/Coyne/Forrest
8 May	Everton	A	L 0-6	..	Lomas	..	..	Ferdinand	Ruddock	..	..	..	..	..	Keller
16 May	Middlesbrough	H	W 4-0	Forrest	Potts	..	..	..	..	Keller 1	..	Sinclair 2	..	..1	Cole
	Worthington Cup														
15 Sep	Northampton T	A	L 0-2	Hislop	Pearce	Ruddock*	Lampard	Potts	Moncur	Sinclair	..	Hartson	Wright	Lazaridis	Breacker
22 Sep	Northampton T	H	W 1-0	..	..	Dicks	Impey	Ferdinand	Potts	..	Abou*	Wright	Lampard 1	Keller	Omoyinmi
	FA Cup														
2 Jan	Swansea C	H	D 1-1	..	..	..1	Lomas	Ruddock	Potts	..	Berkovic*	..	Hartson*	Lazaridis*	Abou/Cole/Omoyinmi
13 Jan	Swansea C	A	L 0-1	..	Breacker*	..	Ruddock	Ferdinand	Lampard	Omoyinmi*	Sinclair	Hartson	Lomas	..	Berkovic/Hall

Hammer of the Year 1998-99
SHAKA HISLOP

	P	W	L	D	F:A	Pts	Pos
Manchester U	38	22	3	13	80:37	79	1st
West Ham	38	16	13	9	46:53	57	5th

1993-1999

CHAPTER 9

Harry Redknapp and his coaching staff would have no time for rest and recuperation during the summer of 1999. The Intertoto Cup was scheduled to kick-off in mid-July and, as usual, there was work to be done in the transfer market. 'We've had a terrific season... All my players are secured, they're under contract so I won't be selling the best of them,' declared Redknapp in May. Unfortunately, circumstance would force the manager's hand, and two months later Eyal Berkovic was sold to Celtic for a Scottish record fee of £5.75m.

The sale of Berkovic had been widely anticipated. There had been frequent speculation that he was unhappy at Upton Park following his well-publicised altercation with John Hartson, and the emergent Joe Cole offered Redknapp an obvious alternative. Nevertheless, the departure of the Israel international left the Hammers squad short of attacking players and the manager acted quickly to remedy the situation, signing Derby County's Costa Rica international striker Paulo Wanchope for £3.5m.

Hammers go Intertoto

A centre-half and a right-back had also been on the Hammers' shopping list, but neither had been purchased by the time the Intertoto Cup kicked off with a home tie against Finnish minnows FC Jokerit at Upton Park on 17 July. A crowd of almost 12,000 was in attendance to watch Paul Kitson score the only goal of the game and give Hammers a slender advantage to take into the second leg in Helsinki. 'We've only had about nine days back... but this will all be worth it if we get a Uefa Cup place,' said Redknapp. A goal from Frank Lampard earned Hammers a 1–1 draw in Finland and booked a place in the fourth round. Lampard would catch the eye throughout the early months of the season, and his fine form continued with a memorable long-range goal in the 1–0 victory over Dutch side Heerenveen, who Hammers defeated 2–0 on aggregate to reach the Intertoto Cup Final.

Paulo Wanchope opens his West Ham goalscoring account with this strike in the 1-0 victory over Heerenveen in the Intertoto Cup, July 1999.

The small matter of a two-legged tie against French team FC Metz was now all that stood between West Ham United and qualification for the Uefa Cup. However, thoughts of Europe were put on hold with the resumption of Premiership action and a derby clash with Tottenham at Upton Park on 7 August. The match against Spurs ended with a deserved 1–0 victory for the Hammers, who took the lead through a Lampard goal on 45 minutes, but it was a fixture most notable for the debut of veteran defender Stuart Pearce. The former England captain had signed on a free transfer from Newcastle United just five days earlier, with Redknapp making his move for Pearce after a similar deal to re-sign Slaven Bilic from Everton had broken down due to injury worries.

'I needed a leader and organiser,' explained Redknapp, 'someone with a bit of personality.' Pearce certainly gave a good account of himself against Spurs, but his debut was marred somewhat by a collision with namesake Ian, who was left nursing a knee injury that would sideline him for 16 months.

With Ian Pearce injured and Stuart Pearce ineligible, West Ham's defensive resources were stretched to the limit for the Intertoto Cup Final first leg against Metz. A flat back four of Scott Minto, Steve Lomas, Rio Ferdinand and Steve Potts struggled to settle against the counter-attacking French forward line, which was spearheaded by Louis Saha. After just 12 minutes Saha struck with a clever header over Hislop to leave the Hammers chasing the game. Seventy-eight minutes of West Ham United pressure followed, but when goalkeeper Lionel Letizi saved Frank Lampard's second-half penalty, the dream of Uefa Cup football began to fade. The game ended 1–0 to Metz, although Redknapp remained optimistic: 'It's not over by any means. We are capable of going there and scoring goals... no way are we out of this tie yet.'

The manager's positive attitude was supported by Hammers' continued good form in the Premiership. A draw away at Aston Villa, with Trevor Sinclair scoring an injury-time equaliser, and a 2–1 home success over Leicester City had taken Redknapp's team to a respectable seventh place after three games.

Against the Foxes, it was Di Canio and Wanchope who scored the goals, and the Hammers would need both their star forwards to be at their unpredictable best for the return match against Metz. It was Di Canio who made the first telling contribution. The Italian broke into the box after 25 minutes, turning his marker before picking out Sinclair with an unerring pass, which the wing-back duly crashed home past Leitizi to bring the scores level on aggregate.

Two minutes before half-time, Di Canio again acted as provider, setting up Lampard to score the goal that sent 4,000 travelling Hammers delirious with joy. West Ham United had a brief scare in the second half, when Nenad Jestrovic pulled back a goal for Metz after 68 minutes, but ten minutes later Wanchope latched onto John Moncur's astute through-ball to put the tie beyond doubt. The football had been breathtaking, and Hammers fluent performance was simply too good for Metz. Captain Steve Lomas collected the egg-cup sized trophy and celebrated his team's Uefa Cup qualification. 'I'm delighted,' beamed Redknapp, 'It's what we deserved anyway after finishing fifth last year. Everyone in England should know now we have a good side.'

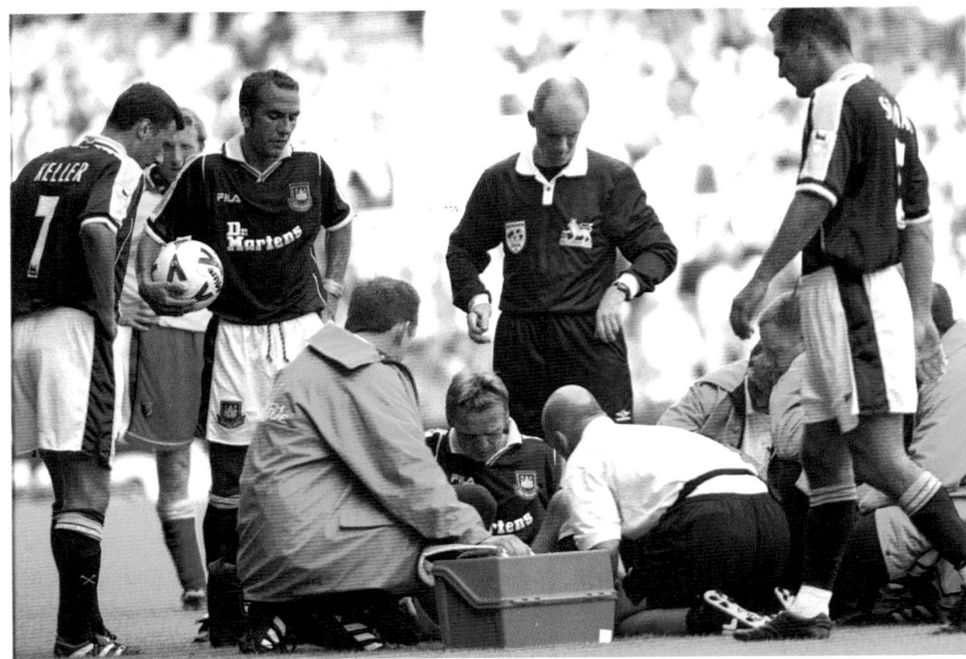

It was indeed true, Redknapp did have a good team, but he was fast running out of defenders. After the Metz game the manager had praised the outstanding contribution of Rio Ferdinand, and it was clear that the 19-year-old sweeper was the player holding together a somewhat makeshift backline. So it was with horror that the Hammers boss watched his star defender limp out of the action in the next match against Bradford City at Valley Parade. An ankle injury would sideline Ferdinand for a month and took much of the sheen off a Di Canio inspired 3–0 victory, which had taken Hammers up to the dizzy heights of fourth place.

Stuart Pearce and Steve Potts were now the only two fit centre-backs in Redknapp's squad, so it was to collective relief that Derby County's experienced Croatia international Igor Stimac signed for £600,000 just prior to the 31 August Uefa Cup deadline. With Stimac onboard, Redknapp did at least have enough defenders to play his preferred 3-5-2 system.

Top: Midfielder Frank Lampard puts the misery of a first-leg penalty miss against FC Metz behind him, as he celebrates scoring in the return. Hammers won 3–1 to clinch the Intertoto Cup and a place in the UEFA Cup.

Above: Hammers physio John Green tends to Stuart Pearce while Marc Keller, Paolo Di Canio and Igor Stimac look on. The prognosis was not good, Pearce had broken his leg and would not play again until 26th February.

However, his plans would again be upset by another freak injury, this time a broken leg sustained by Stuart Pearce in the 1–0 victory over Watford at Upton Park. Pearce, who had returned to the senior England team at the age of 37 just three days earlier, was left nursing a fractured tibia after a clash with Micah Hyde. Redknapp was distraught, 'He's going to be out for a few months, it's heartbreaking... He put his boot back on and said he wanted to give it a go. But I knew as soon as I saw it that his leg was broken. I heard it go.'

Hammers were now up to third in the table and if injuries were dominating the team's defensive performances, then it was the brilliance of Paolo Di Canio that was becoming the theme of their attacking play. The Italian was proving an inspiring presence, and he was again on target when Hammers made their Uefa Cup debut against Croatian team Osijek at Upton Park on 16 September.

Di Canio, however, was suffering from a thigh injury and saw his limelight stolen by an unlikely candidate. Chilean defender Javier Margas had been an unmitigated disaster during his first season with West Ham United, and he had returned to South America muttering about retirement. However, he had unexpectedly arrived back in East London for pre-season training and played a key role in the 3–0 victory against the Croatians.

Igor Stimac had also been impressive against Osijek, and he was confident that his presence would help compensate for the loss of Stuart Pearce, 'We are a bit quiet and I will take the responsibility. It was only my second match but this crowd make it easy to settle.' Unfortunately, the team did not always enjoy the benefits of the Upton Park crowd, and away from home they struggled throughout the season. In September and October, Hammers played five away games in the Premiership and lost all of them, each time without scoring. The only respite from these autumnal away day blues, was provided with a 3–1 victory against Osijek, courtesy of goals from Kitson, Marc-Vivien Foe and Neil Ruddock.

Di Canio outguns Arsenal

At the start of October, West Ham United were already 15 games into a marathon season. The critics argued that their Intertoto Cup exertions were now catching up with them, and a home match against Arsenal would test the theory. The first 28 minutes proved forgettable, but Di Canio took charge thereafter, opening the scoring when the ball fell somewhat fortuitously for him after a mazy run. The Italian added a second goal 18 minutes from the end, and this time it owed nothing to good fortune. A clearance from Hislop was headed on by Wanchope into the path of the Italian, who deftly flicked the ball over Martin Keown and curled a superb shot into the top corner past the desperate dive of David Seaman. Davor Suker pulled back a late goal for the Gunners, but the West Ham United defence held out in the wake of intense Arsenal attacking pressure.

Di Canio's brilliance against the Gunners was, however, overshadowed by an ugly incident that would dominate the following day's papers. The game had exploded into controversy in the second half when Patrick Vieira was shown a second yellow card for a foul on Di Canio. The inevitable red card followed and an ugly mêlée ensued, concluding with Vieira spitting at West Ham United defender Neil Ruddock. The incident provided back-page headlines for a week or more. Gunners manager Arséne Wenger accused Di Canio of kidding the referee and Ruddock of provoking Vieira but the FA, nevertheless, imposed a six match ban on the France international.

Hammers cruised through their next home game, a Worthington Cup tie against AFC Bournemouth, winning 2–0 courtesy of goals from Lampard and Marc Keller. It was Lampard's sixth goal of the season, and the previous Sunday his excellent form had been rewarded with a debut England cap against Belgium at the Stadium of Light. Hammers also had Trevor Sinclair in the senior squad, Adam Newton in the Under-21s and four players (Stephen Bywater, Joe Cole, Ezomo Iriekpen and Michael Carrick) in the Under-18s. The future certainly looked bright at Upton Park, however, one West Ham United player's past was about to come back to haunt the club.

Croatian team Osijek, who Hammers had defeated in the Uefa Cup back in September, had discovered that Igor Stimac had played against them despite an outstanding two-match ban from his time with Hajduk Split. Osijek wanted West Ham United thrown out of the competition, but Uefa dismissed their case because Stimac's name had been omitted from a list of suspended players circulated to all clubs. The Croatian defender would now have to sit out the next Uefa Cup tie, against Romanian side Steaua Bucharest. It would not be the last time an ineligible player caused major problems for the Hammers in 1999.

The first leg of the Steaua tie proved a bizarre encounter. The Romanians won the match 2–0, with the Hammers struggling to find any defensive cohesion. However, it was Danish referee Claus Bo Larsen who did most to make the game memorable. The Dane booked Di Canio in the first half for dissent, and with the Italian growing justifiably frustrated at the lack of protection being given to him, the referee allegedly ordered Redknapp to substitute his star player after 55 minutes. Midfielder John Moncur had been the messenger in this surreal episode and confirmed, 'His actual words were we "should change" Paolo otherwise he would have to send him off.'

Top: Tony Adams lunges in on Di Canio, but the Arsenal defender's efforts are in vain. The Italian, who had already danced his way around Martin Keown, bends his shot over David Seaman and into the net to give the Hammers a 2–0 lead in this derby match. The game ended 2–1 after Davor Suker pulled back a goal for the visiting Gunners.

Above: Patrick Vieira and Neil Ruddock are restrained by teammates after they clash towards the end of West Ham United's 2–1 victory over the Gunners in October 1999.

An exasperated Redknapp was still struggling to understand what had gone on after the game, 'I have never heard that kind of thing before in a professional match. We had no choice but to get Paolo off. The last thing I wanted was for him to miss the second leg.' The Hammers manager remained hopeful that his team could overturn their first leg deficit in the return at Upton Park, 'We are a fantastic home team and it should be an interesting night. I've got to still believe that we can still win the second leg 3–0.'

However, goalscoring form had deserted the Hammers, who had managed to find the net just once in 450 minutes since their victory over Bournemouth. They dominated the second leg against Steaua but a combination of poor finishing and lenient refereeing conspired to scupper their European ambitions. The match finished 0–0 and left Redknapp perplexed: 'I've never seen a team invent so many different ways of going close in 90 minutes.'

Despite the disappointment of their Uefa Cup elimination, there would be no European hangover for the Hammers who immediately embarked on a five-match unbeaten run. The highlight of this upturn in fortune was a 4–3 victory over Sheffield Wednesday at Upton Park, which saw Di Canio made captain for the day.

For the remainder of November, it was two of West Ham United's young stars who attracted most of the headlines. Striker Jermain Defoe had joined the club's youth ranks in May from Charlton and six months later a tribunal ordered the Hammers to pay the South London Club an initial transfer fee of £400,000 rising to £1.65m dependent on appearances. Inevitably, certain papers had a field day with the story. Club secretary, Graham Mackrell remained philosophical, 'If the player makes the progress we hope he's going to make, it's fair to both parties.'

The other young Hammer in the news was Joe Cole, by now a veteran of the back pages. The prodigiously gifted midfielder was now beginning to fulfil his immense potential. Against Birmingham City in the fourth round of the Worthington Cup at St Andrews, Cole scored his first senior goal for the club to help Hammers clinch a 2–1 victory and safe passage into a quarter-final tie against Aston Villa at Upton Park.

In the Premiership, Redknapp's team were still struggling to pick up points away from home. Two goalless draws against London rivals Chelsea and Spurs had gone someway to bucking the trend, but on both occasions a West Ham United player had been dismissed, Margas at Chelsea and Lomas at White Hart Lane. Hammers had now had five players red carded in 28 games and Redknapp was becoming incensed, 'we've had five men sent off this season, and none of them has been for anything sinister.'

Joe Cole celebrates his late winner in the Worthington Cup victory over Birmingham City, November 1999. It was Cole's first senior goal for the Hammers and he later confessed that he had planned an elaborate celebration routine. However, in the elation of the moment he settled for pulling his shirt over his head and running around the goal.

The mood of the West Ham United manager was made bleaker on 11 December when he took his team to Tranmere Rovers' Prenton Park ground for an FA Cup third round match. True to recent away form Hammers lost 1–0 and were left to focus on the Worthington Cup tie against Villa. It was a game that would dominate West Ham United's thoughts for more than a month.

Aston Villa and Manny-gate

Villa sat one place above the Hammers in tenth position in the Premiership table and it was undeniably a meeting of equals. The match started badly for the home team, with the visitors taking a shock lead after just three minutes courtesy of Ruddock's mistake and Ian Taylor's sharp finishing. Hammers piled on the pressure for the next hour and finally got their reward when Ferdinand and Di Canio combined to create a shooting chance for Lampard, who made no mistake from close range.

The game appeared to be heading toward extra time, but with just seconds on the clock Dion Dublin scored to give Villa the lead once more. West Ham United supporters began to drift out of the ground, but they were stopped in their tracks when Gareth Southgate and Gareth Barry conspired to bring down substitute Paul Kitson in the penalty area. Referee Stephen Lodge pointed to the spot, and the nerveless Di Canio stroked the ball past David James.

Extra time came and went without addition to the scoreline, and the tie headed to its inevitable conclusion: a penalty shoot-out. Both teams scored their first three kicks, with Lampard, Lomas and Di Canio all successful for the Hammers, and although Trevor Sinclair had his effort saved, Alan Wright missed too and parity was restored. Ruddock, Marc Keller and Ugo Ehiogu took the score to 5–4 and left Villa needing to score to stay in the shoot-out. Gareth Southgate, still haunted by his penalty miss against Germany in Euro '96 bravely stepped forward, but his weak effort was saved by Hislop. Upton Park duly erupted in whole-hearted celebration, the like of which had not been seen since promotion was clinched on the final day of the 1992–93 season.

However, 48 hours later, as Harry Redknapp began to anticipate a semi-final tie against Leicester City, the buoyant mood was shattered. Aston Villa had lodged an appeal with the Football League over the result of the quarter-final on the grounds that West Ham United had played an ineligible player. Manny Omoyinmi, who came on as a substitute with just eight minutes remaining, was already cup-tied, having played in the second round of the same competition for Gillingham against Bolton Wanderers. The bombshell news had arrived on the eve of the Hammers home match against Manchester United, and

Paolo Di Canio is first to congratulate Shaka Hislop after the Hammers keeper saves Gareth Southgate's penalty to clinch shoot-out victory over Aston Villa and a place in the Worthington Cup semi-finals. Rio Ferdinand and Trevor Sinclair are also quick to show their gratitude.

the supporters clearly felt just as subdued as their manager, who had confessed he was 'too upset to talk' when informed about Villa's appeal.

Alex Ferguson's all-conquering European Champions were the last team West Ham United would have wanted to face after the traumas of the preceding two days. The visitors, true to their reputation, were in ruthless mood and put the dejected Hammers to the sword, racing into a three-goal lead inside 20 minutes. Di Canio led a spirited fightback, scoring twice, but West Ham United lost the game 4–2. 'It ain't been an easy day,' confessed Redknapp. Alas, things would not get any easier for some weeks to come.

Five days after the Villa game, the significance of Omoyinmi's brief appearance became apparent, when it was announced that the quarter-final would have to be replayed. Company secretary Graham Mackrell and football secretary Alison O'Dowd would both resign over the incident, although Mackrell insisted that he had checked with Gillingham that Omoyinmi was not cup-tied. 'It was a little error but unfortunately it has had large consequences for the club,' explained the outgoing Mackrell. Redknapp was flabbergasted by the whole episode, 'I would have thought a fine would have been sufficient,' said the Hammers boss, 'Manny was only on eight minutes and he touched the ball twice.'

Worthington Cup re-run

However, Redknapp's thoughts counted for nothing and his team would face Villa again after Christmas. In the interim, Hammers three games over the festive period all ended in draws. After the sideshow of the Premiership, the main event returned to Upton Park in the shape of the Worthington Cup re-run on 11 January. The first half was a cagey affair with few chances, but two minutes after the interval the game sprang into life when Lampard gave the Hammers the lead with a superb curling chip over the stranded David James. The home team held onto their narrow advantage for the next 32 minutes in assured fashion, so when Ian Taylor equalised with just 11 minutes remaining, Upton Park fell into stunned silence.

Extra-time proved a painful experience for the Hammers. Villa took an early lead through Julian Joachim, and when Di Canio won and missed a penalty shortly afterwards, West Ham United fans knew their chance of a final trip to Wembley had gone. Shortly before the end, Taylor increased Villa's margin of victory but by then, with Neil Ruddock playing in attack, Redknapp's team knew there was no way back.

'Tonight will haunt me forever,' said the war-weary Hammers boss, 'It's not like losing a normal match. We had already won the game once and reached the semi-finals. It's a bitter pill to swallow.'

Paolo Di Canio, who had missed his vital spot-kick, exorcised his Worthington Cup demons by scoring in Hammers' next match, at home to guess who... Aston Villa. The game ended 1–1, the fifth time the two clubs had drawn in the space of 12 months, and will be remembered for an awful miss from Paulo Wanchope, the Costa Rican somehow scooping the ball over the bar from inside the six-yard box.

Wanchope's ungainly style had not endeared him to the Upton Park crowd and he frequently found himself a target for abuse from home supporters. The £3.5m striker did, however, score twice in the 3–1 away victory over Martin O'Neill's Leicester City. Hammers were now up to eighth in the Premiership, and all that was left to play for was a place in either the Uefa or Intertoto Cup. However, consistency was a commodity in short supply throughout the remainder of the season and it seemed Redknapp's team was as likely to lose 5–0 as win by the same scoreline. Convincing victories, like the

5–0 triumph against Coventry and the 2–0 win over Southampton, were set alongside equally emphatic defeats, witness the 1–7 reverse at Old Trafford and the 0–4 debacle at home to Everton.

Nine-goal thriller against Bantams

For Hammers fans, of course, the defeats were quickly forgotten and it was two famous victories that would live longest in the collective memory. The first was an enthralling 5–4 success over lowly Bradford City. The match began badly for West Ham United, when Shaka Hislop broke his leg in a collision with Bantams striker Dean Saunders after two minutes. Eighteen-year-old Stephen Bywater came on for his debut in place of Hislop and endured a torrid afternoon. At half-time the score stood at 2–2 and the goals continued to flow in the second half, with Bradford going 4–2 ahead with a brace from Jamie Lawrence, who profited from mistakes from Hammers' rookie keeper.

With 40 minutes remaining, the home team surged forward but they could not find a way past a blanket Bradford defence. And as the frustration grew, the ever-volatile Di Canio became increasingly incensed with the decisions of referee Neale Barry. In the 55th minute, Barry turned away a penalty appeal from the Italian for the third time in the game and Di Canio decided he could take no more. The striker gestured to the bench that he wanted to be substituted and began to take off his shirt. 'Paolo, you're not coming off. Now get back out there and fight!' said Redknapp. The Italian opted to follow his manager's instruction and later confessed it was just 'the adrenaline injection I craved,' adding 'I was possessed, I was in overdrive'.

Ten minutes later the Hammers finally won a penalty, although this time it was Paul Kitson who toppled in the area. Designated penalty taker Frank Lampard duly collected the ball, but before he could put it on the spot Di Canio had ripped it from his grasp. The Italian made no mistake and the rescue act was completed with goals from Cole, his first in the Premiership, and Lampard. A 5–4 victory had left spectators and players exhausted, but the antics of Di Canio had left the most lasting impression.

Di Canio was also at the centre of the action in another notable West Ham United performance, against Wimbledon at home on 26 March. The Hammers won the match 2–1, but the scoreline does not reveal the emphatic nature of the victory. Frenchman Frederic Kanouté made his debut in the match against the Dons following a loan move from Lyon, and his assured touch and powerful running made him an instant hit with the Upton Park crowd. The 22-year-old scored what proved to be the game's decisive goal and his performance was hailed as a 'fantastic debut... one of the best I have ever seen,' by Redknapp. However, even the dynamic young Frenchman could not outshine the majestic Di Canio.

The Italian opened the scoring against Wimbledon with a goal of sublime quality. Trevor Sinclair's deep, lofted cross from the right wing made its way to the Italian who had pulled into space outside the far post. Di Canio, it seemed, had no angle to shoot for goal and, with Sinclair's cross coming at chest height he had no option but to control the ball and await reinforcements. But West Ham United's no.10 refused the predictable. Di Canio leapt into mid-air and struck an unerring volley into the far corner of Neil Sullivan's net. 'It was a fantastic goal but it was no fluke. He does that every day in training,' declared Redknapp.

Di Canio's effort against Wimbledon was voted Goal of the Season by BBC's Match of the Day panel, and the Italian was also the winner of Carling Opta's Player of the Season award. However, amazingly the former Juventus and AC Milan striker did not feature on the shortlist for either the PFA or Football Writers' awards.

West Ham United's form picked up during April, with consecutive victories over Newcastle, Derby and Coventry, but any thoughts of Europe evaporated when the remaining four games yielded just a single point. It had been a long and difficult season for Harry Redknapp, whose ambitions had not been helped by serious injuries to several of his first-team squad. Stuart Pearce had broken his leg twice, the second occasion after just two games of his comeback, Ian Pearce had

Paolo Di Canio gets himself airborne to crash home a sublime volley in the 2–1 victory over Wimbledon, March 2000. It was the highlight of an unforgettable season for the Italian, and was rightly voted BBC Match of the Day's Goal of the Season.

undergone surgery on his knee and had been out since opening day, while both Joe Cole and Shaka Hislop had seen their seasons ended prematurely by leg fractures.

On a more positive note, the season had also seen the emergence of several young players. Joe Cole had established himself in the first team, while fellow midfielder Michael Carrick had also made good progress after loan spells at Swindon and Birmingham. Rookie keeper Stephen Bywater had recovered well from his traumatic debut against Bradford and kept a clean sheet in the season's final match at home to Leeds United.

The match against Leeds had also been notable for the late sending off of Cameroon international Marc-Vivien Foe. The midfielder had kicked his last ball for the Hammers and was involved in one of the close-season's first transfers when he completed a £6m move to French team Lyon. The deal also saw the impressive Kanouté move permanently to Upton Park along with a cash adjustment.

Despite that move, Harry Redknapp knew that he would not be in a position to spend 'big money' in the summer's transfer market. Arsenal veterans Nigel Winterburn (small fee) and Davor Suker (Bosman free) duly arrived, while Paulo Wanchope departed for Manchester City for £3.5m after a mixed first season at Upton Park. The best news for Hammers fans, however, was that Rio Ferdinand remained at the club despite intense speculation linking him with moves to Leeds, Real Madrid and Barcelona.

2000–2001 Gets Underway

The Premiership's fixture computer had clearly developed a prejudice against the Hammers during the summer of 2000. The first six games of the new season, saw Harry Redknapp's team entertain Manchester United and Liverpool and pay visits to Chelsea, Sunderland and Tottenham. Nevertheless, players, manager and supporters were still optimistic about the club's chances of regaining the heights of 1998–99 and qualifying for the Uefa Cup again.

The season opener at Stamford Bridge pitted a West Ham United team that was without the injured Rio Ferdinand and the suspended Trevor Sinclair, against a Chelsea team that had just invested £25m on three attacking players, Jimmy Floyd Hasselbaink, Eidur Gudjohnsen and Mario Stanic. Predictably, it was the Blues who triumphed, but Hammers contributed greatly to an entertaining game that ended 4–2, with Di Canio and Kanouté on target for the visitors. 'Chelsea are an outstanding side and real championship contenders but we matched them all the way and we can match anybody on our day,' said Redknapp.

The Hammers would fulfil their manager's prophecy in the opening weeks of the season by 'matching' the approach play of every team they came up against, however a combination of defensive mistakes, poor refereeing and, most notably, profligate finishing, would undermine their efforts. A 2–2 draw against Manchester United, courtesy of a stirring comeback from 2–0 down inspired by Joe Cole's prodigious dribbling skills, brought much praise but just a single point. Draws against both Liverpool and Sunderland are also worthy of mention, however, the 1–0 defeats at home to Leicester and away to Tottenham were far more representative of West Ham United's early season fortunes.

The defeat to Peter Taylor's Leicester City was particularly galling. The Hammers had dominated the Foxes completely during the first 45 minutes of the game, but on the stroke of half time Stimac was sent off for a second yellow card and the Midlanders were given a lifeline.

Things got worse for Harry Redknapp and his team in the second half. First Hislop flapped at a cross and watched as Darren Eadie fired the ball home to give City the lead on 54 minutes, and then Kanouté limped out of the game two minutes later. Redknapp had already withdrawn Davor Suker for tactical reasons, so he was left with Di Canio, who looked like he might implode at any time after the injustice of Stimac's sending off, and Paul Kitson in attack. After the match, all the talk was of the unnecessary but pivotal first yellow card shown to Stimac. 'It was harsh,' admitted Peter Taylor, 'I'd have been disappointed if I'd lost a player like that.'

After six games West Ham United were marooned at the foot of the Premiership table with just three points to show from their efforts. However, despite his team's poor start to the season Redknapp refused to be pessimistic, 'What have we got to panic about?', enquired the Hammers boss. 'We've

Above: The goals of the prodigiously talented Jermain Defoe helped the Hammers retain their Under-19 Premier Youth Academy title in 1999–00.

Right: Davor Suker scores with a far from typical far-post header in the 2–2 draw with Manchester United at Upton Park, August 2000. The Croatian would struggle for form and fitness throughout his one and only season with the Hammers.

got enough strong characters and enough belief to know we are a good side and I know we will finish in the top half of the division.'

A season's first win was finally achieved with a 1–0 victory over Walsall in the Worthington Cup. Hammers' goal had arrived in the 84th minute from the boot of 17-year-old striker Jermain Defoe and, although the victory would prove a catalyst for an autumnal upturn in West Ham United's fortunes, Defoe's short-term future lay elsewhere. The England Under-18 forward was soon loaned out to AFC Bournemouth, where he would catch the eye with 18 goals in 26 League games, including an amazing run which saw him score in ten consecutive matches.

The win over Walsall was followed by a 3–0 away success at Coventry City and in 13 games between mid-September and mid-December, West Ham United lost only once; that defeat coming in the 2–1 reverse at home to Arsenal. International recognition duly arrived for the improving Hammers. Joe Cole and Rio Ferdinand were named in Kevin Keegan's England squad for the World Cup qualifiers against Germany and Finland, and both Michael Carrick and Adam Newton received Under-21 call-ups.

Harry Redknapp was, no doubt, delighted with his team's resurgence but he was still trying to improve the balance of his side. A right-back was high on the manager's list of priorities, while a left-sided midfielder or winger was also required. Two players who offered potential solutions to this problem left Upton Park on loan in September, Gary Charles moving to Birmingham City and Marc Keller to Portsmouth. Meanwhile, left-sided striker Kaba Diawara arrived for the remainder of the season from Paris St Germain.

Above: The Hammers claimed their first victory of 2000–2001 with a 3–0 win over Coventry City at Highfield Road in September. Joe Cole fires home Hammers' second goal.

Top: Jermain Defoe scores the only goal in the victory over Walsall in the Worthington Cup. Defoe would spend the remainder of the season terrorizing Second Division defences during a loan spell at AFC Bournemouth.

Right: Leeds United's Alan Smith gives Rio Ferdinand a friendly welcome in the match at Elland Road, November 2000. Hammers won 1–0 but within a week Ferdinand had joined Leeds for a record £18m fee.

Rio departs for record fee

The loan signing of Diawara would fade into the tiniest insignificance when set beside Redknapp's next dealing on the transfer market. For almost six months, speculation had been growing that Rio Ferdinand was set for a move out of Upton Park, with Leeds United tipped as his most likely destination. An impressive performance for England against Italy on 15 November did nothing to stifle the rumours, and three days later Ferdinand was among the Hammers' star performers in the 1–0 victory over Leeds at Elland Road. Whites manager David O'Leary had clearly seen enough and, having previously tabled a £15m offer, added a further £3m to his bid. It was too much for the West Ham United board to turn down and, reluctantly, they accepted what amounted to a world record transfer fee for a defender. Ferdinand duly agreed personal terms and on 26 November completed his move.

'West Ham accepting the bid came as a big surprise to me,' admitted Ferdinand, 'It was a big wrench to leave... West Ham will always have a big place in my heart.'

Harry Redknapp was now left without his defensive lynchpin, although he had boosted the club's coffers considerably after selling a player who had risen through the Upton Park junior ranks. 'It was just an amazing offer – £18m... what can you say to that?' offered Redknapp. However, before the West Ham United manager could start adding to his squad he had

work to do with some of his existing charges. His relationship with Paolo Di Canio was reported to be going through a 'difficult' spell and there was speculation linking several of his top players with moves in the wake of the Ferdinand sale. Lampard and Kanouté were both reported to be leaving, although both were in harness along with Di Canio for West Ham United's first Rio-less match: away to Southampton. The Dell was not usually a happy hunting ground for the Hammers but goals from Kanouté, Stuart Pearce and Sinclair secured a well-deserved 3–2 victory.

Worthington Cup elimination at the hands of First Division strugglers Sheffield Wednesday followed the Southampton victory, but the role of Goliath was not an unfamiliar one to the Hammers. In the Premiership, Redknapp's team continued to make steady progress, with Kanouté in particular catching the eye. 'That centre-forward we've got, what a player!' boasted the Hammers boss, 'He's a bit special. Chelsea have been in for him and Liverpool as well but I can't sell him.'

By the start of December West Ham United had climbed to sixth place in the table, and with new players arriving at a startling rate, dreams of Europe resurfaced. Liverpool's Cameroon international defender Rigobert Song was the first Ferdinand-financed player to arrive at Upton Park, signing in a £2.5m deal in November. Song was soon joined by former-Anfield team-mate Titi Camara for (£1.5m) and Bulgarian striker Svetoslav Todorov (from Liteks Lovech, £750,000); while Defenders Christian Dailly (Blackburn Rovers, £2m), Raggy Soma (Bryne, £800,000), Sebastien Schemmel (FC Metz, loan) and Hannu Tihinen (Viking Stavangar, loan) all arrived in December and January.

A 5–0 win over Charlton Athletic at Upton Park on Boxing Day appeared to vindicate Redknapp's frenzied purchasing, and with the Hammers now comfortably in the top half of the table the manager had few critics. However, football is a notoriously fickle game and victory over Charlton was followed by two months without a win in the Premiership. A 3–1 defeat against Manchester United at Old Trafford on New Year's Day sparked West Ham United's descent down the Premiership table, although January was not without its highlights for Hammers fans.

The FA Cup provided the only remaining hope of silverware in the 2000–01 season, but a third round tie away at Second Division high-fliers Walsall represented a significant obstacle given West Ham United's dismal record against lower division teams. But on this occasion there would be no feast for the tabloid vultures. An early goal from Frank Lampard, who was captaining the side for the first time, settled the nerves and, although Walsall equalised, Frederic Kanouté scored twice to ensure victory despite a second goal and a late rally from the home side.

Above: Scottish international defender Christian Dailly proved himself a versatile and reliable defender following a £1.75m move from Blackburn Rovers in January 2001.

Top: Cameroon captain Rigobert Song was the first post-Ferdinand signing to arrive at Upton Park in the winter of 2000. The versatile former Liverpool defender signed in a £2.5m deal.

Right: Trevor Sinclair scores the goal of the game in Hammers' game of the season, a 5–0 victory over Charlton Athletic at Upton Park on Boxing Day 2000.

Di Canio outfoxes Barthez

Twenty-four hours after the elation of the win over Walsall, West Ham United fans experienced a sudden sinking feeling when the FA Cup fourth round draw handed them a trip to Old Trafford and a clash with the Champions. But those fearing a repeat of the 3–1 reverse from New Year's Day need not have worried. Redknapp had clearly learned much from the previous meeting and he employed a new look system, making five changes to his line-up. The manager's tactics worked perfectly. The back five of Schemmel, Tihinen, Dailly, Pearce and Winterburn were committed, well-organised and restricted Manchester United to just a handful of half chances, while Frederic Kanouté toiled tirelessly at the other end in his role as the team's lone striker.

It was, however, in midfield that Redknapp's side was mot effective. Carrick and Lampard occupied the central positions, while Cole and Di Canio were given innovative roles that saw them play as half wing-back and half inside-forward. All four midfielders earned deserved plaudits, but it was the talismanic Di Canio who struck the game's only goal with 14 minutes remaining. The Italian, who had been upset when his critics had suggested that he feigned injury to avoid playing in big away games, latched on to a clever through ball from Kanouté and broke into space on the right of the Manchester United penalty area. Goalkeeper Fabien Barthez initially began to advance but then stopped and, as the Hammers striker bore down on goal,

his whistle for full time. West Ham United had recorded their first victory at Old Trafford in 12 attempts and had become the first away team to win an FA Cup tie there in 12 years.

'I've taken it on the chin a few times here,' declared a jubilant Redknapp, 'Everyone had a job and they stuck to it. It was a great team effort.' The manager was also fulsome in his praise of Di Canio, 'Barthez was trying to psyche him out. He was trying to kid him that he was offside, but he picked on the wrong person.'

West Ham United's reward for victory against the Reds was a fifth round tie away to Champions League chasing Sunderland. The match was shown live on Sky TV at 12pm, so most travelling fans had to set off at around 6am. Free coach travel provided by the a millionaire supporter, Robbie Cowling, went some way to compensating for the inconvenience of such an early start, but it was Kanouté's 76th-minute winning goal that did most to cheer the travel-weary Hammers supporters at the Stadium of Light. The Frenchman was a real handful to the Black Cats defence throughout the game, and it was only his inability to time his runs more accurately – he was caught off-side ten times – that prevented him from scoring sooner. The game ended 1–0 and, although Kanouté had scored the only goal, Stuart Pearce was the undoubted man of the match. 'The

the Frenchman held up his arm to appeal for offside. Barthez's tactics, whether inspired by gamesmanship or confidence, would have prompted many strikers to hesitate, but not Di Canio. The Italian remained focused, curling a neat shot around the belated dive of the United keeper to send the 9,000 Hammers supporters inside Old Trafford into ecstasy. The celebrations recommenced 19 minutes later when the referee blew

Above: Freddie Kanouté slides the ball past Sunderland keeper Thomas Sorenson to earn Hammers a deserved 1–0 victory in the 5th round of the FA Cup.

Top and left: Di Canio celebrates the goal that earned a 1–0 victory over Manchester United in the FA Cup fourth round. Later he and Hannu Tihinen applaud the contribution of West Ham United's 9,000 travelling fans.

longer the game went on the better he seemed to get,' said Sunderland and Republic of Ireland striker Niall Quinn, 'I first played against him in 1985 and he is still brilliant. He is someone you look up to. I am nearly 35 and I don't look up to many people but he would be one.'

A home match against Tottenham Hotspur was all that now stood between the Hammers and their first semi-final for ten years. Alex Ferguson had said that West Ham United's name might be on the Cup after victory over his team in January, and now many supporters began to believe him. But, in truth, the signs were not good. The Upton Park injury list was growing by the day, with Sinclair and Lomas both out for the remainder of the season and the likes of Stuart Pearce, Carrick, Lampard, Kanouté and Di Canio all less than 100 per cent fit. A 3–0 reverse at Highbury and a 2–0 defeat at home to Chelsea had also done little for confidence in the week prior to the quarter-final. Frustratingly, however, it was individual defensive errors rather than any more significant malaise that cost West Ham United dearly against Spurs.

Joe Cole would be singled out for blame in the after match post-mortem, as it was the young midfielder who was at fault for the goals that put Spurs 1–0 and 3–1 up, but he was not the only player to blame. Freddie Kanouté, for example, had also missed a glorious chance to make the match level at 2–2 and several players were below par on the day. Unfortunately, Spurs keeper Neil Sullivan was not among them, and although Pearce and Todorov did manage to score, a series of acrobatic late saves left West Ham United's Cup dreams in tatters and ensured the match ended 3–2 to Tottenham.

'It's disappointing when you give people jobs to do and they don't do them,' moaned Redknapp, 'I felt we'd win today and it's going to be very hard to lift everyone... I'm very low. I'm bitterly disappointed.' It was a sentiment that most supporters could appreciate.

For the remainder of the season, West Ham United's primary objective was to reach 40 points and guarantee a place in the Premiership for 2001–02. It was a feat that proved harder than most fans had imagined and, after five consecutive defeats in March, Redknapp's team were languishing in 14th place. The Hammers flirtation with the doomed and the desperate continued until the final home game against Southampton on 5 May. A 3–0 win against the Saints ensured top-flight status and enabled supporters to take a well-deserved deep breath. It had been a difficult season, with the victory over Manchester United and the continued progress of Messrs Cole, Lampard and Carrick – who had each become England squad regulars under Sven-Goran Eriksson – providing the only real highlights. Most Hammers followers were glad to see the back of 2000–01, although few can have predicted the news that would arrive on 8 May 2001.

After seven years in charge manager Harry Redknapp left the club by mutual consent, sending shockwaves reverberating throughout English football. West Ham United had had just eight managers in their entire history, and it was generally considered that Redknapp's job was safe for as long as he wanted it. It was not clear whether he had jumped or been pushed, but the plain fact of the matter was the Harry Redknapp was no longer in charge at Upton Park. 'The last eight weeks or so haven't been particularly enjoyable and I feel that, maybe, it's time for a change,' explained the outgoing Hammers boss in somewhat diplomatic fashion.

The real reasons for Redknapp's departure may never be made public, but it seems that a disagreement with chairman Terence Brown at a meeting on 8 May provided the catalyst for change. By his own admission, the meeting had 'gotten out of hand', and the 54-year-old who had first arrived at Upton Park as an apprentice in 1964 later confessed that: 'Leaving the club was the last thing on my mind when I went over this morning'. He revealed that, 'I never dreamed it would happen. After meeting the chairman it all changed and I found myself out of work.'

With the season almost over, and little else happening in the world of football, the news of Redknapp's departure dominated the sports pages for almost a week. Speculation was rife as to why he had left the club and who would replace him.

The end of an era. After seven years in charge, Harry Redknapp's reign as West Ham United manager came to an end.

However, West Ham United still had one fixture to fulfil, and with assistant manager Frank Lampard following his friend and colleague out of the Upton Park exit, the club turned to coach Glenn Roeder to take on the job of caretaker manager. The ex-Watford boss coped admirably, fending off intense media attention while preparing his team for an away match against Middlesbrough. Hammers lost the game 2–1, with Todorov scoring his first Premiership goal, but the result seemed an irrelevance to most supporters, who were more concerned with rumours about who might succeed Redknapp.

Alan Curbishley, George Graham, Alex McLeish and Steve McLaren were all reported as being linked with the job, but after five weeks of deliberation the board made the bold decision to appoint the relatively inexperienced Glenn Roeder as Harry Redknapp's successor on 14 June. It proved a busy day for the Hammers, as the announcement of the new manager coincided with the sale of Frank Lampard to Chelsea for £11m. The board immediately confirmed that Roeder would benefit from the proceeds of the Lampard sale, and Managing Director Paul Aldridge was in optimistic mood after a hectic 24 hours at Upton Park. 'We are delighted to give one of the game's most respected young coaches the opportunity to take the team forward,' declared the West Ham United MD, 'The board wish Glenn every success and look forward to an exciting season ahead.'

The face of the future: Michael Carrick rose to prominence during the 2000–2001 season earning himself a place in the senior England squad.

SEASON 1999-2000 FA CARLING PREMIERSHIP

1 Aug	Tottenham H	H	W	1-0	Hislop	Potts	Minto	Pearce I*	Ferdinand	Pearce S	Lampard 1	Sinclair	Wanchope	Di Canio*	Foe	Keller/Cole
16 Aug	Aston Villa	A	D	2-2	..	..	..*	Moncur*	..	..	..	.. 1	..	..	..	Keller/Kitson (Southgate 1 og)
21 Aug	Leicester C	H	W	2-1	..	..	Lomas	..	..	..	..	..	.. 1	.. 1	..	
28 Aug	Bradford C	A	W	3-0	..	..	..	..	..*	..	..	.. 1	.. 1	.. 1	Keller	Carrick
11 Sep	Watford	H	W	1-0	..	..	..	..*	Stimac	..*	..	..	..	.. 1	..	Margas/Carrick
19 Sep	Everton	A	L	0-1	..	..	..	..	..	Margas	..	..	..	..	..	
25 Sep	Coventry C	A	L	0-1	..	..	..	..	..	Foe	..	..	..	..	..*	Newton
3 Oct	Arsenal	H	W	2-1	..	..	..	..*	..	Ruddock	..	..	..*	.. 2	Foe	Kitson/Margas
17 Oct	Middlesbrough	A	L	0-2	..	Ferdinand	..	..*	..	..	..	..	..	..	Keller*	Cole/Forrest
24 Oct	Sunderland	H	D	1-1	..	..	..*	Cole	..*	Margas	..	.. 1	..*	..	..	Ruddock/Moncur/Kitson
27 Oct	Liverpool	A	L	0-1	..	..	..	..	Ruddock	Potts	..	..	..	Kitson	..	
30 Oct	Leeds U	A	L	0-1	..	..	..	Foe*	..	Margas	..	Moncur	..	..	..	Cole
7 Nov	Chelsea	A	D	0-0	Forrest	..	..	..	Stimac	..	..	Cole*	..	Sinclair	..	Ruddock
21 Nov	Sheffield W	H	W	4-3	Hislop	..	Potts	.. 1	Ruddock	Sinclair	.. 1	..	.. 1	Di Canio 1	..	
27 Nov	Liverpool	H	W	1-0	..	..	Margas	Lomas	..	.. 1	..	..	..*	..	..	Kitson
6 Dec	Tottenham H	A	D	0-0	..	..	..*	..	..	..	..	..	Kitson*	..*	Foe	Potts/Wanchope/Minto
18 Dec	Manchester U	H	L	2-4	..	..	Minto	..	..	Foe	..	Sinclair	Wanchope	.. 2	Keller	
26 Dec	Wimbledon	A	D	2-2	..	..	..	Margas	..	..	.. 1	.. 1	..	..	Cole	
28 Dec	Derby C	H	D	1-1	..	..	..*	..	Potts	..	..	..	..	.. 1	..	Keller
3 Jan	Newcastle U	A	D	2-2	..	..	..	Stimac 1	..	..	.. 1	Carrick	Sinclair	Cole	Keller*	Byrne
15 Jan	Aston Villa	H	D	1-1	..	..	Margas	..	Lomas	Cole	..	Sinclair	Wanchope	Di Canio 1	..	
22 Jan	Leicester C	A	W	3-1	..*	..	..	Ruddock	..*	..	..	..	.. 2	.. 1	..*	Forrest/Carrick/Minto
5 Feb	Southampton	A	L	1-2	Forrest	..	..*	Stimac	..	Charles	.. 1	..	Wanchope	Cole	Minto	Moncur
12 Feb	Bradford C	H	W	5-4	Hislop*	..	Charles*	..	..	Moncur 1	.. 1	.. 1	Di Canio 1	.. 1	Minto	Bywater/Kitson
26 Feb	Everton	H	L	0-4	Illic	..	Pearce S	..	..	..	Cole	..	Wanchope	Kitson	Keller	
4 Mar	Watford	A	W	2-1	Forrest	..	..	..	.. 1	..	Lampard	Foe	.. 1	Sinclair	Minto	
8 Mar	Southampton	H	W	2-0	..	..	..*	..	..	..	..	..	.. 1	.. 1	Cole*	Minto/Di Canio
11 Mar	Sheffield W	A	L	1-3	..	..	Ruddock	..	..	..*	.. 1	..	..	Di Canio	Sinclair	Cole
18 Mar	Chelsea	H	D	0-0	..	..	Minto	..	..	..*	..	..	..*	..	..	Kitson*/Ruddock/Cole
26 Mar	Wimbledon	H	W	2-0	..	..	..	..	..	..*	..	..	Kanouté 1	.. 1	..	Keller
1 Apr	Manchester U	A	L	1-7	..	..	..	Potts	..	..	..	..	..	Wanchope 1	..	
12 Apr	Newcastle U	H	W	2-1	..	..	..	Stimac*	Ruddock*	Cole	..	..	..	Di Canio	Keller*	Charles/Wanchope 2/Margas
15 Apr	Derby C	A	W	2-1	Feuer	..	..	..*	Margas	..*	..	..	Wanchope 2	Di Canio	Sinclair	Charles/Carrick
22 Apr	Coventry C	H	W	5-0	..	..	..*	..	.. 1	Carrick 1	..	Sinclair	..	.. 2	Kanouté 1	Newton
29 Apr	Middlesbrough	H	L	0-1	..	..	Keller	..	..	Foe	..	..	..	..	..	
2 May	Arsenal	A	L	1-2	Bywater	Potts	..	..	Foe	Moncur	Carrick	..	..	.. 1	..	
6 May	Sunderland	A	L	0-1	..	..	Ferdinand	..	..	..	..	..	..	..	..	
14 May	Leeds U	H	D	0-0	..	..	..	..	Margas	Foe	Moncur	..	..	..	..	

Intertoto Cup

17 Jul	FC Jokerit	H	W	1-0	Forrest	Potts*	Minto	Ruddock	Ferdinand	Lomas	Lampard	Sinclair*	Kitson 1	Di Canio	Cole	Wright/Keller
24 Jul	FC Jokerit	A	D	1-1	Hislop	Jones	..	..	..	..	.. 1	..	..	..*	Keller*	Potts/Lazaridis
28 Jul	Heerenveen	H	W	1-0	..	Potts	..	..*	..	..	.. 1	..	Wanchope	..*	..*	Moncur/Kitson/Pearce I
4 Aug	Heereneveen	A	W	1-0	..	Lomas	..	Pearce I	..	Foe	..	Moncur*	.. 1	..*	Sinclair	Cole/Kitson
10 Aug	FC Metz	H	L	0-1	..	Potts	..	Lomas	..	..*	..	..	..	..	..	Kitson
24 Aug	FC Metz	A	W	3-1	..	..	Keller	..	..	..	.. 1	..	.. 1	..*	.. 1	Cole

UEFA Cup

16 Sep	NK Osijek	H	W	3-0	Hislop	Potts	Margas	Stimac	Lomas	Moncur*	Lampard 1	Sinclair	Di Canio 1*	Wanchope 1	Keller	Kitson/Foe
30 Sep	NK Osijek	A	W	3-1	..	..	Ferdinand*	..	..	Foe 1	..	..	..*	Kitson 1	..	Wanchope/Ruddock 1
21 Oct	Steaua Bucharest	A	L	0-2	..	..	..	Ruddock	..	..	..	..	..*	Wanchope	Moncur	Margas
4 Nov	Steaua Bucharest	H	D	0-0	..	Margas	..	..	..	Cole	..	..	..	..	Keller*	Kitson

FA Cup

11 Dec	Tranmere R	A	L	0-1	Hislop	Potts*	Minto	Foe	Ferdinand	Ruddock	Sinclair	Lomas	Di Canio*	Cole	Lampard	Kitson/Wanchope

Worthington Cup

13 Oct	Bournemouth	H	W	2-0	Hislop	Ferdinand	Ruddock	Stimac	Sinclair	Foe	Lampard 1	Cole	Wanchope*	Di Canio	Keller 1	Kitson
30 Nov	Birmingham C	A	W	3-2	..	..	..	Margas*	Charles*	..	..	Lomas	..*	..	Keller	Sinclair/Kitson 1/Cole 1
15 Dec	Aston Villa	H	W	2-2	..	..	..	..	Sinclair	Cole*	..1	..	..*	..1	..	Kitson/Omoyinmi
11 Jan	Aston Villa	H	L	1-3§	..	..	Potts*	Stimac	..*	..	..	..	Foe	..	Minto	Ruddock/Keller

§ Match replayed because West Ham United fielded an ineligible player.

Hammer of the Year 1999-00
PAOLO DI CANIO

	P	W	L	D	F:A	Pts	Pos
Manchester United	38	28	3	7	97:45	91	1st
West Ham United	38	15	13	10	84:76	55	9th

From left to right: Marc Keller, Frank Lampard, Neil Ruddock, Trevor Sinclair, Javier Margas and Manny Omoyinmi celebrate the Worthington Cup quarter final victory over Villa. However, 48 hours later the Hammers were left reeling by the shock news that Villa were appealing against the result of the match on the grounds that Omoyinmi had been cup tied and, therefore, ineligible. The Midlanders won their appeal and the resultant replay.

West Ham United player of the season Stuart Pearce fires home a long range free-kick against Spurs in the FA Cup quarter-final at Upton Park, March 2001. Pearce's goal made the score 2–1 to Tottenham and offered the home side some hope, but Hammers eventually crashed out 3–2.

SEASON 2000-01 FA CARLING PREMIERSHIP

19 Aug	Chelsea	A	L	2-4	Hislop	Lomas	Margas	Stimac	Pearce S	Winterburn	Carrick*	Lampard	Di Canio 1	Suker	Kanouté 1	Cole
23 Aug	Leicester C	H	L	0-1	..	Ferdinand	..*	..	..	..	..	Lomas	..	..*	..*	Cole/Charles/Kanouté
26 Aug	Manchester U	H	D	2-2	..	..*	..*	..	..	..	..	..	.. 1	.. 1	Cole	Bassila/Kitson
5 Sep	Sunderland	A	D	1-1	..	Sinclair	Lomas	..	..	..	..	Lampard	..	.. 1*	..	Moncur
11 Sep	Tottenham	A	L	0-1	..	..	..	Ferdinand	..	..	..	..	..	Kanouté	..	
17 Sep	Liverpool	H	D	1-1	..	..	Stimac	..	..	..	..	Lomas	.. 1	..	..	
23 Sep	Coventry C	A	W	3-0	..	..*	..	..*	..	..	Lampard 1	..	.. 1	..*	.. 1	Carrick/Potts/Diawara
30 Sep	Bradford C	H	D	1-1	..	..	..	..	..	..	Carrick	..	..	..	.. 1	
14 Oct	Ipswich T	A	D	1-1	..	..	..*	..	..	..*	Lampard	..	.. 1	..	..	Potts/Moncur
21 Oct	Arsenal	H	L	1-2	..	..	Lomas	..	.. 1	..	..	Moncur*	..	..	..	Suker
28 Oct	Newcastle	H	W	1-0	..	..	Pearce I	..	..	..*	..	Carrick	..	.. 1*	..*	Suker/Potts/Moncur
6 Nov	Derby C	A	D	0-0	..	Lomas	..	..	..	Sinclair	..	..	..	..*	Suker*	Moncur/Diawara
11 Nov	Manchester C	H	W	4-1	..	Sinclair 1	.. 1	..	..	Winterburn	..	..	.. 1*	..	Lomas 1	Potts
18 Nov	Leeds U	A	W	1-0	..	..	..*	..	..	.. 1	..	..	Diawara	..	..	Potts
25 Nov	Southampton	A	W	3-2	..	.. 1	Stimac	Lomas	.. 1	..	..*	..	Di Canio	.. 1	Diawara	Moncur
2 Dec	Middlesbrough	H	W	1-0	..	Song	Winterburn	Stimac	..	Carrick	..*	Sinclair	..	.. 1	..	Potts/Moncur
9 Dec	Aston Villa	H	D	1-1	..	..	Pearce I	Potts	..	.. 1	..	..	..	..	..*	Moncur
16 Dec	Everton	A	D	1-1	..	..	..	Winterburn	..	..	..	..	..	.. 1	Lomas	
23 Dec	Leicester C	A	L	1-2	..	..	..*	..	..	..	Lampard	..	Camara	.. 1	..	Cole
26 Dec	Charlton A	H	W	5-0	..	..	Winterburn	Lomas	..	..	.. 1	.. 1*	Di Canio*	.. 2	Camara*	Cole /Moncur/Tihinen (1 og)
1 Jan	Manchester U	A	L	1-3	..	..	..	..	..	..	..	..	Moncur*	.. 1	..*	Cole/Tihinen
13 Jan	Sunderland	H	L	0-2	..*	..	..	Tihinen*	..	Lomas	..	..	Di Canio	..	Cole	Forrest/Camara
22 Jan	Charlton A	A	D	1-1	Forrest	Schemmel	..	..	Song	Dailly	..	Carrick	.. 1	..	..*	Moncur
31 Jan	Tottenham H	H	D	0-0	Hislop	..	..	..	Pearce S	..	..	..	..	..	..	
3 Feb	Liverpool	A	L	0-3	Forrest	..*	..	..	..	..	..	..	Camara	..*	..*	Song/Soma/Todorov
12 Feb	Coventry C	H	D	1-1	..	..	..	..	..	..	..	..	Di Canio	..	.. 1	
24 Feb	Bradford C	A	W	3-1	Bywater	..*	..	Stimac	..	..	.. 2	..	..	Camara*	..	Pearce I/Suker
3 Mar	Arsenal	A	L	0-3	Hislop	Song	..	..*	..*	..	..	Soma	Schemmel	Suker	Diawara*	Tihinen/Pearce I/Todorov
7 Mar	Chelsea	H	L	0-2	..	..	Potts	Pearce I	..*	..	..	..	Di Canio	..*	Cole	Schemmel*/Diawara/Bassila
17 Mar	Ipswich T	H	L	0-1	..	..	Schemmel*	..	..	Winterburn	..	Carrick	..	Kanouté	..*	Todorov/Moncur
31 Mar	Everton	H	L	0-2	..	..	Winterburn	Stimac	..	Foxe	..	..	..	..	..	
7 Apr	Aston Villa	A	D	2-2	..	Schemmel*	..	..	..	Song	.. 1	..	..*	.. 1	Moncur	Cole/Soma
14 Apr	Derby C	H	W	3-1	..	Song	..	..	Pearce I	Moncur	.. 1	..	..	.. 1	Cole 1	
16 Apr	Newcastle U	A	L	1-2	..	..	..	..	..	..*	.. 1	..	Schemmel*	..*	..	Dailly/Todorov/Diawara
21 Apr	Leeds U	H	L	2-0	..	Dailly*	..	..	..	..*	..	..	Di Canio	..*	..	Foxe/Diawara/Todorov
28 Apr	Manchester C	A	L	0-1	..	Song	Pearce S	..	..*	Dailly	Winterburn*	..	..	Diawara*	..	Foxe/Suker/Todorov
5 May	Southampton	H	W	3-0	..	..	..	..*	Foxe	..	Cole 1	..	.. 1	Kanouté 1	Todorov*	Bassila/Schemmel
19 May	Middlesbrough	A	L	1-2	..	Schemmel	..	Minto*	..	Song	Dailly	..	Cole	..	.. 1*	McCann/Defoe
FA Cup																
6 Jan	Walsall	A	W	3-2	Hislop	Song	Winterburn	Pearce S	Tihinen	Lampard 1	Sinclair	Cole	Kanouté 2	Camara*	Carrick	Bassila
28 Jan	Manchester U	A	W	1-0	..	Schemmel	..	..	..	Dailly	Lampard	..*	..	Di Canio 1*	..	Soma/Pearce I
17 Feb	Sunderland	A	W	1-0	..	..	..	..	Stimac	..	..	..	.. 1	..	..	
11 Mar	Tottenham H	H	L	2-3	..	..*	..	.. 1	..	..	..	..	..	..	..	Todorov 1
Worthington Cup																
19 Sep	Walsall	A	W	1-0	Hislop	Potts	Winterburn	Ferdinand	Stimac	Pearce S	Lomas	Carrick	Sinclair	Keller*	Cole	Defoe 1
27 Sep	Walsall	H	D	1-1	..	Lomas 1	..	Margas	..	..	Lampard*	..	Di Canio	Kanouté	..	Potts
31 Oct	Blackburn	H	W	2-0	..	Potts	Pearce I	Ferdinand	Sinclair	..	..	..	.. 1	..*	Suker 1	Moncur
29 Nov	Sheffield W	H	L	1-2	..	Song*	Winterburn	Stimac	Lomas	..	.. 1	..	..	..	Sinclair	Suker

Hammer of the Year 2000-01
STUART PEARCE

	P	W	L	D	F:A	Pts	Pos
Manchester United	38	24	6	8	79:31	80	1st
West Ham United	38	10	16	12	45:50	42	15th

INDEX

ACKNOWLEDGEMENTS

The author would like to thank the following: Andrew Deutz for introducing me to the delights of Upton Park; Julian Brown and Trevor Davies at Hamlyn for giving me the opportunity to write this book; Peter Arnold for his advice, encouragement and careful editing; Matthew Smith, a Hammer exiled in Wales, for his friendship and kind loan of research materials; Barry Smith for sharing his memories of following the Hammers in the 1960s; John Helliar for his patience, incredible archive and encyclopaedic knowledge of West Ham United; Pat and the staff at Helliar and Sons for providing a constant supply of tea during my regular visits; Dave Smith for a word when it counted; Peter Stewart at West Ham United for his tolerance and good humour; Richard Scott for his friendship and for allowing access to his extensive archive of programmes and press cuttings; the staff at Stratford Library and the National Newspaper Library in Collindale; Trevor Brooking, Peter Brabrook, Tony Gale and Steve Potts who took the time to share memories, good and bad, of their time with the Club; Marj and Pete Johnson and Harry and Moira Ward for their encouragement and support; and finally to Ernie Gregory, a man with an unrivalled knowledge of West Ham United, who gave me a sense of perspective and an insight into the Club which I could not have otherwise achieved.

Bibliography

Bonzo - An Autobiography, Billy Bonds (Arthur Barker, London, 1988) Trevor Brooking by Trevor Brooking, Trevor Brooking. (Pelham Books, London, 1981) Tony Cottee - My Autobiography - Claret and Blues, Tony Cottee (Independent UK Sports Publications, London, 1995) At Home with the Hammers, Ted Fenton (Nicholas Kaye, London, 1960) Just Like my Dreams - My Life with West Ham, John Lyall (Viking, London, 1989) Harry Redknapp - My Autobiography, Harry Redknapp with Derek McGovern (CollinsWillow, London, 1998) Spot on with Tonka Ray Stewart (1991) West Ham United Who's Who, Tony Hogg and Tony McDonald (Independent UK Sports Publications, London, 1994) West Ham United - A Complete Record 1900-1987, John Northcutt and Roy Shoesmith (Breedon Books, Derby, 1987) West Ham United - An Illustrated History, John Northcutt and Roy Shoesmith (Breedon Books, Derby, 1998) West Ham United - The Making of a Football Club, Charles Korr (Gerald Duckworth and Co. Ltd, London, 1987) West Ham United, From Greenwood to Redknapp - Match by Match, Clive Leatherdale (Desert Island Books, Essex 1997)

Senior Editor: Trevor Davies
Design: Richard Scott
Original design: Birgit Eggers
Picture research: Daffydd Bynon and Liz Fowler
Production Controller: Edward Carter

PHOTOGRAPHIC ACKNOWLEDGMENTS

The Publishers would like to thank the following individuals and organisations for their kind permission to reproduce the photographs in this book:

Allsport 5 right, 5 top left, 5 top right, 122, 138 bottom, 139 top, 139 bottom, 145 top right, 146 bottom left, 147 top right, 149 centre, 153 top, 154, 157 top, 173 main picture, 174 bottom left /Shaun Botterill 140 top, 150 bottom /Clive Brunskill 156, 187 right /David Cannon 135, 136 bottom /Phil Cole 148, 149 top, 150 top /Michael Cooper 153 bottom,/Tom Hevezi 136 top,/Ross Kinnaird 164,/Roger Labrosse 133 bottom /Jamie McDonald 171 bottom /Steve Morton 140 bottom,/Tony O'Brien 168 bottom right, 169 /Gary M Prior 155 top, 158 top, 158 bottom, 168 bottom left /Ben Radford 160 bottom /Anton Want 141, 149

Allsport Historical Collection/MSI 5 bottom left

Alpha 98 bottom left, 126 main picture /Magi Haroun 162, 166

Steve Bacon 108 top, 108 bottom, 109, 110, 112 bottom, 113 centre, 116 top, 118 top left, 118 top right, 118 centre, 119, 120, 121, 125, 130, 131, 132, 137, 142 top, 142 bottom, 143 top, 143 bottom, 152, 155 bottom, 157 bottom, 159 top, 159 bottom, 160 top, 161, 167, 176-186, 187 left, 188-189

Colorsport 4 main picture, 42 main picture, 56 main picture, 57 centre, 61 bottom centre, 63 main picture, 64 top left, 64 bottom right, 67 bottom right, 69 centre right 1, 71 main picture, 79 top right, 79 bottom right, 80 top left, 80 bottom centre, 80-81 main picture, 91 main picture, 95 bottom right, 98 top left, 100, 102 left, 104 top, 106-107, 107 bottom, 113 bottom, 114 top, 114 bottom, 116 bottom, 117 top, 117 bottom, 123, 133 top, 138 top, 144 left, 163, 168 top right, 171 top right

Empics 175 main picture /Chris Cole 165

John Helliar 7 bottom centre, 8 main picture, 11 top, 12 main picture, 13 top centre, 14 top centre, 14 centre left, 24 main picture, 28 top left, 31 main picture, 32 top left, 33 main picture, 34 top centre, 36 main picture, 36 bottom centre, 37 centre right, 38 top centre, 38-39 main picture, 40 main picture, 40 bottom centre, 41 centre right, 44 main picture, 45 bottom centre, 47 main picture, 47 bottom left, 48 main picture, 49 bottom left, 50 main picture, 59, 60 top left, 70 main picture, 73 bottom right, 75 main picture, 80 top right, 82 main picture, 83 main picture, 84 top left, 85 main picture, 86 main picture, 86 bottom left, 87 main picture, 87 top centre, 88 top centre, 88 bottom left, 89 top right, 89 bottom Right, 90 main picture, 92 main picture, 94 bottom left, 95 main picture, 170 top, 170 bottom

Hulton Getty Picture Collection 5 centre right, 19 bottom right, 22-23 main picture, 25 main picture, 57, 66 top left, 68 main picture, 68 top centre, 72 main picture, 76 main picture, 78-79 main picture, 84 bottom left, 93 top right, 94 top centre, 96 top right, 96 bottom, 97 bottom left, 99 main picture, 127 main picture, 128 top left, 128-129 main picture /Evening Standard 101, 103 bottom, 113 top right

Mirror Syndication International 22 main picture, 26 main picture, 34 top right, 34 bottom right /Daily Mirror 104 bottom, 105

Topham Picturepoint 6 main picture, 28-29 main picture, 32-33 main picture

Adam Ward 21 top right, 23 top right, 27 top right, 28 bottom centre, 32 bottom centre, 38 bottom centre, 46, 46 bottom centre, 49 top centre, 62 bottom centre

West Ham Football Club 7 top, 9 bottom right, 15 main picture, 16 main picture, 17 top centre, 17 centre, 17 bottom right, 18 top centre, 18 centre, 18 bottom centre, 19 top centre, 20 main picture, 23 bottom left, 25 top centre right, 25 insert top right, 27 bottom left, 32 centre left, 34-35 main picture, 38 left, 39 bottom right, 45 main picture, 51 main picture, 51 top centre, 52 main picture, 53 centre left, 53 centre right, 53 bottom left, 54 top centre, 54 centre left, 55 main picture, 81 bottom centre, 85 top centre, 86 centre